PRACTICE AND PROCEDURE IN LABOR ARBITRATION

PRACTICE AND PROCEDURE IN LABOR ARBITRATION

OWEN FAIRWEATHER

THE BUREAU OF NATIONAL AFFAIRS, INC., WASHINGTON, D.C.

Copyright © 1973

The Bureau of National Affairs, Inc.

Washington, D.C. 20037

Printed in the United States of America

Library of Congress Catalog Card Number: 73-76162

International Standard Book Number: 0-87179-188-9

Preface

During the last 35 years labor arbitration has grown from a process misunderstood and frowned upon by the courts to one especially protected by them. The encouragement of labor arbitration is now a basic part of our national labor policy.

In the beginning, when the collective bargaining agreement was a relatively primitive document, there was a tendency to think of the arbitrator as a mediator and there developed a cliché—that arbitration was an informal process in which rules of practice or procedure were out of place. In selecting an arbitrator, the parties granted to him the authority to make whatever rules he believed he needed.

At first arbitrators quite naturally nurtured this view—that they had been delegated the right to invent, improvise, and determine without any limitations. But as time passed, arbitrators and the practitioners presenting cases became aware that a body of practice, and, what is more, of law, was developing around the process and it could not be ignored. The arbitrators themselves began to cite decisions of other arbitrators on procedural matters, and state and federal courts, and even the Supreme Court, began to enunciate procedural law applicable to labor arbitration.

It became clear that the time had come to catalogue what arbitrators in fact were doing about many of the practice and procedural problems that they encountered and what the courts did when the rulings of arbitrators on such matters came before them for review.

The process of cataloguing started in various legal memoranda, but the attempt to make a reasonably complete catalogue began in 1967. As material was collected, the risk involved in cataloguing became quite clear. A practice or procedure that is reported might be considered to be endorsed as the preferred practice or procedure. Partly for this reason, an effort was made to report the variety that exists with a conscious effort to avoid editorial identification of the "best" procedure. Some of the flexibility so valuable to the labor arbitration process might inadvertently be dampened if one procedure or another were considered "best." It should also be remembered that much of the procedure followed by arbitrators is not reported by them in their written awards because many practice and procedure problems they confront are resolved before their award writing starts.

The effort to make the collection of information as complete as possible proved to be a bigger task than could be fitted into a busy work schedule. It became clear that if the task was ever to be completed it would have to become a team effort. I am particularly grateful for the efforts of my partners, Ray J. Schoonhoven and Charles J. Griffin, and my associates, Joel H. Kaplan and William R. Sullivan, for rowing laboring oars, and to the following partners and associates who made valued contributions: John Van Aken, Keith R. Reed, Rody P. Biggert, Harry T. Edwards, Joseph Herman, Peter J. Hurtgen, Edward W. Bergmann, Robert E. Mann, George E. Peronas, Dennis R. Homerin, David B. Ross, Anthony J. Crement, Richard Hudlin, John P. Kennedy, and Robert M. Johnson. In addition, I am deeply indebted to Eileen Hickey, my secretary, for the effort she poured into this project.

OWEN FAIRWEATHER

April 1973

Table of Contents

CHAPTER I

The Source of the Procedural Law
in Labor Arbitration

The practice and procedure in labor arbitration involves the manner in which a labor arbitration case is initiated, how the hearing proceeds and what happens after the hearing is concluded. When labor arbitration began to grow in the United States as a result of the rapid unionization of major industries in the early 1930s, most of the practice and procedure in labor arbitration was established and developed by the arbitrator. He used, as his basic standards, the needs and desires of the parties he was servicing since labor arbitration was considered to be a completely private process.

The view that labor arbitration should be controlled or formalized by any body of law made by judges or legislators was repugnant not only to the early arbitrators, but also to the parties who were submitting disputes to arbitration. They rather uniformly believed that judges, legislators, and lawyers did not understand the pragmatic and fast-moving nature of the labor arbitration process and that if the law crept in it would generate rigidities which would make the labor arbitration process less satisfactory to the parties.

In recent years, however, the law has been flowing over the labor arbitration process like a tidal wave and much of this has involved procedural matters. One reason why there was so little law surrounding the labor arbitration process in its infancy was that the courts initially made no effort to accommodate labor arbitration. They considered labor arbitration to be a competitive process with the court system and hence a process that should be thwarted and discouraged.[1] In the early days of labor arbitration, courts ruled that an agreement to submit a dispute to arbitration could be revoked at will by either

---

[1] See generally Sturges and Reckson, *Common Law and Statutory Arbitration: Problems Arising From Their Coexistence*, 46 MINN. L. REV. 819 (1962); 6A A. Corbin, CONTRACTS § 1443 at 388 (1962, Supp. 1964) ("A general agreement to arbitrate all future disputes is contrary to public policy and void"); *United Steelworkers v. Warrior & Gulf Navigation Co.*, 363 U.S. 574, 586-87 (dissenting opinion); *Marchant v. Mead-Morrison Mfg. Co.*, 252 N.Y. 284, 299, 169 N.E. 386, 391 (1929); *Continental Milling & Feed Co. v. Doughnut Co.*, 186 Md. 669, 676, 48 A.2d 447, 450 (1946); *U.S. v. Moorman*, 338 U.S. 457, 462 (1950).

party, even after the arbitration hearing, if the revocation occurred prior to the entry of an award. Agreements to arbitrate were revocable even when they contained an express covenant that neither party to the agreement could revoke it because, the courts held, parties could not make irrevocable agreements which were legally revocable.[2]

The courts' jealousy of arbitration as a competing process and their refusal to enforce agreements to arbitrate on the theory that one or the other party could revoke them disappeared as the state legislatures began to enact arbitration statutes. Twenty-nine states have arbitration statutes specifically applicable to controversies arising out of labor agreements or specific agreements to arbitrate a labor dispute.[3] Sixteen states have general arbitration statutes construed to be applicable to disputes arising out of labor agreements.[4]

---

[2] See, *e.g.*, *Baltimore and Ohio R. Co. v. Standard*, 56 Ohio St. 224, 46 N.E. 577 (1897).

[3] Alabama (ALA. CODE tit. 26, §§ 338-342 (1958)); Alaska (ALASKA STAT. § 23.05.060 (1962)); Arkansas ARK. STAT. ANN. § 81-107 (1960)); Colorado (COLO. REV. STAT. ANN. §§ 80-4-10, 80-4-11 (1963)); Connecticut (CONN. GEN. STAT. REV. § 31-117 (1968)); Illinois (ILL. ANN. STAT. ch. 10, §§ 20 to 30 (Smith-Hurd, 1966), as amended (Supp. 1970)); Iowa (IOWA CODE ANN. §§ 90.1 to 90.14 (1949)); Kentucky (KY. REV. STAT. §§ 336.140, 336.150 (1962)); Louisiana (LA. REV. STAT. ANN. §§ 23:861 to 23:876 (1964)); Maine (ME. REV. STAT. ANN. §§ 881 to 960 (1964)); Maryland (MD. ANN. CODE art. 89, §§ 3 to 13 (1969)); Massachusetts (MASS. ANN. LAWS ch. 150C, §§ 1 to 16 (1965)); Michigan (MICH. STAT. ANN. § 17,454 (10.3) (1968)); Minnesota (MINN. STAT. ANN .§ 179.09 (Supp. 1970)); Montana (MONT. REV. CODES ANN. §§ 41-901 to 41-909 (1961)); Nevada (NEV. REV. STAT. §§ 614.010 to 614.080 (1967)); New Hampshire (N.H. REV. STAT. ANN. §§ 273:12 to 273:27 (1966)); New Jersey (N.J. REV. STAT. §§ 34-13-1 to 34-13-9 (1965)); North Carolina (N.C. GEN. STAT. §§ 95-36.1 to 95-36.9 (1965)); Ohio (OHIO REV. CODE ANN. §§ 4129.01 to 4129.12 (1965)); Oregon (ORE. REV. STAT. §§ 662.405 to 662.455 (1967)); Pennsylvania (PA. STAT. ANN. tit. 43, §§ 211.31 to 211.39 (1964)); Rhode Island (R.I. GEN. LAWS ANN. §§ 28-9-1 to 28-9-26 (1968)); South Carolina (S.C. CODE ANN. §§ 40-301 to 40-307 (1962)); Texas (TEX. REV. CIV. STAT. ANN. arts. 239 to 249 (1959)); Utah (UTAH CODE ANN. § 35-1-16 (1953)); Vermont (VT. STAT. ANN. tit. 21, §§ 501 to 513 (1967)); Washington (WASH. REV. CODE ANN. §§ 49-08.010 to 49-08.060 (1962)); Wisconsin (WIS. STAT. ANN. § 111.10 (1957)).

[4] Delaware (DEL. CODE ANN. tit. 10 §§ 5701 to 5706 (1953)); Florida (FLA. STAT. ANN. §§ 682.01 to 682.22 (Supp. 1969)); Georgia (GA. CODE ANN. §§ 7-201 to 7-224 (1953)); Hawaii (HAWAII REV. LAWS §§ 658-1 to 658-15 (1968)); Idaho (IDAHO CODE ANN. §§ 7-901 to 7-910 (1948)); Kansas (KAN. STAT. ANN. §§ 5-201 to 5-213 (1963)); Mississippi (MISS. CODE ANN. §§ 279 to 297 (1956)); Missouri (MO. ANN. STAT. §§ 435.010 to 435.280 (1950)); Nebraska (NEB. REV. STAT. §§ 25-2103 to 25-2120 (1943)); Nevada (NEV. REV. STAT. §§ 38.010 to 38.240 (1967)); New Mexico (N.M. STAT. ANN. §§ 22-3-1 to 22-3-8 (1953)); New York (N.Y. CIV. PRAC. §§ 7501 to 7514 (McKinney, 1963)); North Dakota (N.D. CENT. CODE §§ 32-29-01 to 32-29-21 (1960)); Tennessee (TENN. CODE ANN. §§ 23-501 to 23-519 (1955)); Virginia (VA. CODE ANN. §§ 8-503 to 8-507 (1950) *as amended* § 8-503 (Supp. 1968)); West Virginia (W.VA. CODE ANN. §§ 55-10-1 to 55-10-8 (1966)). Indiana and Wyoming have enacted the Uniform Arbitration Act supplemented by language making it expressly applicable to labor arbitration: Indiana (IND. ANN. STAT. §§ 3-227 to 3-248 (Supp. 1970); Wyoming (WYO. STAT. ANN. §§ 1-1048.1 to 1-1048.21 (Supp. 1969)). The California statute (CAL. CIV. PRO. CODE §§ 1280-1294 (West, 1955)) excepting from arbitration contracts "pertaining to labor" has been construed to except only contracts relating to the actual hiring of labor and not collective bargaining agreements. *Ulene v. Murray Millman of California,* 175 Cal. App.2d 655, 346 P.2d 494 (1959).

On the federal side of the ledger, Congress enacted the United States Arbitration Act[5] in 1925 to provide for the enforcement of commercial agreements to arbitrate,[6] but parties to collective bargaining agreements began to predicate suits to compel arbitration on this Act.

After the enactment of Section 301 of the Labor Management Relations Act,[7] there developed considerable confusion in the lower federal courts as to whether Section 301 or the U.S. Arbitration Act conferred jurisdiction upon federal courts to compel or stay arbitration or enforce or vacate awards.[8] In *Textile Workers Union v. American Thread Co.,*[9] Judge Wyzanski held that an agreement to arbitrate a dispute concerning the interpretation and application of a labor agreement could be enforced under Section 301, but that the practice under the U.S. Arbitration Act should be "a guiding analogy."[10]

Subsequently, in *Textile Workers Union v. Lincoln Mills,*[11] the Supreme Court, for the first time, identified Section 301 as the source of all law, substantive and procedural, for labor arbitration. In that case, the Fifth Circuit held that an agreement to arbitrate could not be enforced [12] because there was no federal or state common law or statute that required or permitted the enforcement of such an agreement. The Supreme Court, however, reversed and enforced the agreement. Although Justice Douglas, writing the majority opinion, did not refer to the U.S. Arbitration Act, he did say that the Supreme Court's construction of Section 301 was in accord with Judge Wyzanski's decision in *American Thread,*[13] which apparently meant that the Supreme Court accepted the practice under the U.S. Arbitration Act [14] "as a guiding analogy" to be followed in developing the procedural law applicable to labor arbitration.

The Supreme Court again suggested in *General Electric Co. v. Local 205, United Electrical Workers,*[15] that the procedural law

---

[5] 9 USC § 1, *et seq.* (1947).

[6] The U.S. Arbitration Act, as Judge Wyzanski observed, "was drafted a generation ago, prior not only to the Taft-Hartley Act but also the labor situation that has developed since the 1930's." *Textile Workers Union v. American Thread Co.,* 133 F.Supp. 137, 142 (D. Mass. 1953).

[7] 29 USC § 185 (1964).

[8] See generally Cox, *Grievance Arbitration in the Federal Courts,* 67 HARV. L. REV. 591 (1956).

[9] 113 F.Supp. 137 (D. Mass. 1953).

[10] *Id.* at 142.

[11] 353 U.S. 448 (1957).

[12] *Lincoln Mills v. Textile Workers Union,* 230 F.2d 81 (5th Cir. 1956).

[13] 353 U.S. at 451.

[14] See Smith and Jones, *Arbitration and the Courts,* 63 MICH. L. REV. 751, 801-2 n. 120 (1965).

[15] 353 U.S. 547 (1957).

developed under the U.S. Arbitration Act was to be "a guiding analogy." It enforced, under Section 301, an agreement to arbitrate which the Second Circuit had enforced under the U.S. Arbitration Act, noting that the Second Circuit had taken "a different path . . . though we reach the same result."[16] Despite this, in a companion case, *Goodall-Sanford, Inc. v. United Textile Workers Local 1802*,[17] the Supreme Court counselled against full application of the U.S. Arbitration Act as "a guiding analogy" when it held, under Section 301, that an order directing arbitration was a "final decision" that could be appealed, contrary to rulings by lower courts based on the U.S. Arbitration Act. Although, in *Goodall-Sanford*, the Supreme Court made it quite clear that procedural law developed in cases under the U.S. Arbitration Act could no longer be relied upon exclusively as a source of answers to procedural questions in labor arbitration cases, the Court implied that the law developed under the U.S. Arbitration Act should not be ignored by the practitioner. This is a fair inference because where the procedural law developed under 301 is not clear, the law developed under the U.S. Arbitration Act may be considered compatible with the emerging federal law being developed under Section 301, especially by the lower federal courts,[18] and, hence, should be carefully considered when seeking answers to the procedural questions in labor arbitration litigation.

This conclusion was substantiated when a federal district court,[19] fourteen years after the Supreme Court's decision in *Goodall-Sanford*, enforced a subpoena for the appearance of a witness and for the production of certain records issued under a state statute in a labor arbitration proceeding on the basis of the authority vested in the court by the U.S. Arbitration Act. While, the court said it was exercising this power *sua sponte* and added the requirement that the records called for by the subpoena were to be examined by the arbitrator *in camera*, this decision demonstrates that state statutes and the U.S. Arbitration Act, at least to some degree, are still considered a source of procedural law in arbitration.

This is not surprising. It is, after all, now firmly established that the emerging federal law being developed under Section 301 must

---

[16] *Id.* at 548.

[17] 353 U.S. 550 (1957).

[18] See *Aircraft Lodge 703 v. Curtiss-Wright Corp.*, 169 F.Supp. 837 (D.N.J. 1959); *Macneish v. New York Typographical Union No. 6*, 205 F.Supp. 558 (S.D. N.Y. 1962); *Pock v. New York Typographical Union No. 6*, 223 F.Supp. 181 (S.D.N.Y. 1963); *Austin Mailers Union No. 136 v. Newspapers, Inc.*, 226 F.Supp. 600 (D. Tex. 1963); cf. *Western Automatic Machine Screw Co. v. UAW*, 335 F.2d 103 (6th Cir. 1964); *Local 1645, UAW v. Torrington Co.*, 242 F.Supp. 813 (D. Conn. 1965), aff'd, 358 F.2d 103 (2d Cir. 1966).

[19] *Local Lodge 1746, IAM v. United Aircraft Corp.*, 329 F. Supp. 283 (D. Conn. 1971).

also be applied by state courts,[20] and this means that agreements to submit disputes to arbitration are enforceable under Section 301 even in state courts which have not yet changed the contrary common law rule by a statutory provision making such agreements enforceable.[21] This does not mean, however, that state statutes and even the federal Arbitration Act have no relevance in answering procedural questions in labor arbitration. Whether such statutory provisions remain applicable can only be answered by a determination that the provision of the state statute in question or the U.S. Arbitration Act is compatible with federal labor policy and the emerging federal law under Section 301.[22] If it is compatible, then the state or federal court can absorb the provision of the state law or federal act as part of the emerging federal law. The Supreme Court has made it clear that "any state law applied, however, will be absorbed as federal law and will not be an independent source of private rights."[23] If the state or federal court decides the provision of the state law being asserted as applicable is incompatible with the emerging federal law, then it "must give way to principles of federal labor law."[24]

In spite of the uneasy status of state statutory law in suits to compel or stay arbitration, or to enforce or vacate awards, state courts frequently rely on state arbitration statutes to deny requested relief.[25] For example, a request for vacation of an award was denied by a Minnesota court under a provision of a Minnesota statute. The argument that the Minnesota statutory law was not applicable was rejected by the court with this observation: "The controlling substantive law is Federal law," but "state law, if compatible with the purposes of § 301, may be resorted to in order to find the rule that will best effectuate the Federal policy."[26] Following this same easy rationale, many state and federal district courts have required strict compliance with the procedural requirements of the state or federal arbitration

---

[20] *Teamsters Local 174 v. Lucas Flour Co.,* 369 U.S. 95, 102; *Carey v. General Electric Co.,* 213 F.Supp. 276 (S.D.N.Y. 1962), *modified,* 315 F.2d 499 (2d Cir.), *cert. denied,* 377 U.S. 908 (1963).

[21] *Volunteer Electric Cooperative v. Gann,* 41 CCH L.C. ¶ 16,537 (Tenn. Ct. App. 1960); *Local 774 v. Cessna Aircraft Co.,* 186 Kan. 569, 352 P.2d 420 (1960).

[22] *Textile Workers Union v. Lincoln Mills,* 353 U.S. 448, 456-57 (1957). Note, however, that any action arising under Section 301 is controlled by federal substantive law even though it is brought in a state court and removal is but one aspect of the primacy of the federal judiciary in deciding questions of federal law. *Avco Corp. v. Lodge No. 735, IAM,* 390 U.S. 557 (1968).

[23] *Textile Workers Union v. Lincoln Mills,* 353 U.S. 448, 456-57 (1957).

[24] *Teamsters Local 174 v. Lucas Flour Co.,* 369 U.S. 95, 102 (1962).

[25] See generally *Comment, The Applicability of State Arbitration Statutes to Proceedings Subject to LMRA Section 301,* 21 OHIO STATE L.J. 692 (1966); *Local 2131, United Bhd. of Carpenters & Joiners v. Aetna Steel Products Corp.,* 56 SCH. L.R. 141, 36 L.A. 717 (C.P. Schuylkill Co., Pa. 1960).

[26] *Fischer v. Guaranteed Concrete Co.,* 276 Minn. 510, 514, 151 N.W.2d 266, 269 (1967).

statutes.[27] For example, a New York court held that a motion to compel arbitration must be served on the other party in technical compliance with the state statutory requirements.[28] Further a New York federal court held that an action to stay must be filed within the state statutory time limits.[29]

In a more startling development, the Supreme Court adopted the view that a state statute of limitations should control in the filing of a Section 301 suit. In *UAW v. Hoosier Cardinal*,[30] the Court declined to formulate a uniform federal standard by saying that the lack of uniformity in regard to the limitations upon the bringing of a Section 301 suit would not impair the goal of uniformity often enunciated as national labor policy.

The Second Circuit, however, in *West Rock Lodge No. 2120, IAM v. Geometric Tool Co.*,[31] held that the Connecticut statutory rule that an arbitration award not rendered within 60 days after the submission of the parties was invalid and should be vacated was not a rule compatible with the emerging federal law and was not controlling. In so holding, the Second Circuit disagreed with the District Court that the rationale of *Hoosier Cardinal* required the adoption of the rule of the Connecticut statute.

Decisions are cited throughout this volume where courts have asserted some technical procedural rule contained in a state statute to determine a labor arbitration case; hence, this *caveat:* The procedural requirements of the state statute and the U.S. Arbitration Act should be carefully inspected and if possible complied with; otherwise a decision asserting a procedural rule could result, which could only be overcome by an expensive appeal. It is true that neither Act is technically a source of procedural law in labor arbitration, but unless the law emerging under Section 301 on a particular point has been clarified by the Supreme Court, the rules that have developed under both the state law and the federal arbitration act should be

---

[27] *Cf. IAM v. General Electric Co.*, 406 F.2d 1046 (2d Cir. 1969). (Commencement of action to compel arbitration by petition under Section 4 of the U.S. Arbitration Act instead of by complaint under Section 301 is valid in that the Arbitration Act has been recognized as applicable to labor cases.)

[28] *2166 Bronx Park East, Inc. v. Local 32E, Building Service Employees*, 45 Misc.2d 492, 257 N.Y.S.2d 192, 193 (Sup. Ct. 1965) ("Although service by certified mail is permitted for notice of intention to arbitrate and for an application to stay arbitration within 10 days after service of such notice (CPLR 7503(c)), an application to compel arbitration is the commencement of a special proceeding (CPLR 7502(a)) and must be instituted by service in the same manner as a summons (CPLR 403(c)).")

[29] *IAM v. General Electric Co.*, 282 F.Supp. 413 (N.D.N.Y. 1968), *aff'd*, 406 F.2d 1046 (2d Cir. 1969).

[30] 383 U.S. 696 (1966). See also *Howerton v. J. Christenson Co.*, 65 L.C. ¶ 11,569 (N.D. Calif. 1971).

[31] 406 F.2d 284 (2d Cir. 1968).

considered guides since courts can adopt such rules by merely assert-ing they are compatible with the emerging federal law. This rather uneasy qualification concerning the application of the provisions of state statutes and the U.S. Arbitration Act should be remembered when comments about procedural rules based on state statutes or on the U.S. Arbitration Act are made in this volume.

CHAPTER II

The Submission of a Case to Arbitration

A case is submitted to arbitration either pursuant to a provision of a labor agreement providing that future disputes will be submitted to arbitration, or pursuant to a separate agreement to submit a particular dispute to arbitration.

A. SUBMISSION OF A DISPUTE UNDER THE ARBITRATION PROVISIONS OF A COLLECTIVE BARGAINING AGREEMENT

Generally, the obligation to arbitrate is found in a clause in a labor agreement that provides that disputes which cannot be resolved by agreement will be resolved by arbitration. The initiation of arbitration is usually by a "demand," normally in letter form, requesting arbitration concerning a particular grievance.

This normal practice has been codified in Rule 7 of the Voluntary Labor Arbitration Rules of the American Arbitration Association as follows:

"7. *Initiation Under an Arbitration Clause in a Collective Bargaining Agreement*—Arbitration under an arbitration clause in a collective bargaining agreement under these Rules may be initiated by either party in the following manner:

"(a) By giving written notice to the other party of intention to arbitrate (Demand), which notice shall contain a statement setting forth the nature of the dispute and the remedy sought, and

"(b) By filing at any Regional Office of the AAA two copies of said notice, together with a copy of the collective bargaining agreement, or such parts thereof as relate to the dispute, including the arbitration provisions. After the Arbitrator is appointed, no new or different claim may be submitted to him except with the consent of the Arbitrator and all other parties." [1]

The party receiving the demand typically responds by complying

---

[1] American Arbitration Association, VOLUNTARY LABOR ARBITRATION RULES, Rule 7 (1965).

with the contractual procedures for selecting an arbitrator[2] or by submitting the grievance to a previously agreed upon arbitrator.

The submission of a particular grievance claim often takes the form of a joint letter to an arbitrator asking him to determine the merits of the grievance, citing the specific provision of the labor agreement in dispute, and, by reference to the arbitration clause in the labor agreement, advising the arbitrator of the scope of his authority.[3]

In many instances the statement of the grievance, as originally written by the employee or his union steward, is the claim of contract violation that is submitted to arbitration. Although this statement may be inarticulate, the representatives of one or the other party are frequently unable to agree upon a revised statement which poses a more precise question. The failure of parties to frame issues more precisely at this stage seems due to a fear that the representative, if his side does not win, will be blamed for the loss because of his revision in the wording of the grievance.[4]

B. SUBMISSION OF A DISPUTE BY A SUBMISSION AGREEMENT

Sometimes where the labor agreement provides for the submission of future disputes to arbitration, the dispute to be submitted is identified on a "submission agreement." Such an agreement is always necessary where the contract does not provide for the submission of future disputes to arbitration or where it provides for the arbitration of a dispute only if the parties agree to submit a specific dispute.

The "submission agreement" sets forth the question to be resolved, the relief desired, and identifies the arbitrator or the arbitration board that the parties have selected.[5] It usually grants to the arbitrator, or the board, jurisdiction over the subject of the dispute and empowers him or them to decide conclusively all questions of law or fact which must be decided to resolve the dispute.

---

[2] The process of selecting the arbitrator or the board of arbitration to whom the grievance claim will be submitted is discussed in detail in Chapter V.

[3] F. Russell, RUSSELL ON ARBITRATION, 158 (17th ed., A. Walton 1963); P. Prasow and E. Peters, ARBITRATION AND COLLECTIVE BARGAINING, 17-24 (1970); Merrill, *A Labor Arbitrator Views His Work*, 10 VANDERBILT L. REV. 789, 793 (1957); Kagel, *Labor and Commercial Arbitration Under the California Arbitration Statute*, 38 CALIF. L. REV. 799, 804-805 (1950). See also Davey, *Hazards in Labor Arbitration*, 1 IND. & LAB. REL. REV. 386, 398 (1948).

[4] Mentschikoff, *The Significance of Arbitration—A Preliminary Inquiry*, 17 LAW & CONTEMP. PROB. 698, 705 (1952).

[5] Six state statutes require that the submission agreement name the arbitrator or arbitrators. Colorado (COLO. REV. STAT. ANN. ch. 18, Rule 109(b) (Rules of Civ. Pro. 1970)); Georgia (GA. CODE ANN. § 7-201 (1936)); Iowa (IOWA CODE ANN. § 679.2 (1950)); Kentucky (KY. REV. STAT. § 417.020 (1962)); Nebraska (NEB. REV. STAT. § 25-2104 (1943)); and Tennessee (TENN. CODE ANN. § 23-504 (1955)).

Where the jurisdiction and/or remedial powers of the arbitrator or board are limited in the labor agreement, care must be exercised not to incorporate broader definitions in the submission agreement as the submission agreement will control. For example, in *Railway Clerks v. Universal Carloading,*[6] the labor agreement provided that if the charges against the employee were not sustained, the employee shall be reinstated and paid for all time lost. The arbitrator ordered reinstatement, but declined to award back pay. In refusing the union's petition to correct the award, the court held that since the questions submitted to the arbitrator in the submission agreement were whether the company had acted properly when it terminated the employee and "If not, what remedy is ordered?" the submission agreement superseded the labor agreement and the union could not object that no back pay was awarded or that the remedy was not to its liking. On the other hand, in *Food Workers v. A & P Tea Co.,*[7] the court vacated an award which did not reinstate an employee on the ground that the arbitrator's authority had been limited by a letter between the parties because the court held that the contract and the submission agreement determined the authority of the arbitrator, rather than the letter.

C. EFFECT OF THE FAILURE TO BE SPECIFIC

A state court has stayed an arbitration proceeding until the specific issues to be arbitrated were made clear on the ground that the employer is entitled to be apprised of the specific provisions of the agreement sought to be enforced and the nature of the employer's breach.[8] On the other hand, an arbitrator has ruled that where the violation of two clauses is alleged but only one clause was involved, no basis for a claim of nonarbitrability existed.[9] Another arbitrator ruled that it was proper in a particular dispute to redefine the issue after the evidence was presented where such *post hoc* redefinition would not be an "expansion of the issue" that would "prejudice the company by a surprise presentation for which it was unprepared."[10]

---

[6] 1 Cal. App.3d 145, 72 LRRM 2798 (1969). A stipulation may turn out to be too narrow. In *Timm Industries, Inc.,* 9 L.A. 642 (Prasow, 1948), the stipulation limited the arbitrator to the consideration of one particular section of the collective agreement in determining the disposition to be made of the grievance. The company based its case on the management rights section, but the arbitrator stated that the introduction of the management rights provision was extraneous to the issue, as defined in the submission agreement, and he made his decision solely on the basis of the one section specified by the parties in the submission agreement.

[7] 415 F.2d 185 (3d Cir. 1969).

[8] *Unipak Aviation Corp. v. Mantell,* 20 Misc.2d 1078, 196 N.Y.S.2d 126 (1959).

[9] *Textile Paper Products Co.,* AAA Case No. 88-14 (Sanders, 1966).

[10] *Continental Can Co.,* AAA Case No. 45-17 (Sugerman, 1962).

Where the statement of the grievance is ambiguous, the arbitrator will sometimes clarify the issue to be determined. For instance, an arbitrator ruled that the claim by the company in its answer to the grievance that the union had violated the agreement by engaging in an illegal work stoppage became an issue in the case in spite of the union's contention that this claim raised in the answer was a "new and separate matter," not part of the grievance. The arbitrator said:

> " 'Judged by any reasonable standard of grievance interpretation, the company was quite justified in treating the written grievance as having raised two problems, and in seeking to answer both complaints.' . . . 'The company certainly had the right to explain the foreman-refusal to discuss the answer and claim that the men who had shut down their machines to seek such discussion were thereby in violation of the contract. To expect any closer relationship between a grievance and a grievance answer would be to attempt to bestow upon the labor-management grievance procedure a technical character which would equal or exceed even the highly complex struggle over pleadings in court cases, and I do not believe this is either intended or desirable.' " [11]

Similarly, where an arbitration hearing was held, even though the issues submitted were vague, the Sixth Circuit held that a federal district court had erred when it vacated the award on the grounds that the statement of the issue submitted was too vague.[12]

The need for specificity in the statement of the issue in dispute, however, was underscored by the Supreme Court's decision in *Boys Markets, Inc. v. Retail Clerks Union, Local 770.*[13] There, the Court held that a federal district court may enjoin a strike in violation of a no-strike clause if the dispute involved is one that can be submitted to an arbitrator under the labor agreement. This means that before an injunction will issue to enjoin the strike action, a court is required to determine if the issue in dispute is one within the scope of the commitment to arbitrate in the labor agreement.

This new involvement of courts in questions of labor contract interpretation has also involved the courts in the process of clarification of issues for resolution by arbitrators. For example, the Second Circuit in *Ice Cream Drivers Local 757 v. Borden, Inc.*[14] held, relying specifically on *Boys Markets,* that the district court could rephrase and broaden the statement of the issue to be arbitrated to include " 'the disputes between [Borden and the union] arising out of Borden,

---

[11] *Champion Spark Plug Co.,* AAA Case No. 41-17 (Rock, 1961).

[12] *Kroger Co. v. Teamsters Local 661,* 380 F.2d 728 (6th Cir. 1967).

[13] 398 U.S. 235 (1970).

[14] 433 F.2d 41 (2d Cir. 1970).

Inc.'s closing of its manufacturing operations. . . .' "[15] so that the dispute causing the strike which the court enjoined would find its resolution through arbitration.

In addition, the desired relief should be clearly requested in the submission presented to the arbitrator. The problem that can arise when the relief requested is not clear is illustrated by a decision of the Eighth Circuit in *Luggage & Novelty Workers Local 66 v. Neevel Luggage Mfg. Co., Inc.*[16] affirming a trial court's denial of enforcement of an award because the arbitrator granted relief beyond that requested by the submission. The question submitted was whether the layoff of certain employees was "improper under the terms of the contract between the parties." The arbitrator determined that the layoff was improper but then ordered the employees reinstated and paid for time lost. The trial court had denied enforcement of that part of the award granting back pay because the question of back pay was not "specifically submitted for arbitration." In affirming, the court of appeals relied on the *Steelworkers Trilogy,*[17] holding that a party cannot be required to submit to arbitration any dispute which he has not agreed so to submit.[18]

Arbitrators as well as courts have pointed out the need for care in stating the relief desired in the submission. For example, Arbitrator Whitley P. McCoy held in *International Harvester Company, Springfield Works*[19] that a request for retroactive pay for all men in a department affected by a particular breach of contract was too general to permit an award of back pay. He held that if an employee claimed he was denied pay, he was required to file a claim for the specific sum he claimed was due and support his claim with evidence.

While not conclusive, these cases highlight the fact that if care is not exercised in drafting the question to be resolved and the relief requested, the award may not resolve the dispute and the stage may be set for additional litigation.

---

[15] *Id.* at 46.

[16] 325 F.2d 992 (8th Cir. 1964). But see *American Bosch Arma Corp. v. International Union of Elec. Workers Local 794*, 243 F.Supp. 493 (N.D. Miss. 1965). Moreover, the Eighth Circuit decision should not cause one to conclude that an arbitrator does not have broad remedial powers, a topic fully discussed in Chapter XIV.

[17] *United Steelworkers of America v. Warrior & Gulf Navigation Co.*, 363 U.S. 574 (1960); *United Steelworkers of America v. Enterprise Wheel & Car Corp.*, 363 U.S. 593 (1960); *United Steelworkers of America v. American Mfg. Co.*, 363 U.S. 564 (1960).

[18] 325 F.2d 992, 994 (8th Cir. 1964).

[19] Case No. 28 (McCoy, 1949) (unpublished). See also *Geneva Industries, Inc.*, 66-3 ARB ¶ 8852 (Davis, 1966); *Caterpillar Tractor Co.*, 65-1 ARB ¶ 8187 (Dworkin, 1964); *United Engineering & Foundry Co.*, 70-2 ARB ¶ 8644 (Dybeck, 1970).

D. SUBMISSION OF MULTIPLE GRIEVANCES
TO ONE ARBITRATOR

When a union attempts to submit two or more nonrelated grievances to the same arbitrator in the same hearing,[20] a procedural issue often arises. If the labor agreement expressly provides that more than one grievance may be submitted at one hearing to one arbitrator, the answer is found in the agreement. But where the labor agreement is silent or vague on this matter, arbitrators examine the more general language relating to the grievance procedure to find the answer and generally permit a group of grievances, absent other controlling factors,[21] to be submitted at one time.

Arbitrator John F. Sullivan, in *Automatic Division of Yale & Towne*,[22] held that more than one grievance could be submitted to a single arbitrator where the contractual procedure stated that it was intended "to settle grievances in an orderly and expeditious manner." Likewise, Arbitrator Robben Fleming[23] said that a party is required to submit more than one issue in a single arbitration if the other party so desires, where the contract does not specifically deal with arbitration of multiple grievances and where "there is nothing in the past practice of the parties which furnishes a reliable guideline for reaching a decision as to what the parties intended." The fact that the grievance procedure section of the contract referred to "a question" and "the subject" in the singular, "does not indicate that single, rather than multiple, issues were to be heard in the actual arbitration proceeding. . . ." Fleming went on to say that where neither the

---

[20] The term "multiple grievance arbitration" must be distinguished from the term "multiple grievants" which refers to a single grievance involving two or more employees directly affected by a single management action (*e.g.,* assignment of a low-seniority employee to a vacancy when several other employees with higher seniority have bid for the vacancy), or where two or more employees are affected by what is asserted to be the same management action occurring at different times (*e.g.,* temporary transfer of three different employees to the same lower-rated job on three different days).

[21] *Standard Oil Co.,* AAA Case No. 3-3 (Fleming, 1959) (multiple grievances allowed since there was no past practice furnishing a reliable guideline); *West Va. Pulp & Paper Co.,* 71-1 ARB ¶ 8086 (Seinsheimer, 1971) (multiple grievances allowed, but arbitrator noted that a technical case may arise which would require a specially experienced arbitrator and thus would not be subject to combination); *Chamberlain Corp.,* 49 L.A. 355 (Duff, 1967) (multiple grievances must be submitted jointly unless the contract or past practice requires a contrary procedure).

[22] F.M.&C.S. No. 63A/1969 (Sullivan, 1963) (unpublished). See also *Pittsburgh Metallurgical Co., Inc.,* AAA Case No. 6-7 (Luskin, 1959) where it was held that even when the term "grievance" was used in the singular, a union had the right to combine grievances in the absence of express language to the contrary. But *cf. American Mach. & Foundry Co.,* AAA Case No. 28-9 (Norton, 1961) involving the term "grievance" in the singular, but buttressed by a past practice of submitting only one case at a time.

[23] *Standard Oil Co.,* AAA Case No. 3-3 (Fleming, 1959).

contract nor past practice provides a "satisfactory guide," it is fair to assume:

> "[T]hat the parties intended their arbitration clause to have the interpretation commonly accorded such clauses in the day-to-day practice of the industrial relations world. This practice is clearly in favor of multiple issues in a single arbitration proceeding. This practice is so universal that a contrary result should only be reached where the contract specifically indicates that such was the intention of the parties. This contract does not express any such intent." [24]

In *Perfection Biscuit Co.*,[25] on the other hand, Arbitrator O'Malley held that where the labor agreement referred to the processing "of a grievance" to arbitration, more than one grievance could not be submitted simultaneously to one arbitrator over the employer's objection.

Some arbitrators have permitted more than one grievance to be presented over the objection of the employer if the grievances were all processed through the steps of the grievance procedure simultaneously and reached arbitration at the same time.[26] Yet another arbitrator, to the contrary, said that simultaneous processing does not authorize the submission of a group of grievances to one arbitrator.[27] Similarly, a court directed that three factually unrelated grievances should be submitted to three different arbitration boards:

> "To permit an accumulation of disputes and then require that one board pass on all would be like requiring three unrelated matters in court litigation be tried by the same jury. . . . If complaints are of sufficient importance to require arbitration, the saving of some expense cannot outweigh the importance of having experienced and satisfactory arbitrators in each specific problem which they will be summoned to consider.[28]

Generally, courts hold that the arbitrability of multiple disputes before a single arbitrator is an issue which must be resolved by the

---

[24] *Standard Oil Co.*, AAA Case No. 3-3 (Fleming, 1959); see also *Pittsburgh Metallurgical Co.*, AAA Case No. 6-7 (Luskin, 1959); *Hamilton Cosco*, AAA Case No. 32-5 (Fisher, 1961); *Anaconda American Brass Co.*, AAA Case No. 130-16 (Keffe, 1969); *Waller Bros. Stone Co.*, AAA Case No. 22-13 (Luskin, 1960); *Dragon Cement Co.*, AAA Case No. 48-3 (Zack, 1962); *Fuller Co.*, AAA Case No. 63-20 (Unterberger, 1963); *Goodman Mfg. Co.*, AAA Case No. 64-15 (Jaffee, 1963); *Cleveland Pneumatic Tool Co.*, 54 L.A. 371 (Belkin, 1970).

[25] F.M.&C.S. No. 64A/1921 (O'Malley, 1963) (unpublished). See also *Day & Zimmerman, Inc.*, 51 L.A. 215 (Marshall, 1968); *Crown Zellerbach Corp.*, 21 ALAA ¶ 72,508 (Larson, 1964); *Remington Rand Univac*, 42 L.A. 65 (Lockhart, 1964); *Anaconda American Brass Co.*, AAA Case No. 51-12 (Turkus, 1962); *Erwin Mills*, AAA Case No. 88-10 (Porter, 1966); *Macy's New York*, AAA Case No. 91-8 (Rubin, 1966).

[26] *Koppers Co.*, 33 L.A. 392 (Schedler, 1959); *Armstrong Cork Co.*, 23 L.A. 13 (Williams, 1954); *W. Va. Pulp & Paper Co.*, 71-1 ARB ¶ 8086 (Seinsheimer, 1970).

[27] *Cit-Con Oil Corp.*, 24 L.A. 186 (Morvant, 1955).

[28] *Parker White Metal Co. v. Mine Workers Union*, 45 Erie Co. L.J. 315 (C. P. Erie Co., Pa. 1962).

arbitrator.[29] In *UAW v. Robertshaw Controls Co.,*[30] the court refused to grant the UAW's request for an order directing the employer to submit several unrelated grievances to a single arbitrator on the ground that an arbitrator had previously held that the applicable labor agreement did not require that result. Similarly, in *Fitchburg Paper Co. v. MacDonald*[31] and *Teamsters Local 469 v. Hess Oil & Chemical Corp.,*[32] the courts ruled that the procedural issue was one for an arbitrator, not for the courts, to resolve and accordingly ordered the issue to be arbitrated. While one court took judicial notice of the convenience and expediency with which one arbitrator could hear and resolve a series of grievances, it similarly ruled that the issue was one for the arbitrator.[33] In another case, however, it was ordered that all arbitration proceedings instituted by a union be consolidated into one proceeding on the ground that the interests of all the parties involved were common because all the grievances involved an interpretation of a consumer price index contract provision.[34]

Arbitrator Turkus in *Anaconda American Brass Co.*[35] decided against multiple grievance arbitration where the union had submitted nine separate and different grievances to a single arbitrator and where the individual grievances had arisen at various times over an 11-month period. He held that the resolution of the procedural issue required the arbitrator to ascertain the parties' contractual intent. He rejected the view that consideration of efficiency, expedition, and economy should be controlling. Rather he found that one arbitrator did not have authority to hear multiple grievances because (i) references in the grievance procedure were in the singular; (ii) a special procedure was established for "technical" disputes and disputes relating to discharge and discipline cases (indicating the parties did not want

---

[29] That questions of procedural arbitrability are ones for the arbitrator and not the court is settled by *John Wiley & Sons, Inc. v. Livingston,* 376 U.S. 543 (1964), a case that will be frequently cited throughout this book. Of course, the question of what is substantive and what is procedural has always plagued courts, and its resolution is no less difficult in this area than it is elsewhere. Several lower courts have held that whether or not multiple grievances should be arbitrated jointly before a single arbitrator or separately in different arbitration proceedings is a procedural matter of contract interpretation and is for the arbitrator and not the court to decide. *American Sterilizer Co. v. International U. UAW, Local 832,* 341 F. Supp. 522 (W.D. Pa., 1972); *Filchburg Paper Company v. MacDonald,* 242 F. Supp. 502 (D. Mass., 1965); *Teamsters Local 469 v. Hess Oil & Chem. Corp.,* 226 F. Supp. 452 (D. N.J., 1964); *Traylor Eng. & Mfg. Div. of Fuller Co. v. United Steelworkers,* 220 F. Supp. 896 (E.D. Pa., 1963); *Avon Products, Inc. v. International U. UAW, Local 710,* 386 F.2d 651 (8th Cir., 1961).

[30] 63 LRRM 2348 (S.D. Ohio 1966).

[31] 242 F.Supp. 502 (D. Mass. 1965).

[32] 226 F.Supp. 452 (D.N.J. 1964).

[33] *Traylor Eng'r. & Mfg. Div. of Fuller Co. v. United Steelworkers of America,* 220 F.Supp. 896 (E.D. Pa. 1963).

[34] *American Broadcasting Co. v. Brandt,* 72 LRRM 2210 (N.Y. Sup.Ct. 1969).

[35] 39 L.A. 814 (Turkus, 1962).

those kinds of cases, at least to be arbitrated with other types of disputes); and (iii) the parties' consistent past practice had been to arbitrate cases separately and individually. While noting that the parties had, on one occasion, mutually agreed to submit multiple cases to arbitration, he ruled that this one exception was not controlling as to the question of what was acceptable to the parties without mutual agreement.

In *Harshaw Chemical Co.,*[36] the arbitrator decided that multiple grievances could be decided in a single proceeding if (i) the grievances to be arbitrated all reached the arbitration stage at the same time and (ii) they involved issues which are not so dissimilar as to affect the parties' decision as to the arbitrator. Likewise, Arbitrator Dworkin in *Johnson Bronze Co.*[37] required the employer to present multiple grievances to arbitration where the grievances were not numerous and were processed at approximately the same time. The arbitrator went on to say, however, that the union waived its right to insist on multiple grievance arbitration when it sent separate submission letters to the Federal Mediation & Conciliation Service for each grievance. In *American Metal Climax, Inc.,*[38] Dworkin held that considerable weight should be given to past practices and, in the absence of such past practice, the controlling question should be whether a party is unduly prejudiced by the multiple grievance procedure. Dworkin held in that case that three "run-of-the-mill" disciplinary cases were sufficiently similar and that it would not be "burdensome" to the employer to arbitrate them together.

E. THE SIGNIFICANCE OF THE AGREEMENT TO BE BOUND BY THE AWARD

The statutes of five states require that the parties specifically agree, either in the labor agreement or in the submission agreement, to be bound by the award,[39] and in one state it is required that the parties post bonds to guarantee compliance with the award.[40] However, the most important reason why the parties should specifically agree to be bound by the arbitrator's decision is to avoid relitigation of the same issue by the National Labor Relations Board. Thus, the Board has announced that it will refrain from asserting its jurisdiction, even

---

[36] 44 L.A. 97 (Seinsheimer, 1965).

[37] 41 L.A. 961 (Dworkin, 1963).

[38] 69-2 ARB ¶ 8855 (Dworkin, 1969).

[39] Colorado (COLO. REV. STAT. ANN. ch. 18, Rule 109(b) (Rules of Civ. Pro. 1970)); Kentucky (KY. REV. STAT. § 417.020 (1962)); Michigan (MICH. STAT. ANN. § 417.454 (10.3) (1968)); New Mexico (N.M. STAT. ANN. § 22-3-4 (1953)); and Texas (TEX. REV. CIV. STAT. ANN. art. 242 (1959)).

[40] South Carolina (S.C. CODE ANN. § 10-1901 (1962)).

though a charge is filed raising an issue within the Board's jurisdiction, where an arbitrator's award has adequately resolved the issue.[41] More recently, the Board has specifically held that the federal labor law requires the parties to a contract to honor their contractual obligation to arbitrate rather than to ignore their agreed-upon procedure for the sake of pursuing other legal remedies under the LMRA.[42] This deference to arbitration, however, is contingent upon the parties having agreed to be bound by the award. This requirement that there be an agreement to be bound is one of the so-called *Spielberg* requirements set up by the Board in its *Spielberg* decision.[43]

The agreement to be bound can either be in writing in the labor agreement or in the submission agreement, or it can be implied from a uniform practice of submitting disputes to arbitration and complying with them.[44] Where a "claim of reservation" is made by a party about compliance with an award, the Board will not defer to the

---

[41] Section 10(a) of the LMRA provides that the National Labor Relations Board is empowered to prevent any person from engaging in an unfair labor practice and that this power shall not be affected by any other means of adjustment or prevention established by agreement. However, the Act also provides in Section 203(d) that "[f]inal adjustment by a method agreed upon by the parties is hereby declared to be the desirable method for settlement of grievance disputes arising over the application or interpretation of an existing collective-bargaining agreement." The Board has a problem of harmonizing its obligation under Section 10(a) to prevent unfair labor practices with its obligation to promote the private resolution of grievance disputes over matters such as discharges, which may involve matters which might well be considered an unfair labor practice. The balance between these two statutory objectives has been obtained by the development of a Board policy of deferring to an arbitration award previously issued by an arbitrator involving conduct which might constitute an unfair labor practice under Section 8 if the Board finds that the arbitration procedure was fair and regular, that all parties agreed to be bound by the award, and the decision of the arbitrator was not repugnant to the purposes of the Act. These three standards generate procedural considerations in arbitration and are referred to in various places in this study as the Spielberg requirements because the case in which they were first enunciated was *Spielberg Mfg. Co.*, 112 NLRB 1080 (1955). In the case where the union charges the employer has violated Section 8(a)(5) by unilaterally making changes in any condition of employment without complying with the requirements of Section 8(d), the Board has indicated that it will not assert its jurisdiction, in deference to the grievance-arbitration machinery, even where the union has not attempted to use that machinery, provided certain criteria are met. The requirements the Board has set up are that: (i) the contract clearly provides for a grievance and arbitration procedure, (ii) the unilateral action complained of is not designed to undermine the union and is not patently erroneous but rather is based on a substantial claim of contractual privilege, and (iii) it appears that the arbitral interpretation of the contract will resolve both the unfair labor practice issue and the contract interpretation issue in a manner compatible with the purposes of the Act. *Jos. Schlitz Brewing Co.*, 175 NLRB No. 23 (1968).

[42] *Collyer Insulated Wire*, 192 NLRB No. 150 (1971).

[43] *Spielberg Mfg. Co.*, 112 NLRB 1080 (1955).

[44] In *Denver-Chicago Trucking Co.*, 132 NLRB 1416, 1421 (1961), the Board based its finding that the parties had agreed to be bound by a Joint Grievance Committee's statement that the parties had followed the contractual grievance procedure for 18 years, and that no "claim of reservation" had ever been made by any party. See also *Local 18, Operating Engineers*, 145 NLRB 1492 (1964).

award. Thus, in *Hershey Chocolate Corp.*,[45] an attorney for some of the grievants advised the arbitrator of his intention to seek "other legal recourse" should the award be unfavorable, and hence the Board refused to defer to it because the employees had not agreed to be bound by it.

The Third Circuit, however, questioned the Board's refusal in *Hershey Chocolate* to defer, saying it doubted "whether the Board in this instance wisely rejected the arbitrator's decision."[46] Since that decision, the Board has deferred to awards even where one party asserted that the award was "tainted" by the unwillingness of the other party to be completely bound.[47] Hence, the statement that an agreement to be bound to the arbitrator's award is necessary before the Board will defer to the award is somewhat elastic, but, as a matter of practice, the agreement to be bound should always be clear.

F. SECURING PARTICIPATION OF ALL INTERESTED PARTIES

Although a majority of the disputes submitted to arbitration are bilateral, in some situations a union other than a party to the collective bargaining agreement from which the arbitration arose has a direct and substantial interest in the outcome of the proceeding. A court has denied enforcement of an award adversely affecting the interests of a nonparticipating union [48] and arbitrators have dismissed cases on the ground that a binding award could not issue unless another union was a party.[49] Also, the National Labor Relations Board has twice indicated that it would not defer to an award if the rights of a union not a party to the arbitration would be affected.[50]

The most common examples of such trilateral controversies are

---

[45] 129 NLRB 1052 (1960), *enforcement denied,* 297 F.2d 286 (3d Cir. 1961).

[46] *NLRB v. Hershey Chocolate Corp.,* 297 F.2d 286, 293 (3d Cir. 1961).

[47] *Edward Axel Roffman Associates, Inc.,* 147 NLRB 717, 724 (1964); *Insulation & Specialties, Inc.,* 144 NLRB 1540, 1543-44 (1963).

[48] See, *e.g., Jennings v. M. & M. Transportation Co.,* 104 N.J. 265, 249 A.2d 631 (Super. Ct. 1969). (After arbitration award giving one local a certain work assignment, a second local claimed the work. The International Union then made a jurisdictional award to the second local. The court held second award would be controlling.)

[49] *Ametek, Inc.,* AAA Case No. 62-6 (Loucks, 1963) (disputed work assignment was not within the jurisdiction of the arbitrator because the work in dispute had been assigned to a member of union which did not participate in the arbitration); *Pottstown Metal Products-Division of Cochrane Corp.,* AAA Case No. 12-21 (Crawford, 1959). (Grievance concerned promotion to a position in a unit represented by a union other than that to which the grievant belonged. The other union had declined to participate in the arbitration.)

[50] *Warm Springs Lumber Co.,* 181 NLRB No. 90 (1970); *Horn & Hardart Co.,* 173 NLRB No. 164 (1968), *aff'd,* 439 F.2d 674 (2d Cir. 1971).

"jurisdictional disputes."[51] In *Carey v. Westinghouse Electric Corp.*,[52] the Supreme Court ruled that the absence of one of the unions involved in a jurisdictional dispute does not affect the arbitrability of the claim of one of the disputants. As the Court noted, absent the participation of the other union, "an adjudication of the arbiter might not put an end to the dispute. . . . [but] may as a practical matter end the controversy or put into movement forces that will resolve it."[53] Justice Black dissented in *Carey*, stating that the lack of the second union as a party placed the employer in a "helpless position":

> "He is trapped in a cross-fire between unions. All he can do is guess as to which union's members he will be required by an arbitrator, the Labor Board, or a court to assign to the disputed jobs. If he happens to guess wrong, he is liable to be mulcted in damages. . . . [T]he employer cannot make a choice which will be binding on either an arbitrator, the Board, or a court. The Court's holding, thus subjecting an employer to damages when he has done nothing wrong, seems to me contrary to the National Labor Relations Act as well as to the basic principles of common everyday justice." [54]

Black's supposition proved correct in *Carey*, because the National Labor Relations Board subsequently declined to defer to the arbitration award stemming from the Court's decision in *Carey*.[55]

In *Lockheed-California Co.*[56] the arbitrator ruled that he had authority under the contract between the employer and the IAM to offer the United Welders Union, over the IAM's objection, an opportunity to join as a party the arbitration of the IAM's claim over work which the employer had assigned to the United Welders. Upon the Welders' acceptance of the offer, the arbitrator ruled that a "new"

---

[51] The term "jurisdictional dispute" is used here in the broad sense used by the Supreme Court in *Carey v. Westinghouse Electric Corp.*, 375 U.S. 261, 263 (1964), as including: "(1) a controversy as to whether certain work should be performed by workers in one bargaining unit or those in another; or (2) a controversy as to which union should represent the employees doing particular work." See generally Comment, *The Employer As a Necessary Party to Voluntary Settlement of Work Assignment Disputes Under Section 10(k) of the NLRA*, 38 U. Chi. L. Rev. 389 (1971), which deals with the question as to the necessity for an employer to be a party to a type (1) jurisdictional dispute.

[52] 375 U.S. 261 (1964).

[53] *Id.* at 265.

[54] *Id.* at 275.

[55] *Westinghouse Electric Corp.*, 162 NLRB 768 (1967). The arbitration award which the Board did not follow is *Westinghouse Electric Corp.*, 45 L.A. 161 (Feinberg, 1965). The cross-fire in which an employer can be caught when the issue in arbitration is a claim of a union to certain work when the other union is not a party is also illustrated by cases such as *American Sterilizer Co. v. Local 832, UAW*, 278 F.Supp. 637 (W.D.Pa. 1968), where two separate arbitration proceedings under separate collective bargaining agreements resulted in opposite interpretations of identical language in the two contracts. See also *Local 1505, Electrical Workers v. Local 1836, Machinists*, 304 F.2d 365 (1st Cir. 1962), *vacated*, 372 U.S. 523 (1963), with directions to dismiss the cause as moot.

[56] 46 L.A. 865 (Block, 1966).

ponents of this view do not see the problems of duplicative proceedings and inconsistent determinations as critical enough to interject the element of compulsion involved in an interpleader order.

The problems discussed above involve the need for participation of a different union, if its rights or the rights of its members will be affected by the award of the arbitrator. Related to these problems is the need for participation of individuals whose rights may be affected by the award. *Clark v. Hein-Werner Corp.*[68] was a case where a group of supervisors brought an action to enjoin the enforcement of an award that held that the supervisors could not displace employees in the unit in a work force reduction causing them to be laid off. The court enjoined the enforcement of the award on the ground that the supervisors were not represented in the arbitration hearing.

Arbitrators who have reacted to this court-announced view have pointed out that arbitration awards sustaining a claim by one employee that his seniority rights were violated would become invalid unless the junior employee and possibly everyone junior to the grievant received notice of the hearing and was given a right to appear.[69]

The Supreme Court in *Humphrey v. Moore* [70] determined that the relative seniority rights of large numbers of employees can be determined with the union representative without involvement of the individual in an arbitration proceeding. Where the rights affected are between individuals represented by the same union, such a view is consistent with the Supreme Court's views expressed in *J. I. Case* [71] that exclusive representational rights have been granted the union by the National Labor Relations Act. This rationale does not completely resolve the problem that confronted the court in the *Hein-Werner* case.

---

[68] 8 Wisc.2d 264, 99 N.W.2d 132 (1959), *cert. denied,* 362 U.S. 962 (1960).
[69] *Quality Aluminum Casting Co.,* 41 L.A. 580 (Marshall, 1963).
[70] 375 U.S. 335 (1964).
[71] *J. I. Case Co. v. NLRB,* 321 U.S. 332 (1944).

CHAPTER III

Enforcement of Agreements Arbitrate

The enforcement of the agreement to arbitrate future disputes, whether in a collective bargaining contract or in a special submission agreement, would in all likelihood come before a court under Section 301 of the LMRA,[1] but could also be raised under provisions of a state arbitration statute [2] or the U.S. Arbitration Act.[3] As pointed out in Chapter I, however, state and federal arbitration statutes would be applicable in enforcement proceedings only to the extent that they are compatible with the emerging federal law being created under Section 301. This chapter deals with the manner in which courts handle actions to enforce agreements to arbitrate.[4]

A. AN AGREEMENT TO ARBITRATE MUST BE ESTABLISHED

In any enforcement proceeding, an agreement to arbitrate must be established. The burden of proof is on the party urging the existence of such an agreement.[5] For example, where an employer sought to compel a union to arbitrate, a court denied the request on the basis

---

[1] 28 USC § 181 (1964).

[2] An enforcement of a refusal to arbitrate a back pay dispute was obtained under the unique Wisconsin Employment Peace Act, making the refusal to arbitrate a back pay grievance an unfair labor practice. See *Kiekhaefer Corp. v. Wisconsin Employment Relations Board,* 43 LRRM 2520 (Wis. Cir. Ct. 1958).

[3] 9 USC § 1, *et. seq.* (1964).

[4] Where the defense is that the issue is not one encompassed by an agreement to arbitrate, the defense is one of nonarbitrability. This defense is also dealt with in the next chapter because the granting of a stay for lack of arbitrability of the subject matter often involves the same considerations that are involved in the denial of the enforcement of an alleged obligation to arbitrate.

[5] *United Steelworkers of America v. Warrior & Gulf Nav. Co.,* 363 U.S. 564, 583, n. 7 (1960); *Atkinson v. Sinclair Refining Co.,* 370 U.S. 238, 241 (1962). In *Drake Bakeries v. Local 50,* 370 U.S. 254, 256 (1962) the Court held:
   "As was true in *Atkinson, supra,* the issue of arbitrability is a question for the courts and is to be determined by the contract entered into by the parties."
John Wiley & Sons, Inc. v. Livingston, 376 U.S. 543, 546, n. 1 (1964); *Int'l Union of Operating Engineers, Local 150 v. Flair Builders, Inc.,* 406 U.S. 487 (1972). *Torrington Co. v. Metal Products Workers Union, Local 1695,* 347 F.2d 93 (2d Cir. 1965), *cert. denied,* 382 U.S. 940 (1965); *Bethlehem Mines Corp. v. United Mine Workers,* 344 F. Supp. 1161 (D.Pa. 1972).

that the union's negotiator did not possess the power to bind the union to the purported agreement.[6] In another case, a clause in a collective bargaining agreement stating that when the grievance procedure is exhausted without satisfaction the parties "shall further make an effort to agree to dispose of the difference or grievance by means of arbitration," was held not enforceable as an agreement to arbitrate.[7]

Similarly, a company's promise to execute a collective agreement which would contain an agreement to arbitrate was not an enforceable agreement to arbitrate. Concerning the union's demand for arbitration, the court said "the union was seeking arbitration under a collective agreement that was never consummated." [8] Likewise, a company's written assent to be bound by an association agreement that had expired did not obligate the company to arbitrate a dispute under a subsequent agreement to which it had not signed a written assent.[9]

An agreement separate from the collective bargaining contract must be clearly incorporated by reference into the latter before an agreement to arbitrate contained in the basic agreement applies to disputes over the interpretation of the separate agreement.[10] For example, in a memorandum of agreement which provided that "the employer agrees to continue the pension plan in the form presently in existence," this language was held not to be a sufficient reference to show a clear intention of the parties to arbitrate grievances arising under the pension plan:

> "Inasmuch as the pension plan is not incorporated into the collective bargaining agreement, the grievance concerning the administration of its pension plan . . . does not fall within the ambit of paragraph 18 of the collective bargaining agreement which provides that arbitration is to be had concerning 'all grievances hereunder.' " [11]

Similarly, where the dispute arose over sick leave payments from a welfare fund, no agreement to arbitrate was established because the provisions establishing welfare benefits were not in the collective agreement.[12]

Some of the more recent case law, however, indicates that the law is taking a new tact different from that of the older cases. Thus courts,

---

[6] *Warrior Constructors, Inc. v. Operating Engineers, Local 1926*, 383 F.2d 700 (5th Cir. 1967).

[7] *Steelworkers, Local 4264 v. New Park Mining Co.*, 169 F.Supp. 107 (D. Utah, 1959). See also *Fredriksen v. Bornscheuer*, 213 N.Y.S.2d 799 (Sup.Ct. 1961).

[8] *Luggage Workers Union, Local 60 v. Major Moulders, Inc.*, 11 App. Div.2d 668 (N.Y. 1960).

[9] *Local 11, IBEW v. Jandon Electric Co.*, 429 F.2d 584 (9th Cir. 1970).

[10] *United Steelworkers of America, Local No. 1617 v. The General Fireproofing Company*, 464 F.2d 726 (6th Cir. 1972).

[11] *New York Racing Ass'n. v. Ind. Ass'n of Mutuel Employees of New York State*, 32 Misc.2d 867, 869, 224 N.Y.S.2d 784, 786 (Sup. Ct. 1962).

[12] *Pittsburgh Railways Co. v. Amal. Ass'n of Street, Electric Railway and Motor Coach Employees of America, Division 85*, 176 F.Supp. 16 (W.D. Pa. 1959).

in emphasizing that labor peace is promoted by agreements to arbitrate,[13] have been prone to look more carefully for the existence of such agreements. For example, the Eighth Circuit [14] decided that a statement in a letter from an employer to a union when withdrawing its proposals during negotiations that "[W]e will continue handling any grievances that may arise in accordance with the procedure set forth [in the draft agreement]" established an agreement to arbitrate a discharge grievance arising nearly a year later. When the union sought to arbitrate the discharge case, the employer replied that no agreement to arbitrate existed. The court, however, found that the letter to the union 10 months earlier constituted an interim agreement that the company would arbitrate grievance cases even though there had been no final agreement between the parties on the terms of the contract.

B. ENFORCEMENT OF AN AGREEMENT TO ARBITRATE NEED NOT DETERMINE THE MERITS

In an action to compel arbitration, the function of the court should be confined to ascertaining whether the party seeking arbitration is making a claim which is governed by the contract. This was made clear by the Supreme Court in the *Steelworkers Trilogy* [15] where it was held:

"The function of the court is very limited when the parties have agreed to submit all questions of contract interpretation to the arbitrator. It is confined to ascertaining whether the party seeking arbitration is making a claim which on its face is governed by the contract. Whether the moving party is right or wrong is a question of contract interpretation for the arbitrator. In these circumstances the moving party should not be deprived of the arbitrator's judgment, when it was his judgment and all that it connotes that was bargained for." [16]

The Fifth Circuit, reflecting on the *Steelworkers Trilogy,* articulated as follows:

"The merits of a suit to compel arbitration, of course, do not include the determination (1) of the underlying facts and (2) what the ultimate

---

[13] *Retail Clerks v. Lion Dry Goods, Inc.,* 369 U.S. 17 (1962); *Monroe Sander Corp. v. Livingston,* 377 F.2d 6, 9-10 (2d Cir.), *cert. denied,* 389 U.S. 831 (1967); *Columbian Carbon Co. v. International Union of Operating Engineers, Local No. 405,* 360 F.2d 1018 (5th Cir. 1966); *IUE v. General Electric Co.,* 332 F.2d 485 (2d Cir.), *cert. denied,* 379 U.S. 928 (1964). See discussion in Chapter IV, Section E.
[14] *Taft Broadcasting Co., WDAF AM-FM-TV v. NLRB,* 441 F.2d 1382 (8th Cir. 1971).
[15] *United Steelworkers of America v. American Mfg. Co.,* 363 U.S. 564 (1960); *United Steelworkers of America v. Warrior & Gulf Navigation Co.,* 363 U.S. 574 (1960); *United Steelworkers of America v. Enterprise Wheel & Car Co.,* 363 U.S. 593 (1960).
[16] 363 U.S. at 567-68.

outcome of the controversy will be. These, if the matter is arbitrable, are for the determination of the arbitrator. What and all that we must pass on here is the correctness of the district court's determination that an arbitrable controversy is presented.[17]

Where a company was ordered to arbitrate, one court rejected the company's plea that the court delineate the precise issue to be determined, stating that such an intrusion into the arbitration process by the court would be against "the more advanced thinking on arbitration," but others have concluded that delineation is a court's function where the issue is unclear.[18]

C. COMPLIANCE WITH THE GRIEVANCE PROCEDURE AS A PREREQUISITE FOR ENFORCEMENT

Questions of procedural requirements under the grievance procedure are to be determined by the arbitrator. While, at one time, there was variance among many courts as to the resolution of this issue, the Supreme Court in *John Wiley & Sons, Inc. v. Livingston* [19] made clear that "procedural questions which grow out of the dispute and bear on its final disposition should be left to the arbitrator."

Since *Wiley,* courts have consistently refused to look at "procedural" questions, taking the position that *Wiley* has accorded final disposition of such matters to the arbitrator.[20] For example, on the question of timeliness, in *Local 51, IBEW v. Illinois Power Co.,*[21] the Seventh Circuit was faced with the issue of whether a union waived its right to the grievance and arbitration procedure under the collective bargaining contract by not filing its grievance against the employer within the specific time limit provided for in the contract.

---

[17] *Gulf Oil Corp. v. Operating Engineers, Local 715,* 279 F.2d 533, 535 (5th Cir. 1960).

[18] Courts should not delineate: *Retail Shoe & Textile Salesmen's Union, Local 410 v. Sears, Roebuck & Co.,* 185 F.Supp. 558 (N.D. Cal. 1960); see also *General Tire & Rubber Co. v. Local 512, United Rubber Workers,* 191 F.Supp. 911 (D. R.I. 1961). Courts should delineate: *John Wiley & Sons, Inc. v. Livingston,* 376 U.S. 543, 546-47 (1964); *Local 616, IUE v. Byrd Plastics, Inc.,* 428 F.2d 23 (3rd Cir. 1970); *Piano & Musical Instrument Workers v. W. W. Kimball Co.,* 239 F. Supp. 523 (N.D. Ill. 1965). The Illinois court said the arbitrator could not second guess the court on the arbitrability determination, but arbitrators have not felt so constrained. *Wilshire Oil Co. of California,* AAA Case No. 65-9 (Roberts, 1964); *Socony Mobil Oil Co.,* AAA Case No. 72-14 (Turkus, 1965); *Hughes Tool Co.,* AAA Case No. 26-1 (Aaron, 1960); *Berkshire Hathaway Co.,* AAA Case No. 41-1 (Healy, 1961); *Macy's New York,* AAA Case No. 43-6 (Schmertz, 1962); *Celanese Corp. of America,* AAA Case No. 19-4 (Kahn, 1960).

[19] 376 U.S. 543, 557 (1964).

[20] See, *e.g., Radiator Corp. v. Operative Potters,* 358 F.2d 455 (6th Cir. 1966); *Avon Products, Inc. v. UAW,* 386 F.2d 651 (8th Cir. 1967); *Palestine Telephone Co. v. Local 1506, IBEW,* 279 F.2d 234 (5th Cir. 1967). See also *International Union of Operating Engineers, Local 150 v. Flair Builders, Inc.,* 406 U.S. 487, 92 S.Ct. 1710 (1972).

[21] 357 F.2d 916 (7th Cir. 1966), *cert. denied,* 385 U.S. 850 (1966).

On this rehearing of the case the court specifically held that *Wiley* was controlling and that the issue as to timeliness of the grievance was solely for the arbitrator. The same issue was posed in *Teamsters Local 776 v. Standard Motor Freight, Inc.*[22] and in *Chambers v. Beaunit Corp.*[23] In both those cases, the district courts similarly held that the issue of timeliness was for the arbitrator.

A question unanswered by *Wiley* is whether a court should vacate an award where the arbitrator's procedural ruling is particularly egregious. Such a case is *Farkash v. Brach*,[24] which predated *Wiley.* In *Farkash,* the contract provided that if the parties could not agree on a hearing date, the arbitrator could call a hearing on "such notice as he deems appropriate." The day set by the arbitrator for the hearing fell on a religious holiday for the employer. In spite of this, the arbitrator held the hearing. The court vacated the award on the grounds that due process required that the employer be given a chance to attend the arbitration and present his case. Such a court decision appropriately requires that an arbitrator's procedural ruling be in accordance with due process. As such, the court decision is eminently correct. Whether it is in accord with *Wiley,* however, remains to be seen.

The line between substance and procedure, of course, has never been an easy one to draw and this is no less true in applying the *Wiley* rule.[25] For example, where the contract specifically excluded from arbitration disputes over "standards of production established or changed by management," a grievance charging that a production standard was improperly changed by the company was held not arbitrable. The court rejected the union's contention that the provision in the agreement that "[a]ny case appealed to the arbitrator over which he has no power to rule shall be referred back to the parties without decision," excluded the question of arbitrability from court determination.[26]

In a very recent case, where a union waited several years before taking action to challenge an employer's alleged violations of a contract, the union was held by the Supreme Court not to have deprived itself of the right to compel arbitration. Reversing the Seventh Circuit, the Court explained that, while a court has the responsibility to determine whether a union and employer have agreed to arbitration,

---

[22] 260 F. Supp. 269 (M.D. Pa. 1966).

[23] 278 F. Supp. 62 (E.D. Tenn. 1967), *aff'd.,* 404 F.2d 128 (6th Cir. 1968).

[24] 52 LRRM 2334 (N.Y. Sup. Ct. 1963).

[25] See notes 69-70 *infra* and accompanying text.

[26] *Local 73, Amalgamated Meatcutters and Butcher Workmen v. Fred Rueping Leather Co.,* 282 F. Supp. 653 (E.D. Wis. 1968). See also *Beckley Mfg. Corp. v. Electrical Workers, Local 2011,* 296 F. Supp. 117 (D.C. W.Va., 1969).

a claim that particular grievances are barred by laches is an arbitrable question.[27] In dissent, Justice Powell, joined by Chief Justice Burger, argued that the equitable defense of laches, like fraud or duress in the inception of the contract, is a question properly within the province of courts to decide.[28]

The Fourth Circuit has reached the same conclusion, *i.e.,* that the issue of laches should be decided by the arbitrator.[29] The principal argument, in the Fourth Circuit's view, for leaving the issue to the arbitrator is that court litigation involves inordinate delay which is inconsistent with the national labor policy of speedy resolution of employee grievances.

D. EFFECT OF TERMINATION OF THE COLLECTIVE AGREEMENT ON ENFORCEMENT ACTION

As noted earlier, it is essential that there be an obligation to arbitrate before a court will order arbitration. Where the grievance arose during the life of the collective agreement but the demand to arbitrate occurs after the agreement expires, an order to arbitrate will usually issue,[30] for otherwise "a party [could] simply . . . stall the arbitration hearing until after the expiration of the contract and thus not be bound by the award." [31] Where it is not clear that the operative event took place during the term of the agreement, courts have refused to order arbitration.[32] Where four employees were discharged for activities in connection with a strike during a hiatus between two agreements, grievances over the discharges were held arbitrable because:

---

[27] *International Union of Operating Engineers v. Flair Builders, Inc.,* 406 U.S. 487, 92 S.Ct. 1710 (1972). But *cf. Clothing Workers v. Ironall Factories Co.,* 386 F.2d 586 (6th Cir. 1967).

[28] 406 U.S. 487, 92 S.Ct. at 1713-16.

[29] *Tobacco Workers v. Lorillard Corp.,* 448 F.2d 949 (4th Cir. 1971).

[30] *UAW v. White Motor Corp.,* — F. Supp. —, 69 L.C. ¶ 13,060, 81 LRRM 2222 (Minn. 1972); *Honeywell, Inc. v. United Instrument Wkrs.,* 307 F. Supp. 1126 (E.D. Pa. 1970); *Piano & Musical Instrument Workers, Local 2549 v. W. W. Kimball Co.,* 221 F. Supp. 461 (N.D. Ill. 1963), *rev'd,* 333 F.2d 761 (7th Cir.), *rev'd,* 379 U.S. 357 (1964); *Machinists, Lodge 2116 v. Buffalo Eclipse Corp.,* 12 App. Div.2d 875, 210 N.Y.S.2d 214 (1961); *Textile Workers Union v. Newton & Co.,* 394 Pa. 422, 147 A.2d 155 (1958); *Potoker v. Brooklyn Eagle,* 2 N.Y.2d 553 (1957).

[31] *Piper v. Meco, Inc.,* 302 F.Supp. 926, 927 (N.D. Ohio, 1968), *aff'd,* 412 F.2d 752 (6th Cir. 1969); *United Steelworkers of America v. Enterprise Wheel & Car Corp.,* 363 U.S. 593 (1960).

[32] *Teamsters v. Kroger Co.,* 411 F.2d 1191 (3d Cir. 1969); *Austin Mailers Union No. 136 v. Newspapers, Inc.,* 226 F.Supp. 600 (W.D. Tex. 1963), *aff'd,* 329 F.2d 312 (5th Cir.) *petition for cert. dismissed,* 377 U.S. 985 (1964).

"The grievance was action of the Employer in terminating the contractual right to present and future employment. It was these actions by the Employer after the new contract became effective that for the first time had any adverse effect upon the four employees. This was the action complained of, not the reasons given by the Employer for the disciplinary discharge." [33]

A dispute over a lockout which occurred during the period between two agreements, however, was not one that could be arbitrated because no agreement was in force when the dispute arose. The court said: "Whether such a contract exists . . . must be decided by the Court before any authority is conferred upon the arbitrator." [34] Finding no agreement in existence at the time of the grievance, the Sixth Circuit refused to order arbitration. Arbitration was also denied where the activity on which discipline was based, the discipline complained of, and the filing of grievances over such discipline all occurred during the hiatus.[35] But if the parties agree to arbitrate grievances which arise during the interval, they must do so.[36]

Where there is an agreement to arbitrate disputes over the terms of a new contract, the Fourth Circuit in *Winston Salem Printing Pressmen v. Piedmont Publishing Co.*,[37] found it enforceable even though the agreement containing the commitment to arbitrate the new terms had expired prior to receipt of the demand for arbitration. The court acknowledged that its opinion was in conflict with the First Circuit's holding in *Boston Printing Pressmen's Union No. 67 v. Potter Press* [38] that such disputes are not arbitrable after the expiration of the contract, but held that *Potter Press* no longer represented an accurate interpretation of Section 301 in light of *Lincoln Mills* [39] and later Supreme Court decisions, such as *Wiley* and the *Steelworkers Trilogy*.

---

[33] *Boeing Co. v. IAM*, 381 F.2d 119, 122 (5th Cir. 1967). *Contra, IBEW v. Wadsworth Electric Mfg. Co.*, 240 F.Supp. 292 (E.D. Ky. 1965).

[34] *Local 998, UAW v. B & T Metals Co.*, 315 F.2d 432, 436 (6th Cir. 1963). See also *Hilton Davis Chemical Co., Div. of Sterling Drug, Inc.*, 185 NLRB No. 58 (1970); *Teamsters, Local 996, Hawaii Teamsters v. Honolulu Rapid Transit Co., Ltd.*, 343 F. Supp. 419, 68 L.C. ¶ 12,767 (D. Haw. 1972).

[35] *Proctor & Gamble Independent Union of Port Ivory, N.Y. v. Proctor & Gamble Manuf. Co.*, 312 F.2d 181 (2d Cir. 1962), *cert. denied*, 374 U.S. 830 (1963). The NLRB has held that it is not a violation of Section 8(a)(5) to refuse to process a grievance to arbitration which arose during a period between old and new contracts. *Hilton-Davis Chemical Co.*, 185 NLRB No. 58 (1970).

[36] *Taft Broadcasting Co.*, 185 NLRB No. 68 (1970), *enf'd.* 441 F.2d 1382 (8th Cir. 1971).

[37] 393 F.2d 221 (4th Cir. 1968). See also *Div. No. 892, Amalgamated Ass'n Street, Electric Railway & Motor Coach v. MK&O Transit Lines*, 210 F. Supp. 351 (N.D. Okla. 1962).

[38] 141 F. Supp. 553 (D. Mass. 1956), *aff'd*, 241 F.2d 787 (1st Cir. 1957), *cert. denied*, 355 U.S. 817 (1957).

[39] *Textile Workers of America v. Lincoln Mills*, 353 U.S. 448 (1957).

E. ENFORCEMENT OF AN AGREEMENT TO ARBITRATE BY THE SIGNATORY UNION

Generally speaking, the only parties entitled to invoke enforcement of an agreement to arbitrate are the parties to the agreement.[40] In many instances the union will be the sole enforcer because many collective agreements do not allow the employer to present a grievance for arbitration.

In *United Electrical Workers v. Star Expansion Industries*[41] the court held that a union which was decertified after it had initiated the arbitration of a discharge dispute retained the right to process the grievance to a conclusion. The motion of the newly certified union for an injunction restraining the employer and the decertified union from proceeding with the arbitration was denied. The court noted that the arbitrator, when representatives of the newly certified union appeared at the hearing, ruled that the union which had initiated the arbitration could process the grievance to conclusion because "the duty to arbitrate is of contractual origin," and the successor union had no agreement when the grievance arose. "No legal theory is suggested which can permit [the successor union] to assert rights under a contract to which it is a complete stranger."[42] Moreover, "[T]o thrust upon the courts . . . a matter already decided by the arbitrator would be productive of delay and confusion and impair the federal policy in favor of arbitration."[43] It would better serve the "promotion and maintenance of industrial peace and stabilization" to permit the instant arbitration to "proceed untrammeled" to a conclusion.[44]

Likewise, the arbitrator in *Trumbull Asphalt Co.*[45] found that a decertified union retains standing to process grievances to arbitration after its decertification where the grievances arose and were initiated prior thereto.

These decisions, however, seem particularly questionable in light of the Supreme Court's decision in *John Wiley & Sons, Inc. v. Livingston*,[46] allowing a union to arbitrate grievances against a successor employer which never was a signatory party to the collective bargain-

---

[40] See, *e.g.*, *Local 13, Int. Longshoremen's & W.U. v. Pacific Mar. Ass'n.*, 441 F.2d 1061 (9th Cir. *rehearing denied*, 1971); *Vaca v. Sipes*, 386 U.S. 171 (1967); *Black-Clawson Co. v. Machinists*, 313 F.2d 179 (2d Cir. 1962); *Ostrofsky v. Steelworkers*, 171 F. Supp. 782 (D. Md. 1959), *aff'd*, 273 F.2d 614 (4th Cir. 1960), *cert. denied*, 363 U.S. 849 (1960).

[41] 246 F. Supp. 400 (S.D.N.Y. 1964). See also *A. Seltzer & Co. v. Livingston*, 253 F. Supp. 509 (S.D.N.Y. 1966).

[42] 246 F. Supp. at 401.

[43] *Id.* at 402.

[44] *Id.*

[45] 38 L.A. 1093 (Elson, 1962).

[46] 376 U.S. 543 (1964).

ing agreement. Moreover, the Second Circuit in *McGuire v. Humble Oil & Refining Co.*[47] has suggested that such a continuing right of a predecessor union will not be enforced where a merger of bargaining units has occurred and further processing of grievances by the displaced union could adversely affect the ongoing bargaining agent's authority.

A variation of this latter point was at issue in *Glendale Mfg. Co. v. Local No. 520, ILGWU,*[48] where the Fourth Circuit refused to enforce an arbitration award which required an employer to negotiate with a union pursuant to a wage reopening clause. Several days after the award was handed down, the union was decertified. A month later when it requested the employer to negotiate in accordance with the award, the employer refused. Unholding this refusal, the court held that to require the employer to abide by the award would be equivalent to ordering him to violate Section 8(a)(2) of the LMRA by bargaining with a minority union. Since it could not force the employer to commit an unfair labor practice, the court denied enforcement of the award.

F. ENFORCEMENT BY THE SIGNATORY EMPLOYER

If the labor agreement provides for appeals to arbitration by either the company or the union, then the company has the same standing to enforce an agreement to arbitrate as the union.[49] In this connection, the collective agreement involved in *Local 463, United Papermakers v. Federal Paper Board Co.*[50] provided that grievances may be filed by an "aggrieved employee" or the union, but after the grievance case reached the fourth step "either party to the dispute may call upon the American Arbitration Association to select an arbitrator." The court ruled that under this language the company could proceed to arbitration.

Where the agreement's language, however, did not give the employer a right to proceed to arbitration, a federal district court in Michigan held that the employer could not compel the arbitration of individual employee grievances over the objection of the union:

> "[I]t is far from clear that the company has the right to compel the union to arbitrate grievances, not of the company, but of employees. Such a procedure is patently so contrary to experience and common

---

[47] 355 F.2d 352 (2d Cir. 1966), *cert. denied,* 384 U.S. 988 (1966).

[48] 283 F.2d 936 (4th Cir. 1960).

[49] *Kentile Floors, Inc.,* AAA Case No. 103-3 (Sovern, 1967); *Kentile Floors, Inc.,* AAA Case No. 141-15 (Hill, 1967); *The National Cash Register Co.,* AAA Case No. 92-10 (Brandschain, 1966); *Chase Bag Co.,* AAA Case No. 61-15 (Elkouri, 1963); *Drake Bakeries v. Bakery Workers,* 370 U.S. 254 (1962).

[50] 239 F.Supp. 45 (D.Conn. 1965).

sense that in order for a contract to be so interpreted there would have to be the most lucid kind of language. Were the company seeking arbitration of *its* complaints and grievances, the complexion . . . would be very different." [51]

On the other hand, a federal court in Connecticut enforced the demand of United Aircraft Corporation that the union proceed to arbitrate a dispute over a one-day suspension of a union steward when the union had refused the employer's request to arbitrate and had taken the case to the National Labor Relations Board.[52] The court said that compelling the union to honor its contractual duty to arbitrate would not frustrate, invade, or otherwise interfere with the Board's proceeding to determine the union charge that the company engaged in unfair labor practice.

Another problem faced by the employer signatory is whether he is limited only to arbitration to resolve his disputes with the union. More often than not, an employer's grievance against the union revolves around the union's breach of the no-strike clause. In such circumstances, the employer is foreclosed from seeking damages in a court suit under Section 301, and is limited solely to seek redress under the contract's arbitration procedure,[53] unless it can be said with "positive assurance" [54] that the employer is barred access, by the contract, to its grievance procedure. This standard of "positive assurance" has led most courts to require arbitration of an employer's claim for damages resulting from a union's breach of its no-strike clause,[55] for the "positive assurance" test is, as one court noted, "an imposing litany to overcome." [56]

Given this, two late-vintage circuit court of appeals decisions are noteworthy since they appear to present an escape hatch from this "imposing litany." In both *G. T. Schjeldahl Co. v. Local 1680, IAM* [57] and *Boeing Co. v. UAW*,[58] the arbitrability of an employer's claim for damages for breach of a no-strike clause was litigated. While both courts recognized the strong national labor policy favoring arbitration, they also recognized that a claim for arbitration must be premised on a contractual provision. Reviewing the arbitration clauses in

---

[51] *Crescent Brass & Pin Co. v. UAW*, 36 L.A. 643, 644 (E.D. Mich. 1960).

[52] *United Aircraft Corp. v. Canel Lodge 700, IAM*, 314 F.Supp. 371 (D.Conn. 1970).

[53] *Drake Bakeries v. Local 50, American Bakery & Confectionary Workers*, 370 U.S. 254 (1962).

[54] *Atkinson v. Sinclair Refining Co.*, 370 U.S. 238 (1962); see also *United Steelworkers of America v. Warrior & Gulf Navigation Co.*, 363 U.S. 574 (1960).

[55] See, *e.g., ITT World Communications, Inc. v. Communications Workers of America*, 422 F.2d 77 (2d Cir. 1970); *H. K. Porter Co. v. Local 37, United Steelworkers of America*, 400 F.2d 691 (4th Cir. 1968).

[56] *IAM v. General Electric Co.*, 406 F.2d 1046, 1048 (2d Cir. 1969).

[57] 393 F.2d 502 (1st Cir. 1968).

[58] 370 F.2d 969 (3d Cir. 1967).

dispute, both courts concluded that they were "employee oriented" and hence did not allow an employer to demand arbitration.

In *Boeing,* the Third Circuit noted:

"Despite this liberal rule of construction a reluctant party may not be compelled to submit a controversy to arbitration unless under a fair construction of the agreement he is bound to do so. Absent a contractual obligation to the contrary, a reluctant party is free to pursue any available legal remedy to redress its grievances.

" . . .

"It is apparent from a reading of the contract that the grievance procedure is employee oriented. The grievance procedure is available only to the employees as 'the exclusive remedy for the disposition of any claim, dispute or grievance of any kind . . . *Against the Company.'* [Emphasis supplied]. Article VI, § 7. The only arbitrable grievances are those 'involving the interpretation or application of the provisions of [the] agreement which [have] been processed through Step 4 of the grievance procedure,' supra. The entire procedural structure is designed to resolve only the employees' grievances against the company. This seems obvious from a consideration of Article V-A (Grievance Procedure) and Article VI (Arbitration) in their entirety.

"It is our opinion that we have before us a case in which 'it may be said with positive assurance,' as in *Atkinson,* supra, that the arbitration clause is not susceptible of a construction that the plaintiff was bound to arbitrate the issues involved in its action for damages." [59]

Taking the same tack, the First Circuit held in *G. T. Schjeldahl Co.:*

"We recognize that the strong policy favoring labor arbitration requires doubts to be resolved in favor of arbitration. . . . However, where the undertaking in question was in all other respects oriented towards employee grievances only, the mere fact that the agreement contains a clause which might be more broadly construed if it were not limited by specific provisions is not a sufficient ambiguity. Nor is the belief that it would be preferable had the agreement been broader sufficient reason to make it so. That only employee grievances should be arbitrated is not a result absurd on its face. *Cf. Boeing Co. v. International Union,* 3 Cir., 1967, 370 F.2d 969. Our duty to determine whether under a proper construction of the agreement the parties agreed to arbitrate . . . does not require us to do violence to principles of contract interpretation." [60]

These two cases represent an interesting base point for analysis of collective bargaining contracts which, while not specifically excluding an employer's right to arbitrate, can be construed as such. Moreover, they are consistent with the Supreme Court's constant declarations that arbitration, while the preferable forum to resolve industrial disputes, is still only required where the contract so permits.[61]

---

[59] Id. at 970-71.
[60] 393 F.2d at 504-05.
[61] See, *e.g., Atkinson v. Sinclair Refining Co.,* 370 U.S. 238 (1962).

Where a union had ordered employees to refuse to work overtime and the employer could not under the labor agreement submit a grievance objecting to this union conduct to arbitration, a *Boys Markets* [62] injunction was held to be proper. The union claimed that the lack of ability to submit the issue to arbitration should deny to the employer the injunction.[63] The Third Circuit in *Avco Corp. v. Local 787, UAW* [64] said that all that *Boys Markets* requires is that both parties are contractually bound to arbitrate, and does not require that both parties be capable of initiating arbitration.

Another case posing the problem of who can enforce an agreement to arbitrate arose in the context of an employers' association.[65] There, a federal district court held that the association had standing to invoke arbitration on behalf of the member employers. Since the association was the employer's agent in contract negotiations and, therefore, a party to the agreement, the court said it could properly institute arbitration proceedings under a clause stating that either "the Employer or the Union shall submit the grievance to the [arbitration] committee."

G. ENFORCEMENT OF AN AGREEMENT TO ARBITRATE MADE BY A UNION THAT IS A PREDECESSOR, SUCCESSOR, OR A LOCAL UNION

The right of a successor union to represent employees in an arbitration initiated by the predecessor union became the issue in *United Electrical Workers v. Star Expansion Industries, Inc.*[66] The predecessor union had filed a grievance protesting the discharge of an employee; an arbitrator was appointed and a hearing was set. The labor agreement with the predecessor union then expired and the predecessor was displaced through a representation election. The successor union, relying on its certification as the bargaining representative, sought to displace the predecessor union as the representative of the dischargee. The arbitrator refused intervention by the successor union and the district court affirmed, saying that the certification of the successor gave successor no rights under the predecessor's expired contract with the employer since there is "no legal

---

[62] *Boys Markets, Inc. v. Retail Clerks Union Local 770,* 398 U.S. 235 (1970).

[63] The Union's claim was sustained in the District Court, citing *Avco Corp. v. UAW Local 787,* 325 F.Supp. 588 (D.C. Pa. 1971). See also *Stroehmann Bros. v. Bakery Workers Local 1427,* 315 F. Supp. 647 (D.C. Pa. 1970).

[64] *Avco Corp. v. Local 787, UAW,* 459 F.3d 968 (3d Cir. 1972).

[65] *Connecticut Labor Relations Division of New England Road Builders Ass'n v. Hoisting & Portable Engineers Local 478 of Operating Engineers,* 285 F. Supp. 311 (D. Conn. 1968).

[66] Note 41 *supra; contra, Duralite Co. v. Local 485 IUE,* 207 F. Supp. 273 (E.D. N.Y. 1962).

theory . . . which can permit it to assert rights under a contract to which it is a complete stranger." [67] Quite to the contrary, another district court held that a union that was displaced by a successor union in an NLRB election had no standing to bring a suit to compel arbitration of a demand to liquidate a pension plan established under an agreement with the predecessor union because the successor union, upon certification, became the representative of the employees and was therefore entitled to all rights and assumed all representational obligations under the pension plan. [68]

A related problem exists where the local of the union desires to proceed to arbitration and the international does not, or vice versa. It has been held that the local union has no standing to compel arbitration under a labor agreement executed by the international union "on behalf of" the local, [69] because the agreement is between the international union and the employer. In contrast, a district court declared that a dispute over whether a local union, whose request for the appointment of an arbitrator was endorsed by the multi-union unit, is the proper party to represent an aggrieved employee is a procedural question to be decided by the arbitrator. [70]

H. ENFORCEMENT BY AND AGAINST A SUCCESSOR EMPLOYER

In *John Wiley & Sons v. Livingston,* [71] there was a merger of Interscience Publishers, Inc. with the much larger John Wiley & Sons. As a result, Interscience, with whom the union had a collective agreement, ceased to exist as a separate entity. The union maintained, however, that its agreement with Interscience survived the merger and, at least in certain respects, was binding on John Wiley & Sons. The company disagreed; the union sued to compel arbitration; and the case made its way to the Supreme Court.

The Court first made it clear that: "Federal law, fashioned 'from the policy of our national labor laws,' controls." [72] The Court then proceeded to declare the answer dictated by federal labor policy:

> "It would derogate from '[t]he federal policy of settling labor disputes by arbitration,' *United Steelworkers v. Enterprise Wheel & Car Corp.,* 363 U.S. 593, 596 . . . if a change in the corporate structure or owner-

---

[67] 246 F. Supp. at 401.

[68] *Brewery Workers v. Stegmaier Brewing Co.,* 338 F. Supp. 1137 (D.C. Pa. 1972).

[69] *Local 12405, District 40 UMW v. Martin Marietta Corp.,* 328 F.2d 945 (7th Cir.), *cert. denied,* 379 U.S. 880 (1964).

[70] *Electric Boat Div., General Dynamics Corp. v. Bhd. of Carpenters and Joiners, Local 1342,* 242 F. Supp. 617 (D. Conn. 1965). See also *U.S. v. Pilot Freight Carriers, Inc.,* DAILY LAB. REP. No. 59, D-1 (March 24, 1972).

[71] 373 U.S. 543 (1964).

[72] *Id.* at 548.

ship of a business enterprise had the automatic consequence of removing a duty to arbitrate previously established; . . ." [73]

Did the Court reach this result because the parties intended it? Mr. Justice Harlan, writing the unanimous opinion, said no:

"The preference of national labor policy for arbitration as a substitute for tests of strength between contending forces could be overcome only if other considerations compellingly so demanded. We find none. While the principles of law governing ordinary contracts would not bind to a contract an unconsenting successor to a contracting party, a collective bargaining agreement is not an ordinary contract. . . . Central to the peculiar status and the function of a collective bargaining agreement is the fact, dictated both by circumstance . . . and by the requirements of the National Labor Relations Act, that it is not in any real sense the simple product of a consensual relationship. Therefore, although the duty to arbitrate . . . must be founded on a contract, the impressive policy considerations favoring arbitration are not wholly overborne by the fact that Wiley did not sign the contract being construed." [74]

Since *Wiley,* courts have required a successor employer, who purchased only assets, to arbitrate a grievance,[75] and have held a newly acquired company of a corporate buyer bound to arbitrate under the provision in the collective agreement of the seller when continuity of identity between the two is found to exist.[76]

In *McGuire v. Humble Oil & Refining Co.,*[77] however, where the acquiring company had an existing labor agreement, the arbitration clause in the labor agreement of the seller was held not to give the union who represented the employees of the seller the right to force the buyer to arbitrate a grievance under the labor agreement of the seller. The court's holding was predicated upon a ruling by the NLRB that those employees of the seller retained by the buyer were effectively merged into the unit represented by the union representing all the other employees of the buyer. The court distinguished *Wiley* on the ground that in *Wiley* the seller was unionized, but the buyer was not:

"In the light of *Wiley* we do not see how we can arrive at any other conclusion than that to direct arbitration here would disturb the harmony

---

[73] *Id.* at 549.

[74] *Id.* at 549-50.

[75] *Local Joint Executive Board, Hotel & Restaurant Employees Int'l Union v. Joden, Inc.,* 262 F.Supp. 390 (D.Mass. 1966); *Wackenhut Corp. v. United Plant Guard Workers,* 332 F.2d 954 (9th Cir. 1964).

[76] *Monroe Sander Corp. v. Livingston,* 262 F.Supp. 129 (S.D.N.Y.), *modified on other grounds,* 377 F.2d 6 (2d Cir. 1966). In addition to being required to arbitrate, an award requiring action by a predecessor can be enforced against the successor. *Burt Bldg. Materials Corp. v. Teamsters Local 1205,* 18 N.Y.2d 556, 277 N.Y.S.2d 399 (1966); *Morceau v. Gould National Batteries,* 344 Mass. 120, 181 N.E.2d 664 (1962).

[77] 355 F.2d 352 (2d Cir. 1966), *cert. denied,* 384 U.S. 988 (1966).

of the existing body of federal labor law and tend to foster rather than prevent industrial strife and unrest." [78]

Similarly, in *Owens-Illinois, Inc. v. Retail, Wholesale and Department Store Union*,[79] the court held that the purchaser was not bound by the seller's arbitration clause, distinguishing *Wiley* and relying on *McGuire v. Humble Oil & Refining Co.* As in *McGuire*, but unlike *Wiley*, another union was representative of the employees in the *Owens-Illinois* case. In addition to distinguishing the subject case from *Wiley*, the court also distinguished it from *Wackenhut Corp. v. Plant Guard Workers* [80] and *Steelworkers v. Reliance Universal Inc.*[81] In the *Wackenhut* and *Reliance* cases, the court pointed out, the purchaser continued to operate the acquired business with substantially the same employees and officials, while in the instant case the supervisors were different and only seven of the 110 employees had worked for the seller.

While *Wiley* certainly requires a successor-employer to arbitrate disputes of its predecessors, whether *Wiley* goes beyond this was examined by the Supreme Court in *NLRB v. Burns International Security Services, Inc.*[82] In that case, Lockheed Aircraft Company had contracted with the William J. Burns International Detective Agency for its plant protection service to replace the Wackenhut Corporation. At the time of the change, there was in existence a labor agreement between Wackenhut and the United Plant Guard Workers of America. Burns hired certain guards formerly employed by Wackenhut but Burns refused to honor the terms of the labor agreement between Wackenhut and the Union. The NLRB ordered Burns to do so on the basis of *Wiley*.[83] The Second Circuit, however, rejected the Board's ruling [84] and so did the Supreme Court. However, in so doing, the Court left its pronouncement in *Wiley* undisturbed:

> "We do not find *Wiley* controlling in the circumstances here. *Wiley* arose in the context of a § 301 suit to compel arbitration, not in the context of an unfair labor practice proceeding where the Board is expressly limited by the provisions of § 8(d). That decision emphasized

---

[78] *Id.* at 357.

[79] 276 F.Supp. 740 (S.D.N.Y. 1967).

[80] 332 F.2d 954 (9th Cir. 1964).

[81] 335 F.2d 981 (3d Cir. 1964).

[82] 406 U.S. 272, 92 S.Ct. 1571 (1972).

[83] *William J. Burns Int'l Detective Agency*, 182 NLRB No. 50 (1970); see also the three other cases decided with *Burns, Hackney Iron & Steel Co.*, 182 NLRB No. 53 (1970); *Kota Div. of Dura Corp.*, 182 NLRB No. 51 (1970); *Travelodge Corp.*, 182 NLRB No. 53 (1970).

[84] *Burns International Detective Agency v. NLRB*, 441 F.2d 991 (2d Cir. 1971). In *H. K. Porter Co. v. NLRB*, 397 U.S. 99 (1970), the Court refused to enforce a Board order requiring an employer to agree to a checkoff proposal as a remedy for its refusal to bargain. The Court did so because it held such relief compelling agreement was beyond the powers of the NLRB.

'the preference of a national labor policy for arbitration as a substitute for tests of strength before contending forces' and held only that the agreement to arbitrate, 'construed in the context of national labor policy,' survived the merger and left to the arbitrator, subject to judicial review, the ultimate question of the extent to which, if any, the surviving company was bound by other provisions of the contract.

"*Wiley*['s] . . . narrower holding dealt with a merger occurring against a background of state law which embodied the general rule that in merger situations the surviving corporation is liable for the obligations of the disappearing corporation. See N.Y. Stock Corporation Law § 90; 15 FLETCHER, PRIVATE CORPORATIONS (rev. ed. 1961), § 7121." [85]

Whether or not an employer is a successor has been held by some courts to be a question to be resolved by the court and thus the obligation to arbitrate could also be a matter for the court.[86] Other courts have said the question is to be resolved by the arbitrator.[87] Where the question is whether the agreement grants arbitration rights to employees in plants in only one division or in any plant in the company where the union represents the employees, has been held a question to be decided by the arbitrator.[88]

In both pre- and post-*Wiley* cases, where the successor is a trustee in bankruptcy, the trustee has been held not bound by the agreement to arbitrate contained in an agreement between the union and the bankrupt employer. For example, the Sixth Circuit said that enforcement of arbitration of a grievance claim that vacation amounts due were to increase as if the employer was still in business was not required. The bankruptcy court held it was not obligated to surrender jurisdiction to the arbitrator on such a claim since "labor peace was not an issue" and that the employees would be given a chance to prove their grievance claim in the bankruptcy court.[89]

Similarly, the Ninth Circuit approved the dissolution by a federal district court of a state court order compelling arbitration where the employer was bankrupt and its business was terminated. The court said that while federal policy favors arbitration of "ordinary" labor

---

[85] 92 S.Ct. at 1581.

[86] *Monroe Sander Corp. v. Livingston*, 377 F.2d 6 (2d Cir. 1967); *Office Employees Int'l Union, Local 153 v. Ward-Garcia Corp.*, 190 F. Supp. 448 (S.D. N.Y. 1961); *Retail Clerks Union, Local 428 v. L. Bloom Sons*, 173 Cal. App.2d 701, 344 P.2d 511 (1959).

[87] *U. S. Gypsum v. United Steelworkers*, 384 F.2d 38 (5th Cir. 1967). Subsequently, Arbitrator Rolf Valtin held U.S. Gypsum a successor and obligated to arbitrate under the predecessor's labor agreement. See *United States Gypsum Co.*, 56 L.A. 363 (Valtin, 1971), *United Electrical Workers v. Star Expansion Industries, Inc.*, 246 F.Supp. 400 (S.D.N.Y. 1964).

[88] *Teamsters Local 745 v. Braswell Motor Freight Lines, Inc.*, 392 F.2d 1 (5th Cir. 1968).

[89] *Muskegon Motor Specialties Co. v. Davis*, 313 F.2d 841, (6th Cir. 1963). *Cf. Koven & Bro. v. United Steelworkers Local 5767*, 381 F.2d 202 (3d Cir. 1967).

disputes, the bankruptcy court is resolving various controversies between various creditors of a debtor, and the employees' claim is another such claim and not "the type of grievance which is ordinarily the subject of arbitration under a collective bargaining agreement enforced pursuant to § 301(a)." [90]

I. ENFORCEMENT OF THE CONTRACT BY AN AGGRIEVED EMPLOYEE

While some commentators have argued that "the individual employee has rights under the collective agreement, the enforcement of which are not subject to the union's exclusive control," [91] the Supreme Court has expressly rejected this view in *Vaca v. Sipes*.[92] However, the Court held that, in the absence of a breach of its duty of fair representation,[93] the union, as collective bargaining agent, can control the processing of an employee's grievance, including the question of whether to submit it to arbitration:

"Though we accept the proposition that a union may not arbitrarily ignore a meritorious grievance or process it in perfunctory fashion, we do not agree that the individual employee has an absolute right to have his grievance taken to arbitration regardless of the provisions of the applicable collective bargaining agreement. In L.M.R.A. § 203(d), 29 U.S.C. § 173(d), Congress declared that 'Final adjustment by a method agreed upon by the parties is . . . the desirable method for settlement of grievance disputes arising over the application or interpretation of an existing collective-bargaining agreement.' In providing for a grievance and arbitration procedure which gives the union discretion to supervise

---

[90] *Johnson v. England*, 356 F.2d 44 (9th Cir.), *cert. denied*, 384 U.S. 961 (1966); *Riker v. Browne*, 204 N.Y.S.2d 60, 62 (Sup. Ct. 1960) ("A provisional receiver is born by order of the court. . . . He may affirm or reject the rights and obligations of the interest he is caretaking, and it would be inconsistent to compel arbitration . . . against him on obligations antedating his creation."); *Eastern Freight Ways, Inc. v. Local 707, Teamsters*, 300 F.Supp. 1289 (S.D.N.Y. 1969).

[91] Summers, *Individual Rights in Collective Agreements and Arbitration*, 37 N.Y.U. U. L. REV. 362, 384 (1962). See *Serra v. Pepsi-Cola General Bottlers, Inc.*, 248 F.Supp. 684 (N.D.Ill. 1965), as an example of one of the few cases which adopted this view.

[92] 386 U.S. 171 (1967). An exhaustive and excellent study of *Vaca v. Sipes* may be found in Lewis, *Fair Representation in Grievance Arbitration: Vaca v. Sipes*, THE SUPREME COURT REVIEW 81 (1967).

[93] In *Vaca*, the Court defined the concept of fair representation by noting (386 U.S. at 190):
"A breach of the statutory duty of fair representation occurs only when a union's conduct toward a member of the collective bargaining unit is arbitrary, discriminatory, or in bad faith."
In *Humphrey v. Moore*, 375 U.S. 335, 350 (1964), the Court said the union discharged its duty of fair representation if it "took the position honestly, in good faith and without hostility or arbitrary discrimination." See also *Ford Motor Co. v. Huffman*, 345 U.S. 330 (1953); *Steele v. Louisville & Nashville R.R. Co.*, 323 U.S. 192 (1944).

the grievance machinery and to invoke arbitration, the employer and the union contemplate that each will endeavor in good faith to settle grievances short of arbitration. Through this settlement process, frivolous grievances are ended prior to the most costly and time-consuming step in the grievance procedures. Moreover, both sides are assured that similar complaints will be treated consistently. and major problem areas in the interpretation of the collective bargaining contract can be isolated and perhaps resolved. And finally, the settlement process furthers the interest of the union as statutory agent and as coauthor of the bargaining agreement in representing the employees in the enforcement of that agreement. See Cox, *Rights Under a Labor Agreement,* 69 Harv.L.Rev. 601 (1956).

"If the individual employee could compel arbitration of his grievance regardless of its merit, the settlement machinery provided by the contract would be substantially undermined, thus destroying the employer's confidence in the union's authority and returning the individual grievant to the vagaries of independent and unsystematic negotiation. Moreover, under such a rule, a significantly greater number of grievances would proceed to arbitration. This would greatly increase the cost of the grievance machinery and could so overburden the arbitration process as to prevent it from functioning successfully." [94]

In a pre-*Vaca* case, Arbitrator Charles Short held that because the parties to the labor agreement were identified as the "Company" and the "Union," an employee had no right to be represented at an arbitration hearing by his own attorney and ruled that evidence submitted by the employee's attorney after the close of the hearing was inadmissible. Arbitrator Short noted:

"The grievance and arbitration procedure . . . of the collective bargaining agreement is to be enforced by the union and the company and not by individual employees. The union was the proper party to process the grievance . . . and [the grievant] has no right to seek redress individually in this arbitration. In particular, [the grievant] has no right to be represented in this arbitration by private counsel."[95]

There are, however, some situations where an individual employee may, without the consent of the union, seek to enforce his "rights" under a collective bargaining agreement, either in arbitration or by a suit under Section 301. An infrequent example is an appeal to arbitration by the employee made pursuant to an arbitration clause which expressly allows an individual employee to compel arbitration regardless of the desires of the union.[96] An instance where the employee can sue for breach of contract under Section 301 is where there is no grievance and arbitration procedure provided for under the collective agree-

---

[94] 386 U.S. at 191-92.

[95] *Roadway Express,* AAA Case No. 40-18 (Short, 1962). See also *Yale Transport, Inc.,* 41 L.A. 736 (Kerrison, 1963).

[96] *Cf. Black-Clawson Co. v. IAM Lodge 355,* 313 F.2d 179 (2d Cir. 1962).

ment.[97] For example, an action claiming a discharge was a breach of the collective bargaining agreement was maintained in a federal district court by a union and a discharged employee under Section 301 because the agreement contained no arbitration clause.[98]

Individual action by an employee under Section 301 to have his claim resolved by the court may also be warranted when the employer has refused to process the grievance under the contractual procedure so as to, in effect, repudiate that procedure:

> "An obvious situation in which the employee should not be limited to the exclusive remedial procedures established by the contract occurs when the conduct of the employer amounts to a repudiation of those contractual procedures. *Cf. Drake Bakeries, Inc. v. Local 50, Am. Bakery, etc., Workers,* 370 U.S. 254, 260-263. See generally 6A Corbin, Contracts § 1443 (1962). In such a situation (and there may of course be others), the employer is estopped by his own conduct to rely on the unexhausted grievance and arbitration procedures as a defense to the employee's cause of action." [99]

Where arbitration is provided as the exclusive remedy for employee grievances,[100] however, it is well settled that an employee must exhaust the grievance procedure before he can institute a Section 301 action.[101] And the cases are quite clear that such an attempt must be one that conforms to the requirements of the grievance procedure.[102]

---

[97] *Smith v. Evening News Ass'n,* 371 U.S. 195 (1962). One court has held that employees must exhaust administrative remedies provided for in an employment contract before they may resort to the courts, even though it was provided that controversies "may" be submitted to arbitration. The use of the word "may," however, did not provide the employee an option of going to court or arbitration. The Interstate Commerce Commission was required by federal statute to make provisions for the protection of employees adversely affected by the merger of railroads. One of the provisions of the rules of the commission was that any controversy "may" be submitted to arbitration. Although it was not necessary to rule on the meaning of the word "may," the court said: "While the Commission has provided that disputes 'may' be submitted to arbitration . . . the provisions made by the Commission for arbitration are mandatory and not permissive." *Arnold v. Louisville & Nashville R.R. Co.,* 180 F.Supp. 429 (M.D. Tenn. 1960). *Cf. Republic Steel Corp. v. Maddox,* 379 U.S. 650 (1965).

[98] *Bhd. of Telephone Workers v. New England Telephone & Telegraph Co.,* 240 F. Supp. 426 (D. Mass. 1965).

[99] *Vaca v. Sipes,* 386 U.S. 171, 185 (1967).

[100] *Belk v. Allied Aviation Service Co.,* 315 F.2d 513 (2d Cir. 1963).

[101] *Republic Steel Corp. v. Maddox,* 379 U.S. 650 (1965). *Accord, Woodward & Lothrop v. Bowers,* 67 L.C. ¶ 12,495 (1971); *Parsons v. Norfolk & Western R.R. Co.,* 310 F. Supp. 1197 (S.D. W.Va. 1970); *Rhine v. Union Carbide Corp.,* 343 F.2d 12 (6th Cir. 1965); *Giordano v. Mack Trucks, Inc.,* 203 F. Supp. 905 (D.N.J. 1962); *Henderson v. Eastern Gas & Fuel Associates,* 290 F.2d 677 (4th Cir. 1961).

[102] See, *e.g., Broniman v. Great Atlantic & Pacific Tea Co.,* 353 F.2d 559 (6th Cir. 1965), *cert. denied,* 384 U.S. 907 (1966); *Doty v. Great Atlantic & Pacific Tea Co.,* 363 F.2d 930 (6th Cir. 1966). See, however, *Merkle v. Kerrigan,* N.Y. S.Ct. Queens Co., 67 L.C. ¶ 12,479 (1972) where summary judgment dismissing an employee's wrongful discharge suit was denied as factual issues concerning whether a union had refused to timely process the employee's grievance were unresolved by an arbitrator, who had dismissed the employee's grievance as untimely.

For example, where grievances have not been in writing, contrary to the contractual procedure, courts have dismissed Section 301 suits on the grounds that the attempt to exhaust was not proper.[103] Indeed, some courts have also required the aggrieved employee, not only to exhaust the contractual grievance procedure, but his internal union remedies as well.[104]

This exhaustion requirement can be circumvented in a few limited cases. One is where the union has breached its duty of fair representation. If, however, the claim of lack of fair representation is not asserted and established, *Vaca* makes quite clear that the individual employee has no standing to compel arbitration or vacate or modify an award or proceed on the merits under Section 301. Under the test laid down in *Vaca,* it would appear that a union might, in good faith, be quite mistaken about the merits of an employee's grievance and validly deprive the employee of any remedy. The appropriate litigable issue under *Vaca* is whether the union has acted in an arbitrary, dishonest, hostile, discriminatory, or bad faith manner in dealing with the grievance. Absent a showing of one of these conditions by the employee, the union retains the discretion and authority to screen and settle grievances short of arbitration.[105] As noted by one court of appeals,[106] "[T]he union is permitted to exercise its discretion in prosecuting grievances." Indeed, it seems well settled that even a showing of negligence on the part of the union in processing a grievance is insufficient to amount to a breach of duty of fair representation.[107]

To the contrary, and standing against the great weight of authority,

---

[103] *Steen v. UAW Local 163,* 373 F.2d 519 (6th Cir. 1967); *Desrosiers v. American Cyanamid Co.,* 377 F.2d 864 (2d Cir. 1967).

[104] See, *e.g., Bsharah v. Eltra Corp.,* 394 F.2d 502 (6th Cir. 1968); *Foy v. Norfolk & Western Ry.,* 377 F.2d 243 (4th Cir.) *cert. denied,* 389 U.S. 848 (1967); *Neal v. System Board of Adjustment,* 348 F.2d 722 (8th Cir. 1965). But see *Orphan v. Furnco Construction Corp.,* 466 F.2d 795 (7th Cir. 1972).

[105] See, *e.g., Gratien v. Bethlehem Steel Corp.,* — F. Supp. —, 79 LRRM 2870, 68 L.C. ¶ 12,628 (1972); *Bartels v. N. Y. Lithographers & Photo Engravers,* 306 F. Supp. 1266 (S.D. N.Y. 1969); *Donnelly v. United Fruit Co.,* 40 N.J. 61, 190 A.2d 825 (N.J. Supreme Ct. 1963). In *Pfeiffer v. UAW Local 556,* Daily Lab. Rep. No. 216, D-1 (November 4, 1968), the UAW Public Review Board indicated that it will apply a more rigid and objective standard than the Supreme Court requires to determine when the union violates its duty of fair representation. In *Pfeiffer,* the local union declined to take the grievant's case to arbitration because the union attorney predicted that it had only a fifty-fifty chance of winning. The review board awarded the grievant several thousand dollars in lost wages and commented that "the odds here dictated pursuance of the claim." But see *Encina v. Tony Lama Co.,* 316 F. Supp. 239 (W.D. Tex. 1970), *aff'd,* 448 F.2d 1264 (5th Cir. 1971), where the union's decision not to go to arbitration in large measure because of the expense involved was upheld.

[106] *Watson v. Teamsters,* 399 F.2d 875, 880 (5th Cir. 1968).

[107] See, *e.g., Brough v. Steelworkers,* 437 F.2d 748 (1st Cir. 1971); *Bazarte v. United Transportation Union,* 429 F.2d 868 (3d Cir. 1970); *St. Clair v. Teamsters Local 515,* 422 F.2d 128 (6th Cir. 1969).

a New Jersey court concluded that a union's refusal to represent an employee and press his grievance claim is *ipso facto* arbitrary conduct on the part of the union and confers standing to sue in court on the employee.[108] This decision was an apparent attempt to compromise the majority and dissenting opinions in *Vaca*, but this case appears to be *sui generis*, except for one fleeting aberration by the First Circuit.[109]

Another example where exhaustion has not been required is where it would be futile for the employee to be compelled to present his grievance to the union. The most obvious example is where there is evidence of past racial discrimination sufficient to prove a consistent pattern of lack of fair representation so as to indicate that any attempt to exhaust the grievance procedure would be futile. *Glover v. St. Louis-San Francisco Ry. Co.*[110] was such a case. There, the complaint alleged in the clearest possible terms that a formal effort to pursue contractual or administrative remedies would be absolutely futile. As such, the Supreme Court held:

> "The allegations are that the bargaining representatives of the car employees have been acting in concert with the railroad employer to set up schemes and controversies to bar Negroes from promotion wholly because of race. If that is true, insistence that plaintiffs exhaust the remedies administered by the union and the railroad would only serve to prolong the deprivation of rights to which these plaintiffs according to their allegations are justly and legally entitled." [111]

Another example of futility is where an employer-union conspiracy is alleged.[112] It should be pointed out, however, that there exists a

---

[108] *Zalejko v. Radio Corp. of America*, 98 N.J. Super. 76, 236 A.2d 160 (1967). The court relied on *Vaca v. Sipes* holding that even though it may have acted in good faith, a union breached its duty of fair representation when it ignored the employee's offer to produce a conflicting medical opinion and acquiesced in the discharge and refused to press the matter to arbitration.

[109] In *Figueroa v. Puerto Rico Telephone Co.*, 425 F.2d 281 (1st Cir.), *cert. denied*, 400 U.S. 877 (1970), the First Circuit ruled that a union breached its duty of fair representation when it did not process the grievances of several employees. The First Circuit reached this conclusion, in spite of the fact that it found no bad faith on the part of the union, ruled that the union president vigorously sought redress for these and other employees before the NLRB and the courts, and found that the union's chances for redress in the grievance procedure, had it filed these grievances, were virtually nil. The First Circuit seems to have retreated considerably from its tenacious position in *Figueroa* when it ruled, several months later in *Brough v. Steelworkers*, 437 F.2d 748, 750 (1st Cir. 1971) that: "The Labor Management Relations Act imposes upon the exclusive representative only a duty of good faith representation, not a general duty of due care."

[110] 393 U.S. 324 (1969); see also *Transport Workers v. American Airlines*, 413 F.2d 751 (10th Cir. 1969); *Amal. Meat Cutters & Butcher Workmen v. Allen*, 298 F.Supp. 985 (W.D.Mo. 1969).

[111] 393 U.S. at 331.

[112] *Price v. Teamsters*, 46 F.R.D. 18 (E.D.Pa. 1969); *Desrosiers v. American Cyanamid Corp.*, 377 F.2d 864 (2d Cir. 1967).

very thin line between conspiracy and mutual agreement as to the administration of the contract.[113] That a union has a "wide range of reasonableness"[114] in negotiating and administering the contract, and particularly the grievance procedure,[115] should not be ignored.

If an employee is successful in proving the charge of "unfair representation" in a Section 301 suit, the court, rather than decide the merits of the claim, may order the company and union to arbitrate the employee's grievance, at which time the employee could have independent counsel.[116] This remedy has been utilized by the NLRB[117] in cases where the union is found to have violated its duty of fair representation under the National Labor Relations Act.[118] A New York court, however, has held that if the union fails to carry out its duty of fair representation, the employees may not process their own grievances at the arbitration since the union is their exclusive representative.[119] This being so, the only appropriate remedy is against the union for damages, not an action by the employees for the right to represent themselves.[120]

J. ENFORCEMENT BY THIRD PARTIES

In many instances, persons other than employees may be indirectly affected by the terms of the labor agreement and therefore desire to raise a complaint under it. Generally, as noted earlier, persons who are not parties to the agreement have no standing to compel arbitration under the agreement. For example, supervisors who are excluded from the terms of coverage of the agreement, persons who were promised benefits by an employer at a time before they transferred into the

---

[113] *Simmons v. Union News Co.,* 341 F.2d 531 (6th Cir.), *cert. denied,* 382 U.S. 884 (1965); *Union News Co. v. Hildreth,* 295 F.2d 658 (6th Cir. 1961).

[114] *Ford Motor Co. v. Huffman,* 345 U.S. 330, 338 (1953).

[115] *Vaca v. Sipes,* 386 U.S. 171 (1967); *Humphrey v. Moore,* 375 U.S. 335 (1964).

[116] *Cf. Columbia Broadcasting Co. v. American Recording & Broadcasting Ass'n,* 293 F.Supp. 1400 (S.D.N.Y. 1968). The right to independent counsel where there is a showing of unfair representation is fully discussed in Chapter VIII, Hearing, under Section F, *The Parties and the Aggrieved Employee's Rights to Select Counsel.*

[117] An employee is able to process a claim of unfair representation not only before a court, but also before the NLRB. *Miranda Fuel Co.,* 140 NLRB 181 (1962), *enforcement denied,* 326 F.2d 172 (2d Cir. 1963). In *Vaca v. Sipes,* 386 U.S. 171, 186 (1967), the Court "assumed" that breach of the duty of fair representation constituted an unfair labor practice.

[118] *Rubber Workers Local 12,* 150 NLRB 312 (1964), *enforced,* 368 F.2d 12 (5th Cir. 1966).

[119] *Koch v. Met Food Corp.,* 70 LRRM 2408 (N.Y. Sup. Ct. 1969).

[120] *Local 485, I.U.E.,* 170 NLRB No. 1234 (1968); *Port Drum Co.,* 170 NLRB No. 555 (1968), but see *Vaca v. Sipes,* 386 U.S. 171 (1967), *Czosek v. O'Mara,* 397 U.S. 25 (1970), which both indicate that even though a union has breached its duty of fair representation, it cannot be assessed for damages flowing from the employer's breach of contract.

bargaining unit,[121] or retirees [122] have no standing to seek arbitration either independently or through the union.[123]

The same type of analysis denies to civil rights groups and "outside" interest groups any right to submit grievances on behalf of employees and process them to arbitration or represent employees in arbitration who are already covered by an existing labor agreement and represented by a union. To recognize such a group as an employee's representative would be inconsistent with the legal rights of the certified union.[124]

K. ENFORCEMENT OF AGREEMENTS TO ARBITRATE BY THE NLRB

The National Labor Relations Board had ruled that a refusal to arbitrate grievances requesting reinstatement of strikers, discharged for engaging in picketing misconduct, was an unfair labor practice.[125] The Fourth Circuit, however, reversed the Board,[126] holding that the agreement which ended the strike was silent on the question of reinstatement and that the union representatives knew that the employer would not reinstate strikers who were guilty of misconduct. The court held that the terms on which the strike was settled did not include arbitration of disputes over reinstatement of strikers and hence the employer's refusal to arbitrate was not an unfair labor practice.

The Board later concluded that enforcement of agreements to arbitrate is a matter for the courts, not the Board. In *Hilton-Davis Chemical Co.*[127] the Board quoted with approval the following from a Second Circuit opinion:

> "The duty to arbitrate is wholly contractual and the courts have the obligation to determine whether there is a contract imposing such a duty." [128]

---

[121] *J. I. Case Co. v. NLRB*, 321 U.S. 332 (1944); *Ranco, Inc.*, 68-1 ARB ¶ 8197 (Klein, 1968). In *Ranco*, the arbitrator denied standing to arbitrate to employees who sought enforcement of a promise to make a gift of tools if they transferred into the bargaining unit.

[122] In *Van Dyne-Crotty, Inc.*, 46 L.A. 338 (Teple, 1966), the arbitrator denied standing to a "voluntary retiree" to compel arbitration of a grievance which arose after his retirement.

[123] *Flambeau Paper Co.*, 68-2 ARB ¶ 8404 (Hart, 1968).

[124] *Hotel Employers Ass'n of San Francisco*, 47 L.A. 873 (Burns, 1966).

[125] *Community Motor Bus Co.*, 180 NLRB No. 105 (1970).

[126] *NLRB v. Community Motor Bus Co.*, 439 F.2d 935 (4th Cir. 1971).

[127] 185 NLRB No. 58 (1970).

[128] *Proctor & Gamble Independent Union v. Proctor & Gamble Mfg. Co.*, 312 F.2d 181, 184 (1962).

CHAPTER IV

Stays of Arbitration

In the prior chapter, actions to enforce an agreement to arbitrate were considered. Closely related are actions to stay an arbitration.[1] If a request for an order to arbitrate is not granted, the effect is a stay. If the request for a stay is not granted, the effect is an order to arbitrate.[2] In this chapter, we are concerned with what the courts do when claims of procedural deficiency or of nonarbitrability are presented.

A. REQUEST FOR STAYS BECAUSE OF PROCEDURAL DEFICIENCY

When confronted with the claim of lack of arbitrability because of procedural deficiences, courts have held that questions of procedural arbitrability under the Supreme Court's decision in *John Wiley & Sons, Inc. v. Livingston* [3] should be resolved by the arbitrator.[4]

---

[1] As used here, the term "stay" encompasses not only the temporary cessation of arbitration pending the results of other litigation, but permanent termination of the arbitration which can also occur when a suit requesting arbitration for reasons of nonarbitrability or other defects is dismissed.

[2] See generally Rosen, *The Individual Worker in Grievance Arbitration: Still Another Look at the Problem,* 24 MD. L. REV. 233, 258 (1964); Smith, *The Question of "Arbitrability"—The Roles of the Arbitrator, the Court and the Parties,* 16 Sw. L.J. 1 (1962); Weiss, *Labor Arbitration in the Federal Courts,* 30 GEO. WASH. L. REV. 285, 293-301 (1961); Van de Water, *Growth of Third Party Power in the Settlement of Industrial Disputes,* 12 LAB. L.J. 1135, 1143-49 (1961).

[3] 376 U.S. 543, 557 (1964).

[4] *Meat Cutters Local 405 v. Tennessee Dressed Beef Co.,* 428 F.2d 797 (6th Cir. 1970); *UAW Local 864 v. Daniel Radiator Corp. of Texas,* 328 F.2d 614 (5th Cir. 1964); *United States ex rel. Madison v. Rundle,* 422 F.2d 49 (3d Cir. 1970); *Bevington & Basile Wholesalers, Inc. v. Brewery Workers Local 46,* 330 F.2d 202 (8th Cir. 1964); *Meat Cutters Local 195 v. Way,* 238 F.Supp. 726 (E.D. Pa. 1965); *Western Automatic Machine Screw Co. v. UAW Local 101,* 335 F.2d 103 (6th Cir. 1964); *Teamsters Local 776 v. Standard Motor Freight, Inc.,* 260 F.Supp. 269 (M.D. Pa. 1966); *Trailways of New England, Inc. v. Amalgamated Ass'n of Street, Electric Railway and Motor Coach Employees, Div. 1318,* 343 F.2d 815 (1st Cir. 1965); *Rochester Tel. Corp. v. Communications Workers,* 340 F.2d 237 (2d Cir. 1964); *Long Island Lumber Co. v. Martin,* 15 N.Y.2d 380, 259 N.Y.S.2d 142 (1965); *Local 1401, Retail Clerks Int'l Ass'n v. Woodman's Food Mkt., Inc.,* 371 F.2d 199 (7th Cir. 1966); *Brewery Workers Local 366 v. Adolph Coors Co.,* 240 F.Supp. 279 (D. Colo. 1964).

Even prior to *Wiley,* courts recognized that "the essence of arbitration [is] that it be speedy, . . . and . . . if procedural questions are to be passed on by the court it would open the door to all sorts of technical obstructionism." [5] The rule that the arbitrator, rather than the courts, should decide the procedural deficiency questions has been held not to apply to commercial arbitration where the special reasons for expeditious procedure are not present to the same degree as they are in labor arbitration.[6]

In a case concerning whether an employer had waived contractual time limits in the agreement by prior conduct, a federal court held that it was a question of procedural arbitrability which should be decided by an arbitrator, not the court.[7] The court noted that it was "unnecessary" to determine whether there were exceptions to the *Wiley* doctrine, for in deciding what procedural questions are "strictly procedural" would be, in most instances, to open a door closed by the *Wiley* decision.

On the other hand, courts have dismissed arbitration requests where the procedural defect is so clear that to refer the matter to an arbitrator would be an imposition upon all concerned.[8] Where a party admittedly has not complied with plain contractual time limits and offered no mitigating facts or contributory conduct by the opposing side as a defense, the Sixth Circuit in a post-*Wiley* decision has held that it would still be within the court's jurisdiction to bar recourse to arbitration.[9]

A unique procedural question was decided by the court in *Local 616, IUE v. Byrd Plastics, Inc.*[10] An initial arbitration had been dismissed by the arbitrator on the ground that the employee had not signed the grievance form as required by the contract. The grievance was then refiled over the signature of the employee. The employer refused to participate in the second arbitration on the ground that the first arbitration had disposed of the grievance and discharged the employer's duty to arbitrate. The second arbitrator disagreed with this argument and decided on the merits for the employee. The district

---

[5] *Local 748, IUE v. Jefferson City Cabinet Co.,* 314 F.2d 192, 195 (6th Cir. 1963).

[6] *Long Island Lumber Co. v. Martin,* 15 N.Y.2d 380, 259 N.Y.S.2d 142 (1965).

[7] *Brewery Workers Local 366 v. Adolph Coors Co.,* 240 F.Supp. 279 (D. Colo. 1964).

[8] See, *e.g., Boilermakers Local 483 v. Shell Oil Co.,* 369 F.2d 526 (7th Cir. 1966); *Boeing Co. v. UAW Local 1069,* 349 F.2d 412 (3d Cir. 1965). See also *Western Metal Specialty Div.,* 53 L.A. 878 (Solomon, 1969); *Ranco, Inc.,* 50 L.A. 269 (Klein, 1968).

[9] *ACWA v. Ironall Factories Co.,* 386 F.2d 586 (6th Cir. 1967). *International Union of Operating Engineers Local 150 v. Flair Builders, Inc.,* 440 F.2d 557 (7th Cir. 1971); *Amalgamated Clothing Workers of America v. Ironall Factories Co.,* 386 F.2d 586 (6th Cir. 1967). Contra, *Tobacco Workers International Union Local 317 v. Lorillard Corporation,* 448 F.2d 949 (4th Cir. 1971).

[10] 428 F.2d 23 (3d Cir. 1970).

court denied enforcement, but the circuit court reversed, analogizing the result of the first arbitration to a dismissal without prejudice. Although the court agreed with the finding of the second arbitrator that the grievance remained arbitrable, the court did not defer to his decision but reexamined the issue for itself.

B. STAYS BECAUSE OF CONFLICT
WITH THE NLRA AND FLSA

Where the National Labor Relations Board is involved, courts have issued stays of an arbitration proceeding to avoid a possible conflict between the decision of the Board and the award of the arbitrator. For example, a court has ruled that an arbitrator may not determine which of two rival unions is entitled to disputed work when that issue is pending before the Board.[11] There, an employer had filed a charge with the Board alleging that both unions had threatened to strike if their members were not assigned certain work and were, therefore, violating the National Labor Relations Act. One union petitioned the court to compel the employer to arbitrate the dispute over the work assignment and the company asked that the petition be dismissed on the ground that the National Labor Relations Board had exclusive jurisdiction over the issue. The court agreed with the employer, holding:

> "[T]he Board possesses the sole and exclusive jurisdiction to decide which of the rival unions is entitled to an assignment of the work form-ing the basis of the controversy between them, and that the provisions of the collective bargaining agreements with the unions, though among the factors to be considered by the Board, are not conclusive upon it and may be disregarded by it. It must follow that even if arbitration were ordered, pursuant to the collective bargaining agreement, any award made by the arbitrators would not be binding upon the Board, which alone has the jurisdiction to decide which union is entitled to the work. Permitting arbitration to proceed would undoubtedly lead, in many cases, to an award requiring an employer to assign work to one union, only to have the Board direct that the work be assigned to a rival union."[12]

Whether one union was entitled to recognition as the bargaining representatives of employees in a store, was held not arbitrable where a second union was seeking recognition of the same unit of employees under NLRB procedures.[13] The first union had a collective agreement

---

[11] *New York Mailers' Union No. 6 v. New York Times Co.,* 32 Misc.2d 60, 222 N.Y.S.2d 1000 (Sup. Ct. 1961).

[12] 32 Misc.2d at 62, 222 N.Y.S.2d at 1002.

[13] *Local 1357, Retail Clerks Int'l Ass'n v. Food Fair Stores, Inc.,* 202 F.Supp. 322 (E.D. Pa. 1961). See also *Amperex Electronic Corp. v. Rugen,* 284 App. Div. 808, 132 N.Y.S.2d 93 (1954); *Int'l Ass'n of Machinists v. Howmet Corp.,* 466 F.2d 1249, 81 LRRM 2289 (9th Cir. 1972).

with the employer in which it was designated the exclusive representative of the employees and subsequent to entering into this agreement, the employer contracted to supervise the operation of a second
store. The other union filed a petition with the National Labor Relations Board seeking an election in the second store to determine
whether it should be the bargaining representative. When the first
union requested arbitration of this issue, the court said:

> "Such matters cannot be ultimately decided through the grievance resolv-
> ing procedure of collective bargaining agreement where the rights of
> third persons, not parties to the agreement, are involved. Therefore, the
> relief requested by plaintiff cannot be granted by his court." [14]

Similarly, arbitration was enjoined pending conclusion of proceedings before the NLRB where the trial examiner made a preliminary
finding on the very question to be arbitrated.[15] The union initiated an
arbitration through the procedures of the Federal Mediation and Conciliation Service as specified in the collective bargaining agreement.
The employer instituted a Section 301 suit to enjoin the arbitration.
The court, granting the injunction, held that it would be repetitious to
arbitrate the very same issue which the trial examiner had decided.
Likewise, a court ruled that an arbitration initiated by a union would
be stayed where the issue to be referred to the arbitrator had been
ruled on by the Board, for otherwise there might be conflicting decisions on the same issue.[16] And, in *Lanco Coal Co. v. Southern Labor
Union Local 250*,[17] the court refused to enjoin a wildcat strike and
compel arbitration of the dispute, notwithstanding the broad contractual arbitration provisions and the *Boys Markets* decision,[18] because
the dispute was primarily a representation case over the employees'
dissatisfaction with their union and thus one "where the priority position of the National Labor Relations Board should be protected."[19]

At first glance, these decisions would seem to conflict with *Carey v.
Westinghouse Electric Corp.*[20] where the Supreme Court was confronted with a dispute involving a claim by a union that its members
should do certain work while the same work was being claimed by
another union for its members. The company had refused to arbitrate

---

[14] 202 F.Supp. at 324.
[15] *Kentile, Inc. v. Local 457, United Rubber, Cork, Linoleum & Plastics Workers*,
228 F.Supp. 541 (E.D.N.Y. 1964). But see *International Tel. & Tel. Corp. v. Local
400, IUE*, 248 F.Supp. 949, 950-51 (D.N.J. 1965) where the court said:
"The commencement of arbitration will not interfere with the pending decertification proceeding. . . . If the decision on decertification changes the representative
status of the Union the matter may be corrected upon suit to enforce the award."
[16] *Blue Bird Knitwear Co. v. Livingston*, 54 LRRM 2476 (N.Y. Sup. Ct. 1963).
[17] 320 F.Supp. 273 (N.D. Ala. 1970).
[18] *Boys Markets, Inc. v. Retail Clerks Union Local 770*, 398 U.S. 235 (1970).
[19] *United States v. Partin*, 320 F.Supp. at 275.
[20] 375 U.S. 261 (1964).

the claim of one of the unions on the ground that the dispute presented a matter within the jurisdiction of the National Labor Relations Board. The lower court refused to compel arbitration, but the Supreme Court, in reversing, noted that no matter how the dispute was characterized, arbitration should be held because of the strong federal policy favoring arbitration. Moreover, the Court noted, the NLRB's superior power could always be invoked thereafter. The Court articulated its rationale as follows:

> "However the dispute be considered—whether one involving work assignment or one concerning representation—we see no barrier to use of the arbitration procedure. If it is a work assignment dispute, arbitration conveniently fills a gap and avoids the necessity of a strike to bring the matter to the Board. If it is a representation matter, resort to arbitration may have a pervasive, curative effect even though one union is not a party.
> "By allowing the dispute to go to arbitration its fragmentation is avoided to a substantial extent; and those conciliatory measures which Congress deemed vital to 'industrial peace' . . . and which may be dispositive of the entire dispute, are encouraged. The superior authority of the Board may be invoked at any time. Meanwhile the therapy of arbitration is brought to bear in a complicated and troubled area." [21]

While there may appear to be tension between *Carey* and the decisions referred to previously, the latter are generally distinguishable from *Carey* because in the cases where the stays of arbitration were issued by the courts, the superior authority of the Board had already been invoked, thus rendering any arbitration meaningless; whereas, in *Carey,* the superior authority of the Board had not yet been invoked.[22] As for *Lanco Coal Co., supra,* this can be distinguished on the grounds that, unlike in *Carey,* the court felt that arbitration could serve no useful purpose because of the peculiar circumstances present there.

Where the NLRB has already decided the issue, the policy considerations for granting a stay of a demand for arbitration on the same issue are, of course, different.[23] For example, after two unions and the employer had joined in a petition to the National Labor Relations Board for a unit clarification, the Seventh Circuit refused to compel arbitration of a dispute over the unit because the Board's deter-

---

[21] *Id.* at 272.

[22] The superior power of the Board, however, was eventually invoked and its decision was contrary to that of the arbitrator. *Westinghouse Electric Corp.,* 162 NLRB 768 (1967).

[23] *Buchholz v. Local 463, IUE,* 15 App. Div.2d 394, 224 N.Y.S.2d 638 (1962), *aff'd* 15 N.Y.2d 181, 257 N.Y.S.2d 134 (1965). Of course, where the issues before the Board and the arbitrator differ, even though they are related, prior Board action is not a bar to a subsequent arbitration petition. See *Local 12934 of International Union, District 50, United Mine Workers of America v. Dow Corning Co.,* 459 F.2d 221 (6th Cir. 1972).

mination of the unit, adverse to the position of the union petitioning for an order compelling arbitration, fully disposed of the issue. In upholding a lower court's refusal to order arbitration, the court in *Smith Steel Workers v. A. O. Smith Corp.* stated:

> "Arbitration provides an alternative means of resolving disputes over the appropriate representational unit, but it does not control the Board in subsequent proceedings. . . . The court could compel neither arbitration nor enforce any arbiter's award in conflict with the Board's order." [24]

In a situation where the arbitration agreement precluded the filing of unfair labor practices, a court refused to stay the action before the Board, holding that the agreement was unenforceable.[25] This dispute concerned the misconduct of strikers. The union objected to the company action concerning the strikers and it was agreed that the dispute should be arbitrated. The union then filed an unfair labor practice charge with the NLRB which the company claimed it could not do under the agreement. The Second Circuit rejected the company's contentions, holding that such an agreement does not waive the union's right to file unfair labor practices because the rights under the National Labor Relations Act are public ones that cannot be impaired by a private agreement.[26]

Related to the decisions refusing to grant a stay where a claim could be submitted to the National Labor Relations Board and granting a stay when it has, are the cases where the stay of arbitration is asked for because the claim could be processed under the Fair Labor Standards Act. The Third Circuit, in a decision which the Supreme Court declined to review,[27] held that merely because a claim could be brought under the Fair Labor Standards Act, arbitration would not be prohibited. In a different context, the Sixth Circuit ruled that arbitration was mandatory despite the fact that the plaintiff-employee had a cause of action under the Kentucky workmen's compensation statute. The court found that the claim was clearly governed by the labor contract and as such was to be treated as arising under the

---

[24] 420 F.2d 1, 7 (7th Cir. 1969). See also *Local 464, American Bakery and Confectionary Workers International Union, AFL-CIO v. Hershey Chocolate Corp.,* 310 F.Supp. 1182 (M.D. Pa. 1970).

[25] *IAM Lodge 743 v. United Aircraft Corp.,* 337 F.2d 5 (2d Cir. 1964), *cert. denied,* 380 U.S. 908 (1965).

[26] *E.g., Hribar Trucking, Inc.,* 166 NLRB 745 (1967); *Breitling Bros. Construction Co.,* 153 NLRB 685 (1965); *Great Lakes Carbon Corp.,* 152 NLRB 988 (1965).

[27] *Watkins v. Hudson Coal Co.,* 151 F.2d 311 (3d Cir. 1945), *cert. denied,* 327 U.S. 777 (1946). See also *State v. Berry,* 434 P.2d 471 (Ore. Sup. Ct. 1968). *Contra, Andacht v. William Andacht, Inc.,* 183 N.Y.S.2d 62 (1958). See also *U. S. Bulk Carriers v. Arguelles,* 400 U.S. 351 (1971); *Iowa Beef Packers, Inc. v. Thompson, cert. granted,* — U.S. —, 92 S.Ct. 70 (1971). (Iowa Supreme Court held "it was optional whether employees arbitrated their claim for overtime compensation before suing in court under the FLSA.")

Labor Management Relations Act. Accordingly, the court held that arbitration should have been attempted prior to the filing of the suit.[28]

C. STAYS GRANTED FOR LACK OF A GRIEVANCE

A stay was granted where a dispute had not yet crystallized and any award the arbitrator would have rendered would be a request for an advisory opinion.[29] In that case, a union had petitioned to compel arbitration to determine whether the collective agreement should cover vessels which were to be transferred to a company in which the employer owned 26 percent of the stock. At the time the demand was made, the transfer was still contingent upon government approval. The court said that the matter was not arbitrable because "it merely calls for an advisory opinion."

A union received a stay of an arbitration claim that the increase in the union's dues and initiation fee was discriminatory and excessive on the ground that the claim did not establish any issue of discrimination against the employer.[30] When an employer contended, however, that the union violated the collective agreement when it disciplined a foreman who was also a union member and the union in reply contended its disciplinary procedures were internal union concerns, the court concluded there was sufficient merit in both contentions that arbitration should be directed.[31]

Similarly, there was no recognizable grievance against an employer's successor over a vacation pay claim where the union had executed and had delivered a general release discharging the employer and its successor and assigns from all actions in law or in equity which the union "ever had, now has or . . . hereafter can, shall or may have," save one claim unrelated to the controversy.[32] Where a claim is discharged by operation of law, the court held it "may not be subject to arbitration as it is not arbitrable under the collective bargaining agreement."[33] In contrast, another court held that it was for the arbi-

---

[28] *R.F. Rhine v. Union Carbide Corp.*, 343 F.2d 12 (6th Cir. 1965) *rev'g* 221 F.Supp. 701 (W.D. Ky. 1963).

[29] *District 2, Marine Engineers Beneficial Ass'n v. Isbrandtsen Co.*, 226 N.Y.S.2d 883 (Sup. Ct. 1962). See also *Lempco Automotive, Inc. v. IAM Local 1444*, 184 F.Supp. 114 (N.D. Ohio 1960), where settlement of the grievance caused the action to stay arbitration to become moot.

[30] *Stamford Transit Co. v. Teamsters Local 145*, 146 Conn. 467, 152 A.2d 502 (1959).

[31] *Pock v. New York Typographical Union No. 6*, 223 F.Supp. 181 (S.D.N.Y. 1963); see also *Houston Chronicle Publishing Co. v. Houston Typographical Union No. 87*, 272 F.Supp. 974 (S.D. Tex. 1966); *Macneish v. New York Typographical Union No. 6*, 205 F.Supp. 558 (S.D.N.Y. 1962).

[32] *L.O. Koven & Bro. v. Local 5767, Steelworkers*, 250 F.Supp. 810 (D.N.J. 1966).

[33] *Id.*, at 815.

trator, not the court, to determine whether a controversy was moot due to an alleged accord and satisfaction.[34]

A court has also examined the compliance of a union to the time limits for appeal because under many collective agreements the failure of the union to process the grievance within a time limit is evidence that the union accepted the last answer of the employer, and if acceptance has in fact occurred, no grievance remains to be arbitrated.[35] Such a holding, of course, raises serious questions as to whether the court is entangling itself in a procedural matter, contrary to *Wiley*.

Another illustration where a stay was granted for lack of a grievance involved a seniority claim arising out of a layoff.[36] The new collective bargaining agreement omitted the layoff provisions of the prior agreement and a letter accompanying the agreement explained that a joint study committee would be appointed to negotiate a mutually acceptable layoff plan by an agreed date or economic sanctions could be invoked. Since the parties were unable to agree on a layoff plan by the agreed date, a strike ensued. The court rejected the argument that the provision of the old agreement remained in effect during the negotiation period and thus denied the request for arbitration.

In a very recent case, an injunction was granted against the arbitration of a grievance brought by the union where the employer showed that the grievance was the same as a prior one earlier decided by a joint area committee.[37]

D. EFFECT OF A WILDCAT STRIKE ON THE DUTY TO ARBITRATE

Where there has been a strike in violation of the agreement, employers have often requested a stay of arbitration on the basis that the union's pledge not to strike was the *quid pro quo* for the right to arbitrate and the fundamental breach, caused by the strike, terminated the employer's obligation to arbitrate.[38] This view had little acceptance and the Supreme Court has expressly held in *Drake Bakeries*[39] and

---

[34] *Galveston Maritime Ass'n v. South Atlantic & Gulf Coast Dist., Int'l Longshoremen's Ass'n, Local 307*, 234 F.Supp. 250 (S.D. Tex. 1964).

[35] *Hall v. Sperry Gyroscope Co.*, 26 Misc.2d 566, 208 N.Y.S.2d 63 (Sup. Ct. 1960).

[36] *Radio Corp. of America v. Ass'n of Scientists & Professional Engineering Personnel*, 414 F.2d 893 (3d Cir. 1969). See also *City of Hartford, Conn.*, 71-1 ARB ¶ 8090 (Johnson, 1971).

[37] *Drake Motor Lines v. Highway Truck Drivers*, 343 F.Supp. 1130, 80 LRRM 3003 (1972). See *Signal Delivery Service, Inc. v. Teamsters Local 107, Highway Truck Drivers & Helpers*, 345 F.Supp. 697 (D.Pa. 1972).

[38] The Supreme Court has held that an agreement to arbitrate is the *quid pro quo* for a no-strike commitment. *Lucas Flour v. Teamsters Local 174*, 369 U.S. 95, 105 (1962).

[39] *Drake Bakeries v. Local 50, American Bakery & Confectionery Workers*, 370 U.S. 254 (1962).

Needham Packing [40] that arbitration rights under a collective agreement are not forfeited by the breach of the no-strike clause of the agreement. Courts have also refused to stay arbitration of grievances over the seniority rights of wildcat strikers [41] or the discharge of employees who participated in such a strike. [42]

The Second Circuit reexamined the effect of a strike in violation of a no-strike clause upon the right of a union to invoke the arbitration clause in light of, and after, the Supreme Court's decision in *Boys Markets* [43] and concluded that the strike did not cause a forfeiture of such rights. [44] However, there must always be a finding on arbitrability before a *Boys Markets* injunction will issue. [45]

E. STAYS GRANTED FOR NONARBITRABILITY OF SUBJECT MATTER

Before the *Steelworkers Trilogy* [46] there were many attempts to persuade courts to deny arbitration on the ground that the subject matter or issue presented in the grievance claim was one over which the arbitrator had no jurisdiction because it raised an issue which did not involve the interpretation or application of the labor agreement. What the courts have been doing since the *Trilogy* when a request for denial of arbitration is presented depends on the scope of the arbitration clause. The typical arbitration clause authorizing the arbitrator to decide questions of interpretation and application of the labor agreement is referred to herein as a "broad clause." Clauses which specifically exclude certain subjects from arbitration are

---

[40] *Local 721, United Packinghouse, Food and Allied Workers v. Needham Packing Co.*, 376 U.S. 247 (1964).

[41] *Wright Steel & Wire Co. v. Steelworkers*, 346 F.2d 928 (1st Cir. 1965); *Local 120, Textile Workers v. Newberry Mills, Inc.*, 315 F.2d 217 (4th Cir. 1963); *Local 748, IUE v. Jefferson City Cabinet Co.*, 314 F.2d 192 (6th Cir. 1963); *Retail, Wholesale Department Store Union, Local 1085 v. Vaughn's Sanitary Bakery, Inc.*, 196 F.Supp. 633 (M.D. Pa. 1961); *U.S. Pipe & Foundry Co. v. American Arbitration Association, Steelworkers Local 2026, et al*, 67 N.J. Super. 384, 170 A.2d 505 (1961); *Local 239, Molders & Foundry Workers v. Susquehanna Casting Co.*, 283 F.2d 80 (3d Cir. 1960); *National Cash Register Co. v. Wilson*, 7 App. Div.2d 550, 184 N.Y.S.2d 957 (1959).

[42] *Trailways of New England, Inc. v. Motor Coach Employees, Div. 1318*, 343 F.2d 815 (1st Cir. 1965), *aff'g.* 232 F.Supp. 608 (D. Mass. 1964); *Teamsters Local 677 v. Trudon & Platt Motor Lines, Inc.*, 146 Conn. 17, 147 A.2d 484 (1958); *Armstrong-Norwalk Rubber Corp. v. Local 283, Rubber Workers*, 167 F.Supp. 817 (D. Conn. 1958).

[43] See note 18, *supra*.

[44] *Teamsters Local 757 v. Borden, Inc.*, 433 F.2d 41 (2d Cir. 1970).

[45] *Parade Publications, Inc. v. Philadelphia Mailers Union Local 14*, 459 F.2d 369 (3d Cir. 1972).

[46] *Steelworkers v. Warrior & Gulf Navigation Co.*, 363 U.S. 574 (1960); *Steelworkers v. Enterprise Wheel & Car Corp.*, 363 U.S. 593 (1960); *Steelworkers v. American Mfg. Co.*, 363 U.S. 564 (1960).

referred to as "exclusion clauses." There are some unique cases under each heading.

(1) Stays Granted Under Broad Clauses

Courts have generally been reluctant to issue stays since the *Steelworkers Trilogy*.[47] In rare cases, however, stays have been granted. For example, a court has issued a stay in a case where an employee objected to a retirement consistent with a uniform 12-year practice never previously challenged.[48]

When one court examined the specific clauses of a labor agreement and the rights reserved to the management by the agreement, an arbitration was denied.[49] The agreement gave to the employer the right to reduce the work force for a short period without considering seniority and the grievants objected to the employer's disregard of seniority during a short-period layoff. In affirming the district court's declaratory judgment that the grievance over the layoff was not arbitrable, the Third Circuit found that the layoff was an authorized exercise of rights specifically reserved to management and, consequently, an objection to it was not an issue to be submitted to arbitration.[50]

On the other hand, a management rights clause providing that an insurance company has the exclusive right to determine the types and classes of policies to be sold did not prevent the arbitration of a union's grievance over the company's elimination of certain insurance policies and the substitution of others.[51] The federal district court added that if an arbitrator should decide in favor of the union, the arbitrator could grant relief other than requiring the reinstatement of the old policies.

---

[47] *Id.* Some commentators have viewed these three decisions as a reaction to the growing "rush to the court" whenever a colorable claim of doubt as to arbitrability was present. J. Freidin, LABOR ARBITRATION IN THE COURTS, 20 (1952). For a general discussion of these cases, see Smith and Jones, *The Supreme Court and Labor Dispute Arbitration: The Emerging Federal Law*, 63 MICH. L. REV. 751, 755 (1965); Levitt, *The Supreme Court and Arbitration*, 14 N.Y.U. CONF. LAB. 217 (1961). "[B]oth the number and the success of challenges to the [enforcement of the obligation to arbitrate] declined." ABA REPORT ON THE COMMITTEE ON LABOR ARBITRATION AND THE LAW OF COLLECTIVE BARGAINING, LABOR RELATIONS SECTION, 161 (1968). See also Snyder, *What Has the Supreme Court Done to Arbitration*, 12 LAB. L.J. 93 (1961); St. Antoine, *Contract Enforcement and the Courts, Labor Contracts in the Courts*, 15 LAB. L.J. 583 (1964); Davey, *Discussion*, MANAGEMENT RIGHTS AND THE ARBITRATION PROCESS, Proceedings of the Ninth Annual Meeting, National Academy of Arbitrators, 34 (J. McKelvey Ed. 1956).

[48] *Local 30, Philadelphia Leather Workers' Union of Meat Cutters v. Brodsky & Son*, 243 F.Supp. 728 (E.D .Pa. 1964).

[49] *Halstead & Mitchell Co. v. Steelworkers Local 7032*, 421 F.2d 1191 (3d Cir. 1969).

[50] See related discussion in Chapter III Section B.

[51] *United Insurance Co. of America v. Insurance Workers Int'l Union*, 315 F.Supp. 1133 (E.D. Pa. 1970).

Where no language in the agreement can be identified as applicable to the dispute and the arbitrator's jurisdiction is limited to an interpretation and application of the agreement, some courts have issued stays;[52] others have referred the matter to the arbitrator.[53]

(2) Stays Denied Under Broad Clauses

Under broad clauses, courts have referred to arbitration grievances over the omission of names from a seniority list;[54] establishment of new job classifications;[55] obligation to retire and the right to a pension;[56] promotions and reassignments;[57] rights to holiday and vacation pay after a plant closing;[58] the failure to pay overtime premiums;[59] the installation of new equipment;[60] wage payments;[61] a discharge of an employee at the request of the government;[62] the role of supervi-

---

[52] *Radio Corp. of America v. Ass'n of Scientists & Professional Engineering Personnel*, 414 F.2d 893 (3d Cir. 1969); *Boilermakers Local 483 v. Shell Oil Co.*, 369 F.2d 526 (7th Cir. 1966); *Boeing Co. v. UAW Local 1069*, 349 F.2d 412 (3d Cir. 1965); *Torrington Co. v. Metal Products Workers Local 1645*, 347 F.2d 93 (2d Cir. 1965); *UMW Dist. 50 v. Matthiessen & Hegeler Zinc Co.*, 291 F.Supp. 578 (N.D. W.Va. 1968).

[53] *Local 12934, District 50 UMWA v. Dow Corning Corp.*, — F.Supp. —, 69 L.C. ¶ 13,045 (E.D. Mich. 1971); *Monroe Sander Corp. v. Livingston*, 377 F.2d 6 (2d Cir. 1967); *Local 1401, Retail Clerks v. Woodman's Food Market*, 371 F.2d 199 (7th Cir. 1966); *Local 1416, IAM v. Jostens, Inc.*, 250 F.Supp. 496 (D. Minn. 1966); *A.S. Abell Co. v. Baltimore Typographical Union No. 12*, 338 F.2d 190 (4th Cir. 1964); *IBEW Local 702 v. Central Illinois Public Service Co.*, 324 F.2d 920 (7th Cir. 1963); *Fitzgerald v. General Electric Co.*, 23 App. Div.2d 288, 260 N.Y.S.2d 470 (1965).

[54] *United Furniture Workers Local 402 v. Mohawk Flush Door Corp.*, 212 F.Supp. 933 (M.D. Pa. 1963). See also *Southwestern Electric Power Co. v. IBEW Local 738*, 293 F.2d 929 (5th Cir. 1961).

[55] *Carey v. General Electric Co.*, 213 F.Supp. 276 (S.D.N.Y. 1962); *Cutting Room Appliances Corp. v. FLM Joint Board, United Mechanics, 150 Div.*, 75 LRRM 2288 (N.Y. Sup. Ct. 1970).

[56] *Butchers Union Local 229 v. Cudahy Packing Co.*, 59 CAL. REP. 713, 428 P.2d 849 (Sup. Ct. 1967); *United Saw, File & Steel Products Workers of America, Federal Labor Union 22254 v. H.K. Porter Co.*, 190 F.Supp. 407 (E.D. Pa. 1960); *International Tel. & Tel. Corp. v. Local 400 Professional, Technical and Salaried Div., IUE*, 290 F.2d 581 (3d Cir. 1961); *Communications Workers v. Southwestern Bell Tel. Co.*, 415 F.2d 35 (5th Cir. 1969); *Chemical Workers Local 19 v. Jefferson Lake Sulphur Co.*, 197 F.Supp. 155 (S.D. Tex. 1961).

[57] *Palestine Tel. Co. v. IBEW Local 1506*, 379 F.2d 234 (5th Cir. 1967); *Matter of Rollway Bearing Co.*, 11 App. Div.2d 753, 201 N.Y.S.2d 648 (1960); *Communications Workers v. Bell Tel. Laboratories, Inc.*, 349 F.2d 398 (3d Cir. 1965).

[58] *IBEW v. Westinghouse Electric Corp.*, 198 F.Supp. 817 (E.D. Pa. 1961); *Posner v. Grunwald-Marx, Inc.*, 56 Cal.2d 162, 14 Cal. Rep. 297, 363 P.2d 313 (1961).

[59] *Philadelphia Photo-Engravers' Union 7 v. Parade Publications, Inc.*, 202 F.Supp. 685 (E.D. Pa. 1962); *United Brick & Clay Workers and Local 790, United Brick & Clay Workers v. A.P. Green Fire Brick Co.*, 343 F.2d 590 (8th Cir. 1965).

[60] *Taft Broadcasting Co. v. Radio Broadcast Technicians Local 253*, 298 F.2d 707 (5th Cir. 1962); *Cuneo Eastern Press, Inc. of Pa. v. Bookbinders & Bindery Women's Union Local 2*, 176 F.Supp. 956 (E.D. Pa. 1959); *Bhd. of Locomotive Firemen & Enginemen Lodge 844 v. Kennecott Copper Corp.*, 338 F.2d 224 (10th Cir. 1964).

[61] *Socony Vacuum Tanker Men's Ass'n v. Socony Mobil Oil Co.*, 254 F.Supp. 897 (S.D.N.Y. 1966); *Columbian Carbon Co. v. Operating Engineers Local 405*, 360 F.2d 1018 (5th Cir. 1966).

[62] *IAM Local 2003 v. Hayes Corp.*, 296 F.2d 238 (5th Cir. 1961).

sion in employment procedures;[63] eligibility of a discharged employee for employment;[64] a discharge of an employee where there is no reference to discharge in the agreement;[65] discharge of a probationary employee;[66] improper classification of an employee;[67] refusal to reinstate a disabled employee;[68] refusal to displace replacements of strikers desiring to return;[69] assignments of work to an employee in another union;[70] walking off the job;[71] new time value for an incentive standard;[72] refusal of the employer to train an employee for a new skill;[73] scope of the appropriate unit;[74] refusal to pay fringe benefits;[75] lack of work due to suspension of operations because of a strike of another union;[76] discontinuance of employee discounts;[77] readjustment of delivery routes;[78] and subcontracting.[79]

Disputes over the nonpayment or the reduced payment of a small financial bonus, or the failure to provide a turkey at Thanksgiving or Christmas, however, have been held to be nonarbitrable issues under a broad clause.[80] The court explained its reasoning thusly:

"[T]he employer paid the Christmas bonus uninterruptedly over a period of years; yet neither the current collective bargaining agreement nor any

[63] *IAM Local 1416 v. Jostens, Inc.*, 250 F.Supp. 496 (D. Minn. 1966).

[64] *Teamsters Local 782 v. Blue Cab Co.*, 353 F.2d 687 (7th Cir. 1965).

[65] *Local 156, Packinghouse Workers v. Du Quoin Packing Co.*, 337 F.2d 419 (7th Cir. 1964); *IAM Lodge 12, District 37 v. Cameron Iron Works, Inc.*, 138 F.Supp. 144 (S.D. Tex. 1960).

[66] *Local 702, United Ass'n of Journeymen & Apprentices of the Plumbing and Pipe Fitting Industry v. Nashville Gas Co.*, — F.Supp. — ,76 LRRM 2417 (D.C. Tenn. 1970).

[67] *Acme Markets, Inc. v. Retail Clerks Union Local 1357*, 235 F.Supp. 814 (E.D. Pa. 1964).

[68] *Carey v. General Electric Co.*, 213 F.Supp. 276 (S.D.N.Y. 1962).

[69] *IAM Lodge 1652 v. International Aircraft Services, Inc.*, 302 F.2d 808 (4th Cir. 1962).

[70] *Carey v. General Electric Co.*, 213 F.Supp. 276 (S.D.N.Y. 1962).

[71] *International Molders & Foundry Workers Union Local 239 v. Susquehanna Casting Co.*, 184 F.Supp. 543 (M.D. Pa. 1960).

[72] *IUE v. Westinghouse Electric Corp.*, 268 F.2d 352 (3d Cir. 1959).

[73] *Local 459, IUE v. Remington Rand*, 191 N.Y.S.2d 876 (Sup. Ct. 1959).

[74] *Clanebach, Inc. v. Las Vegas Local Joint Executive Bd. of Culinary Workers and Bartenders*, 388 F.2d 766 (9th Cir. 1968).

[75] *Fruit & Vegetable Packers & Warehousemen's Local 760 v. California Packing Corp.*, — F.Supp. —, 54 LRRM 2625 (E.D. Wash. 1963).

[76] *IBEW Local 24 v. Hearst Corp.*, 352 F.2d 957 (4th Cir. 1965).

[77] *IBEW Local 702 v. Central Illinois Public Service Co.*, 324 F.2d 920 (7th Cir. 1963).

[78] *F & M Schaefer Brewing Co. v. Local 49, Brewery Workers*, 420 F.2d 854 (2d Cir. 1970).

[79] *UAW Local 463 v. Weatherhead Co.*, 203 F.Supp. 612 (N.D. Ohio 1962); *Westinghouse Electric Corp v. IAM Local 1790, Dist. 38*, 304 F.2d 449 (1st Cir. 1962); *United Cement, Lime & Gypsum Workers Local 206 v. Celotex Corp.*, 205 F.Supp. 957 (E.D. Pa. 1962); *Application of Morten, Inc.*, 216 N.Y.S.2d 825 (Sup. Ct. 1961); *IUE v. General Electric Co.*, 332 F.2d 485 (2d Cir. 1964); *Cluett, Peabody & Co. v. Clothing Workers*, 17 Misc.2d 582, 188 N.Y.S.2d 695 (Sup. Ct. 1959).

[80] *Boeing Co. v. UAW Local 1069*, 349 F.2d 412 (3d Cir. 1965). *Accord, Progress Bulletin Publishing Co.*, 182 NLRB No. 135 (1970) (contract silent on Christmas bonus, so solution to the dispute does not turn on interpretation of contract).

of its predecessors mentions a bonus or binds the employer to continue it. . . . There is no mention anywhere of bonus or the slightest suggestion that either party contemplated that the Christmas bonus paid voluntarily by the employer was within the provisions of the agreement. It clearly was not and, therefore, may not be made the subject of an arbitrable dispute under it." [81]

On the other hand, the failure to pay a Christmas bonus has been held by other courts to be an arbitrable grievance under a broad arbitration clause. [82]

The courts have adopted some general tests to determine a claim that the subject matter of a dispute is nonarbitrable. Interpreting a contract which excluded from arbitration all questions "involving changes in the terms and provisions of this agreement," the First Circuit held that it would not deny arbitration under such contract language unless it could say " 'with positive assurance' that a decision in the union's favor would necessarily constitute a change in the terms of the agreement." [83]

Another general test used by courts involves the use of bargaining history to determine arbitrability of the subject matter. Courts generally hold that where bargaining history must be referred to in an effort to prove nonarbitrability of the subject matter, then the language of the agreement is not clear enough to foreclose arbitration and the question of arbitrability should be referred to the arbitrator. [84]

There are some interesting post-*Trilogy* decisions in several circuit courts which exemplify that a strict reading of a contract, even under a broad arbitration clause, will lead to a conclusion that a claim is nonarbitrable. In *Independent Petroleum Workers of America, Inc. v.*

---

[81] *Supreme Knitting Machine Co. v. Amalgamated Machine Metal and Instrument Local 485*, 32 Misc.2d 1010, 224 N.Y.S.2d 45 (Sup. Ct. 1962).

[82] *Newspaper Guild of Buffalo Local 26 v. Tonawanda Publishing Co.*, 20 App. Div.2d 211, 245 N.Y.S.2d 832 (1964); *Hirt v. N.Y. Automatic Canteen Corp.*, 295 N.Y.S.2d 142 (Sup. Ct. 1968); *Akron Typographical Union No. 182 v. Beacon Journal Publishing Co.*, — F.Supp. —, 72 LRRM 2362 (N.D. Ohio 1968), aff'd, 416 F.2d 969 (6th Cir.) cert. den'd, 396 U.S. 959 (1969); *Harris Structural Steel Co. v. Steelworkers Local 3682*, 298 F.2d 363 (3d Cir. 1962).

[83] *Camden Industries Co. v. Carpenters Local 1688*, 353 F.2d 178, 180 (1st Cir. 1965).

[84] *IUE v. General Electric Co.*, 332 F.2d 485, 490 (2d Cir. 1964). See also *Communications Workers v. Southwestern Bell Tel. Co.*, 415 F.2d 35 (5th Cir. 1969); *Order of Repeatermen and Toll Test-Boardmen Local 1011, IBEW v. Bell Tel. Co. of Nevada*, 254 F.Supp. 462 (D. Nev. 1966); *Local 483, Boilermakers v. Shell Oil Co.*, 369 F.2d 526 (7th Cir. 1966); *Insurance Workers Int'l Union v. Home Life Insurance Co.*, 255 F.Supp. 926 (E.D. Pa. 1966); *Communications Workers v. Bell Tel. Laboratories, Inc.*, 349 F.2d 398 (3d Cir. 1965); *Acme Markets, Inc. v. Retail Clerks Union Local 1357*, 235 F.Supp. 814 (E.D. Pa. 1964); *A. S. Abell Co. v. Baltimore Typographical Union No. 12*, 338 F.2d 190 (4th Cir. 1964); *Ass'n of Westinghouse Salaried Employees v. Westinghouse Electric Corp.*, 283 F.2d 93 (3d Cir. 1960).

American Oil Co.,[85] the collective bargaining agreement provided that "questions directly involving or arising from applications, interpretations or alleged violations of the terms of this agreement," were subject to arbitration. The Seventh Circuit held that the employer was not required to arbitrate a dispute concerning the subcontracting out of certain work because there was no clause referring to subcontracting and "the mere allegation that the agreement has been violated" did not entitle a party to submit a dispute to arbitration. According to the court, the bargaining history of the parties demonstrated that the union had been unsuccessful in attempting to prohibit the company's right to contract out work.

The *American Oil* case was relied on by the Seventh Circuit in *Local 483, International Brotherhood of Boilermakers v. Shell Oil Co.*[86] The court, in discussing its prior opinion, stated:

> "But fundamentally the question decided there, and here, is that when arbitration is limited in the bargaining agreement to questions involving the application and interpretation of the agreement, and the agreement does not limit the freedom of the employer to contract out work, a court should not compel arbitration. This court there considered the Supreme Court cases (the *Steelworkers Trilogy*) relied upon here and found that those cases did not change the principle 'that compulsory arbitration cannot be properly awarded absent a contract between the parties agreeing thereto.' 324 F.2d at 906. The court there considered as having 'some significance' the bargaining history between the parties, which showed the Union's lack of success in gaining an agreement prohibiting or limiting the company's right to contract out work, and the silence of the contract on the point." [87]

Along these same lines, the Second Circuit said it was error to refuse to accept evidence of bargaining history where the meaning of an exclusionary clause was the issue before the district court.[88]

(3) Stays Granted Under Exclusionary Clauses

A clause excluding a subject matter from arbitration can be construed as an instruction to the arbitrator as well as to a court. When the matter comes first to the court the courts have stated that where the issue is clearly one excluded from arbitration by a specific exclu-

---

[85] 324 F.2d 903 (7th Cir. 1963), *aff'd by an equally divided court*, 379 U.S. 130 (1964). *Accord, Teamsters v. Blue Cab Co.*, 353 F.2d 687 (7th Cir. 1964); *Pacific Northwest Bell Tel. Co. v. Communications Workers*, 310 F.2d 244 (9th Cir. 1962); *Independent Soap Workers v. Proctor & Gamble*, 314 F.2d 38 (9th Cir.), *cert. denied*, 374 U.S. 807 (1963); *Columbian Carbon Co. v. IUE Local 405*, 360 F.2d 1018 (5th Cir. 1966). See *Boilermakers v. Shell Oil Co.*, 369 F.2d 526 (7th Cir. 1966).

[86] 369 F.2d 526 (7th Cir. 1966). See also *Associated Milk Dealers, Inc. v. Milk Drivers Union*, 422 F.2d 546 (7th Cir. 1970).

[87] 369 F.2d at 529.

[88] *Strauss v. Silvercup Bakers, Inc.*, 353 F.2d 555 (2d Cir. 1965).

sion clause, the party asking for the stay order should receive it so as not to be required to go through an arbitration when it bargained not to be so required.

In *Playboy Clubs International v. Hotel & Restaurant Employees & Bartenders Union*,[89] the employer moved for a preliminary injunction staying arbitration proceedings arising during the discharges of "Bunnies" for "lack of Bunny image" because the collective contract (i) restricts arbitration to discharge for union activity and (ii) provides a special three-step procedure, in which the executive vice president of the employer has the right to make the final decision with respect to discharge for any other reason including failing to maintain "the Bunny image." The court found that there was no claim by the union that the 13 discharges in issue were for union activity. The court granted the employer's motion to stay the arbitration proceedings.

When a party argues that grievances over certain subjects cannot be appealed to arbitration because of a clause excluding the subject matter, that party making the argument must realize that the merits of the claim may then be decided by the court. If the arbitrator cannot interpret and apply the agreement, courts do not conclude that an alleged violation of the agreement has no remedy, but rather hold that the court can determine the dispute. In *UAW Local 391 v. Webster Electric Co.*,[90] the employer contracted out janitorial work and thereby displaced three employees. The court held that since there was no arbitration clause, the question of contracting out was for the judiciary and not for an arbitrator. The court concluded by finding that the employer's action violated the union shop provision of the collective bargaining agreement.

In another case, a stay was granted in a dispute over a promotion when the agreement said "in no event" shall a dispute arising out of the promotion clause "be subject to arbitration." The court said the exclusionary language foreclosed arbitration in spite of the Supreme Court decisions establishing a "strong presumption" in favor of arbitration because "it is difficult to imagine a clearer or more direct exclusionary clause." [91]

---

[89] 321 F.Supp. 704 (S.D.N.Y. 1971).

[90] 299 F.2d 195 (7th Cir. 1962). See also *American Motors Corporation v. Wisconsin Employment Relations Board*, 145 N.W.2d 137, 63 LRRM 2226 (Wis. Sup.Ct. 1966); *Allied Oil Workers Union v. Ethyl Corp.*, 341 F.2d 47 (5th Cir. 1965); *Telephone Workers v. New England Telephone & Telegraph Co.*, 240 F.Supp. 431 (D. Mass. 1965).

[91] *Communications Workers v. New York Tel Co.*, 327 F.2d 94, 96 (2d Cir. 1964). See also *Desert Coca-Cola Bottling Co. v. General Sales Drivers, Delivery Drivers & Helpers Local 14*, 335 F.2d 198 (9th Cir. 1964); *Order of Repeatermen and Toll Test-Boardmen Local 1011 v. Bell Tel. Co. of Nev.*, 254 F.Supp. 462 (D. Nev. 1966).

A change in the method of payment from an incentive to a time basis was held not arbitrable since the Wage Plan Agreement provided that the company may cancel production standards or incentive application when changed circumstances "make it impracticable, in the Company's judgment, to accurately measure the operation for incentive application." [92]

When the management rights clause reserves to management a specific authority such as "the right to . . . subcontract work" and the arbitration clause excluded from arbitration the exercise by management of its reserved rights, a grievance protesting the subcontracting of work was held not arbitrable.[93] The Court distinguished *Warrior & Gulf* [94] stating that in *Warrior* the clause excluded matters "which are strictly a function of management" from arbitration without identifying subcontracting as one of those matters, while the instant contract specifically barred subcontracting from grievance procedure and arbitration.

Similarly, where the management rights clause had been interpreted by the parties to exclude from arbitration subcontracting, except disputes over the subcontracting of maintenance work, a dispute over the transfer of work to another plant was held not arbitrable.[95]

One federal district court has held that where it was the established policy to contract out maintenance work and the agreement gave the company the right to continue such policy while excluding from arbitration disputes over the exercise of such policies, a dispute over contracting out was not arbitrable.[96] The court said that in *Warrior & Gulf* the exclusions from arbitration were vague, whereas in the case under consideration "contracting out of maintenance work was a policy of the respondent; . . . the written contract permitted the Company to exercise and continue such policy; and . . . the same was not arbitrable but was specifically excluded from the scope of arbitration." [97] The court's evaluation of *Warrior & Gulf* is not inconsistent with the Supreme Court's decision, for as the Court noted there:

> "A specific collective bargaining agreement may exclude contracting out from the grievance procedure. . . . In such a case a grievance based solely on contracting out would not be arbitrable. Here, however, there

---

[92] *General Drivers, Warehousemen & Helpers Local 89 v. American Radiator & Standard Sanitary Corp.,* 309 F.2d 434 (6th Cir. 1962).

[93] *Rochester Independent Workers Local 1 v. General Dynamics/Electronic Div.,* 54 Misc.2d 470, 282 N.Y.S.2d 804 (Sup. Ct. 1967). See also *Radio Corp. of America v. Ass'n of Scientists & Professional Engineering Personnel,* 414 F.2d 893 (3d Cir. 1969).

[94] *Steelworkers v. Warrior & Gulf Navigation Co.,* 363 U.S. 574 (1960).

[95] *Boeing Co. v. Local 1069, UAW,* 234 F.Supp. 404 (E.D. Pa. 1964).

[96] *Local 725, IUE v. Standard Oil Co. of Ind.,* 186 F.Supp. 895 (D.N.D. 1960).

[97] *Id.* at 902.

is no such provision. . . . In the absence of any express provision excluding a particular grievance from arbitration, we think only the most forceful evidence of a purpose to exclude the claim from arbitration can prevail, ...

". . .

"Whether contracting out in the present case violated the agreement . . . is a question for the arbiter, not for the courts." [98]

Where the agreement specifically excluded from arbitration disputes involving individuals who had been permanently replaced during a strike, a dispute involving such employees was held not to be arbitrable. The court said that an order to arbitrate would be "a perversion of the grievance procedure and an effort by the union to get through the grievance machinery new employment for those persons whose claims were expressly excluded from it." [99]

Because of the presumption in favor of arbitrability, courts have held the following cases to be arbitrable: A dispute over vacation pay where the agreement provided for arbitration of "any dispute or grievance excepting wages";[100] a dispute over a "time value" where the agreement excluded disputes over the job incentive system;[101] a dispute over a change from incentive to time payment for certain work where the agreement excluded disputes over the establishment or change of wage rates;[102] a dispute over a layoff where the agreement excluded disputes over the company's right to schedule shutdowns;[103] a dispute over a discharge for insubordination where the agreement said the employer was to be the sole judge of qualifications;[104] a dispute over a promotion where the agreement said the "employer has discretion and authority in filling job openings";[105] and, a dispute over the denial of merit increase where the agreement

---

[98] 363 U.S. at 584-85. See also *Local 1912, IAM v. United States Potash Co.,* 270 F.2d 496 (10th Cir. 1959); *UAW Local 463 v. Weatherhead Co.,* 203 F.Supp. 612 (N.D. Ohio 1962); *IUE v. General Electric Co.,* 148 Conn. 693, 174 A.2d 298 (1961).

[99] *IUE Local 787 v. Collins Radio Co.,* 317 F.2d 214, 220 (5th Cir. 1963). See also *Storck v. Quaker Oats,* 85 Ill. App.2d 399, 228 N.E.2d 752 (1967).

[100] *Nafi Corp. v. Textile Workers Local 981,* 196 N.E.2d 598 (Ohio Ct. App. 1963).

[101] *IUE v. Westinghouse Electric Corp.,* 169 F.Supp. 798 (W.D. Pa. 1958), *aff'd* 268 F.2d 352 (3d Cir. 1959). See also *Steelworkers Local 4377 v. General Electric Co.,* 211 F.Supp. 562 (N.D. Ohio 1962), *aff'd* 327 F.2d 343 (6th Cir. 1964).

[102] *Steelworkers Local 4377 v. General Electric Co.,* 327 F.2d 853 (6th Cir. 1964). See also *Local 490, Rubber Workers v. Kirkhill Rubber Co.,* 367 F.2d 956 (9th Cir. 1966).

[103] *Local 967, IAM v. General Electric Co.,* 282 F.Supp. 413 (N.D.N.Y. 1968), *aff'd* 406 F.2d 1046 (2d Cir. 1969).

[104] *Operating Engineers Local 3 v. Crooks Bros. Tractor Co.,* 295 F.2d 282 (9th Cir. 1961).

[105] *Nepco Unit of Local 95, Office Employees Union v. Nekoosa-Edwards Paper Co.,* 287 F.2d 452 (7th Cir. 1961).

provided that "[the] arbitrator shall have no authority to change wage rates." [106]

Where there was language that could be construed to bar the arbitrator from establishing or modifying wage rates or job classifications, a court held that grievances relating to those matters should be arbitrated because:

"[T]he canons for construing labor agreements, as set down by the Supreme Court, require that such a broad-reaching exclusion as is urged by the company should be garbed in unmistakably clear language.

" . . .

"Should his decision or the remedy exceed the bounds of his authority as established by the collective bargaining agreement, that abuse of authority is remediable in an action to vacate the award." [107]

Significantly, the court was saying that if after the court's referral of the dispute to arbitration the arbitrator exceeded his jurisdiction when he rendered his award, the court could review the correctness of the arbitrator's award in an action to vacate.[108] This would mean that the standards used to determine, in an action to vacate, whether the arbitrator determined the jurisdiction question correctly are different than those used to determine whether a stay should or should not be issued in the first instance.

On the other hand, some courts hold that the arbitrator's determination that a dispute is arbitrable is binding on the court in an action to vacate even if the reviewing court disagrees with the arbitrator's finding, unless that finding can be shown to be arbitrary and capricious.[109] Another court went so far as to say that a finding by the arbitrator that he has jurisdiction is "insulated from subsequent judicial review." [110]

(4) Stays of Claims for Damages for Contract Breach Strikes Denied Under Broad Clauses

Numerous broad arbitration clauses have supported an employer's petition for an order to arbitrate his claim for damages resulting from violation of a no-strike clause or for denial of the union's request for a stay order to prevent the submission of such a claim to arbitra-

---

[106] Radio Corp. of America v. Ass'n of Professional Engineering Personnel, 291 F.2d 105 (3d Cir. 1961). See also Cleveland Federation of Musicians Local 4 v. Musical Arts Ass'n, — F.Supp. —, 71 LRRM 2855 (N.D. Ohio 1969).

[107] Carey v. General Electric Co., 315 F.2d 499, 507-08 (2d Cir. 1963).

[108] Accord, Foodhandlers Local 425, Meat Cutters v. Pluss Poultry, Inc., 260 F.2d 835 (8th Cir. 1958). But see Meat Cutters Local 385 v. Penobscot Poultry Co., 200 F.Supp. 879 (D. Me. 1961); Local 149, Boot & Shoe Workers v. Faith Shoe Co., 201 F.Supp. 234 (M.D. Pa. 1962).

[109] Federal Labor Union 18887 v. Midvale-Heppenstall Co., 421 F.2d 1289 (3d Cir. 1970).

[110] Camden Industries Co. v. Carpenters Local 1688, 353 F.2d 178 (1st Cir. 1965).

tion.[111] Similarly, court actions by employers for damages for a contract breach strike have been denied on the ground that the employer should have taken his claim for damages to the arbitrator.[112] Courts, however, have been willing to grant an employer damages when the employer is procedurally foreclosed from seeking relief through the arbitration process on his own initiation.

For instance, a union's request for a stay of the court action pending arbitration of the employer's claims for damages from a contract breach strike was denied where the arbitration clause provided that only grievances presented by employees could proceed up the grievance procedure to arbitration. The court, after reading the arbitration clause, said it could say with "positive assurance" that an employer's claim for damages arising out of the contract breach strike was not a grievance that could reach arbitration under the agreement and was, therefore, not arbitrable.[113]

One court mixed the arbitrability and nonarbitrability of various questions arising out of a contract breach strike in an interesting way. The issue of whether the strike was a contract violation is for the arbitrator, the court held, but then if he found that the strike was a violation, the issue of damages was for the court.[114]

F. APPEALS AND REMOVALS IN STAY LITIGATION

If an appeal is taken after a stay of arbitration has been denied, the district court should temporarily enjoin the arbitration to permit the appeal to be completed. The motion for a stay of arbitration pend-

---

[111] *Johnson Builders v. Carpenters Local 1095*, 422 F.2d 137 (10th Cir. 1970); *Howard Electric Co. v. IBEW Local 570*, 423 F.2d 164 (9th Cir. 1970); *ITT World Communications v. Communications Workers*, 422 F.2d 77 (2d Cir. 1970); *H. K. Porter Co. v. Steelworkers Local 37*, 400 F.2d 691 (4th Cir. 1968); *United States Steel Corp. v. Seafarers' International Union*, 237 F.Supp. 529 (E.D. Pa. 1965); *Teamsters Local 70 v. Consolidated Freightways Corp.*, 335 F.2d 642 (9th Cir. 1964); *Fifth Avenue Coach Lines, Inc. v. Transport Workers Local 100*, 235 F.Supp. 842 (S.D.N.Y. 1964); *Yale & Towne Mfg. Co. v. Local 1717, IAM*, 299 F.2d 882 (3d Cir. 1962); *Tenney Engineering, Inc. v. UE Local 437*, 174 F.Supp. 878 (D.N.J. 1959).

[112] *Local 463, Papermakers v. Federal Paper Board Co.*, 239 F.Supp. 45 (D. Conn. 1965); *Franchi Const. Co. v. Local 560, Hod Carriers*, 248 F.Supp. 134 (D. Mass. 1965); *Minn. Joint Board, ACWA v. United Garment Mfg. Co.*, 338 F.2d 195 (8th Cir. 1964); *Evans-Amityville Dairy, Inc. v. Kelly*, 214 F.Supp. 951 (E.D.N.Y. 1963); *Gilmour v. Wood, Wire and Metal Lathers Int'l Union Local 74*, 223 F.Supp. 236 (N.D. Ill. 1963); *Drake Bakeries, Inc. v. Local 50, American Bakery & Confectionery Workers*, 370 U.S. 254 (1962).

[113] *Boeing Co. v. UAW Local 1069*, 370 F.2d 969 (3d Cir. 1967). See also *Old Dutch Farms v. Teamsters Local 584*, 359 F.2d 598 (2d Cir. 1966); *Stroehmann Bros. v. Local 427, Confectionery Workers*, 315 F.Supp. 647 (M.D. Pa. 1970).

[114] *Los Angeles Paper Bag Co. v. Printing Specialties & Paper Products Union, Dist. Council 2*, 345 F.2d 757 (9th Cir. 1965). See *Dist. 50 IAM v. Chris-Craft Corp.*, 385 F.2d 946 (6th Cir. 1967); *Tenney Engineering, Inc. v. UE Local 437*, 174 F.Supp. 878 (D.N.J. 1959).

ing appeal is made under Rule 65(c) of the Federal Rules of Civil Procedure.

An application for a stay of arbitration can be removed to a federal court by a defendant if the requirements for removal are met,[115] but a union which represented the grievant in an arbitration case and filed an application for a stay in a state court could not remove to the federal court because the federal statute authorizing removal of a civil action permits removal only by a defendant.[116]

The enjoining of contemplated action by an employer until the arbitration of a dispute over the action was completed occurred in a dispute over contracting out of work. A district court concluded that the union was entitled to an order restraining the company from subcontracting the work until the merits of the dispute were determined by an arbitrator because there were 60 man-days of work involved.[117]

---

[115] 28 USC § 1441(a) (1971). See also *Avco Corp. v. IAM Aero Lodge 735*, 390 U.S. 557 (1968), holding a § 301 action to be removable from state to federal court.

[116] *Hall v. Sperry Gyroscope Co.*, 183 F.Supp. 891 (S.D.N.Y. 1960). See *Application of Rosenthal-Block China Corp.*, 278 F.2d 713, 714 (2d Cir. 1960); *Old Dutch Farms, Inc. v. Milk Drivers & Dairy Employees Local 584*, 222 F.Supp. 125 (E.D.N.Y. 1963).

[117] *IUE Local 103 v. Radio Corp. of America*, 77 LRRM 2201 (D.N.J. 1971); *Contra, Detroit Newspaper Publishers Ass'n v. Detroit Typographical Union No. 18, Intern. Typographical Union*, 471 F.2d 872 (6th Cir. 1972).

CHAPTER V

Selection of the Arbitrator or the Board

If a party intends to object to a demand for arbitration, that party may waive his objection by participation in the selection of an arbitrator or a board,[1] but a request for an extension of time within which to select an arbitrator does not waive this objection and a party may thereafter move a court for an order to stay the arbitration.[2]

A. PROCEDURES FOR SELECTION OF AN ARBITRATOR OR A BOARD OF ARBITRATORS

The procedure for selecting an arbitrator or a board of arbitrators the selection of an arbitrator for each dispute (*ad hoc* arbitration) procedure is not the procedure used to select the arbitrator or the board and there has been no agreement to a variation in procedure or a waiver, an award rendered by the arbitrator or board may be set aside by a court.[3] The more common selection procedures are by mutual agreement, through use of an agency or through use of an arbitration board.

(1) Selection of an Arbitrator by Mutual Agreement

Approximately 80 percent of those labor agreements providing for the selection of an arbitrator for each dispute (*ad hoc* arbitration) provide that the arbitrator shall be selected by mutual agreement.[4] One

---

[1] *In re New York Shipping Ass'n,* 54 LRRM 2680 (N.Y. Sup. Ct. 1963); *Frank Chevrolet Corp. v. UAW Local 259,* 33 Misc.2d 12, 228 N.Y.S.2d 692 (1962).

[2] *Dana Realty Corp. v. Consolidated Electric Construction Co.,* 21 App. Div.2d 769, 250 N.Y.S.2d 784 (1964).

[3] *Order of Railway Conductors & Brakemen v. Clinchfield Railroad Co.,* 278 F. Supp. 322 (E.D. Tenn. 1967); *Edmund E. Garrison, Inc. v. Local 137, IUOE,* 283 F.Supp. 771 (S.D.N.Y. 1968) (Employer was not entitled to select himself and his attorney as arbitrators under agreements providing that arbitration boards would be composed of two representatives of each party and that parties could not be arbitrators. In so holding, the court noted "[C]ustom in arbitration proceedings dictates that a party may not appoint himself." (283 F.Supp. at 773)).

[4] 165 DAILY LAB. REP. B-7 (August 26, 1965).

observer described the process involved in selecting *ad hoc* arbitrators as follows:[5]

> "It is frequently standard operating procedure when a case arises for each side to scurry about making telephone calls to parties who have appeared in cases before particular arbitrators under consideration, to read all obtainable decisions previously rendered by such arbitrators, to check 'confidential' reports kept by services maintained for the purpose of keeping tab on arbitrators and to check 'black lists' and 'approved' lists of arbitrators maintained by various sources. This haphazard, hit or miss procedure is not only burdensome, time-consuming and frequently ineffective, but it also tends to degrade arbitration and the arbitration process."

In the event the parties deadlock and cannot agree upon an arbitrator, some states allow court appointment of the arbitrator upon application of one of the parties.[6] On the other hand, several states have statutory provisions preventing court appointment of arbitrators.[7] Quite obviously, in such states, the labor agreement should provide a *final* method for selecting the arbitrator to avoid the risk of a deadlock.

Approximately eight percent of the labor agreements in the United States provide for a permanent arbitrator.[8] This procedure, of course, avoids the delays involved in selecting an arbitrator each time a grievance or group of grievances reach the arbitration step of the grievance procedure and, of course, carries no risk of deadlock and possible court intervention. The permanent arbitrator usually serves only as long as he is acceptable to both parties.

A permanent arbitrator is desirable where the agreement covers large number of employees and it is anticipated that a significant num-

---

[5] Levitt, *Lawyers, Legalism, and Labor Arbitration*, 6 N.Y. L. Forum 379 (1960).

[6] State statutes providing for court appointment of the arbitrator are: Ariz. Rev. Stat. Ann. § 12-1503 (Supp. 1965); Cal. Civ. Pro. § 1281.6 (Supp. 1965); Conn. Gen. Stat. § 52-411 (1958); Fla. Stat. Ann. § 682.04 (Supp. 1969); La. Rev. Stat. § 9:4204 (1950); Me. Rev. Stat. Ann. tit. 26, § 954 (1964); Md. Ann. Code art. 7, § 3 (1965); Mass. Ann. Laws ch. 150C, § 3 (Supp. 1965); Mich. Stat. Ann. 27A.5015 (1962); Minn. Stat. Ann. § 572.10 (Supp. 1965); Nev. Rev. Stat. § 38.055 (1963); N.H. Rev. Stat. Ann. § 542:4 (1955); N.J. Rev. Stat. § 2A:34-13 (1952); N.Y. Civ. Prac. Law § 7504 (McKinney, 1963); N.C. Gen. Stat. § 1-547 (1943); Ohio Rev. Code Ann. § 2711.04 (Page, 1953); Ore. Rev. Stat. § 33.250 (1963); Pa. Stat. Ann. tit. 5, § 164 (1963); R.I. Gen. Laws Ann. § 10-3-6 (1956); Tenn. Code Ann. § 23-504 (1955); Tex. Rev. Civ. Stat. Ann. art. 226 (Supp. 1965); Utah Code Ann. § 78-31-4 (1953); Wash. Rev. Code § 7.04.050 (1961); Wis. Stat. Ann. § 298.04 (1958); Wyo. Stat. Ann. § 1-1048.5 (Supp. 1963).

[7] See, *e.g.*, Ala. Code tit. 7, §§ 829, 830 (1958) (the arbitrator is to be chosen by the parties); Ill. Ann. Stat. ch. 10, § 103 (Smith-Hurd, Sup. 1964) ("if the method of appointment of arbitrators is not specified in the agreement and cannot be agreed upon by the parties, the entire arbitration agreement shall terminate"); Kan. Gen. Stat. Ann. § 5-201 (1964) (the arbitrator is to be mutually agreed upon by the parties"); N.M. Stat. Ann. § 22-3-2 (1953) (the arbitrator shall be chosen by the parties); S.C. Code Ann. § 10-1902 (1962) (the arbitrator shall be chosen by the parties).

[8] 165 Daily Lab. Rep. B-6 (August 26, 1965).

ber of grievances will go to arbitration during the term of the agreement. The steel and automotive industries have made extensive use of permanent arbitrators. Stability is sought by having a consistency in the decisions permitting the parties to more accurately anticipate the nature of the award, causing, it is hoped, the withdrawal of grievances as they approach the hearing stage.[9]

A few labor agreements contain a list of several arbitrators from which the parties made a selection in rotation.[10] In some cases, the parties agree to use one of the arbitrators to hear all cases unless he is unavailable, in which case the second arbitrator on the list is called. This method, like the naming of a permanent arbitrator, speeds up the selection process.

(2) Selection Through Use of Agency Procedures

A common method of selecting an arbitrator is an agreement to utilize the services of either the American Arbitration Association (AAA) or the Federal Mediation and Conciliation Service (FMCS). One survey reported that approximately 70 percent of labor agreements require one of these two agencies to appoint an arbitrator if the parties cannot select one of the arbitrators proffered on the agency's list either by ranking their choice and permitting the agency to select an arbitrator acceptable to both parties or by the process of striking names in rotation. Eighteen percent of the labor agreements give one of these two agencies the right to select the arbitrator initially.[11]

The AAA maintains a national panel or roster whose members have been selected for their experience, competence, and impartiality.[12] The FMCS maintains a roster of "arbitrators who are qualified and acceptable and who adhere to ethical standards."[13] The AAA and the FMCS normally will submit lists of arbitrators who are proximate to the location of the parties and who possess special technical knowl-

---

[9] A court maintained consistency by reappointment of arbitrator after lapse in his term in *William Faehndrich, Inc.,* 15 Misc.2d 370, 181 N.Y.S.2d 918 (Sup. Ct. 1959).

[10] See, *e.g.,* Killingsworth, *Arbitration: Its Uses in Industrial Relations,* 21 L.A. 859, 860 (1963); 165 DAILY LAB. REP. B-6 (August 26, 1965).

[11] 165 DAILY LAB. REP. B-7 (August 26, 1965).

[12] A relatively small percentage of the arbitrators listed do the bulk of the arbitration work. For example, a survey in 1964 revealed that only 370 arbitrators out of the 1,400 names then listed with the AAA actually rendered one or more awards during that year. Coulson, *Spring Checkup on Labor Arbitration Procedure,* 16 LAB. L.J. 259, 262 (1965).

[13] 29 CFR § 1404.2, § 1404.4, § 1404.6 (1971). Upon joint request FMCS will supply the parties with the names of seven arbitrators unless a different number is requested by the parties. FMCS will supply a list of arbitrators upon request of one party only if both parties agree (usually in the labor agreement) that one party may request a list of arbitrators.

edge, if so requested by the parties. The AAA charges $50 to each party, whereas the FMCS furnishes panels without charge.[14]

Under the AAA procedures, it is important to distinguish between a simple request for an arbitration panel and an agreement of the parties to proceed under the agency's Voluntary Labor Arbitration Rules. Once the parties agree to be bound by these rules, greater authority resides in the AAA administrator to appoint an arbitrator if the normal procedure does not result in a satisfactory choice. The full procedure is:

(1) Immediately after the filing of the demand or submission, the AAA shall submit simultaneously to each party an identical list of names of persons chosen from the labor panel.

(2) Each party shall have seven days from the mailing date in which to cross off any names to which he objects, number the remaining names indicating the order of his preference, and return the list to the AAA.

(3) If a party does not return the list within the time specified, all persons named therein shall be deemed acceptable.

(4) From among the persons who have been approved on both lists, and in accordance with the designated order of mutual preference, the AAA shall invite the acceptance of an arbitrator to serve.

(5) If the parties fail to agree upon any of the persons named or if those named decline or are unable to act, or if for any other reason the appointment cannot be made from the submitted lists, the Administrator shall have the power to make the appointment from other members of the panel without the submission of any additional lists.[15]

A party cannot delay an arbitration hearing under the AAA rules by refusing to select an arbitrator.[16] The FMCS now has procedural rules providing for selection of an arbitrator upon failure of one or both parties to complete one of the two selection procedures referred to in the rules. A panel of arbitrators is provided by the agency and the parties must either (i) select the arbitrator by alternately striking names or (2) rank the arbitrators in preference order and then the FMCS will select an arbitrator agreeable to both parties.[17]

---

[14] The AAA's fee covers all panel lists provided to the parties in the particular case, in addition to the use of a conference room at the AAA's Regional Office for the hearing. Many state agencies, such as the state department of labor or a state employment relations board, also provide lists of arbitrators.

[15] American Arbitration Association, *Voluntary Labor Arbitration Rules,* Rule 12 (1970).

[16] *Id.,* Rule 27.

[17] 20 CFR § 1404.6; Finnegan, *Federal Mediation and Conciliation Service,* MANAGEMENT RIGHTS AND THE ARBITRATION PROCESS, Proceedings of the Ninth Annual Meeting, National Academy of Arbitrators 96 (J. McKelvey Ed. 1956).

(3) Selection of an Arbitration Board

Some contracts provide that each party appoint one arbitrator and that the two appointed arbitrators are to select the impartial arbitrator or chairman. In Georgia, this procedure is incorporated into a statute requiring that "every arbitration under this Chapter shall be composed of three arbitrators, one of whom shall be chosen by each of the parties and one by the arbitrators chosen by the parties." [18] This statutory procedure was held not to be satisfied where the dispute was submitted to two arbitrators who were given the power to select a third should they disagree.[19] The Texas statute provides for the selection of a five-man board of arbitration, two selected by each party and the fifth selected by the other four.[20] The South Carolina statute calls upon each party to select a "discreet person, both of whom then select the third member of the board." [21] Even a bipartite board can be an arbitration board if the parties so agree.[22] Furthermore, the participation of a party in an arbitration before a board which was not composed of the number of arbitrators specified in the Railway Labor Act constituted a waiver of that party's right to object to an award rendered by that board.[23]

A study of 1,717 labor agreements by the Bureau of Labor Statistics of the United States Department of Labor revealed that 46 percent of the agreements studied provided for tripartite arbitration boards in 1952, but that the percentage had declined to 39 percent by 1962 and to 38 percent by 1965.[24]

The risk of deadlock exists where the appointed arbitrators cannot agree on an impartial arbitrator or chairman, and the applicable labor agreement fails to provide a method for breaking the deadlock. In some states, courts will appoint the arbitrator upon application of one of the parties; in others they will not.[25]

---

[18] GA. CODE ANN. § 7-202 (1936).

[19] *Osborn & Walcott Mfg. Co. v. Blanton,* 109 Ga. 196, 34 S.E. 306 (1899) (refusal to enforce award).

[20] TEX. REV. CIV. STAT. ANN. art. 239 (1959).

[21] S.C. CODE ANN. § 10-1902 (1962).

[22] *Humphrey v. Moore,* 375 U.S. 335 (1964); *Kennedy v. McLean Trucking Co.,* 54 N.J. 533, 149 A.2d 606 (N.J. Super. Ct. 1959). A Joint Local Committee set up by a collective bargaining agreement is a valid arbitration board even though bipartite. See also *Digeorgia v. American Federation of Musicians Local 802,* 17 N.Y. Misc.2d 343, 186 N.Y.S. 2d 517 (Sup. Ct. 1959); *Publishers' Ass'n of New York v. New York Stereotypers Union Number One,* 9 App. Div.2d 110, 192 N.Y.S.2d 18 (1959).

[23] *Order of Railway Conductors v. Clinchfield R.R. Co.,* 407 F.2d 985 (6th Cir. 1969).

[24] U.S. Bureau of Labor Statistics, Dept. of Labor, *Bulletin No. 1425-26,* MAJOR COLLECTIVE BARGAINING AGREEMENTS 36 (1966).

[25] See notes 6 and 7 *supra.*

In spite of the risk of deadlock, the usual practice is for each party to nominate an arbitrator and then the two arbitrators choose a third, the impartial chairman. There has been considerable controversy as to whether the two arbitrators chosen by the parties are expected to maintain the same degree of impartiality as the impartial chairman—or whether they may assume the role of advocates for their nominators. Early guidelines on this question were provided in *American Eagle Fire Insurance Co. v. New Jersey Insurance Co.,*[26] where the court held:

> "[T]he practice of arbitrators conducting themselves as champions of their nominators is to be condemned as contrary to the purpose of arbitrations and as calculated to bring the system of enforced arbitrations into disrepute. . . . [The arbitrator] should keep his own counsel and not run to his nominator for advice when he sees that he may be in a minority. When once he enters into an arbitration, he ceases to act as agent of the party who appoints him. He must lay aside all bias and approach the case with a mind open to conviction and without regard to his previously formed opinions as to the merits of the party or the cause. He should sedulously refrain from any conduct which might justify even the inference that either party is the special recipient of his solicitude or favor. . . ." [27]

This approach was the basis for many early awards.[28]

The trend, however, has been toward the relaxation of strict standards of impartiality for party-nominated arbitrators. For example, in one case, the arbitration clause required each party to select one member "not associated with the Company or the Union," the two so named then to select the chairman from a list furnished by the American Arbitration Association, was interpreted not to disqualify an attorney "most of [whose] clients are labor organizations," who had been counsel for the union on "isolated occasions," and who had served as a union-appointee to arbitration panels for the same parties.[29] Arbitrator Crane said:

> "General experience with tripartite arbitration boards indicates that it is the impartial chairman who decides the disputed issue and that a party-appointed member either concurs or dissents, depending upon whether or not the decision is favorable to the party which appointed him." [30]

New York Civil Practice Law and Rules were specifically amended to provide that only the partiality of an arbitrator appointed as a

---

26 240 N.Y. 398, 148 N.E. 562 (1925).
27 240 N.Y. at 405, 148 N.E. at 564.
28 See, *e.g., Wheeling Gas v. The City of Wheeling,* 5 W.Va. 448 (1872).
29 *Columbus & Southern Ohio Electric Co.,* AAA Case No. 31-13 (Crane, 1961).
30 *Id.*

neutral is a basis for vacating an award.[31] This change "takes cognizance of the common practice of each party appointing his own arbitrator who is not individually expected to be neutral." [32]

This approach was upheld in *Astoria Medical Group v. Health Insurance Plan of Greater New York*.[33] There, it was held that an arbitrator appointed by the parties may be partisan, but he may not be dishonest by being "deaf to the testimony or blind to the evidence presented."[34] The use of nonneutral arbitrators was found not to be objectionable since the arbitration is not strictly a judicial remedy.[35] A motion to vacate, the court held, must be based on "some misconduct on the part of an arbitrator and not simply on his interest in the subject matter or the controversy of his relationship to the party who selected him." [36]

The manner by which the arbitration board is selected is important when the General Counsel of the National Labor Relations Board determines whether to dismiss the charge and defer to arbitration. General Counsel Peter Nash said:[37]

> "Unfair labor practice charges will not be deferred for arbitration unless the applicable contract procedures for the resolution of disputes provides for 'arbitration.' In determining whether the person, persons or body provided in the contract for the last-stage resolution of the dispute are arbitrators or arbitral bodies, and that the contract therefore provides for 'arbitration,' the criteria for this determination which have been developed by the Board in the application of the *Spielberg* [38] policy should be employed. Thus, the absence of a neutral member on a bipartite panel would not necessarily preclude deferral.[39] But where, in addition, it appears that all members of the bipartite panel are or would be arrayed in interest against the charging party, deferral would not be appropriate." [40]

---

[31] *New York Civil Practice Law and Rules,* Section 7511(b) i(ii) (as amended 1963).

[32] N.Y.S. LEGISLATIVE DOCUMENT No. 13 at 146 (1958).

[33] 11 N.Y.2d 128, 227 N.Y.S.2d 401, 182 N.E.2d 85 (1962). See also *Associated General Contractors, Evansville Chapter, Inc. v. NLRB,* 465 F.2d 327 (7th Cir. 1972).

[34] 11 N.Y.2d at 137.

[35] *Id.* at 136.

[36] *Id.* at 137.

[37] Nash, *Arbitration Deferral Policy Under Collyer,* Memorandum of NLRB General Counsel to NLRB Regional Directors and Officers-in-Charge, DAILY LAB. REP. No. 49, A-1, March 10, 1972. (The following three footnotes taken from Nash text.)

[38] *Spielberg Manufacturing Co.,* 112 NLRB 1080 (1955).

[39] *Denver-Chicago Trucking Co.,* 132 NLRB 1416 (1961); *Modern Motor Express, Inc.,* 149 NLRB 1507 (1964). The Board's reference in *Tulsa-Whisenhunt Funeral Homes, Inc.,* 195 NLRB No. 20 (1972), n. 1, to "a forum of third parties" was not deemed sufficient to infer Board rejection of the relevance of the *Denver-Chicago* principle to the *Collyer* deferral policy.

[40] *Roadway Express, Inc.,* 145 NLRB 513 (1963); *Youngstown Cartage Co.,* 146 NLRB 305 (1964).

The management and union representatives on a tripartite board are actually advocates for the respective parties.[41] To label the management and union representatives on the board as "arbitrators" is not only a misnomer, but also raises serious ethical and legal questions.[42] For example, the Committee on Ethics of the National Academy of Arbitrators questioned the wisdom of labeling all of the members of such tripartite boards as arbitrators, as follows:

"If arbitration is a judicial process, the use of tripartite boards of arbitration to determine questions of contract interpretation may involve a problem of ethical content. . . . It is common knowledge that the members designated by the parties almost invariably view the case as partisans, though purporting to sit as impartial judges. . . .

"Is this an 'ethical' arrangement? Whether it is or not, if the decision is to be made by majority vote, it often puts the neutral arbitrator in an impossible position if his function is to decide the case 'judicially.' Yet the parties may have entered into such an arrangement in perfect good faith. They may have sound practical reasons for preferring such an arrangement, uppermost of which is the fear of having an arbitrator unfamiliar with the mores of the particular company-union relationship go off 'half-cocked.' When it is realized that an award in a labor dispute is not merely the decision of a legal issue but may materially affect the day-to-day relationship of an employer and his employees for an indefinite period in the future, the concern of the parties is understandable. Yet serious questions exist as to the propriety of tripartite arbitration in the interpretation of labor contracts—if the arbitration and the judicial processes are indistinguishable." [43]

Absence of one of the three arbitrators from the hearing, unless absence is waived, is grounds for vacating the award.[44] The death of a party appointed as arbitrator after the hearings but before the deci-

41 See *United Ass'n of Journeymen, Plumbing and Pipe Fitting Industry Local 525 v. Eighth Judicial District Court of Nevada,* 412 P.2d 352 (Nev. Sup. Ct. 1966) (where the contract between a union and a contractors' association provided for a tripartite board composed of two members designated by each side and a neutral chairman, the lower court was in error in vacating award of the arbitration board so established on the basis that it was not composed of five unbiased, neutral members). See also *Palizzotto v. Teamster Local 641,* 67 N.J. Super. 145, 170 A.2d 57 (1961).

42 See Levitt, *Lawyers, Legalism, and Labor Arbitration,* note 5 *supra,* at 397.

43 *Standards of Conduct for Labor Arbitrators,* THE PROFESSION OF LABOR ARBITRATION, Selected Proceedings of the First Seven Annual Meetings, National Academy of Arbitrators, 143-44 (J. McKelvey Ed. 1957), quoted in *Associated General Contractors of America, Evansville Chapter, Inc. v. NLRB,* 465 F.2d 327, 80 LRRM 3157 (7th Cir. 1972).

44 *West Towns Bus Co. v. Div. 241, Amalgamated Ass'n of Street, Electric Ry. and Motor Coach Employees,* 26 Ill. App.2d 398, 168 N.E.2d 473 (1960); *Knickerbocker Textile Corp. v. Donath,* 22 Misc.2d 1056, 205 N.Y.S.2d 408 (Sup. Ct.), *aff'd,* 282 App. Div. 680 (1953); *Turner v. Cox,* 16 CAL. RPTR. 644 (Ct. App. 1961); *Bluhm v. Perenia,* 75 N.Y.S.2d 170 (Sup. Ct. 1946).

sion is also grounds for vacating the award.[45] If a party-appointed arbitrator, however, withdraws after the proceedings begin, the remaining two can render the award.[46]

After the hearing, the board members meet in an executive session to review the evidence and the two partisan members attempt to ensure that the neutral chairman understands the position of the party they represent and their view as to the weight and significance of the evidence. Sometimes the executive session is held after the neutral chairman has prepared a draft of his award, and the partisan members are then given an opportunity to correct factual errors and suggest changes in language.

B. DUTY OF THE ARBITRATOR TO DISCLOSE

An arbitrator who has been selected to arbitrate a labor dispute has a duty to disclose to the parties certain types of information concerning his background, associations, and relationships. Rule 3 of the Code of Ethics for Arbitrators promulgated jointly by the American Arbitration Association and the National Academy of Arbitrators states that:

> "Any person whom the parties or the appointing agency choose to regard as qualified to determine their dispute is entitled to act as their arbitrator. It is, however, incumbent upon the arbitrator at the time of his selection to disclose to the parties any circumstances, associations or relationships that might reasonably raise any doubt as to his impartiality or his technical qualification for the particular case." [47]

This rule does not require an arbitrator to disqualify himself for any reason. He simply is required to disclose certain information, and the parties (or the appointing agency) have the option to regard him as qualified or unqualified.

The American Arbitration Association's 1970 Voluntary Labor Arbitration Rules provide in Rule 11 that "[N]o person shall serve

---

[45] *Fromer Foods, Inc. v. Edelstein Foods, Inc.,* 181 N.Y.S.2d 352, 353 (Sup. Ct. 1958):

"In most instances an award by two arbitrators is binding even though a third withdraws before the award is rendered. This is not so, however, when one of the arbitrators dies after the hearing but before the decision has been made or the award rendered. The deceased arbitrator cannot be deemed to be a mere dissenter...."

[46] *Publishers' Ass'n of New York City v. New York Stereotypers' Union No. 1,* 15 Misc.2d 931, 934, 181 N.Y.S.2d 527, 530 (Sup. 1959):

"Obviously the Union's withdrawal from the arbitration during its progress, because the impartial chairman did not agree with its contentions, may not be permitted to defeat the award. Arbitration would be completely undermined if awards could be nullified by such strategy."

[47] American Arbitration Association and National Academy of Arbitrators, *Code of Ethics and Procedural Standards for Labor-Management Arbitration,* Rule 3 (1962).

as a neutral arbitrator in any arbitration in which he has any financial or personal interest in the result of the arbitration, unless the parties, in writing, waive such disqualification." [48] And Rule 17 reads as follows:

"Prior to accepting his appointment, the prospective neutral Arbitrator shall disclose any circumstances likely to create a presumption of bias or which he believes might disqualify him as an impartial Arbitrator. Upon receipt of such information, the AAA shall immediately disclose it to the parties. If either party declines to waive the presumptive disqualification, the vacancy thus created shall be filled in accordance with the applicable provisions of these Rules." [49]

On its face, this Rule does not appear to cover a problem of disclosure which arises subsequent to acceptance of the appointment by the arbitrator, but Rule 46 provides that "The Arbitrator shall interpret and apply these Rules [including Rule 11] insofar as they relate to his power and duties." [50]

The Federal Mediation and Conciliation Service has adopted, in the Code of Federal Regulations,[51] rules which are applicable to arbitrators whose services are obtained through FMCS. Under Section 1404.2(a) "It is the policy of the Service to maintain on its roster only those arbitrators . . . who adhere to ethical standards." With respect to disclosure, Subsection C states that "The arbitrators on the roster are expected to keep the Service informed . . . of any business connections with or of concern to labor or management. . . ." And Section 1404.12 provides that the Service expects ". . . its arbitrators and the parties . . . to be guided by ethical and procedural standards as codified by appropriate professional organizations and generally accepted by the industrial community and experienced arbitrators." This particular regulation is applicable to the actual conduct of an arbitration proceeding.

In 1925, Congress adopted the United States Arbitration Act.[52] Whether this statute applies to arbitration of a dispute under a collective bargaining agreement has been discussed in various contexts in this volume. Nevertheless, for arbitration of controversies coming within its terms, Section 10 provides that an award may be vacated "where there was evident partiality . . . in the arbitrators." [53]

An arbitrator's failure to disclose his previous association with the union was held to be grounds for vacating an award since such non-

---

[48] American Arbitration Association, *Voluntary Labor Arbitration Rules,* Rule 11, Jan. 1, 1970.
[49] *Id.,* Rule 17.
[50] *Id.,* Rule 46.
[51] 20 CFR § 1404.1 *et seq.* (1971).
[52] 9 USC § 1 *et seq.* (1970).
[53] *Id.* § 10 (1970).

disclosure deprived the employer of its rightful opportunity to make a knowledgeable selection of an impartial arbitrator.[54] The facts showed that: (1) the arbitrator was employed as an attorney for the respondent union for a period of several years; (2) less than six months prior to the hearing he listed his address as that of the union; and (3) in 1967 he had been paid over $10,000 by the union for his services. "On this record," the court concluded, "it is reasonable to infer that the prior relationship between the arbitrator and the [union] constituted partiality." [55]

In *Commonwealth Coatings Corp. v. Continental Casualty Co.,*[56] the Supreme Court vacated an arbitration award in a commercial arbitration case. The majority of the Court found that the award should be set aside under Section 10 of the U.S. Arbitration Act because the neutral member of an arbitration board failed to disclose that he had received $12,000 in consultant's fees from one of the parties over a period of four to five years. The neutral arbitrator, in fact, had rendered service as a consultant on the very projects which became involved in arbitration. Justices Harlan, Stewart, and Fortas pointed out in a dissent that the award in question was unanimously adopted by the panel which included an arbitrator chosen by the subcontractor and that there was no claim that the neutral arbitrator actually was partial. The dissent believed that the majority of the court adopted a *per se* rule that if an arbitrator had any prior business relations with one of the parties of which he fails to inform the other party, however innocently, the arbitration award is always subject to being set aside.

Although a determination of what is partiality and bias is difficult, a number of clearly disqualifying criteria have emerged in New York decisions primarily involving commercial arbitration. It has been held that an arbitrator presumably was not impartial when he formed an opinion prior to the hearing,[57] had an interest in the controversy,[58] was related to one of the parties,[59] had relatives employed by one of the parties and had once been employed as a lawyer by the same party,[60] had an undisclosed former business relationship with one of

---

[54] *Colony Liquor Distributors, Inc. v. Teamsters Local 669,* 34 App. Div.2d 1060, 312 N.Y.S.2d 403 (1970).

[55] 34 App. Div.2d at 1062, 312 N.Y.S.2d at 405.

[56] 393 U.S. 145 (1968).

[57] *Flanary v. Sahagian,* 134 N.Y. 85, 31 N.E. 319 (1892).

[58] *Greenspan v. Greenspan,* 129 N.Y.S.2d 258 (Sup. Ct. 1954).

[59] *People ex rel. Union Bag and Paper Corp. v. Gilbert,* 143 Misc. 287, 256 N.Y.S. 442 (Sup. Ct.), *aff'd,* 236 App. Div. 813, 260 N.Y.S. 939 (1932). See also *Cassara v. Wofford,* 55 So.2d 102 (Fla. Sup. Ct. 1951).

[60] *Colony Liquor Dist., Inc. v. Teamsters Local 669,* 312 N.Y.S.2d 403 (App. Div. 1970).

the parties,[61] had a current business relationship with one of the parties,[62] or was attorney for one party.[63]

An important question has been the distinction between actual bias and presumptive bias and, on this issue, the courts have not been consistent. For example, in *Western Union v. Selley*,[64] the New York Court of Appeals removed a court-appointed arbitrator who had previously voiced strong prolabor views and had been a candidate of the American Labor Party, although there was no allegation of actual bias or prejudice. In contrast, another New York court, in *Matter of DiNicola*,[65] held that despite evidence that the arbitrator had renewed a friendship with counsel for one litigant and made a gift to such counsel while the case was pending, evidence of injudicious conduct was insufficient to disqualify the arbitrator and vacate the proceeding.

The question of indebtedness has also been subject of conflicting judgments. It has been held that where a personal unsecured loan was given by one of the parties to the arbitrator, the award he rendered should be vacated.[66] In a later case, however, the same court held that an arbitrator is not disqualified when he is an officer of a corporation which is creditor or debtor of one of the parties, if debt arises out of normal business.[67] In *Katz v. Uvegi*,[68] the court held that the demanding and receiving of fees prior to the completion of the decision of an arbitrator was improper and constituted misconduct.[69]

While earlier courts were quite firm in applying a rule of both complete impartiality and complete freedom from suspicion of partiality,[70] recent rulings have indicated a more liberal view. For example, the courts have refused to vacate awards "as a matter of public policy unless the partiality is clearly established." [71]

Perhaps the best rule for determining partiality was that of the Illinois court in the case of *Giddens v. Board of Education* [72] where it held that "an interest or bias to disqualify [an arbitrator] may be small, but it must be direct, definite and capable of demonstration,

---

[61] *Application of Seigal*, 153 N.Y.S.2d 673 (Sup. Ct. 1956).

[62] *Dukraft Mfg. Co. v. Bear Mill Mfg. Co.*, 22 Misc.2d 1057, 151 N.Y.S.2d 318 (1956).

[63] *Werbsa v. Cobb*, 254 App. Div. 481, 5 N.Y.S.2d 311 (1938).

[64] 295 N.Y. 395, 68 N.E.2d 183 (1946).

[65] 2 App. Div.2d 675, 152 N.Y.S.2d 995 (1956).

[66] *In re Friedman*, 215 App. Div. 130, 213 N.Y.S. 369 (1926).

[67] *E. Richard Meinig Co. v. Katakura & Co.*, 241 App. Div. 406, 272 N.Y.S. 735, aff'd, 266 N.Y. 418, 195 N.E. 134 (1934).

[68] 18 Misc.2d 576, 187 N.Y.S.2d 511 (Sup. Ct.), aff'd, 11 App. Div.2d 773, 205 N.Y.S.2d 972 (1959).

[69] See also *Schecter v. Atlas Shirt Co.*, 86 N.Y.S.2d 220 (Sup. Ct. 1949).

[70] See, *e.g.*, *Smyth v. Bd. of Education*, 214 App. Div. 735, 210 N.Y.S. 922 (1925); *In re Friedman*, 215 App. Div. 130, 213 N.Y.S. 369 (1926).

[71] *Isbrandtsen Tankers, Inc. v. District 2, National Marine Engineers Beneficial Ass'n*, 33 Misc.2d 504, 236 N.Y.S.2d 808 (Sup. Ct. 1962).

[72] 398 Ill. 157, 75 N.E.2d 286 (1947).

rather than remote, uncertain or speculative." [73] In that case, the Illinois Supreme Court refused to overturn an appraisal of the valuation of leased school fund property on the grounds that one of the three appraisers' real estate firm had been employed by the school board as an expert witness in a case 10 years before and that another had been criticized by one of the parties in a prior appraisal.

An objection based on partiality may be waived. It has been held that the mere existence of a possible prejudicial relationship does not demand vacating the award if the parties involved knew of this relationship and failed to make timely objection. [74]

C. DUTY OF THE APPOINTING AGENCY TO DISCLOSE

An appointing agency has a duty to disclose to the parties facts which may determine the qualification of an arbitrator. A federal district court in *Rogers v. Schering Corp.* [75] said:

"[W]hen the Association is informed by a prospective arbitrator in response to its inquiry, of circumstances which are 'likely to create a presumption of bias,' nothing less than a prompt communication of such disclosure to the parties, even where the filling of a vacancy is concerned, provides the affected party with an opportunity to challenge 'for cause.' Nor is it sufficient for the Association to take the position that *it* weighed the disclosure and concluded that it did not affect the eligibility of the proposed arbitrator.

"...

"The failure of the Administrator to communicate to the parties [such] information . . . is more than a loose procedural informality. It goes to the heart of a body designed to resolve controversy—its integrity. In this instance it fails to protect what might be termed 'due arbitration process.' " [76]

In that case an arbitration panel had rendered an award concerning the royalty value of a drug patent. Prior to the award and during the hearing one of the parties to the arbitration discovered that one member of the panel had done business with the other party to the arbitration. This information had been disclosed to the American Arbitration Association which had selected the panel, but had not been relayed to the parties. An objection was raised at the hearing but no change resulted in the make-up of the panel. The court considered the lack of notification irregular and illegal and vacated the award.

---

[73] *Id.* at 167, 75 N.E.2d at 291.
[74] *Avalon Fabrics, Inc. v. Raymill Fabrics, Inc.*, 195 Misc. 267, 89 N.Y.S.2d 166 (Sup. Ct. 1949).
[75] 165 F.Supp. 295 (D.N.J. 1958) *aff'd*, 271 F.2d 266 (3d Cir. 1959).
[76] 165 F. Supp. 300, 301. See also *Advance Trucking Corp. v. Teamsters Local 807*, 38 Misc.2d 618, 240 N.Y.S.2d 203 (Sup. Ct. 1963).

D. LIABILITY OF THE ARBITRATOR FOR MISCONDUCT

It was early established that judges should be immune to civil liability for acts performed in accordance with their duties.[77] This immunity has also been extended to arbitrators. For example, in *Jones v. Brown* [78] it was held that an arbitrator could not be sued for damages as a result of a fraudulent and corrupt act or award. In *Hill v. Aro Corp.*,[79] an employee sued an arbitrator who had decided the employee's grievance against the employee. The employee claimed that the arbitrator had engaged in misconduct during the hearing. The court granted the arbitrator's motion to dismiss:

> "If national policy encourages arbitration and if arbitrators are indispensable agencies in the furtherance of that policy, then it follows that the common law rule protecting arbitrators from suit ought not only to be affirmed, but, if need be, expanded." [80]

Injured parties are, however, not completely without remedy. In *Beaver v. Brown* [81] the court said that while judicial immunity protects arbitrators from civil liability, "it does not allow them compensation for an act rendered useless by their willful misconduct." Evidence of such misconduct could be used to defeat a motion by the arbitrator to recover for his services.

---

[77] See, *e.g.*, *Bradley v. Fisher*, 80 U.S. 335 (1872).
[78] 54 Iowa 74 (1880). See also *Babylon Milk & Cream Co. v. Horvitz*, 151 N.Y.S.2d 221 (Sup. Ct. 1956); *Cahn v. ILGWU*, 203 F. Supp. 191 (E.D.Pa.) *aff'd*, 311 F.2d 113 (3d Cir. 1962).
[79] 263 F.Supp. 324 (N.D. Ohio 1967).
[80] *Id.* at 326.
[81] 56 Iowa 565 (1881).

CHAPTER VI

The Challenges to the Arbitrator That a Dispute Is Not Arbitrable

This chapter considers the authority or jurisdiction of the arbitrator to determine a particular dispute. Stated another way, it reports what arbitrators do when a claim is made that a particular grievance should be dismissed because it is not arbitrable under the labor agreement.

What courts do concerning claims that a particular grievance is not arbitrable has been reported in Chapters III and IV. Often, courts resolve a claim that a particular grievance is not arbitrable by referring the dispute to arbitration, unless the lack of arbitrability is absolutely clear.

The first situation to be examined is where a court refers a dispute to arbitration after one party has claimed before the court that the dispute is not arbitrable, and the claim, rejected by the court, is again made to the arbitrator. Is the arbitrator bound to find the dispute arbitrable because a court has referred the dispute to arbitration, or can he examine the claim of nonarbitrability anew?

The contention that the arbitrator cannot reexamine the claim of nonarbitrability once a court has referred a dispute to arbitration was discussed by Arbitrator Thomas T. Roberts. The Supreme Court of California had referred a case claimed to be nonarbitrable to arbitration, and over the objection of the union, Roberts held that the court's order directing arbitration did not preclude the company from again raising the question of arbitrability before the arbitrator.[1]

Similarly, Arbitrator Burton B. Turkus has said that when a court refers a grievance, claimed to be nonarbitrable, to arbitration, because the Supreme Court has said that courts should resolve doubts over arbitrability in favor of arbitrability, it does not dispose of the claim of nonarbitrability if raised. Arbitrator Turkus said that it would be

---

[1] *Wilshire Oil Co. of California*, AAA Case No. 65-9 (Roberts, 1964).

"utterly inconsistent with the very doctrine or overriding theme upon which the [*Warrior & Gulf*] decision is predicated," and an "abdication of responsibility and independence of judgment" if the arbitrator were to hold a grievance arbitrable merely because under the Supreme Court view it should not be withheld from arbitration.[2]

In a like vein, Arbitrator Benjamin Aaron explained that the import of the *Steelworkers Trilogy* is that they do not require a finding of arbitrability by the arbitrator:

" 'Those cases all dealt . . . with the power of federal courts, rather than with the discretion of arbitrators. Construing those cases in a way most favorable to the Union here involved would lead at most to the conclusion that if the parties had litigated this issue in federal court instead of submitting it to private arbitration, the court would have ruled that the issue was arbitrable; or that, conversely, if the arbitration decision in this case were in favor of arbitrability, the court would decline to vacate it on review. Neither of those contingencies has occurred. The parties elected to resolve this dispute through arbitration, and the decision rests upon the judgment of a majority of the three Arbitrators selected to hear the case. In exercising that judgment we should not, in my opinion, be influenced by any calculation of what a court might do if confronted by the same problem. The dominant theme of the Supreme Court decision referred to above is that courts typically lack the specialized knowledge, experience, and insight to deal wisely with these problems. Whether either this assumption, or the corresponding one that arbitrators typically possess such expertise, is correct is, to put it mildly, a question on which there is considerable disagreement. In any case, the doctrine enunciated in the Supreme Court to uphold claims of arbitrability solely on the ground that a court would do so in like circumstances must be resisted; for to yield would be to abdicate the assumed independence of judgment based on specialized knowledge and experience upon which the Supreme Court doctrine is predicated.' "[3]

Similarly, Arbitrator James J. Healy has said that when the labor agreement provided for arbitration of "any dispute . . . of any nature or character," and even though there " 'probably' was a basis for finding arbitrability . . . under . . . *Warrior & Gulf Navigation Co.*, the union's request for establishment of a differential . . . when certain tasks are performed was not arbitrable."[4] The arbitrator interpreted the decision of the Supreme Court to mean that the union could establish a *"prima facie* case" in a court for its right to proceed to arbitration, but that it still remained for the arbitrator to determine whether he can proceed "to the pure merits" of the claim or dismiss the claim for lack of an arbitral issue.

---

[2] *Socony Mobil Oil Co.,* AAA Case No. 72-14 (Turkus, 1965).

[3] *Hughes Tool Co.,* AAA Case No. 26-1 (Aaron, 1960).

[4] *Berkshire Hathaway Co.,* AAA Case No. 41-1 (Healy, 1961).

A determination by an arbitrator that a grievance is arbitrable does not mean that the grievance has merit. Arbitrator Eric J. Schmertz has noted:

> "The arbitrability of an issue does not require it to be meritorious. A grievance, though wholly lacking in merit, may be arbitrable because it involves as its subject matter a term or condition of employment encompassed by the Collective Bargaining Agreement." [5]

In a similar vein, Arbitrator Mark L. Kahn explained that parties often confuse lack of merit of a grievance as a basis for a claim of nonarbitrability:

> "I find that the Company in this case has similarly (but erroneously) derived a conclusion as to arbitrability from its appraisal of the merits. If the action of the Company that gave rise to this proceeding was within its rights and did not violate either the Agreement or any binding joint understanding then the grievance should be denied—not because it is not arbitrable but because it lacks merit." [6]

Claims of nonarbitrability must turn on the particular provisions of the agreement in issue. There are, however, particular provisions in any agreement which generate disputes over claims of nonarbitrability. For example, the definition of a "grievance" in the labor agreement may create restrictions on the arbitrator's authority. Commonly, the arbitrator is limited to deciding grievances which in turn are defined as claims that a provision of the agreement has been violated by some management action. In such circumstances, a grievance that does not allege some violation of the labor agreement itself will produce a challenge that the arbitrator has no jurisdiction over the matter.

Generally, labor agreements do not provide that the management may file a grievance.[7] Hence, arbitrators often do not have authority to hear a claim by management that the union or an employee has violated the agreement. In some collective bargaining agreements, however, there are special arbitration procedures by which the employer can submit a grievance concerning a violation of the no-strike clause.[8]

---

[5] *Macy's New York,* AAA Case No. 43-6 (Schmertz, 1962).

[6] *Celanese Corp. of America,* AAA Case No. 19-4 (Kahn, 1960).

[7] An exception was the agreement in *Drake Bakeries, Inc. v. Local 50, Bakery and Confectionery Workers,* 370 U.S. 254, 257 (1962), which provided:
"The parties agree that they will promptly attempt to adjust all complaints, disputes or grievances arising between them involving questions of interpretation or application of any clause or matter covered by this contract or any act or conduct in relations between the parties hereto, directly or indirectly."
The arbitration provision gave "either party" the right to refer an unsettled matter to arbitration. The Supreme Court held that this language required the employer to arbitrate his claim against the union based on an alleged breach of the no-strike clause.

[8] See discussion of special arbitration procedures involving violations of the no-strike clause in Chapter XIV, Section K.

The contractual grievance procedure establishes the manner in which a grievance is initiated, the number of steps or union-management conferences through which the grievance is processed, and the time limits between the various steps. These "procedural details" vary greatly in different collective agreements. Nonetheless, failure to follow the procedures will usually provide a basis for objecting to any attempt to present the grievance case to arbitration on the ground that the arbitrator cannot assert jurisdiction over the grievance since it is not properly before him.

In addition to restrictions on arbitral authority contained in the definition of a grievance, labor agreements typically contain express limitations on the arbitrator's authority. The arbitrator is commonly confined to the resolution of grievances or disputes as to "the interpretation or application of the agreement," or of claims of "violation of the agreement." Frequently, he is further enjoined not to "add to, subtract from, or modify any of the terms of the agreement."[9] In the *Ford Motor Company* agreement, the arbitrator is admonished also that he has "no power to substitute his discretion for the company's discretion in cases where the company is given discretion" by the agreement and no power "to provide agreement for the parties in those cases where they have in their contract agreed that further negotiations shall or may provide for certain contingencies."[10]

If the responding party, usually the company, believes the claim presented would require the arbitrator to exceed these or similar limitations, a challenge to the arbitrator's jurisdiction to hear and render an award is often made. This chapter deals with how the various types of challenges to the jurisdiction of the arbitrator are handled by arbitrators.

A. LACK OF JURISDICTION DUE TO PROCEDURAL DEFECTS AND THEIR WAIVER

(1) Late Filing of the Grievance

When a grievance has not been filed within the time limits set forth in the collective bargaining agreement, the arbitrator will gen-

---

[9] It is not uncommon for an agreement to provide that disputes over wage rates, production standards, safety, or other specified matters, may not be presented to arbitration and a right of the union to strike over such disputes is reserved to the union; in others, it is not. Where the issue is not one over which the union can arbitrate, it is one that can be submitted to a court even though this would likely surprise the party, usually the management, that demanded the specific exclusion from arbitration. See Schulman, *Reason, Contract, and Law in Labor Relations,* 68 HARV. L. REV. 999, 1004-05 (1955).

[10] Agreement between *Ford Motor Co. and UAW,* Art. VII, § 16, p. 48 (1970).

erally dismiss the claim as nonarbitrable,[11] unless the opposing party has waived this procedural defect. Since the parties have limited the cases which they agree to arbitrate according to the terms of their agreement, the arbitrator has no authority to hear a claim presented too late because it has not properly entered the procedure and hence has not reached the arbitration "step." Arbitrators have supported the dismissal not only on the ground that the arbitrator must receive his authority to hear the grievance claim from the agreement, but also on the ground that the establishment of a time limit reflects the parties' recognition that grievance matters should be heard promptly and not allowed to fester for long periods permitting evidence to be lost and recollections to be dimmed.[12]

Where the agreement requires that grievances be filed "promptly," the arbitrator has a more difficult task in determining whether this standard has been met.[13]

In cases where the delay in filing the grievance is not substantial, arbitrators have shown great reluctance to dismiss a claim and have taken considerable pains to find a construction favorable to timely filing. For example, under a provision that "all grievances and differences of opinion must be mentioned within 15 days after they are first known to exist," intervening holidays were held not included in the calculation since the policy in favor of prompt settlement of grievances is not compromised by their exclusion.[14] Also, nonworking days as a result of a strike have not been counted on the ground that normal grievance processing is suspended during the strike.[15]

---

[11] See, e.g., Specialty Paper Box Co., 50 L.A. 1220 (Nathanson, 1968); Ekco Products Co., 40 L.A. 1339 (Duff, 1963); American Metallurgical Products Co., 34 L.A. 311 (McDermott, 1959); Creamery Package Mfg. Co., 31 L.A. 917 (Kelliher, 1958); Mosaic Tile Co., 13 L.A. 494 (Cornsweet, 1950); Walker Country Hosiery Mills, 13 L.A. 387 (Holden, 1949); Firestone Tire & Rubber Co., 9 L.A. 518 (Rader, 1948); Standard-Coose-Thatcher Co., 4 L.A. 79 (McCoy, 1946). See also related cases in which new issue could not be raised because of expiration of time limits: Du-Wel Products, Inc., 55 L.A. 891 (Walsh, 1970); Darlington Fabrics, AAA Case No. 92-12 (Rose, 1966); Quinn Wire & Iron Works, 64-1 ARB ¶ 8400 (Doyle, 1964); Continental Can, AAA Case No. 58-16 (Green, 1963); Witco Chemical Co., AAA Case No. 14-12 (Wirtz, 1959); Tappan Co., AAA Case No. 9-14 (Kabaker, 1959); R. H. Osbrink Mfg. Co., 28 L.A. 88 (Phelps, 1957); U.S. Rubber Co., 28 L.A. 704 (Livengood, 1957); John Deere Tractor Works, 18 L.A. 497 (Davey, 1952).

[12] See, e.g., Precision Extrusions, Inc., 49 L.A. 338 (Stouffer, 1967); Kennecott Copper Corp., 35 L.A. 412 (Ross, 1960).

[13] See, e.g., Jones & Laughlin Steel Corp., 30 L.A. 432 (Cahn, 1958); Management Services, Inc., 26 L.A. 505 (Williams, 1956); Combustion Engineering Co., 20 L.A. 416 (McCoy, 1953); Barbet Mills, Inc., 19 L.A. 677 (Maggs, 1952); but see North American Refractories, AAA Case No. 84-13 (Teple, 1955); Celanese Corp. of America, AAA Case No. 32-22 (Dunau, 1961).

[14] Eimco Corp., 41 L.A. 1184 (Dykstra, 1963); see also Schneider's Modern Bakery, Inc., 44 L.A. 574 (Hon, 1965).

[15] Airco Alloys & Carbide Co., 50 L.A. 1223 (Kesselman, 1968).

Furthermore, some arbitrators by analogy to the familiar case law concerning the application of statutes of limitation to fraudulent actions, hold that time limits on filing run only from the time the grievant became aware or should have become aware of his claim. For example, an employee who was terminated from employment while on sick leave and hence had no opportunity to learn of his termination until he attempted to return to work, was not barred under a time limit period running from the date of termination.[16] Arbitrators have generally felt that grievants should have full awareness of their injury before the time limit should start running, but this awareness is held to occur with the first clear and overt act sufficient to give such notice.[17]

Lack of awareness, however, that there exist time limits within which a grievance may be filed does not excuse late filing, since a grievant provided with a copy of the labor agreement is conclusively presumed to be aware of the existence of the time limits.[18] As with all general rules, exceptions have been created. Thus, in *Mutual Plastics Mold Corp.*,[19] an employee who was disqualified from working by the company's doctor filed an untimely grievance asserting that her failure to file earlier should be excused by the fact that she did not know until she later discussed the matter with a union representative that a grievance could be filed on the subject. Accepting this contention, the arbitrator said:

"Under most circumstances, the employee is presumed to know that actions of management are subject to review through the grievance and arbitration procedure. The specific facts of this case, however, render the normal presumption inapplicable. In the Arbitrator's opinion, a rea-

---

[16] *E. F. Hausermann Co.*, 42 L.A. 1076 (Klein, 1964). See also *Garvin's Jersey Farms, Inc.*, 41 L.A. 927 (Stouffer, 1963); but see *Durez Plastics Div. Hooker Chemical Corp.*, AAA Case No. 146-9 (Scheib, 1970); *Standard Steel Treating Co.*, AAA Case No. 146-8 (Walt, 1970); *Singer Co.*, 46 L.A. 382 (Cahn, 1966); *Robertshaw-Fulton Controls Co.*, AAA Case No. 58-16 (Green, 1963); *National Dairy Products*, AAA Case No. 40-20 (Miller, 1962); *United States Pipe & Foundry Co.*, AAA Case No. 33-9 (Seibel, 1961); *E. W. Bliss Co.*, AAA Case No. 19-7 (Teple, 1960).

[17] See, *e.g.*, *Tin Processing Corp.*, 26 L.A. 732 (Morvant, 1956) (union could not object to layoff of an employee according to an erroneous seniority list posted three years earlier); *Ekco Products Co.*, 40 L.A. 1339, 1341 (Duff, 1963) ("Whether or not Union officials had knowledge of the facts concerning Miss N—'s dismissal, Miss N— knew all the relevant facts, and could have brought them to the attention of the Union.").

[18] *Research Parts & Engineering Corp.*, 48 L.A. 594 (Krinsky, 1967). See also *Watson v. Teamsters Local 728*, 399 F.2d 875 (5th Cir. 1968) wherein the grievants claimed unawareness of their being hired as "casuals" to explain their failure to file a grievance protesting that status or to demand seniority status after 30 days employment as provided in the contract. The court concluded it to be highly unlikely that the grievants were actually unaware and, in any event, paid no heed to their subjective state of mind; *Corn Products Co.*, AAA Case No. 103-9 (Edes, 1967); *American Enka Corp.*, AAA Case No. 88-12 (Steel, 1966).

[19] 48 L.A. 2 (Block, 1967).

sonable construction of the three day time limit for filing a grievance as applied to this case is that the time did not begin to run until the Union or employee concerned became aware of the right to file a grievance." [20]

When the running of a time limit on filing starts with "the alleged incident," "cause," "event," ambiguities in the language exist which require interpretation. A grievant might argue, for instance, that the act of actually filling a job vacancy with another employee, rather than the rejection of his own bid for the vacancy, was the incident that started the time limit running.[21] In one case (a grievance claiming pay for work the employee should have been assigned), it was held that the "event" was the date management refused to allow the grievant work rather than the date they refused his subsequent demand for pay —an interpretation which tightened the time restriction.[22]

If the alleged violation can be considered to impose a continuing injury to the grievant, the arbitrator may find that the grievance is a continuing one and that the time limit on the filing of a grievance recommences each day and, hence, a filing of a grievance is never precluded. Damages or back pay in such a case, however, will be awarded only from the date the grievance was filed. A company's failure to discharge an employee who does not join the union within 31 days is never barred because the failure remains as a "continuing violation."[23] The most frequent use of the "continuing violation" doctrine occurs in claims for damages as a result of the employer's failure to pay an employee the rate established for the classification to which he is assigned or the failure to grant him a merit increase.[24]

In addition, arbitrators will not bar a grievance because of late filing if conduct by a management representative makes it unjust or unreasonable to do so on the grounds of estoppel. For example, if the delay in filing was occasioned by an offer by the management representative to settle the claim, not yet formally filed, or to make certain evidence available which the employee claims he needs to file a

---

[20] *Id.* at 8.

[21] *Joy Mfg. Co.,* 44 L.A. 304 (Sembower, 1965) (the act starting the limitation was the unequivocal rejection of employee's bid); *Heckethorn Mfg. & Supply Co.,* 61-1 ARB ¶ 8255 (Warns, 1960) (the "occurrence" was the layoff of the senior, not the recall of a junior, employee).

[22] *Bethlehem Steel Corp.,* 46 L.A. 767 (Strongin, 1966).

[23] *Kerr-McGee Oil Industries, Inc.,* 44 L.A. 701 (Hayes, 1965); *Sargent Engineering Corp.,* 43 L.A. 1165 (McNaughton, 1964); *Standard Oil Co. of Calif.,* AAA Case No. 70-4 (Burns, 1964); *American Meter Co.,* AAA Case No. 61-17 (Teple, 1963).

[24] See, *e.g., Dayton Tire & Rubber Co.,* 48 L.A. 83 (Dworkin, 1967); *Steel Warehouse Co.,* 45 L.A. 357 (Dolnick, 1965); *Taylor-Winfield Corp.,* 45 L.A. 153 (Kates, 1965); *Avco Corp., Lycoming Div.,* 43 L.A. 765 (Kornblum, 1964). See also *Miss. Structural Steel Co.,* 55 L.A. 23 (Boothe, 1970); *Nashville Bridge Co.,* 48 L.A. 44 (Williams, 1967); *Combustion Engineering, Inc.,* 46 L.A. 289 (Murphy, 1966).

proper claim, the employer will be estopped from setting up the contractual time limit as a bar.[25] Similarly, where the parties have not observed time limits in the past, this history together with evidence that the employer was aware that a grievance filing was contemplated, may bar the employer's objection that the grievance was not filed on time.[26] Arbitrators also hold that the time limit objection is waived by the employer if the grievance is processed through the preliminary steps of the grievance procedure without the timeliness being asserted as a defense.[27]

Arbitrator Clair Duff explained that a grievance over the establishment of an incentive rate was not barred from arbitration because it was not filed promptly. Since the employer continued to revise the procedures, the facts basic to the grievance did not become static. He said:

> "Contractual time limits cannot be stringently applied to facts that are shifting. Until the incentive plan applicable to this crew was developed in its final form, and its impact on the earning ability of the employees involved could be reliably determined, the dispute was inchoate. Under such circumstances, the 'grievance occurred' when the final impact of the new incentive could be measured with accuracy which certainly was some weeks after the final revision was adopted." [28]

On the other hand, arbitrators hold that a discussion of a grievance claim on its merits in a preliminary step of the grievance procedure will not waive an objection based on failure to file the grievance within the time limit if the objection is raised by the employer at the first opportunity.[29] Arbitrators usually insist that before they will find a waiver of the objection to their jurisdiction, the waiver must be established by clear and substantial evidence. For example, in *Firestone Tire & Rubber Co.,*[30] the agreement provided that a written grievance must be filed with the company's labor relations department within three days after a discharge or suspension. The union charged that

---

[25] *Weirton Steel Co.,* 54 L.A. 1049 (Kates, 1970); *Interscience Encyclopedia, Inc.,* 55 L.A. 210 (Roberts, 1970); *Russ Maita Distributors,* 51 L.A. 861 (Koven, 1968); *Sanna Dairies, Inc.,* 43 L.A. 16 (Rice, 1964); *Celanese Corp. of America,* AAA Case No. 14-11 (Schedler, 1959).

[26] *Dockside Machine & Boiler Works, Inc.,* 55 L.A. 1221 (Block, 1970); *City Transportation Co.,* AAA Case No. 88-11 (Williams, 1966); *Borg-Warner Corp.,* AAA Case No. 84-21 (Lennard, 1965); *Ward Foods, Inc., Bell Bakeries Div.,* 43 L.A. 608 (Dworet, 1964); *Eastern Racing Association,* AAA Case No. 72-9 (MacLeod, 1964).

[27] *Billingsley, Inc.,* 48 L.A. 802 (Krinsky, 1967); but see *Deep Rock Oil Corp.,* 6 ALAA ¶ 69,376 (Emery, 1953). But see awards listed in note 29.

[28] *H. K. Porter Co.,* AAA Case No. 54-12 (Duff, 1963).

[29] *Elicon Detroit, Inc.,* AAA 54-30-0384 (Walt, 11-15-72); *Pennsylvania Steel Foundry & Machine Co.,* AAA Case No. 94-19 (Boyer, 1966); *Chase Bag Co.,* 42 L.A. 153 (Elkouri, 1963); *American Metallurgical Products Co.,* 34 L.A. 311 (McDermott, 1959).

[30] 9 L.A. 518 (Rader, 1948).

the company had waived the formal filing within this time limit, since its representatives were aware of the discharge and had discussed it with union representatives, leading them to believe that the management was reconsidering the discharge. Arbitrator Rader held the evidence of waiver was insufficient:

> "There is no question legally but that the parties to the contract can waive provisions in it, but this cannot be done by implication unless it be that the implications are of such a nature to create a legal and positive presumption that the same were waived. Otherwise it is necessary that there be a direct waiving by both parties to any given provision in a contract. . . . To rule, without the strongest provocation, that [a] provision of a grievance section of a contract has been waived would be establishment of a precedent which might have far-reaching effects. To use an illustration, it would be like the neglecting of a leak in the dikes of Holland. . . ." [31]

A most significant footnote in the Nash memorandum explaining the policy of the General Counsel to dismiss a charge of an unfair labor practice and defer to arbitration if the claim could be resolved under the labor agreement suggests that such dismissal will occur even when the time limits established in the agreement have run barring a grievance on the same subject matter. [32]

(2) Tardy Processing Through Grievance Steps

After a grievance has been properly filed, failure to process the grievance to the next higher step of the procedure is also often asserted as a bar to arbitration of the grievance on the basis that the arbitrator has no jurisdiction to hear and determine a grievance not properly before him. [33] Often this procedural defect will occur immediately prior to arbitration after the grievance has been processed through all conference steps. [34]

Where a telegram appealing a grievance to arbitration was sent one day late, Arbitrator Lewis M. Gill held the grievance was not

---

[31] *Id.* at 521, 522. See also *Mosaic Tile Co.,* 13 L.A. 949, 950 (Cornsweet, 1950) ("Since the agreement is the 'constitution' of the parties and written by them after negotiation, any waiver of one of its provisions must be proven by clear, convincing and definite evidence"); *Phillips Petroleum Co.,* 7 L.A. 595 (Rader, 1947).

[32] Nash, *Arbitration Deferral Policy Under Collyer,* Memorandum of NLRB General Counsel to NLRB Regional Directors and Officers-in-Charges, DLR No. 49 (3/10/72) n. 11.

[33] *Abex Corp.,* 53 L.A. 79 (Stouffer, 1969); *Chase Bag Co.,* 53 L.A. 612 (Larson, 1969); *Diamond Power Specialty Corp.,* 44 L.A. 878 (Dworkin, 1964).

[34] *Frolic Footwear, Inc.,* 53 L.A. 353 (Seinsheimer, 1969); *Precision Extrusions, Inc.,* 49 L.A. 338 (Stouffer, 1967) (and numerous cases cited therein); *Erwin Mills, Inc.,* 47 L.A. 606 (Stark, 1966); *Management Services, Inc.,* 20 L.A. 34 (McCoy, 1963); *International Harvester Co.,* 10 L.A. 525 (Kelliher, 1948). See also *Massey-Ferguson,* AAA Case No. 84-8 (Cole, 1965); *Cleveland Pneumatic Tool Co.,* 43 L.A. 869 (Dworkin, 1964); *Foster Refrigerator Corp.,* AAA Case No. 56-14 (Santer, 1963).

arbitrable. Rejecting the union's contention that knowledge by the company of the union's dissatisfaction because of comments at a grievance meeting constituted notice of appeal, Gill noted that such an argument had "a great deal of persuasiveness." He held, however:

> "The question before me at this point is quite different; it is whether I have any authority to rule that the grievances are arbitrable under these circumstances, and if so whether I should do so. It seems perfectly clear that I have no such authority. The time limit in question is very plain and unambiguous, and it was unquestionably past by the time the Union's telegram was sent and received. The parties can waive a contractual provision by mutual agreement, but an arbitrator cannot." [35]

Arbitrators dismiss grievances when there is a failure to respect time limits for appeals on policy grounds as well as on the ground of lack of jurisdiction or authority. Arbitrator Stouffer said:

> "The principal reason for strict adherence to contractual time limitations for processing of grievances is so that the grievances will be quickly and efficiently processed. Any relaxation of the time requirements, rather than benefiting any of the parties, actually leads to the ultimate destruction of the utility of the grievance procedure.
>
> "The Company and the Union in consummating the currently-effective Collective Bargaining Agreement expressly agreed to the time limits for processing grievances, and also that an arbitrator would have no authority to add to, subtract from, or change the Agreement. . . ." [36]

In *John Deere Tractor Co.*,[37] Arbitrator Clarence M. Updegraff also explained the benefits of time limits:

> "The union is well-manned by some able full-time and some similarly able part-time officers. If they abandon a grievance at any step, it may well be inferred that they have become convinced of its lack of merit. The time limitations have a part to play similar to those in adjustment of legal rights. Statutes of limitations exist to limit or terminate all sorts of legal rights and procedures since, though 'the law abhors forfeitures' it proceeds upon the principle that, if rights are not pursued while the disputes are reasonably recent or fresh, justice may fail because evidence has disappeared, witnesses have moved off and been lost, or collateral rights entitled to recognition have appeared which rest upon the established status quo." [38]

As with the initial filing of a grievance, arbitrators have demonstrated a similar reluctance to bar a grievance for failure to appeal within a time limit and thus have found, for example, the employer estopped to assert the lack of timely appeal when the union has in the past failed to conform to the time limit on appeal requirements

---

[35] *Lancaster Malleable Castings Co.*, AAA Case No. 9-10 (Gill, 1959).
[36] *Precision Extrusions, Inc.*, 49 L.A. 338, 341 (Stouffer, 1967).
[37] 3 L.A. 737 (Updegraff, 1946).
[38] *Id.* at 743.

without objection from the management,[39] or where the company representatives gave to the union representatives reason to believe there would be another hearing at which an international representative of the union would be present,[40] or where the delay in filing the demand for arbitration was occasioned by the parties' attempt, at the company's suggestion, to formulate the issue.[41]

Some arbitrators have found a waiver where the objection to jurisdiction is based on a failure to appeal a grievance from the last step to arbitration within the time limits, unless the objection is raised before the commencement of the arbitration hearing.[42] Others, however, have held that where time limits on appeal are clear and compliance with these limitations has been required in the past, a party is not obligated to raise his objection before the hearing starts. Arbitrator John Sembower discussed the reasons for such a view in *Joy Manufacturing Company*:[43]

"[I]t is regrettable that the timeliness of the grievance should arise for the first time in arbitration, but still it has to be considered because it is universally held that the jurisdiction of the arbitrator may be questioned at any point, just as may the jurisdiction of a court of law, unless the issue has been expressly waived.

"Aware that parties usually prefer their disputes to be decided upon the so-called merits rather than technicalities, arbitrators usually are rather lenient if there are no specific time elements spelled out in the

---

[39] *Kankakee Electric Steel Co.*, 53 L.A. 178 (Sembower, 1969); *E. W. Bliss Co.*, 45 L.A. 1000 (Lehoczky, 1965); *Collis Co.*, 50 L.A. 1157 (Doyle, 1968). See also *Penn Jersey Boiler & Construction Co.*, 50 L.A. 177 (Buckwalter, 1967); *General Precision, Inc.*, 42 L.A. 589 (Roberts, 1964); *E. J. Lavino Co.*, AAA Case No. 7-15 (Valtin, 1959).

[40] *Southland Paper Mills*, AAA Case No. 32-3 (Singletary, 1961).

[41] *Hammermill Paper Co.*, AAA Case No. 62-22 (Shister, 1963); *Royal McBee Corp.*, AAA Case No. 16-7 (Healy, 1959); but see *Federal-Mogul-Bower Bearings, Inc.*, AAA Case No. 14-20 (Seibel, 1959).

[42] *American Air Filter Co.*, 54 L.A. 1251 (Dolnick, 1970); *Badger Concrete Co.*, 50 L.A. 901 (Krinsky, 1968); *Produce Inc.*, 50 L.A. 453 (Keefe, 1968); *United Engineering & Foundry Co.*, 49 L.A. 1036 (Wagner, 1967); *United States Steel Corp.*, 48 L.A. 1085 (Dybeck, 1967); *Plasti-Line, Inc.*, AAA Case No. 88-16 (King, 1966); *The General Refractories Co.*, AAA Case No. 48-6 (Miller, 1962).

[43] 44 L.A. 304, 306-07 (Sembower, 1965). See also *Textile Paper Products*, 51 L.A. 385 (Hebert, Imp. Arb., 1967); *Nashville Bridge Co.*, 48 L.A. 44 (Williams, 1967); *Erwin Mills*, AAA Case No. 90-5 (Stark, 1966); *Lake Shore Coach Co.*, 44 L.A. 1190 (Geissinger, 1965); *Deep Rock Oil Corp.*, 6 ALAA ¶ 69,376 (Emery, 1953) (no waiver was found where the sole grounds for inferring a waiver was the company's failure to raise earlier its objections to an untimely demand for arbitration); *Wyandotte Chemicals Corp.*, 35 L.A. 783 (Wollett, 1960) (no waiver although the defense of nonarbitrability was not raised until third step); *American Metallurgical Products Co.*, 34 L.A. 311 (McDermott, 1959) (no waiver since timeliness issue was raised prior to arbitration, although not discussed); *Management Services Inc.*, 5 ALAA ¶ 73,002 (McCoy, 1953); *Consolidated Vultee Aircraft Corp.*, 12 L.A. 786, 793 (Aaron, 1949) ("The first two steps are at the shop level; and it would appear to be sound policy to try to settle even untimely grievances on their merits at that stage"); *Columbian Carbon Co.*, 8 L.A. 634 (Potter, 1947) (no waiver merely because company failed to raise defense of timeliness at the earliest possible moment).

contract. But it is different if the parties had agreed upon deadlines, because these are, in effect, self-imposed 'statutes of limitations.' . .

"One possible basis for deviation is if the parties have allowed their schedule to fall into disuse, and both are guilty of repeatedly letting things slide and not living up to the time requirements. . . . However, in this instance there is no evidence of anything but a policy of strict compliance on the part of both parties. . . ."

Under a clause which stated that unsettled grievances "will be considered closed" if not filed for arbitration within 60 days of the origin of the grievance, a grievance was held to be not arbitrable four months after it arose, despite the fact that it was still being negotiated in the grievance procedure.[44] The union's argument that it would be "bizzare" to demand arbitration before it was known that negotiations would be fruitless relates to, the arbitrator said, "the wisdom" of the clause the parties had agreed upon, but does not give the arbitrator the right to disregard that clause. The parties saw fit to impose a time limit "from the time the grievance arose." As this language is "unambiguous and emphatic," the arbitrator held, he "may not uphold the right to arbitrate and disregard the condition qualifying the right which the parties saw fit to state so clearly."[45]

An exception to the more general rule, however, appears to arise when one party appeals a grievance to arbitration after permitting an earlier but identical grievance to be barred by failure to appeal it to arbitration within the time limit. Arbitrator Killingsworth held the objection to the second grievance must be raised prior to the arbitration hearing, or it is waived:

"By any realistic standard, the present grievance is the same as Grievance No. 22-67. Precisely the same reassignment of functions provides the basis for both grievances. Therefore, the Company could have refused to consider the present grievance in the grievance procedure on the ground that the Union's failure to appeal Grievance No. 22-67 to arbitration had settled that grievance on the basis of the Company's Step 4 answer, which denied the grievance. Or the Company could have discussed the whole matter once again, while specifically reserving the right to object to the appeal of the present grievance to arbitration. The Company in fact did neither of these things. . . . In other words, it appears that the Company raised this jurisdictional point for the first time at the arbitration hearing." [46]

---

[44] *Booth Broadcasting Co.*, AAA Case No. 52-14 (Ellmann, 1962).

[45] In *FMC Corp.*, 54 L.A. 807 (Whyte, 1970), time limits arose in a different context. There, the contract required an award to be issued within 15 days "after the matter is finally submitted." When the company requested a stenographic transcript and permission to file a brief, the arbitrator ruled the requests proper and concluded that the 15 days began only after the briefs were filed.

[46] *General American Transportation Corp.*, Grievance No. 16-68, pp. 5-6 (Killingsworth, 1970) (unreported). See also *IUE Local 616 v. Byrd Plastics, Inc.*, 428 F.2d 23 (3d Cir. 1971); *Miehle-Goss-Dexter, Inc.*, AAA Case No. 97-17 (Davis, 1966); *United States Steel Corp.*, 11 STEEL ARB. 8311 (Florey, 1963); *United States Steel Corp.*, 5 STEEL ARB. 2861 (Garrett, 1955).

B. LACK OF JURISDICTION OVER AN ALLEGED OFFENSE BECAUSE OF THE PASSAGE OF TIME

Arbitrators have sometimes held that an alleged offense cannot be processed to arbitration because it has been barred by the passage of time.[47] This concept, known as laches, may be a rationale by the arbitrator for a decision on the merits and may not be a true procedural rule. However, the concept of laches is close enough to a procedural rule to deserve mention. Some arbitrators are actually imposing a "reasonable time" requirement within which grievances must be filed by adopting the equitable principle of laches.[48]

A decision by Arbitrator Raymond R. Roberts illustrates how considerations of laches enter a consideration of the merits.[49] An employee, hired in 1968, stated on his employment application that he had been self-employed at farming since 1961. Two years later, the employer learned that the employee had been working for another company at the time he filled out the application and that the prior employer was not satisfied with his work performance. When this discovery was made, the employee was discharged for violation of the rule against falsification of employment applications. The union protested, claiming that the discharge was improper because it was based on a cause which had occurred two years before. The company argued that the employee would not have been hired if his prior employment had been known and the prior employer's assessment obtained. Arbitrator Roberts upheld the discharge. Roberts noted that essentially two lines of cases have emerged among arbitrators in dealing with problems of this kind—the first, applying limitation periods when the misrepresentation was not serious or it ceased to be relevant or material to the employment; the second, where the misrepresentation was serious and of continuing importance to employment, no limitations period was applied. Applying the standard to the instant case, Roberts found the misrepresentation to be deliberate and material to the employee's continuing employment since his record with the company was seen by the arbitrator as merely a continuation of his previous actions with his former employer.

---

[47] *Acme Hamilton Manufacturing Corp.*, AAA Case No. 86-8 (Dash, 1965); *P. R. Mallory & Co.*, AAA Case No. 19-23 (Stark, 1960).
[48] *Dayton Tire & Rubber Co.*, 48 L.A. 83 (Dworkin, 1967); *Huber Pontiac, Inc.*, 66-3 ARB ¶ 9021 (Traynor, 1966); *New York Racing Ass'n*, 43 L.A. 129 (Scheiber, 1964); *Bethlehem Steel Co.*, 37 L.A. 956 (Seward, 1961); *Warner Electric Brake & Clutch Co.*, 31 L.A. 219 (Kelliher, 1958) (failure to file a grievance promptly cut off back pay even though the grievance was brought within the period of time specified in the agreement); *Rockwell Mfg. Co.*, 25 L.A. 534 (Duff, 1955) (analogy drawn to equitable doctrine of laches); *Hinson Mfg. Co.*, 20 L.A. 688 (Davey, 1953) (a grievance filed six months after the action was barred by laches).
[49] *Tiffany Metal Products Mfg. Co.*, 56 L.A. 135 (Roberts, 1970).

Similarly, Arbitrator Albert Epstein upheld the discharge of a drill press operator who had failed to indicate on an employment application executed eight months earlier that she had a college degree and had been discharged by her last employer. The arbitrator found that the omission was intentional and sustained the discharge.[50]

On the other hand, it was held in *Dayton Malleable Iron Co.*[51] that the employee was improperly discharged where the asserted falsity consisted of failing to reveal that he had earlier been employed by the employer. On the facts, said the arbitrator, it must be found that the claimed falsity was not willful. The employee had also been with the company approximately four years before the falsification was discovered and that falsification consisted of not revealing in his application that he had worked some 25 days for the company previously before quitting. Moreover, the arbitrator found the falsification not to be a material one.

The defense of laches has barred back pay even in situations where the grievance is continuing and hence is not barred. In such a case, the arbitrator said.[52]

> " 'Although the union testified that it was not previously aware of the company's failure to pay the bonus, it cannot be denied that it failed to investigate the matter over an extended period of years. . . . So far as any earlier period is concerned, the defense of laches is applicable.' However, 'the breach of the agreement has been a continuing one, . . . occurring at the end of each payroll period, and it cannot be said that the present grievance was untimely filed. . . .' In view of the 'lack of attention' to this matter on the part of the union for so long a period, . . . back pay was awarded only to the date of the grievance."

C. LACK OF JURISDICTION OVER A CHANGED ISSUE

Some arbitrators have held that their authority is limited to a determination of the merits of the claim of contract violation alleged in the submitted grievance. For example, in *National Lead Co.*, Arbitrator Joseph G. Stashower said:

> "When the dispute is submitted to the Arbitrator, as a result of the appeal of the grievance, the only items which the Administrator may

---

[50] *Powers Regulator Co.*, 56 L.A. 11 (Epstein, 1970). See also *Tiffany Metal Products Mfg. Co.*, 56 L.A. 135 (Roberts, 1971); *Thorsen Mfg. Co.*, 55 L.A. 581 (Koven, 1970); *Midland-Ross Corp.*, 55 L.A. 258 (McNaughton, 1970); *General Cable Corp.*, 54 L.A. 696 (Updegraff, 1970); *Westinghouse Corp.*, AAA Case No. 146-2 (Schmertz, 1970); *Henry Vogt Machine Co.*, AAA Case No. 90-6 (Stouffer, 1966); *Rexall Drug Co.*, AAA Case No. 47-6 (Dworkin, 1962); *General Electric Co.*, AAA Case No. 5-22 (Brown, 1959).

[51] 54 L.A. 1192 (Howlett, 1970).

[52] *American Meter Co.*, AAA Case No. 61-17 (Teple, 1963).

consider are those mentioned in the grievance, unless the parties have by stipulation extended the scope of the Arbitrator's authority to consider addditional items not mentioned in the grievance. Therefore, it must be held in this dispute, that the only items which the Arbitrator may consider are those mentioned in Grievance No. 712." [53]

If the union representatives attempt to broaden the scope of the claim by asserting a different or additional violation at the arbitration hearing, the arbitrator may well hold that a new grievance is being submitted in a manner inconsistent with the agreed upon procedure. Both jurisdictional grounds and policy considerations require that a hearing on such new claims be disallowed.[54] In *Allis-Chalmers Mfg. Co.*,[55] Arbitrator Elmer E. Hilpert succinctly expressed the underlying rationale:

> "[T]he Referee does not treat a grievance, written at the 'shop level,' as a 'pleading' in a court of law. Hence, if any time prior to the Hearing of the matter . . . the Union has 'cured,' or 'corrected' the 'defects,' or deficiencies, in its allegations of necessary facts, in a grievance, the Referee would treat this as a processable grievance, subject only to the postponements necessary to enable the Company to meet the Union's case. However, if the Union changes its whole theory of recovery when it comes before the Referee, such a 'new' grievance must obviously be returned to the prior steps in the parties' 'Complaint and Grievance Procedure.' . . ." [56]

Similarly, where the union submitted to the arbitrator an issue which was different than the issue discussed in the grievance procedure and set forth in the union's demand for arbitration, the arbitrator ruled that he had no jurisdiction to hear the union's new issue. The labor agreement stated that only "such grievance" that has not been "satisfactorily settled" in the grievance procedure "may be appealed to an impartial umpire." Arbitrator James Altieri said:

> "It seems clear that the only question properly before the undersigned is whether the employer as charged, has assigned bargaining unit work

---

[53] 30 L.A. 893, 897 (Stashower, 1958).

[54] See, *e.g.*, *Perfex Plastics, Inc.*, 68-2 ARB ¶ 8638 (Malinowski, 1968); *Lithonia Lighting, Inc.*, 67-1 ARB ¶ 8043 (Holly, 1967); *Decar Plastics Corp.*, 66-3 ARB ¶ 8810 (Solomon, 1966); *Chrysler Corp.*, 1 ALAA ¶ 67,258 (Wolff, 1964); *Tenn-Flake, Inc.*, 60-1 ARB ¶ 8178 (Alexander, 1960); *Bethlehem Steel Co.*, 8 STEEL ARB. 5515, 5519 (Stark, 1959); *National Lead Co.*, 30 L.A. 893 (Stashower, 1958); *Bridgeport Brass Co.*, 30 L.A. 622 (Donnelly Chm., 1958); *American Airlines, Inc.*, 27 L.A. 448 (Wolff, 1956); *Bethlehem Steel Co.*, 5 STEEL ARB. 3419 (Seward, 1956); *Bethlehem Steel Co.*, 4 STEEL ARB. 2373 (Platt, 1954); *Bethlehem Steel Co.*, 2 STEEL ARB. 1293 (Seward, 1953); *Bethlehem Steel Co.*, 17 L.A. 295, 300 (Selekman, 1951); *General Motors*, Umpire Decision No. E-276 (Alexander, 1949); *Chrysler Corp.*, 1 ALAA ¶ 67,258 (Wolff, 1944).

[55] Referee Case No. 57 (Hilpert, 1958) (unpublished).

[56] *Id*. at 16.

to nonbargaining unit personnel. However, the union is presently specifically contending that by reason of the regular performance of experimetal work by [the nonbargaining unit employee] he is not outside the bargaining unit, as the grievance alleges, but, to the contrary, is part of it. The union therefore is no longer protesting that the company is assigning bargaining unit work to a nonbargaining unit employee. . . . The arbitrator has no authority to render declaratory judgment on a claim that asserts no specific violation and that has not been processed through the grievance procedure to arbitration." [57]

When an employer reassigned certain duties between classifications and a grievance was filed claiming that the reassignment violated the local working conditions provision, and then in its prehearing brief (submitted just prior to the arbitration hearing) the union for the first time raised a claim that the reassignment violated the seniority article, Arbitrator David Miller refused to consider the union's new seniority claim because it had not been raised in the prior steps of the grievance procedure:[58]

"Under the Agreement an issue brought to arbitration is framed by the original grievance statement and the facts, arguments and allegations raised by either party in the pre-arbitration steps of the grievance procedure. Unquestionably the obligation for early disclosure of all main facts and pertinent arguments is designed to permit settlement of the issue by the parties and to prevent surprise in the event the matter is submitted to arbitration. The purpose is evident throughout the provisions for 'Adjustment of Grievance'—Section 6. And it is emphasized in the Arbitration Procedure 'ground rules' mutually adopted by the parties' representatives on September 17, 1962. This does not mean that obviously inherent facts and arguments should be excluded from consideration in arbitration by overtechnical appraisal of the presentations in the earlier steps of the procedure. It does mean, however, that either party is entitled to know and consider, in the pre-arbitration steps of the grievance procedure, the essential claims and arguments upon which the other relies.

". . .

"It is my conclusion that this late submission of the question with respect to whether a seniority violation occurred raises a serious procedural issue. Of the several arguments raised by the Union in this case, that alleging violation of Section 12 could conceivably be the most important. To permit its inclusion at this juncture would be to entertain a major alteration in position without benefit of pre-arbitration discussion of the issue by the parties. And to do so would be a disservice to the purposes of Section 6 procedures. The ruling is, therefore, that the matter of violation of Section 12—Seniority is not properly before me."

---

[57] *John Bath & Co.*, AAA Case No. 86-9 (Altieri, 1965).
[58] *United States Steel Corp.*, 12 STEEL ARB. 8490, 8491 (Miller, 1964).

Similarly, in *E. B. Bliss*,[59] the arbitrator ruled that although the union could refer to new sections of the contract in the fourth step of the grievance procedure, additional sections may not be referred to during the arbitration proceedings.

Also, if a party raises a grievance with respect to certain employees, then claims damages at the hearing for other employees similarly situated, but not mentioned in the original grievance, arbitrators will exclude the claims of unnamed grievants because the other party had had no opportunity to investigate those claims or attempt their settlement.[60]

The desire to have both parties deal fully and honestly with each other from the start of the grievance process has been emphasized by many arbitrators as the rationale for refusing to hear an issue that has not been processed through the grievance procedure. As Arbitrator David Wolff observed in an early case:

> "Under a strict, but fair, interpretation of the grievance procedure provided in the contract, the Chairman can find that the Union is bound by, and limited to, the matters contained in the original grievance, inasmuch as any material extension, amendment or modification results, in fact, in another or different grievance. Such a change or shift in position at a date later than the original grievance may not permit either side a fair and full use of the grievance procedure. Not only does it weaken the procedure, but the knowledge that such a loose practice was permitted could easily eventually void the good results which may be expected in the preliminary steps of a well functioning grievance system." [61]

More recently, Arbitrator Arthur Malinowski refused to consider an issue not raised in the prior steps of the grievance procedure, and said:

> "Arbitrators have long held that the procedural steps of the grievance procedure provide an opportunity for possible settlement of the controversies which may arise between the Parties. It is in the atmosphere

---

[59] 7 Steel Arb. 4781, 4783 (Di Leone, 1958). See F. Elkouri & E. Elkouri, How Arbitration Works 139 (BNA Books, 1960):

"[I]f a deviation from what occurred at the pre-arbitral stage actually constitutes the addition of a new issue or dispute that has not been previously discussed by the parties, or the addition of a claim that has not been filed as required by the collective agreement, and if this by-passing of the grievance procedure is objected to by one of the parties, the arbitrator will ordinarily refuse to dispose of the new matter in his award."

See also *Whirlwind, Inc.*, 68-2 ARB ¶ 8525 (Solomon, 1968); *Bethlehem Steel Co.*, 13 Steel Arb. 9898 (Porter, 1966).

[60] See, *e.g., Geigy Chemical Corp.*, 34 L.A. 102 (Morvant, 1959); *Swift & Co.*, 17 L.A. 537 (Seward, 1951). *Compare International Harvester Co.*, 14 L.A. 756 (Seward, 1950) (arbitrator found the abstract contract interpretation arbitrable but would not award back pay for unnamed grievants).

[61] *Chrysler Corp.*, 1 ALAA ¶ 67,258, 67,588 (Wolff, 1944); see also *Bethlehem Steel Co.*, 4 Steel Arb. 2373 (Platt, 1954); *Bethlehem Steel Co.*, 17 L.A. 295, 300 (Selekman, 1951); *General Motors Corp.*, Umpire Decision No. E-276 at 638 (Wallen, 1949).

of discussion, offer and counter-offer that the Parties may resolve their differences in a manner not to interfere with production. The parties in Article II have provided for an elaborate grievance procedure and have further clearly limited the Arbitrator's authority to those matters which have been properly carried through the grievance and arbitration procedure." [62]

Perhaps the most exhaustive discussion of this problem was by Arbitrator Bernard Meltzer in *Borg-Warner Corporation*.[63] The union there challenged the company's right to downgrade an employee. At the hearing, it argued that even if the employee had been properly downgraded, the company should have permitted him to bump into a job for which he qualified. Arbitrator Meltzer refused to consider the bumping argument on the ground that the issue had not been raised in prior steps of the grievance procedure and, therefore, was not ripe for arbitration. His analysis is particularly lucid:

"The arbitrator recognizes that a grievance should not be read like a technical instrument or a common law pleading. Nevertheless, the arbitrator is persuaded that in this case important legal and practical considerations require him to limit the issue to be determined solely to that raised by the written grievance initially signed by the grievant and the Union Steward.

"Under the contract, arbitration is the final step in a complex and formal grievance procedure. Accordingly, the arbitrator's authority to determine a grievance not processed in accordance with the contract is open to serious question. While the parties may waive compliance with the prescribed grievance procedure and alter the original grievance in the course of processing it, the vague and inconclusive evidence regarding a statement concerning 'juggling,' which did not operate as adequate notice of the issues to be raised, is not a sufficient basis, in the circumstances of this case, for finding a waiver.

"These legal considerations reflect and are reenforced by strong practical considerations. Arbitration is a supplement to, and not a substitute for, the grievance process. The arbitrator's function is 'to decide questions which the parties themselves have tried to settle without success.' To treat these two processes as the same is to threaten the integrity and usefulness of both of them. Where, as in this case, there is a multi-step grievance procedure, one of the resultant advantages is that it brings to bear on the solution of a grievance with general implications the different kinds of know-how which exist at different echelons of the Union and the Company. But this advantage is lost or diluted where a new issue is formulated for the first time at the arbitration stage.

"These generalities operate with particular force in this case. The issues in question, crystallized only at the arbitration stage, involve a complex seniority system created by contractual language which is not altogether clear. Witnesses who might have testified as to past prac-

[62] *Perfex Plastics, Inc.*, 68-2 ARB ¶ 8638 at 5218 (Malinowski, 1968).
[63] 27 L.A. 580 (Meltzer, 1956).

tices were either not available at the hearing, or when available, had not collected data which might have been relevant. Under all these circumstances, there is a danger that a determination of these issues in this arbitration might create difficulties which have not been fully explored because of the failure to process these issues through the grievance procedure." (Citations omitted.)[64]

Unless the parties have thoroughly explored an issue in the lower stages of the grievance procedure, it cannot be said to have been "referred" or "appealed" to arbitration. In other words, the determination of the arbitrator's jurisdiction, *i.e.*, of the issues to be resolved by the arbitrator, is for the parties and is not subject to the latitude normally given to an arbitrator concerning other matters. This rule was stated by Arbitrator Robert Howlett:

> "While arbitrators are not bound by the technical procedural rules of the common law or chancery courts . . . , the flexibility afforded an arbitrator in procedure and deciding a case on the merits does not apply to decision of the issue or issues before the arbitrator." [65]

On the other hand, arbitrators seldom refuse jurisdiction of a grievance because the grievant or union representative failed to cite the correct contract provision in support of its claim, even where the agreement so provides, or alter the theories underlying the claim so long as the company was not misled by this failure or change.[66] If the grievance clearly states the relevant facts, arbitrators generally hold that adequate notice concerning the claim has been given, even if the basis for the claim at the hearing varies from the claim asserted at the first step.[67]

D. LACK OF AN AGGRIEVED

Where the agreement requires "the aggrieved" to present his grievance orally in the first step and then to sign a written statement of it in the second step, a grievance signed by the chief steward was challenged as nonarbitrable. The arbitrator held it was arbitrable on the ground that the steward was the employee's representative.[68] However, where the requirement was that the aggrieved employee sign the grievance and there was evidence that he refused to do so, an arbi-

---

[64] *Id.* at 584.

[65] *Wyandotte Chemicals Corp.*, 38 L.A. 808, 817 (Howlett, 1962).

[66] *Anderson Clayton Foods Co.*, 54 L.A. 551 (Feller, 1970); *Hupp Corp.*, 48 L.A. 524 (Hayes, 1967); *Olin Mathieson Chemical Corp.*, 67-1 ARB ¶ 8292 (Getman, undated); *Montgomery Ward & Co.*, 48 L.A. 429 (Gorsuch, 1967); *Package Machinery Co.*, 41 L.A. 47, 48 (Altieri, 1963).

[67] *Monroe Concrete Co.*, 56 L.A. 15 (Weckstein, 1971); *Colson Co.*, 54 L.A. 896 (Roberts, 1970); *Lockheed Aircraft Corp.*, 55 L.A. 14 (Krimsly, 1970).

[68] *Interlake Iron Corp.*, AAA Case No. 76-6 (Gross, 1964); *Flexsteel Industries*, AAA Case No. 68-6 (Abersold, 1964).

trator has held he had no jurisdiction to hear the grievance.[69] Similarly, where eight members of the union committee signed the grievance (none of whom was the aggrieved), the requirement of the labor agreement that a grievance "be reduced to writing and signed by the aggrieved" as a condition for proceeding from the first to the second step of the grievance procedure made the grievance not arbitrable Arbitrator William N. Loucks stated:

"It is perfectly clear that, unless the matter is in writing and is 'signed by the aggrieved,' there is nothing which can proceed from [the first step] onward through the subsequent steps of the grievance procedure of which arbitration is the final step." [70]

Where the grievance was over a demotion, but the grievant had been discharged for other reasons after the grievance was filed but before the arbitration, and its arbitrability was challenged on the ground there was no longer an employee-grievant, Arbitrator Robert McIntosh said an arbitrable issue was presented:

"At the time the grievance was filed, [an employer-employee relationship] existed. That being so, the necessary jurisdiction was established. . . . Certainly an employee who has begun proceedings to clear his employment record is entitled to pursue his remedy until he has exhausted all available avenues and through all available tribunals." [71]

Arbitrator Bert Luskin explained that where the dischargee was a probationary employee a grievance over his discharge presented an arbitrable issue because:

"The issue in question involves the interpretation and application of provisions of the collective bargaining agreement, and to that extent the grievance is arbitrable. A distinction must be made between issues which, by their nature, fall outside the scope of the arbitrator's authority in areas which would prohibit the issuance of an award in cases where the application or interpretation of provisions of the agreement are not involved. The fact that provisions of the agreement permit the Company to exercise its right to terminate a probationary employee would constitute a good and sufficient defense to the claim of the discharged employee; but the issue, however, may be the subject of a grievance with the terminal point of arbitration, since it does in fact involve the application and interpretation of specific provisions of the collective bargaining agreement." [72]

A grievance claiming reinstatement of an individual who had accepted retirement checks was arbitrable because the question of

---

[69] *Symington Wayne Corp.*, AAA Case No. 104-8 (Dash, 1967); *Howell Electric Motors Co.*, AAA Case No. 36-22 (Kahn, 1961).

[70] *Masell Manufacturing Corp.*, AAA Case No. 14-1 (Loucks, 1959). See also *Combustion Engineering, Inc.*, 54 L.A. 1118 (Erbs, 1970).

[71] *Kelsey-Hayes Co.*, AAA Case No. 40-5 (McIntosh, 1961).

[72] *The Electric Storage Battery Co.*, AAA Case No. 17-13 (Luskin, 1959); see also *American Bosch Arma Corp.*, AAA Case No. 66-2 (Greene, 1964).

whether the grievant had actually retired, losing rights under the agreement, was a question of interpretation.[73]

Arbitrator Ralph Seward in *Swift & Company*[74] found the employer had violated a no-discrimination clause by refusing to hire qualified Negro job applicants, but that his award could be applied only to named grievants and could not be extended to additional grievants whose names were furnished to the employer for the first time at the arbitration hearing. He stated in part:

> "The arbitrator's award does not cover the five negro women whose names were first given to the company at the arbitration hearing. The scope of this grievance and of the union's claim for relief was defined when the union furnished the company with the names of thirteen negro women who had allegedly been the victims of discrimination. This list purported to be complete. Prior to the hearing there was no suggestion that additional women might be involved. In the opinion of the arbitrator the union's attempt to expand the grievance at the arbitration hearing to include additional grievants was improper and must fail." [75]

Similarly, in *Geigy Chemical Corp.*,[76] an employee filed a written grievance on a formal grievance report form and said 10 employees were involved. In rejecting the jurisdiction over the claims of the unnamed grievants, the arbitrator explained:

> "On the other hand, it is a misuse of the grievance procedure to permit a brother member to file a grievance and not identify oneself with that grievance if the same injury is suffered. It is wrong because (1) it is unfair to expect one man to carry the fight for others who remain in the background anonymously, (2) it is unfair to the Company because they cannot evaluate the grievance as to a possible compromise settlement when they are ignorant as to how many employees are involved, and (3) it is unfair to the grievance procedure because it was never intended that one of the parties may withhold important facts concerning a dispute while it is being considered in the grievance steps. The primary purpose of the grievance procedure is to settle disputes, and it is only possible to achieve a settlement when all of the facts are known and can be evaluated. Unless both parties are aware of all facts concerning a dispute, which includes the names of the people involved, how then can it be said that all efforts have been exhausted to effect a settlement? By withholding facts the parties are also withholding effort towards reaching a settlement." [77]

---

[73] *Schnadig Corp.*, AAA Case No. 78-12 (Abersold, 1965).

[74] 17 L.A. 537 (Seward, 1951).

[75] *Id.* at 540. See also *City of Hartford, Conn.*, 71-1 ARB ¶ 8090 (Johnson, 1971) (a vague claim of racial discrimination without specifying incidents and grievants did not present an arbitrable issue).

[76] 34 L.A. 102 (Morvant, 1959).

[77] *Id.* at 104-05.

However, where one member of a group signed and the grievance was filed within the time limit, the claims of other employees in the group were not defeated when their names were added after the time had run. Arbitrator Benjamin Wolf said:

"One purpose of the signature requirement is to prevent a grievance from being filed against the employee's wishes. Another is to prevent the filing of a grievance by a person not authorized to do so. In this case, neither of these circumstances applies.

" 'Since the objection raised by the Employer would foreclose the right of an employee to be heard on the merits of his grievance, any doubt with respect to the formality of the filing should be resolved in favor of permitting the grievance to have a hearing on the merits. For this reason, I find that the original grievance was properly signed in detail within the meaning of [the contract].'

"Finally, the delayed signing by some of the grievants was explained by the fact that the employer had said that if the union were serious about the complaints, each individual ought to sign it. Thus, 'these grievances were corrected amendments of the original grievances' and the fact that the individual signing occurred after the five day period does not 'nullify the timeliness.' " [78]

Where four employees signed the grievance and there was no evidence that a fifth withheld his signature because he acknowledged the propriety of the company's action, he was permitted to join as a grievant.[79]

Although an "aggrieved employee" was needed to get a case before the arbitrator and ten employees signed the grievance, an arbitrator permitted three additional grievants to be added at the hearing where the issues involved were the same, saying:

"Since the company is not faced with defending any new or different factual allegations, I see no harm in considering the thirteen grievances as a single question." [80]

E. LACK OF JURISDICTION BECAUSE THE CLAIM IS SETTLED

Where the grievance is merely a refiling of a grievance that was settled previously, arbitrators hold that the second grievance is not arbitrable, even where "both the Union and Company testimony, and documents available at the hearing, support the Grievant's claim" that the work he performed entitled him to an evaluation equal to that of the setup man. The arbitrator "[found] the issue closed" because

---

[78] *A. P. Smith Valve Division of U.S. Pipe & Foundry,* AAA Case No. 139-1 (Wolf, 1970).
[79] *National Vulcanized Fibre Co.,* AAA Case No. 83-6 (Brecht, 1965).
[80] *Smith Plastics Inc.,* AAA Case No. 105-10 (Walt, 1967).

of the settlement of an earlier grievance involving the same basic claim.[81] This rationale involves the application in labor arbitration of the principle of *res adjudicata*, long established in the law, that if the identical claim was previously settled it cannot be relitigated. Even resubmission of a grievance that was continuing in nature after a prior identical grievance was "considered settled," because it was not appealed within the specified time limit, caused an arbitrator to hold that the "new grievance was nonarbitrable.[82] And, where the requested relief has been granted, even though the parties may still dispute the appropriate contract interpretation, the grievance has been dismissed. This is the application of the legal principle that matters that have become *moot* should not be litigated. Arbitrator August Eckhardt explained his lack of authority to render an award after the "demand" was "paid off" to make the issue moot:

> "Until an actual dispute arises together with the related, specific facts, neither party has a right to demand arbitration. For this purpose, the dispute cannot be theoretical and will exist only when one party is demanding some benefit or condition which the other party refuses to give.
> "Furthermore, even though such a dispute does exist at some time, there is no basis for arbitration unless the dispute continues at the time of the award of the arbitrator. A withdrawal or an abandonment of the demand by the one party or the acceding to that demand by the other will terminate the dispute and leave no issue for arbitration. This is true despite the fact that, even at that point, the parties are not in agreement on the interpretation of the clause which gave rise to the dispute.
> "To provide an adequate basis for arbitration, a grievance must be more than an argument over interpretation. It must be also a request for action. Without a demand for relief, there is no reason for arbitration. Those executing the Agreement controlling this arbitration surely so intended when they provided for arbitration as a method of settling 'grievances.' ...."[83]

Likewise, when a union advised a company that a grievance was settled and hence withdrawn from the grievance procedure, the grievance became nonarbitrable even when the union membership by vote attempted to reverse this decision. Arbitrator Saul Wallen said that the withdrawal was a "commitment to a third party, in this case the company," and the failure of the membership to ratify could not have the effect of "rescinding" that action. "The withholding of approval in such circumstances merely constitutes notice of the Executive Board that the membership does not agree with the course it has

---

[81] *Penn-Union Machine Corp.*, AAA Case No. 15-14 (Cummins, 1959). See text associated with note 46 *supra* and cases cited therein.

[82] *Farrel Corp.*, AAA Case No. 84-8 (Cole, 1965).

[83] *Inland Container Corp.*, 29 L.A. 861 (Eckhardt, 1957).

taken. . . ." [84] While Wallen did not bar the particular grievance in dispute, he held that "in future cases" the grievances dropped by the Executive Board would be deemed nonarbitrable.

On the other hand, the withdrawal of a grievance protesting the company's announcement that a job would be awarded to a junior bidder (grievance No. 15) did not bar arbitration of the same grievance (grievance No. 21) several months later when the job was actually filled by the junior. The arbitrator said:

> "It can fairly be said that grievance No. 15 was only grieving an event that might happen. This event did not happen while grievance No. 15 was in active process. Hence, since the event conceivably also might not happen, the grievance complained of contractual hurt and loss . . . where no such hurt and loss yet existed or might never come to exist. . . . It is the arbitrator's opinion that grievance No. 15 was filed anticipatorily, pressing a grievance of employees who then had no basis yet to grieve. Not only was their grieving untimely at the time of filing but their grieving remained untimely all the time the grievance progressed through the appellate steps of the grievance procedure until they were exhausted. The selection of [the junior] became grievable when in fact the company acted on its announced selection. . . . Then a grievance could be properly filed—and it was in the form of instant grievance No. 21." [85]

Similarly, Arbitrator James Healy ruled that when a grievance was withdrawn and corrected to refer to a violation of a different clause of the labor agreement and then refiled, the grievance was arbitrable because the union was not acting capriciously and that:

> "The position taken by the company would seem to be unreasonably inflexible, given the language of the relevant contract provisions. This is not tantamount to a legal case of *res adjudicata*. It is simply a matter of a union having decided that its appellate claim, as originally advanced, was ill-founded. As the contract is written, . . . the union is privileged to alter its allegation and introduce what it deems to be the most valid basis for its complaint. True, the union cannot be allowed to alter capriciously its basis for complaint. Were this to be allowed the company is correct in stating that what it had a right to consider a resolved grievance could be kept alive indefinitely by the union's capricious change of its grievance-basis claim. In the present case, however, there is no reason to conclude that the revised grievance placed the company in any greater jeopardy or that it was otherwise affected adversely by the grievance based on a different contract clause." [86]

Although a failure on the part of the union to properly advance the grievance claim to arbitration may cause the arbitrator to rule he

---

[84] *General Cable Corp.*, AAA Case No. 36-14 (Wallen, 1961).

[85] *Allied Products Corp.*, AAA Case No. 26-20 (Ryder, 1960).

[86] *Chapman Valve Manufacturing Co.*, AAA Case No. 41-11 (Healy, 1961).

has no jurisdiction to grant the claim,[87] a failure of the company to comply with a procedure requirement of the agreement does not similarly cause arbitrators to find that a "settlement" favorable to the claimant has occured. For example, Arbitrator John McGury held that the failure of the company to comply with a contractual requirement that parties submit a written statement of their positions at the arbitration hearing was held not to justify the union's request that its holiday pay grievance be granted for that reason alone. "Forfeitures are to be avoided whenever possible in all legal relationships. This is especially true where the parties have a continuing interest in the resolution of problems on their merits, rather than by deadlines or technicalities." [88] The critical question is whether the party guilty of the procedural defect thereby gained an advantage "in presenting the substantive aspects of the case." In this case, despite the fault, "both parties are able to stand on equal terms in presenting their case at the time of the hearing."

Furthermore, where a procedural defect can be cured, the arbitrator should cure it, not generate a forfeiture. For example, where the union contended that arbitration of the employer's complaint was barred by the fact that no conference between the parties over the alleged violation of the agreement had taken place, Arbitrator Michael Sovern ruled that at most "the union would be entitled to a stay of these proceedings for the holding of the omitted conference. But the union did not request such relief and little purpose would be served by tendering it the opportunity to do so now. I conclude the dispute is arbitrable." [89]

F. LACK OF AN AGREEMENT TO INTERPRET

Most of the claims of lack of jurisdiction of the arbitrator because of the lack of an agreement to arbitrate are made to courts. (See Chapter III, *Enforcement of Agreements to Arbitrate.*) However, such a challenge to the arbitrator's jurisdiction may be made to the arbitrator. For example, a claim was made that an arbitrator's jurisdiction was limited to an interpretation of a labor agreement applicable to a group of plants and that he had no jurisdiction to interpret local "plant level" agreements reached between local union officials and plant managers. The arbitrator rejected this challenge to his jurisdiction, holding that the plant level agreement was the controlling document in connection with a dispute over overtime distribution.[90]

---

[87] See in this chapter Section A(2), *Tardy Processing Through Grievance Steps.*
[88] *Borg-Warner Corp.,* AAA Case No. 62-5 (McGury, 1964).
[89] *Kentile Floors, Inc.,* AAA Case No. 103-3 (Sovern, 1967).
[90] *Continental Can Co., Inc., Houston, Texas,* 69-7 ARB ¶ 8359 (Merrill, 1969).

G. LACK OF JURISDICTION OVER THE SUBJECT MATTER

Collective bargaining agreements establish a set of usually generalized rules to resolve future specific disputes. In this context, no amount of care can eliminate potential ambiguity. If the parties were to attempt to anticipate all variations, negotiations would be endless and even to make the effort would, under most circumstances, be unwise because of the innumerable agreements that would be needed to settle matters that might not arise, thus increasing the chance of deadlock.

The absence of specific language relating to the management conduct complained of in a grievance often leads to the challenge that the grievance involves no issue of contract interpretation over which the arbitrator has either jurisdiction or authority to resolve the particular grievance claim.[91] For example, a grievance requesting that the company fill an assistant foreman job during his vacation did not present an arbitrable issue where the collective bargaining agreement contained no provision concerning the wages, hours, and conditions of employment of supervisory personnel, and the arbitrator "cannot order the company to reactivate a position outside the bargaining unit." [92]

In a case involving the company's right to require employees to take their vacations during a period of plant shutdown and where the labor agreement excluded "any matters of general management questions, management policy, business requirements [or] operations" from arbitration, the arbitrator found that the union's contention that the exclusionary clause did not apply would have merit if the union could demonstrate the company's action was not predicated on operational requirements, but was arbitrarily based on unrelated considerations. However, the arbitrator held that the burden of demonstrating bad faith on the company's part had not been met, and hence, "[t]he dispute would seem to fall four square within the scope of the exclusionary language leaving matters of business requirements, operations, and general management questions outside of the competence of the arbitrator to pass upon." [93] It is submitted that the discussion by Arbitrator Altieri, leading to the conclusion that the dispute was not arbitrable, could easily be the reasoning why the grievance should be denied on its merits, except for the fact that the clause of the agree-

---

[91] See, e.g., *T & M Rubber Specialties Co., Inc.,* AAA Case No. 137-8 (Sembower, 1970); *Arrow Newaygo Foundry Co.,* AAA Case No. 105-5 (Rogers, 1967); *Anaconda American Brass Co.,* AAA Case No. 69-15 (Davis, 1964); *Bell Telephone Co. of Pa.,* AAA Case No. 40-6 (Duff, 1962); but see *William H. Haskell Mfg. Div. of Easco Corp.,* AAA Case No. 141-13 (Yagoda, 1970); *Ostendorf-Morris Co.,* AAA Case No. 35-23 (Teple, 1961).

[92] *American Enka Corp.,* AAA Case No. 84-9 (Holly, 1965).

[93] *E. R. Squibb Co.,* AAA Case No. 30-4 (Altieri, 1961).

ment involved was expressed as an exclusion of subject matter from arbitration.

Similarly, a grievance against the issuance of a memorandum to supervisors, setting forth guidelines for determining improper absenteeism did not present an arbitrable grievance,[94] as it did not relate to any provision of the labor agreement.

In another case, a claim against a company for reinbursement for damage to an employee's tool box was held not arbitrable by Arbitrator Samuel Edes. He said:

> "I cannot relate, directly or indirectly, the practice upon which the Union relies to any express provision of the contract." [95]

Edes explained the relationship of lack of jurisdiction to resolve a grievance and the parol evidence rule discussed in Chapter X when he rejected the union's contention that the company's past practice with respect to repair or replacement of tools made such benefits an "integral part of the contract." "I do not find it necessary," the arbitrator said, "in this case to pass upon whether the past practice of the Company was such as to encompass the replacement of [the grievant's] tool box." Evidence of past practice would be persuasive in interpreting an "ambiguous" or "inept" provision of a contract, but in the absence of any contract provision dealing with the subject matter of the grievance, the arbitrator "cannot decide a controversy based entirely upon practices and customs outside of the obligations assumed in the written terms of the agreement." [96]

However, a grievance by a discharged foreman who had formerly been in the unit but not retransferred upon his termination was an arbitrable one because the issue:

> "[P]osed by the parties on the merits sufficiently involves the possible interpretation and application of [the clause governing return to the bargaining unit] to warrant careful consideration by an arbitrator. Should the employee have been retransferred to a position in the bargaining unit? Are [the recognition clause] and [the clause governing retransfers] entirely consistent? The issue on the merits is not immediately, obviously and grossly beyond the scope of [the retransfer clause]. This is not to say that the grievance . . . and the remedy requested need to have a *prima facie* case but only that it may possibly involve, in a serious way, the interpretation and application of provisions of the agreement." [97]

Where a labor agreement provided for the negotiation of revisions in base rates during its term, and also provided that "all claims, dis-

---

[94] *Boston Edison Co.*, AAA Case No. 132-2 (Rubin, 1969).
[95] *Borg-Warner Corp.*, AAA Case No. 14-21 (Edes, 1959).
[96] *Id.*
[97] *Landers, Frary & Clark*, AAA Case No. 75-7 (Dunlop, 1964).

putes or differences arising out of the terms of this agreement shall be settled in accordance with the procedure provided by the agreement," the inability of the parties to agree upon new base rates did not present an arbitrable issue. "The arbitration of basic wage rates is uncommon in most industries, including aircraft and electronics; it seems most unlikely, therefore, that the parties would have contemplated the arbitration of a wage reopening dispute and yet not have provided specifically in the Agreement for such an eventuality." [98]

Arbitrators do not conclude that merely because the issue in dispute could become a matter of concern under the National Labor Relations Act they do not have jurisdiction if an interpretation and application of the agreement is involved. Concurrent jurisdiction of the NLRB and an arbitrator was asserted by Arbitrator Melvin Lennard [99] when he refused to stay a decision of a submitted dispute, because the same issue was pending before the National Labor Relations Board.

Such challenges to the arbitrator's jurisdiction may be classified as questions of "subject-matter jurisdiction." Every decision by an arbitrator, denying a grievance claim on the ground that there is no contractual restriction on the right of the management to take the action complained of, is in fact a ruling that the subject matter was not covered by the agreement. Where the challenge to the arbitrability of the grievance is a claim that the subject matter in dispute is one over which the arbitrator has no jurisdiction, the claim is not waived by a failure to raise it during the processing of the grievance in the lower steps of the grievance procedure. For example, Arbitrator G. Allen Dash said that where the contract required the parties "to attempt in good faith to adjust all grievances" under methods provided for in the agreement, the employer was "obliged to consider [a grievance] on its merits through the several steps of the Grievance Procedure" and did not forfeit its right to assert the defense of "non-arbitrability" by having failed to question arbitrability during the grievance procedure:

> "There is no need, and there would be no point, for the Company to raise the issue of arbitrability during the several steps of the Grievance Procedure at which the Company is obligated to consider the merits of the grievance." [100]

Furthermore, the employer's right to dispute arbitrability for the first time at the hearing was not affected, as the union asserted, by the

[98] *Hughes Tool Co.*, AAA Case No. 26-1 (Aaron, 1960).

[99] *Burgmaster Corp.*, AAA Case No. 85-11 (Lennard, 1965). *Accord, Aeroil Products Co.*, AAA Case No. 65-18 (Stark, 1964); *Nicolet Industries*, AAA Case No. 18-11 (Rock, 1960).

[100] *Celanese Corp. of America*, AAA Case No. 10-21 (Dash, 1959).

failure to make this defense in the statement answering the demand for arbitration:

> "Under the contract and under the Rules of the American Arbitration Association, the participation of the Company in selecting an Arbitrator to hear a particular grievance does not require it to divulge its defense of non-arbitrability in advance of the arbitration proceedings. . . . By participation in the selection of the Arbitrator to hear and decide a particular grievance, the Company and the Union do commit themselves to having the question of arbitrability decided by the Arbitrator (if that question is raised as a defense by either party), but they do not thereby automatically commit themselves to arbitrate the grievance on is merits unless the Arbitrator rules that the grievance is arbitrable." [101]

Similarly, Arbitrator S. Harry Galfand pointed out that a party can waive a procedural defect which, if not waived, would bar arbitration on the merits, but it cannot waive a lack of jurisdiction over subject matter to create jurisdiction in the arbitrator when jurisdiction does not exist. He said that the failure of the company to indicate in advance of the hearing that it intended to contest arbitrability did not prevent such a claim from being made. "It is a question of whether the arbitrator has the power of jurisdiction to consider the question." If he lacks that power, that lack cannot be overcome, no matter when the defense of nonarbitrability is raised:

> "The doctrine of estoppel—perhaps applicable to the failure to take advantage of a procedural failure—cannot, in my opinion, be applied to the fundamental question of the arbitrator's jurisdiction. It is certainly helpful to harmonious labor-management relations, and courteous to advise that a position of nonarbitrability will be taken, but I cannot hold that the failure to do so constitutes a fatal or disabling defect." [102]

A challenge to the arbitrator's jurisdiction on a subject-matter basis is generally handled as a preliminary matter before a decision on the merits. Since jurisdiction over subject matter and the merits of the claim are very often closely related,[103] and the prevailing view among arbitrators appears to be that a grievance claim will be considered within their jurisdiction if based upon an alleged violation of the agreement [104] and involving an issue not completely foreign to the

---

[101] *Id.*

[102] *Bally Case & Cooler Co.*, AAA Case No. 93-10 (Galfand, 1966).

[103] Arbitrator Byron Abernethy says there may be only a "semantic difference" between ruling that a claim is unarbitrable and ruling that it is an arbitrable claim which is utterly without merit. But he says the union grievance raises a question of application of the agreement to promotions to supervisory status. He decides this is an issue which, "under the terms of this agreement, the union is entitled to have resolved." *Sun Oil Co.*, 52 L.A. 463, 467 (Abernethy, 1969).

[104] A claim based upon an agreement unrelated to the collective agreement and the arbitration provision contained therein is generally held by arbitrators not properly before them. See, *e.g.*, *Ranco, Inc.*, 50 L.A. 269 (Klein, 1968).

traditional scope of labor agreements and arbitration,[105] a challenge to the jurisdiction of the arbitrator to hear the matter creates a risk. If he finds jurisdiction to hear the case on the merits, he may feel compelled to find some provision of the agreement from which to imply a restriction when deciding the grievance on the merits. In view of this, an attack on grounds of subject matter jurisdiction may be inadvisable because the same consideration can be raised when the grievance is being considered on its merits, *i.e.,* does it present a factual basis for a finding of a contract violation?

The risks of attacking subject-matter jurisdiction of the arbitrator are not limited solely to this consideration, however. As one arbitrator noted when he ruled that a grievance not signed by an aggrieved employee was not one within his jurisdiction, this meant that the dispute became one over which the union could conduct an authorized strike under a clause permitting strikes over matters not subject to grievance procedure.[106] This is also underscored by the rule announced by the Supreme Court in *Boys Markets Inc. v. Retail Clerks Union, Local 770,*[107] which produces an often unexpected consequence when the employer wins on a procedural objection basis. Thus, a strike in violation of the agreement over the dispute would not be enjoinable because the grievance is not subject to resolution by arbitration.

H. THE PROCEDURE USED TO RAISE A CHALLENGE TO THE ARBITRATOR'S JURISDICTION

A claim that the arbitrator has no jurisdiction over the subject matter or that the grievance is not properly before him because of a procedural defect, such as untimely filing or appeal, can be presented in one of two ways. The claim may be presented in a separate and advance hearing, where a ruling on jurisdiction is requested. More commonly, the lack of jurisdiction contention is presented as the first part of a hearing on the merits.[108] Unless the parties specifically agree to submit the issue of arbitrability in a separate advance hearing, the arbitrator usually asks both parties to proceed on the merits after the party has presented its jurisdictional objection, defer-

---

[105] *Ethyl Corp.,* 50 L.A. 322 (Dworkin, 1968); *Great Atlantic & Pacific Tea Co.,* 49 L.A. 515 (Crawford, 1967); *New Hotel Showboat, Inc.,* 48 L.A. 240 (Jones, 1967).

[106] *Lummis & Co.,* AAA Case No. 32-22 (Kahn, 1961).

[107] 398 U.S. 235 (1970).

[108] Smith and Jones, *The Impact of the Emerging Federal Law of Grievance Arbitration on Judges, Arbitrators and Parties,* 52 VA. L. REV. 831, 871 (1966); F. Elkouri & E. Elkouri, How ARBITRATION WORKS 119-127 (BNA Books, 1960); Collins, *Arbitrability and Arbitrators,* 13 N.Y.U. CONF. LAB. 449, 451 (1960).

ring his ruling as to jurisdiction until after the record on both the jurisdiction and merits has been completed.[109]

In this connection, courts have held that a defense of nonarbitrability is not lost because the party asserting it participated in a hearing on the merits of the grievance, as long as the party asserts and preserves the defense of nonarbitrability.[110] Some arbitrators, however, are less sure about the effect participation in a hearing on the merits has upon the nonarbitrability defense.[111] Since the issue of nonarbitrability goes to the issue of the arbitrator's jurisdiction, the better rule would appear to be that participation in the arbitration does not constitute waiver. Such a rule would conform to the general judicial rule that lack of subject-matter jurisdiction is never waived.[112]

I. THE IMPLIED JURISDICTION TO INTERPRET AND APPLY THE LAW AS WELL AS THE CONTRACT

To what extent the arbitrator can or should interpret and apply the law as well as the agreement, has been extensively debated and is actually a question of the arbitrator's jurisdiction.[113] Few argue that arbitrators should ignore federal law when a provision is ambiguous and can be interpreted in two ways—one consistent with the law and one inconsistent therewith. Professor Bernard Meltzer has said:

"[W]here a contractual provision is susceptible to two interpretations, one compatible with, and the other repugnant to, an applicable statute, the statute is a relevant factor for interpretation. Arbitral interpretation of agreements like judicial interpretation of statutes, should seek to avoid a construction that would be invalid under a higher law."[114]

---

[109] For an example of a preliminary ruling procedure, see *Central Transformer Corp., Moloney Electric Co. Div.,* 50 L.A. 927 (Lehoczky, 1967). See generally Fuller, *Collective Bargaining and the Arbitrator,* WIS. L. REV. 3, 13-18 (1963).

[110] *Bakery & Confectionery Workers Local 719 v. National Biscuit Co.,* 378 F.2d 918 (3d Cir. 1967) (objection at hearing preserves defense); *Humble Oil & Refining Co. v. Teamsters Local 866,* 271 F. Supp. 281 (S.D.N.Y. 1967) (participation in hearing does not bar defense).

[111] *Phoenix Closures, Inc.,* 49 L.A. 874 (Sembower, 1967) (proceeding on merits renders defense moot); *City of Meriden,* 48 L.A. 137 (Summers, 1967) (arbitrator unsure of effect of award upon reviewing court).

[112] C. Wright, FEDERAL COURTS 244 (West Pub. Co., St. Paul, Minn., 1963).

[113] See generally Meltzer, *Ruminations About Ideology, Law, and Labor Arbitration,* THE ARBITRATOR, THE NLRB AND THE COURTS, Proceedings of the Twentieth Annual Meeting, National Academy of Arbitrators 1, 14-19 (D. Jones Ed. 1967); Howlett, *The Arbitrator, the NLRB, and the Courts, Id.* at 67; Mittenthal, *The Role of Law in Labor Arbitration,* DEVELOPMENTS IN AMERICAN AND FOREIGN ARBITRATION, Proceedings of the Twenty-First Annual Meeting, National Academy of Arbitrators 42 (C. Rehmus Ed. 1968); Meltzer, *Rejoinders, Id.* at 58; Howlett, *A Reprise, Id.* at 64; St. Antoine, *Discussion, Id.* at 75; Sovern, *When Should Arbitrators Follow Federal Law?,* ARBITRATION AND THE EXPANDING ROLE OF NEUTRALS, Proceedings of the Twenty-Third Annual Meeting, National Academy of Arbitrators 48 (G. Somers Ed. 1970).

[114] Meltzer, *Ruminations About Ideology, Law, and Labor Arbitration,* note 113 *supra* at 1, 17.

Where the question is not one of choosing one of two interpretations of an ambiguous provision—one consistent with the law, one inconsistent—arbitrators are clearly entitled to rest their decisions squarely on the law, if the parties have granted to the arbitrator the authority to do so either in the agreement or by specific authority granted at the hearing. For example, where the parties executed a contract which was intended to incorporate the provisions of Title VII of the Civil Rights Act, the arbitrator held that the EEOC guidelines were applicable.[115]

The problem arises when the arbitrator has not been granted specific authority to apply the law [116] and concludes that if he followed the labor agreement and not the law, his award would be in conflict with the law.

The contract principle that illegal bargains are unforceable is applicable to collective bargaining ageeements.[117] Harry Shulman, well-known arbitrator and former dean of the Yale Law School, said provisions which violate statutory prohibitions should be unenforceable. A collective agreement should fit within the framework created by the law, as must any other contract.[118]

Clyde Summers has stated that it should be the responsibility of both arbitrators and courts to excise provisions of collective agreements which are illegal, and to choose that construction of an ambiguous provision which renders it compatible with the law.[119]

To the contrary, Professor Bernard Meltzer believes that arbitrators should respect "the agreement that is the source of their authority and should leave to the courts or other official tribunals the determination of whether [a provision of an] agreement contravenes a

---

[115] Given the extent of federal regulation in the employment area, the law that can be involved in such cases is quite extensive. For example, questions could arise under the 1964 Civil Rights Act, see Edwards & Kaplan, *Religious Discrimination and the Role of Arbitration Under Title VII*, 69 MICH. L. REV. 599, 645 n. 225 (1971); the Fair Labor Standards Act, *Pennsylvania Electric Co.*, 47 L.A. 526 (Stein, 1966); the Military Selective Service Act of 1967, *Pomrening v. United Air Lines*, 448 F.2d 609 (7th Cir. 1971); and the National Labor Relations Act, *Carey v. Westinghouse Electric Co.*, 375 U.S. 261 (1964), to name but a few of the federal statutory schemes which could be enmeshed in an arbitration.

[116] *Alsco, Inc.*, 48 L.A. 1244 (Altrock, 1967); but see *Ridinger v. General Motors Corp.*, 325 F. Supp. 1089 (S.D. Ohio, 1971) which indicates that the law has changed considerably from that applied in *Alsco, Inc.*

[117] The Labor Management Relations Act contains a number of express prohibitions against certain kinds of contract clauses. Section 8(e) prohibits "hot cargo" clauses, Sections 8(a)(3) and 8(b)(2) restrict union security clauses, and Section 302 circumscribes welfare and pension plans. An agreement made between an employer and a minority union is void if it purports to cover all employees, because it restrains the employees rights of self-organization guaranteed by Section 7. See also *Middletown Bd. of Ed.*, 56 L.A. 830 (1971).

[118] See generally, Shulman, *Reason, Contract, and Law in Labor Relations*, 68 HARV. L. REV. 999 (1955).

[119] Summers, *Collective Agreements and the Law of Contracts*, 78 YALE L.J. 525, 556 (1969).

higher law. Otherwise," Meltzer said, "arbitrators would be deciding issues that go beyond not only the submission agreement but also arbitral competence." [120]

An example of the snarl that is produced by a strict application of this latter view is the decision by Arbitrator Harry Platt in *Union Tank Car Co.*[121] The employees working at a new integrated tank car manufacturing plant (known as Plant 1) were represented by the Boilermakers. Due to a reduction in orders for tank cars, production was cut back at another nearby but older facility where the employees were represented by the Oil, Chemical and Atomic Workers. The labor agreement with OCAW provided that if the operations performed at that location were transferred to another location in the area, the contract with OCAW would apply to the employees performing such work.

OCAW claimed that a transfer of work had occurred when certain operations at the older facility were discontinued, but were continued at Plant 1, and filed a grievance claiming that its labor agreement should apply to at least the operations at the new integrated plant previously performed by its members, *i.e.,* the finishing operations, even though the employees performing the finishing work were represented by the Boilermakers. The arbitrator first found that the discontinuance of finishing work at the old facility constituted a "transfer" of operations to Plant 1 and then construed the language in the OCAW agreement to mean the company was obligated to apply the OCAW agreement to the finishing operations, ignoring the legal prohibitions imposed upon the employer by the fact the Boilermakers at that time were the exclusive representative of the employees performing all the work at the new plant.[122] To superimpose another union as their representative and to substitute another agreement would be inconsistent with the National Labor Relations Act. The arbitrator did not face up to these problems but knew they existed:

> "I must decline to decide the legal questions raised. It need hardly be added that, in doing so, those questions . . . are left for resolution, in

---

[120] Meltzer, *Ruminations About Ideology, Law, and Labor Arbitration,* note 113 *supra,* at 1, 14-19; see also *Micro Lectric, Inc.,* 48 L.A. 50 (Wolf, 1967). A Florida court, to the contrary, rejected the employer's contention that if an arbitrator were permitted to decide disputes involving the effect of wage controls on contractually committed wage increases, uniform administration of the wage control law would be undermined. *Local 1115, Nursing Home, Hospital, Senior Citizens Hotel Union v. Hialeah Convalescent Home, Inc.,* — F. Supp. —, 81 LRRM 2312 (S.D. Fla. 1972).

[121] 55 L.A. 170 (1970); see also, *Eaton Mfg. Co.,* 66-3 ARB ¶ 9089 (Kates, 1966).

[122] As the Supreme Court held in *NLRB v. Jones & Laughlin Steel Corp.,* 301 U.S. 1, 44-45 (1937), "The obligation to treat with the true representative [is] exclusive and hence impose[s] the negative duty to treat with no other."

the parties' discretion, in a forum which has responsibility for dealing with such specialized matters." [123]

In his first award, the arbitrator ordered the employer to negotiate with OCAW to determine how the OCAW agreement would be applied to employees represented by the Boilermakers who were performing finishing work at Plant 1, reserving jurisdiction to make a final determination of the parties could not reach agreement.

As soon as discussions with OCAW to find a way to apply its agreement to the employees performing finishing operations at Plant 1 commenced, the Boilermakers filed unfair labor practice charges against the company alleging that it was illegal for the employer to attempt to substitute OCAW for the Boilermakers as the representative of these employees. The Regional Director issued a complaint, alleging that in attempting to comply with the Platt award, the company was violating the National Labor Relations Act.

In the interim, since the parties were unable to reach agreement, Arbitrator Platt issued a final award, providing:[124]

> "(a) Contingent upon a determination by the National Labor Relations Board that it would not violate the provisions of the NLRA, the Company is directed to apply the existing OCAW agreement to the finishing operations performed in Plant No. 1.
> "(b) The Company is directed to reimburse and make whole all OCAW-represented employees for all lost wages and benefits, including health and welfare and retirement benefits, caused by the violation of Article II, Section I as heretofore determined."

Subsequently, the Boilermakers brought a claim against OCAW before Arbitrator David Cole under the AFL-CIO Internal Disputes Plan. The claim was that OCAW, by its actions in impinging on the Boilermakers' unit had violated the Federation's "no raiding agreement." Arbitrator Cole agreed and enjoined OCAW from any further such activities.[125]

Following this withdrawal of the unfair labor practice charges, the employer filed a unit clarification petition. This resulted in the Board's deciding that the Boilermakers were the exclusive representative of all the employees at Plant 1, including those performing the finishing work.[126]

OCAW then filed a complaint in the federal district court asking for enforcement of the Platt award. During the course of this proceeding, it abandoned its claim to represent any employees at Plant 1,

---

123 55 L.A. at 181.
124 *Union Tank Car Co.,* 55 L.A. 170 (Platt, 1970).
125 57 L.A. 318 (Cole, 1971).
126 *Union Tank Car Co.,* NLRB Case No. 13-UC-50 (Apr. 28, 1971).

claiming only that money was due OCAW-represented employees for lost wages and benefits because of the employer's violation of the agreement.

In *Local 7-210, OCAW v. Union Tank Car Company*,[127] Judge Parsons reported the employer's position:

> "The Company argues that since the award required it to apply the OCAW contract [to finishing activity at Plant 1] only if legally permissible . . . it is not liable for damages, having acted in accord with the NLRB ruling that the proper exclusive bargaining representation with whom it must negotiate is the Boilermakers. The thrust of the Company's position is that since it could not be compelled to apply the OCAW contract to Plant No. 1, because to do so would be illegal and violative of the NLRB ruling, it cannot now be compelled to pay damages for refusing to commit an unfair practice act." [128]

The court agreed, holding that "where there is a conflict between an arbitrator's award and a later NLRB ruling, the arbitrator's findings must give way before the superiority of the NLRB decision [and the employer] is not liable for damages," and this decision was affirmed by the Seventh Circuit.[129]

This confusing and burdensome problem arose because the arbitrator failed to read into the clause concerning the application of the OCAW agreement the necessary proviso that the parties by implication meant that the agreement would follow the work only if "it were legal to do so."

Maritime v. Commercial Tankers Corp.,[130] reports another example where expensive and multiforum litigation resulted when an arbitrator failed to assume that the parties intended to enter into a labor agreement that complied with the law, and hence did not intend to incorporate by implication a provision requiring illegal conduct. In this case a ship owned by Commercial Tankers was being sold. Under Commercial's collective bargaining agreement with the NMU, it was obligated in the event of a sale of a ship to obtain from the buyer an agreement that the buyer would recognize the National Maritime Union as the representative of the complement of unlicensed seamen

---

[127] 337 F.Supp. 83 (N.D. Ill., 1971).

[128] *Id.* at 86.

[129] *Id.* at 88, *aff'd, Local 7-210, Oil, Chemical and Atomic Workers International Union, AFL-CIO v. Union Tank Car.* — F.2d —, 82 LRRM 2823 (1973), relying on the Supreme Court decision in *Carey v. Westinghouse Electric Corp.*, 375 U.S. 261 (1964); *Smith Steel Workers v. A. O. Smith Corp.*, 420 F.2d 1 (7th Cir. 1969), and *Dock Loaders v. W. L. Richeson & Sons, Inc.*, 280 F.Supp. 402 (E.D. La. 1968). The court in *International Ass'n of Machinists v. Howmet Corp.*, 466 F.2d 1249, 81 LRRM 2289 (9th Cir. 1972) held that there was no obligation to arbitrate a claim which, if granted by the arbitrator, would require an employer to violate its agreement with another union.

[130] 457 F.2d 1127 (2d Cir. 1972).

who would work on such ship. However, Commercial, the seller, subsequently attempted to sell one of its ships without requiring the aforementioned undertaking from the buyer, because the buyer was a party to a multivessel agreement with the Seafarers International Union.

The National Maritime Union initiated arbitration proceedings claiming before the arbitrator that the refusal to obtain such recognition agreement as a condition of the sale of the ship was a contract violation. The arbitrator, without passing upon the claim that the clause would require illegal conduct, ordered Commercial, the seller, to provide such a recognition agreement. Because Commercial ignored the award, the NMU immediately sought to obtain an injunction from a federal district court enforcing the award, which prohibited the sale until a recognition agreement, required by the collective bargaining agreement, was delivered to the NMU. Commercial argued before the court that the delivery of such a recognition agreement would violate the antitrust laws. The buyer joined in the suit, alleging that the restriction in the collective bargaining agreement violated the "hot cargo" provision of Section 8(e) of the National Labor Relations Act.[131] The court rejected these arguments and granted NMU a preliminary injunction.

The buyer then filed a charge with the National Labor Relations Board alleging that the provision in the collective agreement requiring the delivery of such agreement required a violation of Section 8(e). The Regional Director agreed and petitioned the district court for an injunction which, if granted, would have had the effect of lifting the preliminary injunction that the same court had previously entered against the sale. The court refused to grant the restraining order and an appeal was taken which was merged with the seller's appeal from the injunction blocking the sale. The Second Circuit lifted the injunction, permitting the sale to occur, an action which recognized the illegality of the clause requiring the seller to deliver to the union an agreement that the buyer would recognize the NMU.[132]

All this litigation could have been avoided if the arbitrator had inferred into the agreement the general understanding that parties intend to enter into legal understandings and then had ruled that the clause required an illegal action and was, therefore, unenforceable.[133]

---

[131] 325 F. Supp. 360.

[132] 329 F. Supp. 151.

[133] This is consistent with the well-established principle enunciated in *Von Hoffman v. Quincy*, 71 U.S. 535, 550 (1866):
"The laws which subsist at the time and place of the making of a contract, and where it is to be performed, enter into and form a part of [the contract], as if they were expressly referred to or incorporated in its terms."

To do so would not be a distortion of the real intention of the parties, as it can be assumed they have agreed not to require one or the other to violate the law.[134]

In *Warren Consolidated School*,[135] Arbitrator Robert Howlett said:

"There are arbitrators who take the position that arbitrators may not, or should not, be concerned with constitutional or statutory issues. In my opinion, however, every contract includes all applicable provisions of the law and arbitrators, as well as all other decision making entities, are bound by the law applicable to the contract being construed. . . .
"An award which does not consider the law may result in error." [136]

Thus, Howlett has argued that the arbitrator should always be considered to have the authority to apply the law so as to avoid an award inconsistent with the law.[137] According to Howlett, "each contract includes all applicable law."[138] He infers that an arbitrator charged with construing a contract is also authorized to interpret and apply the applicable law.[139]

Another example of where an arbitrator examined the law to construe a labor agreement is *Gould Inc.*[140] The union asserted that certain card check recognition procedures could be used to gain recognition rights. The group of employees were not production and maintenance employees in a battery plant and battery warehouse, and thus if such recognition was gained by such procedure the employees would be automatically covered by the multiplant agreement. The company contended that such a construction would be legally improper because it would deprive employees in nonbattery plants of their statutory rights to bargain collectively for an agreement to serve their own

---

[134] A union failed to include a paragraph from an employer's offer that it was "based upon the . . . contingency the law will permit the action proposed." The employer refused to sign but was ordered to do so by the court because the failure to include "a statement that the contract was subject to any law then existing . . . had no effect on its acceptance since all contracts are subject to the then existing law." *Davis v. Servis Equipment Co.*, 341 F.Supp. 1298, 68 L.C. ¶ 12,578 (N.D. Texas, 1972).

[135] *Warren Consolidated Schools*, 67-1 ARB ¶ 8228 (Howlett, 1967).

[136] 67-1 ARB at 3800.

[137] Howlett, *The Arbitrator, The NLRB, and the Courts*, note 113 *supra*, at 67, 78-79. Howlett did concede, however, that on occasion the arbitrator may:
"[D]etermine that the General Counsel [of the NLRB] or the [EEOC] Commission, with its power of investigation, is in a better position to secure evidence than is an under- or non-represented employee whose dispute has been submitted to arbitration, he should so advise the parties and withdraw." (pp. 92-3).

[138] *Id.* at 83.

[139] See also *Pennsylvania Electric Co.*, 66-3 ARB ¶ 8842 at 5912-13 (Stein, 1966); *United States Pipe and Foundry Co.*, 68-2 ARB ¶ 8595 (Hon, 1968); *Lockheed-Georgia*, 68-2 ARB ¶ 8769 (Cantor, 1968); *Alsco, Inc.*, 48 L.A. 1244 (Altrock, 1967); *Hall China Co.*, 51 L.A. 1259 (Nichols, 1969).

[140] 72-1 ARB ¶ 8055 (Kelliher, 1972).

special needs. Based on this consideration of the law, the ambiguity in the language was construed to limit the application of the agreement in battery plants and battery warehouses.

However, where the law providing for equal pay for equal work was enacted after the date the labor agreement became effective, Arbitrator S. Harry Galfand would not read the terms of the law into the agreement so as to respond to a grievance claiming that females were being paid less for performing the same work as men. He said:

> "A careful search through the contract fails to disclose any provision, paragraph or clause properly applicable to this question of paying the same rates to female employees as to male employees, even assuming that the work they perform is the same." [141]

The arbitrator noted that in negotiating the current contract, the parties agreed upon a wage increase, but they did not negotiate, "or at least not successfully," for equalization of male and female rates of pay. That the federal equal-pay-for-equal-work law was enacted does not make this requirement "automatically" a part of the contract. "It may be a proper subject for negotiation, even during the term of the contract; but it does not become per se a provision of the agreement subject to application or interpretation by the arbitrator."[142]

Many contracts contain an express clause to the effect that any provision which is found to be illegal shall be unenforceable. This clause should be implied into all agreements. Arbitrator Richard Mittenthal, noting the prevalence of express clauses to this effect, suggests that it is reasonable to assume that parties "do not wish to be bound by an invalid provision. The implication seems clear that the arbitrator should not enforce a provision which is clearly unenforceable under the law." [143] He also pointed out that a party, which has obligated itself to be bound by an arbitration award, will be frustrated if the award orders the party to violate the law:

> "The arbitrator should 'look to see whether sustaining the grievance would require conduct the law forbids or would enforce an illegal contract; if so, the arbitrator should not sustain the grievance.' This principle, however, should be carefully limited. It does not suggest that 'an arbitrator should pass upon all the parties' legal rights and obligations.'
> . . . Thus, although the arbitrator's award may *permit* conduct forbidden by law but sanctioned by contract, it should not *require* conduct forbidden by law even though sanctioned by contract." [144]

---

141 *Bally Case & Cooler Co.*, AAA Case No. 93-10 (Galfand, 1966).
142 *Id.*
143 Mittenthal, *The Role of Law in Labor Arbitration, supra* note 113, at 42, 49.
144 *Id.* at 50; see also Cox, *The Place of Law in Labor Arbitration,* THE PROFESSION OF LABOR ARBITRATION, Selected Papers From the First Seven Annual Meetings of the National Academy of Arbitrators, 1948-1954, 76, 79 (J. McKelvey Ed. 1957). Meltzer has criticized Mittenthal's view:

At least one court has seemingly adopted the Meltzer view. In *Associated Milk Dealers, Inc. v. Milk Drivers Union Local 753*,[145] the court ordered a further hearing of evidence on the question of whether the contractual "most favored nation" clause violated the antitrust law under *United Mine Workers v. Pennington*.[146] The court said:[147]

> "Arbitrators are ill-equipped to interpret the anti-trust laws and their consideration of possible violations would add little. Indeed, an agreement requiring arbitration of private antitrust claims would probably be unenforceable."

Similarly unenforceable, however, is an arbitration award which would require the employer to violate a law because, in such cases, the courts have refused enforcement of the award.[148]

Courts have also refused to deny arbitration on the basis that an award might contravene law.[149] One court explained what could happen if it was assumed that arbitrators could not deal with claims that involved an interaction of the law and the agreement, ruling that the issue of a particular award's consonance with law should be taken up first before the arbitrator:

> "If a court must in every case make a preliminary judicial determination against every defense that the ingenuity of counsel for a recalcitrant party can conceive before an arbitration procedure can go forward, . . . 'the arbitral wheels would very soon grind to a halt.' " [150]

"[Mittenthal's formula] is not supported by the authority conferred on the arbitrator by the parties; or by the expertise imputed to arbitrators and courts; or by the twin desires for finality of arbitration awards and the limitation of judicial intervention. Under Mr. Mittenthal's approach, the role accorded to law would depend on how an employer resolved a controversy and not on its essential character or the functions properly delegated to different adjudicative agencies. In my opinion, such an approach transforms an accidental consideration into a decisive one." Meltzer, *Rejoinders*, note 113 *supra*, at 58, 60.

[145] 422 F.2d 546 (7th Cir. 1970).

[146] 381 U.S. 657 (1965).

[147] 422 F.2d at 552.

[148] *UAW Local 985 v. W. M. Chace Co.*, 262 F.Supp. 114 (E.D. Mich. 1966); *Glendale Mfg. Co. v. Local No. 520 ILGWU*, 283 F.2d 936 (4th Cir. 1960), *cert. denied*, 366 U.S. 950 (1961). See also Dunau, *Three Problems in Labor Arbitration*, 55 VA. L. REV. 427, 439 (1969) ("a court cannot enforce an [arbitration] award which requires the performance of an illegal act even if the contract authorizes it.").

[149] *Stein Printing Co. v. Atlanta Typographical Union No. 48*, 329 F.Supp. 754 (1961) (effect of a Georgia Right to Work Law upon the contractual obligation of foremen to be members of the union referred to arbitration); *Federal-Mogul Corp. v. UAW*, — F. Supp. —, 74 LRRM 2961 (E.D. Mich. 1970); but see *Retail Clerks v. Montgomery Ward & Co.*, 316 F.2d 754 (7th Cir., 1963); *McGuire v. Humble Oil & Refining Co.*, 355 F.2d 352 (2d Cir.), *cert. denied*, 384 U.S. 988 (1966), where the courts refused to compel arbitration because to do so would require the employer to deal with a minority union in violation of the NLRA.

[150] *Carey v. General Electric Co.*, 315 F.2d 499 (2d Cir. 1963).

Under the policy of the National Labor Relations Board to defer to an arbitration award [151] and to dismiss a proceeding if the matter in dispute can be resolved by arbitration,[152] the Board requires that the legal questions, that could be raised before the Board, be raised before the arbitrator and disposed of by him.[153] This is merely another reason why arbitrators should consider the related laws to be part of the agreement.

In a nutshell, there are difficulties either way the arbitrator turns. Given the fact, however, that one of the principal policy reasons behind the favored status of arbitration is its speed in settling contractual differences between the parties, it is more than a bit antithetical to such a policy for arbitration to be only the first step in protracted litigation. The parties themselves should select an arbitrator who, in their view, is competent to grapple with the "legal" questions that impinge on the contractual ones and his jurisdiction to avoid rendering an award inconsistent with the law should be implied.

J. JURISDICTION TO REFORM A MISTAKE

Some arbitrators have said that the jurisdictional limits imposed by most contracts upon the arbitrator prevent him from reforming an agreement, even where mistake is asserted and supported by evidence. For example, Arbitrator David Cole stated:

"Assuming the fact that [one of the parties] understood or believed that there was no obligation . . . the provision agreed upon plainly indicates the contrary. It is elementary that the process of interpreting or enforcing a contract does not include the right to re-write or re-make the agreement, however unwise it may appear to be." [154]

In a similar vein, Arbitrator Thomas Tongue held:

"[T]he function of an arbitrator in deciding disputes arising under written contracts is solely to determine the meaning and application of the terms of the contract and that an arbitrator has no power to decide what the parties *should* have put into their contract or, indeed, what they agreed upon verbally, but did not put into their contract." [155]

---

[151] *Spielberg Manufacturing Co.,* 112 NLRB 1080 (1955).

[152] *Coppus Engineering Corp.,* 195 NLRB No. 113 (1972); *Collyer Insulated Wire,* 192 NLRB No. 150 (1971).

[153] *Air Reduction Co., Inc., Airco Industrial Gases-Pacific Division,* 195 NLRB No. 120, 79 LRRM 1467 (1972). Member Kennedy in a dissent said that the burden is on the grievant to raise the legal question (discrimination because of union activity in this case) and hence deferral should occur even though the discrimination issue was not resolved.

[154] *Sperry Gyroscope Co.,* 18 L.A. 916, 918 (Cole, 1952).

[155] *B. J. John Furniture Corp.,* 32 L.A. 708, 711 (Tongue, 1959). See also *Tanner Motor Livery, Ltd.,* 63-2 ARB ¶ 8664 at 5183 (Roberts, 1963); *Columbia Kleen-Rite, Inc.,* 62-3 ARB ¶ 8884 at 6210 (Duff, 1962); F. Elkouri & E. Elkouri, How ARBITRATION WORKS 242 (rev. ed. 1960).

The relief from a mistake, Arbitrator Harry Casselman asserted. was an action in equity:

> "If either side is claiming mistake, they must seek reformation in a court of common law jurisdiction. The Arbitrator has no such power or jurisdiction." [156]

In agreement with this approach is the Ninth Circuit's decision in *West Coast Telephone Co. v. Local 77, IBEW*.[157] There the employer brought suit under Section 301 to obtain reformation of the agreement because of a mistake. The union moved to submit the reformation issue to arbitration, but the lower court refused to do so. On appeal, the Ninth Circuit held that arbitration was properly denied because the agreement specifically prohibited alteration of its terms by an arbitrator.

On the other hand, if one party can establish that the written agreement is not an accurate transcription of the actual agreement, as in the case of a printer's error, Arbitrator Arvid Anderson held he had the power to reform the agreement:

> "These provisions were entered into in the mistaken belief that the final drafts of the contract correctly spelled out the terms of their bargain. The parties did not intend to gamble on the fortunes or misfortunes resulting from inadvertent errors which might creep into the written document in the course of its preparation. Just the opposite is true. Such clauses exhibit a concern that arbitrators remain faithful to the parties' agreement. . . . In this case, the arbitrator will reform the parties' agreement so that it will read as they intended it should have read. . . ." [158]

---

[156] *Bloomfield Hills Bd. of Educ.*, 69-1 ARB ¶ 8386 at 4318 (Casselman, 1969).
[157] 431 F.2d 1219 (9th Cir. 1970).
[158] *Jacobson Mfg. Co.*, 64-3 ARB ¶ 9097 at 6777 (Anderson, 1964). See comments by Charles K. Hackler, *Problems of Proof in the Arbitration Process*, PROBLEMS OF PROOF IN ARBITRATION, Proceedings of the Nineteenth Annual Meeting, National Academy of Arbitrators 242-43 (D. Jones Ed. 1967):
"[I]f the arbitrator is good enough to settle very important issues on a day-to-day basis, I think it is denigrating to say that this one area, the very limited area of proper reformation where the written document is in error, should be removed from the arbitrator and given to some court or to the Board."

CHAPTER VII

Discovery of Evidence Before the Hearing

In modern litigation, court procedures permit the wide use of pre-trial discovery to compel the production of records and witnesses for depositions.[1] In general, evidence obtained from a party during discovery may be used in a trial [2] for any purpose.[3]

Depositions of a person not a party may be used only for impeachment [4] if that person is a witness and in certain limited circumstances as testimony where the deponent is unavailable as a witness at the trial.[5]

In arbitration, formal prehearing discovery procedures are very limited. Labor arbitrators are sensitive to the need for cautious discovery in the collective bargaining relationship because of the potential adverse effect which broad discovery rules could have where parties deal with each other on a daily basis. An awareness of this unique relationship was recognized in this statement of Arbitrator Edgar Jones:

---

[1] FED. R. CIV. P. 26(b) *(Depositions Pending Action)* provides:
"Any party may take the testimony of any person, including a party, by deposition upon oral examination or by written interrogatories, for the purpose of discovery or for the use as evidence or both."
See also *Id.* at 33 *(Interrogatories to Parties); Id.* at 35 *(Physical and Mental Examination of Persons);* and *Id.* at 36 *(Admission of Facts and of Genuineness of Documents).*

[2] FED. R. CIV. P. 26(d) and FED. R. CIV. P. 33 provide that the rules of evidence govern admissibility.

[3] *Id.* 26(d)(2).

[4] *Id.* 26(d)(1).

[5] *Id.* 26(d)(3) provides:
"The deposition of a witness, whether or not a party, may be used by any party for any purpose if the court finds: 1) that the witness is dead; or 2) that the witness is at a greater distance than 100 miles from the place of trial or hearing, or is out of the United States, unless it appears that the absence of the witness was procured by the party offering the deposition; or 3) that the witness is unable to attend or testify because of age, sickness, infirmity, or imprisonment; or 4) that the party offering the deposition has been unable to procure the attendance of the witness by subpoena; or 5) upon application and notice, that such exceptional circumstances exist as to make it desirable, in the interest of justice and with due regard to the importance of presenting the testimony of witnesses orally in open court, to allow the deposition to be used."

"The needs of the managerial process require a different and more cautious approach than the broad license to probe embodied in the Federal Rules. Furthermore, the constituent nature of a labor union, its political structure, means that discovery without 'good cause' shown would be unwise in those situations in which the union is the object rather than the initiator of discovery remedies. The underlying psychology looks much the same in either case. A certain amount of inscrutability is needed on each side for an effective continuing bargaining relationship to function." [6]

This is not to say, however, that discovery is either unknown or unworkable in arbitration. Quite the contrary, a free flow of information between the parties is needed to enable them to better evaluate their respective positions and perhaps avoid arbitration altogether. This chapter will examine such arbitral discovery procedures and the attendant problems which have arisen.

A. ARBITRATOR'S ENFORCEMENT OF INFORMAL DISCOVERY BY REMANDS TO THE GRIEVANCE PROCEDURE

Perhaps the most common form of arbitral discovery is informal discovery, through exchanges of information, as the grievance claim proceeds through the grievance procedure.[7] This has greatly reduced the need for court-sanctioned discovery procedures in labor arbitration.

Some collective agreements specifically recognize that full exchange of information on an informal, but complete, basis is important. For example, the United States Steel Corporation agreement with the United Steelworkers provides:

"At all steps in the grievance procedure, and particularly at the 3rd Step and above, the grievant and the Union representative should disclose to the Company representatives a full and detailed statement of the facts relied upon, the remedy sought, and the provisions of the Agreement relied upon. In the same manner, Company representatives should disclose all the pertinent facts relied upon by the Company." [8]

Only when both sides know all the facts can either be expected to commit itself to an early settlement. As in collective bargaining, a party must know the facts before he will bind himself. Arbitrator Jones explained the need for free but informal exchange of information in the grievance procedure:

---

[6] Jones, *Labor Board, the Courts, and Arbitration—A Feasibility Study of Tribunal Interaction in Grievable Refusals to Disclose*, 116 U. PA. L. REV. 1185, 1224 (1968).

[7] Jones, *Blind Man's Bluff and the NOW—Problems of Apocrypha, Inc. and Local 711—Discovery Procedures in Collective Bargaining Disputes*, 116 U. PA. L. REV. 571, 573 (1968).

[8] Section 6(D)(1), *General Provisions Applying to Grievances, United States Steel Corp. and United Steelworkers of America* Agreement (August 1, 1971).

"It is obvious that a major purpose of the usual multi-step grievance procedure is to achieve the earliest possible disclosure of the operative facts of the dispute and the dispositive contractual provisions. . . .

". . . Disclosure is thus a normal characteristic of a properly function-grievance procedure. . . . The whole thrust of the grievance procedure is toward early and complete disclosure so that settlement can ensue." [9]

Thus, the parties generally will have obtained knowledge of the facts by an informal discovery process prior to the arbitration hearing. If certain required information is not initially available at the hearing, arbitrators frequently suggest "informal" discovery:

"It is quite common for an arbitrator to suggest in the course of the morning, what we might call, rhetorically, 'lunchbreak discovery'; 'Why don't you dig that out during the lunchbreak and make it available?' The parties generally comply and disclosure is routine when the hearing resumes after luncheon." [10]

Arbitrator Gabriel Alexander explained the policy considerations behind informal discovery in grievance processing:

"[S]ound collective bargaining requires frank and candid disclosure at the earliest opportunity of all the facts known to each party. There will undoubtedly be times when facts are not discovered, and therefore not disclosed, until after the grievance has been partially processed, and problem enough is created by those instances. There is not a scintilla of justification for the withholding of information by either party from and after the time it is discovered." [11]

Arbitrators have responded to these considerations, to the extent that the "general rule" is usually stated as being that new evidence or argument will not be admitted at the arbitration hearing unless some special reason is shown for its not having been brought out before.[12] If the evidence were of a type that should have been exchanged, arbitrators will remand the case to the grievance procedure for reconsideration in the light of the new evidence.[13]

These views were reiterated by Arbitrator Bert Luskin when he explained at an arbitration hearing his position concerning information exchange before the case should come before the arbitrator:

"[I]n the grievance procedure, gentlemen, you ought to put all your cards on the table, and both sides should be aware of what the theories of the other are.

---

[9] Jones, *The Accretion of Federal Power in Labor Arbitration—The Example of Arbitral Discovery,* 116 U. PA. L. REV. 830, 836 (1968).

[10] *Id.* at 842.

[11] *Decisions of the Impartial Umpire, General Motors Corp.,* No. F-97 (Alexander, 1950).

[12] Wirtz, *Due Process of Arbitration,* THE ARBITRATOR AND THE PARTIES, Proceedings of the Eleventh Annual Meeting, National Academy of Arbitrators 1, 14, 15 (J. McKelvey Ed. 1958).

[13] *Bethlehem Steel Co.,* 18 L.A. 366 (Feinberg, 1951).

"I object strongly to the 'ace-in-the-sleeve' technique. I think it is wrong. I think it inhibits the grievance procedure. . . .

". . . [I]f your grievance procedure is going to work, both sides must know in advance what the other is going to say in arbitration. Both should have been able, in the grievance procedure, to explore the whole thing, and everybody should know what is going to come forward." [14]

When however, new evidence that a party desires to introduce merely grows out of a deeper investigation prior to the arbitration hearing, the policy of encouraging a free exchange of facts in the lower steps of the procedure is not applicable and arbitrators do not return the case to the grievance procedure.[15]

Although the exchange of information is usually encouraged by arbitrators, some arbitrators have been reluctant to order witnesses to appear for questioning. In *Menasco Mfg. Co.,*[16] the grievant argued that he should be reinstated to work rather than remaining on a medical leave of absence with disability pay. At the third step of the grievance procedure, the company, referring to a contract clause stating that either party should be given the facts surrounding the grievance with the knowledge of the other party, asked to have the grievant produced for questioning, but the union representatives refused. The arbitrator did not order that the grievant appear for questioning, stating that the company representatives already had knowledge of all of the relevant facts.[17]

When the shoe is on the other foot and the union is seeking information, an arbitrator did not order its production believing that the union already had the information. The union claimed that the denial of requested information denied "procedural due process" to a union steward discharged following a contract breach strike. The arbitrator said that the company's termination letter informed the grievant and the union that he was being penalized for "participation, leadership, and support of an illegal work stoppage." Moreover, he said, everyone was aware that the grievant alone rejected a company request to return to work as a cue for rank-and-file strikers to do the same. Since there was nothing secret about this information there should have

---

[14] Excerpts from transcript of grievance arbitration, *Rockford Clutch Division and UAW,* September 30, 1971.

[15] See, *e.g. Standard Oil Company (Ohio),* 68-1 ARB ¶ 8305 (Anrod, 1968); *United Parcel Service Inc.,* 66-2 ARB ¶ 8703 (Dolson, 1966); *Pittsburgh Steel Co.,* XI STEEL ARB. 8131 (McDermott, 1963); *North American Aviation, Inc.,* 17 L.A. 183 (Komaroff, 1951); *Texas Co.,* 7 L.A. 735 (Carmichael, 1947); *Bethlehem Steel Co.,* 6 L.A. 617 (Wyckoff, 1947); *American Steel and Wire Co.,* 5 L.A. 193 (Blumer, 1946). Wirtz, note 12 *supra,* at 1, 15:
"[U]nless some deliberate attempt to mislead the other party is disclosed, and particularly if the 'new' evidence or argument appears substantially material, most arbitrators will be disinclined to rule the matter out of the proceedings."
[16] 65-2 ARB ¶ 8834 (Boles, 1965).
[17] *Id.* at 6047.

been no doubt in the minds of the union representatives why this employee was singled out for discharge.[18]

B. THE ARBITRATOR'S AUTHORITY TO ORDER FORMAL DISCOVERY

If the collective agreement is silent on the authority of the arbitrator concerning discovery, the question arises whether he obtains his authority (1) from a particular state arbitration act, (2) from the rules of the American Arbitration Association if the parties have agreed to them,[19] (3) from the state statutory discovery procedures on the ground that they are merged into the emerging federal law on labor arbitration,[20] or (4) on an *ad hoc* basis derived from his authority to rule on procedural questions.[21]

Arbitrator Mark Kahn, without relying on any authority other than his right to rule on procedural questions, said that under a contract giving the union the right, "by use of grievance procedure and arbitration," to review the company's determination of evaluation points for new or changed jobs, the company was obligated to respond to the union's request for the point rating for each factor of the job involved

---

[18] *Acme Boot Co.,* 52 L.A. 585 (Oppenheim, 1969).

[19] See, *e.g.,* American Arbitration Association, *Voluntary Labor Arbitration Rules,* Rule 28 (1970) which states:

"28. Evidence—The parties may offer such evidence as they desire and shall produce such additional evidence as the Arbitrator may deem necessary to an understanding and determination of the dispute. When the Arbitrator is authorized by law to subpoena witnesses and documents, he may do so upon his own initiative or upon the request of any party. The Arbitrator shall be the judge of the relevancy and materiality of the evidence offered and conformity to legal rules of evidence shall not be necessary. All evidence shall be taken in the presence of all of the arbitrators and all of the parties except where any of the parties is absent in default or has waived his right to be present."

[20] See discussion in Chapter I. Jones, notes 7 and 9 *supra.* The arguments surrounding this problem are premised, in the first instance, by the decision in *NLRB v. Acme Industrial Co.,* 385 U.S. 432 (1967) where the Supreme Court upheld a Board decision requiring that information sought by a union from an employer should be made available so that the union could determine whether to grieve. Thus, given the right of discovery, the Court's decision in *UAW v. Hoosier Cardinal Corp.,* 383 U.S. 696 (1966) that state statutes of limitations are to govern § 301 actions, indicates that the dichotomy between substance and procedure—see, *e.g., Hannah v. Plumer,* 380 U.S. 460 (1965); *Byrd v. Blue Ridge Rural Electric Co-op, Inc.,* 356 U.S. 525 (1958); *Guaranty Trust Co. of New York v. York,* 376 U.S. 99 (1945); *Erie R. Co. v. Tompkins,* 304 U.S. 64 (1938)—exists under national labor policy and, hence, state law is controlling. It is argued, however, that these state laws are, under *Textile Workers Union v. Lincoln Mills,* 353 U.S. 448 (1957), merged into a uniform federal law. In *Local Lodge 1746, IAM v. United Aircraft,* 329 F.Supp. 283 (D. Conn. 1971) the court enforced a subpoena for the appearance of a witness and production of certain records issued under a state statute on the basis of the authority vested in the court by the U.S. Arbitration Act.

[21] *Teamsters Local 757 v. Borden, Inc.,* 78 LRRM 2398 (S.D.N.Y. 1971); *John Wiley & Sons v. Livingston,* 376 U.S. 543, 555-59 (1964). See generally R. Fleming, THE LABOR ARBITRATION PROCESS 170-75 (1965); Jones, note 9 *supra,* at 830; Jones, note 7 *supra,* at 571.

and other related jobs. He rejected the company's contention that under the contract it was required only to explain to the union the basis for its determination of the evaluation points and not the actual number of points:

> "Since job evaluation is designed to provide a systematic basis for the establishment of an internal wage structure, the point rating received by a particular job, for each of the factors involved in the plan, can only be appraised intelligently on the basis of the point rating assigned to other jobs for these same five factors under the particular plan in effect. . . . It would seem to be necessary . . . that selected factor point ratings for other jobs in which the respective factors rank close to the factors for the job in dispute be supplied." [22]

That Kahn had the authority to order such discovery is supported by case law. Thus, in a recent federal case,[23] a district court ruled that an employer was not required to comply with a subpoena *duces tecum* obtained from a state court because under *Wiley* procedural matters, such as discovery, were to be decided by the arbitrator.[24] The court further pointed out that the arbitrator's ruling on such an issue could be challenged in a proceeding to vacate the award.

It is interesting to note that while the arbitrator would thus appear to have inherent powers to order discovery, such formalized rules as those of the American Arbitration Association do not appear to support the full range of discovery procedures.[25] Although the following decisions concerning prehearing discovery are based on Rule 30 of the American Arbitration Association Commercial Arbitration Rules, that rule is identical to the AAA Labor Arbitration Rule 28.[26] In *Commercial Solvents Corp. v. Louisiana Liquid Fertilizer Co.,*[27] a federal district court held that Rule 30 did not give a party the right to take a discovery deposition of the other party. The court explained why prehearing depositions were not available under these rules:

> "Respondent urges that it is entitled to avail itself of the discovery rules because, save for the agreement to arbitrate, the federal courts would have jurisdiction of the subject matter of a suit arising out of the controversy between the parties and in such a suit the federal discovery rules would obtain. The argument contains its own answer. By volun-

---

[22] *Pennsalt Chemical Corp.,* AAA Case No. 16-15 (Kahn, 1961).

[23] *Teamsters Local 757 v. Borden, Inc.,* 78 LRRM 2398 (S.D.N.Y. 1971).

[24] *Cf. Tappan Co.,* 49 L.A. 922 (Dworkin, 1967), where the arbitrator held that his authority on procedural matters extended to a determination of the proper form in which relevant data on incentive standards and rates should be submitted to the union, even though another arbitrator had denied the union's contention in a previous grievance and no specific challenge to the incentive rates was presented to this arbitrator.

[25] The AAA Rules do, however, allow the arbitrator to "subpoena witnesses and documents" when authorized by state law. See VOLUNTARY LABOR ARBITRATION RULES, Rule 28 (1970). See also Section D. of this chapter *infra*.

[26] See note 19 *supra*.

[27] 20 F.R.D. 359 (S.D.N.Y. 1957).

tarily becoming a party to a contract in which arbitration was the agreed mode for settling disputes thereunder respondent chose to avail itself of procedures peculiar to the arbitral process rather than those used in judicial determination. 'A main object of a voluntary submission to arbitration is the avoidance of formal and technical preparation of a case for the usual procedure of a judicial trial.' 1 Wigmore, Evidence § 4(e) (3d ed. 1940). Arbitration may well have advantages but where the converse results a party having chosen to arbitrate cannot then vacillate and successfully urge a preference for a unique combination of litigation and arbitration. . . .

"The fundamental differences between the fact-finding process of a judicial tribunal and those of a panel of arbitrators demonstrate the need of pretrial discovery in the one and its superfluity and utter incompatibility in the other." [28]

In addition, the court rejected the argument that Rule 81(a)(3)[29] of the Federal Rules of Civil Procedure permitted one party to take a formal discovery deposition of the other party to an arbitration proceeding. Similarly, in another commercial case, *Foremost Yarn Mills, Inc. v. Rose Mills, Inc.,*[30] in rejecting plaintiff's request for a pre-arbitration discovery deposition, the court said:

"[I]n a proceeding before arbitrators neither the statute [U.S. Arbitration Act] nor the rules make available to any party thereto the discovery procedures provided in the Federal Rules of Civil Procedure." [31]

The Pennsylvania Supreme Court in *Harleysville Mutual Casualty*

Co. v. Adair [32] also held that AAA rules did not permit prehearing discovery, even though the state law did.[33] The parties had submitted a dispute under the AAA Commercial Arbitration Rules and the arbitrator ruled that under those rules a set of interrogatories submitted by one party to the other need not be answered. The court affirmed the ruling of the arbitrator, stating that the arbitrator had properly ruled that the other party "was not entitled to discovery under the arbitration rules." The issue, the court said, was:

---

[28] *Id.* at 361-62.

[29] FED. R. CIV. P. 81(a)(3) provides:

"(3) In proceedings under Title 9, U.S.C., relating to arbitration, or under the Act of May 20, 1926, ch. 347, § 9 (44 Stat. 585), U.S.C., Title 45 § 159, relating to boards of arbitration of railway labor disputes, these rules apply only to the extent that matters of procedure are not provided for in those statutes. These rules apply to proceedings to compel the giving of testimony or production of documents in accordance with a subpoena issued by an officer or agency of the United States under any statute of the United States except as otherwise provided by statute or by rules of the district court or by order of the court in the proceedings."

[30] 25 F.R.D. 9 (E.D. Pa. 1960).

[31] *Id.* at 11.

[32] 421 Pa. 141, 218 A.2d 791 (1966).

[33] The AAA rules expressly grant to the arbitrator the power to subpoena documents and witnesses where such power is granted by state law, but the rules do not grant the power to the arbitrator to require prehearing depositions even where such power is granted by state or federal laws to courts. See note 19 *supra.*

"[W]hether pretrial discovery or 'pre-hearing' discovery under the Procedural Rules is available in an arbitration proceeding instituted in accordance with the provisions of the . . . rules of the American Arbitration Association." [34]

The court observed that:

"Appellant knew full well that those [AAA] rules did *not* provide for any pretrial discovery as in action at law." [35]

Although noting that the Pennsylvania statute [36] allowed for depositions in arbitration, the court added:

"When appellant, by its own contract, agreed to abide by the rules of the American Arbitration Association, it voluntarily surrendered the right to invoke any of the procedural devices which would be available in an action at law. The right to discovery is one of these devices which is not obligatory as an essential of due process to a valid arbitration proceeding." [37]

It should, of course, be noted that both *Commercial Solvents* and *Harleysville Mutual* involved instances where there were express agreements to be bound by the AAA rules and hence they should not be considered controlling in labor arbitration cases generally. Nevertheless, they do reflect the notion that arbitration is an entirely different forum than a court for purposes of discovery, a notion consistent with the fear that formal prehearing discovery would chill the free flow of information in the grievance procedure and unduly formalize and rigidify labor arbitration. It should be emphasized that while court litigation is often the terminal point of a relationship between parties, arbitration is only a part of a continuing collective bargaining relationship. Arbitration may indeed be an adversary proceeding, but it is one where the adversaries must keep a watchful eye lest they endanger the parties' larger relationship.

In *Penn Tanker Co. of Delaware v. C.H.Z. Rolimplex, Warszawa*,[38] discovery procedures by oral depositions and written interrogatories were held inappropriate in arbitration proceedings commenced under the U.S. Arbitration Act:

"It is true that in *Commercial Solvents* it does not appear that there was any proceeding instituted under 9 U.S.C. § 8, as there is here, with the Court retaining jurisdiction to direct arbitration. But this would not seem to change the basic policy considerations. The purpose of 9 U.S.C.

---

[34] 421 Pa. at 143-44, 218 A.2d at 793.
[35] *Id.* at 144, 218 A.2d at 794.
[36] PA. STAT. ANN. tit. 5, § 167 (1963).
[37] 421 Pa. at 145, 218 A.2d at 794. Jones, *The Accretion of Federal Power in Labor Arbitration—The Example of Arbitral Discovery*, 116 U. PA. L. REV. 830, 884 (1968).
[38] 199 F. Supp. 716 (S.D.N.Y. 1961).

§ 8 is 'to allow an aggrieved party the benefit of security obtained by attachment.' . . . Thus, in *Empresa Maritima de Transportes, S. A. v. Transatlantic and Pacific Corp., Admiralty No. 197-120* (S.D.N.Y. 1959), a libel had also been commenced under 9 U.S.C. § 8. Thereafter, libelant sought to use discovery and inspection procedure otherwise available in admiralty proceedings. In denying the motion, this Court made clear that a party who elects to arbitrate may not simultaneously invoke the discovery procedure of this Court.

" . . .

"Title 9 does not deal in terms with discovery although sections thereof do deal with 'matters of procedure'; *e.g.*, §§ 4 and 7. An argument could be made that the Federal Rules should be applied to proceedings under Title 9 to the extent to which they are mutually consistent. It may be that there is a limited area for application of discovery procedures to proceedings under Title 9; *e.g.*, on the issue of whether there was an agreement to arbitrate which the Court must decide under § 4 before directing the parties to proceed to arbitration. . . . But I do not think that Rule 81(a)(3) is designed to allow judicially imposed and controlled discovery as to the merits of a controversy which will be referred to arbitration under 9 U.S.C. § 4, except, perhaps, upon a showing of true necessity because of an exceptional situation—which this case does not appear to be." [39]

Therefore, in the commercial arbitration setting, the courts conclude that an agreement to arbitrate precludes a party from availing itself of the discovery procedures which would be available if the proceedings were in a court. [40]

In a case where the parties had agreed that the rules of the American Arbitration Association would prevail, Arbitrator Albert Epstein, in *AFTRA on behalf of Howard Miller and Westinghouse Broadcasting Co.,*[41] denied a request for leave to take a prehearing deposition but did so as an interepretation of the state law. He said:

---

[39] *Id.* at 718.

[40] In *Kallus v. Ideal Novelty and Toy Co.,* 45 N.Y.S.2d 554 (Sup. Ct. 1943), the court denied petitioner's request for pretrial deposition on the basis that such a pretrial examination of witnesses is "utterly incompatable with arbitration." In *Stiller Fabrics v. Michael Saphier Assoc.,* 148 N.Y.S.2d 591 (Sup. Ct. 1956), the court denied a request for leave to conduct a prehearing examination, saying that such pretrial procedures are not compatible with "the whole purpose and methods of procedure in arbitration." See also *In the Matter of Katz,* 3 App. Div.2d 238, 160 N.Y.S.2d 159 (1957); *In the Matter of Schwartz,* 127 Misc. 452, 217 N.Y.S. 233 (Sup. Ct. 1925). In another case, the use of discovery in arbitration proceedings about to be commenced under the rules of the New York Stock Exchange, was denied on the ground it would handicap those proceedings. The Massachusetts court stated:
"We also feel that arbitration, once undertaken, should continue freely without being subjected to a judicial restraint which would tend to render the proceedings neither one thing nor the other, but transform them into a hybrid, part judicial and part arbitrational. We also might add that it seems somewhat incongruous to resort to judicial help for pre-hearing discovery after a voluntary understanding had left the entire matter to the determination of arbitrators."
Cavanaugh v. McConnell & Co., 357 Mass. 452, 258 N.E.2d 561 (1970).

[41] AAA Case No. 51-30-0174-68 (Epstein, 1968).

"I am denying the application for leave to take depositions at this time, under the authority vested in me by the terms of Chapter 10, Section 107 of the Illinois Revised Statutes. There has been no showing at this time that the applicant requires depositions for use as evidence relevant to the proceedings, and counsel for the Company has indicated that upon direction by the Arbitrator during the hearing, the witnesses whose depositions are being sought, will be available to testify at the hearing." [42]

Hence, he did not conclude that the AAA rules should be the exclusive source of procedural rights as did the Pennsylvania court, but he nonetheless reached the same conclusion: The use of formal discovery procedures is not compatible with the arbitration process.

In seeming contrast with these cases is a cryptic decision arising from the Fifth Circuit which allowed discovery in a labor arbitration case. In *Asbestos Workers Local 66 v. Leona Lee Corp.,*[43] the parties had entered into a settlement agreement resolving two lawsuits and an NLRB proceeding which the union later claimed was breached by the company. The union then brought suit to have the question of the breach resolved under the arbitration clause of the parties' collective bargaining agreement. In granting the union's request, the district court also ordered:

"To the extent necessary for the presentation of the matter submitted for trade board and arbitration determination, the discovery process of this Court pursuant to the Federal Rules of Civil Procedure shall be available and enforceable in the Court." [44]

The court of appeals in affirming held:

"Also, the District Court did not err when it specifically made available to the parties federal discovery procedures 'to the extent necessary for the presentation of matters submitted for Trade Board and Arbitration determination.' Such order is consistent with the District Court's retention of jurisdiction and effectuates the policy favoring arbitration." [45]

This is certainly a curious and enigmatic case, difficult to analyze because there appears to be, from the reported facts, no compelling circumstances to justify resort to formal discovery procedures. How such an order "effectuates the policy favoring arbitration" is never articulated and, as has been seen, such a proposition can be seriously questioned. In any event, the court apparently limits the scope of discovery procedures in terms of relevance and materiality, a standard

---

[42] *Id.*
[43] 76 LRRM 2024 (W.D.Tex. 1969), *aff'd,* 434 F.2d 192 (5th Cir. 1970).
[44] 76 LRRM at 2025.
[45] 434 F.2d at 194.

which has been used vis-á-vis subpoenas used in labor arbitration.[46] That it is the court, rather than the arbitrator, which determines the issues of relevance and materiality seems at odds with other case law,[47] and is a surprising result emanating from this generally surprising case.

C. THE USE OF DISPOSITIONS AS EVIDENCE

Section 7(b) of the Uniform Arbitration Act [48] provides:

> "(b) On application of a party and for use as evidence, the arbitrators may permit a deposition to be taken, in the manner and upon the terms designated by the arbitrators, of a witness who cannot be subpoenaed or is unable to attend the hearing."

Thus, this authority would permit an arbitrator to grant an application [49] for the taking of evidentiary depositions of witnesses. An evidentiary deposition, in contrast to a discovery deposition,[50] is taken to preserve evidence and is only permitted after it has been shown to be a necessary procedure and that the evidence sought is relevant. To this extent, it is compatible with effective grievance procedures and practices, and hence is also compatible with the "emerging federal law."

That the arbitrator may require a showing of the relevancy of the evidence sought is illustrated by *Kemikalija Import-Export v. Associated Metals and Minerals Corp.*,[51] a commercial arbitration case where an application to take depositions to preserve evidence was denied because there was no showing of the relevance of the evidence. The court, in affirming the denial, stated:

> "The arbitrators ruled that before they would allow the issuance of commissions to take such depositions, appellant would have to submit some *prima facie* proof of the existence of [the relevant information sought] a sufficient showing to warrant the taking of depositions. Until it did so, the materiality and relevance of the proposed testimony would not be established." [52]

---

[46] See, *e.g.*, *IAM Local Lodge 1746 v. United Aircraft Corp.*, 329 F.Supp. 283 (D. Conn. 1971); *Teamsters Local 757 v. Borden, Inc.*, 78 LRRM 2398 (S.D.N.Y. 1971).

[47] *Id.*

[48] UNIFORM ARBITRATION ACT § 7(b); see, *e.g.*, PA. STAT. ANN. tit. 5, § 167 (1963).

[49] Unlike federal practice, the party must obtain leave of the presiding authority (the arbitrator) before taking a deposition. See FED. R. CIV. P. 26(d)(3), note 5 *supra*, which operates after the deposition has been taken.

[50] For an example explaining the difference, see Illinois Supreme Court Rules 202 and 212, ILL. REV. STAT. ch. 110A, §§ 202 and 212 (1971).

[51] 19 App. Div.2d 868, 244 N.Y.S.2d 115 (1963).

[52] *Id.* at 116.

D. THE SUBPOENA OF DOCUMENTS
AND OTHER EVIDENCE

Occasionally, during an arbitration proceeding, evidence essential to a party's case requires a subpoena to bring it before the arbitrator either in documentary form or in the person of a recalcitrant witness.[53] Many states have statutes allowing the arbitrator to require the production of specified documents or the attendance of specified persons as witnesses.[54] If the arbitrator's request is ignored, enforcement is then available through the courts, not as an enforcement of subpoena powers created by the state statute or by the U.S. Arbitration Act, but as an enforcement of the arbitrator's power to compel production of material evidence under Section 301.

If the request for production of books is too broad, arbitrators and courts will restrict the subpoena.[55] Arbitrator Jules Justin, for example, refused in *I. Hirst Enterprises, Inc.*[56] to grant a request for a subpoena *duces tecum* because the purpose was either a fishing expedition or harassment. In *C.&P. Telephone Co. of W.Va.*,[57] the Arbitrator interpreted Rule 28 of the AAA Voluntary Labor Arbitration Rules concerning the scope of an arbitrator's subpoena power in these words:

"A party may at any time prior to the conclusion of the hearing make a written request to the arbitrator for the production disclosure and

---

[53] The UNIFORM ARBITRATION ACT, § 7, for example, provides:

"§ 7. *Witnesses, Subpoenas, Depositions.*

"(a) The arbitrators may issue (cause to be issued) subpoenas for the attendance of witnesses and for the production of books, records, documents and other evidence, and shall have the power to administer oaths. Subpoenas so issued shall be served, and upon application to the Court by a party or the arbitrators, enforced, in the manner provided by law for the service and enforcement of subpoenas in a civil action.

"(b) On application of a party and for use as evidence, the arbitrators may permit a deposition to be taken, in the manner and upon the terms designated by the arbitrators, or a witness who cannot be subpoenaed or is unable to attend the hearing.

"(c) All provisions of law compelling a person under subpoena to testify are applicable.

"(d) Fees for attendance as a witness shall be the same as for a witness in the . . . Court."

[54] Indiana [IND. ANN. STAT. §§ 3-227 to 3-248 (Supp. 1970)]; Maine [ME. REV. STAT. ANN. tit. 14, §§ 14-5927 to 14-5949 (Supp. 1970)]; Maryland [MD. ANN. CODE art. 7, §§ 1 to 23 (1968)]; Massachusetts [MASS. ANN. LAWS ch. 1500, §§ 1 to 16 (1965)]; Minnesota [MINN. STAT. ANN. §§ 572.08 to 572.30 (Supp. 1970)]; Wyoming [WYO. STAT. ANN. §§ 1-1048.1 to 1-1048.21 (Supp. 1969)]. For other state statutes permitting use of subpoenas, see PA. STAT. ANN. tit. 5, § 166 (1963); N.Y. CIV. PRAC. § 7505 (McKinney, 1963); CAL. CIV. PRO. CODE § 1282.6 (West, Supp. 1965).

[55] *Local 99, ILGWU v. Clarise Sportswear Co.*, 44 Misc.2d 913, 255 N.Y.S.2d 282 (Sup. Ct. 1964). There it was held that the union's right to investigate payroll records and cash disbursements of employer "pertaining to employees" did not give the arbitrator authority to issue a subpoena to produce books and records for information as to merchandise manufactured.

[56] 24 L.A. 45, 47 (Justin, 1954).

[57] 21 L.A. 367 (Dworkin, 1953).

inspection of specific documents and other writings in possession and control of a party to the dispute, which request may be granted by such arbitrator if he determines that the request is proper and that the information requested is relevant and material to the issues in dispute." [58]

In the *C.&P. Telephone* case, the arbitrator did grant the union's request, but limited the scope of the subpoena stating:

"[I]t should extend only to such documents and writings which appear to be relevant and pertinent to the issues presented for ultimate determination. The exercise of the arbitrator's authority should be reasonable, and the party is entitled to be protected against 'fishing expeditions' and the examination of files and records which may not be considered as being pertinent. . . .

"Accordingly, the request for the disclosure of the employment application is denied, as is the request for the reports of the supervisors on the ground that such records would not be of any probative value, and would involve the disclosure of confidential reports, including personal opinions. . . ." [59]

The arbitrator, however, did grant the request for medical records which were "of a documentary character which would be directly related to the issues in dispute." [60] The grievance concerned the propriety of a discharge.

In an arbitration of a dispute concerning incentive rates, the union sought data concerning allowances for personal needs, fatigue or rest. The request was held to have sufficient particularity and sufficient materiality to cause the arbitrator to overrule the employer's motion to quash a subpoena *duces tecum* issued by the arbitrator pursuant to the Illinois statute. The arbitrator held that the statutory requirement of "precise designation" had been met and that the request was not a "dragnet" or "shotgun" request for records.[61]

It should be noted that a court has held that the refusal of an arbitrator to order production of books and records specified in a party's subpoena is insufficient reason to vacate an award. In *Milliken Woolens v. Weber Knit Sportswear*,[62] the arbitrators had issued a subpoena, but, concluding later that the subpoenaed books and

---

[58] *Id.* at 371; see also *Milliken Woolens, Inc. v. Weber Knit Sportswear,* 20 Misc.2d 504, 192 N.Y.S.2d 408 (Sup.Ct. 1959) where, relying on the AAA Commercial Arbitration Rules, Rule 30, the court affirmed an award of an arbitrator who had refused to subpoena records which he found were not material to the hearing.

[59] 21 L.A. at 371.

[60] *Id.*

[61] *Automatic Electric Co. and IBEW,* 42 L.A. 1056 (Sembower, 1964). See also *Food Employer Council, Inc.,* 197 NLRB No. 98, 80 LRRM 1440 (1972), where the Board laid down guidelines within the boundaries of good faith and common sense to be followed in giving the union the information requested.

[62] 20 Misc.2d 504, 192 N.Y.S.2d 408 (Sup. Ct. 1959); but see *Heck Elevator Maintenance, Inc.,* 197 NLRB No. 20, 80 LRRM 1448 (1972), where the Board held that a union was entitled to request information about a company's relation-

records were not material or relevant, refused to compel their production. The court said:

> "It is elmentary that 'mere refusal to receive evidence is not sufficient to vacate; the evidence excluded must be shown to be clearly relevant to the disputed issue'." [63]

In *IAM Local Lodge 1746 v. United Aircraft Corp.*,[64] a federal district court had to determine whether an arbitrator at the request of the union had the power to subpoena a company official to the hearing and also the delivery to the union of certain investigation records in connection with a discharge case. The court ruled that under the U.S. Arbitration Act [65] the court had the authority to enforce a subpoena of a witness and the delivery of records even though the subpoena had been issued under a state law. The court, however, put limitations on the process:

> "This Federal Court does have concurrent enforcement jurisdiction and possesses the necessary statutory authority (9 U.S.C. § 7) to enforce the procedures attendant upon the orderly consummation of this arbitration hearing. *Atlantic Coast Line R.R. v. Bhd. of Locomotive Engineers*, 398 U.S. 281, 296, 90 S.Ct. 1739, 26 L.Ed.2d 234 (1969). Under this aegis, it will act *sua sponte* to sever the Gordian knot which created the impasse. The defendant shall produce forthwith the disputed file material for an *in camera* inspection by the arbitrator.
>
> "Such a procedure will, of course, deny to the plaintiff-Union its claim of a *carte blanche* discovery privilege, to peruse the employer's file. Arbitration has never afforded to litigants complete freedom to delve into and explore at will, the adversary party's files under the pretense of pretrial discovery.
>
> " 'The Court agrees . . . that in a proceeding before arbitrators neither the statute nor the rules makes available to any party thereto the discovery procedures provided in the Federal Rules of Civil Procedure.' *Foremost Yarn Mills, Inc. v. Rose Mills, Inc.*, 25 F.R.D. 9, 11 (E.D. Penn. 1960). See also *International Union of Electrical Radio & Machine Workers v. Westinghouse Electric Corp.*, 48 F.R.D. 298 (S.D.N.Y. 1969); *Commercial Solvents Corp. v. Louisiana Liquid F. Co.*, 20 F.R.D. 359, 361 (S.D.N.Y. 1957).
>
> "It must be assumed that the presiding arbitrator is an experienced person well versed in evaluating the alleged claims of the employer, that some files contain classified security information involving national defense or plant security, personal health records and other similar confidential data. All of this should be screened from the file, except where the arbitrator determines it to be relevant evidence in the dispute. Even in the latter instances, proper safeguards should be ordered, such as

---

ships to and arrangements with a second company, so the union could determine whether it should pursue grievances over the alleged performance of contract work by nonmember employees of this second employer.

[63] 20 Misc. 2d at 506, 192 N.Y.S.2d at 411 (citations omitted).

[64] 329 F.Supp. 283 (D. Conn. 1971).

[65] 9 USC § 7 (1970).

sealing the record or limiting its access to counsel only, so that no unnecessary harm or prejudice or unnecessary embarrassment may be caused to anyone.

" 'Once it is determined, as we have, that the parties are obligated to submit the subject matter of a dispute to arbitration, "procedural" questions which grow out of the dispute and bear on its final deposition should be left to the arbitrator.' *John Wiley & Sons, Inc. v. Livingston,* 376 U.S. 543, 557, 84 S.Ct. 909, 918, 11 L.Ed 2d 898, aff'g 313 F.2d 52 (2d Cir. 1964)." [66]

Another federal court reached a contrary result in a case involving a state-issued subpoena *duces tecum.*[67] In denying enforcement of the state-issued subpoena, however, the court, as did the court in *United Aircraft,* recognized the primary role of the arbitrator in determining such disputes.

In this latter case, after a court had ordered Borden, Inc.[68] to arbitrate disputes arising out of the closing of a manufacturing facility, the union informally demanded of Borden certain books and records. Production was refused and the union asked the arbitrator to issue a subpoena to compel their production. Before acting on the request, the arbitrator took the matter under advisement to determine the relevancy of the requested documents. The union then asked a state court to issue a subpoena pursuant to state statute. Borden then had the case removed to a federal district court. That court held that it was up to the arbitrator to issue the subpoena if he determined that the documents asked for would be relevant. The court explained that the arbitrator derives the necessary power, not from the state statute or from the U.S. Arbitration Act, but from the emerging federal law developing under Section 301. The court held:

> "It is § 301 itself which mandates the application of federal law to this case. In *Textile Workers Union of America v. Lincoln Mills,* 353 U.S. 448, 40 LRRM 2113 (1957), the Court made abundantly clear the principle that federal law is to govern the enforcement of collective bargaining agreements pursuant to § 301. . . .
> " . . .
> "Given the applicability of federal law, we now turn to a clear and consistent line of federal cases holding that it is, at least in the first instance, the duty of the arbitrator to make procedural decisions in the course of an arbitration. . . .
> " . . .
> "The arbitrator in this action has already devoted time and energy to the resolution of this dispute. In so doing he has become familiar with

---

[66] 329 F.Supp. at 286-87.

[67] *Teamsters Local 757 v. Borden, Inc.,* 78 LRRM 2398 (S.D.N.Y. 1971).

[68] *Ice Cream Drivers and Employees Union Local 757 v. Borden Inc.,* 312 F.Supp. 549 (S.D.N.Y. 1970), *aff'd,* 433 F.2d 41 (2d Cir. 1970).

the substantive issues in the case and, under the Labor Management Relations Act and the decisions which have construed it, it is properly his function to determine the relevancy and materiality of the documents requested and whether production should be ordered. The intervention of this court sought by the applicant here *in medias res* can only serve to impair the integrity of the arbitration process." [69]

E. DISCOVERY UNDER THE NLRB'S INTERPRETATION OF SECTION 8(a)(5)

Although informal discovery as a case proceeds up the grievance procedure is widespread, cases do arise where disclosure of information is refused by either the company or the union.[70] The party seeking discovery may, of course, look to the NLRB.

In *NLRB v. Acme Industrial Co.*,[71] the Supreme Court upheld an NLRB decision ordering an employer to supply information because the union needed it in order to evaluate whether or not certain arbitrable grievances existed. The Court established a special "discovery-type standard" which was "the probability that the desired information was relevant," [72] and held that it was proper for the Board to make a "threshold determination of the potential relevance" [73] of the data. Standards set out in *Acme Industrial* are now looked to by the Board in disclosure cases.[74] A ruling, however, that a disclosure should be made is not a determination by the Board as to the merits of the dispute. As one court noted:

"In ordering the employer to furnish requested information under [the *Acme Industrial* standards], the Board does not make a binding construction of the contract but leaves the question of definite and detailed interpretation to the parties' grievance machinery or to the arbitrator." [75]

At least one court prior to *Acme Industrial* held that the NLRB may not determine whether the employer's refusal to furnish economic data to the union constituted bargaining in bad faith where that determination would amount to a decision on the merits of an arbitrable grievance. The court said:

---

[69] 78 LRRM at 2399-2400.
[70] Several examples are set forth in Jones, note 7 *supra*.
[71] 385 U.S. 432 (1967).
[72] *Id*. at 437.
[73] *Id*. See also *NLRB v. Rockwell-Standard Corp.*, 410 F.2d 953 (6th Cir. 1969).
[74] See, *e.g.*, *United States Steel Corp.*, 178 NLRB 444 (1969); *P. R. Mallory & Co.*, 171 NLRB 457 (1968), *enforced*, *P. R. Mallory & Co. v. NLRB*, 411 F.2d 948 (7th Cir. 1969). See also *IT&T Corp. v. NLRB*, 382 F.2d 366 (3d Cir. 1967); *American Oil Co.*, 164 NLRB 29 (1967), where blanket requests for information were denied enforcement.
[75] *P. R. Mallory & Co. v. NLRB*, 411 F.2d 948, 954 (7th Cir. 1969). In *Fafnir Bearing Co. v. NLRB*, 362 F.2d 716 (2d Cir. 1966) the court held that where the labor contract was silent, the union had a right to have its timestudy expert make a study of an incentive rate involved in a grievance.

"Where the parties have prescribed a voluntary grievance procedure for settlement of such controversies, courts are to (a) enforce them fully and (b) stay out of the determination of the intrinsic merits under the guise of determining arbitrability. . . . The courthouse . . . is not the place to work out industrial disputes when arbitration has been prescribed and is available." [76]

Unfortunately, these disclosure disputes are not disposed of in an expeditious manner, because they are raised in an 8(a)(5) proceeding and hence only thwart the entire grievance-arbitration process with its emphasis on prompt settlement of disputes. Arbitrator Jones persuasively argues that this National Labor Relations Board disclosure procedure is too slow, too expensive, and too cumbersome: "[T]he Board . . . simply does not have at its disposal the remedy of discovery." [77] He proposes that the Board refrain from using Section 8(a)(5) as a discovery procedure for grievance arbitration and that requests for disclosure be made to the arbitrator and enforced by a court if need be in an action under Section 301.

---

[76] *Sinclair Refining Co. v. NLRB*, 306 F.2d 569 (5th Cir. 1962). In *Timken Roller Bearing v. NLRB*, 325 F.2d 746, 752-53 (6th Cir. 1963), the Sixth Circuit distinguished *Sinclair* on the grounds that in the latter, the cease-and-desist order was not enforced because the ordered action was not within the subject matter of the collective bargaining agreement; whereas in *Timken* the ordered action was explicitly a part of the collective bargaining agreement. Therefore, the court enforced the Board's order. In *IAM v. United Aircraft Corp.*, 337 F.2d 5, 10, n. 4 (2d Cir. 1964), a case concerned with an attempt to preclude resort to the NLRB through limitations on the right to arbitrate, the Second Circuit said the *Sinclair* case "concerned a dispute over the relevance of information sought by the Union, and not a waiver of the Union's right to admittedly relevant information."

[77] Jones, note 9 *supra*, at 1196, 1211-18.

CHAPTER VIII

The Hearing

An opportunity to present evidence and arguments and to cross-examine witnesses is a fundamental part of the grievance and arbitration process. Many state statutes expressly require a hearing in an arbitration proceeding[1] and other state statutes provide that an arbitrator's refusal to hear all evidence is grounds for the vacation of an award, thereby recognizing that a hearing is essential.[2]

A. THE ARBITRATOR'S CONTROL OF THE HEARING

Generally, it has been held that the arbitrator is in control of all facets of the hearing. Attempts to wrest control of the hearing from him have met with mixed success. For example, even upon a showing of misconduct by the arbitrator, some courts have refused to grant

---

[1] The following statutes expressly protect a party's right to a hearing: ARK. STAT. ANN. § 34-507 (1960); FLA. STAT. ANN. §§ 682.06(2) and 682.13(d) (Supp. 1969); ILL. REV. STAT. ch. 10, § 105(b) (1971); IND. ANN. STAT. §§ 3-233 and 3-240(a)(4) (Supp. 1970); KY. REV. STAT.. § 417.030 (1962); ME. REV. STAT. ANN. tit. 14, §§ 5931(a) and 5938(1)(D) (Supp. 1970); MASS. ANN. LAWS ch. 150C, §§ 5(b) and 11(a)(4) (1965); MICH. STAT. ANN. § 17.454 (10.3)(3) (1968); MINN. STAT. ANN. § 572.12(b) (Supp. 1970); MONT. REV. CODES ANN. §§ 93-201-5 and 93-201-7 (1964); N.J. REV. STAT. § 2A:24-8(c) (1965); N.M. STAT. ANN. § 22-3-7 (1953); N.Y. CIV. PRAC. art. 75, § 7506(c) (McKinney, 1963); OHIO REV. CODE ANN. § 2711.10 (1969). Three states provide that their court rules will apply to arbitration procedure: COLO. REV. STAT. ANN. § 80-4-10 (1964); GA. CODE ANN. § 7-210 (1953); and TEX. REV. CIV. STAT. ANN. § 78-31-16(3) (1953).

[2] CAL. CIV. PRO. CODE § 1288(c) (West, 1955); CONN. GEN. STAT. REV. § 52-418(c) (1968); IDAHO CODE ANN. § 7-907(2) (1948); LA. REV. STAT. ANN. § 9:4210(c) (1964); MD. ANN. CODE art. 7, § 12(a)(4) (1968); MISS. CODE ANN. tit. 3, § 290(c) (1956); MO. ANN. STAT. § 435.100(a)(3) (1952); N.C. GEN. STAT. § 1-559(3) (1969); N.D. CENT. CODE § 32-29-08(3) (1960); PA. STAT. ANN. tit. 5, § 170(c) (1963); UTAH CODE ANN. § 78-31-16(3) (1953); WYO. STAT. ANN. § 1-104(1)(c) (Supp. 1969). Numerous other states also require that arbitrators take oaths that they will act fairly and in an unbiased way. A challenge to the absence of a hearing could be made through these clauses. States that have arbitrator's oaths are: ALA. CODE tit. 26, § 339 (1958); ARK. STAT. ANN. § 34-503 (1960); DEL. CODE ANN. tit. 10, § 5704 (1953); GA. CODE ANN. § 7-207 (1953); IDAHO CODE ANN. § 7-905 (1948); KAN. STAT. ANN. § 5-206 (1964); KY. REV. STAT. § 417.012 (1962); MISS. STAT. ANN. tit. 3, § 283 (1956); MO. ANN. STAT. § 435.030 (1952); N.D. CENT. CODE § 32-29-04 (1960); N.M. STAT. ANN. § 22-3-3 (1953); N.Y. CIV. PRAC. art. 75, § 7506(a) (McKinney, 1963); R.I. GEN. LAWS ANN. § 28-9-10 (1968) (can be waived by consent of parties); S.C. CODE ANN. § 10-1902 (1962); TEX. REV. CIV. STAT. ANN. art. 243 (1959).

a stay once the proceedings have commenced,[3] but other courts have not felt so constrained.[4]

In *In re IAM Republic Lodge No. 1987 and Republic Aviation Corp.*,[5] the court intervened on petition of the union in a proceeding and issued an order that an arbitration concerning vacations be heard promptly, ahead of 15 pending grievances, and decided before the deadline for taking the vacations arrived. The court did not rely on Section 301 of the LMRA, but said that under New York state law it had authority to order an expedited proceeding in view of its power to compel arbitration.

In other situations courts have held that a union may not withdraw from an arbitration proceeding it had instituted, absent the arbitrator's consent. To do so, one court said, would "destroy the whole warp and woof of arbitration." [6]

B. LOCATION OF THE HEARING

As a general rule, selection of the hearing site is left to the parties. Rule 10 of the American Arbitration Association's Voluntary Labor Arbitration Rules provides that "the parties may mutually agree upon the locale where the arbitration is to be held." The Federal Mediation and Conciliation Service has a similar rule.[7]

Sometimes the parties select a "neutral" site (removed from the plant premises) to hold the hearing,[8] but often they prefer that the hearing be held at the plant so that needed records can be quickly obtained.

To prevent a stalemate from occurring over a disagreement on a hearing site, a number of state statutes give the arbitrator the ultimate

---

[3] *Lipman v. Haeuser Shellac Co., Inc.*, 263 App. Div. 880, 32 N.Y.S.2d 351 (1942); *In Re Nadalen Full Fashion Knitting Mills, Inc. and Barbizon Knitwear Corp.*, 206 Misc. 757, 134 N.Y.S.2d 612 (Sup. Ct. 1954).

[4] *Astoria Medical Group v. Health Insurance Plan of Greater New York*, 13 App. Div.2d 288, 216 N.Y.S.2d 906 (1961), where the court removed a party-appointed arbitrator prior to the award, saying ". . . it is inconceivable that a court of equity must sit idly by and permit an arbitration proceeding to continue where, by reason of the surrounding circumstances, any award made in favor of one party is pre-ordained to be vacated. The courts are not that impotent."

[5] 41 Misc.2d 279, 245 N.Y.S.2d 900 (Sup. Ct. 1963).

[6] *Simons v. New York Herald Tribune, Inc.*, 15 Misc.2d 116, 152 N.Y.S.2d 13 (Sup. Ct. 1956).

[7] 29 CFR § 1404.12 (1971).

[8] To help parties find a "neutral" site, both the American Arbitration Association and the Federal Mediation and Conciliation Service maintain hearing rooms in several cities. American Arbitration Association, *Procedural Aspects of Labor-Management Arbitration*, 28 L.A. 933, 943 (1957); 29 CFR § 1404.12 (1971).

right to determine the hearing site.[9] Furthermore, the same power can be inferred from more general provisions of various state statutes.[10] Of course, these statutes are the guides. The rules contained therein become the rules in labor arbitration only when they are adopted by the court as being compatible with the procedural law of labor arbitration emerging under Section 301. Rule 10 of the American Arbitration Association's Voluntary Labor Arbitration Rules directs:

> "[I]f the locale is not designated in the collective bargaining agreement or submission, and if there is a dispute as to the appropriate locale, the AAA shall have the power to determine the locale and its decision shall be binding." [11]

C. NOTICE OF THE HEARING

When the location has been determined, the parties must be notified of the time and place of the hearing. Many state statutes require a formal notice.[12] Some statutes expressly provide that an objection to lack of formal notice is waived when a party appears at the proper time and place.[13]

The National Labor Relations Board has also set some guidelines concerning notice of hearing. It has ruled that if an issue, which could have been brought before the Board, is submitted to arbitration, the Board will defer to the resulting award if certain standards of pro-

---

[9] ALA. CODE tit. 26, § 339 (1958); CAL. CIV. PRO. CODE § 1286 (West, 1955); CONN. GEN. STAT. ANN. § 52-413 (1968); FLA. STAT. ANN. § 682.06 (1969); GA. CODE ANN. § 7-204 (1953); IDAHO CODE ANN. § 7-904 (1948); ILL. ANN. STAT. ch. 10, § 105 (1966); ME. REV. STAT. ANN. tit. 14, § 5931 (Supp. 1970); MD. ANN. CODE art. 7, § 7 (1968); MONT. REV. CODES ANN. § 93-201-4 (1964); N.Y. CIV. PRAC. art. 75, § 7506(b) (McKinney, 1963); N.C. GEN. STAT. § 1-549 (1969); N.D. CENT. CODE § 32-29-03 (1960); OHIO REV. CODE ANN. § 2711.06 (Supp. 1969); R.I. GEN. LAWS ANN. § 28-9-8 (1968); UTAH CODE ANN. § 78-31-6 (1953); VT. STAT. ANN. tit. 21, § 507 (1967); WYO. STAT. ANN. § 1-1031 (1957).

[10] ARK. STAT. ANN. § 34-507 (1960); KY. REV. STAT. § 417.016 (1962); MICH. STAT. ANN. § 17.454(10.3) (1968); TEX. REV. CIV. STAT. ANN. tit. 10, art. 243 (1959).

[11] See also Note, *Labor Arbitration in New Jersey*, 14 RUTGERS L. REV. 143, 173 (1959); Braman, *The 1943 Washington Arbitration Act*, 4 ARB. J. (n.s.) 217, 221 (1949); Sterm & Troetschel, *The Role of Modern Arbitration in the Progressive Development of Florida Law*, 7 MIAMI L.Q. 205, 208 (1953).

[12] ALA. CODE tit. 26, § 339 (1958); ARK. STAT. ANN. § 34-507 (1960); COLO. REV. STAT. ANN. § 80-4-10 (1964); CONN. GEN. STAT. REV. § 52-413 (1968); GA. CODE ANN. § 7-204 (1953); ILL. ANN. STAT. ch. 10, § 105(a) (1966); IND. ANN. STAT. § 3-233(b) (Supp. 1970); KY. REV. STAT. § 417.030 (1962); ME. REV. ANN. tit. 14, § 5931(1) (Supp. 1970); MD. ANN. CODE art 7, § 5(b) (1968); MASS. ANN. LAWS ch. 150C, § 5(a) (1965); MICH. STAT. ANN. § 17.454(10.3)(3) (1968); MINN. STAT. ANN. § 572.12(a) (1968); MISS. CODE ANN. tit. 3, § 281 (1956); MO. ANN. STAT. § 435.050 (1952); N.Y. CIV. PRAC. art. 75, § 7506(b) (McKinney, 1963); N.C. GEN. STAT. § 1-549 (1969); N.D. CENT. CODE § 32-29-03 (1960); R.I. GEN. LAWS ANN. § 28-9-8 (1968); TENN. CODE ANN. § 23-507 (1955); UTAH CODE ANN. § 78-31-6 (1953); VT. STAT. ANN. tit. 21, § 507 (1967).

[13] ILL. REV. STAT. ch. 10, § 105(a) (1971); ME. REV. STAT. ANN. tit. 14, § 5931 (Supp. 1970); MD. ANN. CODE art. 7, § 5(b) (1968); MASS. ANN. LAWS ch. 150C, § 5(a) (1965); MINN. STAT. ANN. § 572.12(a) (Supp. 1970).

cedural regularity and fairness are met. These guidelines are commonly referred to as the *Spielberg* standards[14] and one of them requires that notice of the time and location of the hearing must be given to the individual grievant, unless it can be shown that the individual grievant's interests were fully and adequately represented at the hearing. Thus, in *International Harvester Company*,[15] when the arbitrator held that Harvester had violated the union security provision by refusing to discharge an employee for nonpayment of dues, the Board found that the arbitration award satisfied the *Spielberg* requirements because:

> "[The employee's] interests were vigorously defended there by the Company, which had at all times supported Ramsey's position that he was not legally required to maintain his union membership and stubbornly resisted the Union's efforts to secure his removal from his job. For these reasons, we find no serious procedural infirmities in the arbitration proceedings which warrant disregarding the arbitrator's award. After all is said and done, 'procedural regularity [is] not . . . an end in itself, but [is] . . . a means of defending substantive interests.' " [16]

The court of appeals agreed:

> "There is no statutory or constitutional right of an employee to be present at an arbitration hearing. It appears that the company fully and adequately defended petitioner's position at the hearing." [17]

Similarly, in *Eazor Express, Inc.*,[18] the Board deferred to a decision of a joint grievance committee, upholding an employee's discharge, despite his absence from the hearing, on the ground that the employee's interest was adequately represented at the discharge hearing by the union. If, on the other hand, the employee's position is not sufficiently presented by either management or the union, the Board has required that the employee must have received advance notice of the time and the place of the hearing before it will defer to an award adverse to the employee.[19]

D. RIGHT OF A PARTY TO A CONTINUANCE

Closely related to the questions of notice and personal presence is the right of a party to a continuance of the hearing for proper cause. Generally the arbitrator is considered to have exclusive author-

---

[14] *Spielberg Manufacturing Co.*, 112 NLRB 1080 (1955).

[15] 138 NLRB 923 (1962), *enforced sub nom., Ramsey v. NLRB*, 327 F.2d 784 (7th Cir. 1964).

[16] *Id.* at 928.

[17] 327 F.2d at 788.

[18] 172 NLRB No. 201, 69 LRRM 1081 (1968).

[19] *Roadway Express, Inc.*, 145 NLRB 513 (1963); *Precision Fittings, Inc.*, 141 NLRB 1034 (1963); *Gateway Transportation Co.*, 134 NLRB 1763 (1962); *Ford Motor Co.*, 131 NLRB 1462 (1961); *Hamilton-Scheu and Walsh Shoe Co.*, 80 NLRB 1496 (1948).

ity over the granting or refusing of requests for adjournments of the hearing.[20] However, a court has held that an award should be vacated and the matter remitted for a hearing before a different arbitrator in a case where an adjournment which did not prejudice the other party was requested because a material witness was absent.[21] Another court ordered simply that the award be vacated.[22]

Failure to grant a party's request for an adjournment or a continuance may cause the National Labor Relations Board to disregard the award under *Spielberg*. In *Gateway Transportation Co.*,[23] a discharged employee who had received only two days' notice of the arbitration hearing asked for an adjournment in order to obtain time to arrange for the presence of certain witnesses. The request was denied. The Board refused to defer to the arbitration award on the ground that "such a procedure . . . does not satisfy the required standards of fairness and regularity." Also, in *Raytheon Co.*,[24] the Board refused to defer to an award where one of the grievants had asked for an adjournment of substantial duration due to her illness and the arbitrator granted only one day.

F. THE PARTIES' AND AGGRIEVED EMPLOYEES' RIGHTS TO SELECT COUNSEL

The principle that both parties to an arbitration have the right to be represented by counsel of their own choosing is well established. This right is expressed in the rules of the American Arbitration Association[25] and is usually protected by state statute.[26] An interesting

---

[20] *Kool Air Systems, Inc. v. Syosset Institutional Builders, Inc.*, 22 App. Div.2d 672, 253 N.Y.S.2d 346 (1964).

[21] *Ceseretti v. Trans-Air System, Inc.*, 22 App. Div.2d 27, 253 N.Y.S.2d 409 (1964), *aff'd*, 15 N.Y.2d 844, 257 N.Y.S.2d 950, 205 N.E.2d 871 (1965). See also *Lorenzo v. Beauty Culturists Union Local 150A* (N.Y. S.Ct. Bronx Co., 1971), 67 LC ¶ 57,752.

[22] *S. T. Palay Textile Corp. v. Trio Togs, Inc.*, 36 Misc. 2d 646, 233 N.Y.S.2d 708 (Sup. Ct. 1962). Of course, arbitrators must adjourn the arbitration hearing when served with a notice from a court to stay the arbitration proceeding. *Minkoff v. Scranton Frocks*, 181 F.Supp. 542 (S.D.N.Y.), *aff'd*, 279 F.2d 115 (2d Cir. 1960). *Dalcro Corp. v. Wilkinson*, 30 Misc.2d 456, 213 N.Y.S.2d 661 (Sup. Ct. 1961).

[23] 137 NLRB 1764 (1962).

[24] 140 NLRB 883 (1963), *enforcement denied on other grounds*, 326 F.2d 471 (1st Cir. 1964).

[25] American Arbitration Association, VOLUNTARY LABOR ARBITRATION RULES, Rule 20 (1970).

[26] Some states provide an unwaivable right to an attorney. ILL. REV. STAT. ch. 10, § 106 (1966); IND. REV. STAT. § 3-234 (Supp. 1970); N.Y. CIV. PRAC. art. 75, § 7506(d) (McKinney, 1963). Other state statutes provide a right to an attorney and further say that a prior waiver of that right is ineffective. ME. REV. STAT. ANN. tit. 14, § 5932 (Supp. 1970); MD. ANN. CODE art. 7, § 6 (1968); MASS. ANN. LAWS ch. 150C, § 6 (1965); MINN. STAT. ANN. § 572.13 (Supp. 1970); N.C. GEN. STAT. § 1-552 (1969). Other statutes provide that only the grievant, employee, or a lawyer can represent parties in arbitrations but don't guarantee the right to an attorney as such. UTAH CODE ANN. § 78-31-9 (1953); WYO. STAT. ANN. § 1-1031 (1957).

related California case involved an attempt by employees to obtain a court-appointed counsel to prosecute an action to set aside an arbitration award. The court concluded that there was no merit in and no precedent supporting the employees' "unique position."[27]

An employee has a right to independent counsel in an arbitration case where he makes a claim and showing of proof that the union will not provide fair representation.[28] One court held that an independent employee group should be permitted to intervene in an arbitration proceeding between a union and an employer through counsel of their own choosing because the court found that the union had a history of collusion with the employer. It further stated that the possibility of "chaos and confusion," while present in some cases where intervention is sought, was not a factor in the instant case.[29] Such cases are rare, however, and in the absence of clear evidence that the grievant will not be fairly represented by the union, he may not retain outside counsel to prosecute his claim.[30]

Where the individual employee's interest does not coincide with those of his union, thus giving rise to a question of the adequacy of the union's representation of the employee, the Board will not defer to the arbitration award unless the employee not only had notice of the time and place of the hearing but had the right to be represented by his own counsel. For example, in *Star Expansion Industries Corporation*,[31] the employee who was leading a movement to replace the incumbent union was discharged. The incumbent union filed a grievance protesting his discharge which was processed to arbitration. At the hearing, the employee objected to being represented by the attorney for the incumbent union and requested that he be represented by his own attorney who was present at the hearing. The incumbent union objected to the intervention of the employee's counsel. The arbitrator ruled that since he had been appointed by the incumbent union and the employer, he had no authority to order such a change in counsel or to permit the employee's counsel to participate. After this ruling, the employee and his attorney left the hearing. The arbi-

---

[27] *Archuleta v. Grand Lodge of IAM*, 262 Cal. App.2d 202, 68 CAL. RPTR. 694 (1968). See also *An Outline of Procedure Under the New York Arbitration Law*, 20 ARB. J. (n.s.) 73, 89 (1965); Falls, *Arbitration Under the New Civil Practice Law and Rules in New York*, 17 ARB. J. (n.s.) 197, 210-11 (1962).

[28] See Chapter III, Section J. *supra*.

[29] *Iroquois Beverage Corp. v. Int'l Union of United Brewery, Flour, Cereal, Soft Drink and Distillery Workers*, 14 Misc.2d 290, 159 N.Y.S.2d 256 (Sup. Ct. 1955).

[30] See, *e.g., Yale Transport, Inc.*, 41 L.A. 736 (Kerrison, 1963); but see *Clark v. Hein-Werner Corp.*, 8 Wis.2d 264, 99 N.W.2d 132 (1959) which has been greatly criticized since *Vaca v. Sipes*, 386 U.S. 171 (1967). See also Fleming, *Some Problems of Due Process and Fair Procedure in Labor Arbitration*, 13 STAN. L. REV. 235, 237-38 (1961).

[31] 164 NLRB 563 (1967), *enforced sub nom., United Electrical Workers v. NLRB*, 409 F.2d 150 (D.C. Cir. 1969).

trator upheld the discharge, but the Board refused to defer to the award because of the failure of the arbitrator to permit the employee's counsel to participate, holding that it was unlikely that the discharged employee was effectively represented before the arbitrator.

Whenever an employee has the right to independent counsel because of a risk that there will be a failure by the union to represent him fairly, he has the right to be so represented for the entire proceeding and the employee's counsel cannot properly be excluded during any part of the proceeding. Thus, the Board has refused to defer to an award when the grievant's attorney was excluded during portions of the presentation of the case against the grievant, denying his attorney the right to confront and cross-examine witnesses.[32] The Wisconsin Employment Relations Board refused to enforce an award reinstating a discharged employee because the employer's counsel was excluded from the hearing before a joint-area grievance committee which issued the reinstatement order. The Board stated:

"Tribunals set up by contract to administer and dispense 'industrial justice' must comport to certain customary and traditional standards of fair play in their dispensation thereof. This we believe to be especially true when the decisions of such tribunals are to be given finality." [33]

As the right to counsel has become more and more clearly defined in recent years, the opposition to the use of lawyers in labor arbitration has largely disappeared. Lawyers with experience in labor arbitration realize that the relationship between an employer and his employees is "necessarily a continuing one, and that to win a point in bargaining or arbitration by taking a technical or legalistic position may be as hollow a victory as winning a lawsuit against your wife for bending a fender." [34] Arbitrator Elmer Hilpert said much the same thing:

"But above all, an arbitration is a 'family affair'; and the general demeanor toward the opposite party, or his witnesses, should be such as not to 'win a battle and lose a war.' " [35]

Lawyers however, can add much to the quality of arbitration. For example, Arbitrator Benjamin Aaron has said that where lawyers are the parties' representatives, the arbitration process is improved because lawyers are trained to outline disputes clearly and simply, to come directly to the point at issue, to present evidence in an orderly fashion

---

[32] *Honolulu Star-Bulletin, Ltd.,* 123 NLRB 395 (1959).

[33] *William O'Donell, Inc.,* 54 LRRM 1375, 1376 (Wis. Employ. Rel. Bd., 1963), *aff'd,* 26 Wis.2d 1, 131 N.W.2d 352 (1964).

[34] Livengood, *The Lawyer's Role in Grievance and Arbitration,* 9 LAB. L.J. 495, 499 (1958).

[35] Hilpert, *The Arbitration Process,* Labor Law Institute, Missouri Bar Ass'n, October 4, 1956 (unpublished).

and to sum up arguments, relating them to the record made at the hearing.[36] Similarly, Arbitrator Sylvester Garrett explained that lawyers are most useful in arbitration because they are better able to elicit the facts through examination and cross-examination of witnesses.[37] In fact, several arbitrators have pointed out that lay representatives are often more legalistically technical than lawyers. For example, Arbitrator Maurice Merrill stated:

> "Too many laymen think they are acting like lawyers when they resort to pettifogging objections or fight to the last ditch over each minor incident. The lawyers who have appeared before me have manifested an appreciation of the broader aspects of labor-management relationship, a fairness, an adaptability and a resourcefulness that rebuts completely the objections which some have raised against participation by lawyers in the arbitral process. So far from obstructing it with undue technicality and belligerence, they have helped it to run more smoothly. I hope that we shall have increasing use of lawyers as representatives of both sides in labor arbitration." [38]

F. *EX PARTE* PROCEEDINGS

It sometimes happens that although legally bound to proceed with arbitration, one party to the dispute will refuse to participate in a hearing. In such instances, arbitrators are extremely reluctant to conduct an *ex parte* proceeding and prefer to find some way of arranging to hear both parties to the dispute. For example, if one party refuses to appear because it feels the issue is not arbitrable, the arbitrator might try to circumvent the problem by inducing the unwilling party to enter a "special appearance" to be heard only on the issue of arbitrability.

The reasons for the general reluctance to proceed in the absence of one party to a dispute are obvious. The arbitrator draws his authority to hear grievance disputes from the parties themselves. If one party refuses to submit the dispute to arbitration, doubts necessarily are raised concerning the validity of the arbitrator's power to proceed.[39] Also the absence of one party makes the arbitrator's task in resolving the issue much more difficult. The case presented by the willing party will more than likely be slanted. The arbitrator will not have the benefit of opposing counsel's cross-examination and hence his evaluation of evidence and testimony is made more difficult.[40]

---

[36] Aaron, *Some Procedural Problems in Arbitration*, 10 VAND. L. REV. 733 (1957).
[37] Garrett, *Are Lawyers Necessarily An Evil in Grievance Arbitration*, 8 U.C.L.A. L. REV. 535 (1961).
[38] Merrill, *A Labor Arbitrator Views His Work*, 10 VAND. L. REV. 789, 794 (1957).
[39] Such doubts formed the basis of Arbitrator Whelan's refusal to proceed in an *ex parte* hearing in *A.B.C. Cartage & Trucking Co.*, 42 L.A. 55 (Whelan, 1963).
[40] See *Aleo Mfg. Co.*, 15 L.A. 715, 721 (Jaffee, 1950).

In some instances, however, arbitrators have overlooked these difficulties and have gone forward with *ex parte* proceedings.[41] Some arbitrators have reasoned that a general arbitration clause in an agreement would be rendered meaningless if a party could prevent its implementation by refusing to appear at the hearing. For example, Arbitrator Listen Pope in *Velvet Textile Corp.*[42] stated:

> "The Arbitrator regrets that the representative of the corporation did not see fit to present evidence on the union demand. As a result of this failure, there may well be factors in the corporation's situation of which the arbitrator is not cognizant, which would have modified his decision had they been made known. But it is incumbent on an arbitrator to rule in terms of the evidence presented, and the failure of either party to take advantage of the opportunity offered to present its case does not vitiate or invalidate the arbitration procedure. A general arbitration clause in a contract would be rendered meaningless if its implementation depended on the willingness of each party to the contract to present its case, as the party desiring no change in relationships could nullify arbitration simply by refusing to make an appearance."[43]

An *ex parte* award was approved in *Amalgamated Meat Cutters and Butcher Workmen v. Penobscot Poultry Co.*[44] There, a federal district court held that the union was not required to seek a court

---

[41] See, *e.g.*, *Thompson Fuel Service*, 42 L.A. 62 (Kerrison, 1964); *Velvet Textile Corp.*, 7 L.A. 685 (Pope, 1947). In *Amal. Meat Cutters & Butcher Workmen v. Penobscot Poultry Co.*, 200 F. Supp. 879 (D. Me. 1961), when the parties could not agree on an arbitrator within 10 days, the designation, according to the contract, was to be made by the state board of conciliation and arbitration and that board made an appropriate appointment. Both parties were then notified of the hearings, but the company representatives informed the arbitrator they would not attend as they did not consider the disputed questions arbitrable. When an award was rendered *ex parte* in favor of the union, the court was asked to compel the company to comply with the award. The court granted this relief saying: "Defendant was provided full opportunity to appear before the arbitrator and to be heard. It cannot now complain that it chose to stay away." See also *Joint Bd. of Cloak, Shirt and Dressmakers Union v. Senco Inc.*, 289 F. Supp. 513 (D. Mass. 1968) where an *ex parte* arbitration was enforced in part. The court refused to enforce the monetary damages part of the award because the records necessary to determine such award were in the sole possession of the defaulting party, but the court did enforce the arbitrator's order concerning liquidated damages, fund contributions, relocation of part of the company, and access to certain company records. The arbitrator's finding that the company had violated the labor agreement by dealing with jobbers not under contract with the union was upheld.

[42] *Velvet Textile Corp.*, 7 L.A. 685 (Pope, 1947).

[43] *Id.* at 691.

[44] 200 F. Supp. 879 (D. Me. 1961). To the same effect see *Ulene v. La Vida Sportswear Co.*, 220 Cal. App.2d 335; 34 CAL. RPTR. 36 (1963); *Retail Clerks International Ass'n, Local 1207 v. Seattle Department Stores Ass'n, Inc.*, 62 LRRM 2706 (W.D. Wash. 1966). Where the contractual method for selecting the arbitrator requires the cooperation of both parties, a court refused to enforce an *ex parte* award in *Fuller v. Pepsi Cola Bottling Company of Lexington, Kentucky*, 406 S.W.2d 419 (Ky. Ct. App. 1966), saying:

> "The contract is silent as to the procedure to be followed in the event either party failed to appoint its arbitrator. In such a situation, the remedy of the party not in default was a suit to enforce arbitration, not a suit to enforce a unilateral arbitration award not provided for in the contract."

order compelling an employer to submit to arbitration before proceeding to arbitration. It further stated that the award, which resulted from the *ex parte* hearing, is enforceable in an action brought under Section 301, as long as the arbitrator was designated according to the procedure specified in the contract, and the employer was given full opportunity to appear and be heard and failed to avail himself of this opportunity.

Whatever the basis of the arbitrator's jurisdiction to render an *ex parte* award, it is clear that full notice of the time and place of the hearing must be given to the party who does not participate.[45] Without such notice of the opportunity to be heard, courts will not enforce an *ex parte* award.[46]

Rule 27 of the Voluntary Labor Arbitration Rules of the American Arbitration Association[47] provides:

> "27. *Arbitration in the Absence of a Party*—Unless the law provides to the contrary, the arbitration may proceed in the absence of any party, who, after due notice, fails to be present or fails to obtain an adjournment. An award shall not be made solely on the default of a party. The Arbitrator shall require the other party to submit such evidence as he may require for the making of an award."[48]

It should be emphasized, as the rule notes, that an award cannot be granted on the basis of default alone. Rather, the arbitrator should require the party who does participate to produce adequate evidence to meet the appropriate burden of proof.[49] Since in an arbitration proceeding there are no pleadings upon which an arbitrator could

---

[45] In *Farkash v. Brach,* 52 LRRM 2334 (N.Y. Sup. Ct. 1963), an *ex parte* award was vacated because the arbitrator called a hearing for a time he knew one party would not be present because his attorney would be out of the state due to observance of a religious holiday. In *Smith v. Campbell & Facciolla, Inc.,* 20 Cal. App.2d 134, 20 CAL. RPTR. 606 (1962), an arbitrator rendered an award in favor of one party without giving notice of the hearing to the other side. The court vacated the award; noting that *ex parte* arbitrations are permissible but due notice of the proceedings is required. See also *United Steelworkers v. Danville Foundry Corp.,* 52 LRRM 2584 (M.D. Pa. 1963).

[46] *In re N.Y. Shipping Ass'n,* 32 L.A. 696 (N.Y. Sup. Ct. 1959); *Food Handlers Local 425 v. Pluss Poultry, Inc.,* 260 F.2d 835 (8th Cir. 1958). In *Mercuri v. Ligar,* 225 Cal. App.2d 327, 37 CAL. RPTR. 306 (1964), the court held that failure to give personal service of notice of a motion to vacate defeats the attempt to vacate.

[47] Rule 27 was relied upon in *Aleo Mfg. Co.,* 15 L.A. 715 (Jaffee, 1950), where the arbitrator proceeded to conduct a hearing even though the employer was not present. *Ex parte* awards, based upon Rule 27 of the AAA *Voluntary Labor Arbitration Rules* have been enforced in several cases. See *Steelworkers v. Danville Foundry Corp.,* 52 LRRM 2584, 46 LC ¶ 18,119 (M.D. Pa. 1963); *Local 149, Boot and Shoe Workers v. Faith Shoe Co.,* 201 F.Supp. 234 (M.D .Pa. 1962); *U.S. Pipe & Foundry Co. v. Am. Arb. Assn. & United Steelworkers Local 2021,* 67 N.J. Super. 384, 170 A.2d 505 (App. Div. 1961); *UAW v. Waltham Screw Co.,* 47 LRRM 2196, 42 LC ¶ 16,769 (D. Mass. 1960).

[48] American Arbitration Association, *Voluntary Labor Arbitration Rules,* Rule 27 (1970). To the same effect, see Federal Mediation and Conciliation Service, *Arbitration Policies, Functions, and Procedures,* 29 CFR § 1404.8 (1973).

[49] *Dessy-Atco, Inc. v. Youngest Fashions, Inc.,* 205 N.Y.S.2d 577 (Sup. Ct. 1960).

adjudge the merits of the dispute, and given the usual generality of the statement of the issue in requests for arbitration, this requirement seems to be an absolute necessity.

Some collective bargaining agreements specifically provide for the situation where one of the parties refuses to appear at the arbitration hearing. For example, the Bronx County Pharmaceutical Association's collective agreement provided in part that "in the event of a willful default by any of the parties hereto in appearing before the arbitrator after due written notice shall have been given, the arbitrator is hereby authorized to render a decision upon the testimony of the party appearing. . . ." [50] Under this agreement, an arbitrator held that since the sole reason advanced by the union representatives for not appearing was that they would not appear in the same room with counsel for the Association, their refusal to attend was willful, and that he had jurisdiction to hear the testimony *ex parte* and issue an award.[51]

G. USE OF TRANSCRIPTS IN ARBITRATION HEARINGS

The Voluntary Labor Arbitration Rules of the American Arbitration Association provide that a stenographic record may be taken.[52] Arbitrator Samuel Jaffee explained that a transcript makes the entire arbitration proceeding more convenient for the arbitrator:

"Of course, where there is no reporter, it means that the arbitrator has to work harder at taking notes. It also means that a party's representative or attorney may be somewhat inconvenienced in his own notetaking, especially when he himself is asking the witness questions. . . ." [53]

Arbitrator Elmer Hilpert said concerning transcripts:

"Their value in complex cases hardly needs to be stressed. . . . Their value to the parties in their subsequent dealings is beginning to be recog-

---

[50] *Bronx County Pharmaceutical Ass'n,* 16 L.A. 835 (Singer, 1951). In *Fuller v. Pepsi-Cola Bottling Co.,* 406 S.W.2d 416 (Ky. Ct. App. 1961), an *ex parte* award of a union-appointed arbitrator ordering a reinstatement of a discharged employee, made after a failure of employer to appoint an arbitrator, was not enforceable where a collective bargaining agreement did not contain a provision permitting a party-appointed arbitrator to proceed *ex parte,* nor did it provide an alternative plan of arbitration should one party fail to appoint an arbitrator. In so ruling, the court relied on *Harbison-Walker Refractories v. United Brick & Clay Workers,* 339 S.W.2d 933 (Ky. Ct. App. 1960), where the union had a right if the employer refused to appoint an arbitrator to request the appointment of an arbitrator by the American Arbitration Association—clearly an alternative plan of arbitration.

[51] See generally *Pacific Maritime Ass'n,* 52 L.A. 1189 (Kagel, 1969); *Rides Food Shop,* 4 L.A. 719 (Baskind, 1946).

[52] American Arbitration Association, *Voluntary Labor Arbitration Rules,* Rule 21 (1970).

[53] Jaffee, *Battle Report: The Problems of Stenograph Records in Arbitration,* 20 ARB. J. (n.s.) 97 (1965).

nized. They have the added value in arbitration cases of assisting in maintaining order." [54]

Where there are credibility issues, a transcript enables the arbitrator to observe the demeanor of witnesses free from the distraction of notetaking[55] and permits the conflicts in testimony which are basic to rulings on credibility to be recorded for later comparisons.

Arbitrator Arthur Ross explained that transcripts are taken more frequently when attorneys present the case because when attorneys participate there are usually post-hearing briefs. He further stated that:

> "Certainly I would not argue that attorneys, transcripts and briefs should be avoided because they use more time. The advantages of professional handling cannot be gainsaid, especially when significant issues and interests are involved." [56]

If an arbitration award is submitted to a court for enforcement, vacation, or modification, it is often necessary that a full record be available to the court to resolve the conflicting arguments about what transpired at the arbitration hearing.[57]

The establishment of the *Spielberg* standards by the NLRB also makes the use of transcripts in arbitration hearings more important. The Board has said it will defer to an arbitrator's ruling, even where the Board might have reached a different result, if the arbitrator was presented with the unfair labor practice issue[58] but will not defer if the statutory questions were ignored or dealt with only superficially.[59] As Board Member Brown observed, the major problem in applying this standard is the difficulty in determining whether an arbitrator fully considered the unfair labor practice issue before rendering his award.[60] One obvious aid in resolving this question is a transcript of

---

[54] Hilpert, *The Arbitration Process*, Labor Law Institute, Missouri Bar Ass'n, October 4, 1956 (unpublished).

[55] Aaron, *Labor Arbitration and Its Critics*, 10 LAB. L.J. 605, 607 (1959).

[56] Ross, *The Well-Aged Arbitration Case*, 11 IND. & LAB. REL. REV., 262, 267 (1958).

[57] Jaffee, note 53 *supra* at 98.

[58] *Howard Electric Co.*, 166 NLRB 338, 341 (1967); *Schott's Bakery, Inc.*, 164 NLRB 332, 334-35 (1967); *Modern Motor Express, Inc.*, 149 NLRB 1507, 1511 (1964); *I. Oscherwitz & Sons*, 130 NLRB 1078, 1079 (1961).

[59] *Milne Truck Lines*, 171 NLRB 226 (1968); *John Klann Moving & Trucking Co.*, 170 NLRB 1207 (1968); *Illinois Ruan Transport Corp.*, 165 NLRB 227, 232 (1967); *rev'd on other grounds*, 404 F.2d 274 (8th Cir. 1968); *D. C. International, Inc.*, 162 NLRB 1385 (1967); *Dubo Mfg. Co.*, 148 NLRB 1114, 1116 (1964); *Schreiber Trucking Co.*, 148 NLRB 697, 705 (1964); *Raytheon Co.*, 140 NLRB 883, 884-85 (1963), *enforcement denied on other grounds*, 326 F.2d 471 (1st Cir. 1964); *Ford Motor Co.*, 131 NLRB 1462, 1463-64, 1492 (1961); *IBEW Local 340*, 131 NLRB 260 (1961), *enforced*, 301 F.2d 824 (9th Cir. 1962); *Monsanto Chem. Co.*, 130 NLRB 1097, 1098-99 (1961).

[60] Brown, *The National Labor Policy, The NLRB, and Arbitration*, DEVELOPMENTS IN AMERICAN AND FOREIGN ARBITRATION, Proceedings of the Twenty-First Annual Meeting, National Academy of Arbitrators 83, 85 (C. Rehmus Ed. 1968).

the arbitration proceeding, and the Trial Examiner will frequently refer to the fact that he has examined a transcript in determining whether or not the statutory issues had been raised and submitted to the arbitrator.[61] Of course, it is even more helpful when the arbitrator specifically notes in his written decision that he has considered statutory as well as contractual issues.[62] Thus, a party interested in avoiding the possibility of a second hearing involving the same factual situation, and the risk of an inconsistent result, would find it in his best interests to have a transcript taken at the arbitration hearing.

Some local unions which are opposed to the use of transcripts assert that their principal objections are that transcripts increase the cost of arbitration proceedings and cause needless delay. The first objection is not valid because the cost of a transcript is borne by the party ordering it. Only when both parties order copies is the cost shared by both parties. The Voluntary Labor Arbitration Rules of the American Arbitration Association, Rules 21 and 44, specifically provide that the party or parties requesting a stenographic record of the proceedings shall pay the cost of such transcript. Thus, if only the company orders a transcript, the union does not incur any additional expense.

The objection that delay results when a transcript is taken is also not necessarily valid. While the typing of a transcript may delay a proceeding from two days to two weeks, such a delay is not great when considered as part of the total time elapsing between the filing of the grievance and the issuance of an award. Arbitrators often take longer to write an award when they rely on notes because they hesitate to deal with credibility issues when the testimony cannot be reviewed.

---

[61] *John Klann Moving & Trucking Co.,* 170 NLRB 1207 (1968); *D. C. International, Inc.,* 162 NLRB 1385 (1967); *IBEW Local 340,* 131 NLRB 260 (1961), *enforced,* 301 F.2d 824 (9th Cir. 1962).

[62] In *Monsanto Chem. Co.,* 130 NLRB 1097, 1099 n. 7 (1961), the Board, in refusing to defer to an award, pointed to the arbitrator's specific statement in his award that he had ignored any alleged statutory violations. See also *Airco Industrial Gases-Pacific, Div. of Air Reduction Co., Inc.,* 195 NLRB No. 120 (1972), CCH NLRB ¶ 23, 946 (1972).

CHAPTER IX

Witnesses

The function of an arbitration hearing is to gather the facts needed by an arbitrator to properly resolve the dispute before him. The most common method by which evidence concerning the facts is presented is through the oral testimony of witnesses. This chapter deals with practices concerning witnesses appearing in arbitration proceedings.

A. SWEARING OF WITNESSES

Except where required by statute, witnesses need not testify under oath in arbitration.[1] When oaths are not mandatory, their use is primarily dictated by the wishes of the parties and arbitrators will usually accede to a party's request that witnesses be sworn.[2] Unless there is statutory authority in the particular state for the swearing of witnesses, no prosecution for perjury can be maintained merely because the arbitrator or a notary public, usually the reporter, has administered the oath.[3]

---

[1] See generally Comment, *State Arbitration Statutes Applicable to Labor Disputes,* 19 Mo. L. Rev. 280, 291 (1954). Only three states directly require that all witnesses in an arbitration hearing be under oath: KAN. STAT. ANN. § 5-206 (1963); MISS. STAT. ANN. tit. 3 § 285 (1956); PA. STAT. ANN. tit. 5, § 166 (1963). Colorado follows their rules of civil procedure in this area. COLO. REV. STAT. ANN. § 80-4-10 (1964). This would require all witnesses to be under oath. Numerous states give arbitrators the power to administer oaths but in no way require them to do so. ARK. STAT. ANN. § 34-507 (1960); CAL. CIV. PRO. CODE § 1286 (West, 1955); CONN. GEN. STAT. ANN. § 52-414 (1968); GA. CODE ANN. § 7-215 (1953); ILL. STAT. ANN. ch. 10, § 107(a) (1966); KY. REV. STAT. § 417.030 (1962); MINN. STAT. ANN. § 572.14(a) (Supp. 1970); ME. REV. STAT. ANN. tit. 14, § 5933(1) (Supp. 1970); MO. ANN. STAT. § 435.040 (1952); MONT. REV. CODE ANN. 93-201-4 (1947); NEV. REV. STAT. § 614,050 (1967); N.Y. CIV. PRAC. art. 75 § 7505 (McKinney, 1963); N.D. CENT. CODE 32-29-03 (1960); OHIO REV. CODE ANN. § 2711.06 (Supp. 1969); TENN. CODE ANN. 23-509 (1955); TEX. REV. CIV. STAT. ANN. tit. 10, art. 244 (1959).

[2] Arbitrator Maurice Merrill has stated: "The testimonial oath is desired by some parties and considered unimportant by others. My habit is to follow the wishes of the parties as to whether an oath should be administered to the witnesses." Merrill, *A Labor Arbitrator Views His Work,* 10 VAND. L. REV. 789, 795 (1957). See also Kagel, *Labor and Commercial Arbitration Under the California Arbitration Statute,* 38 CALIF. L. REV. 799, 822 (1950): "[I]f the arbitrator is requested to administer oaths he should accede."

[3] *U.S. v. Curtis,* 107 U.S. 671 (1883).

B. SEQUESTRATION OF WITNESSES

Arbitrators have, on occasion, been asked by one party to instruct the other parties and witnesses not to engage in public discussion concerning the matter in dispute. Arbitration, as a process, is private and this is an advantage it has over court litigation.

The *Code of Ethics and Procedural Standards for Labor-Management Arbitration* prepared by the American Arbitration Association and the National Academy of Arbitrators states that the arbitrator is required to respect the private nature of arbitration proceedings. It should follow that the parties as well should not be permitted to subvert the clear intent of these rules by intentionally appealing to the mass media. The American Arbitration Association explains one important reason for the privacy of arbitration:

> "The good name of a company and the reputation of its product are often its most valuable assets, representing heavy outlays for advertising. These may be lost if, as a result of public trial and regardless of its outcome, the firm's credit standing or business ethics are cast in doubt. . . . Differences are resolved through arbitration without danger that the parties may be hurt by adverse publicity." [4]

Not only may publicity affect the employer, but employees as well. In a discharge case, such as for drunkenness or fighting, certainly any publication or publicity as to who the grievant is could have an adverse impact on the employee's reputation, community standing, and the like. It is not surprising then that in published awards, employees' names often are omitted.

In *AFTRA on behalf of Miller and Westinghouse Broadcasting Co.,*[5] the arbitrator made the following response to a request, known as a sequester order, for no public discussion of the matters involved in the arbitration proceeding:

> "Counsel for Westinghouse Broadcasting Company, Inc. presented a motion for a ruling by the arbitrator that the arbitration proceedings are to be considered private and that there shall be no public comments by any of the parties or statements made for the purpose of reporting by news media, relating to the issues involved in this proceeding.
> "I make no formal ruling in this regard, but under the *Procedural Standards and Code of Ethics of the American Arbitration Association,* the arbitration proceedings are considered private and the parties are requested to maintain the privacy of the proceedings until the hearings have been completed and an Award is issued." [6]

The view that the employee involved in a labor arbitration is obligated to respect the private nature of the proceeding is related to the

---

[4] American Arbitration Association, THE LAWYER AND ARBITRATION 4 (1962).
[5] AAA Case 51-30-0174-68 (Epstein, 1968).
[6] *Id.*

view that all employees owe a duty of loyalty to their employer which is violated when an employee releases statements which would be embarrassing or would expose the employer to ridicule.[7]

A sequester order is sometimes difficult to enforce. One was issued to witnesses in *Transport Workers Union v. Philadelphia Transport Co.,*[8] but was violated by certain witnesses. Because of this, it was contended that the testimony of such witnesses should have been excluded, but the court denied the request, saying:

> "Although arbitration hearings are of a quasi-judicial nature, the prime virtue of arbitration is its informality, and it would be inappropriate for courts to mandate rigid compliance with procedural rules such as sequestration. . . . In effect the petitioner is attacking the credibility of the witnesses and this is a matter peculiarly suitable for the final judgment of the arbitrator.
>
> ". . .
>
> "This Court has reached its decision reluctantly for it believes that the Board's failure to enforce its own order could only serve to weaken its image as an impartial, judicial tribunal. Notwithstanding the Board's failure in this respect its decision is amply supported by the record as a whole. . . ." [9]

C. THE ORDER AND NUMBER OF WITNESSES

Wide latitude is afforded the parties in the selection of, and the manner in which, the evidence is presented through witnesses. Indeed, if the arbitrator imposes too strict a limitation on the presentation of witnesses by a party, the award can be invalidated. For example, in *Harvey Aluminum, Inc. v. United Steelworkers,*[10] the court denied enforcement of an arbitration award because the arbitrator had disregarded material testimony of a witness on the ground that the testimony was introduced in rebuttal and should have been introduced during the proponent's principal case. The court stated:

> "The refusal by the Arbitrator to hear all of the testimony of Officer Gottesman or to consider his testimony in making his Award turned on a rule of evidence which the court concludes should not have been binding on petitioner in the absence of some warning by the Arbitrator as to the evidentiary rules to be followed. The failure to receive and consider

---

[7] The employee's duty of loyalty is explained and discussed in the following awards: *Los Angeles Herald-Examiner,* 67-2 ARB ¶ 8658 (Jones, 1967) (duty breached by informing a rival newspaper of an embarrassing ethical dispute); *Maier Brewing Co.,* 66-2 ARB ¶ 8605 (Somers, 1966) (employee posted a notice criticizing an employer's decision); *General Electric Co.,* 40 L.A. 1126 (Davey, 1963) (printing article accusing employer of "insisting on bad parts"); *Sinclair Oil & Gas Co.,* 39 L.A. 508 (Abernethy, 1962) (organizing a boycott of employer's product).

[8] 283 F.Supp. 597 (E.D. Pa. 1968).
[9] *Id.* at 600.
[10] 263 F. Supp. 488 (C.D. Calif. 1967).

the material and pertinent testimony in the circumstances appears to have denied to the petitioner a fair hearing." [11]

The practicabilities of the arbitral process limit the number of witnesses a party will call. There sometimes is a strong temptation to overwhelm the opposition by sheer weight of numbers, but this usually is a dangerous practice. One arbitrator has noted:

"In actual practice, the technique of parading witnesses testifying to a particular event or incident frequently boomerangs on the party using it. The opposing party, if he is skilled in cross-examination, can produce and then highlight conflicts in the witnesses' testimony, thus casting doubt on the credibility of all." [12]

D. EMPLOYEES WHO ARE MEMBERS OF THE UNION AS COMPANY WITNESSES

Although few restraints are exercised by arbitrators over a party's choice of witnesses and the order of their appearance, some limitations are imposed by the cohesiveness of any employee group. As noted by one arbitrator:

"Experienced practitioners in the field of industrial relations accept without rancor, whether they approve or not, the so-called 'code' which estops one member of an organization and frequently one member of an unorganized working force from testifying against another. Whatever the merit of elements such as these, they exist, and their presence cannot come as a shock in trying to elicit facts." [13]

Consequently, employers will often refrain from calling members of a bargaining unit, except the grievant, as witnesses in grievance arbitrations. While an employer may be reluctant to do so, it should be noted, however, that an employer does have the right to call fellow employees and union officials as witnesses. Thus, in *Jaeger Machine Co.*,[14] Arbitrator Theodore High held that the company had a right to call union officials as witnesses, noting: "There is, of course, no property right in witnesses and anyone who is in the hearing room may be called by either party." [15] When the union officials refused to testify on the basis of the union's instructions, the arbitrator ruled that their refusal could be construed as supporting the company's contentions.

---

[11] *Id.* at 493. *Cf. Teamster Local 560 v. Eazor Express, Inc.*, 95 N.J. Super. 219, 230 A.2d 521 (1967) (where a party requests a substantial departure from the normal procedure without stating a reason, the arbitrator is within his authority in denying the request.)

[12] Davey, *The Arbitrator Speaks on Discharge and Discipline*, 17 ARB. J. (n.s.) 97, 102 (1962).

[13] *General Motors Corp.*, 2 L.A. 491, 502 (Hotchkiss, 1938).

[14] 55 L.A. 850 (1970).

[15] *Id.* at 852.

Employers do not call as witnesses employees who are members of the unit for another very significant reason. Many employees will report information to the employer with the understanding that they will not be involved as witnesses and that the fact that they "informed" on a fellow employee will be kept confidential. This often generates a real problem for an employer. He may be certain that one of his employees stole a fellow employee's property or was selling hard drugs to fellow employees because he has been so informed by credible witnesses, but he also knows that he will be unable to prove his *prima facie* case in arbitration to support a discharge because he is committed not to call the informers as witnesses. Sometimes an informing employee will testify without objection if he is subpoenaed, thereby removing the label "company witness." Upon some occasions, the employer who knows the facts is driven to employing undercover investigators who can make the necessary observations and then testify; however, such a procedure is expensive and an investigator can obtain evidence only if the improper conduct is continuing.

E. PROCEDURES USED TO PROTECT INFORMER WITNESSES FROM REPRISAL

In many situations, a witness will refuse to appear at an arbitration hearing for fear of reprisal. For this reason attempts are often made by the employer to submit the testimony of an informer to the arbitrator, yet keep the identity of the informer secret. Such efforts raise a myriad of evidentiary, procedural, and due process questions for the arbitrator, and no uniform response to such efforts has occurred.

Some arbitrators have summarily rejected the attempt to accept statements of an informer as evidence when the informer is not present at the hearing. In *A. C. and C. Co.*,[16] Arbitrator Israel Ben Scheiber held that the discharge of an employee, based upon the confidential telephone calls of a fellow employee who did not appear at the hearing, could not be sustained. He emphasized:

"[U]nder our American System of Jurisprudence, where these two men could not be convicted of even such minor charges as spitting on the sidewalk or of passing through a red light, without having the chance to face and cross examine the witness to these acts, 'confidential telephone calls' are certainly less than sufficient evidence, on which to base reprimands which might at a later date contribute to both their discharge, and to their difficulty in getting future employment.

"The livelihood of a worker should certainly not be placed at the mercy of an informer, who because of his personal dislike of the man whom he accuses, or because of the informer's desire to improve his

---

[16] 24 L.A. 538 (Scheiber, 1955).

seniority status by the discharge of an accused employee, makes a 'confidential telephone call' secure in the knowledge that he will not have to face the man whom he accuses, because of a Company policy not to embarrass him by compelling him to repeat his charges under oath, in the presence of, and to submit to cross examination by, the man whom he has accused." [17]

Arbitrators have also declined to uphold disciplinary action based on statements of an informer who does not testify. They hold that such statements are hearsay and lack probative value because the correctness of the statement cannot be tested by cross-examination.[18]

On the other hand, various arbitrators have recognized the practical need for keeping the identiy of informers secret and have upheld discharges based on reports of undisclosed informers. The leading case in this area is *Los Angeles Transit Lines* where undercover "spotters" were hired to ride on buses to determine whether drivers were depositing fares into the fare box or were stealing the money. Arbitrator George Hildebrand noted evidence from such investigators was acceptable even though "[t]he system may be odious, but there is no practical alternative." [19]

Arbitrators Willard Wirtz and Robben Fleming have both described procedures devised to bridge the gap between the protective value of cross-examination and the practical need to keep the identity of employee-informers secret.[20] One procedure allows the informant to be cross-examined behind a screen or by conference telephone, but permits the arbitrator to interview the witness face to face. Such a procedure has not always proven satisfactory. Arbitrator Ralph Seward has noted:

"When I first went to General Motors in 1944, I found that they were accustomed—in certain discharge cases where the company was afraid to call members of the bargaining unit as witnesses for fear of what might happen to them—to have the arbitrator interview such witnesses

---

[17] *Id.* at 540. See also *Twin City Rapid Transit Co.*, 62-1 ARB ¶ 8128 (Levinson, 1961); *Hooker Chemical Corp.*, 36 L.A. 857 (Kates, 1961); *Bower Roller Bearing Co.*, 22 L.A. 320 (Bowles, 1954); *Lockheed Aircraft Corp.*, 13 L.A. 433 (Aaron, 1949); *Murray Corp. of America*, 8 L.A. 713 (Wolff, 1947); R. Fleming, THE LABOR ARBITRATION PROCESS 177 *et seq.* (1965) where the author compares such arbitration cases to Supreme Court cases dealing with the dismissal of government employee for alleged security reasons. But *cf. Morton Int'l, Inc.*, 67-2 ARB ¶ 8423 (Merrill, 1967) (right to confront one's accuser does not guarantee right of a grievant to be present at a grievance meeting between the company and the union).

[18] See, *e.g., Duraloy Co.*, 13 L.A. 624 (Blair, 1949); *Lockheed Aircraft Corp.*, 13 L.A. 433 (Aaron, 1949).

[19] 25 L.A. 740, 741 (Hildebrand, 1955). *Accord, Shenango Valley Transportation Co.*, 23 L.A. 362 (Brecht, 1954). See generally Fleming, *Due Process in Arbitration*, 13 STAN. L. REV. 235, 245-48 (1961); F. Elkouri and E. Elkouri, HOW ARBITRATION WORKS 183-84 (1960).

[20] Fleming, note 19 *supra;* Fleming, note 17 *supra,* at 179-81; Wirtz, *Due Process of Arbitration,* THE ARBITRATOR AND THE PARTIES, Proceedings of the Eleventh Annual Meeting, National Academy of Arbitrators 1, 19 (J. McKelvey Ed. 1958).

in private. I changed the rule a bit by requiring some showing of danger to witnesses who testified openly at the hearing, but with this change I went along with the procedure for a time. This made me of course, an independent investigator as well as a trier of the facts. I now think it was an unsound and dangerous procedure even though I am sure that it enabled me to get closer to the truth in some cases than I could otherwise have done." [21]

A variation of some interest occurred in *Walker Mfg. Co.* (Harrisonburg, Va.).[22] The company had gained information that two employees were promoting a slowdown in production. The informing employees feared harassment if the fact they informed became general knowledge. Wishing to prevent retaliation against the informers, the company withheld their identity from the union until the hearing. However, to prevent a charge of unfair surprise, copies of the informants' affidavits (with the signatures obliterated) were given to the union and at the hearing the informers appeared as witnesses and were subject to cross-examination. The arbitrator felt that this procedure did not violate the rights of the grievants because the grievants knew what charges were against them and what evidence the company had to support the charges.

Where an informer was paid 50 dollars to reveal a thievery ring stealing fabric from the employer, his suspension, until he revealed the names, was upheld. The arbitrator did, however, require the company to promise to protect the informer from libel if the information was misused.[23]

For reasons related to the protection of informers, a court, when it enforced a subpoena of company investigation records in a discharge case, specified that the records would be delivered *in camera* for inspection by the arbitrator. The court made this a condition so as not to expose to the union representatives generally any statements from one employee reporting on a fellow employee.[24]

F. THE GRIEVANT AS AN ADVERSE WITNESS

The grievant in a discharge or disciplinary suspension case is an exception to the view that an employer should rarely call bargaining unit employees as witnesses in arbitration cases. Some employers prefer to initiate the presentation of their defense in a disciplinary case by calling the grievant as an adverse witness. This tactic prevents the

---

[21] Wirtz, note 20 *supra*, at n. 18. See also *Lockheed Aircraft Corp.*, 13 L.A. 433, 434 (Aaron, 1949) (employer's proposal of independent investigation by arbitrator rejected).

[22] FMCS File 69A/3891 (Ludenberg, 1969) (unpublished).

[23] *Eisen Merchantile, Inc.*, 58 L.A. 340 (Madden, 1972).

[24] *Local Lodge 1746 v. United Aircraft Corp.*, 329 F. Supp. 283 (D. Conn. 1971).

grievant from adjusting his testimony in light of facts presented as part of the employer's initial case.[25] In *Tectum Corp.*,[26] the arbitrator permitted the company to call the grievant as a witness over the union's objection, stating:

> "This arbitrator's ruling that the grievant should submit to questioning by the Company . . . was based upon the arbitrator's opinion that neither the Company nor the Union should be allowed to withhold relevant and material testimony or other evidence. . . ." [27]

The New York Tripartite Committee found nothing objectionable about calling witnesses from the opposing side which would include calling the grievant as a witness at the opening of evidence in a discharge or disciplinary case. The committee said:

> "It is permissible for a party to call witnesses from the opposing side. The witness may be treated as a hostile witness, but it is incumbent on the arbitrator to insure that the direct examination is proper and that the witness is protected against unfair tactics. (Some members do not consider an adverse witness, *per se,* to be hostile.)" [28]

The Pittsburgh Tripartite Committee, except the labor member, expressed the same view:

> "We see no reason why an adverse witness or party cannot be called, subject, however, to the right of the opposite side to examine the witness on *voir dire* before the witness testifies. We believe that the party calling the witness should be bound by the testimony of that witness.
>
> "An arbitrator is called upon to make findings of fact and in order to perform his tasks properly all known facts should be presented to him. Hence, there should be no objection to calling witnesses from 'the other side.'
>
> "An exception to this general rule, in the opinion of the Labor Members of our Committee, should exist in discipline cases. They insist that the burden should be on the employer to prove his case without having the right to call the grievant as a witness. Based on facts known to the employer, the decision to discipline was made. Hence, the grievant should be allowed to decide whether he desires to testify at a hearing involving discipline meted out to him. Management members argue that the general rule should prevail." [29]

The Chicago Tripartite Committee, on the other hand, was critical of calling the grievant as the first witness in a discharge or disciplinary case:

---

[25] In *International Smelting & Refining Co.,* 45 L.A. 885 (Kornblum, 1965), the arbitrator would not allow the grievant to be excluded from the hearing at any time.
[26] 37 L.A. 807 (Autrey, 1961).
[27] *Id.* at 810.
[28] New York Tripartite Committee, *Problems of Proof in the Arbitration Process,* PROBLEMS OF PROOF IN ARBITRATION, Proceedings of the Nineteenth Annual Meeting, National Academy of Arbitrators 301 (D. Jones Ed. 1967).
[29] Pittsburgh Tripartite Committee, *Id.* at 258.

"Except for unusual cases, such as the situation where the grievant knows best what occurred and the circumstances surrounding the occurrence, an arbitrator should rule that the grievant may not be called as a witness at the outset of the case in a discharge or disciplinary matter. Except for this limitation, no other limitations should be placed by the arbitrator on the parties calling witnesses from the other side." [30]

G. EXCLUSION OF WITNESSES DURING TESTIMONY OF OTHERS

Sometimes one or both of the parties will request that witnesses be excluded from the hearing room while other witnesses are testifying. This practice, which is sanctioned by the rules of the American Arbitration Association, prevents the testimony of a witness from being influenced by the statements of others.[31] However, arbitrators are seldom willing to exclude the grievant,[32] and for this reason, as explained in the prior section, he is often called as the employer's initial witness. Arbitrator Daniel Kornblum refused to apply a specific requirement of the agreement that witnesses "shall appear separately and remain present solely to be heard as witnesses" to a dischargee-grievant, saying:

"In a discharge case, as here, exclusion of the aggrieved employee at this terminal stage of the grievance procedure would be tantamount to a denial of due process. It would be akin to excluding a defendant in a criminal proceeding from his own trial." [38]

Similarly, in *Douglas Aircraft Co.*,[34] the company moved to have the grievant excluded from the arbitration hearing on the ground that it is poor industrial relations practice to allow the grievant to hear adverse testimony by fellow unit employees and his supervisor. Arbitrator E. Jones denied the motion, saying that the grievant had a legal right to be present in the hearing.

H. CROSS-EXAMINATION

Cross-examination has been relied upon to probe a witness' testimony, to make it more complete, or to expose it as false or distorted. It is a procedure that is essential to a fair hearing. The Uniform Arbitration Act provides that "the parties are entitled . . . to cross-examine

---

[30] Chicago Tripartite Committee, *Id.* at 99.

[31] American Arbitration Association, *Voluntary Labor Arbitration Rules*, Rule 22 (1970) cited and discussed in Note, *Labor Arbitration in New Jersey*, 14 RUTGERS L. REV. 143, 176 (1959). One arbitrator, commenting on this procedure, states: "On several occasions, I have observed the effectiveness of this safeguard. . . ." Merrill, *A Labor Arbitrator Views His Work*, 10 VAND. L. REV. 789, 795 (1957).

[32] See, *e.g.*, *Tectum Corp.*, 37 L.A. 807 (Autrey, 1961).

[33] *International Smelting & Refining Co.*, AAA Case No. 86-17 (Kornblum, 1965).

[34] 28 L.A. 198 (Jones, 1957).

witnesses appearing at the hearing." [35] and the American Arbitration Association's procedures recognize the right of parties to cross-examine witnesses.[36] Also, the arbitrator himself may examine a witness.[37]

The New York Tripartite Committee concluded that the scope of the cross-examination need not be limited to the scope of direct examination, but that the arbitrator has discretion to confine the examination when the range of inquiry becomes excessive:

> "Cross-examination need not be restricted to the scope of the direct examination, but the arbitrator should exercise reasonable discretion in this regard. If the questions are related directly or indirectly to the issue or to credibility, a reasonable latitude should be permitted." [38]

The Committee added these observations:

> "The arbitrator is responsible for conducting an orderly hearing and should exercise initiative to that end. Since the principal purpose of the hearing is to provide the arbitrator with relevant and admissible evidence necessary to resolve the issue in an expeditious manner, he should not permit personal attacks, outbursts, argumentative, loud or abusive questioning, hectoring, badgering, refusing to let the witness answer the question, or like behavior.
>
> "The arbitrator must afford each party an adequate opportunity to present its case by evidence and argument. He must determine, in individual situations, how much leeway should be given a witness or representative in testifying or presenting his case. However, he should not permit the hearing to bog down with irrelevant matter or repetitious evidence or argument." [39]

The Chicago Tripartite Committee said:

> "We do not, in general, believe that the scope of cross examination should be restricted to the scope of direct. Where the cross examination appears to be getting into irrelevant matters, and objection is made, the arbitrator would do well to ask for an explanation of the purpose of the questions. Sometimes the zeal of an advocate may take him far afield and he may appreciate being guided back to the issue.
>
> "It is difficult to generalize as to the allowable latitude. Cross examination should not be interfered with unless it appears obvious that the questions have no bearing on the issues before the arbitrator or that the witness is not competent to answer the questions." [40]

It was pointed out that improper cross-examination tactics should be prevented by the arbitrator:

---

[35] UNIFORM ARBITRATION ACT § 5(b).

[36] American Arbitration Association, LABOR ARBITRATION PROCEDURES AND TECHNIQUES 18 (1961).

[37] See, e.g., Code of Ethics and Procedural Standards for Labor-Management Arbitration, Part II, 4(b) at 5 (1962).

[38] See note 28 supra.

[39] Id. at 303, 304.

[40] See note 30 supra, at 102.

"The arbitrator plays a crucial role in the proceedings. He should discourage and shut off improper tactics such as redundant cross examination, abuse or intimidation of witness by threats or otherwise, the putting of involved questions not susceptible of intelligent response, shouting at witnesses, standing over witness, and the making of unseemly gestures.

"In certain situations where tense emotional attitudes develop, it may be necessary for the arbitrator to overlook an emotional outburst. But in general it is the arbitrator's responsibility to prevent the proceedings from degenerating into a donnybrook." [41]

Where a grievant is not present at an arbitration hearing, arbitrators have dismissed the grievance on the ground that the grievance claim thereupon becomes uncorroborated hearsay insufficient to support the claim, and further that by the grievant's failure to appear the employer has been denied his right to cross-examine.[42] There are, however, divergent views concerning the effect of denial of cross-examination. In *Sewanee Silica Co.*,[43] the arbitrator admitted that the union's failure to produce witnesses deprived the employer of its right to cross-examine; but the arbitrator concluded that this did not deprive the employer of a fair hearing, stating:

"At several points in the Company's post-hearing brief . . . the Company noted that the Union presented no witnesses, contenting itself with statements and exhibits, and thus that the Company had no opportunities for cross-examination. I wish to reject any possible implication of unfairness here. . . . An arbitration hearing is not a court; one of its principal values lies in its wide-ranging informality, free from the irksome encrustations of jury procedure. No party has an obligation to present witnesses, or to choose any particular form of procedure other than general decorum and order." [44]

The opposite view was expressed in *Tectum Corp.*[45] There, the arbitrator ruled that a grievant must testify and answer employer questions directly bearing on the issue, and the failure to testify would deny a fair hearing. He stated:

"This arbitrator's ruling that the grievant should submit to questioning by the Company subject to the right of the Union to object to specific questions was based upon the arbitrator's opinion that neither the Company nor the Union should be allowed to withhold relevant and material testimony or other evidence except possibly in special circumstances not here involved such as possible criminal incrimination, trade secrets and classified Defense matters." [46]

---

[41] *Id.*

[42] *Vickers, Inc.*, 39 L.A. 614, 621 (Prasow, 1962).

[43] 47 L.A. 282 (Greene, 1966).

[44] *Id.* at 283.

[45] 37 L.A. 807 (Autrey, 1961). See *Berg Airlectro Products Co.*, 46 L.A. 668 (Sembower, 1966).

[46] 37 L.A. at 810.

Similarly, where the employer fails to produce a witness and attempts to submit written reports or affidavits, arbitrators have held the evidence inadmissible on the grounds that if admitted the union would be denied its right to cross-examination, unless the reports or affidavits merely corroborate testimony which was subject to cross-examination. In *Armstrong Cork Co.,*[47] Arbitrator Ralph Roger Williams said:

> "While the Company's statements taken from witnesses are entitled to weight, the Union had no opportunity to cross-examine these accusing witnesses.
>
> " . . .
>
> "Those discharged are entitled to confront their accusers at the arbitration hearing, and to cross-examine them. . . . Signed statements of employees charging another employee with an offense are not conclusive evidence and must be supported by proof. . . . A written statement which is not supported by the testimony of its maker may be used to corroborate other evidence that was subject to cross-examination, but it should not be considered where it only produces novel evidence, because one test which may be used to determine the credibility of a witness is the demeanor of the witness while he is testifying at the hearing."[48]

I. IMPEACHING THE WITNESS

In the *New York Tripartite Report,* it said:

> "To impeach a witness is to call into question his veracity by means of evidence adduced for that purpose, or the adducing of proof that a witness is unworthy of belief. Ordinarily, a party may not impeach its own witness through his own testimony, except where he is a hostile witness or his testimony can be shown to constitute a surprise. (A hostile witness is one who manifests so much hostility or prejudice under examination that the party who has called him is allowed to cross-examine him, *i.e.,* to treat him as though he had been called by the opposite party.) It is not improper to adduce evidence from other witnesses which contradicts or is inconsistent with the testimony of a prior witness called by the same party. It is not proper to introduce evidence or testimony concerning facts not relevant to the proceeding in order to discredit a witness except evidence of a conviction for perjury."[49]

The Chicago Tripartite Committee said:

> "There should be no limitation in efforts to impeach a witness, particularly where cross examination is used to establish facts which are to be followed up by direct testimony. But impeachment does not mean

---

[47] 70-1 ARB ¶ 8186 at 3634 (Williams, 1969) (citations omitted); but *cf. Block Pontiac, Inc. v. Candando,* 274 F. Supp. 1014 (E.D. Pa. 1967) (receipt of affidavits by arbitrator not grounds for invaliding award).

[48] 70-1 ARB at 3634.

[49] See note 28 *supra,* at 302.

harassment—and an arbitrator has an obligation to protect a witness from excessive badgering or repetitive examination on the same subject matter." [50]

J. PROCEDURE FOR PROTECTING WITNESS IN ARBITRATION FROM UNDUE INFLUENCE AND RETALIATION

It is firmly established that union or management retaliation against employees who file complaints or testify before the National Labor Relations Board is illegal.[51] In *Ebasco Services, Inc.*,[52] however, the Board broadened its rule against retaliation to cover witnesses in arbitration hearings. There, three foremen were demoted because they took time off to appear before a permanent arbitration board that was investigating a grievance. Because of the foremen's absence, the employer had to shut down his operation. As a result the employer demoted the foremen. The trial examiner pointed out that the Board's policy was to encourage the use of the contractual grievance procedure, even to the point of deferring to arbitration awards. That the law as administered by the Board should give witnesses in arbitration proceedings the same protection they would receive if they had been witnesses in a Board proceeding, was held to be a reasonable intention of congressional policy to encourage grievance proceedings. Thus, the employer was held to have violated Section 8(a)(1) of the Act by disciplining these foremen for appearing at the hearing.

The NLRB has also involved itself with the protection of employee witnesses who have appeared in arbitration proceedings. A union-imposed fine of $25 against an employee who testified against a fellow employee's interests in an arbitration proceeding was found by the NLRB to be coercive and violative of the National Labor Relations Act.[53]

The Board also found that an employer's action in changing an employee's assignment was unlawfully motivated because he had received an award from an arbitrator for more pay.[54] In a two to one decision the Board found that the reassignment was punishment for successfully pursuing a grievance. The fact that the employer might have to pay more because of the award was no defense for the reassignment. The Board refused to defer action pending a court review of the arbitration award because it said that the discontinuance of

---

[50] See note 30 *supra*, at 103.

[51] *NLRB v. Syracuse Stamping Co.*, 208 F.2d 77 (2d Cir. 1953). See also *Dugal Ltd.*, 196 NLRB No. 80, (1972), CCH NLRB ¶ 24,108 (1972).

[52] 181 NLRB 768 (1969).

[53] *Teamsters Local 788*, 190 NLRB No. 5, 77 LRRM 1458 (1971).

[54] *Mrs. Baird's Bakeries, Inc.*, 189 NLRB No. 89, 76 LRRM 1696 (1971).

the assignment occurred after the award and, therefore, this action by the employer was not before the arbitrator.

The arbitrator also has an obligation to protect witnesses from undue influence and to protect parties from testimony that is distorted by improper influence. One court has held that an arbitration hearing will not be stayed where witnesses were alleged to have been tampered with or subjected to undue influence.[55] The court said that the witnesses would be available at the arbitration hearing and evidence of the alleged undue influence could be presented to the arbitrator.

K. SUBPOENA OF WITNESSES

Subpoenas ordering witnesses to appear at an arbitration hearing have been issued by courts under state statutes. One federal court enforced a subpoena for the appearance of a witness issued under a state statute on the basis of the authority vested in the court by the U.S. Arbitration Act,[56] considering that Act to be the "guiding analogy" for the law emerging through Section 301 on procedural matters mentioned by the Supreme Court.[57] However, another federal court refused to enforce a subpoena issued by a state court on the ground that under the decisions of the Supreme Court the materiality of the evidence sought was a threshold question which the arbitrator should determine.[58] The second court concluded that a procedure which placed the subpoena power outside the control of the arbitrator was to incorporate state law in a manner incompatible with the "emerging law." This latter decision is compatible with the counsel by the Supreme Court in *Goodall-Sanford, Inc. v. United Textile Workers Local 1802* [59] that procedural rules contained in state or federal arbitration statutes must often be retailored before being incorporated into the procedural law emerging through Section 301.[60]

It would seem to be clear that the arbitrator, without need of statutory power from a state or federal statute, can issue a subpoena for the attendance of a witness, which subpoena would be enforced by a federal court under Section 301. In the next chapter the control that arbitrators have placed on pretrial discovery procedures through their

---

[55] *WMCA v. Radio and Television Broadcast Engineers Local 1212,* 23 Misc.2d 1014, 207 N.Y.S. 2d 321 (N.Y. Sup. Ct. 1960). Similarly another court has held that an award would not be vacated because evidence of tampering with a witness was not accepted by the arbitration board, *Newark Stereotypers Union No. 18 v. Newark Morning Ledger Co.,* 261 F.Supp. 832 (D.N.J. 1966).

[56] *Local Lodge 1746 IAM v. United Aircraft Corp.,* 329 F.Supp. 283 (D. Conn. 1971).

[57] *Lincoln Mills v. Textile Workers Union,* 353 U.S. 448, 451 (1957).

[58] *Teamsters Local 757 v. Borden, Inc.,* 78 LRRM 2398 (S.D.N.Y. 1971).

[59] 353 U.S. 550 (1957).

[60] See Chapter VII, Section D, *The Subpoena of Documents and Other Evidence.*

right to determine the relevancy is explained.[61] Arbitrators usually determine the relevancy of the information sought in advance so as to avoid harassment of one party by another through "fishing expeditions." The apparent development in the law placing the control of subpoenas of witnesses to an arbitration proceeding in the hands of the arbitrator, rather than in the hands of a court under a state or federal statute, should be preferred by both parties. It is not common to subpoena witnesses in arbitration cases. However, sometimes witnesses, who are union members and employees, are subpoenaed by the employer to protect the witness from the accusation by his fellow employees that he appeared voluntarily as a witness for the employer.[62]

---

[61] *Id.*
[62] See related discussion in Section D. of this chapter.

CHAPTER X

Construction Principles

Part of the practice and procedure of labor arbitration are the basic approaches used by arbitrators in construing the collective bargaining agreement. These approaches are considered in this chapter.

A. THE PAROL EVIDENCE RULE

The parol evidence rule in its classic form holds that evidence, whether oral or otherwise, cannot be admitted for the purpose of varying or contradicting written language recording the agreement between two parties.[1] This rule has sometimes been called a rule of substantive law because it causes the rights of the parties to be determined by an interpretation of the words in a written document rather than by evidence outside that document.

In labor arbitration the parol evidence rule is a construction doctrine which is closely related to the view that the scope of an arbitrator's jurisdiction is limited to disputes which involve the interpretation and application of a provision of the written agreement between the parties. In addition, the parol evidence rule is also closely related to the reserve rights construction doctrine which holds that management is restricted by the commitments it has made and recorded within the four corners of the written labor agreement, and that unless so restricted the basic managerial authority remains unrestricted.

The policy considerations fundamental to a strict application of the parol evidence rule in labor arbitration were explained by Arbitrator Archibald Cox:

> "[T]he rule is bottomed on common sense. Many business transactions require long and complicated negotiations during the course of which the parties present many arguments and offer a wide variety of proposals and counterproposals. At the end, if a bargain is struck, both parties may want to be able to draw up a writing setting forth their undertakings so

[1] See 3 A. Corbin, CONTRACTS § 573, 180-81 (rev. ed. 1960); 4 S. Williston, CONTRACTS § 631 (3d ed., W. Jaeger 1961); 9 J. Wigmore, EVIDENCE § 2425 (3d ed. 1940).

that each can say with assurance, 'This is it. Here is the agreement setting forth our obligations.' Business transactions would be unstable gambles indeed if this could not be done—if either party were subject to the risk of having a judge or jury go back over all the give-and-take of the prior negotiations and then tell him that it was not enough to carry out the writing. The parol evidence rule makes it possible for the parties to eliminate the uncertainty, if they wish, by adopting the writing as the complete and final expression of their agreement." [2]

Arbitrator Peter Kelliher explained what would happen if the parol evidence rule were not respected in construing labor agreements:

"[T]here would be no point in reducing contract terms to writing. This is not simply a technical rule, but has a long range importance in the maintenance of good relations between the parties. The collective bargaining agreements between the parties are arrived at only after extended negotiations and create an understanding that covers a suitable period of time. Alleged oral agreements cannot be permitted to vary the terms or to serve as amendments to written agreements." [3]

Similarly, Arbitrator Newton Margulies said:

"The oral agreement [sought to be established by one party] is in flat contradiction of the Main Contract. If the existence of the Oral Contract were to have been proved, its terms would mean that the principal substance of the Main Contract was written for little purpose and the Supplemental Contract was written for no purpose. This is a conclusion which does not recommend itself to any arbitrator interested in sound labor relations. Written contracts should seldom if ever be considered to have been drafted, in part or in whole, for the purpose of misleading employees, management and insurance companies." [4]

---

[2] *United Drill & Tool Corp.*, 28 L.A. 677, 679-80 (Cox, 1957). Arbitrator Cox made this additional observation in another context:
"Possibly it is only lawyers who feel misgivings on observing the tendency of some labor arbitrators to receive testimony from the parties as to what they thought and said during the negotiation of the contract which an arbitrator is seeking to interpret. It is easy to brush aside a principle called the parol evidence rule with the explanation that you are getting to the bottom of the problem. Yet behind the technical label lies the policy of enabling men who sign written undertakings to rely on the pretty plain meaning of an agreement which purports to speak for itself, without speculating as to what a judge or arbitrator will conclude after hearing conflicting testimony on the claims, demands or understanding of this and that party prior to the contract's execution." Cox, THE PROFESSION OF LABOR ARBITRATION 86 (1957). See also *Columbian Carbon Co.*, 70-1 ARB ¶ 8100, 3354 (Brown, 1969); *Hoffman-Taft, Inc.*, 69-2 ARB ¶ 8481, 4640-41 (Roberts, 1969); *Bloomfield Hills Bd. of Educ.*, 69-1 ARB ¶ 8386, 4317 (Casselman, 1969); *Great Lakes Pipe Line Co.*, 26 L.A. 100, 102 (Beatty, 1956); *Tennessee Valley Furniture Indus., Inc.*, 21 L.A. 781, 784 (Sanders, 1953).

[3] *Pillsbury Mills, Inc.*, 14 L.A. 1045, 1048-49 (Kelliher, 1950). It should be noted that the rule, in its classical application, does not apply to agreements concluded after the written agreement in question. See also *American Machine & Foundry Co.*, 61-3 ARB ¶ 8730, 6358 (Sembower, 1961).

[4] *Armstrong Rubber Mfg. Co.*, 19 L.A. 683, 685 (Margulies, 1952). *Accord, Sperry Gyroscope Co.*, 18 L.A. 916, 918 (Cole, 1952); *Miller's Furniture Mkt., Inc.*, 10 L.A. 577, 578 (Cahn, 1948). See also *Sun Rubber Co.*, 28 L.A. 362, 368

(1) Parol Evidence Is Admissible to Construe Ambiguous Language

Parol evidence can be considered if the party offering it can establish, as threshold conditions, (1) that the relevant language in the labor agreement is ambiguous and (2) that such language controls the disputed issue. Arbitrator Thomas Tongue stated this rule as follows:

> "There are . . . situations in which verbal discussions can be considered in determining the meaning of terms in contracts, if ambiguous. . . . But in such cases the verbal discussions can only be considered in determining the meaning of such terms and not to reach a result in any way inconsistent with the terms of the contract." [5]

Similarly, Arbitrator Joseph Jenkins held:

> "It is axiomatic that parol evidence may not be utilized to vary or alter the terms of a written instrument. However, it is also axiomatic that when ambiguities exist, whether patent or latent, that parol evidence may be utilized to resolve those ambiguities." [6]

(2) What Is Ambiguous Language?

The question whether relevant language is ambiguous rests upon the facts of each particular case. As a general rule, Arbitrator Walter Boles explained that:

> "Ambiguous language is language which could reasonably be given more than one meaning by reasonable men." [7]

Interestingly, Arbitrator Benjamin Roberts found an ambiguity in language despite the parties' contentions that the contract language was clear:

> "[C]ontradictory unanimity [on a proposition that the contract is unambiguous] does not establish the absence of an ambiguity." [8]

To the contrary is a decision of a court that an agreement by the

---

(Dworkin, 1957); *Price-Pfister Brass Mfg. Co.,* 25 L.A. 398, 404 (Prasow, 1955); *Bethlehem Steel Co.,* 21 L.A. 579, 582 (Seward, 1953); *Tide Water Oil Co.,* 17 L.A. 829, 833 (Wyckoff, 1952). See also the celebrated case of *Western Union Telegraph Co. v. American Communications Ass'n,* 299 N.Y. 177, 86 N.E.2d 162 (1949). *Accord, Teamsters, Local 986 v. Sears, Roebuck & Co.,* — F.Supp. —, 79 LRRM 2907, 68 L.C. ¶ 12,633 (D.C. Calif. 1972). *Contra,* see note 85 *infra.*

[5] *B. J. Furniture Corp.,* 32 L.A. 708, 711 (Tongue, 1959).

[6] *Sperry Rand Corp.,* 69-2 ARB ¶ 8477, 4621 (Jenkins, 1969). See also *Joseph H. Reinfield, Inc.,* 61-3 ARB ¶ 8760, 6484-85 (Scheiber, 1961).

[7] *American Oil Co.,* 62-1 ARB ¶ 8073, 3279 (Boles, 1961).

[8] *Bell Tel. Laboratories,* 39 L.A. 1191, 1204 (Roberts, 1962).

parties that a contract is unambiguous precludes introduction of parol evidence.[9]

Conversely, Arbitrator George Cheney found a contract term unambiguous notwithstanding the parties' stipulation that it was ambiguous:

> "Both the company and the union take the view, that the Collective Bargaining Agreements are ambiguous with respect to the subject matter mentioned in Section X. The Arbiter is unable to concur in this view. . . . After a full and fair consideration, if the forum charged with the construction and interpretation is able to declare with certainty what the intention of the parties was from the writing itself, no matter how difficult this task may be, the instrument is not ambiguous, and the interpreter may not go outside the four corners of the document to ascertain the intentions of the parties. It is only where the document contains conflicting and inconsistent provisions on a given subject that it is ambiguous and extrinsic circumstances can be availed of in ascertaining the intention of the parties. If the plain and unambiguous wording of a contract permits a complete fulfillment of the obligations assumed, then that construction is to be preferred to one dependent upon forced addition to, or elimination of, the terms of the agreement." [10]

(3) Rules Used to Construe Ambiguous Language

Before an arbitrator need seek evidence outside the four corners of the document to construe ambiguous language, various construction principles are often employed to clarify the meaning of the words used.

The first is that the ambiguous language must be construed so as to be compatible with the language in other provisions of the agreement. This well-known principle was stated by Arbitrator C. G. Hampton:

> "In any interpretation of a Contract, the Contract should be viewed as a whole, not in isolated parts. . . ." [11]

In *Birmingham Post*,[12] Arbitrator Whitley P. McCoy said:

> "It is an elementary principle of law that contracts are to be construed, if at all possible, in such a way as to give effect to every provision. Any interpretation which would result in nullifying completely a provision of the contract is to be avoided." [13]

---

[9] *Pacific Tel. & Tel. Co. v. Communications Workers,* 199 F.Supp. 689 (D. Ore. 1961), *rev'd on other grounds,* 310 F.2d 244 (9th Cir. 1962).

[10] *Andrew Williams Meat Co.,* 8 L.A. 518, 524 (Cheney, 1947).

[11] *Buffalo-Springfield Roller Co.,* 5 L.A. 391, 394 (Hampton, 1946).

[12] 4 L.A. 310 (McCoy, 1946). See also *Fulton Sylphon Co.,* 2 L.A. 116, 118 (McCoy, 1946).

[13] 4 L.A. at 313.

Similarly, Arbitrator Harry Platt said:

> "The primary rule in construing a written instrument is to determine, not alone from a single word or phrase, but from the instrument as a whole, the true intent of the parties, and to interpret the meaning of a questioned word, or part, with regard to the connection in which it is used, the subject matter and its relation to all other parts or provisions." [14]

The second construction principle that is often used by the arbitrator, before seeking evidence of meaning outside the four corners of the document, is the rule that ambiguous language should be construed against the drafter. Arbitrator Russell Smith explained:

> "On this record, and following an established canon of contract interpretation, the Arbitrator is of the opinion that the ambiguity in question should be resolved against the Company. As the proponent of the contract provision, it was incumbent upon the Company either to explain clearly what was contemplated or to use language which would not leave the matter in doubt." [15]

Arbitrator James J. Healy relied on the same principle:

> "It is an established principle of contract law that since the person who is doing the writing can, by exactness of expression, more easily prevent mistakes in meaning than the party with whom he is dealing, the doubts arising from ambiguity of language should be resolved against the former in favor of the latter." [16]

Arbitrator Arthur A. Malinowski has summarized the main rules used to clarify meaning in the order of their application, pointing out that they should be used before evidence external to the agreement is examined:

> "Inasmuch as the dispute concerned the interpretation of the terms in the Labor Agreement, the Arbitrator holds that the generally accepted rules of Contract Law will apply. Among these cardinal rules of interpretation are the following: (1) Every part of a Contract is to be interpreted, if possible, so as to carry out its general purpose, (2) The Contract is to be interpreted in such a way as to effectuate the intention of the Parties and where this intention clearly appears from the words used, there is no need to go further, for in such cases, the words must govern and (3) Words used in a Contract will be given their ordinary meaning where nothing appears to show that they were used in a different sense

---

[14] *Riley Stoker Corp.,* 7 L.A. 764, 767 (Platt, 1947). See also *John Deere Tractor Co.,* 5 L.A. 631 (Updegraff, 1946); *Great Lakes Dredge and Dock Co.,* 5 L.A. 409 (Kelliher, 1946); *Metal & Thermit Corp.,* 1 L.A. 417 (Gilden, 1946).

[15] *Timken-Detroit Axle Co.,* 21 L.A. 197, 198 (Smith, 1953).

[16] *Brown & Sharpe Mfg. Co.,* 11 L.A. 228, 233 (Healy, 1948). Arbitrator Healy relied on the same construction principle in *Federal Paper Board Co.,* AAA Case No. 50-16 (Healy, 1962).

or have a technical meaning, and where no unreasonable consequences will result from doing so." [17]

One other construction rule often relied upon was referred to by Arbitrator Peter M. Kelliher:

"It is a universal rule of contract interpretation that a more specific provision takes precedence over a more general provision, particularly where the specific provision follows the general language. Inasmuch as the phrase in Section 3-B broadly construed is general enough to cover both returned material that is defective and returned material that is not defective and because Section 3-C relates only to defective work, which is the type of work here considered, the Arbitrator must find that the facts of this case are clearly governed by Section 3-C. The Arbitrator is not reading out of the contract the phrase 'to re-work returned material,' because there are instances where material is returned for re-work where the original performance was not defective, such as the cases cited where there has been a change in engineering requirements or customer demand." [18]

(4) Evidence External to the Agreement Used to Interpret Ambiguous Language

(a) *Past Practice*

Evidence of the manner in which the parties to a collective bargaining agreement have carried out the terms of the agreement is indicative of the interpretation that should be given to an ambiguous provision. However, there must be consistency in the practice. Arbitrator Whitley P. McCoy has said:

"[P]ast practice can have no bearing unless it shows a settled construction . . . put upon the contract by the parties themselves." [19]

In *Sheller Manufacturing Corp.*,[20] Arbitrator Robert Matthews said:

"[T]he practice must be of sufficient generality and duration to imply acceptance of it as an authentic construction of the contract." [21]

Typically, arbitrators will reject evidence of practice as being unreliable evidence of the meaning of ambiguous language if the evidence of practice is disputed. As noted by Arbitrator Paul Hebert:

---

[17] *Ordnance Manufacturing Division, Whirlpool Corporation (Evansville, Indiana)*, AAA Case No. 52-30 0298-70 (Malinowski, 1971).

[18] *John Deere Harvester Works*, East Moline, 4 ALAA ¶ 68,773 (1951).

[19] *Consolidated Vultee Aircraft Corp.*, 4 L.A. 24, 30 (McCoy, 1945). See also *The Brown Corp. of Ionia*, AAA Case No. 83-15 (Cole, 1965); *The American Envelope Co.*, AAA Case No. 7-16 (Warns, 1959).

[20] 10 L.A. 617 (Matthews, 1948).

[21] *Id.* at 620.

"The past practice under a disputed contract provision is not controlling where the interpretation of the clause has been the subject of dispute between the parties." [22]

Arbitrator Clarence Updegraff has reached the same conclusion:

"[Since] the matter has been subject to some dispute throughout the period, . . . the practice . . . has therefore not attained the standing of a mutual interpretation of the part of the contract in dispute. . . ." [23]

Where the language in the labor agreement clearly specifies a right, the mere nonuse of that right is not evidence that by practice the employer or the union has abandoned the right. The reason for this rule was stated by Arbitrator McCoy in *Latrobe Steel Co.*:[24]

"But if mere non-use resulted in the loss of a contract right, employees might be denied rights, for example overtime pay, merely because they had never through the years received any overtime pay. The Union would not want any such principle as that established. The Union argues that the Company has always sought agreement with the Union in the past. That is merely good labor relations. If seeking agreement, and abstaining from a right merely for lack of agreement, is going to result in losing the right, Management would be less likely in the future to practice good labor relations." [25]

However, where the language is ambiguous the non-exercise of claimed rights is a relevant consideration. Arbitrator James J. Healy explained:

"[I]t is a widely accepted principle that a party that has 'slept on its claimed rights' over a sustained period may thereby have lost those rights. This would not necessarily be the case if the contract were explicit and unambiguous. But it is particularly applicable in a case such as this because the union waited three and a half years before claiming a violation. 'In that period, embracing two separate contract negotiations, it never once raised a grievance nor did it suggest impropriety in company behavior during negotiations.' " [26]

The readoption of ambiguous language is generally regarded as being evidence of an agreement to follow earlier practices established under such language, especially if such language has been construed by an interpreter. As has been noted:

"When contract language has been interpreted, and the parties readopt the identical language in a renewal contract, they readopt that language with the meaning already established, whether it was established by

---

[22] *Columbian Carbon Co.*, 27 L.A. 762, 766-67 (Hebert, 1956). See also *Reliance Steel Prods. Co.*, 24 L.A. 30 (Lehoczky, 1954).
[23] *Weaver Mfg. Co.*, 11 L.A. 825, 826 (Updegraff, 1948).
[24] 34 L.A. 34 (McCoy, 1960). See also *Kroehler Manufacturing Co.*, 17 L.A. 391 (Lapp, 1951); *Gibson Refrigerator Co.*, 17 L.A. 313, 317 (Platt, 1951).
[25] 34 L.A. at 36.
[26] *Federal Paper Board Co.*, AAA Case No. 50-16 (Healy, 1962).

court decision, by arbitration decision, by grievance settlements, by practice, by verbal agreement, or by written agreement." [27]

(b) Bargaining History

Another form of parol evidence relied upon by arbitrators to interpret ambiguous language is evidence of bargaining history.[28] Such evidence may be oral [29] or documentary,[30] but whatever its form, such bargaining history may be quite helpful in construing ambiguous language. As noted by one arbitrator:

> "While parties attempt to express their intent in collective bargaining agreements, occasionally ambiguity does occur. When such ambiguity arises, documents such as proposals and counterproposals may be helpful in determining the intent of the parties." [31]

Where the evidence demonstrates that one party attempted during bargaining to obtain agreement on specific contract language but was unsuccessful and is urging the arbitrator to interpret ambiguous language in such a way to obtain what it did not obtain across the bargaining table, arbitrators often reject the suggested interpretation. For example, one arbitrator rejected a union's contention that ambiguous language should be construed to credit any unworked but paid holiday hours toward the 40 hours needed for weekly overtime because the union had attempted unsuccessfully during bargaining to obtain a commitment that such hours should be counted in calculating overtime:

> "Accordingly . . . I have no alternative, in the light of the practice and the negotiations, but to reject the Union's argument that a paid but unworked holiday counts toward the forty hours." [32]

Arbitrator Dudley Whiting agrees:

> "When a matter has been the subject of negotiation and one party has been unsuccessful in obtaining a desired provision, it is wholly improper

---

[27] *Swift & Co.*, 67-2 ARB ¶ 8399, 4440-41 (McCoy, 1967). See also *Kennecott Copper Co.*, 32 L.A. 646 (Ross, 1959); *Bethlehem Steel Co.*, 20 L.A. 87 (Seward, 1953). *Cf.*, *A. O. Smith Corp.*, 23 L.A. 27, 32 (Prasow, 1954).

[28] See, *e.g.*, *Southwest Ornamental Iron Co.*, 38 L.A. 1025 (Murphy, 1962); *California Elec. Power Co.*, 21 L.A. 704 (Grant, 1953); *North American Aviation, Inc.*, 19 L.A. 138 (Kamaroff, 1952); *Kohlenberger Eng'r. Corp.*, 12 L.A. 380 (Prasow, 1949); *G. C. Hussey & Co.*, 5 L.A. 446 (Blair, 1946); *Western Pa. Motor Carriers Ass'n., Inc.*, 1 L.A. 190 (Guild, 1945).

[29] *Colonial Baking Co.*, 36 L.A. 1130 (Dworet, 1961); *American Can Co.*, 33 L.A. 809 (Bothwell, 1959); *Bethlehem Supply Co.*, 17 L.A. 632 (Emery, 1951); *Borden's Farm Products, Inc.*, 3 L.A. 401 (Burke, 1945).

[30] *Geneva Steel Co.*, 15 L.A. 834 (Garrett, 1950); *National Malleable & Steel Castings Co.*, 4 L.A. 110 (Blair, 1946); *Hershey Chocolate Corp.*, 1 L.A. 165 (McCoy, 1944).

[31] *Milwaukee Spring Co.*, 39 L.A. 1270, 1272 (Gundermann, 1962).

[32] *Consolidated Paper Box Mfg. Co., Inc.*, 27 L.A. 126, 128 (Jaffee, 1956). See also *Koppers Co.*, 21 L.A. 699, 702-03 (Meredith, 1953).

for an arbitrator to award that party the same result as a necessary implication of other contract provisions." [33]

Similarly, Arbitrator William Murphy held that:

"[I]t is also recognized that bargaining history and pre-contract negotiations between the parties are valuable and proper sources from which to ascertain the meaning and proper interpretation of the language of the contract. Where a specific provision has been regarded as an appropriate one for negotiations, and where one party has attempted but failed to get the provision included in the contract, an arbitrator should not thereafter read such provision into the contract through the guise of interpretation. In this case, the bargaining history of the parties and the negotiations preceding the current contract reveal clearly the Union's continuing dissatisfaction with the long-standing plant practice under which tackwelding was performed by helpers rates, and also the Union's persistent efforts to effectuate a change in this situation through the bargaining process. This repeated resort to the bargaining process to change the situation by changing the contract constitutes a recognition on the part of the Union that the practice was not in violation of the contract." [34]

Arbitrator Jules J. Justin has taken the same approach, holding:

"The Union raised the question during the negotiations leading to the present contract. It was then bargained out. It cannot be 'bargained in' by way of an arbitration, under the guise of interpreting or construing other contract clauses, however related." [35]

The construction principle works in reverse. Where one party proposes that a certain clause be removed from the agreement, the arbitrator should not construe the clause to remove the obligation the party attempted to bargain out. Thus, in *Pittsburgh Plate Glass Co.,*[36] Arbitrator Philip G. Marshall noted:

"The Company showed conclusively that down through the years the Union had made efforts to delete or change the present contractual definition of 'continuous processes' and to make all such employees eligible for overtime benefits on the same basis as employees working

---

[33] *General Aniline & Film Corp.,* AAA Case No. 36-7 (Whiting, 1962). See also *Philadelphia Steel & Wire Corp.,* AAA Case No. 93-2 (Short, 1966).

[34] *Southwest Ornamental Iron Co.,* 38 L.A. 1025, 1028-29 (Murphy, 1962). See also *Higgins, Inc.,* 24 L.A. 224, 228 (Reynard, 1955); *S. Austin Bicking Paper Mfg. Co.,* 8 L.A. 987, 989 (Brandschain, 1947). As was stated in F. Elkouri and E. Elkouri, How ARBITRATION WORKS 213 (rev. ed. 1960):
"If a party attempts but fails, in contract negotiations, to include a specific provision in the Agreement, an Arbitrator will hesitate to read such provision into the Agreement through the process of interpretation."

[35] *American Machine & Foundry Company,* 4 ALAA § 68,697 (Justin, 1950). See also *Consolidated Paper & Box Mfg. Co., Inc.,* 27 L.A. 126 (Jaffee, 1956); *Bethlehem Steel Co.,* 12 L.A. 588, 591 (Selekman, 1949); *West Virginia Pulp & Paper Co.,* 12 L.A. 391 (Copelof, 1949); *Harley Davidson Motor Co.,* 6 L.A. 395 (Lappin, 1947); *Pantasote Co.,* 3 L.A. 545 (Cole, 1946).

[36] 14 L.A. 1 (Marshall, 1950).

on non-continuous operations. They were unsuccessful in such efforts. In view of the clear collective bargaining history of Section 20 no proper question of interpretation or application is involved and hence the Arbitrator is without authority to entertain the request for relief sought by the Union. The grievances are therefore denied." [37]

In *Red Owl Stores, Inc.,*[38] the contract on its face appeared to give the union members the right to prepare all meat sold by the stores. However, in practice, the company had long received certain presliced meats. In the most recent contract negotiations, the union had attempted to get a stronger jurisdictional clause but had failed. In rejecting the grievance, Arbitrator Arvid Anderson emphasized that:

> "The Union should have been clearly on notice during the negotiations that, if it intended to change the Company's pre-pricing practice, and to obtain exclusive jurisdiction over pricing that it should have negotiated a specific limitation on such practice in the contract. The testimony of the representatives indicates that the Union was on notice and did intend to change the practice, if it could do so, by a change in the contract provision. Having failed to secure such change in the negotiations, the Board of Arbitration has concluded that the practice of pre-pricing must not be disturbed in this arbitration." [39]

Where a party, however, has merely attempted to clarify a right already reserved, as in the case of a management seeking to clarify the fact that it has the right to subcontract, the rule has been applied. As stated by Arbitrator Edwin Teple:

> "It is well known that collective bargaining agreements frequently need clarification or elucidation, and the parties may endeavor to strengthen their position on either side of the table by language which is designed to explain, clarify or specifically reaffirm a point notwithstanding the proposing party's conviction that it is already covered by general terms, ncessary implication, or an understanding based upon past practice." [40]

Similarly, Arbitrator Barrett said:

> "When a party requests a modification of a contract, such request often constitutes decisive evidence that the modification was not previously contained in the contract. Such a rule may not be invariably applied, however, inasmuch as the party who requests the modification may in fact already possess the modification which he seeks." [41]

---

[37] *Id.* at 6.

[38] 62-3 ARB ¶ 8938 (Anderson, 1962). See also *FMC Corp.*, 45 L.A. 293 (McCoy, 1965).

[39] 62-3 ARB at 6410-11.

[40] *Broughton's Farm Dairy, Inc.*, 41 L.A. 1189, 1198 (Teple, 1963). See also *American Can Co.*, 33 L.A. 809, 812 (Bothwell, 1959); *Goodyear Tire & Rubber Co.*, 1 L.A. 556 (McCoy, 1946).

[41] *Westinghouse Electric Corp.*, AAA Case No. 47-10 (Barrett, 1962).

B. THE "RESIDUAL RIGHTS" CONSTRUCTION PRINCIPLE: THE SUBSTANTIVE APPLICATION OF THE PAROL EVIDENCE RULE

The "Residual Rights" construction principle is very closely related to the parol evidence rule. The policy reasons for the principle are similar. It is the simple view that management had all necessary rights to manage the plant and direct the working forces before the union became the employees' representative and that after the union negotiates a labor agreement, the rights of managment to manage the plant and direct the working forces, which are not limited by a specific term of the agreement, do not evaporate and hence are retained by management. Arbitrator Dudley Whiting stated the rule very concisely in *Sommers & Adams Co.*:[42]

> "By an overwhelming weight of authority, it is well established that, prior to the designation of a collective bargaining representative or execution of a collective bargaining agreement, an employer has a full and complete right to establish all working conditions and rates of pay. A collective bargaining agreement operates as a limitation upon such right, but that right still exists as to all conditions not established by such collective bargaining agreement." [43]

Arbitrator Wayne Quinlan explained that this construction principle was generally accepted by arbitrators:

> "The generally accepted view among Arbitrators, to which this Arbitrator subscribes, is that management rights are limited only to the extent specified in the Working Agreement. Here, as we have seen, there is no contractual limitation of the type that would take away any of those rights generally and ordinarily considered as inherent in management." [44]

Many arbitrators have articulated this construction principle during the 40 years that labor arbitration has been developing in the United States [45] and this construction principle has been recognized

---

[42] 6 L.A. 283 (Whiting, 1947).

[43] *Id.* at 285.

[44] *American Sugar Refining Co.*, 38 L.A. 714, 718 (Quinlan, 1961). This principle is established "by an overwhelming weight of authority," *Sommers & Adams Co.*, 6 L.A. 283 (Whiting, 1947) and "uniformly acknowledged," *Great Lakes Carbon Corp.*, 19 L.A. 797 (Wettach, 1953).

[45] *Owens-Illinois, Inc.*, 70-2 ARB ¶ 8606, 5000 (Stouffer, 1970); *FMC Corp.*, 70-2 ARB ¶ 8594, 4951 (Whyte, 1970); *Whittaker Corp.*, 70-1 ARB ¶ 8302, 4001 (Geissinger, 1970); *Colson Co.*, 54 L.A. 896, 900 (Roberts, 1970); *Wahl Clipper Corp.*, 69-2 ARB ¶ 8610 (Gaff, 1969); *Corn Products Co.*, 50 L.A. 741 (Kates, 1968); *Packaging Corp. of America*, 68-2 ARB ¶ 8813 (Bauder, 1968); *Olin-Mathieson Chem. Corp.*, 68-2 ARB ¶ 8494 (Talent, 1968); *Goodrich Chem. Co.*, 67-1 ARB ¶ 8178 (McIntosh, 1967); *Bard Mfg. Co.*, 65-2 ARB ¶ 8796 (Uible, 1965); *Olin-Mathieson Chem. Corp.*, 42 L.A. 1025, 1040 (Klamon, 1964); *Union Mills Paper Mfg. Co.*, 64-1 ARB ¶ 8287 (Horlacher, 1963); *Mississippi Steel & Iron Co.*, 63-1 ARB ¶ 8391 (Mitchell, 1963); *KVP Sutherland Paper Co.*, 40 L.A. 737 (Kadish, 1963); *American Sugar Refining Co.*, 38 L.A. 714, 718 (Quinlan, 1961); *Harnishfeger Corp.*, 37 L.A. 685 (Young, 1961); *Texas Portland Cement Co.*,

by European observers as a basic reason why managements in the United States have been able to make rapid changes in manufacturing methods and thereby more rapidly increase productivity than their European counterparts.[46]

The residual rights construction principle can be viewed as a substantive restatement of the parol evidence rule. When an arbitrator relies on this principle he is in effect saying that if there is no negotiated written provision restricting the management's right to take specific action, then there is no restriction upon the right of management to act, nor can parol evidence establish such a restriction not expressed in the agreement. Arbitrators who rely on either the parol evidence rule or the residual rights doctrine are in effect ruling that, in the absence of a contractual limitation, a company's right to manage remains unrestricted.[47]

The residual rights construction principle has been applied in numerous factual situations where managerial functions were exercised. For example, Arbitrator Wayne Quinlan applied the principle in a case involving the right to establish new job classifications, holding:

> "While fully understanding and appreciating the contentions of the Union relative to this new job classification being an alteration of the agreement between the parties, still it must be remembered that it has been generally accepted throughout the United States that management's

---

61-2 ARB ¶ 8343, 4625 (Autrey, 1961); *American Sugar Refining Co.*, 61-1 ARB ¶ 8137 (Singletary, 1961); *Colorado Fuel & Iron Corp.*, 9 STEEL ARB. 5603, 5604 (Alexander, 1959); *Celanese Corp. of America*, 30 L.A. 705 (Reid, 1958); *Diamond Milk Products, Inc.*, 28 L.A. 429 (Stouffer, 1957); *Monsanto Chemical Co.*, 27 L.A. 736, 743 (Roberts, 1956); *Babcock & Wilcox Co.*, 26 L.A. 172, 175 (Kates, 1956); *United Wallpaper, Inc.*, 25 L.A. 188, 191 (Sembower, 1955); *Reynolds Metals Co.*, 25 L.A. 44, 49 (Prasow, 1955); *Armstrong Rubber Mfg. Co.*, 24 L.A. 721, 722-23 (McCoy, 1955); *Celotex Corp.*, 24 L.A. 369, 371 (Reynard, 1955); *National Fireworks Ordnance Corp.*, 23 L.A. 349 (Larson, 1954); *Stewart-Warner Corp.*, 22 L.A. 547, 551 (Burns, 1954); *Lone Star Steel Co.*, 20 L.A. 710 (Smith, 1953); *Great Lakes Carbon Co.*, 19 L.A. 797, 799 (Wettach, 1953); *McKinney Mfg. Co.*, 19 L.A. 291, 293 (Reid, 1952); *Graham Bros.*, 16 L.A. 83 (Cheney, 1951); *Illinois Bell Tel. Co.*, 15 L.A. 274, 280 (Davis, 1950); *Blackhawk Mfg. Co.*, 7 L.A. 943, 945 (Updegraff, 1947); *Sommers & Adams Co.*, 6 L.A. 283 (Whiting, 1947); *Novelty Shawl Co.*, 4 L.A. 655, 656 (Wallen, 1946); *Merck & Co., Inc.*, 1 L.A. 430 (Korey, 1946). See, *e.g.*, *National Distillers Products Corp.*, 24 L.A. 500 (Delehanty, 1953); *Donaldson Co.*, 20 L.A. 826 (Louisell, 1953); *New York Trap Rock Corp.*, 19 L.A. 421 (Giardino, 1952); *Byerlite Corp.*, 12 L.A. 641 (Day, 1949); *M. T. Stevens & Sons Co.*, 7 L.A. 585 (Copelof, 1947).

[46] Fairweather, *A Comparison of British and American Grievance Handling*, DEVELOPMENTS IN AMERICAN AND FOREIGN ARBITRATION, Proceedings of the Twenty-First Annual Meeting, National Academy of Arbitrators 1 (C. Rehmus Ed. 1968).

[47] The residual rights construction principle is also consistent with the scope of the arbitrator's jurisdiction which is ordinarily limited to application of the terms of the written agreement to the facts of a particular grievance. There is usually an express proviso that the arbitrator does not have the power to add to, subtract from, or modify the agreement. See, *e.g.*, *Mallinckrodt Chem. Works*, 38 L.A. 267, 268 (Hilpert, 1961).

rights not specifically surrendered in collective bargaining agreement are reserved to management." [48]

Similarly, Arbitrator Robert K. Burns held, in a case raising the question whether the company might assign work currently performed by bargaining unit employees to other employees:

"A careful examination of the contract fails to reveal any provision that specifically prohibits the Company from making a bona fide transfer, allocation, or assignment of work out of the bargaining unit—which is the issue posed in this particular case. In the absence of a specific prohibition or limitation to the contrary it must be assumed that these are reserved and retained powers of management. . . . Accordingly, the Arbitrator in this case denies the grievance submitted by the Union." [49]

Arbitrator James A. Doyle, referring to a union claim that there were implied limitations on the management rights to assign job duties, said:

"Such a limitation should not be lightly inferred. One arbitrator said the limitation must be express. Others have said it must be specific. Still another said that the limitation must be a clear and forceful statement. In *Congoleum-Nairn, Inc., supra,* the arbitrator stated that where the company's right to eliminate classifications has been limited, 'the limitation has been expressly spelled out in clear fashion, *e.g.,* existing job classifications shall remain unchanged for the life of the agreement.'

"In the present Agreement there is no express, specific or clear and forceful statement to the effect that the Company may not, during the life of the Agreement, eliminate a classification and assign the duties formerly performed by employees in that occupation to other classifications. . . ." [50]

In a case involving a claim that supervision could not perform production work, Arbitrator Joseph M. Klamon stated:

"The review of administrative and legal cases and authorities, which appear in the Company Brief, would alone seem to be conclusive on this point, namely that the recognition of the Union as the proper bargaining agent for its members in no way supports an implied abridgement of the right of the Company to assign work. This is one of the fundamental rights of management, and can only be limited or restricted in direct contract negotiations. Moreover, such a restriction must be stated in the clearest of terms and even then extends only as far as is clearly stated. In this case the Company has agreed in the contract to certain restrictions on supervisory officials performing production work.

---

[48] *Phillips Petroleum Co.,* 33 L.A. 379, 384 (Quinlan, 1960).

[49] *Stewart-Warner Corp.,* 22 L.A. 547, 551 (Burns, 1954). See also *Celotex Corporation,* 24 L.A. 369 (Reynard, 1955).

[50] *Omaha Cold Storage Teminal,* 48 L.A. 24, 31 (Doyle, 1967). See also *Colorado Fuel & Iron Corp.,* 9 STEEL ARB.. 6697, 6699 (Valtin, 1961); *Great Lakes Steel Corp.,* 8 STEEL ARB. 5603 (Alexander, 1959); *Reynolds Metals Co.,* 25 L.A. 44 (1958); *Armstrong Rubber Mfg. Co.,* 24 L.A. 721 (McCoy, 1955).

As indicated, this of course binds the Company as far as the contract language goes and no further." [51]

The residual rights construction principle is employed even where there is no clause in the agreement specifically reserving to management the right to manage. In *Bard Mfg. Co.,*[52] Arbitrator Frank R. Uible said:

> "The current Agreement between the parties does not contain a Management's Rights Clause. Even in the absence of a Management's Rights Clause, the direction of the working force is a Management prerogative, except as such prerogative is abridged by the terms of the Agreement. Within the prerogative of directing the working force is the right to assign employees within a given job classification to particular functions or tasks within such classification as it deems best. We do not find in the Agreement an abridgement of this right." [53]

C. THE JURISDICTIONAL CONSTRUCTION PRINCIPLE

The parol evidence rule and the residual rights construction principle are also other articulations of the view that the arbitrator must find the restriction or rights claimed within the four corners of the agreement because his jurisdiction is limited to the interpretation of the terms of the written agreement and the application of such terms to the facts of a particular grievance.[54]

In this connection it is noteworthy that most labor agreements expressly provide that the arbitrator does not have the authority to add to or subtract from or modify the agreement. For example, in *Mallinckrodt Chemical Works,*[55] Arbitrator Elmer Hilpert held that such jurisdictional provisions precluded him from creating new terms or restricting otherwise unrestricted managerial rights:

> "An arbitrator may give effect to, and, thus, compel continued adherence to, a 'past practice,' under a collective bargaining agreement, by 'interpreting' a term, or provision, in such agreement in conformity with such 'past practice,' only when such term, or provision, is *ambiguous* (*i.e.,* is susceptible to either of the two contended-for meanings); but an arbitrator—whose authority, or 'jurisdiction,' is limited, by such agreement, to applying the terms, or provisions, thereof, or to 'interpret(ing)

---

[51] *Olin Mathieson Chemical Corp.,* 42 L.A. 1025, 1040 (Klamon, 1964). See also *Texas-Portland Cement Co.,* 61-2 ARB ¶ 8343 (Autrey, 1961); *Monsanto Chemical Co.,* 27 L.A. 736, 743 (Roberts, 1956); *McKinney Mfg. Co.,* 19 L.A. 291 (Reid, 1952).

[52] 65-2 ARB ¶ 8796 (Uible, 1965).

[53] *Id.* at 5917.

[54] See related discussion of the jurisdictional limitations imposed on arbitrators in Chapter VI.

[55] 38 L.A. 267 (Hilpert, 1961). See also *Western Greyhound Lines,* 33 L.A. 157 (Kliensorge, 1959); *Coca-Cola Bottling Company,* 31 L.A. 697 (Conn. Bd. of Mediation and Arbitration, 1958).

existing provisions of the Agreement and apply(ing) them to the specific facts of the grievance dispute—may not compel continued adherence to a 'past practice,' *as such.*

"Confusion, in this area of labor-management law, arises from a failure to see the distinction between *statutory-administrative* 'terms and conditions of employment,' which are under the jurisdiction of the National Labor Relations Board, and the terms, or provisions, of a collective bargaining agreement, which, usually, are all that is under the 'jurisdiction' of an arbitrator." [Emphasis in original.] [56]

Arbitrator Marion Beatty similarly observed in *American Sugar Refining Co.*:[57]

"In grievance arbitrations, arbitrators are employed to interpret contracts, not to write them, add to them or modify them. If they are to be modified, that has to be done at the bargaining table. If this Union is to have 'jurisdiction over work,' it must obtain this at the bargaining table in language that fairly imports this.

"Arbitrators are not soothsayers and 'wise men' employed to dispense equity and good will according to their own notions of what is best for the parties, nor are they kings like Solomon with unlimited wisdom or courts of unlimited jurisdiction. Arbitrators are employed to interpret the working agreement as the parties themselves wrote it. "In contract interpretation, we are trying to ascertain the mutual intention of the parties. We must be guided primarily by the language used. Admittedly, certain inferences may be read into it, but they should be only those inferences which clearly and logically follow from the language used and which reasonable men must have mutually intended. To go far afield in search of veiled inferences or ethereal or celestial factors is a mistake, I believe. Labor contracts are much more earthy; they are not written in fancy language purposely containing hidden meanings." [58]

And in *Bethlehem Steel Co.*,[59] Arbitrator Mitchell Shipman said:

"[T]he umpire can, however, do nothing but what the parties, in their agreement, provided. He can only apply the provisions of their agreement. Anything beyond that would constitute extension and enlargement of the agreement. This no arbitrator can do." [60]

The National Railroad Adjustment Board echoed the same view in *Pennsylvania Railroad Co.*:[61]

"The subject matter is not covered in any manner in the existing Agreement. No provision of the Agreement has been violated, and none is before us for interpretation.

---

[56] 38 L.A. at 268.

[57] 37 L.A. 334 (Beatty, 1961).

[58] *Id.* at 337.

[59] 3 L.A. 26 (Shipman, 1945).

[60] *Id.* at 31.

[61] 26 L.A. 749 (1956).

"We are, therefore, inclined to the opinion that the principle enunciated in Award 501 of the Fourth Division holds in the instant case:
 " 'What it was never under any obligation to do it may discontinue at its will.' " [62]

Even where the labor agreement is silent on the scope of the arbitrator's jurisdiction, Arbitrator Maxwell Copelof restricted his jurisdiction, saying:

"While this contract does not specifically say so, it is the Arbitrator's well-considered judgment that as Arbitrator he should not assume any powers of in any way modifying an existing contract. This is clearly stated in many of the contracts between unions and companies, and while not clearly stated in the contract with [naming the company and the union] the Arbitrator is convinced were he to assume any such authority, both the Union and the Company would strenuously object to his so doing, and rightfully so." [63]

D. CLOTHING PRACTICE WITH CONTRACTUAL STATUS

Diametrically opposed to those arbitrators who (1) apply the parol evidence rule so as to require that the claimed right or duty be found within the four corners of the collective agreement, (2) find no limitation on the management's right to take managerial action unless the limitation was agreed upon and expressed in the agreement, and (3) conclude that an arbitrator only has the jurisdictional authority to find that the rights and obligations assumed by one or the other party in the written agreement can be established by the process of interpreting and applying its terms, are those arbitrators who, by one of several various theories, find that unexpressed conditions of employment, referred to as practices, obtain contractual status. This approach was contrasted with the residual rights construction principle by Arbitrator Malcolm D. Talbott:

"Many representatives of Management consider a labor contract to be an instrument by which the Union and the employers secure specifically ceded defined rights in derogation of Management's once absolute prerogatives. Thus Management would retain all but the specifically ceded powers. Unilateral action by Management without consultation with the Union could modify or terminate existing plans or establish new plans not covered by the agreement, at will, under this view.

" . . .
"[Another] view, and the one adopted here, is that parties to a comprehensive labor contract, where no evidence appears to the contrary, are to be presumed to have entered in such a contract with the understanding that major conditions of employment, even though not covered by the

---

[62] *Id.* at 751.
[63] *Selby Shoe Co.,* 9 L.A. 721, 723 (Copelof, 1948).

agreement expressly, will by implied consent of the parties remain *status quo* unless they are changed by mutual agreement.

"To support this, we acknowledge that parties' contract with reference to an existing set of practices even if they are not mentioned in the contract. . . . Matters not covered by the contract may be part of the 'context' of the agreement in holding major working conditions as they were.

" . . .

"A collective bargain is, under the view adopted here, a complete settlement and stabilizing of issues involving cost to Management and income to employees for these are certainly *major* conditions. Thus, the intent of such a comprehensive agreement may fairly be said to be to continue existing conditions.

" . . .

"New action may be taken only by mutual agreement of the parties or at the time of negotiation to accomplish such fundamental changes." [64] [Emphasis in original.]

The view that an arbitrator, for policy reasons (parol evidence, residual rights, or jurisdiction) should be confined to the interpretation and application of agreements was rejected by Arbitrator Robert P. Brecht when a union had asked for a restriction on the management's right to schedule overtime:

"Under an agreement use of the term 'right' conveys a technical sanction. Therefore, the Company's right to require employees to work on regular scheduled overtime Saturdays must stem from its Agreement with the Union. The definition of Company rights under an agreement is determined in one of three ways: (1) by specific sanction or prohibition, (2) by reasonable inference from expressed clauses, or (3) by what may be called the principle of residual rights stemming from a management clause such as Article 1, Section 2 of the present Agreement between the parties.

"This last basis is simply that when an area of control or management right has not been identified in the minds of the parties when the collective bargaining agreement was reached it is a right that remains with management if it is a reasonable extension of the management function as granted in the agreement.

"The Company, quite obviously has relied upon interpretation of somewhat related provisions, upon the management clause, and upon its vocal insistence in negotiations to defend its claim that it has the right to require employees to work on regularly scheduled overtime Saturdays.

---

[64] *General Aniline & Film Corp.*, 19 L.A. 628, 629 (Talbott, 1952). The view expressed in this opinion results in an obligation to consult and reach agreement before making changes, which slows down the rate of change. The deleterious effects of such a view on the rate of productivity improvement in England was explained by H. J. Hebden before the Royal Commission on Trade Unions and Employers' Associations, *Minutes of Evidence* 1004, Her Majesty's Stationery Office, 1966, quoted in Labor Law Developments, Proceedings of the Seventeenth Annual Institute on Labor Law 218-219 (1971).

"It is generally conceded that the present Agreement contains no provision which specifically grants the right in question to the Company or specifically prohibits that right to the Company.

". . . Were this the *first time* the issue was raised under a new Agreement or under a series of consecutive Agreements, the principle of residual rights would be entirely persuasive. If the parties for reasons of their own will not through either positive sanctions or negative prohibitions define management's rights, it can be fairly assumed that any right *not specifically identified* will remain a part of managerial prerogative so long as it represents a legitimate extension of functions necessary to operate the business. But this condition in the present case is most emphatically absent. The parties in negotiations wrestled with the precise right in issue. It is true, of course, that the Company never yielded in its belief that the right in question belonged legitimately among its family of prerogatives; but it is equally true that the Union, pointedly and consistently, refused to concede the point by agreement and insisted that the Agreement as written did not grant positively the right to the Company. . . .

"The conclusion, therefore, is inescapable that the Agreement as written does not cover the point in issue. This question, then, must be settled on its merits. . . ." [65] [Emphasis in original.]

Some arbitrators elevate practice to contractual status where there is no relevant language in the agreement, asserting the lack of relevant language is an ambiguity and hence the arbitrator may look at practice to find the answer to the dispute. Arbitrator Irvine Kerrison said:

"[W]here a contract is silent on a matter at issue, . . . past practice carries most weight." [66]

Some arbitrators have said that practice attains contractual status when it remains in effect under various labor agreements:

"In the light of the decisions, as recited above, it seems to me that the current of opinion has set strongly in favor of the position that existing practices, in respect to major conditions of employment are to be regarded as included within a collective bargaining contract, negotiated after the practice has become established, and not repudiated or limited by it." [67]

---

[65] *Sylvania Electric Products, Inc.,* 24 L.A. 199, 208 (Brecht, 1954).

[66] *Kiamesha Concord, Inc.,* 69-2 ARB ¶ 8586, 5003 (Kerrison, 1969). See *Shell Oil Company,* 24 L.A. 748, 749 (Jones, 1955).

[67] *Phillips Petroleum Co.,* 24 L.A. 191, 194 (Merrill, 1955). *Accord, Kennecott Copper Co.,* 32 L.A. 646 (Ross, 1958); *Minneapolis-Moline Co.,* 17 L.A. 497, 503 (Lockhart, 1951). See also *Fruehauf Trailer Co.,* 29 L.A. 372 (Jones, 1957); *Morris P. Kirk & Son, Inc.,* 27 L.A. 6 (Prasow, 1956); *E. W. Bliss Co.,* 24 L.A. 614 (Dworkin, 1955); *Phillips Petroleum Co.,* 24 L.A. 191 (Merrill, 1955); *Northland Greyhound Lines, Inc.,* 23 L.A. 277 (Levinson, 1954); *International Harvester Co.,* 20 L.A. 276 (Wirtz, 1953); *American Seating Co.,* 16 L.A. 115 (Whiting, 1951); *California Cotton Mills Co.,* 14 L.A. 377 (Marshall, 1950); *Franklin Ass'n of Chicago,* 7 L.A. 614 (Gilden, 1947).

Arbitrator Turkus outlined the factors he relies upon to give prior practice contractual status:

"1. Does the practice concern a major condition of employment?
"2. Was it established unilaterally?
"3. Was it administered unilaterally?
"4. Did either of the parties seek to incorporate it into the body of the written agreement?
"5. What is the frequency of repetition of the 'practice'?
"6. Is the 'practice' a long standing one?
"7. Is it specific and detailed?
"8. Do the employees rely on it?" [68]

Those arbitrators who espouse the view that past practice *per se* attains contractual status would prohibit an employer from unilaterally changing conditions or practices not mentioned in the labor agreement.[69] The reasoning relied upon by these arbitrators begins with the proposition that the parties, when they negotiate a collective agreement, do not set down on paper the whole of their agreement. "One cannot reduce all the rules governing a community like an industrial plant to fifteen or even fifty pages." [70] They therefore conclude that the agreement includes not just the written provisions stated therein, but also the conditions and practices which have developed over the years. Hence, if a particular practice or condition is not repudiated during negotiations, it is implied from the silence of the negotiators that the agreement was entered into upon the tacit understanding that the practice or condition would continue in force. For example, Arbitrator Douglas B. Brown said:

"The agreement, no matter how short, does provide a guide to modes of procedure and to the rights of the parties on *all* matters affecting the conditions of employment. Where explicit provisions are made, the question is relatively simple. But even where the agreement is silent, the parties have, by their silence, given assent to a continuation of the existing modes of procedure." [71]

This implication, of course, should not be possible if it conflicts with the express language of the agreement. For example, if the agreement said "the written provisions constitute the entire agreement of the parties," it would seem to be improper to imply that the parties

---

[68] *Jacob Ruppert*, 35 L.A. 503, 504 (Turkus, 1960).
[69] *E. W. Bliss Co.*, 24 L.A. 614 (Dworkin, 1955); *Phillips Petroleum Co.*, 24 L.A. 191 (Merrill, 1955); *Northland Greyhound Lines, Inc.*, 23 L.A. 277 (Levinson, Chm., 1954); *International Harvester Co.*, 20 L.A. 276 (Wirtz, 1953); *Ryan Aeronautical Co.*, 17 L.A. 395 (Kamaroff, 1951); *Libby, McNeill & Libby*, 5 L.A. 546 (Prasow, 1946); *Pullman-Standard Car Mfg. Co.*, 2 L.A. 509 (Courshan, 1945).
[70] Cox, *Reflections Upon Labor Arbitration*, 72 HARV. L. REV. 1482, 1499 (1959).
[71] D. Brown, *Managements Rights and the Collective Agreement*, PROCEEDINGS OF THE FIRST ANNUAL MEETING OF THE INDUSTRIAL RELATIONS RESEARCH ASSOCIATION 145-55 (IRRA 1949).

meant to make practices and conditions not recorded in the agreement a part of the agreement.

Most of the arbitrators who espouse this view predicate their right to do so on the views expressed by Archibald Cox, the original and strongest advocate of the view that past practices and conditions of employment obtain contractual status and, hence, cannot be changed by the employer unless he first obtains the agreement of the union. In asserting that the words of the agreement are not the exclusive source of rights and duties, Cox said:

> "Within the sphere of collective bargaining, the institutional characteristics and the governmental nature of the collective-bargaining process demand a common law of the shop which implements and furnishes the context of the agreement. We must assume that intelligent negotiators acknowledged so plain a need unless they stated a contrary rule in plain words." [72]

Arbitrator Harry Shulman espoused a contrary view. He viewed the assumption that parties by their silence agree to freeze all practices and conditions of employment as unrealistic:

> "It is more than doubtful that there is any general understanding among employers and unions as to the viability of existing practices during the term of a collective agreement. . . . I venture to guess that in many enterprises the execution of a collective agreement would be blocked if it were insisted that it contain a broad provision that 'all existing practices, except as modified by this agreement, shall be continued for the life thereof, unless changed by mutual consent.' . . . The reasons for the block would be, of course, the great uncertainty as to the nature and extent of the commitment, and the relentless search for cost-saving changes. . . ." [73]

Therefore, in Shulman's view the assumption upon which the Archibald Cox implication theory of construction is based is not valid. He elaborated his view in a decision he rendered when he was the Ford Company umpire:

> "But there are . . . practices which are . . . mere happenstance, that is, methods that developed without design or deliberation. Or they may be choices by Management in the exercise of managerial discretion as to convenient methods at the time. In such cases there is no thought of obligation or commitment for the future. Such practices are merely present ways, not prescribed ways, of doing things. The relevant item of significance is not the nature of the particular method but the managerial freedom with respect to it. Being the product of managerial determination in its permitted discretion such practices are, in the absence of contractual provision to the contrary, subject to change in the same

---

[72] See note 70 *supra*.
[73] Shulman, *Reason, Contract and Law in Labor Relations*, 68 HARV. L. REV. 999, 1011 (1955).

discretion. . . . But there is no requirement of mutual agreement as a condition precedent to a change of a practice of this character.

"A contrary holding would place past practice on a par with written agreement and create the anomaly that, while the parties expend great energy and time in negotiating the details of the Agreement, they unknowingly and unintentionally commit themselves to unstated and perhaps more important matters which in the future may be found to have been past practice." [74]

Arbitrator Russell Smith appears to align himself with those arbitrators who adopt the Archibald Cox assumption that the parties intended to contractually freeze the status quo—*i.e.,* all past practices and conditions—when they entered into a collective agreement.[75] Smith, however, recognizes that when past practices and conditions attain contractual status, the union is given a veto over all changes, including changes that the management would make to improve productivity.[76] This prospect forced Smith to seek some limitation to be placed upon the Cox "assumption-implication" theory that would otherwise contractually freeze the status quo. He said:

"Think of the difficulty one might encounter in trying to establish that the unstated assumption of the negotiators on both sides of the table was to continue existing practices. The [Archibald Cox] approach, on the other hand, comes close to engrafting a 'past practice' clause onto the typical collective agreement without regard to the actual assumptions of the negotiators. Their silence at the bargaining table is presumed to constitute assent to existing conditions, whether they thought of this or not.

" . . .

---

[74] *Ford Motor Co.,* 19 L.A. 237, 242 (Shulman, 1952). See also *International Harvester Co.,* 20 L.A. 276 (Wirtz, 1953).

[75] R. Smith, L. Merrifield and D. Rothschild, Collective Bargaining and Labor Arbitration (1970).

[76] An observer from Great Britain reported to a Royal Commission the effect on national productivity that can be found in the manner in which labor agreements are construed:

"The major difference between the [industrial relations] system in North America and the system in the U.K. is that the method of collective bargaining in North America assigns to management a precise and specific management function which it may exercise during the term of the contract, subject only to the right of the union to file grievances for processing by the grievance procedure culminating in arbitration. . . .

"The effect is that . . . management is able to produce change at a much faster rate than we are able to do in this country. For example, any change consistent with the terms of the contract may be introduced by management immediately. . . . In the U.K. because there is no enforceable recognition of management's specific functions, management must be prepared to negotiate every time it wishes to make a change. The result is that we tend to have to bargain under pressure all the time. . . . Because of this there is a tendency for the U.K. compromise to be less efficient than the North American equivalent action by management. . . ."

Great Britain, Royal Commission on Trade Unions and Employers' Associations, *Minutes of Evidence 25, Witness: Massey-Ferguson (U.K.), Ltd.* (London: Her Majesty's Stationery Office, 1966), p. 1004, Testimony of H. J. Hebden.

"Those of us who accept the principle that an agreement may require the continuance of existing practice recognize that this principle cannot be allowed to freeze *all* existing conditions. For instance, the long-time use of hand-controlled grinding machines could hardly be regarded as a practice prohibiting the introduction of automatic grinding machines. Or the long-time use of pastel colors in painting plant interiors could not preclude management from changing to a different color scheme. Plainly, not all practices can be considered binding conditions of employment. Thus, while we are willing to imply that practices are a part of the agreement, we are apprehensive of the breadth of the implication. What seems correct from a theoretical point of view does not always make sense from a practical point of view. Arbitrators, accordingly, have accepted the implication but sought to limit it to just certain kinds of practices. The difficulty is to determine what kind of rational line, if any, can be drawn between those practices which may be incorporated into the agreement and those which may not." [77]

Some arbitrators seeking to find some limitation that will not freeze the status quo and prevent needed change have stated that they will enforce only "major practices" as contrasted to "minor conditions." [78] However, Arbitrator Smith points up the weakness in the "major-minor" distinction when he said:

"What is *major* to one group of employees may be *minor* to all the others; what is *major* from the standpoint of morale may be *minor* from the standpoint of earnings and job security. There is no logical basis for distinguishing between *major* and *minor* conditions. . . . More important, this kind of test encourages arbitrators 'to commence their thinking with what they consider a desirable decision and then work backward to appropriate premises, devising syllogisms to justify that decision. . . .' [79] That is, if an arbitrator decides to enforce the practice he calls it a *major* condition, and if he decides otherwise he calls it a *minor* condition. To this extent, the test provides us with a rationalization rather than a reason for our ruling." [80] [Emphasis added.]

Another rationale to limit the freezing of the status quo that would result from the Archibald Cox construction theory was one suggested by the Elkouris. [81] Smith explains their view and then explains its inadequacy:

"They [the Elkouris] would enforce only those practices which involve 'employee benefits'; they would not prohibit changes in practices which

---

[77] See note 75 *supra*, at 256-257.

[78] *Pan Am Southern Corp.*, 25 L.A. 611, 613 (Reynard, Chm., 1955); *Phillips Petroleum Co.*, 24 L.A. 191, 194 (Merrill, 1955); *Continental Baking Co.*, 20 L.A. 309, 311 (Updegraff, 1953); *General Aniline & Film Corp.*, 19 L.A. 628, 629 (Talbott, Chm., 1952). See Cox & Dunlop, *The Duty to Bargain Collectively During the Term of an Existing Agreement*, 63 HARV. L. REV. 1097, 1116, 1117 (1950).

[79] Frank, *Experimental Jurisprudence and the New Deal*, 78 CONG. REG. 12412, 12413 (1934).

[80] See note 75 *supra*, at 258.

[81] F. Elkouri & E. Elkouri, note 34, *supra*, at 274-275.

involve 'basic management functions.' This test, however, is no more convincing than the major-minor test. It [the Elkouris' rationale] suffers from the same defects. It too encourages the arbitrator to work backward from his decision, thus providing him with a rationalization rather than a reason for his ruling. To enforce a practice all he need say is that it concerns employee benefits, But the fact is that most practices which create such benefits are likely to impinge upon some basic management function. Consider a situation where the employer wishes to reduce a long-established crew size based upon a recent engineering survey of his plant. How is the crew size practice to be characterized? It involves the direction of the working force and the determination of methods of operation, customary management functions, but it also involves the job security of one or more members of the crew, a very real employee benefit." [82]

The tension between the construction theories which cause past practice to become contractually frozen and the more traditional construction principles which cause the arbitrator's authority to be limited to the enforcement of the written agreement is, of course, substantial. As noted by Arbitrator George Cheney, when all past practice is given contractual status, the parol evidence rule is effectively emasculated:

"Furthermore, evidence of usage and custom is not permissible to restrict or enlarge the explicit terms of an instrument or otherwise control the apparent intention of the parties. It is recognized that to permit a written and express contract to be thus controlled, varied, or contradicted by a usage or custom would not only amount to admitting parol evidence to vary a written instrument but also would allow more presumptions or implications arising, in the absence of positive proof expressions of intention, to control, vary, or even contradict the most formal and written declarations of the parties." [83]

Similarly, Arbitrator Marion Beatty said:

"This past practice could throw light on how the parties interpreted their own working agreement if there were a contract provision in point and which needed some clarification, but here there is no contract provision which comes close to providing for the exercise of seniority rights to the extent contended for here." [84]

In contrast, however, some arbitrators have carried the "practice obtains contractual status" theory so far that even where the practice is contrary to the clear words of the agreement they hold the written agreement should be amended or reformed to conform to the

---

[82] See note 80, *supra*.
[83] *Inspiration Consolidated Copper Co.,* 7 L.A. 86, 88 (Cheney, 1947).
[84] *Gas Service Co.,* 35 L.A. 637, 640 (Beatty, 1960). To the same effect see *Spenzer Container Corp.,* 69-1 ARB ¶ 8124, 3419 (Krimsly, 1968); *American Meter Co.,* AAA Case No. 61-17 (Teple, 1963); *Castle & Cook Terminals, Ltd.,* 40 L.A. 62 (Kagel, 1963); *Wallace Barnes Co.,* 27 L.A. 662 (Stutz, 1956).

practice. For example, in *General Controls Corp.,*[85] Arbitrator Edgar A. Jones asserted:

"Even language which by its clear terms brooks no interpretation but one can be effectively amended, even repealed, by a course of contrary interpretation indulged by the Parties over a significant period of time." [86]

The view that a practice in conflict with clear language should be considered an amendment to the agreement was sharply criticized by Arbitrator Saul Wallen:

"The proposition that past practice can be used 'to modify or amend what is seemingly unambiguous' rests on a . . . dubious foundation. Those who argue that it is often permissible, when an arbitrator is confronted with a conflict between an established practice and a seemingly clear and unambiguous contract provision, to regard the practice as an amendment to the agreement rest their argument on the legal theory of reformation. They maintain that the parties' day-to-day actions, when they run counter to the plain meaning of the contract's words, evidence an intent to substitute that which they actually do for that which they said in writing they would do. . . .

"But this approach, it seems to me, is in derogation of an important function of the collective bargaining agreement.
" . . .
"[T]here is much to be said for the idea that the collective agreement's clear language should be considered as the lodestar that enables the top management of the company or the union to correct the deviations from course introduced by subordinates during their day-to-day operations. If the deviations are regarded as evidence of an intent to modify the clear terms of the agreement, the agreement's value as an instrument of control is thereby diminished. At best, this reformation theory must be approached warily and, if invoked at all, applied only where the course of conduct that runs counter to the language was known to and approved by those with the power to contract." [87]

Arbitrator Harry Shulman criticized the view that:

---

[85] 31 L.A. 240 (Jones, 1958). To the same effect see *Borg-Warner Corp.,* 36 L.A. 961 (Mishne, 1961); *Smith Display Service,* 17 L.A. 524 (Sherbow, 1951); *International Shoe Co.,* 2 L.A. 201 (Klamon, 1946). *Contra, National Lead Co.,* 28 L.A. 470, 474 (Roberts, 1957); *Metropolitan Coach Lines,* 27 L.A. 376, 383 (Lennard, 1956); *Smith Display Service,* 17 L.A. 524, 526 (Sherbow, 1951); *Gibson Refrigerator Co.,* 17 L.A. 313, 318 (Platt, 1951); *Texas-New Mexico Pipe Line Co.,* 17 L.A. 90 (Emory, 1951); *Bethlehem Steel Co.,* 13 L.A. 556, 560 (Killingsworth, 1949); *Merrill-Stevens Dry Dock & Repair Co.,* 10 L.A. 562, 563 (Douglas, 1948); *Pittsburgh Plate Glass Co.,* 8 L.A. 317, 322 (Blair, 1947).

[86] 31 L.A. 242.

[87] Wallen, *The Silent Contract vs. Express Provisions: The Arbitration of Local Working Conditions,* COLLECTIVE BARGAINING AND THE ARBITRATOR'S ROLE, Proceedings of the Fifteenth Annual Meeting, National Academy of Arbitrators 117, 121-22 (M. Kahn Ed. 1962). See Arbitrator Wallen's holding in *United States Steel Corp.,* 40 L.A. 636 (Wallen, 1963).

"[W]ould place past practice on a par with written agreement and create the anomaly that, while the parties expend great energy and time in negotiating the details of the agreement, they unknowingly and unintentionally commit themselves to unstated and perhaps more important matters which in the future may be found to have been past practice." [88]

Arbitrators have said that giving contractual status to prior practice *per se* can be a violation of the arbitrator's jurisdictional limitations. For example, Arbitrator Carl Warns said:

"Where as in this case the contract is completely silent on job assignments there is nothing for the practice (the grievance settlement) to relate to or for the history of the negotiations to clarify. In other words, for me to use the settlement of grievance No. 1113 as a principle upon which to resolve the issue before me would be to 'add' to the contract which is not within my authority to do. . . . [A]s arbitrator authorized only to construe an existing contract and without authority to make one for the parties, I can consider what the parties have done since the signing of the contract only as an aid in resolving ambiguities in negotiated language. In other words, where written language is not clear, as pointed out, I can consider bargaining table statements and practices including the settlement of grievances as aids to interpretation. But I cannot without exceeding my authority accept such evidence to add duties and responsibilities which the parties did not agree to at the bargaining table." [89]

And Arbitrator Harold W. Davey explained another incongruous result that occurs when prior practice is given contractual status:

"In other words, the Company's past practice (which has been discontinued and which the Union seeks to have restored) was in my judgment contrary to both the letter and the spirit of (the contract). Therefore, it cannot be argued successfully that a change of practice which in effect brings it into line with contract requirements is at the same time a violation of the contract." [90]

There are, of course, many labor agreements that contain a clause giving contractual status to practices beneficial to the employee so long as the underlying conditions basic to the practice remain unchanged. The famous 2B Clause, known as the "local working conditions clause," in the basic steel agreements is an example. Decisions of arbitrators under such clauses are not, of course, examples of the elevation of past practice to contractual status because in such agreements past practice has been given contractual status by an

---

[88] *Ford Motor Co.*, 19 L.A. 237, 242 (Shulman, 1952).

[89] *Kroger Co.*, 31 L.A. 82, 84 (Warns, 1968). To the same effect see *Mallinckrodt Chemical Works*, 38 L.A. 267, 268 (Hilpert, 1961).

[90] *John Deere Des Moines Works*, 22 L.A. 628, 631 (Davey, 1954). *Accord, Carnegie Illinois Steel Corp.*, 12 L.A. 217 (Seward, 1949).

agreement of the parties.[91] The significance of the lack of a "past practice clause" in the agreement upon a grievance claim was pointed out by Arbitrator Bert L. Luskin:

> "The Collective Bargaining Agreement does not contain a 'local working conditions' clause that would give contractual status to an established practice. There are specific terms and provisions of the Agreement that govern the matter of lunch periods. The payment of lunch money to a Driver is not a matter of contract, and a practice in that respect cannot achieve contractual status." [92]

---

[91] A typical interpretation of 2B is found in *National Tube Division, United States Steel Co.*, 2 STEEL ARB. 1187 (Garrett, 1953).

[92] *The Maytag Company*, Grievance No. P1-D18-3-65 (1966).

CHAPTER XI

The Burden and Quantum of Proof Requirements

A. ARBITRATION—APPELLATE REVIEW OR TRIAL *DE NOVO?*

Arbitrators articulate in their opinions legal principles that they borrow from trial court practice. Their use of the borrowed doctrines of "burden of proof," and "quantum of proof" required to sustain the burden is reported in this chapter.

Some arbitrators are not as prone to borrow the time tested principles that are used daily in trial court practice as are others. Their reluctance may well stem from an instinctive worry that the analogy between what a trial judge does and what they, as arbitrators, do is not close enough to permit them to borrow the trial court principles indiscriminately and without some reshaping. This worry is justified because sometimes an arbitrator is acting as a trial judge and at other times he is acting as an appellate judge.

For example, an arbitrator may be asked by a union to upset a managerial determination that one employee has greater ability than another when the two employees are competing for a promotion or to upset a management determination that an employee engaged in conduct that was "just cause" for his discharge or suspension, or that the work content of a certain job classification should rank higher than the work content of another, etc. Arbitrators quite generally recognize that a manager is employed to make initial determinations concerning these matters. They say that it is not the role of the arbitrator to substitute his judgment for that of the manager and upset the determination unless it is established that the determination was "capricious or arbitrary." [1]

If the management determination is shown to have been made in haste, not based upon all pertinent facts, or if it involved an improper analysis of the facts, the arbitrator will more often conclude that the determination was arbitrary than when it is shown to be based on a

---

[1] See discussion under Section D., "The Required Quantum of Proof," in this chapter.

complete factual analysis and a detached review by higher management. Arbitrator Bert L. Luskin explained that the basis for a determination must be examined to ascertain whether the determination was arbitrary or not. In *Southwestern Bell Telephone Co. v. Communications Workers of America*,[2] he said:

> "The Arbitrator, however, cannot agree with the contention of the Company that the application of the standards of 'just cause' would permit an arbitrator to indiscriminately substitute his judgment for that of the Company in all instances. In effect, the action taken by the Company must be examined *in the light of the basis upon which the Company made its determination;* and if the events would indicate that the Company determination was *based upon the exercise of reason, judgment and discretion,* the action of the Company must be sustained, unless it can be demonstrated that the decision was either discriminatory, arbitrary, capricious or based upon *error of fact.* The Arbitrator should not lightly disturb the Company's determination merely because he does not personally agree with the judgment exercised by the Company; nor should he substitute his judgment for that of the Company on the basis that different persons exercising judgment and discretion based upon the same facts might come to a different conclusion."[3] (Emphasis added.)

Similarly, Arbitrator Bernard Meltzer explained in *Kellogg Co.*:[4]

> "Where, as in this case, *there has been a fair hearing and a good-faith consideration of all the circumstances by management,* management's determination as to the appropriate penalty should not be disturbed unless it was clearly unreasonable. The question involved is not whether the Board would have imposed the same penalty. The question is whether the penalty is within the reasonable range of discretion which management must have in order to discharge its primary responsibility for safe and efficient operations. . . ."[5]

The above quotations indicate that arbitrators are not only reviewing the determination made by the manager, but also the basis for his determination. Was the determination "below" made after all the pertinent evidence was collected? Was this evidence properly weighed where there were conflicts? Was the determination based on rank hearsay, rumor, or on substantial evidence?

When the union is asking that a managerial determination be upset, the arbitrator's role is more analogous to that of a judge in an appellate tribunal than one in the trial court. Judges in a review tribunal will study the evidentiary record upon which the trial judge made his determination to determine whether it was supported by substantial

---

[2] AAA Case No. L-25262 DAL-L33-59 (Luskin, 1960) (unreported).

[3] *Id.* at 6.

[4] 28 L.A. 303 (Meltzer, 1957).

[5] *Id.* at 308.

evidence or was "clearly erroneous" (a test essentially the same as the "capricious or arbitrary" test used by arbitrators).

The arbitrator's role becomes more analogous to that of a trial court judge when it is shown that the managerial decision "below" was made in haste before all the evidence, some possibly conflicting, was collected and analyzed. Then the arbitrator's role becomes more analogous to a trial judge hearing evidence *de novo*.[6] When the role of the arbitrator shifts toward that of the trial court, he must then weigh evidence where there is conflict, evaluate the worth of the hearsay evidence and the like, to a greater extent than he will when he is reviewing determinations made "below" after all the evidence has been collected into an evidentiary record.

The shift in the arbitrator's role from that of an appellate judge reviewing a record to that of a trial judge determining the facts *de novo* can be observed in the awards of many arbitrators. It is however explained with sparkling clarity by Arbitrator Carroll Daugherty who often attaches to his opinion in a disciplinary case an explanation of the arbitrator's role which states in part:

> "The arbitrator's hearing is an appeals proceeding designed to learn whether . . . the employer, as a sort of trial court, had conducted, before making his decision, a full and fair inquiry into the employee's alleged 'crime'; whether from the inquiry said trial court had obtained substantial evidence of the employee's guilt; whether the employer, in reaching his verdict and in deciding on the degree of discipline to be imposed, had acted in an even-handed, non-discriminatory manner; and whether the degree of discipline imposed by the employer was reasonably related to the seriousness of the proven offense and to the employee's previous record. In short, an arbitrator 'tries' the employer to discover whether the latter's own 'trial' and treatment of the employee was proper. . . ." [7]

Daugherty expresses the typical view that an arbitrator "is not supposed to substitute his judgment . . . for that of the company unless there is compelling evidence that the company abused its discretion in words that are consistent with his analogy to an appellate review by saying that he applies this rule, "even though the arbitrator, if he had been the original 'trial judge,' [the manager] might have imposed a lesser penalty." [8]

Daugherty explains why he, like an appellate judge, is concerned with the evidentiary record upon which the management made its determination. A sound determination should be made only after all of the facts are known:

---

[6] "A new trial or retrial had in an appellate court in which the whole case is gone into as if no trial whatever had been had in the court below," BLACK'S LAW DICTIONARY (4th ed. 1951), p. 1677.

[7] *Whirlpool Corp.,* 58 L.A. 421, 427 (Daugherty, 1972).

[8] *Id.* at 427.

"The company's investigation must normally be made *before* its disciplinary decision is made. If the company fails to do so, its failure may not normally be excused on the ground that the employee will get his day in court through the grievance procedure after the exaction of discipline. . . ." [9]

Daugherty's concern that the management's determination be supported by substantial evidence is similar to the concern of an appellate judge that the trial judge's determination be supported by substantial evidence. His concern is reflected in these words:

"At his hearing the management 'judge' should actively search out witnesses and evidence, not just passively take what participants or 'volunteer' witnesses tell him.

"At the investigation did the company 'judge' obtain substantial and compelling evidence or proof that the employee was guilty as charged?

"It is not required that the evidence be fully conclusive or 'beyond all reasonable doubt.' But, the evidence must be truly weighty and substantial and not flimsy or superficial." [10]

Arbitrator Daugherty's analogy between the role of the arbitrator and that of an appellate judge would not be applicable where the dispute is over a contractual interpretation. The arbitrator's role in such a case could be analogous to a declaratory judgment proceeding before a court. This is mentioned here merely to cause one to recognize that the arbitrator's role may vary in different cases—increasing the need for care when borrowing practice and procedure concepts from trial courts.

B. THE BURDEN OF PROOF REQUIREMENTS

Arbitrators Clarence Updegraff and Whitley McCoy wrote nearly 25 years ago concerning the concept of evidential burdens, "This is so sensible and logical a principle that no one, understanding it, would disagree." [11] These authors have explained, in disarmingly simple terms, that concepts relating to "burden of proof" mean that "the party holding the affirmative of an issue must produce sufficient evidence to prove the facts essential to his claim." [12] Needless to say, the burden of proceeding with further evidence will typically shift once the party who bears the initial burden has discharged it. Arbitrator Hugh Babb explained in *Allis Chalmers Mfg. Co.*:[13]

[9] *Id.* at 429.
[10] *Id.* at 428.
[11] C. Updegraff & W. McCoy, ARBITRATION OF LABOR DISPUTES 97 (1946).
[12] *Id.* at 161 (2d ed. 1961). See also F. Elkouri and E. Elkouri, HOW ARBITRATION WORKS 189 (1960); Chambers, *Burden of Proof in Labor Arbitration*, 3 DUKE L.J. 127, 128 (1953); Beck, *Evidence, Burden and Quantum of Proof*, WASH. U. L.Q. 85, 89 (1949).
[13] 29 L.A. 356 (Babb, 1957).

"While the burden of proof remains on the party affirming a fact in support of his case and does not change in any aspect of the cause, the weight of the evidence shifts from side to side as the hearing proceeds, according to the nature and strength of the proofs. . . ." [14]

Burden of proof is, in reality, a composite of several elements which have been termed the burden of proceeding, the burden of persuasion, and the quantum of proof. Presumptions may be relied upon by the party charged with any one of the above burdens and they are also used by arbitrators.

(1) Situations Where the Initial Burden of Proof Is Placed on the Union

The general rule followed by labor arbitrators in nondisciplinary proceedings is that the grieving party—typically the union—bears the initial burdens of proceeding and proof. It is therefore usually up to the union to demonstrate that the action taken by the management is inconsistent with some limitation, contractual or otherwise. In a case involving a challenge of certain layoffs, Arbitrator F. M. Ingle said:

"In any hearing that seeks to adjust or settle differences between people or companies, such as an arbitration, the doctrine of burden of proof should prevail. I do not attempt to hold that the strict rules of law apply in an arbitration matter, but there are certain rules and regulations which must be followed if an arbitration can be handled intelligently. The doctrine of burden of proof simply means that the party who asserts a claim or right against another party has the burden or responsibility of proving it. That is true in this case. The Union recognizes that the Company may have to make layoffs from time to time because of lack of work. Since it must be conceded that the Company has the right to lay off employees and to determine the respective ability of such employees, then their decision stands until such time as the aggrieved employee has produced evidence which would show that the employer or Company had abused the right, had discriminated against an employee or had not acted in good faith in the layoff." [15]

Similarly, Arbitrator Vernon Stouffer wrote in *Columbus Bottlers, Inc.:*[16]

"Nothing is found in the Agreement charging the employer with the responsibility of bearing the burden of proof and showing that its closing

---

[14] *Id.* at 358.

[15] *Combustion Engineering Co.,* 9 L.A. 515, 517 (Ingle, 1948). See also *Local 761, International Union of Electrical Workers v. General Electric,* DAILY LAB. REP. No. 109, A-5 (June 5, 1972) (D.C. W.Ky. 1972) where the court affirmed a previous arbitration award wherein the arbitrator imposed upon the union the burden of proving that a strike, precipitated by 63 maintenance employees, was legal. Text writers generally concur. See, *e.g.,* note 11, *supra:*
"The logical method of proceeding is for the one who has advanced the grievance to state and prove it."

[16] 44 L.A. 397 (Stouffer, 1965).

of the Plant is or was for lack of work. The Union is the complaining party and in the absence of provisions to the contrary, it follows that the burden of proof rests with it to show that the Employer's closing of the Plant constituted a violation of the Agreement or an abuse of discretion." [17]

Where the labor agreement states that the management shall make the initial determination of an issue, arbitrators often state that this determination will be presumed to be correct unless shown by the union to be improper.

For example, Arbitrator Paul Hebert wrote, in a case raising the question whether the management had properly evaluated abilities:

"Since Management is responsible for running the plant and for seeing that it is operated productively, economically and efficiently, contract provisions such as here involved have been interpreted to mean that the initial determination as to the qualifications of an employee for a job must be made by Management. The decision of Management on the matter of qualifications will be upheld if it is reasonably supported by the evidence and if the initial decision is not arbitrary, capricious, or made in bad faith. . . .

"After Management has made its determination on the issue of qualifications the burden of proof is on the Union to upset it by proving that the Company acted arbitrarily, capriciously, acted with discrimination or made an error in judgment." [18]

Similarly, in *Corn Products Co.*,[19] Arbitrator Harold Gilden said:

"Where, as here, the Union questions the Company's appraisal of an employee's competency for a given task, the Union has the burden of supporting such allegation by clear and convincing proof." [20]

There is some published opinion, principally among text writers, opposed to the foregoing views.[21] The cases in which arbitrators have cast upon the management an affirmative burden of proving the cor-

---

[17] *Id.* at 400.

[18] *Koppers Co., Inc.*, 63-1 ARB ¶ 8376 at 4241 (Hebert, 1963).

[19] 14 L.A. 620 (Gilden, 1950).

[20] *Id.* at 622. Other cases in which the above principle is restated include: *Celotex Corp.*, 66-2 ARB ¶ 8523 (Boothe, 1966); *Christy Vault Co.*, 42 L.A. 1093 (Koven, 1964); *Green River Steel Co.*, 41 L.A. 132, 136 (Stouffer, 1963); *United States Steel Corp.*, 41 L.A. 777 (Florey, 1963); *Great Atlantic & Pacific Tea Co.*, 61-1 ARB ¶ 8034 (McCoy, 1961); *General Box Co.*, 35 L.A. 867, 869 (Caraway, 1960); *Standard Oil Co.*, 34 L.A. 285, 290 (Anrod, 1959); *Kroger Co.*, 32 L.A. 296 (Schmidt, 1959); *Allied Chemical & Dye Co.*, 29 L.A. 395 (Reid, 1957); *Weber Showcase Co.*, 27 L.A. 40 (Prasow, 1956); *Aveo Mfg. Co.*, 24 L.A. 268 (Holly, 1955); *Fruehauf Trailer Co.*, 11 L.A. 495 (Whiting, 1948); *Merrill Stevens Drydock & Repair Co.*, 6 L.A. 838 (Marshall, 1947).

[21] See, *e.g.*, Howard, *The Role of the Arbitrator in Determination of Ability*, 12 ARB. J. 14 (1957).
"In the opinion of the writer, there is much to commend the position of those arbitrators who feel that the company should be prepared to shoulder the burden of proving that it correctly determined ability. . . ."

rectness of its action under the contract are, however, typically predicated upon contract language to that effect.[22]

(2) Situations Where the Initial Burden of Proof Is Placed on the Management

(a) Reliance on the Exception to the General Rule

When the company is relying on an exception to the general rule set forth in the labor agreement, the burden is on the company to prove the exception. For example, under a provision granting reporting pay to employees who report to work but find no work available, and relieving the employer of this obligation when certain conditions are met, the union establishes a *prima facie* case with a showing that employees did, in fact, report for work without having been told not to. From that point on, the burden rested with the company to prove that the contractual exception applied.[23]

(b) Disciplinary Action

Since the typical collective bargaining agreement expressly, or implicitly, creates in the dischargee a contractual right to employment unless he has engaged in misconduct justifying his discharge for cause (variously stated as "just cause" or "proper cause"), the managerial right to discharge an employee has in a sense been limited to those situations where the employee's misconduct makes him an exception to this contractual right, thus justifying the termination of the employee's employment relationship. Accordingly, labor arbitrators, with considerable uniformity, require management to establish, *prima facie,* the cause for the discharge action taken. Arbitrator McGury, for example, stated that:

> "In a discharge case, it is usually assumed that the Company has the burden of proving a reasonable cause for the discharge under the contract. . . . [I]f the Company has made the necessary minimal showing of adequate cause . . . [and] the grievant makes no response at all, . . . the Company's original case must stand and the discharge must be upheld." [24]

Similarly, Arbitrator John Larkin noted:

---

[22] See, *e.g., Columbia Steel Co.,* 13 L.A. 666, 668 (Whitton, 1949); but see *Lionel Corp.,* 7 L.A. 121 (Shipman, 1947).

[23] *Walworth Co.,* AAA Case No. 58-15 (James, 1963); see also *Southwestern Bell Telephone Co.,* AAA Case No. 58-18 (Oppenheim, 1963).

[24] *American Maize Products Co.,* 39 L.A. 1165, 1168 (McGury, 1963). See also *Celotex Corp.,* 24 L.A. 369 (Reynard, 1955); *American Optical Company,* 4 L.A. 288, 292 (Whitton, 1946).

"It is generally held by arbitrators that the burden of proceeding first, to establish proof of cause for discharge, is upon the Company." [25]

Once the company has introduced evidence of cause for the discharge, however, the burden of proceeding passes to the union which must, if it is to prevail, successfully rebut the management's case establishing "cause," prove mitigating circumstances, or show that, notwithstanding the existence of "cause," the management action was nevertheless illegally discriminatory or otherwise arbitrary:

"While we have held that the burden of first proceeding, and the burden of proof, are upon the company to prove a reasonable cause for discharge, the making of a *prima facie* case discharged the burden of first proceeding and cast upon the union a burden of rebutting that *prima facie* case." [26]

Similarly:

"In the instant case the Company made the necessary showing that the grievants illegally walked off the job. Having established this fact, the burden of proving that there were mitigating circumstances passed to the grievants and to the Union." [27]

In *Mississippi Lime Co.*,[28] Arbitrator Clarence Updegraff stated:

"As a preliminary matter it should be stated that while the burden of proof is on an Employer to prove a discharge was justified when it occurs under a contract that the Employer will not terminate an Employee 'without just cause' . . . the claim that a man was wrongfully discharged despite making 'reasonable requests' and 'excuses' requires that he establish the reasonableness of his requests and the truth of his excuses for being absent from work. It would be obviously wrong to require that the employer disprove a vague and undefined claim of sickness by an employee. The latter, having affirmatively asserted sickness under all rules of procedure must be expected and required to offer proof of it. To hold otherwise would permit the absent employee to assert any fantastic reason for absence which might occur to the imagination and challenge the Employer to disprove it. To require the employee to establish that his claim of illness is well founded is only to require proof of the person likely to be in touch with all the evidence and able to produce it, if his claim is correct. He is likely to be defeated on such an endeavor only if his claim is not correct. Clearly this is why it is established procedure to require the absentee employee to prove his excuse when its correctness is challenged. . . ." [29]

---

[25] *Borg-Warner Corp.*, 49 L.A. 882, 886 (Larkin, 1967). See also *Avco Mfg. Co.*, 24 L.A. 268 (Holly, 1955); Gorske, *Burden of Proof in Grievance Arbitration*, 43 Marq. L. Rev. 135 (1959).

[26] *Southern Bell Tel. & Tel. Co.*, 26 L.A. 742, 746 (McCoy, Chm., 1956).

[27] *Ingersoll Products Div., Borg-Warner Corp.*, 49 L.A. 883, 886 (Larkin, 1967). See also *Western Greyhound Lines*, 36 L.A. 261 (Lennard, 1960).

[28] 29 L.A. 559 (Updegraff, 1957).

[29] *Id.* at 561.

There are arbitrators, however, who maintain even where a discharge has been challenged that the burden of proof is on the union. For example, Arbitrator Clark Kerr has held that unions challenging disciplinary action must affirmatively establish lack of cause, or risk denial of the grievance:

> "The Company has the basic right to discharge. The Union may challenge discharges on the grounds that there was no adequate cause, or that proper notice was not given. If the Union makes no challenge, the action of the Company stands. If the Union does make a challenge, it must show why the challenge is a merited one. There is no presumption that the action of the Company is wrong until proved right; but quite the contrary. The contract does not read: 'The Company may not discharge until cause for discharge has been proved.' If the contract did read that way, then the Company would need to carry the burden of proof." [30]

The basis for placing the initial burden of proof on the management in the discharge case is in part the fact that the employee has a contractual right to employment (the general rule) unless it is shown he is guilty of improper conduct (*i.e.*, a proper basis for an exception to the general rule). Arbitrators have, however, often refused to follow the general rule on burden where the contract does not establish a "right to employment" [31] or a risk to third parties is involved. [32]

Where the discipline is less than discharge, various arbitrators have said that the burden rests properly on the union. [33] These cases usually show, however, that the arbitrators rested their decisions in the first instance upon an employer's showing of cause. In any event, the clear weight of authority is that management bears the initial burden of establishing "cause" for its action. [34]

The types of conduct which will be held to constitute "cause" for disciplinary action, and the defenses sufficient to overcome a showing of cause are matters of substantive industrial relations which are beyond the scope of this text on practice and procedure. Once management has proven its case of conduct injurious to the employer-employee relationship, the burden of proof that management's action

---

[30] *Wholesale Bakers' Ass'n of Sacramento,* 4 ALAA ¶ 86,641 at 71,433 (Kerr, 1950).

[31] *American Oil & Supply Co.,* 36 L.A. 331 (Berkovitz, 1960).

[32] *United Airlines, Inc.,* 19 L.A. 585 (McCoy, 1952) (public transportation company has duty to remove a pilot from his position if he is discovered to be unqualified because the safety of the public is of paramount importance).

[33] *Dayton Malleable Iron Co.,* 27 L.A. 242 (Warns, 1956); *Walter Butler Shipbuilders, Inc.,* 2 L.A. 633 (Gorder, 1944).

[34] See, *e.g., Lockheed Aircraft Corp.,* 27 L.A. 709 (Maggs, 1956); *St. Joseph Lead Co.,* 16 L.A. 138 (Hilpert, 1951); *Armen Berry Casting Co.,* 17 L.A. 179 (Smith, 1950).

was arbitrary, capricious, or unreasonable switches to the union.[35] As noted in one case:

"Under the generally accepted rule, if management's original decision in the matter was not arbitrary, capricious or unreasonable, or based on mistake of fact, its decision should stand. Furthermore, the boundaries of reasonableness should not be so narrowly drawn that management's judgment must coincide exactly with the arbitrator's judgment. If the penalty imposed is within the bounds of what the arbitrator can accept as a range of reasonableness, it should not be disturbed.

"A common mistake of some employees is the belief that they can, by appealing the disputed matter to arbitration, take the matter completely away from management and place it into the hands of a third party or board for an independent decision, based on sympathy or on standards different from those customarily used in industrial relations."[36]

On the same basis, arbitrators have typically shown an unwillingness to overrule managerial discretion in the matter of degree of discipline imposed for admittedly improper conduct:

"While recognizing the Board's authority to pass on the question of whether there was 'just cause' for the specific penalty imposed, the Chairman also recognizes that this authority is limited. Where, as in this case, there has been a fair hearing and a good-faith consideration of all the circumstances by management, management's determination as to the appropriate penalty should not be disturbed unless it was clearly unreasonable. The question involved is not whether the Board would have imposed the same penalty. The question is whether the penalty is within the reasonable range of discretion which management must have in order to discharge its primary responsibility for safe and efficient operations. . . ." [37]

C. THE *PRIMA FACIE* CASE

A *prima facie* case is generally defined as a presentation of evidence, sufficient in quality and quantity to warrant a ruling by the arbitrator in favor of the presenting party *if no contrary evidence* is proffered by the opposing party.[38] Thus, if in a particular case an arbi-

---

[35] *Industrial Chemical Co.*, 64-2 ARB ¶ 8481 (Larkin, 1964); *Packaging Corp. of America*, 37 L.A. 338 (Teple, 1961); *Robertshaw Fulton Controls*, 36 L.A. 4 (Hilpert, 1961); *Yunker Mfg. Co.*, 9 ALAA ¶ 70,745 (Duff, 1958); *Chesapeake & Potomac Tel. Co.*, 21 L.A. 367 (Dworkin, 1953); *Corn Products Ref. Co.*, 21 L.A. 105 (Gilden, 1953); *Morris Paper Mills*, 20 L.A. 653 (Anrod, 1953); *Cities Service Oil Co.*, 17 L.A. 335 (Larkin, 1951); *Ideal Cement Co.*, 13 L.A. 943 (Donaldson, 1950); *National Lead Co.*, 13 L.A. 28 (Prasow, 1949); *National Lock Co.*, 12 L.A. 1194 (Rader, 1949); *Sherwin-Williams Co.*, 12 L.A. 239 (Gregory, 1949); *Walter Kidde & Co., Inc.*, 10 L.A. 265 (Justin, 1948); *Stockham Pipe Fittings Co.*, 1 L.A. 160 (McCoy, 1945).

[36] *Trans World Airlines, Inc.*, 41 L.A. 142, 144 (Beatty, 1963).

[37] *Kellogg Co.*, 28 L.A. 303, 308-9 (Meltzer, 1957). *Accord, Arkla Air Conditioning*, 45 L.A. 156 (Larkin, 1965); *Bendix Aviation Corp.*, 62-3 ARB ¶ 8777 (Doyle, 1962); *National Lead Co.*, 13 L.A. 28 (Prasow, 1949); *Perkins Oil Co.*, 1 L.A. 447 (McCoy, 1946).

[38] 1 B. Jones, EVIDENCE § 205 (5th ed. 1958, Supp. 1971).

trator chooses to apply a standard requiring a high quantum of proof, this may cause the arbitrator to find that a party has failed to establish its *prima facie* case in spite of the fact that the party has proffered some evidence on every essential point, and its opponent has refused to offer any evidence at all. For example, in *John Deere Waterloo Tractor Works* [39] the management presented the testimony of the grievant's foreman and that of a fellow worker that the grievant was guilty of reckless driving to support the propriety of a one-week suspension. The union rested its case without presentation of a single witness. Nevertheless, Arbitrator Davey said, "I do not find the proof sufficient to sustain the specific charge that Lee was driving recklessly and that his truck was out of control." [40]

In *I. Hirst Enterprises, Inc.,*[41] the union charged the company with a breach of its obligation to sign individual contracts with performers, in accord with the master collective bargaining agreement; the company denied the charge. Neither party put in any evidence. Arbitrator Jules Justin, in order to resolve the dispute, first entertained a *presumption* of compliance with the contract obligation. He then went on to hold that, since the union offered no evidence to substantiate its claim, or to overcome the presumption [*i.e.,* since it had not discharged its burden of proof], the grievance was denied:

> "[T]he party who claims that the contract has been violated must be prepared to offer to the Arbitrator material and evidentiary facts to support or justify its claim. . . . It cannot . . . impose upon the disclaiming party the responsibility of disproving the alleged claim. . . .
>
> "In this case the Association claimed that the Company had violated Article V . . . without offering any fact or proof to sustain that claim. The Company met that claim by asserting that it had not violated the contract. . . .
>
> " . . .
>
> "In light of these facts, therefore, the Arbitrator has no alternative but to find that the proof wholly fails to sustain the Association's claim. . . .
>
> "Accordingly, the Arbitrator finds and Awards that the Company has not . . . violated Article V of the contract. . . ." [42]

Similarly, Arbitrator Elmer Hilpert found that a union had not overcome the presumption against inferring a contract breach:

> "[I]n order to establish a *prima facie* violation of the parties' overtime provision, the union must allege and prove *by facts* that (1) on a given,

---

[39] 20 L.A. 583 (Davey, 1953).
[40] *Id.* at 585.
[41] 24 L.A. 44 (Justin, 1954).
[42] *Id.* at 47. See also Gorske, *Burden of Proof in Grievance Arbitration,* 43 MARQ. L. REV. 135, 138-39 (1959). For a detailed exposition of these issues as they are treated in court proceedings, see 9 J. Wigmore, EVIDENCE § 2497 (3d ed. 1940).

identified overtime assignment, or given, identified overtime assignments; (2) the particular, identified grievant, or grievants, was or were (a) qualified to do the very work that was performed on such very assignment, or assignments, (b) was or were available, and (c) was or were then low in overtime hours; (3) and that he, or she, or they was or were not asked to work that overtime assignment, or those overtime assignments. . . . But, until the Union establishes a *prima facie* case of a violation—as outlined above, the Company is under no duty to go forward with any evidence to 'defend,' or 'explain,' its overtime assignment, or assignments, on this occasion, or these occasions." [43]

D. THE REQUIRED QUANTUM OF PROOF

The quantum of proof question arises most frequently when the union is claiming, for example, that a management determination that one employee has greater ability than another or that one job classification should be ranked higher than another, is being challenged in an arbitration proceeding. The quantum of proof necessary to upset such a determination is usually said to be proof sufficient to show that the determination was arbitrary, capricious, and unreasonable. Because it is management's function initially to make such determinations in its direction of the employees, it is a basic view of most arbitrators that the employer need not affirmatively justify each managerial determination.

Arbitrator Thomas Reynolds discussed these fundamentals in a case involving a determination of the ability of two employees:

"Who shall decide that the difference between two employees is great, or is so small as to make them equal for all practical purposes? The instant case perfectly illustrates the dilemma. The Union complains that, besides seniority, there is no objective yardstick which can be applied to measure relative ability and aptitude. The Company agrees that these matters cannot be measured with perfect objectivity, but insists that experienced supervisors can reliably judge men. . . . [T]o accept the Union's thesis here would amount to saying: . . . that when the Union disagrees with the Company's judgment it may have the decision reviewed by a third party. This way lies general confusion. Aside from its internal contradiction, the proposition is defective in its faulty assumption that outside parties, unfamiliar with the employees involved, could make better judgments as to their relative abilities and aptitudes than could the supervisors (assuming good faith on the part of the latter)." [44]

Since, as Arbitrator Reynolds observed, an arbitrator, as a third party, is generally incapable of being as sensitive to legitimate managerial needs as is the management, arbitrators typically will not reverse a management determination unless it is shown to be arbi-

---

[43] *Allis-Chalmers Mfg. Co.* (Hilpert, 1958) (unreported).
[44] *Hercules Powder Co.,* 10 L.A. 624, 626 (Reynolds, 1948).

trary, capricious, and without reasonable foundation, or so clearly erroneous as to suggest reliance upon invidious factors:

"The employer is best fitted to judge in such matters which employee is more valuable to him, and the Arbitrator does not believe that he should substitute his own judgment therefor in the absence of any evidence that the employer's determination was exercised arbitrarily or capriciously." [45]

Arbitrators have followed this standard in other types of cases. For example, Arbitrator Vernon Stouffer held, in a case involving work assignments:

"Management is entitled in the first instance to determine whether it has the required machinery, tools and equipment to perform a job. . . . If it be ultimately found that Management's judgment was arbitrary, capricious, unreasonable or made in bad faith, then its decision may be set aside. However, a mere error in judgment is not in itself sufficient reason to set the same aside, provided it is made in good faith." [46]

Similarly, in incentive standard and job evaluation cases:

"It is, of course, true that ordinarily when a job rate is determined by a formalized classification and evaluation procedure the results of the evaluation as made by management should not be overridden or changed by an arbitrator in the absence of clear proof of arbitrariness. . . ." [47]

In addition to the quantum of proof standard used when a management determination is being challenged, arbitrators have, over the years, evolved certain verbal formulae as a shorthand means of identifying the quantum of proof needed in various situations. Caution is required in dealing with these formulae, however. As one arbitrator has noted:

"[I]t may be wise to warn inexperienced attorneys not to rely upon certain words of art that arbitrators use carelessly in their opinions. When an arbitrator writes that the company or the union has proved a particular point 'by a preponderance of the evidence,' he may be implying the conscious application of a standard of proof; much more likely, however, he is simply using an expression which comes trippingly off

---

[45] *Hershey Chocolate Co.*, 1 ALAA ¶ 67,169 at 67,361 (Lichliter, 1946). See also *Christy Vault Co.*, 42 L.A. 1093 (Koven, 1964); *General Box Co.*, 35 L.A. 867 (Caraway, 1960); *Allied Chemical & Dye Corp.*, 29 L.A. 395 (Reid, 1957); *Weber Showcase & Fixture Co.*, 27 L.A. 40 (Prasow, 1956); *Ingram-Richardson Mfg. Co.*, 3 L.A. 482 (Whiting, 1945). See C. Updegraff & W. McCoy, Arbitration of Labor Disputes 299 (2d ed. 1961):
"Arbitrators quite generally hold that the decision of such a matter is one primarily for management, subject to being set aside only upon satisfactory proof that the decision was not a *bona fide* exercise of judgment and discretion but was the result of bias, favoritism, anti-union prejudice, or such like matter, or was the result of a clear mistake."
[46] *Green River Steel Corp.*, 41 L.A. 132, 136 (Stouffer, 1963). See also *United States Steel Corp.*, 41 L.A. 777 (Florey, 1963).
[47] *Kroger Co.*, 33 L.A. 296, 298 (Schmidt, 1959).

the tongue and which has no real connection with the degree of proof he will require in future cases of the same type." [48]

Nonetheless, since arbitrators tend to articulate certain standards in some types of cases more than others, it is worthwhile to examine the meaning of these verbal formulations. Furthermore, the NLRB has also scrutinized these verbal formulations in grappling with its rules of deferral to arbitration under the *Spielberg* [49] doctrine. Thus, in *Stevens Sash & Door, Inc.*,[50] the Board refused to dismiss a complaint alleging unlawful discharge of an employee pending the outcome of an arbitration. The Board refused on the basis that the contract narrowly restricted the arbitrator to accepting the employer's decision if supported by substantial evidence and precluded him from making a decision on the preponderance of the evidence.

The strictest quantum of proof imposed in labor arbitration is "proof beyond a reasonable doubt." This standard is typically applied to the proof which management offers in order to establish that an act, warranting discharge, has been committed. Generally, arbitrators agree that it should be applied only in a limited class of those cases— where the employee was discharged for criminal or morally reprehensible conduct.[51] Where an employee is discharged for misconduct criminal in nature, commentators feel the higher burden of proof is justified by the social stigma attaching to the worker. As one arbitrator has noted:

> "It is not alone a question of breaking the plant rules, the customary type of case dealt with in labor arbitration, but also the breaking of the law of society against taking someone else's money. It follows, therefore, that a decision against the individual would have more far reaching results than breaking plant rules, in that it would brand her for the rest of her life as an ordinary thief before her associates, friends and neighbors. Considering the gravity of the consequences, it follows logically to my mind that the evidence should not leave the shadow of reasonable doubt in order to rule against Mrs. Z." [52]

---

[48] Aaron, *Symposium on Arbitration; Some Procedural Problems in Arbitration,* 10 VAND. L. REV. 649, 743 (1957).

[49] 112 NLRB 1080 (1955).

[50] 178 NLRB 154 (1969).

[51] See, *e.g., Allied Chemical Corp.,* 50 L.A. 616 (Turkus, 1968); *Geo. H. Dentler & Son,* 42 L.A. 954 (Boles, 1964); *Ames Harris Neville Co.,* 42 L.A. 803 (Koven, 1964); *American Smelting & Refining Co.,* 7 L.A. 147 (Wagner, 1947); *Bethlehem Steel Co.,* 2 L.A. 194 (Shipman, 1945). A district court held the "reasonable doubt" standard was met in a discharge case in *Alonso v. Kaiser Aluminum,* 345 F. Supp. 1356 (S.D.W.Va., 1971), aff'd, — F.2d —, 81 LRRM 2057, 69 LC ¶ 13,001 (4th Cir., Aug. 15, 1972).

[52] *Amelia Earhart Luggage Co.,* 11 L.A. 301, 302 (Lesser, 1948).
"[O]ne who faces social stigma and ostracism for the commission of an act is entitled to all the safeguards which industrial jurisprudence has established. Perhaps not the strictest proof of 'beyond reasonable doubt' as contrasted with the 'preponderance of evidence'—but very little short of it." *Braniff Airways, Inc.,* 44 L.A. 417, 420-21 (Rohman, 1965).

Arbitrator Burton Turkus in *Great Atlantic & Pacific Tea Co.*,[53] contrasted two quantum of proof standards he employs:

"The proof upon which the discharge is predicated, when grievous misconduct involving moral turpitude . . . is the basis, should establish guilt thereof beyond a reasonable doubt.

"In other types of overt misconduct such as (a) illegal strikes . . . (b) refusal to perform job assignments . . . (c) fighting . . . and (d) other offenses likewise constituting a breach of peace inside the plant or other challenge to the authority of management and its right to maintain morale, discipline and efficiency in the work force, the requisite quantum of proof may not fall short of a clear and convincing demonstration of the commission of the offense. . . .

"The dereliction relied upon for termination of employment may, of course, be predicated upon less dramatic forms of misconduct such as (a) incompetence . . . (b) absenteeism . . . (c) loafing . . . intoxication or gambling on Company time, and (d) violation of safety or other reasonable rules or regulations. In such instance the degree of proof required must likewise achieve the requisite clear and convincing demonstration of the commission of the misconduct, offense or dereliction of duty upon which the discharge is predicated." [54]

In *National Bedding and Furniture Industries, Inc.*[55] Arbitrator Ralph Hon stated:

"On the other hand, the accused is entitled to be presumed innocent until proved guilty. . . . More specifically, to uphold a discharge on grounds which will not only terminate an employee's present means of livelihood but may well affect his chances of obtaining a job with another employer in his line of work, arbitrators insist that the employer prove his case beyond a reasonable doubt. Where this burden is sustained, the employee may be discharged in order to protect the interests of the Company, fellow employees and society. Where the burden is not sustained, the discharge is likely to be revoked. In other words, in order for the discharge to be upheld, the proof must be so conclusive that impartial, reasonable and experienced persons would be morally certain of the guilt of the accused. Dishonesty cannot be assumed, it must be proved." [56]

This "beyond a reasonable doubt" has been criticized by other arbitrators, even in cases involving alleged moral turpitude. Arbitrator Jacob Seidenberg observed:

"We are constrained to state as a preliminary matter, that neither the acquittal nor the conviction of the Grievant in a court of law would have been dispositive of the issue before us for determination. Such matters as the burden of proof and the rules of evidence are different than

---

[53] 63-1 ARB ¶ 8027 (Turkus, 1962).
[54] *Id.* at 3089.
[55] 67-1 ARB ¶ 8356 (Hon, 1967). See also *Budd Co.,* AAA Case No. 146-13 (Greenlee, 1970).
[56] 67-1 ARB at 4283.

those which guide a third party neutral interpreting a voluntary agreed upon collective bargaining contract." [57]

In *Westinghouse Electric Corp.*,[58] the Arbitrator admitted into evidence a statement signed by one person to the effect that he and the grievant had committed an unlawful act; the statement would have been excluded as hearsay in a court of law. Arbitrator Simkin noted:

> "[T]he Arbitrator has permitted the introduction of some testimony and evidence in these proceedings that probably would not be admissible in court. For these reasons, it is important to note that what may amount to a finding of guilt or absence of guilt by the Arbitrator in a specific incident should not be construed as any indication that a court would make the same findings. Similarly, a 'not guilty' or 'guilty' finding in a court proceeding is not necessarily a compelling reason for the Arbitrator to make the same finding in the instant cases. A court decision is a finding as to whether an individual is guilty or innocent of violation of some particular statute. That is not the issue in these proceedings. The question here is whether there is 'just cause' for discharge or suspension." [59]

Leading text writers are in accord with the foregoing view:

> "At stake is not only the matter of justice to an individual employee, important as that principle is, but also the preservation and development of the collective bargaining relationship. . . . [The arbitrator] can . . . make some contribution to the enduring relationship between the parties by refusing to apply rigid and abstract standards of proof to situations in which they are obviously inapplicable. . . . The case of the employee sleeping on the job, or of the worker accused of punching another man's time card—these and many others are often incapable of proof beyond a reasonable doubt, and the most the arbitrator can say is that, more likely than not, the penalty was justified." [60]

Similarly, another writer argues strongly that proof beyond a reasonable doubt should not be required in even this limited class of cases: "The standard of proof in civil litigation when commission of a crime is directly in issue is proof by a preponderance of the evidence. . . . An employer who could successfully sue an employee for an intentional conversion of the employer's property should probably not be required to retain the individual in his employ merely because a case cannot be proved beyond a reasonable doubt." [61]

---

[57] *Morgan Millwork Co.*, 62-2 ARB ¶ 8557 at 5084 (Seidenberg, 1962). See also *Madison Gas & Electric Company*, 69-1 ARB ¶ 8094 (Slavney, 1969); *Allied Chemical Corp.*, 50 L.A. 616 (Turkus, 1968); *Service Trucking Co.*, 41 L.A. 377 (Turkus, 1963); *Hennis Freight Lines*, 44 L.A. 711 (McGury, 1965); *Sun Drugs Co., Inc.*, 31 L.A. 191 (Marcus, 1958).

[58] 26 L.A. 836 (Simkin, 1956).

[59] *Id.* at 842.

[60] See note 48 *supra*, at 741.

[61] Gorske, note 42 *supra*, at 135, 156.

The minimum quantum of proof acceptable in most arbitration cases may be called a "preponderance of the evidence." Abstractly, this test requires the party bearing the burden of persuasion to convince the tribunal that, more likely than not, its version of the facts is correct. This test has been applied in a great many arbitral contexts, and appears to be the criterion employed in the countless cases wherein burden of proof is never mentioned.

Somewhere between "preponderance of the evidence" and "beyond a reasonable doubt" lies a third evidentiary standard sometimes employed by arbitrators. This may be called the "clear and convincing evidence" rule:

> "It should be clear to all that, in order to decide a factual question such as the one above stated, an Arbitrator must be furnished with something more than protestations and mere assertions of an employee's general ability to work in a plant and that what is necessary in a case of this kind is that there be clear and convincing evidence which relates to the grievant's capacity for the specific job to which he seeks promotion. . . ." [62]

The "clear and convincing evidence" standard appears to find its most frequent application in cases involving some sort of reprehensible conduct on the part of the company, such as discrimination. In *Pan American Petroleum Corp.*,[63] Arbitrator McCoy stated:

> "[A] strong case must be made out before an arbitrator would be justified in attributing the discharge to an alleged motive to discourage union activity."[64]

---

[62] *McLouth Steel Co.*, 11 L.A. 805, 809 (Platt, 1948).

[63] 2 L.A. 541 (McCoy, 1946).

[64] *Id.* at 544. See Gorske, note 42 *supra,* at 148 n. 53, where the author states: "[W]here the union alleges discrimination, or persecution in discipline cases, arbitrators consistently hold that the union bears the burden of proof. Because of the seriousness of the charge, it has been held that proof of discrimination must be 'substantial.' . . ."

CHAPTER XII

Rules of Evidence Generally

Labor arbitrators usually adopt a liberal attitude toward the admission of evidence because they believe that the therapeutic aspect of the arbitration process is enhanced if witnesses are allowed to tell their story freely and without the confusion of technical objections foreclosing part of an employee's testimony. On the whole, arbitrators conclude that the rules of evidence which are applied quite strictly in court cases to keep improper evidence away from a jury need not be applied in arbitration matters because the arbitrator is confident of his own competence to weigh evidence and disregard evidence that would be considered improper if introduced in a jury case.

One guideline useful in the arbitration process is the *Code of Ethics and Procedural Standards for Labor-Management Arbitration,* prepared jointly by the American Arbitration Association and the National Academy of Arbitrators, and approved by the Federal Mediation and Conciliation Service. Section 4(e) of the Code states:

"The arbitrator should allow a fair hearing, with full opportunity to the parties to offer all evidence which they deem reasonably material. He may, however, exclude evidence which is clearly immaterial. He may receive and consider affidavits, giving them such weight as the circumstances warrant, but in so doing, he should afford the other side an opportunity to cross-examine the persons making the affidavits or to to take their depositions or otherwise interrogate them." [1]

Although the Code cautions the arbitrator to allow full opportunity for the parties to offer all evidence which they deem "reasonably material," he may exclude evidence which he deems "immaterial." No other exclusionary rule, other than materiality, is specifically mentioned.

The Voluntary Labor Arbitration Rules of the American Arbitration Association is another well-recognized guideline:

---

[1] *Code of Ethics and Procedural Standards for Labor-Management Arbitration,* Part II, 4(e) at 6 (1962).

"Evidence—The parties may offer such evidence as they desire and shall produce such additional evidence as the Arbitraor may deem necessary to an understanding and determination of the dispute. When the Arbitrator is authorized by law to subpoena witnesses and documents, he may do so upon his own initiative or upon the request of any party. The Arbitrator shall be the judge of the relevancy and materiality of the evidence offered and conformity to legal rules of evidence shall not be necessary. All evidence shall be taken in the presence of all of the Arbitrators and all of the parties except where any of the parties is absent in default or has waived his right to be present." [2]

Courts have held that arbtirators are not bound by the rules of evidence controlling judges in state or federal courts [3] and have rejected attempts to vacate awards on the ground that the arbitrator did not follow court rules concerning the admission or exclusion of evidence.[4] On the other hand, where there has been an exclusion of evidence which has, in the opinion of the reviewing court, denied a party a fair hearing, awards have been set aside. For example, in a case [5] involving misconduct on a picket line the company representative asked a police officer to testify about some rock throwing. The arbitrator refused to hear the testimony asserting that it should have been part of the company's case in chief, but the reviewing court rejected this technical ruling and vacated the award, quoting Arbitrator Benjamin Aaron:

"Despite the generally accepted principle that arbitration procedures are necessarily more informal than those in a court of law, objections to evidence on such grounds that it is hearsay, not the best evidence, or contrary to the parol evidence rule, are still frequently raised in *ad hoc* arbitration. To the extent that these and similar objections are intended to exclude proferred evidence, they generally fail. The arbitrator is interested in gathering all the relevant facts he can, his principal objective is to render a viable decision, and any information that adds to his knowledge of the total situation will almost always be admitted." [6]

---

[2] American Arbitration Association, *Voluntary Labor Arbitration Rules*, Rule 28 (1970).

[3] *Newark Stereotypers' Union No. 18 v. Newark Morning Ledger Co.*, 397 F.2d 594, 599 (3d Cir. 1968), *cert. denied*, 393 U.S. 954 (1968).

[4] *Ficek v. Southern Pac. Co.*, 338 F.2d 655, 657 (9th Cir. 1964), *cert. denied*, 380 U.S. 988 (1965); *Western Oil Fields, Inc. v. Rathbun*, 250 F.2d 69, 71 (10th Cir. 1958).

[5] *Harvey Aluminum, Inc. v. United Steelworkers*, 263 F. Supp. 488 (C.D. Cal. 1967), where the court vacated an award on the ground that the arbitrator's exclusion of certain evidence as cumulative denied a fair hearing to the party presenting the evidence, even though the exclusion would have been proper in a judicial proceeding. The court noted that the arbitrator had not announced, prior to the hearing, that traditional rules of evidence would be followed nor did the parties' agreement to arbitrate specify that legal rules would be followed. See also *Smaglio v. Firemen's Fund Ins. Co.*, 432 Pa. 133, 247 A.2d 577 (1968).

[6] *Harvey Aluminum v. United Steelworkers of America*, 263 F.Supp. at 491, quoting from Aaron, *Some Procedural Problems in Arbitration*, 10 VAND. L. REV. 733, 743-44 (1957).

Because arbitrators are not legally required to admit or exclude evidence,[7] some observers label all such rules "legalisms" which have no place in arbitration. The use of the cliché "legalism" to describe such rules conjures up visions of complicated technical maneuvers, frustrated witnesses, surprise evidence, courtroom stage play, and the like. No one, of course, would seriously advocate that such matters should be introduced into labor arbitration hearings. Certain tested legal principles, however, have been followed by many arbitrators to introduce order, clarity, and simplicity into arbitration proceedings. Hence, rules of evidence should not be condemned merely because these principles have been borrowed from rules used in the courts. The principles behind many such rules are grounded in time-tested experience. Arbitrator Archibald Cox explained:

"When legal principles are invoked in arbitration proceedings it is well not to brush them aside impatiently but to recall, that behind them lies the weight of thought tested by experience. If the policy behind the legal rule holds true, the case should turn upon it. If a policy is unimportant, the legal law may safely be disregarded." [8]

This chapter attempts to catalogue the evidentiary principles which are utilized by arbitrators.

A. "COLLATERAL ESTOPPEL" AS A RULE OF EVIDENCE

"Collateral estoppel" is a doctrine which is as appropriate in arbitration as it is in courts to prevent the introduction of evidence to prove that a determination of the same factual issue in a prior proceeding was incorrect. Lord Kenyon, in his explanation of the legal maxim that "one alleging contrary or contradictory things is not to be heard," said:

"[A] man should not be permitted 'to blow hot and cold' with reference to the same transaction, or insist, at different times, on the truth of each of two conflicting allegations, according to the promptings of his private interest." [9]

---

[7] *Newark Stereotypers' Union No. 18 v. Newark Morning Ledger Co.,* 261 F.Supp. 832 (D.N.J. 1966), *aff'd,* 397 F.2d 594 (3d Cir.), *cert. denied,* 393 U.S. 954 (1968); *Isbrandtsen Tankers, Inc. v. National Marine Engineers' Beneficial Ass'n,* 236 N.Y.S. 2d 808 (Sup.Ct. 1962); FMCS Procedures, 29 CFR § 1404.13 (1971); American Arbitration Ass'n, *Voluntary Labor Arbitration Rules,* Rules 28-30 (1970).

[8] Cox, *The Place of Law in Labor Arbitration,* THE PROFESSION OF LABOR ARBITRATION, Selected Papers From the First Seven Annual Meetings of the National Academy of Arbitrators 86 (J. McKelvey Ed. 1957).

[9] H. Broom, A SELECTION OF LEGAL MAXIMS (2d ed. 1950).

In *Lockheed Aircraft Corp.,*[10] Arbitrator James Willingham applied the principle of "collateral estoppel" to a case where an employee had two garnishment judgments against him and was discharged for violating a plant rule:

"Although the grievant may not in fact have owed the bill, it is an elementary principle of law that a judgment cannot be attacked collaterally. . . ."[11]

In *Wheeling Steel Corp.*[12] Arbitrator Mitchell Shipman stated that he was compelled as a matter of law to accept the findings of the Industrial Commission concerning the physical condition of the grievant:

"Accepting the Industrial Commission's findings and decision that the grievant's disability did not arise out of or in the course of his employment with the Company, which must, from the state of record proof, be done, the Umpire would, were he to find that the grievant continued physically unable to return to work on April 16, 1954, be required to hold that his employee status terminated on said date.

"Examining all of the other evidence in the case, certain parts of it stand out as most persuasive against the grievant's claim. One of them is his workmen's compensation claim application of February 26, 1954, wherein he affirms that as of that date, he continued to have 'a temporary total disability.' It is difficult, indeed, to square these statements of the grievant with his contention that he was, on January 8, 1954, physically able to return to work. . . . [T]he only conclusion that can fairly and properly be reached is that he was not physically able to return to work on each of the dates of his request for reemployment or on April 16, 1954, the end of the one year period of his absence. Such a finding would, on all sound and accepted principles of evidence, be mandatory. . . ."[13]

Arbitrator Lennart Larson, on the other hand, would excuse a grievant if his testimony in the arbitration case is different from what it was in the workmen's compensation case:

"When a claim for permanent disability under a workmen's compensation act is made, the employee is likely to find himself in a position where his interests conflict. He wants to receive all the compensation that he is entitled to, and he states fully his pains and disabilities. At the same time, in most cases, he wants to get back to work as soon as possible. In pursuing this interest he must say that he is able to perform his job. He knows that returning to work is material evidence bearing on the degree of incapacity eventually found.

". . .

---

[10] 28 L.A. 411 (Willingham, 1957).
[11] *Id.* at 413.
[12] 25 L.A. 68 (Shipman, 1955). See also *Odanah Iron Co.,* 24 L.A. 299 (Graff, 1955); *Missouri Water Co.,* 7 ALAA ¶ 69,979 (Beatty, 1955); *Jersey Central Power & Light Co.,* 7 L.A. 560 (Copelof, 1947).
[13] 25 L.A. at 73.

"The Company has argued at length that the doctrine of collateral estoppel defeats Barnett's grievance. The proposition is that Barnett, having obtained a verdict and judgment for 50% permanent partial disability because of injury to his back, is estopped to deny that he is disabled from performing the blacksmith helper's job. . . .

"   . . .

"The Arbitrator appreciates fully the merits and policy behind the doctrine of collateral estoppel. But the doctrine cannot be held to operate in the present proceeding. The lawsuit and the arbitration hearing dealt with different fact issues. In the lawsuit the issue was the degree to which Barnett had suffered depreciation in his earning capacity. In the arbitration proceeding the question was whether Barnett could do his job as blacksmith helper in a satisfactory manner without unreasonable risk to his well being and safety." [14]

B. ADMISSION OF HEARSAY EVIDENCE

"Hearsay evidence," as classically defined, is the report of a statement (written or oral) made by a person who is not a witness in the proceeding and introduced to prove the truth of what is asserted.[15]

The hearsay evidence rule is not an absolute rule even in courts and exceptions are made if there are special circumstances surrounding a particular declaration which render the statements more reliable. One example of an exception is testimony which was given under oath at a prior proceeding where the parties and issues were the same. The assumption here is that the opposing party already had the opportunity to cross-examine. Admissions of an individual or a representative (assuming he is a party to the suit in the same capacity) are admissible on the theory that it would be incongruous for a party to challenge the truthfulness of his own declaration.[16] Business records and oral reports that are made to a superior in the regular course of business are regarded as reliable on the theory that the need for regularity in the business will act as a check on their accuracy.[17]

Labor arbitrators are not constrained by the same strict rules of evidence that are followed by the courts and they seldom reject any evidence that is relevant to a material issue in the case.[18] The receipt

---

[14] *General American Transportation Corp.* (Larson, 1957) (unpublished). But see *Sinclair Refining Co.* (Hebert, 1957) (unpublished); *Great Atlantic & Pacific Tea Co.*, 6 ALAA ¶ 69,810 at 74,480 (Baskind, 1955).

[15] J. Wigmore, Evidence § 1361 (3d ed. 1940).

[16] Courts and arbitrators generally refuse to receive evidence of compromise offers, which are clearly admissions, for a purely policy reason: The parties should not be discouraged from attempting to settle. F. Elkouri & E. Elkouri, How Arbitration Works 195-96 (1961). This exception to the hearsay rule is frequently confused with the exception related to out-of-court declarations of a nonparty witness against the interest of the witness. See also note 15 *supra*, at 1455-57. *Cf. General Motors Corp.*, 2 L.A. 491, 503 (Hotchkiss, 1938).

[17] See note 15 *supra*, at 1370-71, 1386-89.

[18] Shulman, *Reason, Contract and Law in Labor Relations*, 68 Harv. L. Rev. 999, 1017 (1955).

of hearsay evidence may be necessary for the arbitrator to get a full understanding of the facts in issue.[19]

Some disagreement exists over the extent to which hearsay evidence, inadmissible in courts, should be admitted in labor arbitration. The *New York Tripartite Committee Report* stated:

> "a. Any evidence qualifying in courts of law as an exception to the hearsay rule should be admissible in arbitration.
>
> "b. In addition, hearsay may be admitted by the arbitrator, at his discretion, if there are persuasive reasons for not requiring the presence of persons quoted and if there is reasonable ground to believe that the statement quoted is trustworthy and if the evidence is of a nature that can be readily refuted if contested.
>
> "(Some members would state instead: 'In addition, hearsay may be admitted by the arbitrator, at his discretion, in exceptional cases, if there is powerful reason for not requiring the presence of the person quoted, and if there is reason to believe that the statement quoted is trustworthy.')" [20]

The informality and speed of the arbitration process would suffer if the introduction of hearsay evidence were limited as tightly as it is in a court. Longer periods of preparation would be required; more witnesses would be needed; and lawyers who are familiar with the hearsay rules would be needed to prepare and present arbitration cases.

Though the rules of evidence should concededly be applied more liberally in arbitration cases, reasonable limits should be imposed on the use of hearsay evidence in order that the opposing party may have an adequate opportunity to rebut statements made in the absence of direct testimony:

> "[A] practice which deserves some comment is the acceptance of evidence by the arbitrator, 'for what it is worth.' When evidence is accepted 'for what it is worth,' it adds incalculable components. The opposing counsel, not knowing what worth the arbitrator will put upon the evidence, is compelled to explore every ramification of the testimony. In reply, the other similarly must counter the opposing evidence and argument. It frequently imposes an unproductive exercise for both parties. It may mean that the hearings are unnecessarily extended. It is suggested that this acceptance of proof 'for what it is worth' be avoided." [21]

---

[19] See *Fenwick Fashion, Inc.,* 42 L.A. 582 (Elbert, undated). See also *United Instrument Workers Local 116 v. Minneapolis-Honeywell Regulator Co.,* — F.Supp. —, 54 LRRM 2660 (E.D. Pa. 1963).

[20] New York Tripartite Committee, *Problems of Proof in the Arbitration Process,* PROBLEMS OF PROOF IN ARBITRATION, Proceedings of the Nineteenth Annual Meeting, National Academy of Arbitrators 297-98 (D. Jones Ed. 1967).

[21] Roberts, *Precedent and Procedure in Arbitration Cases,* PROCEEDINGS OF NEW YORK UNIVERSITY SIXTH ANNUAL CONFERENCE ON LABOR 149, 156 (E. Stein Ed. 1953).

Arbitrators Clarence Updegraff and Whitley McCoy take a different view of this problem:

"[T]he usual practice, where the evidence sought to be elicited is clearly hearsay, is to rule that it will be admitted 'for what it is worth.' Such ruling usually satisfies both parties: It satisfies the offerer of the testimony because he is getting the evidence in; it satisfies the objector because of the clear implication that the arbitrator knows the worthlessness, in most instances of pure hearsay." [22]

Arbitrator Aaron has drawn some general boundaries to the phrase "for what it's worth":

"[A] competent arbitrator may be depended upon substantially to discount some kinds of hearsay evidence that he has admitted over objection. He will do so selectively, however, and not on the assumption that hearsay evidence, as such, is not to be credited. If, for example, a newly appointed personnel manager, or a recently elected business agent, offers a letter to his predecessor from a third party, the arbitrator is likely to ignore the fact that the evidence is hearsay; if satisfied that the document is genuine, he will give it such weight as its relevancy dictates. On the other hand, hearsay testimony about statements allegedly made by 'the boys in the shop' or by executives in the 'front office,' though perhaps not excluded from the record by the arbitrator, probably will have no effect on his decision." [23]

Arbitrators, while accepting hearsay testimony, often wonder why better evidence is not brought forward, and when an arbitrator finds the hearsay evidence unpersuasive, he should advise the parties and ask for better evidence. In *General Tire & Rubber Co.,*[24] Arbitrator Donald Crawford noted:

"The Company relies on [A.'s] account of what [T.] said to the State Police when they interviewed the grievant and [T.]. The Union objected strenuously to the introduction of this hearsay testimony. The important point in arbitration is not whether the hearsay is admitted but its criticalness and what, if any, weight is given to it. (The parties are entitled to know the arbitrator's weighing of the hearsay.) In this case the hearsay could have been critical to the decision because its purpose was to establish the grievant's intent to participate in a theft. The Company was therefore asked to get the direct evidence." [25]

Affidavits of individuals not attending the hearing and hence not subject to cross-examination are sometimes introduced as evidence in arbitrations and are often admitted subject to the same limitations

[22] C. Updegraff & W. McCoy, ARBITRATION OF LABOR DISPUTES 193 (2d ed. 1961) [hereinafter cited as Updegraff & McCoy]. See also American Arbitration Association, A MANUAL FOR COMMERCIAL ARBITRATORS 15 (1964); Aaron, *Some Procedural Problems in Arbitration,* 10 VAND. L. REV. 733 (1957).

[23] Aaron, note 22 *supra,* at 733, 744.

[24] 68-1 ARB ¶ 8186 (Crawford, 1968).

[25] *Id.* at 3649.

that apply to all hearsay evidence.[26] In disciplinary cases, however, arbitrators often rule that affidavits are inadmissible because they deprive one of the parties of his right to cross-examination in a situation where careful evaluation of evidence is important.[27] At least one arbitrator has held that an affidavit of a nonwitness could be introduced to corroborate other evidence that was subject to cross-examination, but was inadmissible if it produced new evidence not testified to by other witnesses.[28]

Medical evidence is often presented in the form of affidavits or certificates. Full weight, in the absence of contradictory evidence is often given to such evidence.[29] Where, however, the medical condition of the grievant is the central point of the case, less weight should be given to an affidavit than to the testimony of a doctor who is exposed to cross-examination.

C. RULES CONCERNING THE CREDIBILITY OF EVIDENCE

In disciplinary cases, many arbitrators have recognized the fact that, as between employees—whose interests or those of their fellows are intimately involved in the arbitration—and a managerial representative, there is a presumption in favor of the latter's credibility which does not exist with respect to the former. Arbitrator William Dolson explained the underlying reasons for this presumption:

> "With respect to the problem where it is the supervisor's word against the grievant's, Arbitrator Harry Shulman at Ford Motor Co., laid down the following rule followed by many arbitrators:
> " '[A]n accused employee is presumed to have an incentive for not telling the truth and that when his testimony is contradicted by one who has nothing to gain or lose, the latter is to be believed.' " [30]

Similarly, Arbitrator Earl Miller held:

> "It was not probable that Foreman [M.] would have made up this story out of whole cloth and promptly reported it to Superintendent [X.]. The normal policy of a young foreman is to avoid antagonizing the men under him. Concocting such a lie against a Union member would be the worst way to achieve his own success. Furthermore, there was no back-

---

[26] See, *e.g., Borden Co.*, 20 L.A. 483 (Rubin, 1953); Updegraff & McCoy, note 22 *supra*, at 193, 200.

[27] *Quaker State Oil Refining Corp.*, 68-1 ARB ¶ 8313 (Wood, 1968); *Jessop Steel Co.*, 68-1 ARB ¶ 8004 (Wood, 1967); *Ward Baking Co.*, 33 L.A. 791 (Marcus, 1959).

[28] *Milgram Food Stores, Inc.*, 68-2 ARB ¶ 8622 (Murphy, 1968).

[29] *White Motor Co.*, 28 L.A. 823 (Lazarus, 1957); *Southern Cotton Oil Co.*, 26 L.A. 353 (Kelliher, 1956).

[30] *United Parcel Service, Inc.*, 66-2 ARB ¶ 8703 at 5432 (Dolson, 1966), quoting L. Stessin, EMPLOYEE DISCIPLINE 44 (1960), paraphrasing the rule in *Ford Motor Co.*, 1 ALAA ¶ 67,274 (Shulman, 1945).

ground of trouble between Foreman [M.] and the grievant, which would have established a motive for such action." [31]

Arbitrator Robert Mueller also recognized the validity of this presumption:

"Another criterion employed to a large extent by arbitrators, is to assess the motives to be served by the respective witnesses. The following example illustrates the general application of this criterion in a discharge case: G, the grievant, testifies that fact X did not exist. F, the foreman, testifies contra that fact X did exist. Solely on these facts, the testimony of grievant would not be afforded as much credibility as the foreman's testimony because the grievant would be more likely to perjure himself to save his job. Grievant has more at stake and therefore the motive is greater. The foreman, on the other hand, *prima facie,* has no motive to testify one way or the other, and presumably would not be inclined to perjure himself. If a strong motive can be shown on the part of the foreman or that the foreman harbors ill-will or malice toward the grievant, the findings more often will be for the grievant." [32]

Arbitrator Arthur Ross said in *Pacific Gas & Electric Co.:*[33]

"Considerable weight should be given to bona fide conclusions of supervisors when supported by factual evidence. In the first place, a supervisor is responsible for the efficient performance of his unit and has a legitimate concern that employees be properly assigned to achieve this objective. In the second place, he has a deeper and more intimate acquaintance with the men under his charge than an arbitrator is able to acquire in a brief hearing." [34]

Accordingly, arbitrators generally require that a union corroborate its interested witnesses' testimony when it is in conflict with the testimony of managerial witnesses.[35]

D. PRESUMPTIONS AND INFERENCES

(1) Knowledge of Rules, Practices and Policies

Often a critical facet of the management's *prima facie* case in a disciplinary proceeding is proof that the employee had knowledge of the rule he allegedly violated. Generally, however, arbitrators indulge in an evidentiary presumption of knowledge if the rule violated is one

---

[31] *Cadillac Gage Co.,* 66-3 ARB ¶ 8969 at 6381 (Miller, 1966).

[32] *Western Condensing Co.,* 37 L.A. 912, 914 (Mueller, 1962). See also *Jones & Laughlin Steel Corp.,* 8 Steel Arb. 5885, 5886 (Alexander, 1960); *Firestone Tire & Rubber Co.,* 33 L.A. 206 (McCoy, 1959); *Pennsylvania Greyhound Lines, Inc.,* 19 L.A. 210, 211 (Seward, 1952).

[33] 23 L.A. 556 (Ross, 1954).

[34] *Id.* at 558. See also *Hercules Powder Co.,* 10 L.A. 624, 625 (Reynolds, 1948).

[35] *Active Products Co.,* 68-1 ARB ¶ 8103 (May, 1967); *American Smelting & Refining Co.,* 67-2 ARB ¶ 8409 (Leonard, 1967).

of common knowledge or the rules have been distributed. Thus, Arbitrator Milton Schmidt noted:

"It is implicit in the employer-employee relationship that an employee must conform to certain well known, commonly accepted, standards of reasonable discipline and proper conduct while engaged in his work. . . . Among these obligations are the duty to perform his work as directed and to remain in his work station instead of wandering around . . . the duty to explain his absence from his work station for an unreasonably long period of time upon inquiry from a management representative, the duty to refrain from the use of foul abusive and profane language, particularly directed toward supervisory personnel. . . .

"Published rules and regulations are not necessary to inform an employee that misconduct of the nature above described may subject him to discharge from the company's employ. Every employee . . . is presumed to know that the [business] cannot operate without a reasonable measure of discipline. . . ." [36]

As to the effect of published rules and regulations, Arbitrator Robert Howlett has held:

"[I]n the arbitrator's opinion a conscious remembering of a rule at the time an act is taken is not necessary in order that a discharge may be for proper cause. If such were the rule every discharge could be reversed by the testimony of a grievant (necessarily a subjective test) that he did not remember the rule which he was violating at the time he did so. The test with respect to a rule clearly communicated to employees must, of necessity, be determined by objective evidence. Unless strong reason is shown, every employee should be charged with knowledge of rules clearly communicated, whether he actually remembers them or not." [37]

And Arbitrator Donald Lee commented on the effect of prior warnings:

"The written warnings placed both the grievant and the Union on notice that drastic action might follow. No appeal was taken from these notices; consequently, the Employer could rightfully assume that the grievant and the Union were fully aware of the situation." [38]

Similarly, as to provisions of the collective bargaining agreement, Arbitrator Vernon Stouffer noted:

"If any education regarding the contents of the Agreement is necessary, that is the duty of the Union, which is recognized and acts as the Bargaining Agent for all unit employees. Ignorance of provisions of the Agreement is not an acceptable reason or excuse for not calling to report absences." [39]

---

[36] *Ross Gear & Tool Co.*, 35 L.A. 293, 295-96 (Schmidt, 1960).

[37] *Valley Steel Casting Co.*, 22 L.A. 520, 527 (Howlett, 1954).

[38] *Badger Concrete Co.*, 64-3 ARB ¶ 9145 at 6962 (Lee, 1964).

[39] *A. O. Smith Corp.*, 66-3 ARB ¶ 8848 at 5937 (Stouffer, 1966).

Finally, as to past practices and policies, Arbitrator Sam Tatum held:

"[The Company] has consistently since 1947 refused to permit a leave for this purpose, and it has only permitted one who had gone out for maternity reasons to return as a new employee. To this the Union has acquiesced until the filing of this grievance. The argument by the Union [stated] that it did not know of the practice of the Company because such had not been communicated to it by the members. It must be concluded that the employees through the years have known of the policy of the Company and the knowledge of the employee must be the knowledge of the Union; and, too, in the plant the Union has its officials or committeemen who are in daily contact with the employees. Therefore, through the years the committeemen must have known of the position of the Company. The knowledge of the committeemen must be the knowledge of the Union." [40]

(2) Presumptions to Establish Responsibility for a Contract Violation Strike

Arbitrators, following the lead of Judge Goldsborough in *United States v. United Mine Workers*,[41] have used a presumption in lieu of evidence to determine the leadership of and responsibility for a strike in violation of a no-strike pledge. For example, in *General American Transportation Corp.*,[42] Arbitrator Harry Pollock wrote:

"It is generally safe to say that members of unions do not act in concert without leadership. This rule is proven by experience. Since this

---

[40] *Chattanooga Box & Lumber Co.*, 44 L.A. 373, 376 (Tatum, 1965). See also *Bell Aircraft Corp.*, 9 L.A. 65, 66 (Jaffee, 1947):
"[I]n a matter so open and so universal as vacation pay, at least the Union's leadership is charged with knowledge of how the contract is being administered." But see *Olson v. Mall Tool Co.*, 346 Ill. App. 9, 104 N.E.2d 665 (1952) where it was held that a rule disqualifying an employee for vacation pay for quitting immediately after a vacation and before receiving her pay was not binding on the employee unless there was evidence that the employee had read the rule booklet or had been instructed to do so.

[41] 77 F. Supp. 563, 566-67 (D.D.C. 1948), *aff'd*, 177 F.2d 29 (D.C. Cir.), *cert. denied*, 338 U.S. 871 (1949):
"The Court thinks the principle is this: that as long as a union is functioning as a union it must be held responsible for the mass action of its members. It is perfectly obvious not only in objective reasoning but because of experience that men don't act collectively without leadership. The idea of suggesting that from 350,000 to 450,000 men would all get the same idea at once, independently of leadership, and walk out of the mines, is of course simply ridiculous."
". . . So that, in general, this Court announces a principle of law. The Court has no means of knowing whether higher courts will adopt the principle or not, but the Court has no doubt about its soundness, not any—that a union that is functioning must be held responsible for the mass action of its members."
See also *United Textile Workers v. Newberry Mills, Inc.*, 238 F.Supp. 366, 373 (W.D.S.C. 1965); *Operating Engineers, Local 926*, 196 NLRB No. 103 (1972). A concerted refusal to work overtime when it had been regularly scheduled and worked is presumptively strike action. *Elevator Mfr's Assn. v. Elevator Constructors*, 342 F.Supp 372, 80 LRRM 2165 (1972).

[42] 42 L.A. 142 (Pollock, 1964).

local was functioning and there was apparently no schism, the union leadership must be held responsible for the acts of its members." [43]

In *Mueller Brass Co.*,[44] Arbitrator David Wolff upheld discipline imposed upon the union officials who participated in an unauthorized strike, stating:

"The fact that all those who participated in the lines were not punished is understandable. From all the testimony, it appears to the arbitrator that the company disciplined only those persons . . . who were union officials. Such action on its part was not discriminatory. It had a right to assume that, when union officials participated in unauthorized activities, they were acting as leaders." [45]

(3) Presumption That the Facts Reported in Unchallenged Prior Disciplinary Warnings Are Correct

Arbitrator McCoy advised the parties during an arbitration hearing that he would employ a presumption that the facts stated in warning notices previously given the employee were correct to prevent a hearing on a discharge case from becoming a hearing on the merits of prior disciplinary warnings:

"Some companies have a system of personnel reports on employees that go into their personnel file. For example, if a man does a negligent piece of work, for which he ought to receive a warning, do you make out a slip, and give him a copy, and send a copy to the labor relations office?

"I have ruled in other arbitrations that where a company does have that system they cannot bring into evidence any previous offenses to help justify a subsequent disciplinary layoff or discharge unless a written record was made of the previous offense.

"In addition, if under such a system a man has a chance to file a grievance to take such a reprimand off his record then the employee cannot claim that he did not engage in the conduct reported in the reprimand warning, unless he has filed such a grievance. In other words, if a man deserves a warning and is given it and is given a slip reporting the offense and doesn't protest it with a grievance, then at a subsequent hearing it must be taken as an admitted offense. In such a case, there is no need for testimony about the prior incident. . . .

"This is the only way that I can see to keep a hearing concerning a discipline or discharge case from becoming a hearing about a thousand incidents." [46]

---

[43] *Id.* at 143-44.

[44] 3 L.A. 285 (Wolf, 1946). See also *Trane Co.*, 71-1 ARB ¶ 8089 (Turkus, 1971).

[45] 3 L.A. at 285-86.

[46] Quoted in *Lectures on the Law and Labor Management Relations*, MICHIGAN UNIV. LAW SCHOOL, SUMMER INSTITUTE FOR INTERNATIONAL AND COMPARATIVE LAW 216-17 (1951).

(4) Presumption That Expert Medical Opinion Is Correct

Medical testimony which is not arbitrary or unreasonable and is given in good faith has been presumed to be correct by arbitrators. For example, in *Great Lakes Spring Corp.,*[47] the company refused to reemploy an employee who had suffered a heart attack as a result of lifting a heavy object in the plant and who was awarded compensation on the basis of total permanent disability. Arbitrator Charles Gregory considered the determination not to reemploy was a valid one when it was shown that the company acted on advice of its doctor, who had extensive knowledge of the nature of the work in the plant and whose judgment could not be shown to be arbitrary, unreasonable, or given in bad faith. In this regard, the arbitrator stated:

"Certainly an employer could hardly be said to be unreasonable or arbitrary following the advice of a physician whom it retains permanently to pass on matters of the sort involved here, especially when that physician, through years of familiarity with the plant's problems and available jobs, has acquired a fairly thorough working knowledge of what jobs are available and of the nature of such jobs. The only possible attack on the Company's position is that the doctor in question is himself arbitrary or unreasonable or is acting in bad faith. Concerning these possibilities, however, there is no evidence in the record." [48]

In *International Shoe Co.,*[49] Arbitrator Saul Wallen said:

"The proper use of this power will be evident if the facts in a particular case show that management's action was taken in good faith, was based on reasonably adequate medical testimony and evidence, and was not taken against a background that would indicate a discriminatory purpose. If these facts exist, there is a presumption of validity that favors the plant physician's medical testimony. This presumption arises out of the fact that the plant physician has a knowledge of both the employee's health and the job conditions. On the other hand, if in a given case there is evidence that management's good faith is lacking, that its physician's conclusions are not well supported by the medical findings, or that there are circumstances surrounding the case tending to support a claim of discrimination, then there would be grounds to set management's action aside or at least cause the case to be submitted to impartial medical inquiry." [50]

In a slightly different situation, Arbitrator Maurice Merrill held that a company could rely on the opinion of its own doctors even though contrary medical evidence was presented by the grievant. The employer had discharged an employee because his physical condition resulting from a brain tumor operation was such as to endanger

---

[47] 11 L.A. 159 (Gregory, 1948).
[48] *Id.* at 160.
[49] 14 L.A. 253 (Wallen, 1950).
[50] *Id.* at 255.

himself and others. Holding that the company was entitled to rely upon the opinions of its own medical advisors so long as they were reasonable, he held:

> "In view of the direct conflict in the medical testimony, with nothing to swing the balance preponderantly on one side or the other, I think that the Company is entitled to rely on the views of its own medical advisers, if it has given Mr. Stone fair notice and opportunity to overcome those views before reaching a final decision. . . . I think that the Company has shown 'good and legitimate reasons' for refusing to re-employ Mr. Stone in the absence of available light work, provided it has observed the due process required by the contract in the separation procedure." [51]

(5) Presumptions That Writings Which Are Delivered Are Authorized, and if Mailed Are Received

Arbitrators Arthur Stack and Robert Feinberg report that the following presumptions are most useful in labor arbitration:

> "Any writing of the company or the union which is published or delivered by an official or authorized representative of the company or union shall be presumed to have been authorized.
> "Any writing which is published or delivered by an official or authorized representative of any other organization or third party shall similarly be presumed to have been authorized.
> "When it can be shown that a letter has been mailed by U.S. mail, it shall be presumed to have been received." [52]

E. EXPERT TESTIMONY

The function of expert testimony in contested proceedings is to assist the trier of fact to draw proper inferences from the proven facts which the trier might be incompetent to draw himself. Arbitrators appreciate expert testimony presented by one or the other party and will sometimes on their own motion call in specialists to resolve disputed technical questions.[53] The arbitrator, however, should not seek expert advice without informing the parties. The Chicago Tripartite Committee said:

> "The committee was of the opinion that it is improper for an arbitrator to seek expert advice without informing the parties. There are situations, however, where the arbitrator may suggest the use of an expert when the parties' experts are in conflict. This is particularly true in cases

---

[51] *Ideal Cement Co.,* 20 L.A. 480, 482 (Merrill, 1953).

[52] See note 20 *supra,* at 295, 297.

[53] *Chrysler Corp.,* 21 L.A. 573, 577 (Wolff, 1953) (engineer consulted to determine whether employer had control over power failure); *Container Co.,* 6 L.A. 218, 219-20 (Whiting, 1946) (incentive rates and an impartial study of plant operations by technical commissioners).

involving incentives or job evaluations. He should not, however, use such an expert without the consent of the parties, and should permit the parties to have access to whatever opinion is offered by the expert selected by him and to comment on the opinion before reaching his decision." [54]

Occasionally, after examination of witnesses, the necessary conclusions from the facts may be difficult to make. Most frequently, this situation arises when expert opinion should have been provided. In such cases, with the agreement of the parties, an arbitrator may himself obtain the needed expert. When this rare procedure is followed, the expert's testimony or report should be presented to the parties with an opportunity for rebuttal given, before the award is rendered. [55]

It is not necessary to qualify as expert in labor arbitration to the same extent required in a court proceeding. The Pittsburgh Tripartite Committee said:

> "The function of a witness is to relate what he has seen and heard, not to draw inferences from these observations or from other facts. This rule does not apply to the 'expert.' The 'expert' is allowed to draw inferences and conclusions because, in theory, his knowledge is superior to that of the person having to resolve the issue, be it judge, jury, or arbitrator.
>
> "Example #8—'Company Attorney: We will present Mr. Jones, a qualified Industrial Engineer, to testify as to the proper classification and rate for this job.'
>
> "*Ruling:* Clearly admissible evidence. One cornerstone of labor arbitration is the supposed expert knowledge of the arbitrator himself concerning the issues in dispute. Hence, the value of expert witnesses correspondingly diminishes, and the probability of substantial error involving misplaced reliance on expert testimony is minimized. This logic does not apply where the expert is discussing medical or other non-industrial specialties.
>
> "Experts frequently are presented in cases involving job evaluation, incentive, and medical matters. Once the competence of the witness is established, there remain few valid objections to his testimony. If an arbitrator is not strong in this area of knowledge, he should question the witness for his own benefit." [56]

The Chicago Tripartite Committee said:

> "Expert testimony should, of course, be received. There was general agreement that the strict court rules for establishing the qualifications of

---

[54] Chicago Tripartite Committee, *Problems of Proof in the Arbitration Process,* Problems of Proof in Arbitration, Proceedings of the Nineteenth Annual Meeting, National Academy of Arbitrators 86, 108 (D. Jones Ed. 1967).

[55] See Kagel, *Labor and Commercial Arbitration Under the California Arbitration Statute,* 38 Calif. L. Rev. 799, 823 (1950).

[56] Pittsburgh Tripartite Committee, *Problems of Proof in the Arbitration Process,* Problems of Proof in Arbitration, Proceedings of the Nineteenth Annual Meeting, National Academy of Arbitrators 245, 253 (D. Jones Ed. 1967).

the expert need not be insisted upon, although, as a practical matter, most parties offering an expert witness will take pains to lay a detailed foundation for claiming that he is an expert. In weighing the testimony of an expert, attention should be given especially to the opportunity of the expert to have access to data which would give him a basis for expressing an opinion. Obviously an expert who testifies on the basis of what someone else has told him, in other words, on the basis of hearsay and not personal knowledge, is not entitled to have as much weight given to his testimony. Again primary reliance must be placed by the arbitrator on cross examination." [57]

In labor arbitration proceedings, since it is the arbitrator himself who is chosen for his expertise in construing labor agreements, expert evidence concerning the construction of the agreement would be out of place. The Chicago Tripartite Committee said:

"There is one area in which an arbitrator can justifiably refuse to receive opinion evidence. It occurs where the issue before the arbitrator is one of interpretation of an agreement and the opinion evidence offered goes to the witness' opinion as to what the contract means. But here again little harm will result from receiving the evidence. The arbitrator is not bound to give it any weight." [58]

F. DEMONSTRATIVE AND DOCUMENTARY EVIDENCE

The problems that arise when documentary evidence is offered usually involve the "best evidence" rule and authentication. The "best evidence" rule in this context is sometimes called the "original document" rule and is the requirement that the original document rather than a copy of it should be the evidence submitted.[59] McCormick in his treatise on evidence has stated the rule as follows:

"[I]n proving the terms of a writing, where such terms are material, the original writing must be produced, unless it is shown to be unavailable for some reason other than the serious fault of the proponent." [60]

Behind every rule of evidence there is some reason justifying its existence. McCormick lists the three reasons basic to the original document rule:

"(1) that precision in presenting . . . the exact words of the writing is of more than average importance, particularly as respect operative . . . instruments, such as . . . contracts, since a slight variation in words mean a great difference in rights, (2) that there is a substantial hazard of inaccuracy in the human process of making a copy by handwriting or

---

[57] See note 54 *supra,* at 86, 94-95.
[58] *Id.* at 94.
[59] 4 J. Wigmore, Evidence § 1232 (3d ed. 1940); 2 B. Jones, Evidence § 560 (5th ed. S.Gard 1958).
[60] C. McCormick, Evidence § 196 (1954).

typewriting, and (3) as respects oral testimony purporting to give from memory the terms of a writing, there is a special risk of error, greater than in the case of attempts at describing other situations generally." [61]

The application of the rule in labor arbitration was stated as follows:

"Where objection is made to the introduction of evidence of a secondary nature on the ground that it is not the best evidence, the original document should be produced unless it is shown, for reasons satisfactory to the arbitrator, that it is not available. Reproductions of original documents shall be deemed the best evidence unless the authenticity of the purported original documents is significantly in question." [62]

The reasons that justify the introduction of secondary evidence in court hearings apply with equal validity in arbitrations. The reasons include:

"[L]oss, destruction, refusal to produce the original by an opponent, detention by a third person who will not surrender possession, physical or legal impossibility of removing the original, as for example, a notice which is pasted on a wall, the inconvenience of removing business records that are in constant use and may not be conveniently removed and voluminous documents the production of which would be wasteful time. Recollection testimony should be permitted where neither the original nor a copy is available if this testimony can give the substance of the document." [63]

The Pittsburgh Tripartite Committee made these comments about "best evidence" in labor arbitration:

"This rule, invented to prevent error, requires submission of the most authoritative source for the information sought to be introduced. Two phases are illustrated below:
"Example #5—'Witness: The written agreement reached by the parties provides that double time is to be paid for all hours over eight (8) in a work day.'
"*Ruling:* Since the testimony concerns a written instrument and its contents, the evidence should not be admitted by oral testimony unless the written instrument cannot be obtained because of its destruction, etc.
"Example #6—'Attorney: I offer into evidence this carbon copy of the agreement reached by the parties in connection with overtime rate.'
"*Ruling:* All carbon copies are really 'duplicate originals.' The mere fact that the original document is not introduced should not bar admission of the copy unless one of the parties expressly challenges the accuracy or correctness of the copy." [64]

The New York Tripartite Committee agreed that secondary evidence should be considered valid when it has been established that the

---

[61] *Id.* at § 197.
[62] See note 20 *supra,* at 299-300. See also Updegraff & McCoy, note 22 *supra,* at 167-69.
[63] See note 54 *supra,* at 92.
[64] See note 56 *supra,* at 252. See also for less restrictive view, note 54 *supra,* at 92.

original evidence cannot reasonably be presented at the arbitration proceeding.[65]

When documentary evidence is submitted, each document should be properly identified as to its source and authenticated.[66] Business records receive special considerations in courts. McCormick states:

> "It is generally held that business records may be authenticated by the evidence of one familiar with the books of the concern, such as a custodian or supervisor, who has not made the record or seen it made, that the offered writing is actually part of the records of the business." [67]

And this rule is particularly important in labor arbitration. It permits, for example, a supervisor in the payroll department to verify an employee's incentive production record even though he did not actually compile the record.

Some arbitration awards have distinguished between formal and informal business records. Both are generally admissible, but, in recognition of the accuracy of original business records, greater weight may be given to data taken from such business records than from informal records or estimates.[68] In this connection, it is of interest that evidence accumulated on a computer was admitted to prove that a grievant had falsified production reports.[69]

Demonstrative evidence consists of tangible things, such as machines, tools, finished products, models, blueprints, and photographs, submitted to the arbitrator to enable him to more easily understand the testimony of the witnesses. For example, in a job evaluation dispute, the arbitrator was furnished photographs of employees operating their machines.[70] The rules which regulate the use of such evidence in court hearings are applicable in labor arbitration.[71] Accordingly:

> "[T]he demonstrative evidence must first be authenticated by testimony of a witness who testifies to facts showing that the object has some connection with the case which makes it relevant." [72]

Thus, if a company desires to show that a particular product is constructed in a certain manner, it may introduce into evidence a blueprint of the item, and place the foreman in charge of producing this item on the stand for the purpose of identifying the blueprint.

---

[65] See note 20 *supra*, at 299-300.
[66] See note 60 *supra*, §§ 185-95.
[67] *Id.*, § 187.
[68] *Jonco Aircraft Corp.*, 22 L.A. 819, 823 (Merrill, 1954).
[69] *American Chain & Cable Co.*, 68-2 ARB ¶ 8374 (Fitzgerald, 1968).
[70] *Brown & Sharpe Mfg. Co.*, 21 L.A. 461, 463-70 (Waite, 1953). See also *Westinghouse Elec. Corp.*, 26 L.A. 836, 842 (Simkin, 1956).
[71] H. J. Wigmore, EVIDENCE §§ 1150-69 (3d ed. 1940).
[72] See note 60 *supra*, § 179.

G. INSPECTION BY THE ARBITRATOR

Another form of demonstrative evidence consists of visits to the plant by the arbitrator.[73] The values of such visits were explained by Arbitrator William Simkin:

"The eye is better than the ear in many aspects of disputes, or at least is a valuable supplement to oral or written evidence. A plant visit is a simple device by which the arbitrator can secure a better understanding of the background of a case. In some instances a plant visit either before or during the hearing will serve to avoid voluminous testimony. The award may be more realistic and therefore acceptable because the plant visit fills part of the gap in the arbitrator's knowledge." [74]

In certain relationships, such visits to obtain familiarity with the setting where the problem which caused the grievance arose, are commonplace. When an arbitrator makes an inspection he is visually exposed to evidence which does not find its way into the record of the proceeding, and when he is accompanied by a representative of one of the parties or even both, he is often given lengthy explanations during his inspection which are in the nature of arguments. The following report contrasts views concerning the propriety of such inspections:

"[T]here is a general, and often incorrect, assumption by the parties that an arbitrator is familiar with the industry in which the case arose and the particular operations involved in particular. Insistence upon a general tour of the employer's operation by the arbitrator, accompanied by a representative of each party, with special attention given to the immediate area involved in the grievance, might prove valuable. It is possible that such a tour would reduce costs by eliminating certain testimony which might otherwise be essential to the arbitrator's grasp of the situation.
  ". . .
"[There is a question] of visual inspection of the premises or the subject of the dispute. In most instances where inspections are requested, arbitrators do invest the time and effort to comply with the requests of either party. However, in a recent arbitration, the arbitrator upon company objection declined such inspection. In that proceeding, an inspection would have avoided the necessity of any formal hearings and the production of witnesses, documents, etc. I believe that where inspection is requested, it should be mandatory on the part of the arbitrator and the parties to inspect the premises in the presence of the parties unless the request is frivolous." [75]

While inspection of the premises may be considered important by

---

[73] *Brown & Sharpe Mfg. Co.*, 21 L.A. 461, 463 (Waite, 1953).

[74] W. Simkin, Acceptability as a Factor in Arbitration Under an Existing Agreement 24 (1952).

[75] Committee on Labor Arbitration, *Report*, 1963 Proceedings, Section of Labor Relations Law, American Bar Association, Part II, 190-91 (1964).

one or the other party, a refusal to make an inspection is not grounds for setting aside an arbitrator's award. The discretion of the individual arbitrator in this regard is protected by the courts even if the particular arbitrator had previously agreed to make inspections.[76]

H. JUDICIAL NOTICE

Arbitrators as well as courts take judicial notice of facts widely known or capable of irrefutable proof, such as dates, addresses, and statutes, as a means of expediting the proceeding. The use of judicial notice in labor arbitration was described by the New York Tripartite Committee:

"1. Arbitrators should take judicial notice of any facts or law which the courts of law would generally notice. (These would include: (a) specific facts so notorious as not to be the subject of reasonable dispute; and (b) specific facts and propositions of generalized knowledge which are capable of immediate and accurate demonstration by resort to easily accessible sources of indisputable accuracy.)

"2. Considerations of fairness would seem to require that: (a) the parties notify the arbitrator and each other of facts concerning which they desire the arbitrator to take notice; or (b) in the absence of such notification, the arbitrator advise the parties of facts concerning which he will take notice." [77]

In arbitration proceedings, however, some arbitrators go beyond such limited use of judicial notice and include certain propositions, particularly industrial practices, as matters that can be assumed to be true. For example, in *Duluth Restaurants*,[78] the arbitrator said that he took "judicial notice" of the fact that the parties to labor agreements are generally in agreement that reopener clauses temporarily remove the bar against strikes and the use of other economic pressure.

I. EXCLUSION OF IMMATERIAL AND IRRELEVANT EVIDENCE

Arbitrators rarely deny a party the opportunity to present evidence on the basis that it is immaterial or irrelevant except where the presentation of such evidence is an imposition on the time and patience of both the other party and the arbitrator and could interfere with the maintenance of an orderly hearing. Exclusions of such evidence occur only infrequently because many arbitrators espouse the view that

---

[76] *Colasante v. Bridgehampton Road Races Corp.*, 16 Misc.2d 923, 185 N.Y.S.2d 203 (Sup. Ct. 1959).

[77] See note 20 *supra*, at 297.

[78] 20 L.A. 658, 662-63 (Lockhart, 1953). See generally Emerzian, *Standards in Labor Arbitration Awards*, 6 LAB. L.J. 743, 759 (1955):
"Arbitrators are usually selected because of their special knowledge in connection with the matter in dispute. They may take notice of general practice in the area of industrial relations, even though no evidence or testimony was offered at the hearing. . . ."

the freedom of the parties to present a full story has a therapeutic effect. Furthermore, where the parties are free to tell a full story, they may present helpful facts and often admissions. Arbitrator Harry Shulman said:

> "The more serious danger is not that the arbitrator will hear too much irrelevancy, but rather that he will not hear enough of the relevant. Indeed, one advantage frequently reaped from wide latitude to the parties to talk about their case is that the apparent rambling frequently discloses very helpful information which would otherwise not be brought out." [79]

The handling of objections to the materiality and relevancy of evidence is an individual matter with each arbitrator and varies to such a degree that documentation as to what arbitrators actually do would be of little value here. However, it should be noted that frequently arbitrators are chosen on the basis of their ability to quickly ascertain material facts in a case and to guide the parties so that they will produce evidence which is relevant to those material facts and not drag out the proceedings with irrelevant testimony.

As labor arbitration has evolved, certain exclusionary rules which are not grounded on materiality or relevancy considerations, but on policy considerations, have evolved which have gained general acceptance. In addition to the exclusionary rules discussed in this chapter, certain exclusionary rules have evolved that are based on due process considerations. These are discussed in the next chapter.

J. EXCLUSION OF, REMAND AND ADJOURNMENT FOR UNDISCLOSED EVIDENCE

Arbitrators take a flexible approach to the introduction of new evidence at the hearing in support of alleged contract violations which have been properly raised in the prior grievance procedure. Arbitrators take very seriously their duty to protect the grievance resolution process.[80] When either party is withholding evidence which might have produced a settlement in the lower steps if it had been presented,

---

[79] See note 18 *supra*.

[80] The failure of the company to reveal evidence that a disputed overtime assignment had been given to a probationary employee rather than to the grievant because the grievant was not qualified to perform the work caused Arbitrator J. P. Horlacher to grant the grievant monetary compensation for the lost overtime assignment despite his admitted inability to do the work on the ground that this odd result was justified by the "necessity to protect the integrity of the grievance procedure. . . . Both the company and the union have a duty to fully disclose all the facts in the processing of a grievance. Absent a showing—and there is none in the present instance—that it was not reasonably possible to discharge this duty to disclose, the party who has not met its obligation must be prepared to accept the appropriate consequences." *Chamberlain Corp.*, AAA Case No. 120-11 (Horlacher, 1968). Fleming, *Some Problems of Due Process and Fair Procedure in Labor Arbitration*, 13 Stan. L. Rev. 235 (1961).

arbitrators have refused to accept the evidence.[81] Arbitrator Willard
Wirtz summarized the views of many arbitrators in this regard as
follows:

> "There are obvious interests, from the standpoint of the parties' con-
> tinuing relationship, in keeping such matters out. It is important to the
> efficient functioning of the grievance procedure that the company and
> the union representatives do their job below. The Industrial Relations
> Manager insists properly that he must, as a matter of operating effi-
> ciency, be in a position to rely on what the union committee has found
> out and decided at least by the third step meeting, and the committee
> has a commensurate interest in being fully informed by that time of
> what the basis is for the company's position. The grievance procedure
> will work better, furthermore, if any practice of saving the best ammuni-
> tion for the hearing before the arbitrator is discouraged.
>
> "Arbitrators have responded to these considerations, to the extent
> that the 'general rule' is usually stated as being that new evidence or
> argument will not be admitted at the arbitration hearing unless some
> special reason is shown for its not having been brought out before." [82]

The view of Umpire Gabriel Alexander is shared by many
arbitrators:

> "[S]ound collective bargaining requires frank and candid disclosure at
> the earliest opportunity of all the facts known to each party. There will
> undoubtedly be times when facts are not discovered, and therefore not
> disclosed, until after the grievance has been partially processed, and
> problem enough is created by those instances. There is not a scintilla
> of justification for the withholding of information by either party from
> and after the time it is discovered." [83]

Some arbitrators, rather than exclude the evidence and remand the
case, will accept the evidence and then grant an adjournment to permit the surprised party an opportunity to evaluate it and collect
rebuttal evidence for presentation. Arbitrator Earl Miller discussed
the problems caused by surprise evidence in *Cadillac Gage Co.*:[84]

> "With regard to the Union objection that at the arbitration hearing
> the Company had brought in secret and surprise witnesses, it should be

---

[81] See related discussion concerning the remanding of cases to the grievance
procedure to force disclosure and consideration of new evidence, a form of informal
discovery procedure essential to a properly operating grievance procedure in Chapter
VII. See *Bethlehem Steel Co.*, 18 L.A. 367 (Feinberg, 1951), where testimony of
union's principal witness was rejected as evidence because it was withheld during
the grievance meetings. For comments on the admissibility of new evidence, see
R. W. Fleming, THE LABOR ARBITRATION PROCESS 144-51 (1965); F. Elkouri &
E. Elkouri, How ARBITRATION WORKS 178-81, 185 (rev. ed. 1960); various *Area
Reports*, PROBLEMS OF PROOF IN ARBITRATION, Proceedings of the Nineteenth Annual
Meeting, National Academy of Arbitrators 86 *et seq.*

[82] Wirtz, *Due Process of Arbitration*, THE ARBITRATOR AND THE PARTIES, Proceedings of the Eleventh Annual Meeting, National Academy of Arbitrators 1, 14-15
(J. McKelvey Ed. 1958).

[83] General Motors Umpire Decision No. F-97 (Alexander, 1950). See also note
54 *supra*, at 104.

[84] 66-3 ARB ¶ 8969 (Miller, 1966).

noted that when [S.] was first called as a witness by the Union, several hours before the Company called [Z.] and [W.], the Union was aware that they would be called and was aware of the statements they would make. . . .

"In any event, there is nothing in the Agreement or in the law governing arbitration requiring either party to reveal all its evidence to the other party before coming to an arbitration hearing. Material submitted by the Union indicates that in the steel industry agreements have been reached to reveal all evidence before arbitration, but no understanding existed between the parties in this case. Absent such an agreement between the parties, the course open to either party is to request a continuance of the hearing in order to rebut surprise evidence. The Arbitrator believes that if there is merit in such a request, it should be granted." [85]

When, however, new evidence merely grows out of a deeper investigation prior to the arbitration hearing, the policy of encouraging a free exchange of facts in the lower steps of the procedure is not applicable and the arbitrator will not return the case to the parties unless the newly discovered evidence creates a surprise prejudicial to the opposing party.[86]

On the other hand, it has been said that many prearbitral grievance meetings are informal, and as Arbitrator Williard Wirtz has observed, the "company, for its part, may very reasonably not have made the thorough investigation it will properly consider warranted if the union ultimately decides to take the case seriously enough to go to arbitration." [87] For these reasons, arbitrators will often receive relevant evidence which one party claims should not be received because it is new evidence that should have been presented at the lower steps of the procedure.[88]

K. EXCLUSION OF EVIDENCE JUSTIFYING BREACH OF AGREEMENT

Arbitrators typically will not accept evidence to prove the assertion that unresolved grievances justified wildcat strike activity. Arbitrators have pointed out that if employees can present such evidence

---

[85] *Id.* at 6380.

[86] *Borg-Warner Corp.,* AAA Case No. 14-21 (Edes, 1959); *Bethlehem Steel Co.,* 18 L.A. 366 (Feinberg, 1951).

[87] See note 82 *supra,* at 15. Wirtz indicated:
"[U]nless some deliberate attempt to mislead the other party is disclosed, and particularly if the 'new' evidence or argument appears substantially material, most arbitrators will be disinclined to rule the matter out of the proceedings."
See also *Pittsburgh Steel Co.,* 11 STEEL ARB. 8131 (McDermott, 1963).

[88] *Standard Oil Co.,* 68-1 ARB ¶ 8305 (Anrod, 1968); *United Parcel Service, Inc.,* 66-2 ARB ¶ 8703 (Dolson, 1966); *C. V. Hill Co.,* AAA Case No. 23-10 (Rock, 1960); *North American Aviation, Inc.,* 17 L.A. 183 (Komaroff, 1951); *Texas Co.,* 7 L.A. 735 (Carmichael, 1947); *Bethlehem Steel Co.,* 6 L.A. 617 (Wyckoff, 1947); *American Steel & Wire Co.,* 5 L.A. 193 (Blumer, 1946).

(on the grounds that the breach of the no-strike clause can be justified), the grievance-arbitration mechanism for handling grievances will fall into disuse and the no-strike pledge will be rendered a nullity. As noted by Arbitrator Saul Wallen:

> "The lesson to be drawn from this unfortunate case is that grievances real or fancied, must be handled through the orderly procedures of the contract and not by 'hitting the bricks.' Not only management but Union members are entitled to rely on the contract negotiated for the parties' joint benefit as an instrument that promotes stability and order. This is its purpose. The grievance procedure may appear to take longer than it should but its end result is justice through reason. The wildcat strike can lead only to frustration." [89]

Similarly, another Arbitrator has said:

> "While the Company bears a considerable responsibility, therefore, for the development of the situation which led to the walkout, this is not a defense for the actions of those who took part in the work stoppage in violation of the contract. Grievance and bargaining procedures exist for this very purpose. These are part of the orderly processes of collective bargaining. Even if the Company takes an action which clearly violates the contract the remedy lies in the grievance procedure, not in mob action, or gangland techniques. This is what the Union, and the employees collectively and individually, contracted to do." [90]

The reason why an employee was insubordinate, or engages in a prohibited refusal to work, is typically not considered by the arbitrator to be material or relevant to the question whether his employer had just cause to terminate him.[91] Thus, Arbitrator Schmidt, responding to a claim that a grievant's verbal attack on his supervisor was prompted by personal problems, held that evidence of personal problems should not be accepted since such evidence was not material.[92] The refusal to permit evidence of personal problems is based in part on the concept that management must be allowed to evaluate employee conduct by objective standards rather than becoming concerned with subjective considerations.[93]

---

[89] *Borden Chemical Co.*, 34 L.A. 325, 328 (Wallen, 1959).

[90] *Vickers, Inc.*, 33 L.A. 594, 602 (Bothwell, 1959). See also *American Potash & Chemical Co.*, 67-2 ARB ¶ 8606 (Meyers, 1967); *McGraw Edison Co.*, 62-3 ARB ¶ 8775 (Howlett, 1962). The exception to this rule—again, a substantive issue—is where employee safety is being imperiled. See, *e.g., Wilcolator Co.*, 44 L.A. 847 (Altieri, 1964). As pointed out in *Wilcolator*, however, the union must prove that the safety problem was acute and that normal dispute-resolution channels were ineffective.

[91] *Cf. Mastro Plastics Corp. v. NLRB*, 350 U.S. 270 (1956) where the Court held that, under the National Labor Relations Act, a contract waiver of the right to strike was unenforceable where employer unfair labor practices generated the strike action.

[92] *Ross Gear & Tool Co.*, 35 L.A. 293 (Schmidt, 1960).

[93] See, *e.g., Ohio Packing Co.*, 30 L.A. 1021, 1024 (Stouffer, 1958); *Aspinook Corp.*, 15 L.A. 593, 595 (Shapiro, 1950); *Goodyear Clearwater Mills No. 2*, 11 L.A. 419 (McCoy, 1948).

L. EXCLUSION OF EVIDENCE OF PRIOR
UNRELATED DISCIPLINARY INCIDENTS

Questions concerning relevancy often arise when the management party submits in evidence prior disciplinary records. Such records are relevant when the employee is disciplined for careless work when the prior offense was similar because a pattern of careless work is being demonstrated, whereas, if the single instance were viewed alone, the management's action might seem trivial and unreasonable. Prior discipline, however, is sometimes considered irrelevant, where the former offense is unrelated to the matter in issue,[94] but has, by other arbitrators, been admitted over the objection from the union.

Arbitrator Louis S. Belkin discussed various aspects of the admissibility of evidence of prior discipline in *Harshaw Chemical Co.*[95] An employee had been discharged for insubordination and use of profane language to a supervisor. The Union's objection to the admissibility of the employee's past work record on the ground that the employer was bound by the language of the termination notice which stated the cause of discharge was overruled. He said:

"The question of the use of the employee's past work record by the company in making its determination to discharge him is one which has several ramifications. In the opinion of the undersigned it would be inconceivable that the company do anything else. We have here a matter of equity and fairness. In order to be fair and equitable the totality of an employee's record, good or bad, must be weighed. This would certainly be applicable where the record is good. It must also apply where the opposite is true. It must also apply insofar as an arbitrator is concerned.

"I could not decide this matter if I had no knowledge of an employee's work performance and work record. This is a matter of discharge or reinstatement and thus transcends the realm of the ordinary grievance. I shall hold therefore that despite the wording of the notice the company may show evidence of the employee's record.

"This does not mean nor is it intended to mean that the union is barred from asserting its claim that the notice shows that the company's use of the employee's work record is an afterthought. The union may offer proof, if it can, that when the employee was discharged the foreman did not know of his past record and thus only the immediate inci-

---

[94] *Grief Bros. Cooperage Corp.*, 42 L.A. 555, 558-59 (Daugherty, 1964); *Givaudan Corporation*, 62-3 ARB ¶ 8934 (Pierce, 1962); but see *United States Steel Corp.*, 62-1 ARB ¶ 8144 (Rock, 1962); *Cities Service Oil Co.*, 17 L.A. 335 (Larkin, 1951). Typically, the relevancy of such disciplinary records is restricted to the question of penalty and not the issue of cause. *Borg-Warner Corp.*, 22 L.A. 589 (Larkin, 1954). See *Chicago Newspaper Publishers Ass'n*, 38 L.A. 491 (Sembower, 1962); *Bird & Son, Inc.*, 30 L.A. 948 (Sembower, 1958); *Capital Airlines, Inc.*, 27 L.A. 358 (Guthrie, 1956).

[95] 32 L.A. 23 (Belkin, 1958). See also *National Malleable & Steel Casting Co.*, 12 L.A. 262 (Pedrick, 1949); *Lake Shore Tire & Rubber Co.*, 3 L.A. 455 (Gorder, Chm., 1946); *Mueller Brass Co.*, 3 L.A. 285 (Wolf, 1946).

dent was in his mind. It may offer proof, if it can, that this is the first time an employee's record of absenteeism or tardiness was used in a discharge for insubordination.

"These, however, are matters of evidence going to motivations. They are matters of proof and issues for argument. They do not and cannot obviate the requirement and necessity for viewing the whole record of performance." [96]

Some arbitrators in nondiscipline cases hold that evidence of prior discipline has no relevancy and should not be admitted. For example, when the question in issue is the ability of the grievant to perform a higher skilled job which the employee seeks as a promotion, weighing the employee's discipline record as part of a consideration of relative ability might cause a denial of the promotion to become a second penalty for the same offense.[97] On the other hand, other arbitrators have held that evidence of prior disciplinary action is at least one measure of fitness for promotion and hence is admissible.[98]

Arbitrators usually consider the entire disciplinary record relevant to an evaluation of the reasonableness of the determination by management of the amount of discipline to be imposed, particularly when the grievant has been discharged.[99] One case illustrating this point is *Lone Star Cement Corp.*[100] where Arbitrator Leonard Oppenheim found discharge an appropriate penalty for falsifying work records when evaluated in the light of the employee's past record:

"While all arbitrators have not agreed upon this matter of past work records, some consideration is generally given to the past record of any disciplined or discharged employee. Thus a good past record may result in the mitigation of an offense and a bad past record may aggravate it. An employee's past record may often be an important factor in the determination of a proper penalty for an offense." [101]

The reasons why the employee's entire record is material as to the question of the amount of discipline was explained by Arbitrator John Seybold:

---

[96] 32 L.A. at 24-25.

[97] *St. Mary's Kraft Corp.*, 40 L.A. 365 (Duncan, 1963); *Waller Bros. Stone Co.*, 34 L.A. 852 (Dworkin, 1960).

[98] *Penn Controls, Inc.*, 45 L.A. 129 (Larkin, 1965); *International Smelting & Refining Co.*, 65-1 ARB ¶ 8052 (Justin, 1964).

[99] *Foremost Dairies, Inc.*, 44 L.A. 148 (Tatum, 1965); *American Forest Products Corp.*, 44 L.A. 20 (Lucas, 1965). Concerning the admissibility and significance of grievant's record after the disciplinary action but prior to the arbitration, see *Robertshaw-Fulton Controls Co.*, 36 L.A. 4 (Hilpert, 1961); *Westinghouse Electric Corp.*, 26 L.A. 836 (Simkin, 1956); *Southern Bell Telephone & Telegraph Co.*, 25 L.A. 270 (McCoy, 1955).

[100] 39 L.A. 652 (Oppenheim, 1962). See also *Columbus Auto Parts Co.*, 49 L.A. 686, 688 (Seinsheimer, 1967); *Ebinger Baking Co.*, 47 L.A. 948 (Singer, 1966); *Foremost Dairies, Inc.*, 44 L.A. 148 (Tatum, 1965); *Wheland Products Div.*, 43 L.A. 634, 636 (Volz, 1964); *Coast Pro-Seal & Mfg. Co.*, AAA Case No. 48-14 (Komaroff, 1962); *A. E. Staley Mfg. Co.*, AAA Case No. 24-24 (Dolnick, 1960).

[101] 39 L.A. at 653.

"Generally speaking, if the employee is guiltless then his past record, good or bad, is irrelevant. But if he did commit the offense which gave rise to the disciplinary action or discharge, it is entirely right and proper to look at his entire employment record. . . . To fail to look at this record would require that we judge each episode in a vacuum and would deprive an employee of the opportunity of capitalizing upon a past record of good performance and behavior which should be 'cash in the bank' to him. But if we are to accept the good, in mitigation of an offense, we must also be prepared to examine that which is not so favorable." [102]

The union in this case contended that to permit consideration of prior offenses would put it in the position of having to file an excessive number of grievances. The arbitrator replied:

"It is this arbitrator's opinion that it is in fact incumbent upon the union to form a judgment in each case as to whether there is some basis for the warning slip or action. If no basis at all exists, it should contest it. If the basis is arguable it should establish that, while it does not concur it will not contest." [103]

M. EXCLUSION OF EVIDENCE OF MISCONDUCT DISCOVERED AFTER THE DISCHARGE

Where a discharge occurs, its propriety must be determined from an analysis of the cause for the discharge and evidence of misconduct discovered after the discharge cannot be presented to justify the discharge action. Arbitrator William N. Loucks so ruled even though he recognized that the employer might well discharge the employee immediately upon his reinstatement, stating that the arbitrator's obligation is "to judge the merits of the discharge as of the date the discharge took place, and on the basis of the specific charge then brought by the company against the employee." [104]

This principle was not applied, however, when the evidence being submitted involved a successful rehabilitation of an employee from alcoholism after his discharge. Arbitrator Aaron Horvitz said:

"If . . . the case must be viewed and should be decided solely as to the facts as they existed as of the date of discharge, I would have no choice but to sustain the employer's action. But the company's position, it seems to me, is not sound under the circumstances and is in conflict with the weight of estimable arbitrable authority. . . . [M]edical authority . . . agrees that alcoholism is a disease in the same sense as many other afflictions which are beyond the capacity of the individual to control

---

[102] *Treadwell Corp.*, AAA Case No. 86-3 (Seybold, 1965).
[103] *Id.* See also Section D(3) of this chapter.
[104] *Surety Co.*, AAA Case No. 50-15 (Loucks, 1962). See also *Westinghouse Electric Corp.*, 26 L.A. 836 (Simkin, 1956); *Southern Bell Telephone & Telegraph Co.*, 25 L.A. 270 (McCoy, 1955).

except through outside help and treatment. If the grievant had been discharged for excessive absenteeism and poor work caused, let us say, by an aggravated ulcer condition, which condition had been cured or relieved by surgery between the time of discharge and the time of arbitration, it is clear to me that I would have the right to consider the prognosis as of the time of the arbitration in reaching a decision." [105]

Horvitz explained that if the arbitrator could not consider evidence of post-discharge conduct in such a case, "it would render rehabilitation, in many cases, a meaningless effort." Horvitz held that since the grievant has since his discharge "been making a strenuous effort to effect a cure," and has "apparently . . . been successful," he should be reinstated without back pay "predicated on his ability to maintain this favorable record." [106].

In connection with back-pay determination, an arbitrator has the right to consider conduct following the date that the incident causing the discipline occurred if it is relevant to the fashioning of the remedy. In *Link-Belt Co.*[107] the arbitrator refused to reinstate the grievant as a remedy in a discharge dispute because the grievant had engaged in interim conduct that would also justify discharge. The grievant's intervening conduct was, therefore, considered by the arbitrator and taken into account in upholding the discharge. A similar decision is *Robertshaw-Fulton Controls Co.*[108] where the arbitrator considered post-incident conduct to negate mitigating factors urged as a reason for reducing the penalty.

N. EXCLUSION OF EVIDENCE OF SETTLEMENT OFFERS

As in court-litigated proceedings, arbitrators typically regard evidence of prehearing settlement discussions as being inadmissible. Thus, Arbitrator Alpheus Marshall held that:

"[T]here may be many considerations in getting a grievance settled by negotiation rather than bringing it to arbitration. But more important than this is the fact that no agreement was reached at the time, and it would be very arbitrary for an arbitrator to decide a case by considering the offers and counter-offers of the parties in an attempt to reach a settlement." [109]

Arbitrator Clair Duff explained the basis for this assumption as to relevancy:

"Settlement offers made in a spirit of compromise do not bind the offering party as admitting that his arguments are weak or incorrect. Har-

---

[105] *Hooker Chemical Corp.*, AAA Case No. 81-2 (Horvitz, 1965).
[106] *Id.*
[107] 17 L.A. 224 (Updegraff, 1951).
[108] 36 L.A. 4 (Hilpert, 1961).
[109] *Stylon Southern Corp.*, 24 L.A. 430, 436 (Marshall, 1955).

monious labor relations are encouraged by such compromises and it is understandable if a party makes an offer to compromise to attain better, or continue good, labor relations even though, in fact, he does not agree with the offeree's view of the Grievance. If offers of compromise and settlement may be used to determine the merits of Grievances, no exploratory offers of settlement would be made, negotiations will become more cautious, disputes will be prolonged and the number of cases that will ultimately reach arbitration will be increased. In our consideration of the dispute we have completely ignored any offers of settlement mentioned in the Arbitration Hearing." [110]

In *Fulton-Sylphon Co.*,[111] Arbitrator Greene said:

"[I]t is clear that any offer made by either party during the course of conciliation cannot prejudice that party's case when the case comes to arbitration. It is the very essence of conciliation that compromise proposals will go further than a party may consider itself bound to go, on a strict interpretation of its rights." [112]

Another reason for excluding evidence of settlement offers was noted by Arbitrator Jerome Klein:

"[I]t should be mentioned that the arbitrator excluded evidence offered by the union relative to an offer of settlement which was rejected by [the grievant]. It is common knowledge that a company or union may make an offer of settlement to avoid the cost and difficulty of processing a matter to arbitration even though the party making the offer may believe that the probability of its action being sustained by the arbitrator is excellent." [113]

The Pittsburgh Tripartite Committee strongly echoes that evidence of offers in compromise must be excluded:

"Most arbitrators and advocates agree that the exclusion rule should be absolute in arbitration cases. Successful solution of grievances short of arbitration is vital to the process. Anything which imperils this philosophy must be avoided. Additionally, parties normally have neither inclination nor skill sufficient to cloak their settlement offers protectively. There are many reasons why offers of settlement are made, and they do not necessarily imply that the offering party admits it was wrong." [114]

O. PRIVILEGED MEDICAL EVIDENCE

The New York Tripartite Committee stated that an arbitrator should exclude evidence concerning the grievant's communications

---

[110] *Koppers Co.*, 61-1 ARB ¶ 8041 at 3193-94 (Duff, 1960).
[111] 8 L.A. 993 (Greene, Chm., 1947).
[112] *Id.* at 996.
[113] *Cleaners Hanger Co.*, AAA Case No. 51-8 (Klein, 1962).
[114] Pittsburgh Tripartite Committee, *Problems of Proof in Arbitration,* Proceedings of the Nineteenth Annual Meeting, National Academy of Arbitrators 253 (D. Jones Ed. 1967).

with his physician in any situation where the same claim for exclusion could properly be made in court with these qualifications:

"An employee asserting a claim or defense based on a physical condition may assert the privilege. However, the consequences of nondisclosure are for the arbitrator to determine.

"The disclosure of the fact of a communication with a physician is not privileged, even though the content of a communication may be privileged.

"If an employee's employment or continued employment is, by contract, controlling practice, or company rule, conditioned on his physical condition, he may not claim the privilege.

"If an employee's employment or continued employment is not explicitly or implicitly, by contract, controlling practice, or a company rule, conditioned on his physical condition, he may claim the privilege." [115]

The Tripartite Committee also recommended a procedure which would bring necessary medical information before the arbitrator without making it public knowledge:

"In the event that an employee desires, for some special reason, to avoid the general disclosure of his communication with his physician, the arbitrator may, at his discretion, limit such disclosure to selected representatives of the parties." [116]

The Chicago Tripartite Committee made a special comment concerning the admissibility of doctor's statements:

"(b) *Doctor's Statements.* It was agreed that doctor's certificates should be admissible in recognition of the difficulty of a busy doctor taking time to come to a hearing. There are occasions where the medical issue may become the central point of the case and here the arbitrator must be quite careful in determining whether the statement should be admitted. In general, the committee would admit the certificate of the doctor with the qualification that, absent the opportunity for cross examination, such evidence is entitled to less weight than medical evidence given in person by a doctor." [117]

P. MISCELLANEOUS PRIVILEGES TO HAVE EVIDENCE EXCLUDED

The New York Tripartite Committee said that witnesses need not testify concerning certain privileged communications:

---

[115] New York Tripartite Committee, *Problems of Proof in Arbitration,* Proceedings of the Nineteenth Annual Meeting, National Academy of Arbitrators 298-99 (D. Jones Ed. 1967).

[116] *Id.* at 299.

[117] Chicago Tripartite Committee, *Problems of Proof in Arbitration,* Proceedings of the Nineteenth Annual Meeting, National Academy of Arbitrators 107-08 (D. Jones Ed. 1967).

"b. *Husband-Wife*—A confidential communication between spouses is privileged where a witness is, at the time of testifying, one of the spouses.

"c. *Grand Jury*—A witness is privileged to refuse to disclose a communication made to a grand jury by a complainant or witness unless the findings of the grand jury have been made public by virtue of having been filed in court or otherwise.

"d. *Classified Information*—A witness who, in the course of his duties, acquired official information, such as classified information not open or disclosed to the public relating to the internal affairs of a government, is privileged to refuse to disclose such information. However, if the arbitrator has government clearance for access to such classified information, the privilege may not be claimed.

"e. *Union and Employer Communications*—Intra-union and intra-employer communications are not privileged.

"f. *Grievance Discussions*—Evidence concerning grievance discussions, other than offers of settlement or compromise, is not privileged unless the parties have explicitly agreed otherwise. (The labor members would limit such evidence to admissions and statements of position unless the contract provides for some type of reporting of grievance discussions.)

"g. *Witness-Attorney*—Communications between a union member testifying on behalf of a union and a union's attorney, or between a company employee and a company's attorney, are privileged." [118]

The Pittsburgh Tripartite Committee was not unanimous in its view concerning whether illegally acquired evidence was admissible but noted a method of avoiding the problem:

"9. *Admissibility of Illegally Acquired Evidence*

"In general, the courts have refused to admit evidence improperly acquired in violation of the constitutional protection against illegal search and seizure. The issue in arbitration cases tends to relate to information which the company regards as confidential, such as inter-office memos, production records, etc.

". . .

"Where the authenticity of the evidence is not in question, and the sole issue is whether the party offering such evidence came into possession of it by 'unauthorized means,' then the cause of justice is probably best served by admitting the evidence. The problem can be avoided, and the probative value of the evidence increased, where the party seeking to introduce the evidence requests the other party to produce it." [119]

Arbitrators have granted witnesses the right to not reply to questions concerning views regarding the meaning of contract language expressed by mediators during negotiations. The other party has the

---

[118] See note 115 *supra,* at 299.
[119] See note 114 *supra* at 261-62.

corollary right to have objections to such questions sustained. The rule can be expressed as follows:

> *Communications With Mediators.* Offers of evidence concerning a conversation with a mediator to prove the meaning of an agreement clause or the views of the other party to an agreement are rejected by arbitrators. Arbitrators agree that the introduction of evidence obtained in this matter affects the confidentiality and privilege that should surround such conversations with mediators.[120]

---

[120] See *Management Services, Inc.,* 58 L.A. 552 (Nicholas, 1972); *Day Care Council,* 55 L.A. 1130 (Glushein, 1970); *Air Reduction Chemical & Carbide Co.,* 41 L.A. 24 (Warns, 1963).

CHAPTER XIII

Due Process Considerations Affecting Admissability and Weight of Evidence

Most arbitrators endeavor to give meaning and application to "due process" considerations in labor arbitration. Yet, while recognizing that "due process" arguments are not to be regarded lightly,[1] many find that the strictures which result from too free borrowing of "due process" principles from the criminal law are out of place in the "shirt sleeves business of arbitration."[2] Abram Stockman, for example, has identified some of the problems of "loose borrowing":

"I think it would be generally agreed that in an arbitration proceeding something less than the ultimate in the protection afforded those accused of crime is apt to be the measure of the protection afforded employees for acts of misconduct committeed during the employment relationship. For there is undeniably a fundamental distinction between a criminal prosecution and an arbitration proceeding. Because our society has seen fit to require that every possible protection be extended to those accused of crime in order to insure that no one will be deprived of his liberty unjustly, it does not follow that an employee is entitled to protection in the same degree for the purpose of determining whether he is to be subjected to job discipline or even deprived of his job. Notwithstanding fre-

---

[1] *Congoleum-Nairn, Inc.,* 63-2 ARB ¶ 8843 (Short, 1963). On search without warrant by either plant or regular police, see *International Nickel Co.,* 68-1 ARB ¶ 8229 (Shister, 1967); *Hennis Freight Lines,* 44 L.A. 711 (McGury, 1964); *Lockheed Aircraft Corp.,* 27 L.A. 709 (Maggs, 1956); *Campbell Soup Co.,* 2 L.A. 27 (Lohman, 1946). On self-incrimination, see *Weirton Steel Co.,* 68-1 ARB ¶ 8249 (Kates, 1968); *United Parcel Service, Inc.,* 45 L.A. 1050 (Turkus, 1965); *Simoniz Co.,* 44 L.A. 658 (McGury, 1964); *Jones & Laughlin Steel Corp.,* 29 L.A. 778 (Cahn, 1957); *Republic Steel Corp.,* 6 STEEL ARB. 3945 (Platt, 1957); *Southern Bell Tel. & Tel. Co.,* 26 L.A. 742 (McCoy, 1956).

[2] Jones, *Evidentiary Concept in Labor Arbitration: Some Modern Variations on Ancient Legal Themes,* 13 U.C.L.A. L. Rev. 1241, 1286-90 (1966); R. Fleming, THE LABOR ARBITRATION PROCESS 181-86 (1965); Fleming, *Some Problems of Due Process and Fair Procedure in Labor Arbitration,* 13 STAN. L. REV. 235 (1961); F. Elkouri & E. Elkouri, How ARBITRATION WORKS 183-84 (1960); Stockman, *Due Process in Arbitration,* THE ARBITRATOR AND THE PARTIES, Proceedings of the Eleventh Annual Meeting, National Academy of Arbitrators 39-40 (J. McKelvey Ed. 1958); Wirtz, *Due Process of Arbitration, Id.;* The Pittsburgh Tripartite Committee, *Problems of Proof: Report on the Pittsburgh Area,* PROBLEMS OF PROOF IN ARBITRATION, Proceedings of the Nineteenth Annual Meeting, National Academy of Arbitrators 273-79 (D. Jones Ed. 1967).

quent resort to the euphemism, 'economic capital punishment,' I submit that incarceration is punishment of greater severity than loss of work and its concomitant effects." [3]

It has been noted that in labor arbitration there are group rights as well as individual rights that need protection. Most of the rights which are basic to an employee's claim in arbitration are acquired for the group as well as the individual via the collective bargaining process. The group has independent rights which must be protected by the union and also by the employer and hence, "due process," to the extent it involves a balancing of interests, must take on a different meaning in labor arbitration than it does in a criminal case in a court. In criminal cases, however, where the contestants are the individual and the state, a different balance is to be struck.

The differences between judicial and arbitration proceedings vis-à-vis due process considerations, has been well noted in one commentary:

"That the analogy between judicial and arbitral decisions breaks down at times should be neither surprising nor troubling. Due process of law in the judicial system involves a balancing of interests. . . . The defendant accused of the commission of a crime struggles against his accuser, the state, with its overwhelming powers and sanctions threating his life and liberty. His survival or defeat primarily affects only him. He may well demand that society subordinate some of its powers and rights to the protection of those of his rights that 'history, reason, [and] the past course of decisions' have recognized as immutable and fundamental. The subject matter and the necessities of the situation determine the balance of interest in his favor.

"The grievant on the other hand is part of an industrial community. The group to which he belongs is not merely a vessel containing the sum total of the individual interests of its members. It has independent rights and interests of its own which may be deeply affected by his actions. Moreover, a large part of the 'rights' claimed by the grievant owe their existence to the group. Nevertheless, he can demand that they be given recognition and protection. But the subject matter and the necessities of the situation strike a different balance, because they have to take into account those independent rights and interests of the group. Due process of law here has a different content than due process of law in the courts. Both require fairness, but 'fairness is a relative, not an absolute concept,' and in the overall scheme of the tripartite relationship greater subordination does not seem to violate that principle." [4]

This difference in the relationship of an accused versus the state and the relationship of a grievant to the total work group and to his employer must be fully appreciated if the reasons why arbitrators do not blindly infiltrate criminal law "due process" rules into the arbi-

---

[3] Stockman, note 2 *supra*.
[4] *Industrial Due Process and Just Cause for Discipline: A Comparative Analysis of the Arbitral and Judicial Decisional Processes*, 6 U.C.L.A. L. REV. 603 (1958-59).

tration process are to be understood. Thus, in discussing the Fourth Amendment (search and seizure), the Supreme Court in *Burdeau v. McDowell*[5] stated that its "origin and history clearly show that it was intended to be a restraint upon the activities of sovereign authority, and was not intended to be a limitation upon other than governmental agencies."[6] For these reasons arbitrators have said that constitutional rights can only be asserted against the Government, not against an employer.[7]

Requiring an employer to follow the strict rules imposed on government prosecutors can easily produce a strained relationship between the employer, the employees, and the union. It may be argued that if the rules applicable to prosecutors are applied to the employer, the employer's representatives will be encouraged to act as prosecutors, a role that is neither appropriate nor one most employers are prepared to assume.

This chapter reports how arbitrators have reacted to assertions that the "due process" rules associated with criminal law should be applied.

A. ADMISSIBILITY OF AND WEIGHT GIVEN TO ADMISSIONS AND CONFESSIONS

Under traditional views expressed in arbitral law, a confession or admission of wrongdoing by an employee to his employer is usually sufficient without more to establish the guilt of the employee.[8] Unions have argued that an employee's admission can be invalidated by his having been placed in fear of discipline by company investigators or by the absence of union representation during the interrogation at which the admission occurred. Such a contention was made in the *Weirton Steel Co.,* case.[9] Based on an anonymous tip, company investigators had found stolen property at the grievant's home.[10] The

---

[5] 256 U.S. 465, 475 (1921).

[6] *Id.* at 475.

[7] See, *e.g., Hennis Freight Lines,* 44 L.A. 711 (McGury, 1964); *Simoniz Co.,* 44 L.A. 658 (McGury, 1964); *Lockheed Aircraft Corp.,* 27 L.A. 709 (Maggs, 1956). *Accord, Wright v. United States,* 224 A.2d 475 (D.C. App. 1966); *United States v. Viale,* 312 F.2d 595 (2d Cir. 1963); *Sackler v. Sackler,* 15 N.Y.2d 40, 255 N.Y.S.2d 83, 203 N.E.2d 481 (1964); but see *Thrifty Drug Stores Co.,* 50 L.A. 1253 (Jones, 1968). The arbitrator there was particularly impressed with the Supreme Court's sweeping dictum in *Miranda v. Arizona,* 384 U.S. 436, 467 (1966), wherein the Court opined:

"Today, then, there can be no doubt that the Fifth Amendment privilege is available outside of Criminal Court proceedings and serves to protect persons in all settings in which their freedom of action is curtailed in any significant way from being compelled to incriminate themselves."

[8] *Phelps Dodge Copper Products Corp.,* 66-1 ARB ¶ 8031 (Dworkin, 1965); *Western Electric Co.* (Kelliher, 1965) (unreported).

[9] 68-1 ARB ¶ 8249 (Kates, 1968).

[10] *Cf. Lankford v. Gelston,* 364 F.2d 197 (4th Cir. 1967), in which it was ruled that an anonymous tip was not probable cause upon which to permit a search.

company interrogated the grievant without a union representative present and told him that he could be arrested when, in fact, the statute of limitation for a criminal prosecution had run. When confronted with the evidence obtained through the search, the grievant admitted the theft. He later recanted his confession at the hearing and the union argued that his confession was not admissible as evidence. Arbitrator Samuel Kates accepted the evidence of the confession and discussed the union's contentions concerning it in his award:

"I do not subscribe to the doctrine that purity must always envelop those engaged in attempting to acertain the truth, or that subterfuge or pretense is always improper in a truth-seeking endeavor. Each such case must, I believe, be judged upon its own facts." [11]

Concerning the union's contention that the threat of arrest made the admission of the confession unreliable, Arbitrator Kates said:

"The evidence does not warrant any holding that the grievant's fear of possible arrest . . . affected the truth of his express oral admission . . . ." [12]

On the other hand, circumstances can exist where testimony concerning an alleged confession has been viewed by the arbitrator with greater caution. In *Gardner-Denver Co.,*[13] the arbitrator concluded that the grievant's discharge was the result of a supervisor's "search for some evidence on which to base a discharge," and therefore that the supervisor's testimony that the grievant confessed to him the wrongdoing basic to the discharge was found to be wholly incredible. This case suggests that when a supervisor (who has authority to discipline the employee) testifies that an employee has "confessed" to the alleged act of misconduct and the employee denies it at the hearing, the resulting issue is really one of credibility rather than of due process.

Criminal law due process rules were applied in *Thrifty Drug Stores Co.*[14] which involved theft of company merchandise. An employee confessed to his own wrongdoing and informed on two other employees. He then acted as a witness at the arbitration hearing and again identified the two fellow participants in the theft and was subjected to cross-examination. The arbitrator, however, became concerned about the setting in which the informer was originally interrogated—in a small security cubicle without the benefit of union

---

[11] 68-1 ARB ¶ 8249 at 3861-62.
[12] *Id.* at 3862.
[13] 8 DAILY LAB. REP. A-5 (Ray, 1969).
[14] 50 L.A. 1253 (Jones, 1968).

representation and under the threat of discipline. In this connection, he said:

> "Therefore when interrogations occur in which discipline is a prospect and without the presence of a union representative, the statements then elicited must be regarded with skepticism and given weight only when other evidence corroborates their substance." [15]

The *Thrifty Drug* case may have involved credibility issues, but not problems of due process. The company was not attempting to prove the guilt of the grievants by hearsay statements of an informer, for the informer was called to testify at the hearing and was subject to cross-examination. Nor did the company rely on an allegedly coercive confession of an accused. Therefore, reliance on two Supreme Court cases—*Miranda v. State of Arizona*[16] and *Garrity v. State of New Jersey*[17]—which declare that in criminal cases involuntary or coerced confessions may not be used to establish the guilt of the confessor, was wholly misplaced. Furthermore, Arbitrator Jones misapplied the *Miranda* rule because he applied the right against self-incrimination to the informer, not to the accused.[18]

In *Armco Steel Corp.,*[19] Arbitrator Sidney Cahn overturned the discharge of an employee for theft on the basis of the unreliable "confessions" given by his two alleged accomplices. Arbitrator Cahn initially explained that the testimony of the informers was fraught with inconsistencies and incredible. If lack of credibility were the basis for reinstatement, the decision could not be challenged, but the arbitrator also relied on stringent criminal law rules to further justify his holdings:

> "Even were I to apply the criminal law of evidence in effect in the State of Texas, I would be compelled to find X innocent, for under the law of that State, in felony cases, the existence of a conspiracy concerning one defendant cannot be proved by the acts or declarations of another. In other words, a conviction cannot be had on the testimony of an accomplice alone, but there must be other evidence tending to connect the accused with the crime so that his conviction will not rest entirely upon the testimony of the accomplice. . . . The testimony of an accomplice implicating an accused must be corroborated by other evidence tending to connect the defendant with the commission of the offense and the corroborating testimony must be such as to be beyond reasonable doubt in order to convict." [20]

---

[15] *Id.* at 1262.
[16] 384 U.S. 436 (1966).
[17] 385 U.S. 493 (1967).
[18] See *Hoffa v. United States,* 385 U.S. 293 (1966) where the Supreme Court held that testimony by a witness of the accused's conversation with that witness did not violate the accused's Fifth Amendment right against self-incrimination.
[19] 48 L.A. 132 (Cahn, 1967).
[20] *Id.* at 135.

In contrast to *Thrifty Drug* and *Armco Steel* is the decision in *Eastern Air Lines.*[21] An airline pilot was discharged for drinking within 24 hours of his next flight. The co-pilot, who had also been drinking (and who was discovered by the security officer in a stewardess' hotel room late at night), gave a written confession "under the pressure of the circumstances"[22] which implicated the pilot. The arbitrator upheld the discharge of the pilot primarily because he had been previously warned about drinking and he admitted at the hearing that he had been drinking on the evening in question. To reach this result, the arbitrator reviewed "the procedural rights of due process of the Grievant." He ruled that (1) the interrogation of the grievant without union representation was not by itself undue pressure violative of due process, and (2) the co-pilot's statement, although given in a "compromising situation did not constitute the sort of duress and coercion which might under certain circumstances invalidate the proceedings."[23]

Thrifty Drug and *Armco Steel* should also be contrasted in approach with *Braniff Airways, Inc.*[24] There, two airline mechanics were discharged for stealing liquor from an airplane; a mechanic gave a written confession implicating another and, except for some circumstantial evidence, there was no other first-hand evidence against the accused, who denied participation. The confession was admitted in evidence and the informer was not called to testify. The arbitrator was troubled by the "due process" considerations and reduced the penalty, saying:

"The question which disturbs me, however, is whether on the basis of this type of proof—a confession, without confrontation, by an alleged accomplice and some circumstantial evidence—discharge was the proper punishment? Of course, seldom is one who participates in a theft ever caught red-handed. Here, the evidence presented certainly does not come close to meeting the standard described as being beyond a reasonable doubt. Furthermore, it appears to be a travesty on justice to permit the one who instigated, planned and executed the theft to be completely exonerated because of a technicality; then draw the full measure of blood from another individual who was duped into the crime and compel him to bear the entire brunt. Parenthetically, Y had been employed by the Company for approximately nine years without having been previously reprimanded or disciplined.

"Although I am completely in accord with the right of management to discourage pilferage, I, nevertheless, believe that in this instance, discharge under all the circumstances prevalent .herein, is too harsh a

---

[21] 46 L.A. 549 (Seidenberg, 1965).
[22] *Id.*
[23] *Id.* at 554-55. In *Sterling Optical Co., Inc.,* AAA Case No. 162-10 (McKelvey, 1972) the arbitrator found a confession was obtained by "coercion" bordering on "entrapment" and discipline modified.
[24] 44 L.A. 417 (Rohman, 1965).

punishment. I am, therefore, sustaining the grievance to the extent that the discharge is reversed, and, instead, Y shall receive disciplinary suspension, without pay, through February 7, 1965." [25]

B. THE INTERACTION OF RULES AGAINST SELF-INCRIMINATION AND THE EMPLOYEE'S DUTY TO COOPERATE IN AN INVESTIGATION OF MISCONDUCT

That no man can be compelled to be a witness against himself is a fundamental principle in criminal law, and despite the language of the Fifth Amendment which purports to limit the privilege against self-incrimination to criminal cases, it has been extended to judicial or official hearings, investigations, or inquiries where persons are called upon formally to give testimony.[26] Self-incrimination has little application in labor arbitration unless possibly when the discipline offense also constitutes a serious crime.[27] Arbitrator Douglas B. Maggs has said that the privilege against self-incrimination is not applicable to grievance arbitrations.

"[T]he constitutional privilege against self-incrimination is available only against the Government. If, in a hotel, arsenic has been discovered in food served in the dining room and also in the bedroom shared by the chef and one of the hotel's private detectives, and the latter refuses to tell management something he admittedly knows about how the arsenic got into the room, surely management would have just cause for discharging him." [28]

An employee has a duty to cooperate with an employer's efforts to make investigations. The principle has been stated:

"It is manifest that an employee has an obligation arising from operational necessity, to make reasonable disclosures to his employer of facts which are relevant to the employer's operations. If an employer is honestly seeking facts rather than really just probing for a confession, he is entitled to the cooperation of his employee in achieving reasonable disclosure of his activities or observations while on the job, and this is an incident of the employment relationship. For it unreasonably to be withheld by an employee would make him vulnerable to discipline, so that obstreperous union representation could disserve an employee being interrogated just as an unreasonable withholding of information relevant to the employer's operations would render him subject to discipline.

---

[25] *Id.* at 421.

[26] McCormick, EVIDENCE § 123 (1954).

[27] The New York Tripartite Committee stated:

"A witness may invoke his constitutional privilege to refuse to disclose any matter or information which would tend to incriminate him. The term 'incriminate,' in this context, refers to a statutory crime." PROBLEMS OF PROOF IN ARBITRATION, Proceedings of the Nineteenth Annual Meeting, National Academy of Arbitrators 300 (D. Jones Ed. 1967).

[28] *Lockheed Aircraft Corp.*, 27 L.A. 709, 712-13 (Maggs, 1956).

Even so, it does not follow that he can be compelled to disclose by the threat or the reality of discharge for refusing to make disclosures when to do so might expose him to criminal prosecution." [29]

In *Kammerer v. Board of Fire and Police Commissioners of the Village of Lombard*,[30] the Illinois Supreme Court held that if a public employee refuses to answer questions concerning a matter about which his employer is entitled to inquire, he may be discharged for insubordination. Although the decision involved a public employer, it is grounded on the view that an employer has the right to require an employee to answer questions relating to his fitness for further employment and that a failure to answer is a violation of the duty of the employee to cooperate with the employer in the investigation.

Arbitrators have upheld such a discharge in the case of editorial writers who invoked the Fifth Amendment[31] where the plant was engaged in defense work,[32] where there was unrest in the plant,[33] where the employee invoking the Fifth Amendment had been acquitted of criminal charges for thievery, but the arbitrator upheld his discharge for refusing to cooperate with the employer in stopping thievery in the plant,[34] and where the grievant refused to be finger-printed to negate or verify suspension for theft.[35]

Arbitrator Whitley P. McCoy came to the conclusion that a refusal of an employee to cooperate with an investigation would not support a discharge because it constituted an attempt by the company to shift the burden of proving alleged misconduct to the employee. The question was whether the employee was moonlighting in violation of a plant rule. The employee was asked whether he had or had not violated the rule and was told that if he had violated the rule but promised to stop doing so, there would be no discipline. The employee balked. He was fired for his refusal to answer. McCoy reinstated him, saying:

> "I know of no principle, or decided case, upholding a company's right to compel an employee, under pain of discharge, to admit or deny a rule violation or other offense. Such a principle would contradict all our Anglo-American principles, particularly the one that a man is pre-

---

[29] *Thrifty Drug Stores Co.*, 50 L.A. 1253, 1262-63 (Jones, 1968). See *Simoniz Co.*, 44 L.A. 658 (McGury, 1964) and *Allen Industries, Inc.*, 26 L.A. 363 (Klamon, 1956) both upholding discharge for refusal to cooperate. *Contra*, an arbitrator reinstated an employee who refused to say whether he was working for a competitor because the employer was then unable to prove the rule violation. *Exact Weight Scale Co.*, 50 L.A. 8 (McCoy, 1967).
[30] 44 Ill.2d 500, 256 N.E.2d (1970).
[31] *Los Angeles Daily News*, 19 L.A. 39 (Dodd, 1952).
[32] *Bethlehem Steel Co.*, 24 L.A. 852 (Desmond, 1955).
[33] *Burt Mfg. Co.*, 21 L.A. 532 (Morrison, 1953).
[34] *General Tire & Rubber Co.*, referred to in Wirtz, note 2 *supra*, at 1, 20.
[35] *Colgate-Palmolive Co.*, 68-1 ARB ¶ 8357 (Koven, 1968).

sumed innocent until he is proved guilty, and that the burden of proof is on the one alleging an offense." [36]

On the other hand, Arbitrator Burton B. Turkus had this to say concerning an employee who refused to cooperate because of an analogy to the right against self-incrimination:

"As broad and comprehensive as it so properly is in the protection of the innocent as well as the guilty when the privilege of self-incrimination is invoked, the Constitution, however, neither guarantees to a grievant, exercising the privilege, the right to his job nor his reinstatement to employment, when evidence sufficient to satisfy a reasonable mind of guilt of 'proven dishonesty' is *independently* established." [37]

Arbitrator John P. McGury in a case where the employee was terminated for refusal to cooperate in the investigation of a theft and who had "taken the Fifth Amendment" pointed out:

"The grievant, out of confusion, or overzealous protective measure against criminal prosecution, or reluctance to involve co-workers, took a position which went beyond the need of his own security and unreasonably infringed upon the right of the Company to make a thorough investigation of the incident, to the substantial disadvantage of the Company.

"The grievant had a right to make himself 200 percent secure against criminal involvement, but he cannot simultaneously protect his rights to future employment when his position frustrated the legitimate right and interest of the Company." [38]

Another kind of industrial surveillance lies in the observations made by members of supervision of production and maintenance operations in their normal course of work. It is only by personally circulating about his area of responsibility that a supervisor can effectively witness what is going on. Surveillance in this context is more frequently an allegation that the supervisor has taken wrongful action on the basis of his observations rather than a claim that he has no right to see what is going on.

Arbitrator Nathan Cayton said this in reply to the contention that a foreman was excessively supervising an employee:

"The basic position stated in the Union's brief is that the Company discriminated against [the grievant] by giving orders through [the foreman] to observe [the grievant] and make notes on him, while no such orders had been given with reference to six or seven other men under the same supervisor. The short answer to this is that the other men had not given reason for criticism or complaint." [39]

---

[36] *Exact Weight Scale Co.,* 50 L.A. 8-9 (McCoy, 1967).

[37] *United Parcel Service, Inc.,* 45 L.A. 1050, 1052 (Turkus, 1965).

[38] *Simoniz Co.,* 44 L.A. 659, 663-64 (McGury, 1964).

[39] *Aro, Inc.,* 70-1 ARB ¶ 8278, 3921 (Cayton, 1969).

Arbitrator George H. Hildebrand discussed the admissibility as evidence of reports of a spotter in the case of a bus driver who was discharged for allegedly violating company rules governing collection of fares. He said that a spotter's report should meet the requirements of the California Uniform Business Records as Evidence Act and added that beyond this:

> "(1) It must be shown that the reports were prepared before the decision to discharge had been taken and the issue joined between the parties. . . . (2) There must be no tangible basis for believing that the company is biased against the employee and has set out to get him." [40]

In *Colgate-Palmolive Co.*[41] (where the grievants were discharged for refusing to submit to a fingerprint test to verify or negate suspicion of theft) the union contended that a request to give fingerprints or be discharged was the same as a request to submit to a lie detector test.[42] The arbitrator upheld the discharges, ruling that if there were a reasonable basis to suspect the grievants, management could require them to cooperate in investigative tests. In so ruling, the arbitrator rejected the view that the privilege against self-incrimination voided the grievants' obligation to cooperate with their employer.

A different consideration was involved in *Scott Paper Co.,*[43] where the arbitrator ruled that "in the absence of a clear plant rule requiring it, an employee may not be required to give evidence against himself, or to submit to a search of his person, or to disclose the contents of his pockets." There it was held that a request by the grievant's supervisor that the grievant empty his pockets to verify or refute reports that he was carrying a gun was an improper request by the supervisor and its refusal was not insubordination. The ruling by the arbitrator was made in spite of a plant rule that employees could be searched as they entered and left the plant if theft was suspected.

The *Scott Paper* decision raises several questions. Should an employer be free to protect the members of its employment community from employees with guns or should he not? If an employer has information from a reliable source that an employee is carrying a gun, is it not the employee's duty to cooperate with his employer when asked to disclose the contents of his pockets or suffer discharge?

The opposite approach to the question was well enunciated in *Maremont Corp.*[44] A grievant, accused of being drunk, refused to

---

[40] *Los Angeles Transit Lines,* 25 L.A. 740, 745 (Hildebrand, 1955).
[41] 68-1 ARB ¶ 8357 (Koven, 1968).
[42] See Section E. *infra,* "Admissibility of Evidence Acquired Through Polygraph Testing."
[43] 69-2 ARB ¶ 8470 (Williams, 1969). See also *Congoleum-Nairn,* AAA Case No. 54-3 (Short, 1963).
[44] *Maremont Corp.* (Meltzer, 1969) (unreported).

take a breath analyzer test as provided in the collective bargaining agreement. The union representatives asserted that the right against self-incrimination meant that no adverse inference could result from the refusal to take the test. Arbitrator Bernard Meltzer, rejecting this contention, held:

"[T]he Union's contention raises the question of whether the privilege operates in an arbitration proceeding to bar evidence of a grievant's refusal to take an intoxication test when the only purpose and effect of that evidence relates to the propriety of Company discipline. For the reasons that follow, this arbitrator answers 'No' to that question.

"The privilege against self-incrimination operates to protect individuals in their relations with government, and, specifically, is designed to provide protection against the risk of criminal penalties arising from compulsion of government. See McCormick, Evidence 268 (1954). The relationship between an employer and his employees is significantly different from the relationship between a state and its citizens. . . . The penalties imposed by the state for criminal offenses are also materially different from discharge by the employer, despite the seriousness of discharge in some situations.

"When, as in this case, the disputed evidence bears only on conduct or omissions occurring prior to the arbitration proceeding and when nothing that occurred in that proceeding increased the defendant's risk from the criminal law, there is no occasion for applying the privilege so as to exclude relevant evidence. In this connection, it should be noted that even exponents of the general position that the privilege is applicable to arbitration hearings, would admit evidence of a grievant's failure to reply to relevant questions asked by his employer during an investigation of alleged misconduct for the purpose of determining appropriate discipline. . . .

"There is plainly no basis for distinguishing between a grievant's refusal to answer and this grievant's refusal to take a test under the circumstances here involved. In this connection, it is appropriate to note that the test was reliable and objective, had been agreed to by the parties, involved no actual or claimed risk of pain or danger, and was to have been administered in the presence of Union representatives. Nothing in this privilege, its purpose, its policy, or its provisions, calls upon the parties or an arbitrator to ignore the evidentiary significance of such a refusal in determining the propriety of industrial discipline."

A closely related question to the manner in which the so-called privilege not to testify is handled in labor arbitration is the question of the inferences that are drawn from a refusal to testify. Arbitrators do draw inferences from the failure of a grievant to testify at a hearing.[45] What that inference might be, however, is subject to some debate.

---

[45] *Commercial Solvents Corp. v. Louisiana Liquid Fertilizer Co.*, 20 FRD 359 (S.D.N.Y. 1937); Problems of Proof in Arbitration, Proceedings of the Nineteenth Annual Meeting, National Academy of Arbitrators 99, 258, 301 (D. Jones Ed. 1967).

In *Southern Bell Telephone & Telegraph Co.*[46] Arbitrator Whitley P. McCoy held:

"I think that the inferences justifiable from such refusal cannot be extended to an inference of guilt of the very act with which the man is charged. . . . In other words, I think that the inferences to be drawn from a refusal to testify are limited to evidentiary *facts,* and do not extend to the ultimate *conclusion* of guilt or innocence which must be drawn from evidentiary facts. Inferences may be resorted to in aid of evidentiary facts; they cannot supply facts of which there is no evidence. Findings of fact must be based on credible evidence. The failure to deny or refute incredible evidence does not change the character of that evidence from incredible to credible."

In *Brown Shoe Co.,*[47] Arbitrator Joseph M. Klamon commented thusly on the failure of the grievants to come forward, appear and testify:

"[I]t is the duty of the men involved to come forward and give the true explanation of what they were doing when they were where they had no right to be. The fact that they did not do so at the time of discharge and did not appear at the hearing coupled with the auditory evidence and the previous pattern of behavior abundantly sustains the Company's position and contention." [48]

On the other hand, some arbitrators have said that no inferences may be drawn from such a refusal. Arbitrator John Sembower, in *American International Aluminum Corp.,*[49] said:

"The Arbitrator disregards any adverse inferences which might be drawn from the Grievant's not being present at the hearing. While this is in no sense a criminal matter, there is an inescapable analogy between the absence from an arbitration hearing of the Grievant in a disciplinary case and the rule of law that a defendant in court may not be required to take the stand if he chooses not to do so, and it shall not be held against him if he does not."

---

[46] 25 L.A. 270, 273 (McCoy, 1955).

[47] 16 L.A. 461 (Klamon, 1951).

[48] *Id.* at 466. *Accord, Pilot Freight Carrier, Inc.,* 22 L.A. 761 (Maggs, 1954). See *International Harvester Co.,* 23 L.A. 64 (Cole, 1954), where the arbitrator dismissed the grievance because the grievant did not appear:
"The failure of a grievant to appear and testify at the hearing of his grievance may be one of the factors leading to the arbitrator's conclusion that the grievance is without merit."
F. Elkouri & E. Elkouri, note 2 *supra,* at 182.

[49] 68-2 ARB ¶ 8591 at 5045 (Sembower, 1968). *Accord, Milgrim Food Stores, Inc.,* 68-2 ARB ¶ 8622 (Murphy, 1968), and *United Parcel Service, Inc.,* 45 L.A. 1050 (Turkus, 1965) where a mere refusal to answer questions was said to be insufficient to discharge someone as that would entail a presumption of guilt from silence. See also *Exact Weight Scale Co.,* 68-1 ARB ¶ 8128 (McCoy, 1967); *RCA Communications, Inc.,* 29 L.A. 567 (Harris, 1957); *Pratt & Whitney Co.,* 28 L.A. 668 (Dunlop, 1957); *J. H. Day Co.,* 22 L.A. 751 (Taft, 1954); *United Press Ass'n,* 22 L.A. 679 (Spiegelberg, 1954).

In spite of the two views, however, the failure of the grievant to testify is detrimental to his position because the testimony against him is then uncontradicted.

C. ADMISSIBILITY OF EVIDENCE OBTAINED WITHOUT A SEARCH WARRANT

With rare exception, arbitrators have adopted the view that the Fourth Amendment's protection against illegal searches and the use of evidence obtained thereby is not applicable in labor arbitration.[50] The U.S. Supreme Court said in *Burdeau v. McDowell*[51] that the Fourth Amendment's "origin and history clearly show that it was intended to be a restraint upon the activities of sovereign authority, and was not intended to be a limitation upon other than governmental agencies."[52] The restraint in the Amendment applies to criminal and quasi-criminal proceedings, and not to litigation in civil cases between individuals.[53]

Therefore, arbitrators have uniformly upheld disciplinary actions and discharges of employees who refused to permit a search of lunch boxes,[54] lockers,[55] and purses.[56] Similarly, evidence obtained from searching an employee's person,[57] an employee's hotel room,[58] and even his garage[59] has been used in arbitration for supporting a discharge.

In *International Nickel Co.*,[60] Arbitrator Shister set forth the typical rationale concerning personal rights of employees when improper search is asserted as a reason for excluding evidence (a foreman had a janitor open employee lockers in the search for missing company property):

> "We are not here dealing with a sweeping, indiscriminate search lacking in reasonable and specific foundation. Quite the contrary. The lockers were unlocked in response to a definite problem—namely, the missing clipboards (Company property). True, as the Union agrees, the Company could have asked the employees which of them had put the clipboards in their lockers. But that would have imposed adminis-

---

[50] See, *e.g.*, *Hennis Freight Lines*, 44 L.A. 711 (McGury, 1964); *Simoniz Co.*, 44 L.A. 658 (McGury, 1964); *Lockheed Aircraft Corp.*, 27 L.A. 708 (Maggs, 1956).

[51] 256 U.S. 465 (1921).

[52] *Id.* at 475.

[53] *People v. Johnson*, 153 Cal. App.2d 870, 315 P.2d 468 (1957); *Walker v. Penner*, 190 Or. 542, 227 P.2d 316 (1951).

[54] *Fruehauf Corp.*, 49 L.A. 89 (Daugherty, 1967).

[55] *International Nickel Co.*, 50 L.A. 65 (Shister, 1967).

[56] *Alden's Inc.*, 68-2 ARB ¶ 8814 (Kelliher, 1968).

[57] *Jones & Laughlin Steel Corp.*, 29 L.A. 778 (Cahn, 1957).

[58] *Eastern Airlines*, 46 L.A. 549 (Seidenberg, 1965).

[59] *Weirton Steel Co.*, 68-1 ARB ¶ 8249 (Kates, 1968).

[60] 68-1 ARB ¶ 8229 (Shister, 1967).

trative inconvenience and delay, which the Company was not contractually obliged to assume in the light of the past practice already alluded to." [61]

In *Aldens Inc.,*[62] Arbitrator Peter Kelliher held that two women were properly discharged when they refused to allow a female security guard, pursuant to a company rule, to examine the contents of their oversized purses. In response to the union's argument that the search was an improper invasion of privacy and violated the employees' constitutional rights, Arbitrator Kelliher said:

> "It was not disputed that the Company here has a serious problem with reference to thefts. The rule established by the Company is entirely reasonable. No Company could stay in business and continue to provide job opportunities for the membership of this Union unless it protected itself against loss by theft. The Company rule is directed at large purses which could be used to secrete Company merchandise. The Union, on the other hand, is properly concerned, as it stated here, with the protection of the privacy and dignity of employees under the circumstances of an inspection. The record, however, shows that the Company took all reasonable procedural precautions to assure this protection to the employees.
>
> " . . .
>
> "When an employee brings a large purse on to the premises, she must expect that she will be subject to such an inspection. It would be unreasonable and totally unrealistic for the Company to attempt to get a search warrant." [63]

The admissibility in arbitration of evidence obtained by a search of lockers, lunch boxes, or purses without the search warrant required in a criminal case presents problems related to those discussed above.[64] As Arbitrator Kelliher said in *Aldens, Inc.,* to require an employer to obtain a search warrant to examine an employee's purse or his locker, or to ask him to disclose the contents of his pockets, could be an unrealistic restriction to impose on the employer. Moreover, fear of unrestricted use of such searches is unrealistic, for the employee is protected by the fact that the employer has many business reasons to be considerate of his employees. Hence, the search of person, locker, or lunch box only occurs when a need for such a search exists.

---

[61] *Id.* at 3787.

[62] 68-2 ARB ¶ 8814 (Kelliher, 1968). But see *Campbell Soup Co.,* 2 L.A. 27 (Lohman, 1946).

[63] 68-2 ARB ¶ 8814 at 5822.

[64] In *Air Line Pilots,* 97 NLRB 929 (1951), the Board said:
"It has been Board practice to admit allegedly purloined documents unless it is established that an agent of the government has been a party to their unlawful seizure."
See also *General Engrg., Inc.,* 123 NLRB 586 (1959); *accord,* 8 Wigmore Sec. 2184A(U) (*cf. Hoosier Cardinal,* 67 NLRB 49 (1946), where connivance of Board agent was found).

The difficulties of applying the rules of the criminal law to the employment situation, some of which were suggested in the *Aldens* case, were also discussed in *Hennis Freight Lines*:[65]

"It may be argued that the spirit of the Constitutional prohibition against unreasonable search and seizure is violated, when the fruits of what has been judicially determined to be an illegal arrest and, therefore, an unreasonable search and seizure, are nevertheless allowed to be considered by the Company or an arbitrator for discharge.

"There is an essential difference between procedural and substantive rights of the parties. The constitutional principles may keep the grievants out of jail but do they guarantee them their jobs in the face of Company knowledge of extremely strong proof of dishonesty involving Company property?" [66]

Similarly, in *Weirton Steel Co.*,[67] company investigators searched the grievant's garage after they misrepresented to the grievant's 14-year-old son the reason for the search. The arbitrator ruled that the investigators' testimony concerning the discovery of stolen goods during the search was admissible evidence and distinguished the lack of admissibility of evidence obtained during searches in criminal investigations. The Arbitrator said:

"In my opinion, the comments made by the Company's security officers and their police associates, for the purpose of ascertaining the truth, and the occurrences leading to and resulting in the grievant's admission of guilt and the redelivery of the Company's property, did not fall to such levels as could truly be said to have wrongfully pierced the grievant's constitutional shield. I do not consider that the strict rules or vigorous practices under which the State or Federal constitution is applied to criminal investigations necessarily apply with equal force to private investigations by an employer into the conduct of an employee." [68]

Another good demonstration of the difference between the criminal law rules and those employed in labor arbitration is found in *Congoleum-Nairn, Inc.*[69] There, an employee's discharge for possession of gambling slips was based on evidence gathered by police officers pursuant to a search warrant, subsequently quashed by the court. The arbitrator, over the union's objection, admitted into evidence the seized material and permitted the police officers to testify regarding the arrest of the grievant. The arbitrator said:

"Company counsel called the two police officers as witnesses. The Union attorney objected that any testimony by Patrolman [M.] or

---

[65] 44 L.A. 711, 713 (McGury, 1964).
[66] *Id.* at 713.
[67] 68-1 ARB ¶ 8249 (Kates, 1968).
[68] *Id.* at 3861-62. See also *Sun Drug Co.*, 31 L.A. 191 (Marcus, 1958).
[69] 63-2 ARB ¶ 8843 (Short, 1963). *Contra* 58 L.A. 1213 (McGury, 1972).

Sergeant [B]., as a result of an illegal search, would be improper and unconstitutional and deprive [P.] of a very valuable property right, since his job was at stake. Union counsel argued that since the Court had suppressed the seized evidence and quashed the search warrant, such evidence thereby became a nullity, as if it had never happened, and to permit testimony concerning the articles which had been seized would give life and vitality to what a Court has decreed has no vitality.

"The arbitrator overruled these objections to the extent of permitting testimony relating to the information and basis upon which Management acted in reaching the decision to terminate the employment of [P.]. . . ." [70]

The arbitrator, however, had some grave misgivings about the use of the evidence in the arbitration illegally obtained under criminal law standards. His misgivings were enhanced by the peculiar factual development which he described:

"At the arbitration hearing on November 14th counsel for the Union served upon Patrolman [M.] and Sergeant [B.], who were present as witnesses for the Company, an order signed by the Honorable Clifton C. Bennett, Judge of the Superior Court of New Jersey [to quash the illegally obtained evidence]. . . .

"The officers asked for a recess to consider the Order. Upon returning from the recess, Sergeant [B.] announced that the officers would comply with the Court Order. Thereupon [the gambling slips] were turned over to [P.], who was asked if the articles were his. In the course of [P.'s] examination of the returned articles, the officers placed him under arrest for possession of numbers slips and took him to the Hamilton Township Police Station. [P.] was released on his own recognizance and returned to the arbitration hearing, which was then resumed." [71]

The grievant was placed in the following awkward position: if he refused to testify, he would let stand without contradiction the evidence put in by the employer; if he took the stand and attempted to explain away his possession of the gambling slips, whatever he said might have been used against him in a subsequent criminal hearing. The arbitrator noted:

"Notwithstanding the distinction between a criminal proceeding, as such, and an arbitration relating to the discharge of an employee, the present proceeding is somewhat novel in that some aspects of the public proceedings became intertwined with the arbitration proceeding." [72]

Because of the close relationship of the criminal case and the arbitration case, the arbitrator said:

"If equity is proper for the Arbitrator's consideration, the 'clean hands' maxim requires consideration, for equity will never assist the harsh

---

[70] 63-2 ARB at 5723.
[71] *Id.* at 5722-23.
[72] *Id.* at 5725.

assertion of legal rights. Moreover, the constitutional protection against unlawful search and seizure is of little value if evidence ordered suppressed may be recaptured by public authorities and used against an accused in a collateral arbitration proceeding without risking possible self-incrimination in a related judicial proceeding." [73]

Because of the unusual circumstances of the case, however, the Arbitrator reinstated the employee without back pay.

D. ADMISSIBILITY OF EVIDENCE OBTAINED BY INTERROGATING EMPLOYEES WITHOUT UNION REPRESENTATION

A few arbitrators express concern over the admission of evidence obtained at an investigation interview after the employee had asked for and had been denied the presence of his union steward or committeeman during the interview. [74] These arbitrators conclude that an employee has a right to have a union representative present during such an interview by analogizing the employee to an individual arrested by the police. They reason that since the latter has the right to have an attorney present when he is being questioned by the police concerning his possible involvement in a crime, so should an employee be entitled to have a representative present. [75]

Other arbitrators espouse the views that whatever right to union representation exists and can be enforced by an arbitrator must be found in the terms of the collective agreement. [76] Unless the parties have agreed that an employee is to be entitled to union representation during an investigation interview, evidence obtained at such an interview is admissible because there is no other ground on which to base the claim for the right to union representation during such interrogation.

---

[73] *Id.* at 5727.

[74] See, *e.g., City of Port Huron, Mich.,* 68-2 ARB ¶ 8788 (Keefe, 1968); *Dow Chemical Co.,* 68-2 ARB ¶ 8647 (Davis, 1968); *Thrifty Drug Stores Co.,* 50 L.A. 1253 (Jones, 1968); *American Enka Corp.,* 68-2 ARB ¶ 8558 (Pigors, 1967). See also *Humble Oil & Refining Co. v. Ind. Industrial Workers Union,* 337 F.2d 321 (5th Cir. 1964), holding an employer's refusal to permit a union representative to attend interrogation of employee was a grievance subject to arbitration.

[75] *Miranda v. Arizona,* 384 U.S. 436 (1966); *Escobedo v. State of Illinois,* 378 U.S. 478 (1964).

[76] *South Central Bell Telephone Co.,* 59 L.A. 134 (Seward, 1972); see, *e.g., F. W. Dwyer Mfg. Co.,* 69-1 ARB ¶ 8361 (Bothwell, 1968); *North American Aviation, Inc.,* 19 L. A. 565 (Komaroff, 1952). See also *Sterling Drug, Inc.,* 68-1 ARB ¶ 8358 (Stein, 1968), where the grievant requested that the entire union committee be present at his discharge hearing, as provided in the collective agreement. His request was denied because in prior discharge cases no employee had ever requested the presence of the entire committee at the discharge hearing. The arbitrator ruled that the discharge of the grievant was for good cause, but because he was denied the requested representation at his discharge hearing, which he had a right to have under the terms of the agreement, his discharge was commuted to suspension without pay.

Sometimes the claim to representation during an investigatory conference is based on the terms of the National Labor Relations Act and the Board has given credence to such view in its *Mobil Oil Corporation* decision.[77] This decision is in contrast to early ones holding that a denial of representation during the investigation stage before discipline has occurred was not improper.[78] Also the Board had previously dismissed a complaint where an arbitrator had determined that the labor agreement did not permit an employee to have union representation during an investigation conference.[79]

Unions have also argued that the right of representation can be implied from the recognition clause found in all labor agreements, but several arbitrators have rejected such a contention. For example, in *International Harvester*,[80] the arbitrator pointed out that:

> "The clear right of the Union, under Article IV, Section 1, to represent the employees in the bargaining unit 'for the purpose of collective bargaining with respect to rates of pay, wages, hours of employment and other conditions of employment' does not carry with it a prohibition against any direct conversation between Management and its employees carried on without the participation or consent of Union officials." [81]

A grievance, another arbitrator reasoned, does not come into being until there is a formal protest against a management action:

> "And it is usually in connection with the first hearing on such a formal complaint or grievance, which takes place between the aggrieved employee and his Foreman, that provision is made for the Employees' Steward to be present. But all of this depends on there first being in existence a formal grievance or complaint often required to be in writing to be processed at all, before any of the contract grievance procedure hearings or steps are appropriate." [82]

A board of arbitration chaired by Arbitrator Peter Kelliher held in *Western Electric Co.*:[83]

> "The Company clearly does have a right under the Contract to conduct interviews or interrogations without according the employee a right to have a Union Representative present. Employees, however, are not to

---

[77] 196 NLRB No. 144 (1972); see also *Quality Manufacturing Co.*, 195 NLRB No. 42, but see *NLRB v. Ross Gear & Tool Company*, 158 F.2d 607 (7th Cir. 1947); *Texaco Inc.*, 408 F.2d 142 (5th Cir. 1969).

[78] *Chevron Oil Co.*, 168 NLRB 574 (1967); *Jacobe-Pearson Ford, Inc.*, 172 NLRB No. 84 (1968); *Dobbs Houses, Inc.*, 145 NLRB 1565 (1964).

[79] *Western Electric Co.*, 197 NLRB No. 82 (1972).

[80] 14 L.A. 925, 928 (Seward, 1950).

[81] *Id.* at 928.

[82] *E. I. duPont de Nemours & Co.*, 29 L.A. 646, 650 (Gregory, 1957). See also *American Can Co.*, 57 L.A. 1063 (Kerrison, 1972).

[83] *Western Electric Co.* (Kelliher, 1965) (unpublished).

be subject to interrogations of an unreasonable length. The Union certainly has a right to advise its members that they should not sign written confessions where they have any reservations as to their being guilty of the offense charged. . . ."

Later in another *Western Electric* case arising at the same plant, a board of arbitration, chaired by Arbitrator Dudley Whiting, held:

"The Union contends that any employee is entitled to Union representation when interrogated in connection with suspected misconduct which might result in disciplinary action. A prior Board of Arbitration rejected that contention because the contract does not provide for such representation until the Company has decided to discipline an employee or terminate his employment. . . . The achievement of such an extension of the Union's right to represent employees can only be accomplished by negotiating a provision therefor into the contract." [84]

Arbitrator Kates in *Weirton Steel Co.*[85] specifically rejected the view that the rules promulgated by the Supreme Court in its *Escobedo* and *Miranda* decisions have application in arbitration:

"The Union has contended that the Company was obligated to provide the grievant with Union representation while questioning him.

"Until contrary authority shall have been pointed out, whether contractual, statutory, judicial or logical, I feel constrained to hold that, in the absence of a specific request for Union representation, the *Escobedo* and *Miranda* doctrines do not obligate an employer to refrain from interrogating an employee about alleged misconduct except in the presence of a Union representative." [86]

Arbitrator Jones, however, in *Thrifty Drug Stores Co.*[87] adopted the diametrically opposite view, relying on *Escobedo* and *Miranda*. He said:

"Therefore when interrogations occur in which discipline is a prospect and without the presence of a union representative, the statements then elicited must be regarded with skepticism and given weight only when other evidence corroborates their substance. Particularly is this so when the employee being interrogated requests union representation and is refused. It is not compatible with the Parties' contractual commitment to fair grievance procedures for the employer to bar union representation when the interrogation foreseeably is aimed at securing disclosures which may result in the discipline of the employee being subject to it." [88]

Thrifty Drugs suggests that whenever an employee is interrogated by a company representative to determine his involvement or lack thereof in an alleged wrongful act, he is entitled to the presence of a

---

[84] *Western Electric Co.* (Whiting, 1966) (unpublished).
[85] 68-1 ARB ¶ 8249 (Kates, 1968).
[86] *Id.* at 3862.
[87] 50 L.A. 1253 (Jones, 1968).
[88] *Id.* at 1262. See also *American Enka Corp.*, 68-2 ARB ¶ 8558 (Pigors, 1967).

shop steward or committeeman because the union is the bargaining agent for employees. But, it should be noted, shop stewards and committeemen are not legally trained and, therefore, the best advice that they could offer would be to tell the employee to say nothing.[89] Such advice not only would frustrate the investigation process, but could lead to the discipline of the employee for refusing to cooperate in a management investigation.[90]

The view that *Escobedo* has application in an industrial setting has also been criticized on the ground that the presence of a union representative would soon be insisted upon at every discussion between an employee and a supervisor. Thus, Arbitrator Gregory rejected the view that there is a right to representation at investigatory discussions, observing that:

> "[A]ny other view would seem to entitle a unit man to have a Steward present at his request whenever a supervisor undertook to have any communication with him about anything to do with his work. Clearly this would result in an impossible situation, since it is the traditional function of the supervisor to transmit orders and criticisms to unit men. Indeed, the Impartial Arbitrator would go even further than this. He believes that under all grievance procedures he has seen, including that in the present contract, a supervisor is entitled to question a unit man with a view to disciplining him, and may go ahead and discipline him, without a Steward present." [91]

A similar result was reached in *United Air Lines, Inc.*[92] There, a large scale investigation was initiated into the disappearance of scrap from a maintenance base. All employees were scheduled for interviews and all but two cooperated. These two demanded union representation at the investigation and their request was denied. A grievance was filed stating that the company violated the contract by denying the employees the requested representation at the fact-finding interview. The arbitrator denied the grievance, holding that union representation is available only after the employee is given discipline. The arbitrator stated:

> "We think the Company had a right to interrogate X__, Y__, or any other employee in an attempt to ascertain what was happening to its

---

[89] In one instance, the president of a union at an arbitration hearing wanted to have a union representative present at an investigation interview not to cause them not to talk but to find out who does talk:
"These employees should be named. We want to know who they are for the purpose of determining whether or not *these employees are typical stool pigeons.* . . . Now, this is something we must know." [Emphasis added.] *Western Electric Co.* (Kelliher, 1965) (unpublished).

[90] See *Colgate-Palmolive Co.,* 68-1 ARB ¶ 8357 (Koven, 1968), where the discharge of two employees was upheld for their failure to cooperate in a theft investigation by management.

[91] *E. I. duPont de Nemours & Co.,* 29 L.A. 646, 650 (Gregory, 1957).

[92] 28 L.A. 179 (Wenke, 1956).

scrap metal and, while doing so, such employees were not, as a matter of right, entitled to have union representatives present. . . ." [93]

E. ADMISSIBILITY OF EVIDENCE ACQUIRED
THROUGH POLYGRAPH TESTING

The admissibility of polygraph results is controlled more by practical considerations than by the concept of "due process." This is true because the rejection of such evidence has usually been predicated upon its unreliability[94] rather than because such a test encroaches upon protected rights. Arbitrators have usually followed the general rule of courts and have either prohibited the introduction of polygraph evidence voluntarily obtained,[95] or have received it but have required the proof of misconduct to be established with other evidence.[96]

Controversy involving the use of polygraph evidence has arisen over the propriety of the discipline of an employee under investigation who refuses to submit to a polygraph test, and over the admissibility or weight to be given to polygraph evidence obtained by the employer where the employee has consented to the test.

The decision of Arbitrator Daniel Lewis in *Town and Country Food Co.,*[97] exemplifies the reasoning of many arbitrators that the refusal of an employee to take the test is not a sound reason for the discharge of the employee:

"Inasmuch as polygraph test results are generally inadmissible, it follows that refusal to take such a test cannot constitute a proper and just cause for discharge predicated upon insubordination. We cannot draw an inference of guilt against employees who refuse to take a 'lie detector' test."

The National Labor Relations Board takes a contrary view. An employer had insisted that two employees who had previously been given keys to a safe, take lie detector tests after a burglary of the safe. The Board said that such a request was understandable and permissible in view of the suspicious nature of the crime. Therefore,

---

[93] *Id.* at 180. See also *North American Aviation, Inc.,* 19 L.A. 565 (Komaroff, 1952).

[94] McCormick, in his treatise on evidence, criticizes this rationale: C. McCormick, EVIDENCE 371-73 (1954).

[95] See *Louis Zahn Drug Co.,* 40 L.A. 353 (Sembower, 1963) and cases cited therein; *Continental Air Transport Co.,* 38 L.A. 778 (Eiger, 1962); *Coronet Phosphate Co.,* 31 L.A. 515 (Vadakin, 1958). But see *Allen Industries, Inc.,* 26 L.A. 363 (Klamon, 1956).

[96] See, *e.g., Bowman Transportation, Inc.,* 59 L.A. 283 (Murphy, 1972); *American Maize-Products Co.,* 45 L.A. 1155 (Epstein, 1965); *Saveway Inwood Service,* 44 L.A. 709 (Kornblum, 1965); *Spiegel, Inc.,* 44 L.A. 405 (Sembower, 1965); *Westinghouse Electric Co.,* 43 L.A. 450 (Singletary, 1964).

[97] 39 L.A. 332, 335 (Lewis, 1962). See *Colgate-Palmolive Co.,* 50 L.A. 441 (Koven, 1968); *Allen Industries, Inc.,* 26 L.A. 363 (Klamon, 1956).

the discharge of the employees for refusing to take the test was lawful. The Board disagreed with its trial examiner who had found that, although the suspensions pending investigation were lawful, discharging the employees for refusing to take the lie detector test was not.[89]

Other bases for exclusion of polygraph evidence are that the test itself is not subject to cross-examination and that the polygraph procedure violates concepts of the right against self-incrimination and the right to privacy.[99] These objections are not valid when there has been consent. Some courts have in fact admitted polygraph results into evidence where there has been consent.[100]

Other arbitrators have gone beyond the reliability considerations. For example, in *Marathon Electric Mfg. Corp.*,[101] Arbitrator Clair V. Duff first questioned the reliability of the test results, but then recognized that the tests may have evidentiary value when there is a stipulation that the results of the test can be introduced:

"[V]oluntary stipulations would undoubtedly make [polygraph test results] admissible in arbitration proceedings." [102]

Since voluntary stipulation does not affect the reliability of the test results nor the ability of the opposite party to cross-examine the test result, the willingness to accept the test results where there is agreement indicates that the reluctance to accept the results without the stipulation is involved as much with the due process considerations as it is with questions of reliability.

A polygraph test voluntarily obtained has been found to be admissible to corroborate other testimony. Arbitrator A. T. Singletary admitted evidence for such purpose in *Westinghouse Electric Corp.*:[103]

"The arbitrator does not pass upon the reliability of the report of the polygraph examination, but observes that the conclusions reached by the examiner are corroborated by the conclusions reached by this arbitrator from evidence other than those tests." [104]

---

[98] *American Oil Co.*, 189 NLRB No. 2 (1971); but *cf. National Food Services, Inc.*, 196 NLRB No. 52 (1972), where an NLRB Trial Examiner held that the refusal of three employees to take a lie detector test was protected activity under the Act.

[99] See, *e.g.*, *State v. Valdez*, 91 Ariz. 274, 371 P.2d 894 (1962); *Kaminski v. State*, 63 So.2d 339 (Fla. Sup. Ct., 1953). See also Fleming, *Some Problems of Evidence before the Labor Arbitrator*, 60 MICH. L. REV. 133, 163-67 (1961), wherein the author suggests that the exclusionary rule is sound as a matter of arbitral policy, but not because polygraph test results are unreliable.

[100] *People v. Sims*, 395 Ill. 69, 69 N.E.2d 336 (1946). See *U.S. v. Ridling*, — F.Supp. —, 41 U.S. LAW WEEK 2191 (E.D.Mich. 1972).

[101] 31 L.A. 1040 (Duff, 1959).

[102] *Id.* at 1042.

[103] 43 L.A. 450 (Singletary, 1964).

[104] *Id.* at 453.

Likewise, in *Koppers Co., Inc.*,[105] Arbitrator Kates held that the results of a polygraph examination could be utilized to corroborate the testimony of a supervisor. In this regard, Arbitrator Kates stated:

"With respect to the polygraph, (lie detector) test given to supervisor [h.], I consider the results of this test to be *one element* tending to support [h.'s] story." (Emphasis added)[106]

Thus, although the test results were not accepted as conclusive of innocence or guilt by some arbitrators, they have said that the test results can be admitted and can be used to weigh other evidence.

For polygraph tests to be usable and admissible on credibility issues, certain conditions should be met: (1) The examiner should be qualified; (2) the test should be administered promptly after the incident; (3) the test should be voluntary; and (4) the examiner *and* his records should be present for cross-examination.[107]

Where polygraph examinations results have been denied admittance as evidence or have been given no weight, the absence of one of the factors noted about has been asserted as the reason. Thus, in *Coronet Phosphate Co., Inc.*,[108] Arbitrator Vadakin admitted the results of the polygraph examination but gave them no weight because (a) the union was not notified of the test, (b) the questions were prepared by the company alone; and (c) the test was given 11 days after the incident. Likewise, in *McDonnell Aircraft Corp.*,[109] polygraph evidence was admitted but given no weight because (a) there was a failure to present the examiner for cross-examination at the hearing; (b) the test was administered 17 days after the incident; and (c) the union was not notified of the test.

The attitudes of arbitrators toward polygraph test results as evidence vary. Where the test results are admitted, they are not afforded great evidentiary weight and are usually accorded weight only where the results support *other* admissible and independent evidence.

---

105 68-1 ARB ¶ 8084 (1967). See also *Wilkof Steel & Supply Co.*, 63-1 ARB ¶ 8026 (Maxwell, 1962); *Illinois Bell Telephone Co.*, 39 L.A. 470 (Ryder, 1962).

106 *Id.*

107 Reid and Inbau, TRUTH AND DECEPTION: THE POLYGRAPH ("LIE-DETECTOR") TECHNIQUE, 257 (1966) said the following four requirements should be met before the results of a polygraph examination should be admitted as evidence:

". . . (1) That the examiner possess a college degree. (2) That he has received at least six months of internship training under an experienced, competent examiner or examiners with a sufficient volume of case work to afford frequent supervised testing in actual case situations. (3) That the witness have at least five years experience as a specialist in the field of Polygraph examinations. (4) That the Examiner's testimony must be based upon Polygraph records that he produces in Court and which are available for cross-examination purposes."

108 31 L.A. 515 (Vadakin, 1958).

109 66-1 ARB ¶ 8236 (McKenna, 1965).

Where the collective agreement states that all employees shall be subject to polygraph testing, an employee's refusal to take the test is a violation of the employee's duty to cooperate.[110]

F. THE USE AND ADMISSIBILITY OF ELECTRONICALLY OBTAINED EVIDENCE

The question of admissibility of evidence obtained by electronic surveillance, either by visual or oral recording, is a serious question in the arbitration context. Attorney Lee M. Burkey has written numerous articles asserting that the employee's right of privacy and dignity should cause arbitrators to refuse to admit evidence of wrongdoing which was obtained by an electronic device.[111] He has said:

"I believe our constitutional safeguards, which I am well aware are largely designed to safeguard persons in criminal proceedings, should be carried over not only into civil matters pending before the courts, but should also be extended to industrial relations." [112]

Burkey's emphasis of due process considerations was challenged by Attorney Evan J. Spelfogel:

"There are many such as Mr. Burkey who sincerely believe in their cause as one of principle, yet, one wonders whether the intensity of union opposition to the lie detector, closed-circuit TV, and other scientific advances described above is not in direct proportion to the effectiveness of such devices in uncovering and preventing theft." [113]

Two reported cases deal with the admissibility of evidence obtained through electronic surveillance. In *Sun Drug Co.*,[114] the arbitrator admitted the recording of a telephone conversation between the grievant and a bookie during which he placed bets. When the recorded conversation was played back to the employee in his supervisor's

---

[110] See *Warwick Electronics, Inc.,* 46 L.A. 95 (Daugherty, 1966); but see *Lag Drug Co.,* 39 L.A. 1121 (Kelliher, 1962); *Brass-Craft Mfg. Co.,* AAA Case No. 27-4 (Kahn, 1961). There are at least five states which statutorily forbid the employer to make submission to a lie detector test a condition of employment and in 1971, a bill to the same effect was introduced into Congress which, if enacted, would apply to all private and federal employment (S. 2156). ALASKA ANN. STAT. ch. 36, § 1 (1964); CAL. LAB. CODE, § 432.2 (West Supp. 1967); MASS. GEN. LAWS ANN. ch. 149, § 19B (1963); ORE. REV. STAT. ch. 659 (1969); R.I. GEN. LAWS ch. 28-6.1 (1968).

[111] Burkey, *Privacy, Property and the Polygraph,* 18 LAB. L.J. 79 (1967); Burkey, *Employee Surveillance: Are There Civil Rights for the Man on the Job?,* PROCEEDINGS OF NEW YORK UNIVERSITY TWENTY-FIRST ANNUAL CONFERENCE ON LABOR 199 (T. Christensen Ed. 1967); Burkey, *Lie Detectors in Labor Relations,* 19 ARB. J. 193 (1964).

[112] Burkey, *Employee Surveillance: Are There Civil Rights for the Man on the Job?* note 111 *supra,* at 214.

[113] Spelfogel, *Surveillance and Interrogation in Plant Theft and Discipline Cases,* PROCEEDINGS OF NEW YORK UNIVERSITY TWENTY-FIRST ANNUAL CONFERENCE ON LABOR 183-84 (T. Christensen Ed. 1967).

[114] 31 L.A. 191 (Marcus, 1958).

office, he admitted the placing of bets by telephone. The arbitrator considered the question of admissibility of the recording and, following the general view, distinguished arbitration hearings from a criminal trial, saying:

"Suffice it to say that while the legality of the means by which information has been gathered is for other authorities to determine, it is sufficient for the purpose of arbitration, based upon the uncontroverted facts in the instant case, for the Arbitrator to sustain the discharge." [115]

In *Needham Packing Co., Inc.*,[116] Arbitrator Harold Davey refused to admit a tape recording of a telephone conversation between a company attorney and a union official. The case involved the disciplining of employees for engaging in a strike in violation of a no-strike clause. The recorded phone conversation was kept secret until the last day of the arbitration proceedings. The arbitrator excluded it on the ground that the union official had not consented to the recording of the conversation and that all of the parties to the conversation were present at the hearing and able to testify concerning what had transpired. In effect, the arbitrator based his decision concerning admissibility on concepts of best evidence, rather than on criminal "due process."

Several reported cases deal with visual surveillance, but do not involve the question of admissibility of evidence. They involved the right to install visual surveillance equipment without first obtaining the agreement of the union. In *Elco, Inc.*,[117] under an agreement which had no management rights clause, but did have a preservation of beneficial working conditions clause, the company installed a television monitoring system in its plant. Arbitrator Hubert T. Delany held that the company had violated the agreement because the use of television destroyed a beneficial working condition.

But, in *FMC Corp.*,[118] Arbitrator Richard Mittenthal reached the opposite result. The company installed closed-circuit television to decrease pilferage and increase efficiency. The union grieved, arguing

---

[115] *Id.* at 194. See R. Fleming, THE LABOR ARBITRATION PROCESS (1965). Fleming used the facts in the *Sun Drug* case as a hypothetical question to poll arbitrators and reported:
"[The arbitrators] were badly split in their responses. Many said that they would not admit evidence which had been illegally obtained; others said that they would follow the law of the particular state as to admissibility; and still others pointed out that illegal methods used in securing evidence did not impair its truth or relevancy. . . ." (at 191).
See also *Fontaine Truck Equip. Co.*, 193 NLRB No. 30 (1971), where the Board held that a tape recording made at the employee's discharge interview, unknown to the employee, should have been admitted in evidence.
[116] 44 L.A. 1057 (Davey, 1965).
[117] *Id.* 563 (Delany, 1965).
[118] 46 L.A. 335 (Mittenthal, 1966).

(1) that the company's nonuse of television in the past created a beneficial working condition, (2) that the company had not established sufficient need to warrant a change from nonuse to use of television, and (3) that being monitored by television created a serious burden on the employees. Arbitrator Mittenthal, discussing the assertion that lack of television monitoring was a beneficial working condition much more fully than did Delany, found no violation of the agreement, holding that prior nonuse of television did not establish a beneficial working condition unless there was mutual agreement concerning the prior nonuse practice, and that management had under the agreement the exclusive right to make the decision. Mittenthal further held that, in the absence of a specific contract restriction, management can change its methods of supervision without mutual agreement, citing the reservation of powers clause in the agreement.

A similar result was reached in *Ford Motor Co. of Canada*,[119] where the arbitrator upheld the company's right to install closed circuit television cameras at the plant gates. Analogizing such cameras to the presence of plant guards, the arbitrator held:

> "The company is entitled to know who comes into its plant, and to observe those who are approaching. It may observe them carefully or carelessly, and I see no reason to restrict it from taking advantage of whatever technological aids which may be available to it to assist in this regard. Whether such aids are effective or not is a matter for the company to determine." [120]

Another pertinent decision related to this area is *Thomas v. General Electric Co.*,[121] where an employee objected on right-of-privacy grounds to an employer's continuing his long-standing practice of taking motion pictures of employees at work, by which it established work standards, improved methods, and safety procedures. The court in dismissing the employee's complaint did not base its decision on a lack of a right-of-privacy issue, but instead held that so long as the employer's purpose in taking the pictures was to improve efficiency and promote safety, it could take motion pictures at its discretion.

In *Caproco, Inc.*[122] the employer installed a closed-circuit television system to study the performance of incentive workers and a grievance resulted. Arbitrator John Day Larkin denied the grievance. The employer, he said, has the responsibility to run an efficient operation, and the evidence showed that performance, and incentive earnings had

---

[119] 57 L.A. 914 (Weatherill, 1971).

[120] *Id.* at 916. *Cf. United States Steel Corp.*, 49 L.A. 101 (Dybeck, 1967), where a discharge for theft was upheld based on an observation from a concealed position in the plant adjacent to the locker room where the theft occurred.

[121] 207 F.Supp. 792 (W.D.Ky. 1962).

[122] 56 L.A. 65 (Larkin, 1971).

improved with the new system. Moreover, the union acknowledged that nothing in the agreement restricted the company's choice of instruments for making time studies.

In 1968, Congress passed the Omnibus Crime Bill, which included a chapter entitled, "Wire Interception and Interception of Oral Communications."[123] This statute places broad restrictions upon electronic eavesdropping and provides that evidence obtained in violation of the statute is inadmissible "before any court, grand jury, department, officer, agency, regulatory body, legislative committee, or other authority of the United States, a State, or a political subdivision thereof." In addition to the federal statute, many states have adopted comprehensive legislation regulating electronic eavesdropping and restricting the admissibility of evidence obtained illegally.[124]

The federal and state statutes are concerned with the interception of oral communications.[125] They place no restrictions on the admissibility of evidence obtained through visual surveillance by television cameras or other equipment. Further, these statutes place no limitations upon the admissibility of intercepted oral evidence in an arbitration proceeding. Whether an arbitrator might exclude electronic evidence based on an analogy with the statutory rule undoubtedly will depend in part on what the issue is. If the employer intercepted a tele-

---

[123] 82 Stat. 212, 18 U.S.C. § 2510-20 (1968). Prior to the passage of the Omnibus Crime Bill, the principal statute governing electronic surveillance was the Federal Communications Act, 48 Stat. 1104 (1934), 47 U.S.C. § 605 (1958), which prohibited the interception of certain communications. Evidence obtained from the illegal interception of communications as inadmissible in criminal cases in both state and federal courts. Whether the prohibition extends to civil cases in state courts is an open question. See generally *Lee v. Florida,* 392 U.S. 378 (1968); *Mapp v. Ohio,* 367 U.S. 643 (1961).

[124] See ALASKA STAT. §§ 11.60.290-11.60.350 (Supp. Sept. 1970); ARIZ. REV. STAT. ANN. §§ 13-1051-13-1059 (Supp. 1970); CAL. PEN. CODE ANN. §§ 630-637-2 (West 1970); COLO. REV. STAT. ANN. §§ 40-4-26, 40-4-30, 40-4-33 (Supp. 1969); CONN. GEN. STAT. ANN. § 52-184a (Supp. 1970) and §§ 189-91 (Pen. Code; West 1969); FLA. STAT. ANN. §§ 934.01-934.10 (Supp. 1970); GA. CODE ANN. §§ 26-3001-26-3010 (Supp. 1970); HAWAII SESS. LAWS ACT 209 (1967); ILL. ANN. STAT. ch. 38 §§ 14-1-14-7 (Smith-Hurd, 1964); KAN. GEN. STAT. ANN. §§ 21-4001-21-4002, 22-2513 (Supp. 1970); MD. ANN. CODE Art. 35 §§ 92-99, Art. 27 §§ 125A-125D (1957); MASS. GEN. LAWS ANN. ch. 272 § 99 (1970); MICH. STAT. ANN. §§ 28.807(1)-28.807(9) (Supp. 1970); MINN. STAT. ANN. §§ 626A.01-626A.23 (Supp. 1970); NEB. REV. STAT. §§ 86-701-86-707 (Supp. 1969); NEV. REV. STAT. §§ 200.610-200.690 (1969); N.H. REV. STAT. ANN. §§ 570-A:1-570-A:11 (Supp. 1969); N.J. STAT. ANN. §§ 2A:156A-1-2A:156A-26 (Supp. 1970); N.Y. PEN. LAW §§ 250 *et. seq.* (Supp. 1970) and N.Y. CIV. PRAC. LAW § 4506 (Supp. 1970); OHIO CODE ANN. § 2933.58 (Page; Supp. 1970); ORE. REV. STAT. §§ 41.910, 141.720-141.990, 165.535-165.545 (1969); S.D. COMP. LAWS 1967 ANN. §§ 23-13A-1-23-13A-11 (Supp. 1970); WASH. REV. CODE ANN. §§ 9.73.030-9.73.100 (Supp. 1970); WIS. STAT. ANN. §§ 968.27-968.33 (Supp. 1970).

[125] The statutes rejecting evidence collected by a wiretap usually apply to court proceedings, but in three states they apply to a "proceeding" and could be construed to reject such evidence in an arbitration proceeding. See CAL. PEN. CODE ANN. §§ 631(c), 632(d) (West, 1970); MINN. STAT. ANN. § 626A.11(1) (Supp. 1970); NEV. REV. STAT. § 200.680(1) (1969).

phone call to a hard drug seller or a syndicate gambling agent working in the plant, the duty of the employer, and for that matter the union, to protect the group from exploitation would arguably override the due process considerations being urged by analogy with the state and federal statutes.

In this connection, Arbitrator J. H. Marcus said in *Sun Drug Co.*, that it was not for the arbitrator to determine admissibility of such evidence as "the legality of the means by which information has been gathered is for other authorities to determine."[126]

G. ADMISSIBILITY OF EVIDENCE DEALING WITH CRIMINAL PROSECUTION OR PAST RECORD AND THE DEFENSE OF DOUBLE JEOPARDY

Another criminal "due process" consideration which occasionally arises in the arbitration setting is the right to be protected from double jeopardy. This doctrine has been asserted to thwart the introduction of evidence in an arbitration proceeding or as a basis for the claim that the discipline imposed is improper.

Often, an employer has suspended an employee during the investigation of a criminal charge and then discharged him if he is convicted. Such discharges are sustained if the crime involves conduct which would cause the retention of the employee in employment to be an unusual risk to the employer or to the employees, or where the criminal conduct involved the employer or fellow employees.[127]

In *Consolidated Badger Cooperative*,[128] the grievant had been convicted of the crime of fornication and the union claimed that discipline by the employer for the same reason would amount to double punishment. After determining that the employee's conviction hampered his effectiveness as an employee and resulted in detrimental publicity affecting the employer's business, the arbitrator discussed the double jeopardy defense, saying:

> "The double jeopardy argument has been advanced in numerous cases before arbitrators and the undersigned is in accord with the majority of other arbitrators to the effect that while the law provides the civil or criminal punishment for any given case the resultant penalties which often result are many times more severe than the penalty itself. . . . The real criterion, however, in double jeopardy arguments is not the fact that two penalties may be assessed for the same cause but whether or not the act of said employee did in fact substantially affect his relation-

---

[126] 31 L.A. at 194.

[127] *Pearl Brewing Co.*, 48 L.A. 379 (Howard, 1967); *Cities Service Oil Co.*, 41 L.A. 1091 (Oppenheim, 1963); *Great Atlantic & Pacific Tea Co.*, 45 L.A. 495 (Livengood, undated).

[128] 36 L.A. 965 (Mueller, 1961), see cases cited therein.

ship with the Employer as an employee and if such is found to be the case any resultant discipline or even discharge which may follow therefrom is based upon his rights as derived from the contract. It must be remembered that without the contract the Employer could discipline or discharge the employee at will. . . ." [129]

For example, in *Westinghouse Electric Corp.*,[130] the arbitrator considered the defense that to discipline an employee for an act for which he could be criminally prosecuted violated the prohibition against double jeopardy. In that case the grievants were discharged for acts of violence during a strike. The arbitrator said:

"I am unable to agree with the union's argument of double jeopardy which is based upon the claim that the discharges were for acts which were also violations of the criminal laws and for which grievants were or could be prosecuted. An employer is not precluded from imposing discipline upon employees for acts which are violations of the penal code and which take place in or about the plant premises or are connected with the employment relationship. Nor, conversely, is punishment by the employer, as authorized by the collective bargaining agreement, any defense to prosecution of the employee by state authorities for a criminal offense based upon the same act." [131]

Arbitrator Ralph Seward rejected a double jeopardy claim when the employer relied upon prior conduct for which discipline had been previously given in determining the amount of discipline to be given for subsequent improper conduct. He said:

"As for the Union's 'double jeopardy' claim, the Umpire does not believe the latter doctrine has any application herein. Obviously, an employee's past record may not be used by itself to justify the discharge penalty, where there has been no new offense—*i.e.* no new disciplinary 'event'—to warrant disciplinary action. But where a fresh offense has been committed, the magnitude of the penalty to be applied may certainly be determined not only by the new offense, alone, but in the perspective of the employee's record as a whole. Indeed, where the employee's record has been good, the Union would be the first to claim that it should be considered as a mitigating circumstance in setting a penalty." [132]

H. DUE PROCESS CONSIDERATIONS RELATING TO THE "AGREED" AWARD

In the course of an arbitration proceeding the parties often decide to settle their dispute, and may ask the arbitrator, as part of the

---

[129] *Id.* at 968.

[130] 40 L.A. 1169 (Schmidt, 1963).

[131] *Id.* at 1173.

[132] *Bethlehem Steel Co.*, 41 L.A. 890, 892 (Seward, 1963). See also *American Airlines, Inc.*, 46 L.A. 737 (Sembower, 1966); *Arden Farms Co.*, 45 L.A. 1124 (Tsukiyama, 1965).

mechanism of settlement, to include the stipulated settlement in his award. This procedure has its counterpart in civil litigation where judgment may be entered upon stipulation of the parties, and comports with the *Code of Ethics and Procedural Standards for Labor-Management Arbitration* prepared by the American Arbitration Association and National Academy of Arbitrators.[133] For these reasons commentators have found no ethical problem in such procedure.[134]

A situation more difficult to evaluate in terms of due process can arise, however, when the parties have agreed beforehand that they want the arbitrator to decide a case in a certain way and the representatives of the two parties want to conceal their agreement from either the grievant, the union membership, or from other company officials.

In court proceedings the lawyers representing the two parties to the litigation often confer together with the judge in chambers on various matters and may upon such an occasion communicate to him a result that the lawyers for the two parties have agreed would satisfy each. In labor arbitration, so long as the representatives of both parties are present in a "chambers" conference with the arbitrator, a similar communication should not raise any more serious questions of ethical conduct than does the parallel chambers conference in a court proceeding,[135] except that there is possibly more uneasiness when an arbitration involves a discharge. One observer, however, believes any type of "agreed award" is harmful to the reputation of the arbitration process. He said:

> *"The 'sweetheart' arbitration*—From time to time over the years there have been a few reports of instances where Union and management agreed upon the decision which the arbitrator should reach and then transmitted their decision to the arbitrator for effectuation by him. Such cases arise in many different settings. For example, the Union may agree that a discharged employee deserves to be fired but refuses to accept the responsibility of agreeing with the employer publicly or the issue involved may be one in which the parties agree but for which neither wants to take specific responsibility insofar as either the employee body

---

[133] CODE OF ETHICS AND PROCEDURAL STANDARDS FOR LABOR-MANAGEMENT ARBITRATION, prepared by The American Arbitration Association and The National Academy of Arbitrators.

[134] See generally Fleming, *Some Problems of Due Process and Fair Procedure in Labor Arbitration,* 13 STAN. L. REV. 235 (1961). Wirtz, *Due Process of Arbitration,* THE ARBITRATOR AND THE PARTIES, Proceedings of the Eleventh Annual Meeting, National Academy of Arbitrators 1, 26-32 (J. McKelvey Ed. 1958); *The "Agreed Case: A Problem in Ethics,* 20 ARB. J. 41-48 (1965).

[135] Fleming, note 134 *supra,* at 235, 248-251, also published in ARBITRATION AND PUBLIC POLICY, Proceedings of the Fourteenth Annual Meeting, National Academy of Arbitrators (1961) at 87-90. For an earlier study, see Wirtz, note 135 *supra,* at 26-32; but see to the contrary Hays, *Labor Arbitration—A Dissenting View,* 74 YALE L.J. 1019, 1033 (1965).

or the general public are concerned. While such instances are rare, it is believed that such 'agreed' or 'sweetheart' arbitrations in which the result is pre-ordained by the parties and the arbitrator acts merely as a rubber stamp are unwise and do serious harm to the integrity of the arbitration process. If the parties have reached agreement on a proposition, they should not seek to make it appear that the decision is not theirs but that of the arbitrator; nor should the arbitrator lend himself to such perversion of his functions." [136]

Because collusion is rarely, if ever, involved unless a grievance claim is an objection to discipline or discharge, many commentators see no objection to private joint communication by representatives of both parties in cases that do not involve discharge or discipline. [137] Where it becomes evident that there is unfair representation, the award would be set aside by a court on that ground. Arbitrator Herbert L. Sherman, Jr., reported that:

"Where the Union representative does not ask the arbitrator to make a prior commitment on the decision that he will render but simply tells the arbitrator that a hearing must be held for 'political' reasons even though the Union representative agrees with the Company's position, the prevailing view among arbitrators (except in the South) is that there is no duty of disclosure. Most Union and Company representatives also believe that there is no duty of disclosure in this situation in which the arbitrator has not been asked to make a commitment on how he will decide the case and in fact he has made no such commitment.

". . . [T]he Union representative may hint, after the hearing, that he expects to lose the case. Most respondents to my questionnaire believe that an arbitrator has no duty to disclose that on a plant visit, after the hearing, the Union representative, who presented the Union's case, indicates that he has done his best in presenting the case but that he will understand if the arbitrator rules in favor of the Company under the contract." [138]

These views are consistent with the view of the Ninth Circuit. In *Local 13, ILWU v. Pacific Maritime Assn.*[139] that court said that an "agreed" award is not improper if not motivated by an improper hostility toward the individual member. The court explained that on occasion there are strong political reasons for union representatives to submit a grievance and yet want the award to be in favor of the employer. While such actions by the union could well be free of hostile motivation toward the individual, some observers have believed that the very fact that a representative "agreed" to an award would be *prima facie* evidence of hostility toward the individual.

---

[136] Levitt, *Lawyers, Legalism, and Labor Arbitration, Symposium on Labor,* 6 NEW YORK LAW FORUM 398 (1960).

[137] See note 2 *supra.*

[138] H. Sherman, Jr., *Arbitrators Duty to Disclose—A Sequel,* 32 U. PITT. L. REV. 167, 181 (1970).

[139] 441 F.2d 1061 (9th Cir. 1971).

Implicitly, the Ninth Circuit rejected the view that evidence of an agreed award was *prima facie* evidence of hostility and required the proponent of vacation to show additional evidence of hostility. The court said:

> "We agree with appellees that a breach of the duty of fair representation would not be established merely by proof that the International Union 'swapped' a concession that section 17.81 applied to union officials for acceptance by the employers' association of the position that the contract limited the individual packing of sacks. In this practical world such issues, susceptible of no absolutely 'right' solution, are often resolved by accommodation. . . . If the choice were motivated by a good-faith balancing of interests of different elements within the International union, it might well fall within the 'wide range of reasonableness . . . allowed a statutory bargaining representative in serving the unit it represents.' " [140]

I. FAILURE TO COMPLY WITH CONTRACTUAL PROCEDURE

In certain collective bargaining agreements a procedure is described that the employer is to follow before discharging an employee. For example, in the labor agreements between the United Steelworkers and the steel producing companies and many fabricating companies the employer is required to suspend the employee for five days and hold a hearing before determining whether to discharge the employee.

In *Republic Steel Corp.,*[141] Arbitrator Stashower, in overturning a discharge for failure to provisionally discharge an employee prior to final termination, said:

> "While I agree that substantially Zeller was afforded the protection intended by the clause when he asked for and was given a hearing within the time limits contained in the Contract, it must be concluded that the procedural requirement as to the provisional discharge was not complied with by the Company. Its failure to so comply constituted a violation of the Contract.
> "In view of this finding, it is unnecessary to discuss the merits of the discharge and the grievance must therefore be upheld." [142]

Because of similar language in the Armco Steel Corporation agreement an employee, who was arrested for taking indecent liberties with a nine-year-old girl and who subsequently pleaded guilty and was sent to a mental hospital and then sentenced to jail for a year,

---

[140] *Id.* at 1067.
[141] 3 STEEL ARB. 1833 (Stashower, 1953). See also *Shop Rite Foods, Inc.,* 55 L.A. 281 (Hayes, 1970); *Northern California Growers Assn.,* 53 L.A. 85 (Eaton, 1969); *Zenith Radio Corp.,* 47 L.A. 257, 258 (Griffin, 1966); *United Air Lines, Inc.,* 47 L.A. 910 (Sembower, 1966); *Decor Corp.,* 44 L.A. 389, 391 (Kates, 1965); *Kroger Co.,* 36 L.A. 1386 (Barnhart, 1961); *Baldwin-Lima-Hamilton Corp.,* 19 L.A. 177 (Day, 1952); *Babcock & Wilcox Co.,* 41 L.A. 862, 867 (Dworkin, 1963).
[142] 3 STEEL ARB. at 1834.

was reinstated by the Arbitrator because he was notified of his discharge while in the hospital rather than being notified of a five-day suspension with the intention to discharge. Due to the Company's use of the wrong words, Arbitrator Kates held that the discharge was ineffective, explaining:

"The parties in their collective bargaining agreement have gone into considerable detail to assure bargaining unit members of so-called 'due process' before being severed from their employment. Due process is often as important in the protection of a man's means of livelihood as with reference to his freedom from imprisonment.

"Any action taken by an employer to terminate a man's employment status, if in violation of agreed contractual procedures which have not been waived, must ordinarily be deemed invalid.

". . .

"In my opinion, the Company violated the 'due process' specified by the contract in its actions in terminating the grievant's employment." [143]

Thus, some arbitrators conclude that a failure by the employer to follow a contractual procedure nullifies the discharge or discipline, irrespective of what wrongful conduct was engaged in by the employee.

To the contrary, however, other arbitrators take the position that a procedural defect by the employer, such as a notice orally given rather than in writing, or the use of the word "discharge" rather than "suspension with intention to discharge" in the notice cannot wipe away the industrial misconduct engaged in by an employee. These arbitrators do consider it their duty to provide the discharged employee all of the protections that the procedural steps set forth in the agreement were designed to provide him, but they do not treat these procedural matters as conditions precedent to an effective discharge, and hence hold that some technical noncompliance does not require reinstatement.

Arbitrator John Day Larkin espoused this viewpoint in a case where an employee participated in a strike in violation of the agreement. The employee was told to return to work or he would be discharged. Upon his failure to return to work he was "indefinitely suspended" instead of receiving a preliminary suspension for five days as provided for in the Agreement. In upholding the discharge Arbitrator Larkin said:

"The record shows that Mr. Garono did not receive the usual 'pink slip' or specific form used in discharge cases, wherein he was notified that he was suspended for 'five (5) calendar days excluding Sundays and holidays. . .', after which his discharge was to take effect. . . . Instead he got a letter stating that his suspension was 'indefinite,' but that the

---

[143] *Armco Steel Corp.,* 43 L.A. 977, 979 (Kates, 1964). See also *Michigan Fleet Equipment,* 72-2 ARB ¶ 8381 (Belkin, 1972) where back pay was ordered for an employee suspended for refusal to wear safety glasses because the foreman neglected to offer a copy of his suspension notice before he left the plant.

termination would be in accordance with the provisions of the Agreement. Because of this disparity in form and language, it is now argued that Mr. Garono is being denied his procedural rights. It is said that he was summarily discharged.

"With this we cannot agree. Mr. Garono was privileged to file a grievance. He was given a hearing locally. And the matter was taken up with Union officials from the District office. From these hearings, the matter was appealed to arbitration. Under the terms of the parties' Agreement, no discharge is final until all steps in the grievance procedure have been exhausted. Therefore, Mr. Garono's case is not concluded until this arbitration award is released. In short, until this report is completed and in the hands of the parties, Mr. Garono's discharge is still provisional. A discharge brought about in this way cannot be considered a preemptory discharge. Or, to use the langage of Article VIII, Mr. Garono has not been 'pre-emptorily' discharged; he was only suspended, pending the process prescribed by the parties in their Agreement. Therefore, any claim to his restoration under the provisions of Article VIII is simply without foundation.

    ". . .

"Suffice it to say that both Mr. Garono's warning notice and his suspension notice assured him that he would be accorded his full rights under the Agreement. And in spite of some slight variation in form and language, we believe that he was given a proper procedural treatment under the circumstances then prevailing." [144]

Similarly, in *Frito-Lay, Inc.,*[145] a discharge for an unsatisfactory ourse of conduct by a salesman was upheld even though the advance otice of discharge requirement of the contract was not complied 'ith. After finding that the company had made out a *prima facie* ase justifying discharge in substantive terms, the arbitrator held:

"I have concluded in the instant case that the delay in the communication should not result in the reversal of the Company's action. As the facts reveal, efforts were made to inform the Union in advance of the discharge, and word was left at the Union's office to return the Company's call. While other means of communication could have been employed, the efforts made to [sic] reflect that the Company was not striving to circumvent the intent of the contract. . . . Furthermore, it is clear that the Company's decision was not made in haste or in anger. In such a setting it is difficult to conclude that notice to the Union in advance of the termination could have stayed the results. It is also significant that notice was conveyed very shortly after the discharge, and thus the delay constituted no hurdle to the investigation of facts or to the implementation of the grievance proceedings. . . ." [146]

In *Thompson Bros. Boat Mfg. Co.,*[147] a truck driver was discharged for serious misconduct during the course of his employment. The

---

[144] *Valley Mold & Iron Co.,* Grievance No. 8, 54-56 (Larkin, 1954) (unreported).
[145] 52 L.A. 1213 (Dykstra, 1969).
[146] *Id.* at 1216-17.
[147] 56 L.A. 973 (Schurke, 1971).

union sought his reinstatement because the company failed to provide the union with written notice of the discharge as required by the agreement. In sustaining the discharge, Arbitrator Schurke stated:

> "There is no evidence that either the Union or the grievant has been prejudiced or that the grievance settlement machinery created by the collective bargaining agreement has been obstructed by the lack of a separate letter to the Union, separately delivered. It is apparent that the grievant promptly transmitted the letter addressed to him to the Union. . . . Since there has been actual notice to the Union and since there is no evidence of prejudice requiring remedy, the undersigned will proceed to the merits of the case. . . ." [148]

Arbitrator George Carroll likewise held in a case where the company neglected to provide the union with written notice of the reasons for discharge before it occurred that it was a procedural defect, but was not a sufficient reason for reinstatement. The employee had been discharged for striking another worker with a heavy metal object and when the case came to arbitration the grievant's only defense was that the company had neglected to give the union the required written notice. Arbitrator Carroll said that the purpose of the notice-of-discharge provision was to inform the employee of the reasons for the discharge, but that since there was "uncontroverted testimony" that both the employee and the union understood fully the reason for the discharge, the lack of the notice was no detriment to the employee.[149]

Arbitrator Hillard Kreimer similarly refused to reinstate a dischargee where the company, contrary to the agreement, gave the employee only an oral rather than written notice of the reasons for his discharge. In reaching his conclusion the Arbitrator stated:

> "The oral notice in no way affected his substantive rights. Certainly, in the rush and pressure of attempting to settle the work stoppage, the Company can be forgiven a procedural oversight.
>
> " . . .
>
> "During the discussions to end the work stoppage, Grievant and the Union were both fully aware that the Company already felt Grievant was involved in it. The suspension was inflicted before the men returned to work, so that everyone had the opportunity to present information on that issue. . . . Although the contract requires that the reasons for suspension or discharge be specified, it also indicates reinstatement should take place if *further* investigation proves an injustice has been done." (emphasis in original)[150]

---

[148] *Id.* at 977.

[149] *Minerals and Chemicals Corp.,* AAA Case No. 13-23 (Carroll, 1959). See also *Wilson & Company, Inc.,* 50 L.A. 807 (Eaton, 1968); *Neway Uniform and Towel Supply of Florida, Inc.,* 66-1 ARB ¶ 8126 (Kuvin, 1966); *United Engineering & Foundry Co.,* 37 L.A. 1095 (Kates, 1962).

[150] *Mead Corp.,* 53 L.A. 342, 344 (Kreimer, 1969). *Contra, Huffman Mfg. Co.,* 38 L.A. 882 (Stouffer, 1972).

One arbitrator did not treat a procedural error as a condition precedent that had to be met before the discharge could be effective, but to encourage future compliance converted a discharge of an employee for insubordination to a five-day suspension because, among other reasons, the employer had failed to follow the contractual requirement that he notify the union of the discharge.[151]

Other arbitrators encourage future compliance by the employer with the procedural rules in another way. Where the company failed or was late in complying with a procedural step such as a failure to give the union notification of the dismissal,[152] the refusal of an employee request to call a foreman to the hearing despite the contractual right to have him called,[153] the failure to give a required written statement of reasons,[154] the failure to hold a required predischarge hearing in the presence of union representatives,[155] arbitrators have sustained the discharges because they were predicated upon sufficient cause, but the dischargees were awarded pay from the date of discharge to the date of the award, or some other appropriate date, as a penalty against the employer for noncompliance.

The position taken by arbitrators in discipline and discharge cases where the employer makes a procedural mistake was summarized by Arbitrator Fleming in these words:

> ". . . (1) that unless there is strict compliance with the procedural requirements the whole action will be nullified; (2) that the requirements are of significance only where the employee can show that he has been prejudiced by failure to comply therewith; or (3) that the requirements are important, and that any failure to comply will be penalized, but that the action taken is not thereby rendered null and void. . . ."[156]

Arbitrator Fleming was very critical of the arbitrators who permit form to control substance (the first group). He said:

> "The procedural irregularity may not have been prejudicial in any sense of the word, the emphasis upon technicalities would be inconsistent with the informal atmosphere of the arbitration process, and the end result could on many occasions be quite ludicrous. If, for instance, an employee gets drunk on the job and starts smashing valuable machinery with a sledge hammer, it would hardly seem appropriate to nullify his discharge on the sole ground that it was in violation of a contractual requirement that the union be given advance notice. . . ."[157]

---

151 *Ranney Refrigerator Co.,* 5 L.A. 621 (Lappin, 1946).

152 *National Lead Co.,* 13 L.A. 28 (Prasow, 1949).

153 *Pittsburgh Plate Glass Co.,* 8 L.A. 317 (Blair, 1947).

154 *Schreider Trucking Co.,* 5 L.A. 430 (Blair, 1946).

155 *Torrington Co.,* 1 L.A. 35 (Courskon, 1945).

156 R. Fleming, The Labor Arbitration Process, 139 (1965).

157 *Id.*

CHAPTER XIV

Remedies

An arbitrator's award normally is accompanied by an opinion setting forth the basis for the decision and the remedy considered necessary to rectify the violation if one is found to exist.[1] Arbitrators have sometimes been asked by one party to issue an award without a remedy, but generally refuse to do so absent an express agreement between the parties.[2]

A. THE BASIS OF THE ARBITRATOR'S REMEDIAL AUTHORITY

Generally speaking, arbitrators rule that their appointment carries with it an implicit power to specify the appropriate remedy.[3] This position was given court approval in the New York case of *Utility Laundry Service, Inc. v. Sklar*[4] where the court emphasized that:

> "An agreement to arbitrate 'all controversies' arising under a contract will be construed as affording 'authority to assess the damages against the party in default.' . . . The issue must turn upon the intent of the parties as expressed in their agreement, and the general submission of 'any dispute' has been held to confer power to award damages. . . ."[5]

The view that a union could not in an arbitration proceeding obtain wages due the employees because the labor agreement did not provide for money awards was rejected by a federal court shortly after *Lincoln Mills*.[6] The court viewed *Lincoln Mills* as "a retreat" from the line of cases relied upon by the company that since a union could not sue

---

[1] See generally F. Elkouri and E. Elkouri, How Arbitration Works 19-28 (rev. ed. 1960); Stein, *Remedies in Labor Arbitration*, Challenges to Arbitration, Proceedings of the Thirteenth Annual Meeting, National Academy of Arbitrators 41 (J. McKelvey Ed. 1960). But see Freidin, *Discussion on Remedies in Arbitration*, Labor Arbitration—Perspectives and Problems, Proceedings of the Seventeenth Annual Meeting, National Academy of Arbitrators 201 (M. Kahn Ed. 1964).

[2] *City of Dearborn, Mich.*, 69-2 ARB ¶ 8442 (Keefe, 1969); *U.S. Steel Corp.*, 35 L.A. 453 (Crawford, 1960).

[3] See, *e.g.*, *Vanette Hosiery Mills*, 17 L.A. 349 (Emery, 1961); *International Harvester Co.*, 9 L.A. 894 (Wirtz, 1947); *Warren City Mfg. Co.*, 7 L.A. 202 (Abernethy, 1947); *Glenn L. Martin Co.*, 6 L.A. 500 (Brecht, 1947).

[4] 300 N.Y. 255, 90 N.E.2d 178 (1949).

[5] 90 N.E.2d at 180. See also *Texas Gas Transmission Corp. v. Chemical Workers Local 187*, 200 F.Supp. 521 (W.D. La. 1961).

[6] *Textile Workers Union v. Lincoln Mills of Ala.*, 353 U.S. 448 (1957).

to recover unpaid wages owed to individual employees, it could not, under Section 301 of the Taft-Hartley Act, obtain an enforcement of an arbitration award directing the company to pay unpaid wages to employees.[7]

This, of course, is a proper view of the remedial scope available under *Lincoln Mills*. Speaking of the remedial authority of courts under Section 301 (which would include the authority to enforce arbitration awards), Justice Douglas emphasized that courts should resolve the problems presented by "looking at the policy of the legislature and fashioning a remedy that will effectuate that policy. The range of judicial inventiveness will be determined by the nature of the problem."[8]

In striking contrast, however, the Eighth Circuit in *Luggage & Novelty Workers Local 66 v. Neevel Luggage Mfg. Co., Inc.*[9] affirmed a trial court's denial of enforcement of an award because the arbitrator granted back pay to an employee he found had been laid off improperly because the remedy of back pay had not been requested in the submission.

This view that the remedial power of the arbitrator is limited to the remedies requested in the submission appears to be inconsistent with the much broader power which the Supreme Court has said resides in the arbitrator.[10] In *Steelworkers v. Enterprise Wheel & Car Corp.*,[11]

---

[7] *Local 130, Electrical Workers v. Mississippi Valley Electric Co.*, 175 F.Supp. 312 (E.D.La. 1959).

[8] See note 6 *supra*, at 448, 457.

[9] 325 F.2d 992 (8th Cir. 1964) distinguished in *American Bosch Arma Corp. v. IUE*, 243 F.Supp. 493 (N.D. Miss. 1965). Usually the authority to award back pay to a reinstated employee is contained in the collective bargaining agreement and such authority is also incorporated by reference in all labor agreements that refer to the American Arbitration Rules. American Arbitration Association, *Voluntary Labor Arbitration Rules*, Rule 9 (1965). See *Stanlinski v. Pyramid Elec. Co.*, 6 N.Y.2d 195, 160 N.E.2d 78 (1959), where the court said the agreement to arbitrate under the American Arbitration Association rules empowered the arbitrator to grant specific performance of a personal service contract.

[10] "It is apparent that in order to carry out the Congressional policy in favor of the arbitrability of labor disputes, arbitrators must be vested with broad power to fashion appropriate remedies in the cases before them. The need for such broad power has generally been recognized by the federal courts which have usually held that in the absence of restrictive language in a collective bargaining agreement the arbitrator has power to fashion a remedy appropriate to the case before him." Dannell, *Norris-LaGuardia and Injunctions in Labor Arbitration Cases*, REPORT OF THE SIXTEENTH ANNUAL NEW YORK UNIVERSITY CONFERENCE ON LABOR 275-76 (M. Kahn Ed. 1957). See generally Comment, *Labor Law: Authority of Arbitrator to Determine Remedy for Violation of Collective Bargaining Agreement*, 43 MARQ. L. REV. 260 (1959); Cornfield, *Developing Standards for Determining Arbitrability of Labor Disputes by Federal Courts*, 14 LAB. L.J. 564, 573 (1963); Fleming, *Arbitrators and the Remedy Power*, 48 VA. L. REV. 1199 (1962); *Labor Arbitration in the Federal Courts: Excerpts from a Report of the Subcommittee on Labor Arbitration Law of the Section on Labor Relations Law, American Bar Association*, 15 ARB. J. 113 (1960).

[11] 363 U.S. 593 (1960).

the Supreme Court held that under Section 301 courts should recognize that the arbitrator has powers to formulate remedies that are compatible with national labor policy.

> "When an arbitrator is commissioned to interpret and apply the collective bargaining agreement, he is to bring his informed judgment to bear in order to reach a fair solution of a problem. *This is especially true when it comes to formulating remedies.* There the need is for flexibility in meeting a wide variety of situations. The draftsmen may never have thought of what specific remedy should be awarded to meet a particular contingency." (Emphasis added.)[12]

Indeed, to underscore the broad remedial powers of an arbitrator, the Court in *Enterprise Wheel* enforced an arbitrator's award which granted back pay to discharged employees beyond the expiration date of the contract.

Taking a cue from this case, courts have enforced broad remedies fashioned by arbitrators. For example, in *Selb Mfg. Co. v. Machinists,*[13] the Eighth Circuit upheld an award ordering a company:

> "(1) [T]o return to their plants in St. Louis machinery, equipment and work they had transferred to the plants in Arkansas and Colorado, and (2) to recall all their St. Louis employees laid off since September 23, 1960, and to reinstate them without loss of seniority or loss of pay."[14]

Likewise, in *Machinists v. Cameron Iron Works, Inc.,*[15] the Fifth Circuit, also taking its cue from the Supreme Court, reversed its prior position[16] that, absent express contractual authority, an arbitrator was not authorized to award damages. The court explained the abruptness of its reversal:

> "Likewise, whether it is thought to be a part of the substantive right or more a part of the grievance procedure, in the absence of clearly restrictive language, great latitude must be allowed in fashioning the appropriate remedy constituting the arbitrator's 'decision.'
>
> ". . . [W]e find no such positive declaration as would exclude from the arbitrators the power to determine whether the award of back pay is or is not within the terms of the agreement, and if so, whether it is or is not an appropriate remedy."[17]

---

[12] *Id.* at 597.

[13] 305 F.2d 177 (8th Cir. 1962).

[14] *Id.* at 179.

[15] 292 F.2d 112 (5th Cir.), *cert. denied,* 368 U.S. 926 (1961). See also *Texas Gas Transmission Corp. v. Chemical Workers,* 200 F.Supp. 521 (W.D. La. 1961).

[16] See, *e.g., Refinery Employees Union v. Continental Oil Co.,* 268 F.2d 447 (5th Cir.), *cert. denied,* 361 U.S. 896 (1959).

[17] 292 F.2d 112, 119 (5th Cir. 1961). The wide range of remedies available to the arbitrator is further evidenced by the Uniform Arbitration Act, which provides in Section 12(a)(5) that:

> "[T]he fact that the relief was such that it could not or would not be granted by a court of law or equity is not ground for vacating or refusing to affirm the award."

Act Relating to Arbitration and to Make Uniform the Law with Reference Thereto, 9 UNIFORM LAWS ANNOTATED 39 (Supp. 1967).

However, there is a limit to the arbitrator's power to fashion a remedy. A district court explained that a remedy fashioned by Arbitrator Rolf Valtin exceeded his authority and was not enforceable.[18] Valtin had determined that when the United States Gypsum Company purchased a plant from the United Cement Company it became bound by the labor agreement between United Cement and the union. This agreement contained a provision reopening wages for negotiation but Gypsum refused to negotiate. Valtin concluded it would be fruitless to order negotiations under this clause four years later so he directed in his award that Gypsum pay a retroactive increase that he calculated would have resulted if there had been negotiations. In holding this remedy improper, the court said that the labor agreement provided for negotiation on wages—not arbitration of a disagreement about the subject; and violates the remedial standards enunciated in *H. K. Porter*.[19] In that case, the Court held that under the Taft Act the National Labor Relations Board cannot prescribe the substantive provisions of the labor agreement.

B. REMEDIES IN DISCIPLINARY CASES

Disciplinary cases constitute the largest single group of cases which are brought to arbitration, and a wide variety of special remedies in such cases have been fashioned by arbitrators. Arbitrators have noted that the contractual right of the employer to discipline and discharge employees for "just cause" requires the arbitrators to make two determinations: (i) whether a cause for discipline exists and (ii) whether the amount of discipline was proper under the circumstances. For example, in *Great Atlantic & Pacific Tea Co.*,[20] Arbitrator Burton Turkus explained:

> "In applying the test of 'just cause' the arbitrator is generally required to determine two factors: (a) has the commission of the misconduct, offense or dereliction of duty, upon which the discipline administered was grounded, been adequately established by the proof; and (b) if proven or admitted, the reasonableness of the disciplinary penalty imposed in the light of the nature, character and gravity thereof—for as frequently as not the reasonableness of the penalty (as well as the actual commission of the misconduct itself) is questioned or challenged in arbitration.

---

[18] *Steelworkers v. U.S. Gypsum Co.*, 79 LRRM 2833 (D.C.Ala. 1972).

[19] 397 U.S. 99 (1970). See also *Ex-Cell-O Corp. v. NLRB*, 449 F.2d 1058 (C.A. D.C. 1971); *Tiidee Int'l Union of Electrical, Radio & Machine Wkrs. v. NLRB*, 426 F.2d 1243 (C.A.D.C. 1970). See also on remand *Tiidee Int'l*, 194 NLRB No. 198 (1972) and 196 NLRB No. 27 (1972); *Braswell Motor Freight Lines*, 196 NLRB No. 10 (1972).

[20] 63-1 ARB ¶ 8027 (Turkus, 1962).

> "In the absence of contract language expressly prohibiting the exercise of such power, the arbitrator, by virtue of his authority and duty to fairly and finally settle and adjust (decide) the dispute before him has the inherent power to determine the sufficiency of the cause and the reasonableness of the penalty imposed." [21]

As Arbitrator Turkus noted, some labor agreements deny the arbitrator the power to modify the penalty if "just cause" for the discipline is established, and this limitation on an arbitrator's remedial power is considered below.

(1) Reinstatement

Where an arbitrator finds that a discharge was not for "just cause," an essential part of the remedy is reinstatement. [22] It is, however, a matter of historical interest that as late as 1936 courts held that an order of reinstatement was unenforceable since the common law forbids the specific performances of an employment contract; *i.e.,* forcing an employee by court order to work for a particular employer, or forcing an employer to continue in employment a particular employee. [23] The employee's right to employment unless he is guilty of misconduct constituting "just cause" for discharge is a contractual right based on the collective bargaining agreement, which is paramount to the individual contract of employment. [24] Reinstatement by order of an arbitrator was a very fundamental change in the United States labor relations system. Collective labor agreements enforced by arbitration became an almost universal part of the employer-union relationship under the stimulus of the War Labor Board established in World War II. No doubt remains about the authority of an arbitrator, acting under the usual provision of the collective agreement that employees may be discharged only for a just cause, to direct reinstatement as the remedy for a discharge he finds to have not been for just cause. Such an arbitration award is enforceable in the courts, like any other, notwithstanding the old common-law doctrine that a court may not order a contract of personal service to be specifically performed.

(2) Conditional Reinstatement

Where an award reinstated a union steward discharged for alleged insubordination with the condition that "upon his return to work he will resign his position as shop steward and will not act in any capacity

---

[21] *Id.* at 3090. See also Davey, *The Arbitrator Speaks on Discharge and Discipline,* 17 ARB. J. 98 (1962).

[22] See *Reece v. Westmoreland Coal Co.,* 340 F.Supp. 695 (W.D.Va. 1972).

[23] *Louisville & Nashville R.R. v. Bryant,* 263 Ky. 578, 92 S.W.2d 749 (1936). See generally C. Gregory, LABOR AND THE LAW (1946).

[24] *J. I. Case Co. v. NLRB,* 321 U.S. 332 (1944).

as a union representative in the plant for a period of one year,"[25] a California court modified the award to remove the conditions on the ground that the conditions on the reinstatement were remedies beyond the arbitrator's authority. However, to the contrary,[26] a New York court reviewed an award reinstating a steward with a proviso that he could not hold a union office for three years. The court held that both the quantum of the penalty and whether the discharge was for just cause were both within the authority of the arbitrator.

In an application of the *Spielberg* doctrine, the Board dismissed a complaint where a reinstatement was conditioned upon the dischargee passing a proficiency test.[27] The employee failed the test and the discharge became final.

(3) The Authority to Reduce the Discipline

Often the language of the labor agreement concerning the arbitrator's authority to change the amount of disciplinary penalty imposed by the management, once cause for discipline has been established, is not clear and, hence, the arbitrator's authority to change the amount of the discipline is often a hotly contested issue. This debate often involves the question of whether the agreement limits the arbitrator (i) to either upholding the discipline imposed by the management or making the employee whole by reinstating him with full back pay, even though cause for some discipline exists but in the arbitrator's opinion is not sufficient cause to support the discipline imposed, or (ii) grants to him the remedial power to direct some intermediate form of penalty.

Since some employers believe that to grant to the arbitrator the power to convert a discharge to a disciplinary suspension causes some arbitrators to reinstate dischargees without back pay under circumstances where the arbitrator would not reinstate the employee with full back pay if he did not have the power to convert the discharge to a disciplinary suspension, they insist that the agreement clearly state that the arbitrator does not have the power to convert the discipline. Even where the agreement language would seem to clearly remove from the arbitrator the right to convert a discharge to a disciplinary layoff, some strange and inconsistent results have occurred. The Michigan Supreme Court held that a discharged employee who was reinstated without back pay could sue the employer for back pay

---

[25] *Arterberry of Lodge 120 IAM v. Lockheed Aircraft Service*, 33 L.A. 292 (Cal. Super.Ct. 1959).

[26] *Consolidated Edison Co. v. Rigley*, 73 LRRM 2220 (N.Y. Sup.Ct. 1970). Arbitrators have occasionally penalized employees in discipline cases with a stated loss of seniority. *Butler Mfg. Co.*, 55 L.A. 451 and 55 L.A. 1214 (Purdom, 1970); *Sam Shainberg Co.*, 54 L.A. 135 (Caraway, 1970).

[27] *Terminal Transport Co.*, 185 NLRB No. 96 (1970).

since the contract expressly provided that in the event the discharge was found to be without just cause the employee would be reinstated "with full seniority and shall receive pay for all time lost from work."[28]

In contrast, the Fourth Circuit has held that an arbitrator did not exceed the scope of his authority when he reinstated a dischargee without back pay under an agreement which stated:

> "In the event it should be decided [by the arbitrator] that an injustice has been dealt the discharged employee, the Company shall reinstate such employee to his former position and pay full compensation for time lost." [29]

In reaching its conclusion, the court felt that the terms of the collective bargaining agreement could be construed to allow the arbitrator the discretion to find that the employee had engaged in "culpable conduct" warranting some "disciplinary sanction," but that he could also find that discharge was an "excessive" penalty and therefore unjust. The court rejected the company's argument that once there was a finding of misconduct the amount of discipline could not be changed as being too rigid an interpretation of arbitral authority.

In another case an arbitrator reduced a penalty for the violation of a management rule that carried with it a penalty of a one-week suspension. The agreement reserved to management the right to promulgate disciplinary rules, and a court on a motion to vacate the award ruled that the arbitrator was precluded from modifying the penalty prescribed by management for violating the rule despite mitigating circumstances.[30]

In a rather unique interaction between a court and an arbitrator over the treatment of a discharge, a Pennsylvania court ordered a hearing by an arbitrator on the issue of wrongful discharge and then provided that the employee was "to be continued on the payroll and removed off the premises." The arbitration award reinstated the dischargee but directed the grievant to repay to the company the money paid to him from the day of his discharge to the date of his reinstatement "during which time he did nothing to earn it." On a motion to confirm the award, the court struck from the award the repayment order. The court held that the previous court order, directing arbitration and specifically stating the employee was to remain on the payroll, was a restriction on the arbitrator's remedial authority.[31]

---

[28] *Carr v. Kalamazoo Vegetable Parchment Co.,* 354 MICH. REP. 327, 92 N.W.2d 295 (1958).

[29] *Lynchburg Foundry Co. v. Steelworkers, Local 2556,* 404 F.2d 259, 260 (4th Cir. 1968).

[30] *Local 217, Int'l Union of Electrical Workers v. Holtzer-Cabot Corp.,* 277 F.Supp. 704 (D.Mass. 1967).

[31] *Sley System Garages v. Transport Workers Local 700,* 178 A.2d 560 (Pa. Sup.Ct. 1962).

In other labor agreements, the question of power to convert a discharge to a disciplinary layoff is not answered, nor do the parties agree at the hearing whether the arbitrator has the power to convert. The matter is left to the arbitrator's determination. Where the agreement language was not clear, a court sustained an award which reinstated an employee discharge for allegedly starting a rumor, with less than full back pay. The court stated that it was within the arbitrator's authority to determine not only the existence of misconduct, but also the fitness of the discipline.[32]

Where an arbitrator found that the employer had given a disciplinary suspension (not a suspension pending investigation) for particular misconduct and then discharged the employee, the penalty was reduced to suspension on the ground that the discharge constituted double jeopardy. Arbitrator M. David Keefe explained:

"It is axiomatic in the administration of disciplinary enforcement that a penalty, once issued, cannot be increased on reconsideration of the same offense. . . . The company action in sending the grievant home with a pass, directing him to remain away until he decided to comply with instructions, can only be described as imposing a time-off penalty." [33]

However, where a foreman, not aware that an employee had already received the contractual reprimand for a first offense of leaving work without permission, issued a first offense violation slip for another such offense, it was proper for the company, upon discovering the error, to issue a corrected slip advising the grievant of a two-day suspension as provided in the labor agreement for a second offense.[34]

One general limitation on the remedial powers of the arbitrator to reduce the discipline imposed is the principle that an arbitrator should not substitute his judgment as to the appropriate penalty for that of management's unless the arbitrator finds that the discipline imposed was arbitrary, capricious, or discriminatory.[35] This limitation on the arbitrator's authority was succinctly set forth in a frequently cited statement by Arbitrator Whitley P. McCoy:

"Where an employee has violated a rule or engaged in conduct meriting disciplinary action, it is primarily the function of management to decide

---

[32] *Gulf States Telephone Co. v. Local 1692 IBEW*, 416 F.2d 198 (5th Cir. 1969). *Accord, Local 2130 IBEW v. Bally Case & Cooler, Inc.*, 232 F.Supp. 394 (E.D.Pa. 1964).

[33] *Gibson, Inc.*, AAA Case No. 103-11 (Keefe, 1967).

[34] *Combustion Engineering Inc.*, AAA Case No. 143-7 (Walt, 1970).

[35] For a few of the numerous decisions where this principle is explained, see *Kaiser Aluminum & Chemical Corp.*, 48 L.A. 449 (Koven, 1967); *Randall Co.*, 66-2 ARB ¶ 8692 (Wissner, 1966); *West Virginia Pulp & Paper Co.*, 65-2 ARB ¶ 8665 (Daugherty, 1965); *Union-Tribune Publishing Co.*, 64-2 ARB ¶ 8626 (Prasow, 1964); *Baugh & Sons Co. of Ohio*, 62-3 ARB ¶ 8771 (Baldwin, 1962); *Davison Chemical Co.*, 31 L.A. 920 (McGuinness, 1959); *S. A. Shenk & Co.*, 26 L.A. 395 (Stouffer, 1956); *Bauer Bros. Co.*, 23 L.A. 696 (Dworkin, 1954); *Corn Products Refining Co.*, 21 L.A. 105 (Gilden, 1953).

upon the proper penalty. If management acts in good faith upon a fair investigation and fixes a penalty not inconsistent with that imposed in other like cases, an arbitrator should not disturb it. The mere fact that management has imposed a somewhat different penalty or a somewhat more severe penalty than the arbitrator would have, if he had had the decision to make originally, is no justification for changing it. The minds of equally reasonable men differ. A consideration which would weigh heavily with one man will seem of less importance to another. A circumstance which highly aggravates an offense in one man's eyes may be only slight aggravation to another. If an arbitrator could substitute his judgment and discretion for the judgment and discretion honestly exercised by management, then the functions of management would have been abdicated, and unions would take every case to arbitration. The result would be as intolerable to employees as to management. The only circumstances under which a penalty imposed by management can be rightfully set aside by an arbitrator are those where discrimination, unfairness, or capricious and arbitrary action are proved—in other words, where there has been abuse of discretion." [36]

This principle was followed by a court when it vacated an award reinstating an employee who had been discharged for dishonesty when there was no finding that discharge for the misconduct was arbitrary, capricious, or discriminatory.[37]

Likewise, one court considered an arbitrator's reinstatement of a discharged employee to a lower position as an improper remedy. The court reasoned that the award recognized that there was cause for discipline, but improperly substituted a reinstatement with a demotion for the discharge given by the employer.[38] In effect, the court held that the arbitrator cannot substitute his judgment for that of the management on the extent of the discipline once cause for discipline is established.

Some arbitrators do not accept this limitation on their right to modify the amount of discipline. Instead, they hold that where the agreement does not impose a clear limitation on the arbitrator's power, he may substitute his own judgment concerning the amount of discipline for the employer's[39] and modify the amount of discipline even if it was not found to be an arbitrary, capricious, or discriminatory penalty.

---

[36] *Stockham Pipe Fittings Co.*, 1 L.A. 160, 162 (McCoy, 1945).

[37] *Truck Drivers & Helpers Local 784 v. Ulry-Talbert Co.*, 330 F.2d 562 (8th Cir. 1964). See also *Textile Workers v. American Thread Co.*, 291 F.2d 894 (4th Cir. 1961); *Sverdlove v. Karlan & Bleicher, Inc.*, 41 L.A. 1064 (N.Y. Sup.Ct. 1963).

[38] *Gulf Oil Corp. v. Guidry*, 32 L.A. 937 (Texas Sup. Ct. 1959).

[39] *McGraw-Edison Co.*, 62-3 ARB ¶ 8775 (Howlett, 1962). See, *e.g.*, *Interstate Bakeries Corp., Blue Ribbon Div.*, 62-2 ARB ¶ 8633 (Frey, 1962); *Todd Shipyards Corp.*, 61-2 ARB ¶ 8328 (Williams, 1961); *Cincinnati Tool Co.*, 61-1 ARB ¶ 8026 (Sembower, 1960); *Gold-Tex Fabrics Corp.*, 32 L.A. 103 (Jaffee, 1959); *Detroit Harvester Co.*, 30 L.A. 820 (Stashower, 1958); *Kellogg Co.*, 28 L.A. 303 (Meltzer, 1957); *Barcalo Mfg. Co.*, 28 L.A. 65 (Levy, 1956); *Weyerhaeuser Timber Co.*, 25 L.A. 634 (Wyckoff, 1955).

As a practical matter, the decisions of arbitrators who express their remedial authority more broadly and those who accept the limitation that they can modify the amount of discipline only if it is arbitrary, capricious, or discriminatory may not differ significantly. When the arbitrator finds that the disciplinary action taken by the management varies from the action which he himself feels would be justified, he can find that the management acted in a capricious or arbitrary manner and reach the same result that would be reached if he had said that he had the authority to modify the amount of discipline without such finding. The difference in approach may well be only one of semantics.[40]

(4) Remedies Where the Employee Breaches the Agreement

The typical labor agreement provides that employees may be discharged only for "just cause." The type of misconduct which constitutes "just cause" for discharge may vary from plant to plant because arbitrators generally conclude that unless an employer is "even handed" in his disciplinary determinations, the discharge is capricious and is subject to modification.

To determine whether the employer's disciplinary determination is "even handed," arbitrators typically examine the types of misconduct for which employees have been discharged in the past. If the misconduct, basic to the discharge, is completely out of pattern with the misconduct of those previously discharged, or is no greater than the misconduct of others not discharged, the arbitrators, unless there are other important considerations, will generally reinstate the grievant or reduce his discharge to a suspension.

The authority for such a remedy is found in the simple fact that the discharge action taken by the employer is not effective to sever the employment relationship because, when tested against the "just cause" standard established in the agreement, there is insufficient cause to support the discharge action. For this reason, arbitrators have held that the employment relationship was not terminated. The appropriate remedy is then reinstatement.

When, however, the employee engages in conduct which is described in the labor agreement as conduct which terminates the employment relationship, arbitrators are not dealing with actions initiated by the employer, nor are they called upon to determine whether the conduct in question constitutes "just cause" for discharge.

A quit, an absence for three working days without notification to the employer, accepting employment elsewhere when on leave of

---

[40] A good example of this type of reasoning may be seen in *Fruehauf Trailer Co.,* 16 L.A. 666 (Spaulding, 1951).

absence, failing to report in the first working day after the expiration of a leave of absence or vacation, failing to return within a specified time when recalled from a layoff are types of conduct often listed in collective bargaining agreements as conduct which terminates the participant's employment.[41] Arbitrator Harry Dworkin pointed out the distinction between termination for being absent for three days without notice to the employer and termination by discharge:

> "There is no evidence in the instant case that the grievant was disciplined through application of either 'a suspension, layoff or discharge' for any specific act of misconduct or infraction which would warrant disciplinary action. There is not here involved an incident of discipline for just cause in accordance with the accepted principles of disciplinary procedure. The grievant was terminated and his seniority ceased pursuant to the notice of January 23, 1969, due to his absence for three consecutive days without notifying the company of a reason to justify such absence. The situation is distinguished from one of discharge or suspension for misconduct. Article XV, is a comprehensive provision dealing with application of length of service in a variety of situations. As regards its application to the instant case, Section 3 specifically provides for a number of situations that may result in termination of seniority. . . ." [42]

When the employment is broken by an act of the employee which constitutes a breach of the agreement, an arbitrator would have no authority to reinstate the employee. This is because the remedial powers of arbitrators do not include the authority to require an employer to hire an individual. However, when the employer discharges an employee, considerations such as his work record and the degree of punishment accorded to other participants in the same act of misconduct become pertinent when determining whether the employee's conduct supports the penalty of discharge. The authority to reinstate a discharged employee is based upon a finding that the discharge by the employer was not effective because it was not for just cause.

Where an arbitrator is being asked to reinstate employees who participated in a strike in violation of a no-strike clause, the arbitrator's remedial authority is more closely related to those cases where the termination occurs by an action of the employee (*i.e.*, quit) rather than by an action of the employer (discharge).

Many labor agreements define the arbitrator's remedial power where there has been a termination of employment because of participation

---

[41] *Midland-Ross*, 49 L.A. 283 (Larkin, 1967); *U.S. Corrugated Fibre Box Co.*, 41 L.A. 804 (Shister, 1963); *Bassick Co.*, 38 L.A. 279 (Seitz, 1962). See also *Brush Beryllium Co.*, 55 L.A. 709 (Dworkin, 1970).

[42] *Brush Beryllium Co.*, note 41 *supra*. (This case is of interest in connection with the contract breach situation because the employee was absent on a "one man strike.")

in a contract breach strike. For example, an arbitrator concluded he had no authority to reinstate 21 strikers who were not permitted to return to work even though several hundred participants were permitted to return because the agreement in express language limited any grievances arising out of violations of the no-strike provision to the question of whether the employee "did or did not . . . participate" in the action charged, and prohibited the arbitrator from substituting "his judgment or discretion for that of management."[43]

Where there is no special language limiting the arbitrator's remedial authority, arbitrators have taken differing positions. Some equate a termination of employment for participation in a strike in violation of the agreement to a discharge for just cause. In these cases, the arbitrators employ the same standards as those used in other discharge cases; other arbitrators consider the termination of employment to be the result of the employee's breach of the agreement analogous to a quit.

When arbitrators treat participation in a contract-breach strike as simply grounds for discharge by the employer, the "even handed" discipline principle creates a quandary. An employer can hardly be required to discharge all of his employees in an attempt to satisfy the "even handed" discipline mandate. Yet, if he does not treat all participants in the same manner, what remedial action can he expect from this group of arbitrators?

The arbitrators who subscribe to the "even handed" discipline principle in the cases in which an employee has breached the no-strike provision almost uniformly hold that an employer may employ selective discipline in such cases. In a conceptually unsatisfying attempt to cling to the notion that employees who breach the contract by participating in a wildcat strike are actually being discharged, the arbitrators state that the selective process employed by employers must not be capricious or discriminatory. For example, Arbitrator Ralph T. Seward stated:

> "The union is right in its contention that employees with a similar degree of guilt should be similarly penalized and that a few should not be arbitrarily chosen to serve as examples for the many." [44]

---

[43] *Magnavox Co.*, AAA Case No. 111-8 (Oppenheim, 1967). See also *Masonite Corp.*, 54 L.A. 633 (Stouffer, 1970); *Randall Co.*, 66-2 ARB ¶ 8692 (Wissner, 1966); *Philips Industries, Inc.*, 66-1 ARB ¶ 8042 (Stouffer, 1965); *Yale & Towne Mfg. Co.*, 41 L.A. 1100 (Wallen, 1963); *Chrysler Corp.*, 9 L.A. 789 (Wolf, 1947); *Borg-Warner Corp.*, 4 L.A. 4 (Updegraff, 1945).
[44] *General Motors Corp.* (Seward) quoted in *Stockham Pipe Fittings Co.*, 4 L.A. 744, 746 (McCoy, 1946). See also *Kaye-Tex Mfg. Co.*, 36 L.A. 663 (Horlacher, 1960); *South Side Dye House, Inc.*, 10 L.A. 533 (Myers, 1948); *Brewer Dry Rock Co.*, 9 L.A. 845 (Copelof, 1948); *Art Metal, Inc.*, 8 L.A. 340 (Kirsh, 1947); *Simplicity Pattern Co.*, 7 L.A. 180 (Wolff, 1947); *Stockham Pipe Fittings Co.*, 4 L.A. 744 (McCoy, 1946); *Argonne Worsted Co.*, 4 L.A. 81 (Copelof, 1946).

Arbitrators have upheld employers in "discharging" employees who led, instigated, or most actively participated in wildcat strikes. Even this standard can lead to an unsatisfying result. In many instances, the employer will not know which employees were most at fault for an illegal work stoppage, or will make errors when he selects those he thinks were the most active. Arbitrator Leonard Oppenheim noted the absurd result that could occur if the "capricious" test were carried to its logical extreme, and indicated that a wise tolerance must be allowed in applying the capricious test. He stated:

"In passing on disciplinary action after a strike in breach of the labor agreement and which has subverted the no-strike commitment of the Union, Arbitrators have held that in these situations the Employer may properly engage in selective discipline. Thus, an employer who is the victim of such a strike is not required to deprive itself of all employees participating in the strike and it may select those for punishment for the offense as it sees fit, provided such selection is not capricious." [45]

Arbitrator John P. Horlacher recognized that the even-handed principle can create a trap that could well make the prohibitions in the "no-strike clause" now enforceable by employee discipline, if an employer was required to identify *all* the instigators, *all* those who were active in the strike, etc. He proposed the following standard in this area:

"3. An interpretation making the no-strike clauses of the Agreement a nullity must be rejected. Something short of a universal flat penalty is permissible provided *the basis of selection makes sense and is not patently and avoidably unfair.*" (Emphasis added.) [46]

Arbitrator Horlacher explained the reasons for the wide tolerance in the selection standard:

"2. Adoption of the Union view that the Company must equally penalize everyone who participated in the walkout—using participation in its simplest sense as failure to report for work during the two days of the stoppage—would convert the no-strike provisions of the contract into a nullity. The entire work force participated, in the sense indicated. A three-day suspension for the whole group would mean a three-day loss of production on top of the two days of the wildcat. This would be so grievous for the Company it would decline to apply such a penalty." [47]

For these reasons, Arbitrator Horlacher, like Arbitrator Seward, would not approve discipline of employees on a capricious standard such as "those whose names start with K, L, or M, or only those who are six feet tall," but would approve a selection that is the "most

[45] *Magnavox Co.,* AAA Case No. 111-8 (Oppenheim, 1967).
[46] *Kaye-Tex Mfg. Co.,* 36 L.A. 660, 663-64 (Horlacher, 1960).
[47] *Id.* at 663.

reasonable that can be devised under the circumstances." In this selection, "the company is not under a duty to be absolutely just regardless of how feasible this is. It is only under a duty to be as just as is reasonably possible under the circumstances.[48] In attempting to explain what he meant, Arbitrator Horlacher pointed to Arbitrator Lehoczky's approval of the discharge of "the first major group who walked off" even though this was the "sole difference between them and the rest of the three hundred [who participated in the strike]."[49]

The requirement that there be some logic to the selection of the group of participants to be discharged from the large group of participants has often caused employers to discharge union stewards and officers if they participate in the strike, not because the employer can prove that each steward and officer individually instigated the strike, but because, as union officers, they are presumed to be the leaders unless they can prove who were, and are also presumed to know better than the other employees the obligations created by the labor agreement, making their participation a more serious industrial offense.[50]

To avoid the problems that flow from the view that all participants should be given an equal penalty, one employer discharged all participants and then reemployed those individuals he chose to reemploy.[51] Such an action, taken to establish identical discipline for all participants, results in the loss of seniority of all reemployed employees, because they reenter as new hires.

Some courts and arbitrators avoid the confusion that the equality-of-discipline principle produces in the contract-breach strike situations by holding that by participating in the strike action an employee severs the employment relationship. In other words, the status of a contract-breach striker is the same as that of an individual who quits. The Supreme Court and several courts of appeals line up with this second view. In *NLRB v. Sand Mfg. Co.,*[52] the Supreme Court said:

"Respondent rightly understood that the men were irrevocably committed not to work in accordance with their contract. It was at liberty to treat them as having severed their relations with the company because of their breach. . . ."[53]

Likewise, the Seventh Circuit, in *NLRB v. Columbian Enameling and*

---

[48] *Id.* at 665.

[49] *Goodyear Atomic Corp.,* 27 L.A. 321, 324 (Lehoczky, 1956).

[50] *General American Transportation Corp.,* 42 L.A. 142 (Pollock, 1964).

[51] *National Lock Co.,* Grievances No. 195, 196 (Rader, 1949) (unpublished).

[52] 306 U.S. 332 (1939).

[53] *Id.* at 344.

Stamping Company,[54] explained that employees who strike, in violation of their contract, engage in an act that breaks the employment relationship:

"What is the status of a group of employees who in the face of such a definite agreement left their employment? . . .
". . .
"[A]t the time they went on strike . . . the employees acted in the face of their agreement—'There shall be no stoppage of work by either party to the contract, pending decision by the Committee of Arbitration.'
"In the face of such an agreement, were they strikers, that is, was there an employer-employee relationship existing, when they quit work? Did the status of employer-employee continue as to them after they quit?
"We must answer this question in the negative. . . ." [55]

Another court of appeals said:

"In our view the strike of April 25 was a breach of the 1946 contract which was still in force on that date.
". . .
"[T]he Company was at liberty to treat the employees as having severed their relations with the Company because of their breach of contract. . . ." [56]

And still another court said:

"If the strike was one in violation of the Union's contract with the Respondent . . . there was no duty on the part of the Respondent to consider the strikers as employees. . . ." [57]

Hence, under the law, as promulgated by the Supreme Court and developed by other courts, a contract-breach striker acquires essentially the same status as a *quit*. Thus, the doctrine of equality of penalty developed in discharge cases where the severance of the employment relationship is a result of an action by the employer, should not be considered by arbitrators when ruling upon the requested remedies. For example, Arbitrator Francis Hauser said in *Interstate Plating Co.*: [58]

"Curtis and Mendal by participating in an unauthorized strike terminated their employee relations with the Company, and so did the other participants. Management's discretion with respect to rehiring the strikers was not restricted by the terms of the collective agreement; it could rehire none, or all, or—as has been the case—reemploy those who reported for work up to a certain date, while refusing to hire latecomers." [59]

---

[54] 96 F.2d 948 (7th Cir. 1948).
[55] *Id.* at 953.
[56] *Boeing Airplane Co. v. NLRB,* 174 F.2d 988, 991 (1949).
[57] *NLRB v. Deena Artware,* 198 F.2d 645, 651 (1952).
[58] 7 L.A. 583 (Hauser, 1947).
[59] *Id.* at 585.

Arbitrator Hauser is essentially stating that an order of "reinstatement" of a contract-breach striker would actually be an order to "rehire," a remedy which is beyond the authority of the arbitrator.

The fact that other employees who participated in a contract-breach strike are not terminated from employment, does not eliminate the fact that another participant is guilty of a breach of the agreement. This was pointed up by Arbitrator Herbert Blumer in *Carnegie-Illinois Steel Corp.*,[60] who said, in response to the claim that the employer's penalties were unequal:

> "[T]he participation of other employees in the work stoppage and strike lessens in no way the fact that the aggrieved employee committed an unquestioned violation of the agreement." [61]

Section 9(F) of the *Carnegie-Illinois* agreement provided that an employee could be discharged only for "proper cause." Blumer held that since participation in a work stoppage "is unambiguously in violation of the agreement, the company would have contractual grounds for discharge without resorting to Section 9-F." [62] This meant that the arbitrator need not determine whether "proper cause" for a discharge by the employer existed, since participation in the strike constituted a breach of the agreement.

If the employment relationship is broken by an action of the employee (*i.e.*, strike participation, quit, etc.), a reinstatement order by an arbitrator is an order to hire an employee. Arbitrator Charles O. Gregory explained that such remedial order is beyond the arbitrator's remedial power:

> "How can he [the arbitrator] require the company to reemploy someone whom it has not unjustifiably discharged. No part of the contract gives him the right to do this or gives the union the right to demand it as far as the arbitrator can see. Whom the company either employs or does not employ is its own affair, as long as it does not violate the law of the land such as the National Labor Relations Act. Regardless of any personal feelings the arbitrator may have in this matter, he thinks it would be an impertinance for him even to suggest that it would be a gracious thing for the company to reemploy . . . in some capacity in the plant in view of the ultimate turn of events. . . . For it must be plain that the status of this case at present is that Nelsen's employment with the company was terminated once and for all; and the company's obligation to hire him anew is no greater than it is to hire any applicant for employment.
>
> "In view of the terms of the contract between the parties, the arbitrator concludes that he has no power to . . . require the company either to employ or reemploy Nelsen." [63]

---

[60] 5 L.A. 363 (Blumer, 1946).
[61] *Id.* at 368.
[62] *Id.* at 369.
[63] *Swift & Co.*, 7 L.A. 703, 705 (Gregory, 1946).

Whether the arbitrator adopts the position (i) that participation in an illegal strike is an action by the employee that severs the employment relationship or (ii) that such participation is an industrial misconduct which may be proper basis for discharge by the employer, depends upon the words used in the agreement and upon how fundamentally the arbitrator views the commitment that employees will not engage in illegal strike action. In *U.S. Rubber Co.*,[64] Arbitrator James J. Healy was asked to reinstate (or rehire) employees who violated a no-strike clause. In refusing to do so, he said:

> "The arbitrator has no way of knowing what type of thinking motivates the members of a bargaining unit who walk off their jobs whenever they feel like it. But the time has certainly arrived when they should be appraised in the most forceful manner possible that they have entered into a contract with a company, one of the specific provisions of which denies them the privilege of such individual action. . . . In the instant case, employees who consider themselves aggrieved seek relief when they themselves have violated the contract. . . ."[65]

(5) Back Pay Awards

Arbitrators hold that the power to decide that there is insufficient cause to support the discipline imposed includes the power to award back pay to remedy the wrong.[66] In *Cincinnati Cleaning & Finishing Machinery Co.*,[67] Arbitrator Fred Whitney rejected a company argument that he did not have authority to award back pay to an employee he found to have been discharged without proper cause because the labor agreement did not contain a provision granting him authority to award retroactive pay:

> "In this case, the Company violated Section 6 of the Labor Agreement when it discharged the grievant without proper cause. Under these circumstances, the grievant deserves a meaningful remedy which is reinstatement on the job and with back pay. Indeed, if the parties actually intended that employees discharged without proper cause are only to be reinstated to the job, but without back pay, they would have adopted unambiguous language to accomplish this objective. Language such as the following would be required:
>
> ". . . '[I]f an arbitrator finds that an employee is discharged without proper cause, the arbitrator shall reinstate such employee to his job, but without back pay.'
>
> ". . .

---

[64] 8 L.A. 44 (Healy, 1947).

[65] *Id.* at 48.

[66] See generally Wolff, *The Power of the Arbitrator to Make Monetary Awards,* LABOR ARBITRATION—PERSPECTIVES AND PROBLEMS, Proceedings of the Seventeenth Annual Meeting, National Academy of Arbitrators, 176, 178-80 (M. Kahn Ed. 1964).

[67] 66-3 ARB ¶ 8876 (Witney, 1966); see also *Minute Maid Co. v. Citrus, Cannery, Food Processing and Allied Workers, Local 444,* 331 F.2d 280 (5th Cir. 1964). See also *Local 130, Electrical Workers v. Mississippi Valley Electric Co.,* 175 F.Supp. 312 (E.D. La. 1959).

"No such restrictive language, of course, appears in either Section 6 or in Section 20 of the Labor Agreement. Therefore, the Arbitrator finds that he has the authority to award back pay under the circumstances of this case. To hold otherwise would fly in the face of a most settled principle of the arbitration process. It would be as if in a civil proceeding a court would find for the plaintiff, but refuse to award monetary damages so as to make the plaintiff financially whole for an injury caused by the defendant. . . ." [68]

Arbitrator Archibald Cox observed in his award in *Electric Storage Battery Co.* that back pay awards, when a dischargee is reinstated, are punitive as well as compensatory because:

"[T]he company pays twice when it improperly discharges a man or violates his seniority. It pays back wages and also pays the person who took the grievant's place. And the 'only justification for an award of back pay is that there is no method of doing perfect justice.' Thus the dilemma lies in being forced to choose between denying the employee an adequate remedy or forcing the employer to pay twice for the same work. When the employer causes the loss, however innocently, it is more just that he should bear the cost of making the employee whole than that the employee should be forced to suffer a denial of contract rights without a remedy." [69]

(a) Reductions in Amount of Back Pay

Arbitrators have reduced the amount of back pay in cases even though the discharge is found to be without just cause when (i) the grievant or the union was guilty of unusual delay in seeking arbitration or in selecting the arbitrator,[70] (ii) where the grievant has had outside wage earnings which are deducted,[71] and (iii) when the dischargee

---

[68] 66-3 ARB at 6045. See also *American Oil Co.,* 37 L.A. 487 (Edelman, 1961); *Jeffrey Mfg. Co.,* 34 L.A. 814 (Kuhn, 1960); *Elberta Crate & Box Co.,* 32 L.A. 228 (Murphy, 1959). The principle of these decisions has been sustained in several court cases. See, *e.g., Minute Maid Co. v. Citrus Workers,* note 67 *supra; Lodge 12, District 37 IAM v. Cameron Iron Works, Inc.,* 292 F.2d 112 (5th Cir.), *cert. denied,* 368 U.S. 926 (1961).

[69] *Electric Storage Battery Co.,* AAA Case No. 19-22 (Cox, 1960). See also *Charles Taylor Sons Co.,* AAA Case No. 35-16 (Sanders, 1961).

[70] *Koppers Co.,* 65-1 ARB ¶ 8013 (Loucks, 1964); *U.S. Industrial Chemical Co.,* 62-2 ARB ¶ 8666 (Nichols, 1962); *Gulf States Utilities,* 62-2 ARB ¶ 8548 (Autrey, 1962); *Valve Corp. of America,* 61-2 ARB ¶ 8591 (Stutz, 1961); *Hale Bros. Stores,* 32 L.A. 713 (Ross, 1959). But see *Thorsen Mfg. Co.,* 55 L.A. 581 (Koven, 1970); *W. Va. Pulp & Paper Co.,* 62-3 ARB ¶ 8753 (Stark, 1962).

[71] See, *e.g., Keystone Steel & Wire Co.,* 65-2 ARB ¶ 8786 (Dougherty, 1965); *Gulfport Shipbuilding Corp.,* 64-3 ARB ¶ 9233 (Ray, 1964); *Bethlehem Fabricators, Inc.,* 63-2 ARB ¶ 8728 (Schedler, 1962). But see *United States Steel Corp.,* 40 L.A. 1036 (McDermott, 1963). In *Steelworkers v. Enterprise Wheel & Car Corp.,* 363 U.S. 593 (1960), the court held that the grievant should be reinstated with back pay for the time lost but with a deduction for amounts received by the grievant from other employment. The duty of an employee unlawfully discharged under the National Labor Relations Act, to mitigate his damages in a back-pay award was affirmed in *Phelps Dodge Corp. v. NLRB,* 313 U.S. 177 (1941). See also Teele, *But No Back Pay is Awarded . . . ,* 19 ARB. J. 103, 107 (1964); Gorske, *Arbitration of Back-Pay Awards,* 10 LAB. L.J. 18 (1959).

failed to seek other employment which would have mitigated the amount of back pay due.[72]

In reducing back pay awards by the amount of an employee's interim earnings, arbitrators have disagreed, however, as to how much outside pay should be deducted. It has been held that the deduction should not include overtime earnings which the dischargee earned from another employer;[73] and where an employee worked part-time at another company prior to his discharge and then began working full time, only those hours worked in excess of his regular working hours could be used to mitigate damages.[74] The expense incurred in seeking other employment may be offset against wages earned when calculating the deduction.[75] The calculation of back pay, if it is awarded, will normally include overtime and shift premiums which would have been earned.[76]

Arbitrators have struggled over the question of whether unemployment compensation during the period of layoff or suspension should be deducted from a back pay award.[77] Under one view, unemployment compensation is a financial benefit and should be deducted. The view was aptly stated by Arbitrator Ted T. Tsukiyama as follows:

> "Under the Hawaii Employment Security Law, benefits are paid out of a fund contributed to only by the employer and not the employees, hence the benefits are not as 'collateral' or indirect as may appear at first blush. . . . From the standpoint of the employee involved, payments received, whether by way of paycheck or by unemployment compensation, represent good, sound American dollar values in the pocket, either way. Thus, the classification of unemployment compensation pay-

---

[72] See, e.g., Master Carbide Co., AAA Case No. 140-5 (Cole, 1970); Allegheny Airlines, Inc., 67-1 ARB ¶ 8244 (Kelliher, 1967); Flintkote Co., 66-3 ARB ¶ 8895 (Merrill, 1966); E. F. Hauserman Co., 66-3 ARB ¶ 8887 (Gibson, 1966); Hall-Omar Baking Co., 62-3 ARB ¶ 8926 (Hampton, 1962); General Tel. Co. of Ind., AAA Case No. 50-1 (Chalfie, 1962); but see Crowell-Collier Broadcasting Corp., 65-2 ARB ¶ 8739 (Jones, 1965). The NLRB, with the affirmance of the courts, has also held that an employee should not be entitled to full back pay where there is a willfully incurred loss. NLRB v. Mastro Plastics Corp., 354 F.2d 170 (2d Cir. 1965), cert. denied, 384 U.S. 972 (1966).

[73] Foote Bros. Gear & Machine Corp., 1 L.A. 561 (Courshon, 1945).

[74] American Iron & Machine Works Co., 19 L.A. 417 (Merrill, 1952).

[75] A. H. Bello Corp., 65-2 ARB ¶ 8711 (Abernethy, 1965).

[76] See, e.g., Towmotor Corp., 66-3 ARB ¶ 9028 (Kates, 1966) (shift premium); Allen Warehouse Co., 63-2 ARB ¶ 8623 (Koven, 1963) (overtime would regularly have been worked); Brass-Craft Mfg. Co., 61-3 ARB ¶ 8743 (Kahn, 1961) (bonus payments). But cf. Shenango, Inc., 66-3 ARB ¶ 8748 (McDermott, 1966) (regular rate, not rate of probable assignments).

[77] See generally Back Pay Awards and Unemployment Insurance Benefits, 4 ARB. J. 268 (1949); Gorske, note 71 supra, at 26-27. In the 1971 can industry and aluminum industry settlements with the United Steelworkers, the parties agreed that "earnings or money" received by the employee between his discharge or suspension and reinstatement are not deductions if back pay is awarded. Agreement between Reynolds Metals Co. and United Steelworkers, June 1, 1971, Article XI, Section 4; agreement between American Can Company and United Steelworkers, February 15, 1971, Article 15.5.

ments as being 'collateral' rather than a direct benefit appears too fine and esoteric a distinction to make in deciding this controversy, particularly when the controlling test or criteria in attempting to make an employee 'whole' is to make him 'FINANCIALLY WHOLE', . . ." [78]

Other arbitrators have treated unemployment compensation as a collateral benefit which is not deductible from back pay for time lost. Thus, in *National Rejectors, Inc.,*[79] Arbitrator Wagner said:

"To the employee who receives them, the benefits are income. To the employer of the employee, they represent costs since the fund [sic] from which they are paid are built up by employer contributions. Yet the payments are made by a public agency to carry out a public policy. In this sense, they are not payments made by the employer for work performed by an employee. They are collateral benefits and not earnings and therefore should be disregarded in a situation in which an employee is to be made whole by the employer just as collateral costs are disregarded for the same purpose." [80]

Certainly if the intent of back pay is to make the grievant financially whole, unemployment compensation payments should be deducted. This is especially true given the fact that these payments are indirectly based on employer contributions.

Some arbitrators have handled the issue by following the method provided in state refunding statutes. For example, the Pennsylvania statute provides:

"[I]n the absence of misrepresentation or nondisclosure of a material fact, no recoupment shall be had if such overpayment is created by reason of . . . (2) a retroactive allocation of wages pursuant to an award of a labor relations board arbitrator or the like, unless such award provides for the repayment of unemployment compensation benefits received during the period to which such payments are allocated." [81]

Full pay back was not awarded to a grievant discharged following a report of the company doctor that he was suffering from a disabling heart condition subsequently proven to be an incorrect find-

---

[78] *Hawaiian Telephone Co.,* 65-2 ARB ¶ 8695 at 5559 (Tsukiyama, 1965). See also *Mueller Industries, Inc., Love Bros. Div.,* 45 L.A. 751 (Solomon, 1965); *Gusdorf & Sons,* 64-1 ARB ¶ 8043 (Stix, 1963); *American Chain & Cable Co.,* 40 L.A. 312 (McDermott, 1963); *Continental Can Co.,* 39 L.A. 821 (Sembower, 1962); *Pittsburgh-Des Moines Steel Co.,* 38 L.A. 148 (Wood, 1962); *Kroger Co.,* 12 L.A. 1065 (Blair, 1949).

[79] 38 L.A. 1091 (Wagner, 1962).

[80] *Id.* at 1092. See also *Littleford Bros.,* 62-3 ARB ¶ 8840 (Warns, 1962); *International Harvester Co.,* 16 L.A. 376 (Seward, 1951). These cases rely on *NLRB v. Gullett Gin Co.,* 340 U.S. 361 (1951), which held unemployment compensation payments were "collateral benefits" and hence not deductible from an NLRB back pay order. See also *Machinists, Local Lodge 790 v. Champion Carriers, Inc.,* 69 L.C. ¶ 13,237, — F.2d —, 82 LRRM 2160 (10th Cir. 1972).

[81] PA. STAT. tit. 43, § 874 (1964); see Wolff, note 66 *supra,* at 185.

ing. The arbitrator held that the date back pay should start was the date the company received the report of the employee's personal doctor, because after that date there was a "strong preponderance of medical evidence" against the company doctor's finding that a disability did exist. The arbitrator rejected the union's contention that back pay should start at the time the grievants were recalled from layoff, under a clause providing for back pay in case of unjust discharge:

> "The injustice to the employee from the standpoint of back pay occurred when he was kept from working after the Company was told of his doctors' reports; after the Company was aware that the doctors disagreed and after the Company had had a chance to consider the Union's proposal to settle the disagreement by an impartial examination by a specialist." [82]

Similarly, in a case where an employee was discharged because a fainting spell at his home revealed a cardiovascular condition, but the evidence that the probability of death or permanent injury from a resumption of his duties at the plant was insubstantial, was presented for the first time at the arbitration hearing, the employee was reinstated, but no back pay was awarded. Arbitrator Millard L. Midonick explained why back pay was not ordered:

> "The medical evidence favoring the employee's contentions as presented at the hearing in this arbitration are much more impressive than the earlier presentations of expert opinion evidence made by the Union to the Company at any time prior to these hearings. . . . The Company . . . had a right to rely upon the only substantial scientific medical opinion available to it at the time of discharge." [83]

Similarly, Arbitrator John F. Sembower held that no back pay was due an employee sent home by a supervisor who in good faith concluded the employee was intoxicated, even though the evidence did not support the supervisor's judgment conclusion.[84] Sembower analogizes his refusal to award back pay to the inability of a driver of an automobile, arrested by a police officer for driving after drinking, to sue authorities for the false arrest even though it is later established that the arrested driver had not been drinking. The company, Sembower said, cannot be penalized when the supervisor has probable cause for his judgment decision and hence the loss of pay must be considered an "unfortunate consequence" of an incident for which no one is technically to blame.

---

[82] *Shahmoon Industries*, AAA Case No. 19-8 (Hogan, 1960).

[83] *Carborundum Co.*, AAA Case No. 35-11 (Midonick, 1961).

[84] *Cleveland Cliffs Iron Co.*, 52 L.A. 435 (Sembower, 1969).

(b) *Interest*

Another area of disagreement involves awarding interest on the back pay awarded. In *Allied Chemical Corp.*,[85] Arbitrator Hilpert ordered that interest be paid in a case where it was requested, saying:

> "Although interest on the monetary relief, due to a wrongfully suspended, or wrongfully discharged, employee has seldom been awarded, it has also seldom been requested; but it is a part of the 'common law' damages for wrongful suspension or discharge; and, in the absence of language in a collective bargaining agreement to the contrary (as there may be, here, respecting a wrongfully discharged employee), the arbitration process should, and does, recognize the 'common law' relief.
>
> "Hence, the Chairman concludes that the Arbitration Board may award [H.] interest, on his monetary award, at the rate of 6% per annum, computed from the day the involved wages would otherwise have been paid to him to the day the check to him is issued." [86]

The opposite position was taken by Arbitrator Sanford H. Kadish in *Intermountain Operators League:*

> "The important point is that it is not customary in arbitrations for the arbitrator to grant interest on claims which he finds owing. If the contract or submission agreement had expressly authorized the arbitrator to grant interest, the matter would be different. In view, however, of the almost unanimous practice on the part of arbitrators not to grant interest, and the failure of the parties to authorize the arbitrator to do so here, I would think it highly inappropriate to do so. Certainly the Union has presented no reason for awarding interest in this case which can not be said to apply equally in any arbitration where a sum of money is involved." [87]

An intermediate position was taken by Arbitrator Thomas J. McDermott in *American Chain & Cable Co.*[88] to the effect that interest should be assessed where there is evidence of employer arbitrariness. Where this element is not present, the fact that payment is made when no work is performed makes lack of interest equitable:

> "The demand for payment of interest on the monies due is one that is only occasionally raised in arbitration cases, which involve damages. It is, however, a demand that can only be granted under very special circumstances. As an example, if it can be shown that a Company acted

---

[85] 66-3 ARB ¶ 9022 (Hilpert, 1966).

[86] *Id.* at 6550. See also *Reynolds Metals Co.*, 54 L.A. 1187 (Purdom, 1970); *All States Trailer Co.*, 44 L.A. 104 (Leflar, 1965); *General Electric Co.*, 39 L.A. 897 (Hilpert, 1962). See generally the remarks of David Feller, former Steelworkers General Counsel, who rejects the view that back pay is an award of money damages, *Discussion*, Labor Arbitration—Perspectives and Problems, Proceedings of the Seventeenth Annual Meeting, National Academy of Arbitrators (M. Kahn Ed. 1964); Youngdahl, *Awarding Interest in Labor Arbitration Cases*, 54 Ky. L.J. 717 (Summer, 1966).

[87] 26 L.A. 149, 154-55 (Kadish, 1956).

[88] 40 L.A. 312 (McDermott, 1963).

in a very arbitrary fashion in its handling of a case, so that the logical conclusion could be drawn that the Company was deliberately trying to injure the affected employees, an arbitrator might find cause for inclusion of interest as a part of damages. In the instant case I can find no evidence of a lack of good faith. The delay in the resolution of the case has resulted from a failure of the parties to agree, and not for any other motive.

"Also, while the workers being recompensed in this case are receiving at the most only what they would have gotten had the cut-back not taken place, they still are obtaining a monetary return for which they did not actually work. Therefore, while these workers have had to suffer a delay in the receipt of their compensation, this loss of time is offset by the above gain." [89]

(c) The Amount Due

The arbitrator need not compute back pay of each grievant in his award, it being sufficient that he supply a specific formula. One court said that the arbitrator need not have:

"[G]one through the accounting process of computing precisely how much back pay each aggrieved employee is entitled to receive, or how much must be deducted by reason of wages earned elsewhere during the period these employees were wrongfully deprived of employment. A good faith compliance with the award by both parties eliminates the necessity of the arbitrator considering such petty, ministerial computations." [90]

In *Pelletier v. Auclair Transportation, Inc.*,[91] an arbitration board ordered the company to reinstate and make two employees whole for such earnings opportunities as may have been available to them under the contract, and to report back as to the settlement made. No settlement was made, and the dispute was again submitted to arbitration for determination of the amounts due. The arbitration board awarded each employee $1,000. The employees sought to set the award aside on the grounds that it was a compromise rather than a determination of actual amounts due; that the employees' evidence showed that they were due $9,209.24 and $7,683.25, respectively; and that the employer's own evidence showed that they were entitled to more than $1,000 each. The employees contended that the arbitrators exceeded their authority when they established an even amount and the same amount for both employees. The court sustained the award holding that the submission to determine the amount due was

---

[89] *Id.* at 315. In *Isis Plumbing & Heating Co.*, 138 NLRB 716 (1962), *rev'd on other grounds*, 322 F.2d 913 (9th Cir. 1963), the NLRB reversed its longstanding policy by awarding interest.

[90] *Steelworkers v. Enterprise Wheel & Car Corp.*, 168 F.Supp. 308, 311 (S.D. W.Va. 1958).

[91] 250 A.2d 834 (N.H.Sup.Ct. 1969).

a general one which permitted the arbitrators to decide upon "principles of equity and good conscience" and hence that the arbitrators had not exceeded their powers.

C. MAKE-WHOLE MONEY AWARDS IN NONDISCIPLINARY CASES

Arbitration is a force for the recompense of both an aggrieved individual and aggrieved party to the collective bargaining agreement. The money awards (damages) imposed by the arbitrator generally seek to make the injured person or party whole for the loss sustained as a result of a breach of the labor agreement.[92] Arbitrator Thomas T. Roberts has noted:

> "[I]t is almost universally accepted that Arbitrators have the power (the Courts would say jurisdiction) to fashion remedies where a violation of the Collective Bargaining Agreement submitted to their consideration is found to exist. This remedial power includes the assessment of compensatory damages, or to use a phrase more commonly invoked, 'the power to make the wronged party whole.' " [93]

Arbitrator Ralph T. Seward has likewise stated:

> "The ordinary rule at common law and in the developing law of labor relations is that an award of damages should be limited to the amount necessary to make the injured party 'whole.' Unless an agreement provides that some other rule should be followed, this rule must apply." [94]

One of the keys to affirmative relief is proof of loss. On this point, Arbitrator John R. Abersold has said:

> "[U]nless it can be shown that the employees suffered some *actual* loss, which the Company was not justified under another provision of the Labor Agreement in requiring them to take, they have no recourse." [Emphasis in original] [95]

---

[92] See generally note 66 *supra*, at 176; Fleming, *Arbitrators and the Remedy Power*, 48 VA. L. REV. 1199 (1962); Smith & Jones, *The Impact of the Emerging Federal Law of Grievance Arbitration on Judges, Arbitrators, and Parties*, 52 VA. L. REV. 831 (1966).

[93] *California Brewers Ass'n*, 65-2 ARB ¶ 8603 at 5247 (1965). For a few of the many cases where money awards were made in nondisciplinary cases, see *PPG Industries, Inc.*, 68-2 ARB ¶ 8807 (Vadakin, 1968); *Sears, Roebuck & Co.*, 39 L.A. 567 (Gillingham, 1962); *Standard Oil Co.*, 61-1 ARB ¶ 8013 (Karlins, 1960); *Jeffrey Mfg. Co.*, 34 L.A. 815 (Kuhn, 1960); *Oregonian Publishing Co.*, 33 L.A. 574 (Kleinsorge, 1959). This view has generally been supported by the courts. See, *e.g., Hiller v. Liquor Salesmen's Union, Local 2*, 226 F.Supp. 161 (S.D.N.Y.), *rev'd on other grounds*, 338 F.2d 778 (2d Cir. 1964); *Texas Gas Transmission Corp. v. Chemical Workers*, 200 F.Supp. 521 (W.D.La. 1961). But see *Bhd. of Railroad Trainmen v. Denver & Rio Grande Western R.R. Co.*, 338 F.2d 407 (10th Cir. 1964), which held employees could only recover nominal damages in the absence of proof of an actual loss.

[94] *Intl. Harvester Co.*, 15 L.A. 1, 1 (Seward, 1950). The computation of damages is often left to the parties. See *Mallinckrodt Chemical Works*, 69-1 ARB ¶ 8352 (Goldberg, 1968); *Five Star Hardware & Electric Corp.*, 44 L.A. 944 (Wolff, 1965).

[95] *Bearings Co. of America*, 35 L.A. 569, 573 (Abersold, 1960).

And, Arbitrator Philip G. Marshall has held:

> "It is equally clear that no one was hurt or damaged by the mis-
> assignment made; no one was laid off; no one lost any time; and no
> one was deprived of overtime opportunities." [96]

However, a request for a money award to make a party whole has
been denied by arbitrators where the proof of loss is considered too
speculative.[97]

Somewhat related to the impropriety of a money award when the
proof of loss is too speculative was a court's refusal to enforce a
money award fashioned by Arbitrator Rolf Valtin ordering *U.S.
Gypsum* to pay retroactively a wage increase he concluded that Gypsum would have agreed upon if it had engaged in collective bargaining with the union as required by the labor agreement he found was
binding upon Gypsum.[98]

D. CLAIMS CONSIDERED *DE MINIMIS*

The *de minimis* doctrine is a principle recognized by arbitrators
when fashioning a remedy. Awards which find violations but decline
to grant damages because the violation is trivial, or awards which
determine an incident to be so trivial that it is not even a violation,
are examples of an application of the *de minimis* doctrine and are
not uncommon.

But when is a grievance claim *de minimis?* There is no simple
answer. *Maui Pineapple Co.*[99] considered a claim of trimmers and
packers, who processed pineapples into a ginaca machine, for pay
because twice daily they donned hairnets, powdered their hands and
slipped them into rubber gloves before the start of their shift a *de
minimis* claim. The arbitrator observed that the practice had been
in existence for ten years and the claim for payment had never been
raised in collective bargaining. Dismissing the claim as trivial, Arbitrator Harold Burr relied heavily upon the Supreme Court opinion
in *Anderson v. Mt. Clemens Pottery Co.*[100] which pointed out that a
wage claim under the Fair Labor Standards for a walk from the

---

[96] *National Lead Co.*, 36 L.A. 962, 964 (Marshall, 1961).

[97] See, *e.g., Walker Mfg. Co.*, 42 L.A. 632 (Anderson, 1964); *Sylvania Electric
Products, Inc.*, 37 L.A. 458 (Jaffee, 1961); *Sears, Roebuck & Co.*, 35 L.A. 757
(Miller, 1960); *Permutit Co.*, 19 L.A. 599 (Trotta, 1952). But see *Mallinckrodt
Chemical Works*, note 94 *supra*. See also *Schneider v. Electric Auto-Lite*, 456 F.2d
366, 79 LRRM 2825 (6th Cir. 1972).

[98] *Steelworkers v. U.S. Gypsum Co.*, 79 LRRM 2833 (D.C.Ala. 1972).

[99] 31 L.A. 442 (Burr, 1958). See also *Foote Mineral Co.*, AAA Case No. 12-26
(Seibel, 1960).

[100] 328 U.S. 680 (1946).

time clock through the plant to a work station could be a *de minimis* claim:

> "We do not, of course, preclude the application of a *de minimis* rule where the minimum walking time is such as to be negligible. The workweek contemplated by [the Act] must be computed in light of the realities of the industrial world. When the matter in issue concerns only a few second or minutes of work beyond the scheduled working hours, such trifles may be disregarded." [101]

On the other hand, Arbitrator Sam Tatum in *Wheland Co.*[102] held that supervisory performance of production work for a 10-second period each day was sufficient to violate the agreement. In that case, the work involved pressing three electric buttons to start up a compressor at the beginning of a shift. Management argued that such work was patently inconsequential, but the arbitrator pointed out that the agreement provided that no supervisor at any time, other than for emergency or instructional purposes, could perform bargaining unit work and in the face of that decision he could not consider the violation *de minimis*.

The effect of contract language upon the application of *de minimis* was pointed out in *Air Mod Division of Cook Electric Co.*[103] Arbitrator Eli Rock observed:

> "It seems clear that the amount of work done by the foreman here was so small and *de minimis* in nature as to make extremely difficult any meaningful remedy to the union, absent a clause which strongly outlaws bargaining work by supervisors." [104]

Similarly, in *Acheson Dispersed Pigments Co.*,[105] Arbitrator E. E. Hale said:

> "Even should it be assumed this was Mechanic's work, the senior qualified Operator . . . would have lost so little pay as a result of [a supervisor] doing it as to be inconsequential. *De minimis non curat lex.*"

And Arbitrator James J. Healy in *New York & Pennsylvania Co.*[106] said:

> "[I]t seems absurd to have some men idle and to be unable to use them for a few minutes on work other than their own, but which nevertheless they are entirely competent to do. But the union in this case is more preoccupied with principle, and technically, the union is correct and must be sustained in the basic complaint. However, the undersigned

---

[101] *Id.* at 692.

[102] 34 L.A. 904 (Tatum, 1960). See also *Imco Container Co.*, AAA Case No. 100-11 (Schmertz, 1967).

[103] AAA Case No. 24-9 (Rock, 1960).

[104] *Id.*

[105] 36 L.A. 578, 583-84 (Hale, 1960).

[106] *New York & Pennsylvania Co.*, AAA Case No. 33-16 (Healy, 1961).

cannot bring himself to award any damages because of the *de minimis* nature of the violation."

But, Arbitrator A. August Lanna, in *Gulf States Paper Corp.*,[107] rejected reliance on *de minimis* in a case involving a supervisor performing bargaining unit work:

"It was argued that the work took only a few minutes and that because the time was so miniscule and that the skills required were minimal that the supervisor therefore was not taking away from the covered employees work which they normally enjoyed. Under different circumstances the *de minimis* theory might apply. The Arbitrator, however, could not hold to this because there was adequate time for the work to be performed."

The doctrine of *de minimis* is held not to apply when there have been repeated violations. Thus, in *Foote Mineral Co.*,[108] Arbitrator Samuel Jaffee said:

"Even if the fifteen or twenty minutes involved may be considered *de minimis* I do not think that the principle has application where, as here, violations of this character (presumably also *de minimis*) have occurred repeatedly, and especially when an award to that effect has previously been issued. . . . The little *de minimis* 'acorns' have by this time grown into an 'oak' of some size."

E. PUNITIVE DAMAGES AND PENALTIES

Arbitrators have generally been unwilling to award punitive or exemplary damages.[109] This view is premised on the theory that punishment and retribution, which are inherent in the punitive damage concept, are foreign to the need for amicable and continuing settlement of disputes via the grievance procedure and arbitration process.[110] In *Publishers Assn. of New York City*,[111] where a union refused to operate printing presses at speeds directed by the employer, Arbi-

---

[107] *Gulf States Paper Corp.*, AAA Case No. 34-2 (Lanna, 1961). See also *Marion Power Shovel Co.*, 34 L.A. 709 (Stouffer, 1960); *Kroger Co.*, 33 L.A. 188 (Howlett, 1959); *Electric Auto-Lite Co.*, 30 L.A. 449 (Marshall, 1958).

[108] *Foote Mineral Co.*, AAA Case No. 36-6 (Jaffee, 1961). See also *Foote Mineral Co.*, AAA Case No. 19-26 (Seibel, 1960); *Budd Co.*, AAA Case No. 10-8 (Gill, 1959); *Minneapolis-Honeywell Regulator Co.*, 31 L.A. 213 (McCormick, 1958).

[109] See generally Bernstein, PRIVATE DISPUTE SETTLEMENT 584-91 (1968). Note, *Mandatory Default Provision in Arbitration Contract Held Not a Penalty*, 5 SYRACUSE L. REV. 111 (1953); Note, *Arbitration—Confirmation of Penal Awards for Breach of Contract*, 27 ST. JOHN'S L. REV. 346 (1953); Note, *Arbitration and Award*, 66 HARV. L. REV. 525 (1953).

[110] For a few of the many cases which have refused to issue an award of punitive damages, see *Corn Products Co.*, 46 L.A. 1073 (Rezler, 1966); *Weyerhaeuser Co.*, 46 L.A. 707 (Kelliher, 1966); *Walker Mfg. Co.*, 64-2 ARB ¶ 8634 (Anderson, 1964); *Celanese Fibers Co.*, 64-2 ARB ¶ 8585 (Howard, 1963); *Philip Carey Mfg. Co.*, 37 L.A. 134 (Gill, 1961); *A. O. Smith Corp.*, 33 L.A. 365 (Updegraff, 1959).

[111] 37 L.A. 509 (Seitz, 1961).

trator Peter Seitz, in rejecting a request for punitive damages, emphasized:

> "When and where punitive damages are awarded, I assume that the award would be based on the theory (a) of pure punishment (of the eye for an eye and a tooth for a tooth variety) or (b) of providing a deterrent to future similar insupportable conduct. I have never considered previously that *lex talionis* was part of the arsenal of remedies normally available to an arbitrator and am unprepared, at this time, to grasp in my hand and to wield unflinchingly, the avenging sword. It seems to me (although I am open to conviction to the contrary) that such blood-letting and sword-wielding might better be done in other tribunals and authorities than by arbitrators." [112]

In an early New York case, *Publishers' Assn. of New York City v. Newspapers and Mail Deliverers Union of New York and Vicinity,*[113] which involved the same association as in the Seitz arbitration, the court refused to enforce an award for punitive damages even where the labor agreement provided for such damages. The court held that it could not enforce the punitive damages remedy because the court itself would have been unable under state law and public policy to make such an award if the case on the merits had come initially before the court.[114]

More recently in *United Shoe Workers v. Brooks Mfg. Co.,*[115] the district court awarded the union $50,000 in punitive damages from an employer who moved his plant in violation of his contract with the union.[116] The Third Circuit reversed the lower court's decision, noting that there are no provisions for punitive damages in Section 301 and reasoning that the statute is generally remedial rather than punitive.[117]

In contrast to this usual reluctance to award punitive damages disguised as compensatory, is the remedy in an award by Arbitrator Rolf Valtin discussed previously in this chapter. He found that U.S. Gypsum Company was obligated to observe the provisions of a labor agreement between a union and United Cement Company, a company that Gypsum had purchased, and then ordered Gypsum to pay a wage increase of 10 cents per hour from the date of a wage reopener, offsetting a 6-cent increase voluntarily granted by Gypsum seven months later.[118] In essence, the arbitrator granted the union what he believed

---

[112] *Id.* at 519-20.
[113] 280 App. Div. 500, 114 N.Y.S.2d 401 (1952).
[114] See *Wilko v. Swan,* 346 U.S. 427 (1953) (dictum). But see *East India Trading Co., Dada Haji Ebrahim Halari,* 280 App. Div. 420, 114 N.Y.S.2d 93 (1952).
[115] 298 F.2d 277 (3d Cir. 1962).
[116] 187 F.Supp. 509, 512-13 (C.D.Pa. 1960).
[117] 298 F.2d at 283-86.
[118] *U.S. Gypsum,* 56 L.A. 363 (Valtin, 1971); reversed by *Steelworkers v. U.S. Gypsum Co.,* 79 LRRM 2833 (D.C.Ala. 1972).

it would have received in wage increases if the company had honored the contract and bargained with the union under the wage reopener. This remedy is particularly interesting in light of the fact that the NLRB has held that it could not grant such a remedy.[119]

A few arbitrators have awarded punitive damages in certain limited situations because the employer was found guilty of a willful violation of the contract.[120] An interesting example of an award of punitive damages occurred in the second of two Bethlehem Steel arbitrations. In the first, the company had changed the dates normally set for vacations and argued that inasmuch as the employees did get their vacations, albeit at an earlier date, this shift in no way affected their total earnings. The union demanded additional vacation pay for those employees affected, but this was denied by Arbitrator Ralph T. Seward. The arbitrator, while sympathizing with the employees affected, did not believe he could establish a monetary value for grievant's "mental discomfort." But, he did issue a warning to the company that he:

> "[W]ould see nothing unreasonable or unfair in a holding that if the Company deliberately forced an employee to take an accelerated vacation in order to avoid layoffs, *knowing* that its action violated the Agreement, it would not thereby have discharged its obligations to the employees . . . and could properly be required to give the employee either a further vacation on the proper dates or pay-in-lieu thereof." (Emphasis in original)[121]

There was a sequel to this award. The employer again rescheduled vacations. Arbitrator Rolf Valtin granted double vacation pay, holding that since Seward's warning, "all concerned have known—or should have known" that forced earlier vacations were violations.[122]

Punitive damages have been approved by courts in spite of contrary decisions reported earlier. A federal district court in *Sidney Wanzer & Sons v. Milk Drivers Union, Local 753*[123] refused to dismiss

---

[119] *Ex-Cell-O-Corp.*, 185 NLRB No. 20 (1970).

[120] See, *e.g.*, *Yale & Towne, Inc.*, 46 L.A. 4 (Duff, 1965). Punitive damages were denied on ground that violation was not willful in *Vulcan Mold & Iron Co.*, 29 L.A. 743 (Reid, 1957); see also *Hearst Consolidated Publications, Inc.*, 26 L.A. 723 (Gray, 1956); *Universal Glass Products Co.*, 24 L.A. 623 (Duff, 1955); *Timken-Detroit Axle Co.*, 6 L.A. 926 (Marshall, 1947).

[121] *Bethlehem Steel Co.*, 31 L.A. 857, 858 (Seward, 1958).

[122] *Bethlehem Steel Co.*, 37 L.A. 821, 824 (Valtin, 1961).

[123] 249 F.Supp. 664, 671 (N.D.Ill. 1966); see also *Patrick v. I. D. Packing Co.*, 308 F.Supp. 824 (S.D. Iowa 1969). But see *Local 127, United Shoe Workers v. Brooks Shoe Mfg. Co.*, 298 F.2d 277 (3d Cir. 1962); *Texas Gas Transmission Corp. v. Chemical Workers, Local 187,* 200 F.Supp. 521 (W.D.La. 1961). See generally Bernstein, PRIVATE DISPUTE SETTLEMENT 591 (1968); Note, *Damages—Punitive Damages For Breach of Collective Bargaining Agreement May Be Awarded Under Section 301 of Taft-Hartley Act,* 52 VA. L. REV. 1377 (1966).

a claim for punitive or exemplary damages, although it explained that normally excessive sanctions are prohibited as being punitive rather than remedial:

> "[W]here the award is a uniquely effective device for changing a specific pattern of illegal conduct by a party before the court, it comes within the remedial purpose of the labor laws, even though the defendant may suffer as if he had been 'punished' for other reasons." [124]

The court cautioned, however, that:

> "Such an award is extraordinary and should be reserved for those labor-management situations which cannot be pacified by other remedies." [125]

The distinction between a "make whole" money remedy and "punitive damages" often clearly arises in labor arbitration in cases where the company has violated the requirement in the agreement to distribute overtime "equally" among employees in a classification or other group. Where employees are not scheduled for overtime in regular rotation and a grievance is filed, the employer will usually say that the injury to the employee's earnings can be corrected by scheduling the employee passed over in the rotation for future overtime to bring his amount of overtime back into equality. The union will reply that such a remedy means that the employer can with impunity fail to comply with a clear commitment in the agreement. In spite of this argument, numerous arbitrators have held that if the employer recreates equality of distribution within a reasonable time, no further remedy is necessary.[126]

The reason arbitrators do not award pay where the agreement provides that overtime will be distributed equally and has been technically violated by not scheduling an employee when it is his turn, was explained by Arbitrator Clarence Updegraff in *A. O. Smith Corp.*:[127]

---

[124] 249 F.Supp. at 671.

[125] *Id.*

[126] See, *e.g., Beryllium Corp.,* 68-2 ARB ¶ 8641 (Hardy, 1968); *Butler Mfg. Co.,* 42 L.A. 304 (Johnson, 1964); *Morton Salt Co.,* 42 L.A. 525 (Hebert, 1964); *Kimberly-Clark Corp.,* 34 L.A. 792 (Hawley, 1960); *Singer Mfg. Co.,* 35 L.A. 526 (Cahn, 1960); *Reed Roller Bit Co.,* 30 L.A. 437 (Hebert, 1958); *Fruehauf Trailer Co.,* 27 L.A. 834 (Seligson, 1957); *Goodyear Atomic Corp.,* 27 L.A. 634 (Shister, 1956); *Celanese Corp. of America,* 24 L.A. 168 (Justin, 1954); *Goodyear Tire & Rubber Co., of Ala.,* 5 L.A. 30 (McCoy, 1946). Sometimes recreating equality of overtime is the remedy specified in the agreement as in *Olin Mathieson Chemical Corp.,* 62-2 ARB ¶ 8566 (McGury, 1962). But see *U.S. Industrial Chemicals Co.,* 33 L.A. 335 (Sullivan, 1959); *Pittsburgh Plate Glass Co.,* 32 L.A. 622 (Sembower, 1958), to name but two cases in which arbitrators have granted monetary damages for breach of an equal distribution of overtime provision.

[127] 33 L.A. 365, 366 (Updegraff, 1959).

"[O]rdinarily the assessment of damages by a court or by an arbitrator requires clear proof that the person to benefit from the payment of damages has actually suffered by the amount to be reimbursed. In the present case, there would normally be many instances where the person who was not called in his turn might first collect for the shift which he failed to work as is claimed here, and subsequently obtain his full share of the overtime of the month or quarter or year, as also was the case here.

"It is of course possible for parties to draft a contract authorizing an arbitrator to assess penalty payments, but since, as has very often been stated, the law abhors penalties, the language should be clear, definite, and positive or the award of the arbitrator granting a penalty rather than damages would quite likely be set aside by a court reviewing the same. It is to be noted that one of the positions taken by management in this case was the positive one that there is no authorization in the contract between the parties providing for the awarding of a penalty against the Company in situations like the present, or in any other."

This same principle was stated by Arbitrator George Cheney in *Mode O'Day Corp.*:[128]

"A party claiming a forfeiture or penalty under a written instrument has the burden of proving that such is the unmistakable intention of the parties to the document. In addition, the courts have ruled that a contract is not to be construed to provide a forfeiture or penalty unless no other construction or interpretation is reasonably possible. Since forfeitures are not favored either in law or in equity, courts are reluctant to declare and enforce a forfeiture if by reasonable intepretation it can be avoided."

In *Celanese Fibers Co.,*[129] the arbitrator said that punitive damages could only be justified in an overtime distribution violation case where the action is a willful attempt to injure the other party:

"Although the Union, in effect, asks for punitive damages for violation of the cited provision, in the opinion of the undersigned arbitrator, punitive damages are out of place in the arbitration process absent a showing of a wilful attempt to injure the other party by violating the Agreement. In the case at issue, the question of violation of Article 12(A) was at worst an honest difference of opinion over the Company's responsibility in this regard." [130]

That the law abhors penalties is an important guide in fashioning remedies in arbitration. Even a past practice of paying penalties has been held to be insufficient to justify an arbitrator awarding a penalty payment:

---

[128] 1 L.A. 490, 494 (Cheney, 1946).
[129] 64-2 ARB ¶ 8585 (Howard, 1963).
[130] *Id.* at 5062-63.

"The Company is not required to pay anyone a penalty for time not worked. A past practice in which the Company has sometimes done so and then very often has refused to do so, can in no way be relied upon to modify the Contract. There is nothing in the Contract, as we have said, that permits the Union to claim pay for time not worked, in an emergency overtime situation such as this." [131]

The principle of construction—that an agreement should not be construed to require a penalty, if any other construction is possible—has also been applied by an arbitrator to reject a construction urged by an employer. In *Alpha Cellulose Corp.*,[132] Arbitrator Peter M. Kelliher stated:

"In essence the Company is attempting to declare a forfeiture of this 'double time' premium as a penalty where the employees fail to meet the conditions of Section 1. As Courts and Arbitrators have frequently stated, if an Agreement is susceptible of two constructions, one which would work a forfeiture and one which would not, the Board must adopt the interpretation which will prevent the forfeiture.

"The party urging a forfeiture or a penalty under a written instrument has the burden of proving that such was the unmistakable intentiton of the parties to the document. A Contract, is not to be construed to provide a forfeiture or penalty unless no other construction or interpretation is reasonably possible. Forfeitures are not favored either in law or in equity and Courts as well as Arbitrators are reluctant to declare and enforce a forfeiture if by reasonable interpretation it can be avoided."

The assessment of a penalty as a remedy was, however, upheld by an arbitrator who said that an employer had the right to deduct from an employee's weekly salary amounts that were proportional to the employee's lateness where the employee was guilty of "repeated and unjustified lateness" after frequent warnings. The union's contention that the deductions constituted a wage cut penalty in violation of the agreement was rejected:

"Repeated and unjustified lateness may be good and sufficient cause for dismissal. The [employer] has the right to discharge for good and sufficient cause. Discharge is the maximum penalty an employer might invoke. A pro rata deduction from an employee's salary for repeated and unjustified lateness is a lesser penalty and may be invoked by the employer rather than the extreme penalty of dismissal." [133]

Another unusual remedy which has overtones of punitive damages was an award of four months' back pay to a dischargee who was not reinstated by the arbitrator.[134] The employee had been discharged for

---

[131] *Gas Service Co.*, 43 L.A. 982, 995 (Klamon, 1964).

[132] 27 L.A. 798, 800 (Kelliher, 1956).

[133] *Hearst Corp., New York Mirror Div.*, AAA Case No. 23-12 (Mintzer, 1960).

[134] *Thorsen Mfg. Co.*, 55 L.A. 581 (Koven, 1970).

failing to include in his job application the fact that he had been fired by one previous employer for insubordination and by another employer for unsatisfactory work. Back pay was awarded, however, because the company left the grievant in doubt as to his status for a longer time than was normal because of the presentation of needless and unprovable charges. The arbitrator said:

"What I have said above amply demonstrates that the grievant deserved to be discharged because of the false statements contained in his employment application. However, there are some unusual aspects about this case. The Company presented two other grounds for discharge at the hearing which they were unable to sustain. Furthermore, the Company also charged the grievant with stealing and that charge was dropped at the Arbitration hearing. Because of the multi-charges and a very complicated record, an inordinate amount of time has passed from the date of discharge to the time of this decision, and this time lapse was not the fault of the grievant or his Union. The passage of time has left the grievant in doubt of his status for a substantial period. To compensate for this uncertainty and possible hardship, the grievant is awarded four months' straight-time pay at his normal wage rate." [135]

F. MONEY DAMAGES FOR VIOLATION OF NO-STRIKE AGREEMENTS

Arbitrators have awarded monetary damages where no-strike provisions of the collective bargaining agreement have been violated and these awards have been enforced by the courts.[136] Arbitrator Sidney Wolff reasoned as follows:

"If we justify an award of damages to an employee for a contract breach on the theory of implied power to formulate a remedy, why must we insist upon a specific grant of authority to award damages for violation of the no-strike covenant?" [137]

In *PPG Industries, Inc.*,[138] Arbitrator James C. Vadakin rejected the union's argument that damages should be denied since there was

---

[135] *Id.* at 585. See also *Magnavox Co. of Tenn. v. IUE Local 748*, 410 F.2d 388, 389 (6th Cir. 1969).

[136] *Machinists v. Cameron Iron Works, Inc.*, 292 F.2d 112, 119 (5th Cir. 1961); *Texas Gas Transmission Corp. v. Chemical Workers*, 200 F.Supp. 521, 528 (W.D.La. 1961). The award of money damages for violation of a no-strike clause was seemingly given approval in *Drake Bakeries, Inc. v. American Bakery & Confectionery Workers, Local 50*, 370 U.S. 254 (1962).

[137] See note 66 *supra*, at 185. But see *Baldwin-Lima-Hamilton Corp.*, 30 L.A. 1061 (Crawford, 1958). See generally Fleming, *Arbitrators and the Remedy Power*, 48 VA. L. REV. 1220; Smith, *Arbitrators & Arbitrability*, LABOR ARBITRATION AND INDUSTRIAL CHANGE, Proceedings of the Sixteenth Annual Meeting, National Academy of Arbitrators 75 (M. Kahn Ed. 1963).

[138] 68-2 ARB ¶ 8807 (Vadakin, 1968).

no provision in the agreement granting the arbitrator the right to do so. He emphasized that:

"When parties enter into a collective bargaining contract, each is assured of specified rights and each, in turn, assumes definite responsibilities. Unless the machinery for enforcement of the contract includes damages or other affirmative remedies for the benefit of an injured party, said remedies designed to make him whole in the face of the breach by the other party, the contract becomes a nullity." [139]

Arbitrator H. H. Rains imposed liability upon the union treasury when the employee members breached their agreement by engaging in strike action, stating:

"The crux of the issue before the Arbitrator is that a breach of the contract between the Company and Union took place and that the Company claims appropriate remedies for that wrongful breach. The responsibility of the Union . . . for such wrongful breach is clear and a failure to apply proper effective remedies in form of prohibition orders, assessment of penalties, and award of damages claimed by the aggrieved party would have the effect of freeing the Union and its members from liability for their actions. Such failure could only militate against the desirable ideal of 'Union responsibility.' Assessment of penalties and award of damages payable to the aggrieved party is a step in direction of preserving 'Union responsibility' and its integrity as the 'responsible party' to the collective bargaining agreement." [140]

Because of the language of many agreements,[141] courts have held that damages for a union breach of a no-strike clause are matters for the court rather than the arbitrator. One court said:

"I find that the contract between the parties did not expressly contemplate that such issue of damages was a dispute or controversy to be settled by grievance and arbitration procedures. Further, since this strike concerns a violation of the no-strike clause it is not a grievance referable to arbitration. . . .

---

[139] *Id.* at 5795. See also *Master Builders Ass'n of Western Pa., Inc.*, 68-2 ARB ¶ 8561 (McDermott, 1968); *American Pipe & Construction Co.*, 43 L.A. 1126 (Ladar, 1964); *Publishers' Ass'n of New York City*, 42 L.A. 95 (Berkowitz, 1964); *Publishers' Ass'n of New York City*, 39 L.A. 564 (Moskowitz, 1962); *Regent Quality Furniture, Inc.*, 32 L.A. 553 (Turkus, 1959).

[140] *Brynmore Press, Inc.*, 7 L.A. 648, 658 (Rains, 1947). See also *Publishers' Ass'n of New York City*, 39 L.A. 564 (Moskowitz, 1962); *Oregonian Publishing Co.*, 33 L.A. 574 (Kleinsorge, 1959); *Regent Quality Furniture Co.*, note 139 *supra*; *Canadian General Electric Co., Ltd.*, 18 L.A. 925 (Laskin, 1952); *cf. Hoffman Beverage Co.*, 18 L.A. 869 (Sheridan, 1952), in which the arbitrator said the company could have recovered damages for a contract breach strike had it requested them.

[141] Where, of course, the employer has a right to use the grievance and arbitration procedure to challenge the breach of the no-strike clause, it is precluded from a damage suit in court. *Drake Bakeries, Inc. v. American Bakery & Confectionery Workers, Local 50*, 370 U.S. 254 (1962).

"As I have found that the Union breached the contract when it induced the work stoppage, as the trier of the fact I shall determine the amount of damages to which the company is entitled." [142]

However, another branch of the same court held in *Tenny Engineering, Inc. v. UE Local 437*,[143] that the arbitration clause rendered arbitrable the issue concerning the union's alleged violation of the no-strike clause and the damages arising therefrom.

The amount of damages that an arbitrator (or a court) should award where there is a strike in violation of a no-strike clause has been determined by a variety of different formulas which are set out below:

(1) *Average daily "overhead cost"* was the formula used in *Structural Steel Ass'n v. Shopmens Local 545*.[144] The strike continued for only one and one-half days. The court appears to have held that the employer could recover the expenses that would be incident to the maintenance of a plant during an unworked holiday period of one and one-half days. The nonoperating expenses were totaled for the first nine months of the year (excluding travel, entertainment, and chariable contributions), divided by the number of days within the period, and multiplied by one and one-half.

(2) *Overhead, plus overtime premium charges,* was the formula used in *International Union of Operating Engineers v. Dahlem Construction Co.*[145] The addition of the expense of the overtime premiums paid to employees making up the lost production would, of course, rule out a damage claim for lost production during the strike. A company could not logically recover the premiums paid regaining the lost production on an overtime basis and also claim it was damaged by a loss of production during the strike.

(3) *Overhead and stand-by expenses* was the formula used in *United Electrical, Radio and Machine Workers Union v. Oliver Corp.*[146] Stand-by expense included the salaries paid to watchmen and supervisory employees who were retained to protect the plant

---

[142] *Structural Steel & Ornamental Iron Ass'n of New Jersey, Inc. v. Shopmen's Local 545 of Int'l Ass'n of Bridge, Structural & Ornamental Iron Workers,* 172 F.Supp. 354, 360 (D.N.J. 1959). The same view was expressed by Arbitrator Donald Crawford in *Baldwin-Lima-Hamilton Corp.,* 30 L.A. 1061, 1064 (1958):

"Damages for strikes and lockouts in violation of the contract is a remedy normal to the Courts—but not to arbitration. When parties seek such extra-arbitral remedy, the proper tribunal is, and has been, the courts—unless the contract specifically authorizes the arbitrator to invoke such a remedy in a strike or lockout situation. And this contract does not. Thus the Company's proper procedure for damages for this illegal strike is with the courts—a course open to it without any prejudice by this finding."

[143] 174 F.Supp. 878 (D.N.J. 1959).
[144] 172 F.Supp. 354, 360-62 (D.N.J. 1959).
[145] 193 F.2d 470, 472 (6th Cir. 1951).
[146] 205 F.2d 376, 387-89 (8th Cir. 1953).

during the period of the strike. There was then added 47.5 percent of the daily fixed overhead because production during the strike had been reduced to 52.5 percent of normal.

A claim for supervisors' salaries was also not satisfactorily established when a company refused to produce "figures on actual supervisors' salaries," and submitted no proof "concerning the amount of time really spent doing nothing on the part of supervisors." Moreover, the arbitrator said that the company could have "mitigated damages" by cancelling shifts for supervisors who, it was known, would have nothing to do. "To compute damages under these circumstances would be intuitive speculation." Arbitrator Wildebush allowed damages of $227.12 and then said:

> "Because the Union was found culpable in abetting the strike, it could have been assessed damages in the full amount claimed by the Company, namely $77,946.41, if such damages were proved. Fortunately for the Union, the proof was not sufficient or was lacking except for the claims allowed. . . . As an unnamed philosopher once said, 'once warned, twice careful.' " [147]

(4) *Fair rental value of idle machinery* was the formula used in *Denver Building Trades Council v. Shore.*[148] This was considered "loss of use."

(5) *Loss of profits* as a formula was seemingly approved in *Textile Workers v. Newberry Mills,*[149] where it was established by proof that the union "participated, condoned, authorized and supported the strike" and hence was liable for damages caused thereby. The court, however, found that no damage was proved because no profit and loss information was introducd by the company.

In *Denver & Rio Grande R.R. v. Bhd. of Railway Trainmen,*[150] however, the court granted the employer damages for an unlawful strike in an amount equal to profits lost because the Ford Motor Company diverted shipments from the railroad due to the threat that a strike stopped by a temporary restraining order might commence once again. Thus, if an employer can connect a customer's diversion of business with a union's strike in breach of contract, he should recover from the union the profits lost because of the customer's change in buying habits.

The proof-of-injury difficulties were well illustrated by Arbitrator Joseph F. Wildebush[151] who held that the union violated the contract by instigating, promoting, and encouraging an "overtime strike,"

---

[147] *Kentile, Inc.,* AAA Case No. 78-10 (1965).
[148] 132 Colo. 187, 287 P.2d 267 (1955).
[149] 238 F.Supp. 366 (W.D.S.C. 1965).
[150] — F.Supp. —, 58 LRRM 2568 (D.Col). 1965).
[151] Note 147 *supra.*

and having found that the union did promote and encourage the work stoppage examined the company's claim for damages. Arbitrator Wildebush said:

> "The company claim for loss of production of tile amounting to $42,480.10 was not substantiated. Loss production is not an item of damage unless it can be related directly and specifically to lost orders and accounts. . . . There were no records of loss of customers or orders. There certainly was a loss of production intended for inventory but no proof of actual damages incurred. This claim for damages is rank speculation and is therefore disallowed."

Arbitrator Sam Kagel, after finding that the strike was in breach of the agreement, remanded to the parties the question of compensatory damages, if any, but retained jurisdiction in the event that resolution is not reached between the parties.[152] The strike started when two mechanical grapepickers were used and ended approximately two weeks later. If some of the grapes were lost because they were not harvested during this period, the measure of compensatory damages would include loss of product.

G. THE AWARDING OF COSTS

Arbitrator Robben Fleming noted the danger of awarding costs when he said:

> "For a number of reasons strong policy considerations militate against an award of costs in the above type of case. In the first place, it is well known that there are contracts which provide that the losing party shall pay the costs of the arbitration. A clause of that kind would have taken care of the problem, but it was not included and, on the contrary, the usual clause providing for the division of costs was included. Secondly, the legal question of the arbitrator's power to award a remedy assigning all costs of the arbitration to the company is sufficiently questionable as to almost certainly bring forth a court test which would be both costly and time consuming. Thirdly, there is Harry Shulman's famed question as to whether, when their autonomous system breaks down, the parties might not better be left to the usual methods for adjustment of labor disputes rather than to court actions on the contract or on the arbitration award?"[153]

Somewhat to the contrary is Arbitrator Sidney Wolff who has stated:

> "I suggest that, should a case arise that might tempt the arbitrator to impose a penalty when not authorized by the contract, he consider assessing the costs of the proceedings upon the intentional violator, be

---

[152] *Almaden Vineyards, Inc.,* 56 L.A. 425 (Kagel, 1971).
[153] Fleming, note 137 *supra,* at 1199, 1218.

it the company or the union unless barred by the contract. This might tend to prevent a repetition of a violation that does not cause monetary loss." [154]

Assessment of costs, however, may arguably be beyond the arbitrator's authority. In one case,[155] the union's request that the entire cost of the arbitration, including witnesses' expenses and counsel fees, be assessed against the company, on the ground that the company was "motivated by malice and indifference" in prosecuting the matter, was denied by Arbitrator Jacob Seidenberg as "outside the authority" of the arbitrator. He said an arbitrator's "jurisdiction" must be distinguished from his "authority" and that even if the arbitrator believed that the union was "entitled to the extraordinary relief" requested he would still be "lacking in the authority to grant it" because under the parties' contractual arbitration procedure, they expressly agreed to share its costs. "To change this provision would be a clear and deliberate rewriting of an important part of the contract." He further noted that there are contracts which provide for the losing party to pay the costs of the arbitration or which provide for the "assessment of punitive damages." But:

> "[T]o introduce these provisions by construction into an agreement where there is not the slightest suggestion that either party desired or intended them is to distort the canons of construction and to subvert the underlying principle of voluntary arbitration." [156]

H. THE AWARDING OF INTEREST

The awarding of interest is usually reserved to disciplinary cases,[157] but there are examples where interest has been awarded in nondisciplinary cases as well. In *Oscar Joseph Stores, Inc.,*[158] Arbitrator Dudley E. Whiting, in awarding interest in addition to the amount of an improperly withheld wage increase, noted:

> "It appears that six per cent is the legal rate of interest on money due under contracts which do not specify some other rate. Here there is no question about the money being due for payroll periods after February 1, 1963. Thus, it must be considered as a liquidated claim then due and bearing that legal rate of interest under this contract. In cases of unliquidated or undetermined obligations interest would accrue legally only after the award, but there is no question of the amount due nor when it becomes due in this case." [159]

---

[154] See note 66 *supra,* at 191.

[155] *Brunswick Corp.,* AAA Case No. 74-14 (Seidenberg, 1964).

[156] *Id.*

[157] See discussion of interest on back pay awards, *supra,* in this Chapter Section B(4)(b).

[158] 41 L.A. 567 (Whiting, 1963).

[159] *Id.* at 567-68.

I. AWARDING OF ATTORNEYS' FEES

In *Mercer, Fraser Co.*,[160] the arbitrator denied an employer's claim that the union should pay attorney fees sustained in an effort to obtain injunctive relief where a violation of a no-strike clause had occurred. Similarly, in *Yellow Cab Co.*[161] a grievant was denied attorney fees. The employer had discharged a cab driver asserting he assaulted a passenger. The driver was charged with a felony, later reduced to a misdemeanor. The driver claimed he acted in self-defense and the charge was dismissed when the passenger did not appear for the trial. The arbitrator awarded reinstatement to the driver, but without back pay and denied his claim for attorney fees for the court part of the case. A court has also said that a union that won in arbitration was not entitled to reimbursement of attorney's fee since the employer's position was not totally without justification.[162] However, a union was entitled to recover costs and attorney's fees incurred opposing a suit to compel arbitration that had resulted in the erroneous issuance of an injunction.[163]

J. DECLARATORY JUDGMENTS

Whether a request for declaratory judgment is arbitrable depends largely on the contractual definition of a grievance.[164] One court has said that a request that an arbitrator render a declaratory judgment "is just as desirable here as in any other legal proceedings, inasmuch as it may avert constant bickering of specific grievances,"[165] and an arbitrator has noted that a grievance requesting a "declaration of rights" or "declaratory judgments" concerning certain work assignments raised an arbitrable issue.[166]

K. INJUNCTIVE RELIEF TO HALT VIOLATION OF NO-STRIKE CLAUSE

Arbitrators occasionally issue a remedial order where a strike in violation of a labor agreement is occurring directing the employees to stop their breach and the union officers to direct the employees to

---

[160] 54 L.A. 1125 (Eaton, 1970).

[161] 55 L.A. 590 (Helbling, 1970).

[162] *Retail Clerks v. Employers Committee*, — F. Supp —, 81 LRRM 2671 (D.Ore. 1972).

[163] *United States Steel Corp. v. Mine Workers*, 456 F.2d 483 (3d Cir. 1972).

[164] See cases in Chapters IV Section C. and VI Sections D. and E. to the effect that an actual grievance is necessary to create jurisdiction in the arbitration.

[165] *Application of Columbia Broadcasting System, Inc.*, 26 Misc.2d 972, 205 N.Y.S.2d 85 (1960).

[166] *United States Pipe & Foundry Co.*, AAA Case No. 67-20 (Koven, 1964).

return to work. In these situations,[167] the collective bargaining agreement contains a no-strike clause and the grievance and arbitration procedures of the contract are invoked under special stipulations that avoid any question of the arbitrator's authority on jurisdictional grounds and permit the dispute to be promptly heard. The arbitrator then promptly makes an award to the effect that the strikers are violating the agreement and orders all picketing to cease and all employees to return to work. In the event that the strike action does not then cease, the employer may petition a court for enforcement pursuant to the provisions of the state arbitration act, if it, as does the Uniform Arbitration Act,[168] contain a provision for confirmation of the arbitrator's award in a decree by the court.[169] The remaining states are presently without a statutory basis for the prompt and efficient enforcement of an arbitrator's cease-and-desist order in a wildcat strike. However, with injunctive relief now available in federal court,[170] and with the enforcement of award powers arising from Section 301 applicable in both state and federal courts,[171] there is no need for a state statutory procedure to obtain enforcement of an injunctive type award.

One of the problems in securing the confirmation of an arbitration award ordering the cessation of a wildcat strike is the confusion that arises when the state statute or the court rules of procedure require certain steps to be taken prior to issuing a confirmation order. For example, the court might allow the normal time for filing an answer which would delay the needed remedy.

By applying rules of procedure which allow a party to delay the confirmation of an award by filing an answer to the application for confirmation or using other procedural devices, a court would be thwarting the intent of the parties to secure as expeditiously as possi-

---

[167] See, e.g., Ford Motor Co., 63-2 ARB ¶ 8491 (Platt, 1963); General American Transportation Corp., 41 L.A. 214 (Abrahams, 1963). For other cases in which arbitrators granted employers injunctive relief, see New Orleans Steamship Ass'n v. ILA Local 1418, 389 F.2d 369 (5th Cir.), cert. denied, 393 U.S. 828 (1968); Ruppert v. Egelhofer, 3 N.Y.2d 576, 148 N.E.2d 129 (1958); Cloak, Suit & Shirt Mfrs., Inc., 5 L.A. 372 (Poletti, 1946).

[168] See, e.g., ILL. REV. STAT. ch. 10 §§ 101-23 (1963); OHIO REV. CODE ANN. ch. 4129.

[169] FLA. STAT. ANN. § 682.12 (Supp. 1970); ME. REV. STAT. ANN. tit. 26, § 957 (1964); MONT. REV. CODES ANN. §§ 93-201 (1964); NEB. REV. STAT. §§ 25.2116 (1964); NEV. REV. STAT. § 614.040 (1964); N.D. CENT. CODE § 32-29-07 (1960); R.I. GEN. LAWS ANN. § 28-9-71 (1969); TENN. CODE ANN. § 23-513 (1955); W.VA. CODE ANN. § 55-10-3 (1966); WYO. STAT. ANN. § 1-1048.13 (Supp. 1969).

[170] Boys Markets, Inc. v. Retail Clerk's Union, Local 770, 398 U.S. 275 (1969). See also Pacific Maritime Ass'n v. Longshoremen's & Warehousemen's Union, CA-9, 67 LC ¶ 12,313 where the court enforced an arbitrator's award that the union cease engaging in a work stoppage in violation of an agreement since the case was not distinguishable from Boys' Markets.

[171] See, e.g., New Orleans Steamship Ass'n v. General Longshore Workers, 389 F.2d 369 (5th Cir.), cert. denied, 393 U.S. 828 (1968).

ble both arbitral and judicial relief against a strike or lockout in violation of a collective bargaining agreement. Moreover, the application of such rules of procedure can well be considered contrary to the Supreme Court's decision in *Boys Markets, Inc. v. Retail Clerk's Union, Local 770.*[172] In *Boys Markets,* the Court recognized that "the peaceful resolution of labor disputes" is a fundamental principle of national labor policy. This principle is weakened if disputes are not settled quickly. Most court rules providing for time for filing answers were never intended to deal with the problem of securing confirmation of an injunctive type award to reestablish industrial peace where there is a strike in violation of the agreement. Thus, in cases involving the confirmation of awards dealing with wildcat strikes, courts should apply "federal law" which allows new rules to be devised to obtain the objectives of federal labor policy as now reflected in *Boys Markets.*

If the award is confirmed by the court, an injunction decree will issue from the court incorporating the arbitrator's injunctive award. In one case, for example, the decree read:

> "[The union], its officers and members shall forthwith cease and desist from engaging in such a strike; that they shall cease to picket the [plant]; and that they cease and desist directly or indirectly from inducing, persuading, encouraging, or permitting any employees to refrain from working or to strike." [173]

Once the arbitration award is incorporated into a decree of the court, all of the court's enforcement machinery, including the powers of the sheriff's office, become available and contempt can be sought if the decree is not honored.

Usually when the process discussed above has been used, the instructions of the international union to the striking employees to return have been ignored and the union officials then cooperate to speed up the arbitration and court confirmation processes. Without this cooperation, this injunctive award procedure would not be effective because of the delay between steps in the grievance procedure, unless the labor agreement contains a special provision, to eliminate the normal delay in this type of case. An example of such a special provision, sometimes referred to as a "quickie" arbitration clause, is the following:

> During the term of this Agreement the Union agrees that there shall be no strikes, work stoppages, slowdowns, or interferences with work on the part of the Union, any of its agents or any of its members. Any employee participating in such activity shall be subject to discipline

---

[172] 398 U.S. 275 (1969).
[173] *Ford Motor Co.,* 62-2 ARB ¶ 8491 at 4622 (Platt, 1963).

including discharge. The parties further agree that in the event of an alleged violation of this Section, the issue arising therefrom may be submitted immediately by the Company to the permanent arbitrator to be heard by said arbitrator as soon as possible after such submission. If the arbitrator finds that the Agreement has been violated, he shall order that the party or parties in violation cease and desist from such conduct and any other conduct inducing said breach or causing it to continue and shall have authority to grant any further relief he deems proper. Said order by the arbitrator shall be in writing and shall issue at the conclusion of the arbitration hearing. The arbitrator shall have authority to retain jurisdiction in such a case to assess damages but the hearing on the question of damages shall occur after the contract violation has terminated.

The most expeditious means of enjoining a wildcat strike may be to circumvent the grievance procedure and seek an injunction directly in Federal Court. In *Boys Market*,[174] the Supreme Court overturned its much criticized decision in *Atkinson v. Sinclair Refining Co.*[175] which had held that violations of no-strike clauses were not grounds for issuing injunctive relief.[176] The Supreme Court in *Boys Markets* ruled that an employer could obtain injunctive relief when the dispute involved is covered by the arbitration clause of the collective bargaining agreement. The Court said:

> "We conclude, therefore, that the unavailability of equitable relief in the arbitration context presents a serious impediment to the congressional policy favoring the voluntary establishment of a mechanism for the peaceful resolution of labor disputes, that the core purpose of the Norris-LaGuardia Act is not sacrified by the limited use of equitable remedies to further this important policy, and consequently that the Norris-LaGuardia Act does not bar the granting of injunctive relief in the circumstances of the instant case." [177]

The Court was quick to limit its ruling, stating:

> "Our holding in the present case is a narrow one. We do not undermine the vitality of the Norris-LaGuardia Act. We deal only with the situation in which a collective bargaining contract contains a mandatory grievance adjustment or arbitration procedure. Nor does it follow from

---

[174] *Boys Markets, Inc. v. Retail Clerk's Union, Local 770*, 398 U.S. 275 (1969).
[175] 370 U.S. 238 (1962).
[176] Even before the Supreme Court's decision in *Boys Markets*, suits to enforce injunctive relief issued by an arbitrator were generally successful in both state and lower federal courts against the claim that the same injunctive relief could not be issued by a court because of the restrictions of the Norris-LaGuardia Act. *Pacific Maritime Ass'n v. ILWU*, 304 F.Supp. 1315 (N.D.Calif. 1969); *New Orleans Steamship Ass'n v. General Longshore Workers*, 389 F.2d 369 (5th Cir.), *cert. denied*, 393 U.S. 828 (1968); *Ruppert v. Egelhofer*, 3 N.Y.2d 576, 148 N.E.2d 129 (1958). But see *Tanker Serv. Comm. Inc. v. Int'l Organization of Masters, Mates & Pilots; Maritime Serv. Comm. Inc.*, 269 F.Supp. 551 (E.D.Pa. 1967); *Philadelphia Marine Trade Ass'n v. Int'l ILA Local 1291*, 365 F.2d 295 (3d Cir. 1966), *rev'd on other grounds*, 389 U.S. 64 (1967).
[177] 398 U.S. at 253.

what we have said that injunctive relief is appropriate as a matter of course in every case of a strike over an arbitrable grievance." [178]

This case will no doubt vastly diminish the use of the "quickie arbitration procedure," since a remedy in court is now available if the issue involved in the strike is an issue subject to arbitration. The strict guidelines for the issuance of an injunction by a district court, however, should not be overlooked:

> " 'A District Court entertaining an action under § 301 may not grant injunctive relief against concerted activity unless and until it decides that the case is one in which an injunction would be appropriate despite the Norris-LaGuardia Act. When a strike is sought to be enjoined because it is over a grievance which both parties are contractually bound to arbitrate, the District Court may issue no injunctive order until it first holds that the contract *does* have that effect; and the employer should be ordered to arbitrate, as a condition of his obtaining an injunction against the strike. . . .' " [179] (Emphasis in original)

Finally, while arbitrators have issued "cease and desist orders" and have required unions to pay damages to an employer in wildcat strike situations, in one case a request by an employer that the union be ordered to pay the employees the wages they lost, was denied on the ground that such a remedial order was beyond the authority of the arbitrator. Arbitrator Lee Epstein said:

> "Whether such loss should fall on the union (and thus indirectly on its members) or directly on the members is really a question of internal union policy, . . . in any event, it is questionable whether this issue is within the scope of the submission." [180]

L. INJUNCTIVE RELIEF IN GENERAL

Arbitrators are often called upon to issue injunctive relief in disputes involving issues other than breach of no-strike provisions and improper discharge of employees. Arbitrators have ordered employers to do many specific acts, such as to reopen plants and return machinery to plants in cases where operations have been moved to other

---

[178] *Id.* at 253-54.

[179] *Id.* at 254. Courts have had difficulty locating the limit set by the Supreme Court on their authority to enjoin strikes in violation of agreements. In *General Cable Corp. v. IBEW, Local 1644*, 331 F.Supp. 478, 77 LRRM 3053 (D.Md. 1971), the court denied injunctive relief because the cause of the strike was picketing by a sister local and the court concluded this was not an arbitral issue, whereas in *General Cable Corp. v. IBEW, Local 1798*, 333 F.Supp. 331, 77 LRRM 3123 (W.D. Tenn. 1971), another district court came to exactly the opposite conclusion. The search of other courts for the limits set by *Boys Markets* is reported in *Ourisman Chevrolet v. Automotive Lodge*, — F.Supp —, 77 LRRM 2084 (D.D.C. 1971); *Simplex Wire & Cable Co. v. Local 2208, IBEW*, 314 F.Supp. 885 (D.N.H. 1970).

[180] *United Jewish Appeal*, AAA Case No. 87-19 (Epstein, 1965).

cities;[181] to establish a new system for filling job vacancies where improper methods were used previously and return employees to their former positions;[182] to reclassify employees who were improperly classified;[183] to engage in bargaining;[184] and to post a performance bond.[185] And an arbitrator has ordered a union to undertake immediately to bring into its membership 100 new journeymen and take other steps to meet the critical manpower shortage, as well as to instruct members by letter that they must work overtime.[186]

Furthermore, the enforcement by a federal court of an injunctive order of an arbitrator cannot be blocked on the ground that the court cannot under the Norris-LaGuardia Act issue or enforce injunctive orders against labor unions. For example, when an employer "set back gangs of longshoremen" after an arbitrator ruled he had the contractual right to do so and a work stoppage resulted, the subsequent order of the court enforcing the award was held not to be in the nature of an injunction violating Norris-LaGuardia, but an order that the union affirmatively comply with the award.[187]

Where the request for specific relief is not the enforcement of the agreement, but a request for an addition to or modification of it, the remedy has been ruled beyond the authority of the arbitrator to grant. For example, requests for an extra week of vacation,[188] modification of an existing wage rate schedule,[189] change in existing fringe benefits,[190] modification of the grievance procedure,[191] and to keep certain incentive payment records,[192] have been denied as beyond the arbitrator's remedial authority.

---

[181] See, e.g., Jack Meilman, 34 L.A. 771 (Gray, 1960); cf. Selb Mfg. Co. v. IAM, District 9, 305 F.2d 177 (8th Cir. 1962).

[182] See, e.g., W. Va. Pulp & Paper Co., 48 L.A. 657 (Rubin, 1966); Ohio Edison Co., 46 L.A. 801 (Alexander, 1966); Sohio Chemical Co., 44 L.A. 624 (Witney, 1965).

[183] American Brake Shoe Co. v. Local 149 UAW, 285 F.2d 869 (4th Cir. 1961). In Hotel Employers Ass'n, 47 L.A. 873 (1966), Arbitrator Robert Baines ordered an employer to cease giving effect to a contract the employer had negotiated with a civil rights group following numerous demonstrations, sit-ins, and threatened violence on the ground that a union had the exclusive representational rights.

[184] See, e.g., American Bakeries, Inc., 46 L.A. 769 (Hon, 1966).

[185] Park-Pitt Building Co., 47 L.A. 235 (Duff, 1966). But see Magnavox Co., 35 L.A. 237 (Dworkin, 1960).

[186] Sheet Metal Contractors v. Local 28, 301 F.Supp. 553 (S.D.N.Y. 1969).

[187] Philadelphia Marine Trade Ass'n, supra note 174.

[188] Board of Education, City of New York, 44 L.A. 929 (Scheiber, 1965).

[189] See, e.g., United States Steel Corp., 44 L.A. 774 (McDermott, 1965); Pittsburgh-Des Moines Steel Co., 40 L.A. 577 (Koven, 1963); Sparta Ceramics Co., 62-1 ARB ¶ 8034 (Nichols, 1961); Waukesha Bearings Corp., 33 L.A. 831 (Slavney, 1959). But see St. Regis Paper Co., 66-3 ARB ¶ 8839 (Peck, 1966).

[190] See, e.g., Marathon City Brewing Co., 45 L.A. 453 (McCormick, 1965).

[191] Northwest Natural Gas Co., 46 L.A. 606 (Merrick, 1966).

[192] McLouth Steel Corp., 47 L.A. 1150 (Ryder, 1966).

M. REMEDY FOR THE NONGRIEVANT

Difficult questions of remedial relief are posed where a contract is breached, but the employee actually hurt by the breach does not grieve. Not surprisingly, the results have been diverse in such cases. For example, where the steward and only four of the five employees involved in the identical distribution-of-overtime grievance signed the grievance, and where there was no evidence to support the employer's contention that the fifth employe withheld his signature because he acknowledged the propriety of the company's action, the arbitrator ruled that the award would apply to the fifth employee as well as to the other four.[193] In another decision where management admitted that it erred in assigning an office employee to do bargaining unit painting for one week of the two-week plant vacation shutdown, the grievant, who had signed up for vacation shutdown work but had not been assigned, was entitled to one week's pay, notwithstanding that other bargaining unit employees who had not grieved, may have had a superior right to the work.[194]

In *Shahmoon Industries v. Steelworkers*,[195] an arbitrator had ruled that the employer had violated its collective bargaining agreement by using the results of physical examinations of recalled employees to unilaterally restrict them to certain jobs and granted back pay to all affected employees, although only one had actually grieved. The employer moved to set aside or modify the award, partly on the basis that the arbitrator had no power to award back pay to employees other than the individual who signed the original grievance. The court, however, found that the grievance had raised a challenge to the employer's practice or policy relating to such other employees as well as the grievant, and confirmed the award of back pay to the whole group.

It should be emphasized, however, that the general rule is that an arbitrator has no jurisdiction to issue an award granting relief to a nongrievant.[196]

N. REMEDIES SHOULD BE COMPLETE

Awards have been vacated if the remedial order is not self-executing and hence incomplete. In vacating such an order, a court said:

---

[193] *National Vulcanized Fibre Co.*, AAA Case No. 83-6 (Brecht, 1965).

[194] *Jamestown Malleable Iron Div.*, AAA Case No. 140-3 (Kates, 1970).

[195] 263 F.Supp. 10 (D.N.J. 1966).

[196] See Chapter III Section J. where attempts of persons not party to the grievance to obtain relief through arbitration is discussed.

"By its terms the decision reserves to the parties the practical application of the general rules which it states. Thus, the decision constitutes an interpretation of the Contract, which becomes a part of the Contract, and if the parties cannot agree upon the application of that interpretation there would seem to be a basis for a new grievance and fresh invocation of the grievance machinery." [197]

Similarly, where claims of violations during a definite period were presented to an arbitrator who rendered a "partial award without prejudice to the union proceeding . . . as to violations . . . during this period other than those herein presented" the award was vacated for lack of finality.[198] However, in another case where the arbitrator's award said that further proceedings before the arbitrators might be necessary before the dispute could be finally resolved, the award was not vacated.[199] Similarly, the court in *Bakery Workers Local 719 v. National Biscuit Co.*[200] enforced the arbitration award despite the arbitrator's recognition of the possibility that later experience might prove a portion of the award erroneous. There the employer initiated certain quantitative standards for production and the standards were contested by the union at arbitration. Some were upheld in part by the arbitrator and he did not render a decision as to others because the evidence was insufficient. The arbitrator noted that because some evidence was unclear, if experience under the standard demonstrated that the decision was in error, this would be grounds for a subsequent grievance. The court held the award to be within the arbitrator's remedial powers.

---

[197] *District 50, Mine Workers v. Revere Copper & Brass, Inc.,* 204 F.Supp. 349, 352 (D.Md. 1962).

[198] *Rosenblum v. Burton Mfg. Co.,* 15 Misc.2d 445, 182 N.Y.S.2d 641 (1958).

[199] *Quill v. Fifth Ave. Coach Lines, Inc.,* N.Y. L.J. June 10, 1963, p. 16, col. 6.

[200] 378 F.2d 918 (3d Cir. 1967).

CHAPTER XV

Post-Hearing Procedures

A. RECEIPT OF EVIDENCE AFTER THE HEARING

Under Rule 32 of the Voluntary Labor Arbitration Rules of the American Arbitration Association and pursuant to general arbitral practice, a hearing may be reopened[1] "by the Arbitrator on his own motion, or upon application of a party for good cause shown, at any time before the award is made."[2] The most common reason for reopening the hearing is a request of a party to introduce new evidence.

A federal district court[3] has ruled that an arbitrator has the power to reopen a case so that evidence can be added to the record where the record was closed inadvertently by the arbitrator before the new evidence was received and the adverse party would in no way be disadvantaged by the acceptance of the new evidence. In that case, the arbitrator mistakenly closed the hearing before acting on the union's request for a subponea *duces tecum*. Recognizing his mistake, the arbitrator reopened the hearing and granted the union's request for the subpoena. In upholding the award, the court noted:

"As soon as the arbitrator's error was discovered, the petitioner's motion to reopen was made and the adversary party notified. . . . [T]he Company's posture was not prejudiced and no hardship was imposed. Under such circumstances, the arbitrator acting pursuant to his own discretion had the right, as well as the obligation, to reopen the hearing

---

[1] Rule 31 provides that the hearing is not closed until the submission of briefs, if briefs are to be filed; however, the cases show that the "hearing" is considered closed for the purpose of introducing evidence when the formal process of eliciting oral testimony has ended. In *Gateway Products Corp.*, 61-3 ARB ¶ 8639 (Marshall, 1961), the arbitrator granted a motion for rehearing that was requested "[a]fter the hearing had been concluded and before the time of filing post-hearing briefs had expired."

[2] VOLUNTARY LABOR ARBITRATION RULES OF THE AMERICAN ARBITRATION ASSOCIATION, Rule 32 (New York, 1970).

[3] *Local Lodge 1746 v. United Aircraft Corp.*, 329 F.Supp. 283, 77 LRRM 2596 (D.C.Conn. 1971). See *Full-Fashioned Hosiery Mfrs.*, 15 L.A. 452 (Taylor, 1950), where the arbitrator reopened the hearing on his own motion because he concluded that he needed additional evidence before he could render a proper award.

sua sponte to receive any evidence, which he deemed necessary and relevant to a fair, just, and knowledgeable disposition of the issues.

" . . .

"The arbitrator's reopening of the hearing and his subsequent issuance of the subpoena corrected his prior oversight and procedural mistake, in prematurely closing the evidentiary hearing. An arbitration hearing closed under a mutual mistake of fact of the arbitrator and the parties, is not closed at all and the arbitrator's subsequent actions to correct the error were well within his jurisdiction. The employer's objection to the production of its investigation file because the arbitrator was without jurisdiction when he issued the subpoena is without merit." [4]

Arbitrators have varied greatly in their willingness to admit evidence into the record after the hearing has been concluded.[5] They do agree, however, that no new evidence should be admitted subsequent to the hearing without affording the other party an opportunity to agree to the reopening or to explain its objections.[6]

Unless there is an agreement admitting evidence into the record subsequent to the close of the hearing, or the hearing has been formally reopened by the arbitrator, new evidence should not be received. Arbitrator Harry Dworkin in *Ohio Steel Foundry Co.*[7] explained why he was required to ignore evidence submitted by a union in its post-hearing brief:

"It is a fundamental principle which governs arbitration proceedings that evidence may only be presented in the presence of both parties. It is essential that the arbitrator hear testimony from the witnesses themselves, wherever possible. The opposing side is entitled to the opportunity of cross-examining the witnesses and to submit responsive evidence. Arbitrators consistently adhere to the principle that no new evidence may be offered or considered after the close of the hearing. It is therefore improper to inject evidentiary matter in a post-hearing brief. Where such 'evidence' appears in the brief, inadvertently or otherwise, the arbitrator is required to disregard such, and this must necessarily be the course which the arbitrator will follow in the instant case." [8]

Similarly, Arbitrator John Sembower refused to accept a new medical statement after the hearing had been closed, and stated:

---

[4] 77 LRRM at 2598.

[5] New evidence often is submitted by separate letter or, occasionally, is included in the post-hearing brief. New evidence is not permitted in post-hearing briefs under international arbitral procedures. Carlston, *Codification of International Arbitral Procedure,* 47 AM. J. INT'L. LAW, 203, 245 (1953).

[6] Pittsburgh Tripartite Committee, *Problems of Proof in the Arbitration Process,* PROBLEMS OF PROOF IN ARBITRATION, Proceedings of the Nineteenth Annual Meeting, National Academy of Arbitrators, 261 (D.Jones Ed. 1967).

[7] 61-2 ARB ¶ 8429 (Dworkin, 1961).

[8] *Id.* at 5038. See also *Bendix-Westinghouse Automotive Air Brake Co.,* 36 L.A. 724 (Schmidt, 1961).

"The arbitrator really has no choice in this matter, for it is entirely clear that once a record is closed, new matter may not be introduced by either side in the absence of agreement to that effect." [9]

A modified version of the Sembower position was adopted by Arbitrator Harold Davey in *Geo. A. Hormel Co.*[10] There newly discovered evidence was admitted where the existing record was defective or incomplete. In emphasizing the need for "compelling" reason to reopen the record and the hearing, Davey stated:

"It is . . . well established that if one of the parties does introduce new material in his post-hearing brief, a formal objection by the other party to its consideration should be honored by the arbitrator unless he finds compelling circumstances causing him to conclude that the hearing should be re-opened, *e.g.*, a finding that the hearing record was incomplete or defective in some fashion." [11]

Arbitrator Marshall, relying on the rules of the American Arbitration Association, concluded that pertinent evidence should be accepted after the hearing, whether or not it was available at the time of the hearing. Moreover, he found that the stricter rules relating to newly discovered evidence applied in court cases are not per se binding the arbitrator. He explained:

"While it is true that in an ordinary case of law it is exceedingly dubious as to whether the Company would be granted a motion to reopen the trial of a law suit on the basis of newly discovered evidence within the framework of the fact situation herein involved, the arbitrator nonetheless rules that the affidavit together with the accompanying documentary evidence are admissible and allows them as part of the record of these proceedings. There is little need to belabor the differences which surround an arbitration proceeding as against an ordinary court action. The arbitrator is not bound by technical rules of evidence and the sole object of an arbitration proceeding is to secure a fair and equitable resolution of differences which arise in the administration of the collective bargaining agreement. While rules of evidence are suggestive of what constitutes a fair hearing and a fair appraisal of the evidence, to follow them slavishly could only result in a distortion of the collective bargaining relationship not only because of the essential difference between a labor contract and an ordinary commercial contract but also because of the completely different climate in which the contract is given effect and the further fact that quite commonly cases are

---

[9] *North Shore Gas Co.,* 40 L.A. 37, 43 (Sembower, 1963); *Printing Industry of Washington, D. C.,* 40 L.A. 727 (McCoy, 1963). See *Continental Can Co.,* 29 L.A. 67, 73 (Sembower, 1956) where the arbitrator stated:
"Matters of fact should properly be confined to the hearing stage, with post-hearing briefs reserved for argument, interpretation, and evaluation."
See also *Code of Ethics and Procedural Standards for Labor-Management Arbitration,* Part III, § 6, 15 L.A. 961-66 (1950), republished 1962.
[10] 63-2 ARB ¶ 8462 (Davey, 1963). See also *Borden Co.,* 33 L.A. 302 (Morvant, 1959); *Madison Institute,* 18 L.A. 78 (Levy, 1952).
[11] 63-2 ARB ¶ 8462 at 4524 (Davey, 1963).

not only presented by non-lawyers but in many instances heard by non-lawyers as well." [12]

In support for this view, the arbitrator cited two rules of the American Arbitration Association: Rule 32—Reopening of the Hearing[13] and Rule 29—Evidence by Affidavit and Filing of Documents.[14] Arbitrator Marshall, reading these rules together, noted that they envision:

> "[T]he possibility of not only the submission of affidavits and controverting affidavits during the hearing, but after the hearing as well where good cause is shown." [15]

Although Marshall made no attempt to explain what is "good cause," it is apparent that he gave the term a liberal interpretation. The evidence he received was a timecard that was available at the time of the hearing but had not been introduced because it was not known in advance that a certain witness was to testify. The timecard proved that a witness was not even at work at the time he said he received a telephone call.

Arbitrator Byron Abernethy adopts a middle view which allows for the admission of newly discovered evidence if it can be shown that the evidence could significantly affect the outcome of the case and that it was not available at the time of the hearing. He explained his test in *United States Potash Co.*: [16]

---

[12] *Gateway Products Corp.,* 61-3 ARB ¶ 8639 at 5927 (Marshall, 1961).

[13] American Arbitration Association, Voluntary Labor Arbitration Rules, Rule 32, p. 6 (1965).
"*Reopening of Hearings*—The hearings may be reopened by the Arbitrator on his own motion, or on the motion of either party, for good cause shown, at any time before the award is made, but if the reopening of the hearing would prevent the making of the award within the specific time agreed upon by the parties in the contract out of which the controversy has arisen, the matter may not be reopened, unless both parties agree upon the extension of such time limit. When no specific date is fixed in the contract, the Arbitrator may reopen the hearings, and the Arbitrator shall have 30 days from the closing of the reopened hearings within which to make an award."

[14] American Arbitration Association, Voluntary Labor Arbitration Rules, Rule 29, p. 5 (1965).
"*Evidence by Affidavit and Filing of Documents*—The Arbitrator may receive and consider the evidence of witnesses by affidavit, but shall give it only such weight as he deems proper after consideration of any objections made to its admission.
"All documents not filed with the Arbitrator at the hearing but which are arranged at the hearing or subsequently by agreement of the parties to be submitted, shall be filed with the AAA for transmission to the Arbitrator. All parties shall be afforded opportunity to examine documents."

[15] *Gateway Products Corp.,* 61-3 ARB ¶ 8639 at 5926.

[16] 30 L.A. 1039 at 1042-43 (Abernethy, 1958). The admission of new evidence after the close of an arbitration hearing has been approved in *Lodge 71, IAM v. Bendix Corp.,* 218 F.Supp. 742 (W.D.Mo. 1963). See also *In re Zuckerman,* note 2 *supra,* allowing for reopening of the hearing where the employer failed to appear at the first hearing.

"But once a hearing has been closed, after both parties have been afforded a full opportunity to present all their evidence and argument, and where one of the parties opposes the reopening of the case, as the Company does here, the interest in an expeditious settlement of disputed matters such as are involved in this case, dictates that an Arbitrator should grant a petition to reopen only upon a very substantial showing of the pertinence of the additional information to be adduced, a showing that the party filing the petition could not with reasonable diligence have produced the evidence at the time of the hearing, or that the party has been prevented, without fault on his part, by fraud, accident, etc., from making out his case. Such substantial showing of relevancy or pertinence has not been made. There is no claim that through any accident, mistake or fraud, the petitioner was prevented from making his case at the hearing. It is true that the Union could not have produced this evidence with reasonable diligence. But the reason it could not have done so was that the evidence simply did not exist, not only at the time of the incident under consideration, but not even at the time of the hearing several months later. The very reason why the evidence could not be produced at the hearing thus goes far toward establishing its irrelevancy."

In *Madison Institute,*[17] Arbitrator Edward A. Levy granted a request made "after the hearing was concluded' to reopen the hearing and introduce new pertinent evidence. He stated:

"Ordinarily where a hearing has been had in which all parties have participated, and have presented all evidence, and have stated on the record that they have nothing further to offer, the matter is deemed to be officially closed for the taking of evidence. However, where certain evidence is evidentiary and of material import and the admission thereof will probably affect the outcome of a cause, is unavailable at the time of the hearing, and if the same is produced subsequently without seriously affecting any substantial right, and it is shown that reasonable grounds existed for its non-production at the time of the hearing, the arbitrator may, in his discretion, reopen the arbitration for the introduction of such evidence only. The reason for this rule is to afford to each of the parties full opportunity to present such material evidence as will assist the arbitrator in ascertaining the truth of all matters in controversy." [18]

Similarly, in *Borden Co.,*[19] the union continued to investigate the facts after the hearing had been closed, and in its post-hearing brief discussed certain new findings and asked that the hearing be reopened. Arbitrator R. H. Morvant stated that the arbitration process was less formal than court procedure and that new evidence could be submitted if pertinent:

"Generally new evidence submitted by one of the parties after the hearing has been closed should be ignored, or stricken from the record,

---

[17] 18 L.A. 78 (Levy, 1952).
[18] *Id.* at 81.
[19] 33 L.A. 302 (Morvant, 1959).

because the other party is unable to refute it, or have his day in court. Still, even in courts of law, new trials are ordered when it is discovered that new evidence has been uncovered which has a bearing on the case and which might result in a different result or decision. This same privilege should exist for arbitration cases as well. Perhaps even more leniency should be shown in arbitration cases than in courts of law, because the parties are not always versed in the law nor are they always astute in case preparation. To close the door of justice on such individuals would not serve the purpose for which the arbitration procedure was established and intended. Consequently, allowances should be made which would protect the less astute and permit him to present his case to the best of his ability and leave him with the feeling that he has had his full day in court." [20]

In so ruling, however, he stated that the additional evidence was not pertinent and would not "necessitate further hearings or briefs."[21]

The rulings of most arbitrators are similar to the Regulations of the National Labor Relations Board which provide, in part, that:

"A party to a proceeding before the Board may, because of extraordinary circumstances, move for reconsideration, rehearing, or reopening of the record after the Board decision or order. A motion for reconsideration shall state with particularity the material error claimed and with respect to any finding of material fact shall specify the page of the record relied on. A motion for rehearing shall specify the error alleged to require a hearing *de novo* and the prejudice to the movant alleged to result from such error. A motion to reopen the record shall state briefly the additional evidence sought to be adduced, why it was not presented previously, and that, if adduced and credited, it would require a different result. Only newly discovered evidence, evidence which has become available only since the close of the hearing, or evidence which the Board believes should have been taken at the hearing will be taken at any further hearing." [22]

The refusal of the arbitrator to reopen a hearing and receive "newly discovered" evidence, however, will not support a court order directing the arbitrator to do so. One court has said that such an order would undercut the finality and therefore the usefulness of arbitration as an expeditious and generally fair method of settling disputes.[23] Moreover, the court added, "Arbitrators are not and never were intended to be amendable to the 'remand' of a case for 'retrial' in the same way as a trial judge." [24]

---

[20] *Id.* at 307.

[21] *Id.*

[22] National Labor Relations Board, RULES AND REGULATIONS AND STATEMENTS OF PROCEDURE SERIES 8, AS AMENDED (1969), Section 102.48(d)(1) (1969).

[23] *Newspaper Guild Local 35 v. Washington Post Co.,* 442 F.Supp. 1234, 76 LRRM 2274 (D.C.Cir. 1971).

[24] *Id.* at 2277.

B. POST-HEARING BRIEFS

It is well established in arbitration that either or both parties may file a post-hearing brief.[25] In a case where a union made a specific objection to the filing of a post-hearing brief, an arbitrator said that "either party had a right to file a post-hearing brief and that the other party could file a brief also, or waive [its] right to file. . . ." In so ruling, the arbitrator distinguished between "evidence," which, under the contract, must be presented at the hearing, and "arguments," as to the meaning of evidence, which may be presented in a post-hearing brief.[26] However, it is an accepted principle in labor arbitration that post-hearing briefs should be limited to argument and should refer only to testimony and evidence adduced at the hearing itself.[27] The general practice is for the arbitrator to exchange the parties' briefs when he has received both, rather than for the parties to serve one another. Since, unlike court litigation where briefs are generally filed sequentially, arbitration briefs are generally filed simultaneously, such an exchange by the arbitrator prevents one party from having the advantage of seeing the opposing brief if it is filed early.

Most arbitrators, such as Benjamin Aaron, believe that post-hearing briefs are necessary and that opposition to them on cost or delay grounds is "unwise." He explained his position as follows:

"Oral summation at the conclusion of the hearing is not—save in the simple cases—an adequate substitute; the parties have not had sufficient time for reflection and for organization of their arguments and the arbitrator may be too tired to derive much benefit from what is being said. One must sympathize with complaints against over-written briefs and against tedious and time-consuming procedures of rebuttals and surrebuttals, but a single, concise, written summary of position, submitted shortly after the conclusion of the hearing, is worth its weight in gold. As a matter of fact, disputes over the interpretation of specific provisions of collective agreements which do not raise issues of fact can often be resolved speedily and economically on the basis of briefs alone."[28]

A contrary view has been expressed by Arbitrator Maurice Merrill, who believes that many post-hearing briefs are merely summaries of the evidence, but he does acknowledge that such a brief can be helpful if the arbitration involves a difficult question of contractual inter-

---

25 Horton, *The Arbitration of Discharge Cases*, 9 Sw. L.J. 332, 337 (1955).

26 *Borg-Warner Corp.*, AAA Case 62-5 (McGury, 1964).

27 *Geo. A. Hormel Co.*, 63-2 ARB ¶ 8462 (Davey, 1963).

28 Aaron, *Labor Arbitration and Its Critics*, 10 Lab. L.J. 605, 608 (1959).

pretation or an issue around which a body of arbitral doctrine has been building up if it is reported and analyzed in the brief.[29]

Arbitrators must occasionally decide what consideration, if any, should be given to new arguments, as opposed to new evidence presented for the first time in a brief of one of the parties. Arbitrator Robben Fleming reports the diversity of opinion among arbitrators on this matter:

> "Some arbitrators take the view that there is nothing wrong with a new argument advanced in the brief, and that as long as the other side receives a copy the arbitrator is not even under any obligation to ask the second party to comment. Other arbitrators feel that any time a substantial new argument is advanced in the brief, comment from the other party should be requested even if it has previously received a copy of the brief and made no comment. Some arbitrators qualify either view by saying that it 'depends on the kind of case and the kind of argument which is made.' "[30]

Arbitrator John Sembower has said that the failure of the company to mention at the hearing an argument later discussed in its post-hearing brief is significant because the union will not be afforded an opportunity to meet the argument.[31] In order to avoid the problem of new arguments, one arbitrator "asks the parties at the end of the hearing to state the grounds on which they will rely in their briefs so that there can be no surprise." Another arbitrator "suggests to the parties that they indicate before the conclusion of the hearing what reported cases they will rely upon in their briefs so that the other side may respond.[32]

These positions seem quite rigid. The rules excluding evidence and particularly arguments should not be so enforced that the flow of facts and arguments into the record is impeded. There is no reason why all arguments must be placed before the arbitrator before the hearing closes. Furthermore, parties to an arbitration proceeding often waive closing arguments stating that arguments will be presented in a brief. No surprise can, consequently, result from a procedure agreed upon in advance.

---

[29] Merrill, *A Labor Arbitrator Views His Work*, 10 VAND. L. REV. 789, 796-97 (1957).

[30] Fleming, *Problems of Procedural Regularity in Labor Arbitration*, 1961 WASH. U.L.Q. 221, 242 (1961).

[31] *Pittsburgh Railways Co.*, 33 L.A. 862, 867 (Sembower, 1959).

[32] Fleming, note 30 *supra*, at 242 (the arbitrators were not named by the author).

CHAPTER XVI

The Award

Arbitration awards follow a general pattern that has developed over the years, influenced to some extent by the requirements of state statutes and by what courts have said when awards have been reviewed. Normally, arbitration awards are written and signed. At common law, the parties could agree that the award would be written or oral, but most state statutes now require that awards be written.[1]

Whatever its form, an award must be clear. The Supreme Court considered the need for clarity in *International Longshoremen's Ass'n v. Philadelphia Marine Trade Association*.[2] There, it reversed a lower court order that a union comply with an award because the award did not contain an "operative command capable of enforcement" and was "too vague to be sustained as a valid exercise of judicial authority." The award had stated that the agreement allowed the employer to "set back" (dismiss) gangs with a one-hour payment. Whether the union's contention that such privilege existed only when a vessel did not arrive at the expected time was not clearly answered. Because of the award's lack of clarity, the Supreme Court held it should be vacated on the ground it was not consistent with the requirement that injunctive orders be specific.[3]

---

[1] See, *e.g.*, *Kenney v. McLean Trucking Co.*, 32 L.A. 323 (N.J. Sup. Ct. 1959), N.J. STAT. 2A:24-7; TEX. REV. CIV. STAT. ANN., art. 231 (1959) (in writing, but no signature). See also Dougherty & Graff, *Should Texas Revise Its Arbitration Statutes?*, 41 TEXAS L. REV. 229, 245 (1962); Feldman, *Arbitration Modernized— The New California Arbitration Act*, 34 S. CAL. L. REV. 413, 429 (1961); Weinstein, *Notes on Proposed Revision of the New York Arbitration Law*, 16 ARB. J. 61, 75-76 (1961); Note, *Commercial Arbitration in Indiana and the Proposed Uniform Act*, 31 IND. L.J. 401, 405-6 (1956); Emery, *Commercial Arbitration Under the Utah Arbitration Act*, 4 UTAH L. REV. 174, 188 (1954); Kellor, *Standards of Practice for Arbitration*, 4 ARB. J. 46, 50 (1949); American Arbitration Association, *Voluntary Labor Arbitration Rules*, No. 38 at 6-7 (1965) ("The award shall be in writing and shall be signed either by the neutral Arbitrator or by a concurring majority if there be more than one Arbitrator. . . .").

[2] 389 U.S. 64 (1967).

[3] Arbitrators generally agree that their awards should be clear enough to resolve the dispute and avoid further litigation. See *Sears, Roebuck & Co., Inc.*, 39 L.A. 567 (Gillingham, 1962); *Universal-Rundle Corporation*, 61-1 ARB ¶ 8092 (Horlacher, 1961). Another reason for a clearly reasoned decision is the unwillingness of the National Labor Relations Board to defer to an arbitration award unless the arbitrator made it clear he considered the issue that would otherwise have been decided by the Board.

Frequently arbitration cases are decided by a board of arbitrators consisting of one management representative, one union representative, and one impartial member who acts as the chairman and is usually a professional arbitrator. At common law, unless the submission agreement expressly or impliedly authorized the board to decide by majority vote, all members of the arbitration tribunal were required to concur before a valid award could be rendered.[4] Today, most statutes, arbitration submissions, and labor agreements provide that an award agreed upon by a majority of the board is acceptable.[5] While there are no reported decisions, it is probable that, absent agreement or statute to the contrary, an award concurred in by a majority of the board would be enforceable under Section 301 of the Labor Management Relations Act.

Usually the impartial chairman prepares a "suggested" award and opinion. It is then concurred in by the satisfied party and dissented to by the dissatisfied party, who may prepare a dissenting opinion. However, if the two board members dissent, the award would not be effective unless the parties decide to treat it as the decision of a single arbitrator. No case has been found that discusses what occurs when the two partial members of a three-member arbitration board file dissents to the award prepared by the impartial chairman. However, an award by a board signed only by one member, was held not to be so irregular that it should be vacated.[6]

A. SUPPORTING OPINIONS BY THE ARBITRATOR

Although most awards are written, statutory requirements for reasoned elaborations are not common. The American Arbitration Association and National Academy of Arbitrators Code of Ethics provides that: "If either party requests the arbitrator to prepare an opinion, such request should be followed."[7] When commercial arbitration awards have been challenged because the arbitrator did not state the reasons for his award, courts have stated that the lack of

---

[4] See 6 S. Williston, A Treatise on the Law of Contracts, § 1929 (rev. ed. 1938); *Creter v. Davis*, 30 N.J. Super. 60, 103 A.2d 392 (Ch. Div.), *aff'd*, 107 A.2d 17 (App. Div. 1954). Unanimity is required in Soviet arbitration procedure. Zawodney, *Grievance Procedures in Soviet Factories*, 10 Ind. & Lab. Rel. Rev. 532, 545 (1957).

[5] See, *e.g.*, Pa. Stat. Ann. tit. 43, § 726 (1964).

[6] *Carpenters & Joiners, Local 642 v. De Mello*, 67 L.C. ¶ 12,447 (Cal. Ct. App. 1972).

[7] American Arbitration Association and National Academy of Arbitrators, Code of Ethics and Procedural Standards for Labor-Management Arbitration 7 (1963).

reasons are not grounds for vacating the award.[8] In the same tradition, the Supreme Court said in *United Steelworkers of America v. Enterprise Wheel & Car Corp.*:[9]

"Arbitrators have no obligation to the court to give their reasons for an award. To require opinions free of ambiguity may lead arbitrators to play it safe by writing no supporting opinions. This would be undesirable for a well-reasoned opinion tends to engender confidence in the integrity of the process and aids in clarifying the underlying agreement." [10]

Where the arbitrator is selected under American Arbitration Association Rules, there is no need for him to make findings of fact in his award even where the state law requires them, since Section 41 of the Association's Rules does not require them.[11]

The efforts of some unions and the American Arbitration Association to foster a high-speed arbitration process by dispensing with a written opinion become somewhat questionable even in discharge cases which usually turn on factual determinations, because the question of discrimination in violation of Section 8(a)(3) of the Act could well lurk in the background. Unless the arbitrator in his written opinion makes the basis for his findings clear, the National Labor Relations Board will not defer to his award.

In the vast majority of labor arbitration cases the award is accompanied by reasoned decision. Most management and union representatives contend that opinions are desirable, except in those isolated instances where it is important that the delay required for the writing of an opinion should be eliminated.

Arbitrator Harry Shulman had this to say about the value of a written opinion:

"It has been urged by some that an arbitrator's award should be made without opinion or explanation in order to avoid the dangers of accumulating precedents and subjecting arbitration to the rigidities of *stare decisis* in the law. Perhaps this view has merit when the particular arbitration is regarded as solely a means of resolving the particular stale-

---

[8] *John Gibbs Agency, Inc. v. Beatty*, 31 Misc.2d 876 (N.Y. Sup. Ct. 1961) ("There is no requirement that the award state the reasoning upon which it was based."). *Application of Harris*, 337 P.2d 832 (Cal. Ct. App. 1959); *Pacific Vegetable Oil Corp. v. C.S.T., Ltd.*, 29 Cal.2d 228, 232 (1946); *Interinsurance Exchange of the Automobile Club of Southern California v. Bailes*, 33 CAL. RPTR. 533 (Cal. Ct. App. 1963); *Willow Fabrics v. Carolina Freight Carriers Corp.*, 20 App. Div.2d 864, 248 N.Y.S.2d 509 (1964); *Colletti v. Mesh*, 23 App. Div.2d 245, 260 N.Y.S.2d 130 (1965); *Linwood v. Sherry*, 178 N.Y.S.2d 492 (Sup. Ct.), *aff'd*, 181 N.Y.S.2d 772 (N.Y. App. Div. 1958).

[9] 363 U.S. 593, 598 (1960).

[10] See *Haddon Craftsmen, Inc. v. Bookbinders*, 281 A.2d 713, 78 LRRM 2525 (Pa. Super. Ct. 1971) (award in which arbitrator had given no reasons could not be overturned in absence of fraud, corruption, or duress since arbitrators have no obligation to give reasons for their awards).

[11] *Hale v. Friedman*, 281 F.2d 635 (D.C. Cir. 1960); *General Construction Co. v. Hering Realty Co.*, 201 F. Supp. 487 (E.D.S.C. 1962).

mate and nothing else. It is an erroneous view for the arbitration which is an integral part of the system of self-government and rule of law that the parties establish for their continuing relationship.

". . . In this system opinions are necessary, first, to assure the parties that the awards are based on reason applied to the agreement. . . ." [12]

B. TIME LIMITS ON SUBMISSION OF AWARD

Many state statutes specify a specific time period after the close of the hearing during which the award must be completed. For example, in Pennsylvania[13] and Connecticut,[14] the statutes require that a written decision shall be rendered within 60 days, and in Washington[15] within 30 days, after the close of the hearing. Similarly, the rules of the American Arbitration Association establish a time limit of 30 days following the close of the hearing, unless the parties agree to the contrary.[16] About one-half of the state statutes give specific power to the parties by agreement to limit the time within which the award must be rendered.[17]

A reading of the labor agreement language, the language of the American Arbitration Association Rules, and the language of the statutes would indicate that the failure to adhere to such time limits could well be grounds for setting aside an award or refusing to follow it. For example, by statute in New York, a late award is unenforceable[18] unless the agreed upon time is waived or extended.[19]

---

[12] Shulman, *Reason, Contract, and Law in Labor Relations,* 68 HARV. L. REV. 999, 1020 (1955).

[13] PA. STAT. ANN. tit. 43, § 213.12 (1964); see Ehrlich, *Labor Arbitration in Pennsylvania,* 24 TEMP. L.Q. 107, 118 (1950); *Damon v. Berger,* 155 A.2d 388 (Pa. Sup. Ct. 1959).

[14] CONN. GEN. STAT. REV. § 52-416 (1968).

[15] WASH. REV. CODE ANN. § 7.04.090 (1961).

[16] American Arbitration Association, *Voluntary Labor Arbitration Rules* No. 37 at 6 (1965). In the CODE OF ETHICS AND PROCEDURAL STANDARDS FOR LABOR-MANAGEMENT ARBITRATION, the American Arbitration Association and the National Academy of Arbitrators state that "the arbitrator should render his award promptly and must render his award within the time prescribed, if any." See generally Ross, *The Well-Aged Arbitration Case,* 11 IND. & LAB. REL. REV. 262, 270-1 (1958); McCassey, *Code of Ethics for Arbitrators,* 1 ARB. J. (n.s.) 206, 213 (1946).

[17] Comment, *State Arbitration Statutes Applicable to Labor Disputes,* 19 MO. L. REV. 280, 292 (1954). See Kagel, *Labor and Commercial Arbitration Under the California Arbitration Statute,* 38 CAL. L. REV. 799, 823 (1950).

[18] N.Y. CIV. PRAC. art. 75 § 7507 (McKinney, 1963). *In re Manhattan News Co.,* 146 N.Y.L.J. 6, 43 L.C. ¶ 50,307 (Sup. Ct. N.Y. Co. 1961).

[19] *Newspaper & Mail Deliverers' Union of N.Y. v. Publishers' Assn' of N.Y. City,* 155 N.Y.L.J. 16, 54 L.C. ¶ 51,539 (Sup. Ct. N.Y. Co. 1966); *Broadway-Fortieth Street Corp. v. President and Directors of Manhattan Co.,* 296 N.Y. 165, 71 N.E.2d 451 (1947). See also *District Lodge No. 71, IAM v. Bendix Corp., Kansas City Div.,* 218 F.Supp. 742, 749 (W.D. Mo. 1963):
"A party to a grievance who is charged with knowledge that an arbitrator's power to decide may have expired should not be permitted to await the decision and then to void the decision if unfavorable."
Lodge No. 725, IAM v. Mooney Aircraft, Inc., 410 F.2d 681 (5th Cir. 1969) (although the collective bargaining agreement provided that arbitrator's decision was to be rendered 44 days after hearing, the company's failure to object to the delay prior to receipt of an adverse award constituted a waiver of objection).

In spite of the clarity of the language, late awards are enforceable if they arise out of a labor agreement. A federal court in *Local Union 560 Teamsters v. Anchor Motor Freight, Inc.*[20] enforced an arbitrator's award in spite of the fact that it was rendered nearly seven months after the 30-day time limit. The Third Circuit rejected the lower court's view that the arbitrator lost his authority under the statute to render a binding award after the time limit expired, noting that neither the company nor the union had been injured by the late award.

Hence, it is quite clear that the emerging federal law of labor arbitration would not countenance the vacation of an award because it was issued after a contractual or statutory time limit. As a practical matter, however, time limits are waived or extended by the parties when the arbitrator advises the parties he is pressed for time. The only value of contractual time limits would appear to be in cases where back pay or similar liability continues to run. The failure to adhere to such time limits would arguably toll back-pay liability.

C. AWARDS AS *STARE DECISIS*

Arbitration awards involving *different parties* but similar issues are not considered to have the precedential value judicial decisions have.[21] However, many rules and principles involving the applica-

---

[20] 415 F.2d 220 (3d Cir. 1969). *Accord, West Rock Lodge No. 2120, IAM v. Geometric Tool Co.,* 406 F.2d 284 (2d Cir. 1968).

[21] F. Elkouri and E. Elkouri, How ARBITRATION WORKS 243-61 (rev. ed. 1960). Manson, *Substantive Principles Emerging from Grievance Arbitration: Some Observations,* PROCEEDINGS OF INDUSTRIAL RELATIONS RESEARCH ASS'N 136-49 (1953); Davey, *Labor Arbitration: A Current Appraisal,* 9 IND. & LAB. REL. REV. 85, 88-89 (1955); Syme, *Opinions and Awards,* 15 LAB. ARB. 953, 959-61 (1950). See also *Timken Roller Bearing Co.,* 32 L.A. 595, 598 (Boehm, 1958); *Pan American Refining Co.,* 9 L.A. 731, 732 (McCoy, 1948). Of course, questions of *stare decisis* would be rather moot in the absence of published awards. The publication of awards is not required by statute, as is the case with appellate judicial decisions, but they are published in substantial number nonetheless. The substantial number of published awards occurs because the award is sent in for publication by one of the parties or by the arbitrator. When sent in by the latter, it is with consent of the parties. Paragraph 8(b) of the CODE OF ETHICS AND PROCEDURAL STANDARDS FOR LABOR-MANAGEMENT ARBITRATION published by the American Arbitration Association and the National Academy of Arbitrators provides:
"There should be no disclosure of the terms of an award by any arbitrator until after it is delivered simultaneously to all parties and *publication or public disclosure* should be only with the parties' consent." (Emphasis added.)
A similar policy has been set by the Federal Mediation and Conciliation Service in 29 CFR § 1404.11 (1968):
"It is the policy of the Service not to release arbitration decisions for publication without the consent of both parties. . . ."
See generally Cherne, *Should Arbitration Awards be Published?,* 1 ARB. J. (n.s.) 75 (1946); Taylor, *Reporting of Labor Arbitration: Pro and Con,* 1 ARB. J. (n.s.) 420, 422 (1946); Levenstein, *Some Obstacles to Reporting Labor Arbitration,* 1 ARB. J. (n.s.) 425 (1946). See also McPherson, *Should Labor Arbitrators Play Follow-the-Leader?,* 4 ARB. J. (n.s.) 163 (1949). Management and union representatives generally believe awards should be published. Warren & Bernstein, *A Profile of Labor Arbitration,* 4 IND. & LAB. REL. REV. 200, 217 (1951).

tion and interpretation of language commonly found in collective bargaining agreements have evolved from the myriad of the published awards. One observer has noted:

> "Increased reliance upon precedent will result in the reasoned development of the law. Already there is emerging a body of industrial case law which reflects the enlightened thinking of arbitrators. The labor relations community is recognizing that many problems are capable of a uniform, nationwide solution." [22]

One arbitrator put it very candidly:

> "As to arbitral decisions rendered under other contracts between parties not related to those in the case at hand, usefulness depends upon similarity of the terms and of the situations to which they are to be applied. They must be weighed and appraised, not only in respect to these characteristics, but also with regard to the soundness of the principles upon which they proceed. Certainly, an arbitrator may be aided in formulating his own conclusions by knowledge of how other men have solved similar problems. He ought not to arrogate as his own special virtues the wisdom and justice essential to sound decision. In at least two instances in recent months I have found by investigation that a strong current of arbitral decisions had overborne my first impression of the implications of particular language. To yield to this 'common sense of most,' especially as, on examination, the reasoning on which it was based carried plausibility, was neither to evade my responsibility nor to sacrifice my intellectual integrity. . . .
>
> ". . . This resort to precedent in aid of interpretation and application does not deserve the scornful appellation of 'playing follow-the-leader.' " [23]

In *S. H. Kress & Co.*,[24] Arbitrator Arthur Ross analyzed past awards extensively in a decision involving a company's right to retire employees at a certain age. He explained that "published awards are not binding on another arbitrator, but the thinking of experienced men is often helpful to him."[25] Arbitrator Carl Warns in *Cochran Foil Co.*,[26] a case involving an employer's right to unilaterally eliminate a job classification, reviewed awards by others and said:

> "Of course, other arbitration decisions are not binding on me, but it is

---

[22] Tobias, *In Defense of Creeping Legalism in Arbitration,* 4 IND. & LAB. REL. REV. 596, 602 (1960). See *Holland Suco Color Co.,* 43 L.A. 1022 (Geissinger, 1964); *Butler Mfg.,* 42 L.A. 304 (Johnston, 1964). *Cf. Union Carbide Corp.,* 46 L.A. 517 (Cahn, 1966) and *Allegheny Ludlum Steel Corp.,* 43 L.A. 1041 (Wallen, 1964).

[23] Merrill, *A Labor Arbitrator Views His Work,* 10 VAND. L. REV. 789, 797-98 (1957).

[24] 25 L.A. 77 (Ross, 1955).

[25] *Id.* at 79.

[26] 26 L.A. 155 (Warns, 1956).

obvious that in arbitration as in other fields, respect must be paid to accumulated wisdom and experience." [27]

A similar view was expressed by Arbitrator M. David Keefe in *Hydromation Engineering Company:*[28]

"The responsibility of the arbitrator, in each case, is to exercise independent and impartial judgment on the issues before him. He has an obligation to consider the reasoning and basis which led to conclusions reached in cited awards. But, nevertheless, his fundamental duty is to make a decision which squares up with his own convictions as to where equity lies in the case which he is to decide."

Arbitrator Harry H. Platt in *Braniff Airways, Inc.*[29] noted that the principle of *stare decisis* is coming into labor arbitration requiring that where a principle has become settled in a series of well-reasoned decisions it should be followed in a similar case.

Arbitrator Elkouri said:

"I am personally convinced that considerable use of precedents in arbitration is inevitable. I am personally convinced also that development of substantive principles through arbitration is likewise inevitable and, I might add, desirable. Most arbitrators, able though they be, do not possess enough of Solomon's wisdom to justify rule by man instead of rule by principle. Not all cases can best be decided in a vacuum. . . .

". . . [I]ssues being arbitrated . . . frequently have counterparts in reported awards. It is indeed comforting to any arbitrator to know that his decision finds support in other awards, or to know at least that his decision does not vary drastically from what others have decided.

". . . [No] arbitrator, and especially the experienced, can eliminate the influence of what he knows others have done. No arbitrator can serve long without becoming aware of the existence of certain more or less generally recognized principles. . . ." [30]

Arbitrator Sanford H. Kadish made the following statement:

---

[27] *Id.* at 157. *Accord, Marathon Electric Mfg. Co.,* 29 L.A. 518 (Thompson, 1957); *National Lead Co.,* 28 L.A. 470 (Roberts, 1957); *Western Gear Corp. of Texas,* 26 L.A. 84 (Boles, 1956); *Philadelphia Transportation Co.,* 25 L.A. 379, 381-83 (Scheiber, 1955); *Cooper-Bessemer Corp.,* 25 L.A. 146, 149 (Reid, 1955); *Bethlehem Steel Co.,* 20 L.A. 91 (Seward, 1953); *Safe Bus Co.,* 21 L.A. 456, 460 (Livengood, 1953); *Great Lakes Carbon Corp.,* 19 L.A. 797, 799 (Wettach, 1953); *Coca-Cola Bottling Works Co.,* 19 L.A. 432, 434 (Schmidt, 1952). See Justin, *Arbitration: Precedent Value of Reported Awards,* 21 LRRM 8 (1947).

[28] *Hydromation Engineering Company v. Sheet Metal Workers' Int'l Assoc., Local 566,* 67-1 ARB ¶ 8037 (Keefe, 1966).

[29] *Braniff Airways, Inc. v. International Air Line Pilots Association.* 70-1 ARB ¶ 8214 (Platt, 1969). See also *Muskogee Iron Works,* 29 L.A. 504, 507 (Singletary, 1957); *Sun Rubber Co.,* 28 L.A. 362, 369 (Dworkin, 1957); *Virginia-Carolina Chemical Corp.,* 23 L.A. 228, 233 (Marshall, 1954); *Jonco Aircraft Corp.,* 22 L.A. 706, 707 (Merrill, 1954); *St. Louis Terminal Warehouse Co.,* 19 L.A. 807, 808 (Treiman, 1952); *Coca-Cola Bottling Works Co.,* 19 L.A. 432, 434 (Schmidt, 1952).

[30] Elkouri, *Development of Substantive Principles Through Arbitration,* COLLECTIVE BARGAINING AND THE LAW 249-54 (1959).

"While I am moved by the foregoing reasons and not precedent, it is nonetheless reassuring to observe that the overwhelming majority, indeed if not the unanimity, of arbitrators who have faced this very issue . . . have reached this same conclusion. . . ." [31]

Arbitrator Elkouri also said:

"[I]t should be recognized that when we speak of development of principles for widespread application we are not too much concerned with the 'authoritative' or 'binding' force which awards often exert in subsequent cases involving the same parties and the same contract. Rather, we are much more concerned with the 'persuasive' or 'guiding' force that awards under *other* contracts often exert. Arbitration awards under other contracts *are* important as precedents, and I suggest that anybody who refuses to recognize this is simply playing ostrich: . . . We need only glance through recent volumes of reported arbitration decisions for strong evidence of the very frequent citation, discussion, and use of such precedents." [32]

However, Arbitrator Steven Carter decided that another arbitrator's award on an identical premium pay issue interpreting the same labor agreement did not bind him to rule the same way, even though he agrees that earlier awards, though not technically binding, should be followed where possible to promote stable industrial relations. But, this rule will not stand up where the prior award was "clearly erroneous." [33]

D. AWARDS AS *RES JUDICATA*

When a prior arbitrator has rendered an award in a dispute between the *same* employer and the *same* union, the precedential effect of

---

[31] *Thermoid Western Co.,* 29 L.A. 424, 427 (Kadish, 1952). See also *Mississippi Lime Co.,* 29 L.A. 559, 562 (Updegraff, 1957); *Stockton Automotive Corp.,* 25 L.A. 687, 690-91 (Whitton, 1955); *American Smelting & Refining Co.,* 24 L.A. 857, 860-61 (Ross, 1955); *Carson Electric Co.,* 24 L.A. 667, 672 (Howard, 1955); *Cherry Growers, Inc.,* 24 L.A. 232, 237 (Howlett, 1955); *National Fireworks Ordnance Corp.,* 23 L.A. 349, 352-53 (Larson, 1954); *Bachman Uxbridge Worsted Corp.,* 23 L.A. 596, 602 (Hogan, 1954); *Allied Arts Corp.,* 23 L.A. 338, 340 (Smith, 1954); *American Wood Products Corp.,* 17 L.A. 419, 423 (Livengood, 1951); *International Harvester Co.,* 16 L.A. 307, 311 (McCoy, 1951); *Bethlehem Steel Co.,* 16 L.A. 111, 113 (Killingsworth, 1951); *Struthers-Wells Corp.,* 17 L.A. 483, 485 (Stashower, 1951); *Grand Sheet Metal Products Co.,* 17 L.A. 388, 390 (Kelliher, 1951).

[32] F. Elkouri and E. Elkouri, How ARBITRATION WORKS 193-200 (1952). See also *Pratt & Whitney Co.,* 28 L.A. 668, 672 (Dunlop, 1957); *Marathon Electric Mfg. Co.,* 29 L.A. 518, 523 (Thompson, 1957); *National Lead Co.,* 28 L.A. 470, 474 (Roberts, 1957); *Western Gear Corp. of Texas,* 26 L.A. 84, 87 (Boles, 1956); *Philadelphia Transp. Co.,* 25 L.A. 379, 381 (Scheiber, 1955); *Cooper-Bessemer Corp.,* 25 L.A. 146, 149 (Reid, 1955); *S. H. Kress & Co.,* 25 L.A. 77, 79 (Ross, 1955); *Safe Bus Co., Inc.,* 21 L.A. 456, 460 (Livengood, 1953); *Great Lakes Carbon Corp.,* 19 L.A. 797, 799 (Wettach, 1953); *Coca-Cola Bottling Works Co.,* 19 L.A. 432, 434 (Schmidt, 1952).

[33] *The Coleman Co., Inc.,* 59 DLR A-6 3/27/69 (Carter, 1969). (See text relating to note 49 in Section D. of this chapter.)

the prior award tends to move from that of *stare decisis* to that of *res judicata*. When the same parties are involved, arbitrators are willing to follow prior awards even though they would not have rendered the same award if they had heard the prior case.[34] In such cases, it is often held that adherence to precedent is desirable in order to maintain stable labor-management relations.[35]

For example, in *Union Pacific Railroad Co.*[36] the chairman of the special board of adjustment admitted that the grievance under consideration logically dictated an award in favor of the union but the board, nevertheless, was required to abide by prior awards where the same issue was arbitrated under the same collective bargaining agreement. The difficult problem for the arbitrator faced with such a case is well illustrated in *Magnavox Co.*:[37]

> "If this had been a matter of first impression, the Arbitrator is not entirely sure how he would have answered the problem. The only certainty he feels is that the answer would not have been an easy one. He is certainly not prepared to conclude that the determination made by the previous arbitrator is clearly erroneous.
>
> ". . . In the Arbitrator's opinion, the only correct answer lies in the rule that once an identical issue between the same parties has been settled through arbitration, the former determination should not be lightly set aside."

The arbitrator's dilemma here is clear: his thinking may be taking him in a direction other than that followed by his predecessor, but if his choice is just that—personal opinion of the best interpretation —then he should follow the prior award in the interest of continuity of interpretation. Arbitrator Roy Ray succinctly put it in *General Portland Cement Co.*:[38]

> "If one Board says no and another says yes, what will a third Board say sometime in the future when the same dispute arises once more? The parties will be right back where they started."

The necessity for finality was emphasized by Arbitrator Langston Hawley in *Mead Corp.* where he held that answers to questions obtained through arbitration should "not be overturned by subse-

---

[34] *Cf. Paramount Transport Systems v. Teamsters, Local 150,* 64 L.C. ¶ 11,527 (E.D. Cal. 1970), where, in a suit by an employer for damages allegedly suffered as a result of an unlawful secondary boycott engaged in by two unions, the determination of the NLRB that such an unfair practice had occurred was considered *res judicata* and therefore binding on a federal district court.

[35] *Brewers Board of Trade, Inc.,* 38 L.A. 679 (Turkus, 1962); *City Service Oil Company,* AAA Case No. 13-13 (Wirtz, 1959).

[36] 62-3 ARB ¶ 8946 (McDermott, 1962).

[37] 70-1 ARB ¶ 8002 at 3009 (Teple, 1969).

[38] 62-2 ARB ¶ 8611 at 5273 (Ray, 1962).

quent proceedings unless there are powerful and compelling reasons for doing so."[39]

The corollary of this necessity of finality is the need for consistency in contractual interpretation stressed by many arbitrators in upholding prior awards.[40] Arbitrator Saul Wallen in *Allegheny Ludlum Steel Corp.* stated:[41]

"I am constrained, both by the parties' essential agreement on the point and by my own recognition of the need for consistency in the interpretation of agreements, to regard the [prior] decision as the settled law of the case and to apply it to the extent it is applicable to the facts at hand."

Arbitrator Whitley McCoy set the guideline for many arbitrators in *Pan American Refining Company:*[42]

"But where, as here, the prior decision involves the interpretation of the identical contract provision, between the same company and union, every principle of common sense, policy, and labor relations demands that it stand until the parties annul it by a newly worded contract provision."

The need for consistency has caused a decision rendered under a multi-employer agreement at one company to be extended to an identical situation at another company covered by the same provisions,[43] and also has been stressed in the mutual application of contractual interpretations rendered at different plants of the same employer who has contracts with several local unions containing identical language.[44] However, at least one arbitrator has refused to hold a subsidiary bound by the interpretation of an applicable master contract provision rendered in a dispute involving the parent company,[45] holding that the required identity of parties and facts was not sufficiently established.

The policy of finality and consistency was combined by the arbitrator in *General Portland Cement Company,*[46] who determined

---

[39] 43 L.A. 391, 394 (Hawley, 1964). *Accord, Owens-Illinois Glass Co.,* 43 L.A. 715 (Dworkin, 1964). See also *Lawson Milk Co.,* 46 L.A. 709, 710 (Gibson, 1966); *Hi-Torc Motor Corp.,* 40 L.A. 929, 930 (Kerrison, 1963); *Atlas Foundry, Incorporated,* 69-2 ARB ¶ 8774 (Bradley, 1969); *Lewin-Mathes Co.,* 37 L.A. 119 (Moore, 1961); *Kennecott Copper Corp.,* 32 L.A. 646 (Ross, 1959).

[40] See, *e.g., Board of Education, City of New York,* 45 L.A. 43 (Rock, 1965).

[41] 43 L.A. 1041, 1042 (Wallen, 1964).

[42] 9 L.A. 731, 732 (McCoy, 1948).

[43] *American-Saint Gobain Corp.,* 62-3 ARB ¶ 8882 (McCoy, 1962).

[44] *National Lead Co.,* 28 L.A. 470 (Roberts, 1957).

[45] *Wallingford Steel Co.,* 34 L.A. 385 (Healy, 1960).

[46] 62-2 ARB ¶ 8611 (Ray, 1962). Another arbitrator said that he did not adopt a strict *res judicata* rule which would prevent the union from re-arguing bargaining history before him, but that the union would have to show by a "preponderance of credible evidence" that the labor agreement should be construed differently than it was by the prior arbitrator. *Board of Education of City of New York,* AAA Case No. 78-8 (Horvitz, 1965).

that although he was not legally bound to follow an earlier award involving the same parties and contractual provisions, a proper regard for the arbitral process required the application of the prior decision since no clear error was perceived[47] and refusal to do so would leave unresolved and unsettled the problem covered by the prior decision.[48] The integrity of the prior decision is frequently the determinative factor in choosing to follow the prior award, even though the present arbitrator might have reached a different decision in the initial case. The criteria for upsetting the prior award has been variously stated as "clearly wrong,"[49] "clearly and significantly wrong,"[50] and "so plainly and palpably erroneous as to be upset."[51]

The language of the collective bargaining agreement is basic to many decisions regarding the effect of prior awards. This is because many agreements provide that the arbitrator's award shall be "final and binding." [52] In *Mead Corp.*, this language caused the arbitrator to state:

"Thus, unless the facts, the contract, and/or the relevant conditions upon which the prior decisions were reached have materially changed, it is the view of this arbitrator that he is bound by the awards which have been previously rendered." [53]

Similarly, in *Holland Suco Color Co.*[54] the arbitrator held:

"The final sentence of Article X, Step 4, provides: 'The award of the arbitrator shall be final and binding.' In other words, the [prior] decision is *'res judicata'* meaning that the point, question, or subject matter which was in controversy or dispute has been authoritatively and finally settled by that decision."

Other arbitrators rely on the contract indirectly by invoking the premise that the past award interpreting its terms has become a part of the terms, and is therefore binding until the parties themselves amend the language.[55] This approach has gained such wide acceptance as to allow the arbitrator in *Stewart-Warner Corp.* to state:

---

47 62-2 ARB at 5273, citing *O & S Bearing Co.*, 12 L.A. 132 (Smith, 1949).
48 62-2 ARB at 5273, citing *Inland Steel Co.*, 1 ALAA ¶ 67,121 (Blumer, 1944).
49 *Neches Butane Products Co.*, 68-1 ARB ¶ 8361 (Merrill, 1968); *Flintkote Co.*, 41 L.A. 268 (Merrill, 1963); *The Coleman Co., Inc.*, 59 DLR A-6 3/27/69 (Carter, 1969).
50 *Brewers Board of Trade*, 38 L.A. 679 (Turkus, 1962).
51 *Lawson Milk Co.*, 46 L.A. 709 (Gibson, 1966).
52 See, *e.g.*, *Atlas Foundry Inc.*, 69-2 ARB ¶ 8774 (Bradley, 1969); *Union Carbide Corp.*, 46 L.A. 517 (Cahn, 1966); *Hi Torc Motor Corp.*, 40 L.A. 929 (Kerrison, 1963); *U.S. Industrial Chemicals Co.*, 41 L.A. 348 (Geissinger, 1963).
53 43 L.A. 391, 394 (Hawley, 1964).
54 43 L.A. 1022, 1024 (Geissinger, 1964).
55 See, *e.g.*, *Pan American Refining Co.*, 9 L.A. 731 (McCoy, 1948). See generally F. Elkouri & E. Elkouri, How ARBITRATION WORKS 254, 255 (rev. ed. 1960).

"It is a well established principle in arbitration processes that arbitration opinions are not precedents; that each case stands upon its own feet. However, it also appears to be a well established principle that the interpretation of contract language embodied in an award becomes a part of that contract language." [56]

The incorporation theory is strengthened where the parties to an award subsequently readopt the same language.[57] Arbitrator Rolf Valtin stated this proposition succinctly in *Alegheny Ludlum Steel Corp.*:[58]

"It is a generally recognized principle that the interpretation of contract language embodied in an award becomes a part of that contract language. If the parties fail to negotiate a change of the language in future contracts, but readopt the same language, that language having received an interpretation is presumed to be readopted with that interpretation."

Similarly, the failure of the adversely affected party to even raise the issue of change in subsequent negotiations has been held to constitute a presumption of acquiescence.[59] This presumption of contractual assimilation could quite properly be considered a form of estoppel whereby the parties are entitled to rely upon the continued efficacy of the prior decision.

Thus, while the strict classical judicial formulations of *res judicata,* that is, that parties should be bound by prior determinations to avoid repetitive litigation, may be somewhat out of place in the less formalistic process of industrial arbitration, there is adequate evidence that arbitrators using various guises have permitted the ideas basic to that doctrine to thrive.[60]

Since the effects of an application of *res judicata* are so conclusive, encompassing matters that were, or could have been, raised, the

---

[56] 33 L.A. 816, 818-819 (Uible, 1960).

[57] *Magnavox Company,* 70-1 ARB ¶ 8002 (Teple, 1969); *Gorton-Pew Fisheries,* 16 L.A. 365 (Wallen, 1951); *Pan American Refining Corp.,* 9 L.A. 731 (McCoy, 1948).

[58] 30 L.A. 1011, 1013 (Valtin, 1958); *Day and Zimmerman, Inc., Lone Star Div.,* 70-2 ARB ¶ 8624 (Caraway, 1970). See also *Ford Motor Co.,* 30 L.A. 46 (Platt, 1958); *Federal Bearings Co., Inc.,* 22 L.A. 721 (Justin, 1954).

[59] *U.S. Industrial Chemicals Co.,* 41 L.A. 348 (Geissinger, 1963). See *Magnavox Company,* 70-1 ARB ¶ 8002 (Teple, 1969) and cases cited therein. See also *Armstrong Cork,* 34 L.A. 890 (Morvant, 1960); *Butler Manufacturing Co.,* 42 L.A. 304 (Johnston, 1964).

[60] In *Clover v. The Columbus Retail Merchants Delivery, Inc.,* 185 N.E.2d 658 (Ohio Ct. App. 1962), the court quoted with approval the following statement from 4 Ohio Jurisprudence 2d 697:
"The decision of the arbitrators on all matters of fact and law is conclusive, and all matters in the award are thenceforth *res judicata,* on the theory that the matter has been adjudged by a tribunal which the parties have agreed to make final, a tribunal of last resort for that controversy."
In *Blumenthal Print Works, Inc. v. Johnson,* 173 N.E.2d 698 (Ohio Ct. App. 1960), the Ohio court held that an arbitration award rendered in New York prevented a relitigation of the same issue in Ohio.

rule necessarily operates upon a narrow basis of exact identity of parties, issues, and causes of action.[61] Thus, the relitigation situation most frequently encountered by arbitrators is where the subsequent case arises from somewhat different circumstances between the same parties[62] and is sufficiently distinguishable to preclude the strict invocation of *res judicata*.[63]

For example, where a prior arbitrator dismissed a grievance because the union had filed it without having the grievant sign it, as required by the labor agreement, and a subsequent arbitrator granted the grievance after it was signed by the grievant and reprocessed, the Third Circuit held the dismissal of the grievance by the first arbitrator was for a procedural reason and was not *res judicata* on the merits of the claim.[64]

On the other hand, in *Reeves v. Tarvizian*,[65] the First Circuit held that an award was *res judicata* on the issues decided in the arbitration even though an employee was not contractually bound to arbitrate the dispute. Similarly, the Sixth Circuit upheld an employer's plea of *res judicata* against an attempt by a union to rearbitrate a case where an earlier award over the same issues had resulted in a favorable award for the company, but a part of the award not dealing with the issues at bar, had been vacated because the arbitrator had exceeded his authority.[66]

Granting that most arbitrators will give great, and sometimes controlling, weight to prior awards involving the same issue between the same parties, there are situations where arbitrators feel compelled to refuse to apply a prior award. Arbitrator Ray, in *General Portland Cement Co.* enumerated these situations as follows:

"(1) The previous award was clearly an instance of bad judgment; (2) the decision was made without benefit of some important and rele-

---

[61] *Drake Motor Lines, Inc. v. Teamsters Local 107, Highway Truck Drivers & Helpers,* 343 F.Supp. 1130 (D.Pa. 1972); *UAW, Local 463 v. The Weatherhead Co.,* 203 F.Supp. 612 (N.D. Ohio, 1962); *Frank Chevrolet Corp. v. UAW Local 259,* 32 Misc.2d 1057, 224 N.Y.S.2d 928 (Sup. Ct. 1961); *Clemens v. Central Railroad Company of New Jersey,* 399 F.2d 825 (3d Cir. 1968); *Goldblatt v. Board of Educ. of the City of New York,* 275 N.Y.S.2d 550 (Sup. Ct. 1966); *Todd Shipyards Corp. v. Marine and Shipbuilding Workers of America,* 242 F.Supp. 606 (D.N.J. 1965).

[62] In *Nix v. Spector Freight System, Inc.,* 264 F.2d 875 (3d Cir. 1959), the court dismissed an attempt by employees not party to an arbitration to attack the award which determined seniority rights. The majority opinion characterized the plaintiff(s) as:
". . . one who was not even a party to the arbitration proceeding [and who] seeks relief which requires the invalidation of the award in a suit in which the beneficiaries of the award are not present or in any way represented."

[63] *Pittsburgh Railways Co. v. Amal. Association of Street, Electric Railway and Motor Coach Employees of America, Division 85,* 176 F.Supp. 16 (W.D. Pa. 1959).

[64] *Local 616, IUE v. Byrd Plastics, Inc.,* 428 F.2d 23 (3d Cir. 1970).

[65] 351 F.2d 889 (1st Cir. 1965).

[66] *IAM v. Jeffrey Galion Mfg. Co.,* 350 F.2d 512 (6th Cir. 1965).

vant facts; (3) the decision was based upon an obvious and substantial error of fact or law; (4) a full and fair hearing was not afforded in the prior case." [67]

Courts have held that determinations in arbitration awards are conclusive when an effort is made to relitigate the same issue in a court proceeding. The Sixth Circuit in *Dewey v. Reynolds Metals Co.* held:[68]

> "We know of no good reason why an award of an arbitrator should not be binding on both parties, the same as a judgment of a court.
> "It is difficult for us to believe that any employer would ever agree to arbitration of a grievance if he knew that the employee would not be bound by the result.
> ". . . The purpose of arbitration is thwarted if the awards are held by the courts to be binding on employers only and not on employees."

In *Dewey,* the employee's claim was that he was discharged because of his religious beliefs and that his Title VII action was not barred by a prior contrary arbitration award which found that the employee was properly discharged for failing to work required overtime irrespective of the employee's religious beliefs. The court, rejecting this argument, held that there was no "national policy for ousting arbitrators of jurisdiction to finally determine grievances initiated by employees, based on alleged violations of their civil rights."[69]

The court reasoned that if the arbitration award was not final, binding, and conclusive on the grievant, the efficacy of the arbitration process would be substantially undermined. If the award had been in favor of Dewey instead of the company, the company would not be permitted to relitigate the award in the courts. "This is the teaching of the *United Steelworkers Trilogy,* which clearly defined the respective function of the courts and the arbitrator."[70] In *Dewey,* the court discussed the role of arbitrators in cases involving alleged civil rights violations in the following manner:

> "The arbitration involved an interpretation of the collective bargaining agreement with respect to Dewey's claims that he had been laid off and discharged because of his religious beliefs. In arbitration proceedings, frequently questions of law and fact are resolved by the arbitrator. Where the grievances are based on an alleged civil rights violation, the parties consent to arbitration by a mutually agreeable arbitrator, in our judgment the arbitrator has a right to finally determine them. Any other

---

[67] 62-2 ARB ¶ 8611 at 5273 (Ray, 1962).
[68] 429 F.2d 324, *rehearing denied,* 429 F.2d 334, 337 (6th Cir. 1970), *aff'd by an equally divided court,* 91 S.Ct. 2186 (1971). For an excellent analysis of *Dewey* and the interaction between arbitration and Title VII of the 1964 Civil Rights Act, see Edwards & Kaplan, *Religious Discrimination and the Role of Arbitration Under Title VII,* 69 Mich. L. Rev. 599 (1971).
[69] 429 F.2d at 332.
[70] *Id.* at 331.

construction would bring about the result present in the instant case, namely, that the employer, but not the employee, is bound by the arbitration.

". . . This result could sound the death knell to arbitration of labor disputes, which has been so usefully employed in their settlement. Employers would not be inclined to agree to arbitration clauses in collective bargaining agreements if they provide only a one-way street, *i.e.*, that the awards are binding on them but not on their employees.

". . . The tremendous increase in civil rights litigation leads one to the belief that the Act will be used more frequently in labor disputes. Such use ought not to destroy the efficacy of arbitration." [71]

Contrariwise are decisions in the Fifth and Seventh Circuits[72] holding that an arbitration award or settlement at an intermediate stage of the grievance procedure does not operate so as to bar a Title VII suit over the identical claim in a federal court.[73]

These decisions are based on the view that "determination under a contract grievance-arbitration process will involve rights and remedies separate and distinct from those involved in judicial proceedings under Title VII."[74] These two courts reasoned that since the National Labor Relations Board is not bound under a doctrine of election of remedies or *res judicata* to accept an arbitral determination affecting rights and duties under the NLRA,[75] a court need not be bound to accept an arbitrator's decision on a racial discrimination claim raised under Title VII as conclusive.

However, the typical claim that a discharge was not for just cause because of racial discrimination involves a single issue—whether the aggrieved employee was or was not discriminated against on account of race or color when he was discharged. This is the same issue of fact that would be decisive in a Title VII suit. As Arbitrator Harry S. Platt said, "No published arbitration cases have been found where the alleged racial discrimination was solely in violation of Title VII and not also violative of a contract provision." [76] The arbitrator has the expertise to resolve the single issue; in fact his expertise may be greater

---

[71] *Id.* at 332. *Accord, Edwards v. North American Rockwell Corp.*, 291 F.Supp. 199 (C.D. Cal. 1968); *Washington v. Aerojet General Corp.*, 282 F.Supp. 517 (C.D. Cal. 1968).

[72] Even in the Sixth Circuit, there is a serious question following *Dewey* whether arbitration awards will bar a subsequent Title VII suit. See, *e.g.*, *Newman v. Avco Corp.*, 4 EPD ¶ 7549 (6th Cir. 1971); *Spann v. Kaywood Div., Joanna Western Mills Co., Inc.*, 3 EPD ¶ 8314 (6th Cir. 1971).

[73] *Hutchings v. U.S. Industries, Inc.*, 2 FEP Cases 725 (5th Cir. 1970); *Bowe v. Colgate-Palmolive Co.*, 416 F.2d 711 (7th Cir. 1969).

[74] *Hutchings v. U. S. Industries, Inc.*, 2 FEP Cases at 731.

[75] *Carey v. Westinghouse Elec. Corp.*, 375 U.S. 261 (1964).

[76] Platt, *The Relationship Between Arbitration and Title VII of the Civil Rights Act of 1964*, 3 GA. L. REV. 398, 408 (1969).

than that of either the EEOC or the federal court because of his greater knowledge of industrial practice.[77]

On the other hand, it has been well argued that the arbitration process with its emphasis on group rather than individual rights may, at times, be at odds with the fundamental policies of Title VII.[78] Thus, some form of deferral, rather than an election of remedies may well be more appropriate.[79]

E. THE EFFECT OF A CONFIRMATION OF THE AWARD ON ITS *RES JUDICATA* EFFECT

The collateral estoppel or *res judicata* effect of an award should not in theory be any different whether or not it is confirmed by a court.[80] However, as a practical matter, a confirmed award, because it becomes an order of court, has a more direct effect if the same court is asked to enforce a contrary award by a different tribunal. This was illustrated when an arbitration award upholding the discharge of an employee who left work early on Friday for religious reasons at the Avco Lycoming Division of Avco Corporation was affirmed by a Connecticut court.

A proceeding was then initiated by the discharged employee before the Connecticut Commission on Human Rights and Opportunities. This tribunal found that the employee had been discriminated against on account of her religion and ordered her reinstated, and the company then appealed to the same superior court. The court declared that the decision of the Connecticut Commission must be "in all respects annulled and set aside."[81] The court-affirmed arbitration award made the matter "res judicata" so far as the Human Relations Commission was concerned and a contrary decision by that Commission could not be enforced.

If a claimant persists in seeking to relitigate the same issue decided by the arbitrator and confirmed by the court, the court has power to enjoin such a claimant for attempting such relitigation on the ground that such an action would be vexatious.[82]

---

[77] *Id.* at 408.

[78] Edwards & Kaplan, *Religious Discrimination and the Role of Arbitration Under Title VII*, 69 MICH. L. REV. 599, 641-54 (1971).

[79] *Id.* at 641-54.

[80] Confirmation is a simple proceeding. For example, it is mandatory in Ohio upon the court to confirm and enforce the award. *Brennan v. Brennan*, 164 Ohio St. 29, 128 N.E.2d 89, 90 (1955).

[81] *Corey v. Avco-Lycoming Division, Avco Corporation*, 2 EPD ¶ 10,259 (Conn. Super. Ct., 1970).

[82] *Laursen v. Lowe*, 50 Ohio App. 103, 197 N.E. 597 (1935).

F. MODIFICATION AND CORRECTION OF AN
AWARD BY THE ARBITRATOR

At common law, an arbitrator did not have authority to modify or correct an award once it had been rendered because of the doctrine of *functus officio, i.e.,* having rendered his award, the arbitrator's task has been fulfilled.[83] Similarly, an arbitrator had no authority to commence a subsequent hearing. For example, the court stated in *Mercury Oil Refining Co. v. Oil Workers Int'l Union:*

"It is a general rule in common law arbitration that when arbitrators have executed their award and declared their decision they are *functus officio* and have no power or authority to proceed further. . . ."[84]

Arbitrator Adolph Koven applied this rule when a company requested him to determine whether the company fulfilled its obligations under a prior award rendered by him. He said that such a request "amounts to asking him to enforce his original award, thereby going beyond his authority in this case."[85]

The common law rule was revised by the Uniform Arbitration Act.[86] That Act provides in Section 9 that the arbitrator can modify or correct his award upon the application of a party:

"On application of a party or, if an application to the court is pending under Sections 11, 12 or 13, on submission to the arbitrators by the court under such conditions as the court may order, the arbitrators may modify or correct the award upon the grounds stated in paragraphs (1) and (3) of subdivision (a) of Section 13, or for the purpose of clarifying the award. The application shall be made within twenty days after delivery of the award to the applicant. Written notice thereof shall be given forthwith to the opposing party, stating he must serve his objections thereto, if any, within ten days from the notice. The award so

---

[83] See Seitz, *Problems of the Finality of Awards or Functus Officio and All That,* LABOR-ARBITRATION—PERSPECTIVES AND PROBLEMS, Proceedings of the Seventeenth Annual Meeting, National Academy of Arbitrators 165 (M. Kahn Ed. 1964).

[84] 187 F.2d 980, 983 (10th Cir. 1951). *Accord, Indigo Springs, Inc. v. New York Hotel Trades Council,* 59 LRRM 3024 (N.Y. Sup. Ct. 1965); *Shippers Express Co. v. Teamsters,* 59 LRRM 2744 (Cal. Sup. Ct. 1965); *Mole v. Queen Insurance Co.,* 14 App. Div.2d 1, 217 N.Y.S.2d 330 (1961). See also *Elgin, Joliet & Eastern Ry. Co. v. Brotherhood of Railroad Trainmen,* 196 F.Supp. 158 (N.D. Ill. 1961). This result has been reported to be the "accepted" view by Arbitrator Robben Fleming who stated that "the arbitrator's decision becomes final once he signs it," and thus, there is no right to a rehearing as in the courts. Fleming, *Problems of Procedural Regularity in Labor Arbitration,* WASH. U. L.Q. 221, 247 (1961). See generally Justin, *Arbitrability and the Arbitrator's Jurisdiction,* MANAGEMENT RIGHTS AND THE ARBITRATION PROCESS, Proceedings of the Ninth Annual Meeting, National Academy of Arbitrators 1, 17 (J. McKelvey Ed. 1956).

[85] *Uarco, Inc.,* 43 L.A. 1060, 1063 (Koven, 1964).

[86] Indiana (IND. ANN. STAT. §§ 3-227 to 3-248 (Supp. 1970)); Maine (ME. REV. STAT. ANN. tit. 14, §§ 14-5927 to 14-5949 (Supp. 1970)); Minnesota (MINN. STAT. ANN. §§ 572.03 to 572.30 (Supp. 1970)); Wyoming (WYO. STAT. ANN. §§ 1-1048.1 to 1-1048.21 (Supp. 1969)).

modified or corrected is subject to the provisions of Sections 11, 12, and 13." [87]

The grounds for such modification or correction do not involve objections to the merits of the award, but correction of miscalculation of figures, mistakes in descriptions, removal of portions of the award exceeding submission but not affecting merits, and corrections of form not affecting the merits.

In several states where the Uniform Arbitration Act has not been enacted, the statute allows an arbitrator to modify or correct his award upon application of a party.[88] Such provisions are similar to the Uniform Arbitration Act as they only permit arbitrators "to correct formal errors or clarify their intent but not to . . . alter the [merits of the] decision."[89]

The theory that an arbitrator's function is exhausted and that he becomes "functus officio" after he submits an award was specifically rejected by the court of appeals in *Enterprise Wheel & Car Corp. v. United Steelworkers:*

> "[T]he award directed the Corporation to reinstate the grievants and compensate them for the time lost less the ten-day suspension period and less such amounts as they may have received from other employment; but the arbitrator failed to include in the award the amounts which had actually been earned or, by the exercise of due diligence, could have been earned by the grievants in other employment. It has generally been held that a final award must be certain in its terms or provide means and data by which it may be made certain by mathematical calculation, and that if it is deficient in this respect it must be vacated since the powers of the arbitrator are exhausted and the award cannot be resubmitted to him for correction or amendment. . . .

---

[87] 24 L.A. 886, 887 (1955).

[88] ARIZ. REV. STAT. ANN. §§ 12-1501 to 12-1517 (Supp. 1969) (does not apply to collective bargaining agreements); CAL. DIV. PRO. CODE § 1284 (West. Supp. 1968-69). For a detailed discussion of the California statute see Comment, *Some Problems Relating to Enforcement of Arbitration Awards Under the New California Arbitration Act,* 9 U.C.L.A. L. REV. 422 (1962). ILL. REV. STAT. ANN. ch 10, §§ 101-123 (Smith-Hurd, 1969); MD. ANN. CODE, art. 7 §§ 1-23 (1968) (only applies to collective bargaining agreements if express provision is made in the agreement subjecting it to the Act); IND. ANN. STAT. §§ 3-227 to 3-248 (Supp. 1970). ME. REV. STAT. ANN. tit. 14, §§ 14-5927 to 14-5949 (Supp. 1970); MASS. ANN. LAWS ch. 150C, §§ 1-16 (1965); WYO. STAT. ANN. §§ 1-1048.1 to 1-1048.28 (Supp. 1969); MINN STAT. ANN. §§ 572.08 to 572.30 (Supp. 1970); FLA. STAT. ANN. § 682.10 (Supp. 1969) (statute applies to all agreements unless the parties specifically provide otherwise); N.Y. CIV. PRAC. LAW § 7509 (McKinney, 1963). See also Weinstein, *Notes on Proposed Revision of the New York Arbitration Law,* 16 ARB. J. (n.s.) 61, 76 (1961); TEX. REV. CIV. STAT. ANN. art. 232 (1968-9) (Act does not apply to collective agreements). See also Dougherty and Graf, *Should Texas Revise Its Arbitration Statutes?* 41 TEXAS L. REV. 229, 246-7 (1962); WASH. REV. CODE ANN. § 7.04.170 (1961) (Act does not apply to collective bargaining agreements).

[89] *Legis, Studies & Rep.,* N.Y. CIV. PRAC. LAW § 7509 at 587 (McKinney, 1963); *Historical and Practice Notes,* ILL. ANN. STAT. ch. 10, § 109 at 694 (Smith-Hurd, 1966).

". . . If this rule were given effect in the pending case the award would be set aside, for it is obviously so incomplete that disputes may well arise as to the amounts of back pay which the employer is obliged to make to the discharged workers. We think, however, that the rule forbidding the resubmission of a final award, which was developed when the courts looked with disfavor upon arbitration proceedings, should not be applied today in the settlement of employer-employee disputes. As pointed out in *Textile Workers Union of America v. Lincoln Mills,* 353 U.S. 448, Congress has clearly indicated that the arbitration of grievance disputes for the preservation of industrial peace is to be encouraged and the Supreme Court has directed the federal courts to fashion a federal substantive law in accordance with this policy. This may readily be done in the pending case by requiring the parties to take steps to complete the arbitration so that the amounts due the grievants for loss of time will be definitely ascertained. . . ." [90]

The Supreme Court reversed that part of the court of appeals' ruling in *Enterprise* which had held that back pay could not be awarded for discharge in breach of the collective bargaining agreement for a period after the expiration of the agreement.[91] But it sustained the ruling quoted above stating: "We agree with the Court of Appeals that the judgment of the District Court should be modified so that the amounts due the employees may be definitely determined by arbitration. . . ."[92]

Even before the decision in *Enterprise,* a court pointed out that the *functus officio* doctrine has no application to a permanent arbitrator for the reason that "he [is] not merely an arbitrator for the specific controversy."[93] In that case, the court held that the question as to the amount of back pay due an employee, whom the permanent umpire held was wrongfully discharged, could be submitted to the same permanent arbitrator as a reopening of the discharge case after the award because he would hear the dispute over the back pay calculation if it became a new grievance.[94]

A California court in *Union Local 679 v. Richmond-Chase Corp.*[95] rationalized the common law rule that an arbitration board loses jurisdiction after rendering an award with the need for a rehearing. The court vacated an award which a permanent arbitration board had issued on the ground that the board had no power to order a rehearing to clarify its award. The court, however, ordered a rehearing since it held that the California arbitration statute did not bar a

---

[90] 269 F.2d 327, 331-332 (4th Cir. 1959). See generally Busch, *Does the Arbitrator's Function Survive His Award?,* 16 ARB. J. 31 (1961); Jones, *Arbitration and the Dilemma of Possible Error,* 11 LABOR L.J. 1023 (1960).

[91] 363 U.S. 593, 597-98 (1960).

[92] *Id.* at 599.

[93] *In re Wagner,* 11 L.A. 1173 (N.Y. Sup. Ct. 1948).

[94] *Id.*

[95] 191 Cal. App.2d 841, 13 CAL. RPTR. 341 (1961).

court from ordering a rehearing when the contract did not fix a time period for the rendering of an award.

Prior to the *Enterprise* decision, some arbitrators clung to at least part of the *functus officio* doctrine stating that they would honor a request for modification or correction of an award only if both parties to the case involved joined in the request,[96] although the prevalence of this practice presently is uncertain. The *functus officio* doctrine, long considered by a great many arbitrators as the correct rule to follow,[97] is incompatible with the function of the labor arbitration process because it requires parties to go to court to obtain corrections of errors or to obtain an order referring the case back to the arbitrator so he can consider the request for correction. Arbitrator Whitley McCoy some 25 years ago noted the inadequacy of the doctrine of *functus officio*.[98] Although he said the doctrine was based on the "presumed intent of the parties" and "upon the public policy which dictates that there be a definite point where litigation shall end and the rights and obligations of disputants be definitely and for all times settled," the doctrine is subject to an exception:

> "The parties to an arbitration cannot be presumed to have intended that an award that contains on its face, or on the face of the record, fundamental mistakes of fact, as distinguished from errors of judgment, causing a miscarriage of justice, should be irremediable. Nor is public policy subserved by a principle that would perpetuate a miscarriage of justice in an arbitration award any more than in a judgment." [99]

In accordance with his opinion, Arbitrator McCoy amended the award based on corrections of certain errors in the record. The company's member of the arbitration board strongly objected, stating that the neutral arbitrator had no authority to amend the award and that the assumption of such power was "mischievous" and "calculated to do irreparable harm to arbitration." McCoy answered:

> "[I]t is far more in the interest of arbitration, and of peaceful labor relations, that arbitrators have the power to correct impeachable awards, than that it be necessary for a Company to apply to the courts, and thus precipitate a strike, as happened recently in Springfield, Ill., or that a

---

[96] Kellor, *Standards of Practice for Arbitration,* 4 Arb. J. (n.s.) 46 (1949). By appearing at a hearing on a petition to clarify an arbitration award, a union was held to have waived its right to object to any clarification ruling, even though its position was that the original award was not ambiguous and needed no clarification. *Textile Workers v. Courtaulds North America, Inc.,* 68 L.C. ¶ 12,865 (S.D. Ala. 1972).

[97] See Fleming, *Problems of Procedural Regularity in Labor Arbitration,* Wash. U. L.Q. 221 (1961).

[98] *Twin City Rapid Transit Co.,* 7 L.A. 845 (McCoy, 1947).

[99] 7 L.A. at 866.

union, in protest of an award go on strike, as happened even more recently in St. Louis." [100]

Where an award is unclear and the parties cannot agree on how to apply it, one court said the remedy is not vacation on the grounds that the award is indefinite or reformation by the court, but resubmission to the arbitrator by the parties.[101] It is pointed out in the next chapter that more and more courts, rather than reform awards where error or ambiguity is shown, have ordered the case to be resubmitted to the arbitrator for clarification of the award.

---

[100] *Id.* at 869.

[101] *National Brotherhood, Packinghouse and Dairy Workers, Local 52 v. Western Iowa Pork Company,* 247 F.Supp. 663 (S.D. Iowa, 1965).

CHAPTER XVII

Actions to Enforce, Vacate, or Correct Awards

Judicial review of an arbitrator's award is generally obtained either on a motion to confirm and enforce an award, or on a motion to modify or vacate an award.[1] The court may also have occasion to review an arbitration award where the losing party has sued on the original claim, and the prevailing party has pleaded the award in defense.[2]

The court's jurisdiction to entertain a suit to confirm or vacate or modify a labor arbitration award falls within the purview of Section 301.[3] This was made clear in *Textile Workers Union v. Cone Mills Corp.*,[4] where the Fourth Circuit ruled that Section 301 applied to suits brought to enforce arbitration awards. Any doubt that Section 301 was the vehicle to enforce or vacate arbitration awards was removed by *Enterprise Wheel & Car Corp. v. United Steelworkers.*[5] There, the Supreme Court, after stating that the award should be remitted to the arbitrator solely to make certain computations, said: ". . . in all other respects we think the judgment of the District Court [enforcing the award] should be affirmed."[6] This necessarily affirmed the ruling upholding jurisdiction of a suit to enforce an

---

[1] The courts have uniformly rejected the contention that a losing party must await suit by the prevailing party in order to raise the issue of the alleged invalidity of the arbitrator's award. See, *e.g., Central Packing Co. of Kansas v. Packinghouse Workers, Local 36,* 195 F.Supp. 188 (D. Kan. 1961).

[2] *Cf. IAM v. Jeffrey Galion Mfg. Co.,* 350 F.2d 512 (6th Cir. 1965) (court upheld employer's plea of *res judicata* against an attempt by a union to rearbitrate a case in which an earlier arbitration award had been vacated by a court).

[3] 29 USCA § 185(a) (1970). See generally *Underwood Corp. v. Electrical Workers Local 267,* 171 F.Supp. 102 (D. Conn. 1957); *Central Packing Co. v. Packinghouse Workers,* 195 F.Supp. 188 (D. Kan. 1961); *Central Metal Products Co. v. UAW Local 1249,* 195 F.Supp. 70 (E.D. Ark. 1961); *Local 971, UAW v. Bendix-Westinghouse Automotive Air Brake Co.,* 188 F.Supp. 842 (N.D. Ohio 1960) (jurisdiction exercised over suit to vacate award without discussion of jurisdictional issue).

[4] 268 F.2d 920 (4th Cir. 1958), *cert. denied,* 361 U.S. 886 (1959).

[5] 363 U.S. 593 (1960).

[6] *Id.* at 599. See also *Pacific Maritime Assn. v. Longshoremen's and Warehousemen's Union,* 454 F.2d 262 (9th Cir. 1971).

award under Section 301 which had been sustained by the court of appeals and constitutes a Supreme Court holding on the point.

The district court in *Enterprise* had noted that the arbitration resulting in the award in that case had been compelled in a suit under Section 301,[7] but it would be absurd to assume that a prior suit to compel arbitration is a prerequisite for federal jurisdiction over the enforcement of the award. This would only encourage otherwise needless litigation to compel arbitration in order to assure jurisdiction to enforce the award. The Supreme Court, in its brief mention of the question of jurisdiction, noted that the court of appeals had agreed with the district court that there was ". . . . jurisdiction to enforce an arbitration award under a collective bargaining agreement,"[8] and this view has become established as part of the emerging law being formulated by the courts under Section 301.[9]

A suit to enforce or to vacate may be initially instituted in either a state court or a federal court, since state courts have concurrent jurisdiction in actions brought under Section 301.[10] An application to modify or vacate an award is removable, however, to a federal court.[11] Neither the arbitrator[12] nor the individual employee involved in the grievance[13] is an indispensable party to such suits.

---

[7] 168 F.Supp. 308, 309-10 (S.D. W.Va. 1958).

[8] 363 U.S. at 596.

[9] *Mississippi Valley Elec. Co. v. IBEW*, 285 F.2d 229, vacating, 278 F.2d 764 (5th Cir. 1960). See also *Textile Workers, Local 1386 v. American Thread Co.*, 291 F.2d 894 (4th Cir. 1961); *American Brake Shoe Co. v. Local 149, UAW*, 285 F.2d 869 (4th Cir. 1961); *Local 971, UAW v. Bendix-Westinghouse Automotive Air Brake Co.*, 188 F.Supp. 842 (N.D. Ohio 1960); *cf. Humhprey v. Moore*, 375 U.S. 335 (1964). Curiously, in spite of these holdings, some federal courts still assume that the U.S. Arbitration Act is basic to their jurisdiction in suits to confirm, vacate, or modify arbitration awards. See, *e.g.*, *Bakery Workers Local 719 v. National Biscuit Co.*, 252 F.Supp. 768 (D. N.J. 1966), aff'd, 378 F.2d 918 (3d Cir. 1967); *Newark Stereotypers Union v. Newark Morning Ledger Co.*, 261 F.Supp. 832 (D. N.J. 1966). See also *Food Handlers Local 425 v. Pluss Poultry, Inc.*, 260 F.2d 835 (8th Cir. 1958).

[10] *Charles Dowd Box Co. v. Courtney*, 368 U.S. 502 (1962). See also *Avco Corp. v. IAM Aero Lodge 735*, 390 U.S. 557 (1968); *Espino v. Volkswagen de Puerto Rico, Inc.*, 289 F.Supp. 979 (D. P.R. 1968); *Lodge 2120, IAM v. Geometric Tool Co.*, 406 F.2d 284 (2d Cir. 1968); *Central Metal Products, Inc. v. Local 1249, UAW*, 195 F.Supp. 70 (E.D. Ark. 1961).

[11] *Avco Corp. v. Aero Lodge 735 IAM*, 390 U.S. 557 (1968); *Kracoff v. Retail Clerks Local 1357*, 244 F.Supp. 38 (E.D.Pa. 1965).

[12] *Honeywell, Inc. v. United Instrument Workers Local 116*, 307 F.Supp. 1126 (E.D.Pa. 1970).

[13] When a company brought an action against a union and an individual employee to enforce an arbitration award, the latter moved to dismiss the action against him. Discussing the scope of coverage of Section 301, the court held it "was not intended to embrace actions by or against individuals." *Red Ball Motor Freight, Inc. v. Teamsters General Drivers Local 961*, 202 F.Supp. 904, 905 (D. Colo. 1962). To the extent that the court held that individuals cannot bring § 301 suits under any circumstances, it is, of course, wrong. See, *e.g.*, *Vaca v. Sipes*, 386 U.S. 171 (1967); *Humphrey v. Moore*, 375 U.S. 335 (1964); *Smith v. Evening News Ass'n*, 371 U.S. 195 (1962). See also *Atkinson v. Sinclair Refining Co.*, 370 U.S. 238 (1962), where the court implied that individual union members could not be held liable for damage under § 301 for breach of a no-strike clause.

However, as explained in Chapter I, the substantive law which should be applied by either the federal or state court in determining whether an award should be vacated, enforced, or modified is federal law, not state law. While the Supreme Court did not foreclose the vacation of an award because it did not conform to one of the standards established in a state arbitration act, the provisions of such acts remain effective as a basis for a challenge of an award only if the particular court concludes they are compatible with federal labor policy, which is still a very uneasy standard. If the state arbitration act provision relating to enforcement, vacation, and modification of awards is considered compatible by the particular court, it is absorbed by that court as part of the emerging federal law, but if the state law is considered incompatible it is not applied, on the ground that it is not compatible with the emerging federal law.

In this connection, the Second Circuit's decision in *IAM West Rock Lodge 2120 v. Geometric Tool Co.*[14] is particularly instructive. There, the union sought to set aside an arbitration award sustaining the discharge of an employee on the ground that the award had not been rendered within the mandatory 60 days following the hearing required by the Connecticut Arbitration Act. The district court vacated the award, but the Second Circuit refused to apply the state law, stating that the situation was one in which there was "a very strong need for federal uniformity."[15] Hence the court refused to apply the state's statutory rule on the time limit for rendering the award.

Somewhat in contrast to the rejection of state law in *Geometric Tool* is the now clear rule that the state statute of limitations governs suits brought under Section 301. In *UAW v. Hoosier Cardinal Corp.*,[16] the Supreme Court held that state statutes of limitations were applicable to suits for enforcement of collective bargaining agreements under Section 301 and it should follow that the limitations in such statutes would also apply to suits to enforce or vacate awards. The courts said that the lack of uniformity of the limitations in the various state statutes was acceptable since " . . . [l]ack of uniformity in this area is . . . unlikely to frustrate in any important way the achievement of any significant goal of labor policy. . . ."[17]

State law was also used in *Howerton v. J. Christenson Co.*,[18] where a federal district court, relying on *Hoosier Cardinal*, applied a state

---

[14] 406 F.2d 284 (2d Cir. 1968).
[15] *Id.* at 286.
[16] 383 U.S. 696 (1966).
[17] *Id.* at 702.
[18] 76 LRRM 2937 (N.D. Cal. 1971). See also, *In re American Federation of Television & Radio Artists,* 72 LRRM 2865 (N.Y. Sup.Ct. 1969) (N.Y. statute for enforcing arbitration award within one year ran from date award was received, not mailed).

statute requiring petitions to vacate an arbitration award to be filed within 100 days after its issuance.

A. THE REASONS FOR VACATING OR NOT VACATING AN AWARD

Under this heading only the more general reasons why courts have vacated or have refused to enforce awards will be discussed. Throughout the volume there are citations to cases where vacature has been granted or denied for other reasons. For example, vacation of awards for failure of arbitrators to hear material evidence or because they relied on evidence not in the record would be discussed in the chapter on evidence, along with the discussion of evidentiary rules in arbitration.

(1) Vacation for No Agreement to Arbitrate

Where the grievance procedure in the labor agreement did not provide for arbitration, an award by a joint area cartage committee was not enforceable by a court on the ground there was no agreement to arbitrate.[19] Another court found that there was no agreement to arbitrate a dispute because it involved individuals who were not covered by the collective agreement.[20]
Both of these cases are grounded squarely on a contractual deficiency —the first because there was no arbitration provision, and the second because the "grievants" had no right to have their claim arbitrated as they were not covered by the agreement.

(2) Awards Exceeding the Scope of the Arbitrator's Jurisdiction

The Supreme Court has said that courts have the powers to vacate an award where the arbitrator exceeds the authority granted him by the labor agreement. The Court stated:

> "[A]n arbitrator is confined to interpretation and application of the collective bargaining agreement; he does not sit to dispense his own brand of industrial justice. He may of course look for guidance from many sources, yet his award is legitimate only so long as it draws its essence from the collective bargaining agreement. When the arbitrator's words manifest an infidelity to this obligation, courts have no choice but to refuse enforcement of the award." [21]

---

[19] *General Drivers, Warehousemen & Helpers, Local 89 v. Riss & Co.,* 298 F.2d 341 (6th Cir. 1962).
[20] *Capitol Airways, Inc. v. The Airline Pilots Association International,* 237 F.Supp. 373 (M.D. Tenn. 1963).
[21] *United Steelworkers of America v. Enterprise Wheel and Car Corp.,* 363 U.S. 593, 597 (1960).

However, in the same decision the Supreme Court stated that "[t]he federal policy of settling labor disputes by arbitration would be undermined if courts had the final say on the merits of the awards," and that ". . . the refusal of courts to review the merits of an arbitration award is the proper approach to arbitration under collective-bargaining agreements."[22]

(a) The Award Must Draw Its "Essence" From the Agreement

Another court, however, relying on the first view expressed in *Enterprise* was quite frank to assert that it had power to vacate an award on its merits for erroneous rationale if the error was extreme:

> "[T]he perverse misconstruction must be more than an egregious error of law before it satisfies the statute; it must be one which is so divorced from rationality that it can be accounted for only by one of the kinds of misbehavior recited in the statute. In that event, the vacatur is granted not for error of law or misconstruction of documents but for misconduct under one or more of the permitted categories, which misconduct has been established. Nothing like that was established in this case." [23]

In *H. K. Porter Co. v. United Saw, File & Steel Products Workers*,[24] the vacation of an award by the court would appear to be based on the court's disagreement with the reasoning used by the arbitrator. The grievance concerned the eligibility of employees, terminated in a plant removal situation, to a pension. The arbitrator held that, notwithstanding the express contractual eligibility requirements of age 65 and at least 25 years of service for a pension, employees under age 65 with 25 or more years of service terminated as a result of the plant removal were entitled to full pensions, and employees over 65 with less than 25 years of service similarly terminated were entitled to a prorated pension. Because of evidence before the arbitrator indicating that the age requirement had not been strictly applied in the past, the court upheld and enforced the first portion of the award, but vacated the second portion because it found no evidence was presented to the arbitrator that the years-of-service requirement had ever been relaxed. The court criticized the arbitrator for attempting to administer "his own brand of industrial justice,"[25] yet the court, rather than vacating the award on the grounds that the arbitrator's

---

[22] *Id.* at 596.

[23] *S & W Fine Foods, Inc. v. Office Employees Int'l Union, Local 153*, 185 N.Y.S.2d 1021, 8 App. Div.2d 130 (1959). See also *Cynthetex Corp., v. Automobile Workers*, 68 L.C. (CCH) ¶ 12,737 (W.D.Ky. 1972).

[24] 333 F.2d 596 (3d Cir. 1964).

[25] *Id* at 600, quoted from *United Steelworkers of America v. Warrior & Gulf Nav. Co.*, 363 U.S. 574, 581-582 (1960).

authority was limited to an application of the terms of the agreement, reviewed the merits and revised the award.[26]

Still another district court in St. Louis, guided by this statement, set aside an award that Olin Mathieson Chemical Corporation could not require, as a condition of continued employment, that certain employees wear metatarsal shoes for safety reasons.[27]

Alleging that the corporation failed and refused to comply with the arbitrator's decision, the union sued for an order to compel the employer to comply. However, the court agreed with the company that the arbitrator, in making his decision, disregarded the clear provisions of the employer-union contract. Looking back to the guidelines the Supreme Court laid down in *Enterprise,* District Judge James H. Meredith decided that the arbitrator here did not confine himself to the interpretation and application of the bargaining agreement but went outside its clear language.

In this regard, the decision of the Eighth Circuit in *Truck Drivers Union v. Ulry-Talbert Co.*[28] is of interest. There, the arbitrator found an employee guilty of the conduct for which he was discharged, but reinstated him without back pay on the ground that the penalty was too severe. The court held that since the collective agreement provided that ". . . the arbitration board shall not substitute its judgment for that of management," the arbitrator had exceeded his authority when he converted the discharge to a disciplinary suspension, and refused to enforce the award.

In *Torrington v. Metal Products Workers,*[29] the Second Circuit affirmed the lower court's vacation of an arbitration award directing the employer to pay employees for time lost while voting in national elections because of an alleged past practice of paying for such lost time. The labor agreement was silent on the issue and hence the Court concluded that the award did not draw its essence from the collective bargaining agreement.

---

[26] *Cf. Baldwin-Montrose Chemical Co. v. Rubber Workers,* 383 F.2d 796 (6th Cir. 1967) (award upheld granting vacation pay to employees who had not met eligibility requirements due to plant shutdown).

[27] *International A. of M. & A. W. v. Olin Mathieson Chem. Corp.,* 335 F.Supp. 212 (1971).

[28] 330 F.2d 562, 564 (8th Cir. 1964). An award reinstating 28 employees striking in violation of the agreement because discharge and offer to rehire as new employees was too harsh, is vacated because employer could determine penalty under agreement. *Amanda Bent Bolt Co. v. UAW Local 1549,* 451 F.2d 1277 (6th Cir. 1971). Compare *Kansas City Luggage Workers v. Neevel Luggage Mfg. Co.,* 325 F.2d 992 (8th Cir. 1964) (back-pay award vacated because issue of back pay was not specifically submitted to arbitrator) with *Minute Maid Co. v. Citrus Workers,* 331 F.2d 280 (5th Cir. 1964) (back-pay award held proper, although contract silent on the matter).

[29] 362 F.2d 677 (2d Cir. 1966).

These vacations should be contrasted with the overwhelming number of cases where courts have refused to vacate awards based on the claim that the arbitrator exceeded his jurisdiction.[30] Generally courts hold that since the arbitrator had the authority to interpret the agreement and had assumed jurisdiction, the construction of the scope of his authority should not be upset absent an express provision excluding the subject matter from arbitration or other forceful evidence that he lacked jurisdiction.[31] An illustration of the respect the court will give to the arbitrator's interpretation is *Local 77, American Federation of Musicians v. Philadelphia Orchestra Association.*[32] The arbitrator was asked "whether under the collective bargaining agreement the musicians may be required to fly."[33] The award, challenged by the union, held that the Philadelphia Orchestra Association could require orchestra members to travel by airplane during a scheduled South American tour. Although the collective bargaining agreement made no mention of intercontinental travel, the court refused to vacate the award, holding that it drew "its essence from the contract with respect to the submitted question." [34] Since there was nothing in the agreement concerning the matter in dispute it can be seen that of the two views expressed in *Enterprise* a court adopts one depending in large part upon the subjective views of the court about the issue.

---

[30] See, *e.g., Meat Cutters Local 641 v. Capitol Packing Co.,* 413 F.2d 668 (10th Cir. 1969); *San Francisco-Oakland Tribune Newspaper Guild v. Tribune Publishing Co.,* 407 F.2d 1327 (9th Cir. 1969); *Machinists District 8 v. Campbell Soup Co.,* 406 F.2d 1223 (7th Cir. 1969); *Honold Mfg. Co. v. Fletcher,* 405 F.2d 1123 (3d Cir. 1969); *Anaconda Co. v. Great Falls Mill & Smeltermen's Union,* 402 F.2d 749 (9th Cir. 1968); *Safeway Stores v. Confectionery Workers Local 111,* 390 F.2d 79 (5th Cir. 1968); *Pulp, Sulphite & Paper Mill Workers, Local 874 v. St. Regis Paper Co.,* 362 F.2d 711 (5th Cir. 1966); *Palacios v. Texaco Puerto Rico Inc.,* 305 F.Supp. 1076 (D.P.R. 1969); *Sheet Metal Contractors Ass'n v. Local 28, Sheet Metal Workers,* 301 F.Supp. 574 (S.D.N.Y. 1969); *Graham v. Acme Markets, Inc.,* 299 F.Supp. 1304 (E.D.Pa. 1969); *Federal Labor Union No. 18887 v. Midvale-Heppenstall Co.,* 298 F.Supp. 574 (E.D.Pa. 1969); *Mine Workers District 50 v. Tenn Clad Industries,* 297 F.Supp. 52 (E.D.Tenn. 1969); *Medo Photo Supply Corp. v. Livingston,* 274 F.Supp. 209 (S.D.N.Y. 1967); *Textile Workers v. Cone Mills Corp.,* 188 F.Supp. 728 (M.D.N.C. 1960); *Drivers Local 75 v. Verifine Dairy Products Corp.,* 70 LRRM 3323 (E.D.Wis. 1969).

[31] *Confectionery Workers v. National Biscuit Co.,* 252 F.Supp. 768 (D.N.J. 1966); *Communications Workers v. American Tel. & Tel. Co., Long Lines Dept.,* 76 LRRM 2208 (S.D.N.Y. 1970).

[32] 252 F.Supp. 787 (E.D.Pa. 1966).

[33] *Id.* at 792. Other cases in which courts held that the arbitrator did not exceed his authority are *Lynchburg Foundry Co. v. Steelworkers Local 2556,* 404 F.2d 259 (4th Cir. 1968) (the arbitrator did not exceed authority in ordering reinstatement of employee without back pay); *Safety Electrical Equipment Corp. v. IUE, Local 299,* 53 LC ¶ 11,306 (D. Conn. 1966) (the arbitrator did not exceed his authority in holding the company's long standing practice of requiring employees returning after accidents to sign waivers under the Workmen's Compensation Act to be a violation of the labor agreement).

[34] 252 F.Supp. at 792.

Just as the award must be related to the contract, the remedy granted by the arbitrator should also relate closely to the relief requested. However, in one case where the arbitrator granted pay for one day when the grievance requested pay for another, the award was not vacated:

"[I]t has never been required that grievances be submitted in language comparable to that used in formal court proceedings. . . .

"It has never been the proper function of courts in cases such as this to look over the shoulder of an arbitrator and relitigate in detail all or any of the issues properly submitted to him for his decision. . . ." [35]

On the other hand, where no request for pay was included in a submission and pay was ordered by the arbitrator, the award was vacated.[36] And, where the question submitted was "Was employee disciplined for just cause . . .?," a reinstatement without back pay established that there was cause for discipline and the award was vacated because the arbitrator's remedy went beyond the specific question submitted.[37]

(b) *The Award Must Not Exceed the Scope of the Question*

Where the parties have submitted a specific question to the arbitrator he must confine his award to an answer to that question. For example, in *UAW Local 1078 v. Anaconda American Brass Co.,*[38] the parties submitted to arbitration the question of whether the employer's "present operating practice" of having foremen perform certain production work violated the collective agreement. Instead of answering this question "yes" or "no," the arbitrator ruled that the agreement was not violated "so long as the work involved does not occupy the major portion of the foremen's time." The court vacated the award on the ground that the arbitrator went beyond his authority. Likewise, in *Sperry Division of the Sperry Rand Corp. v. Electrical Workers, IUE Local 445,*[39] an arbitration award, ruling that technical employees were not covered by a collective bargaining agreement but were governed by the terms of employment in the agreement, was modified to strike the ruling on terms of employment, since the only issue submitted for arbitration related to coverage.

---

[35] *American Bosch Arma Corp. v. IUE, Local 794,* 243 F.Supp. 493, 494 (N.D. Miss. 1965).

[36] *Kansas City Luggage & Novelty Workers Union, Local 66 v. Neevel Luggage Mfg. Co.,* 325 F.2d 992 (8th Cir. 1964). But see *American Bosch Arma Corp. v. IUE, Local 794,* 243 F.Supp. 493 (N.D. Miss. 1965), where *Neevel Luggage* was given a rather narrow reading by the court.

[37] *Polycast Corp. v. Local 8-102, Oil Chemical & Atomic Workers,* 27 Conn. Super. 334, 237 A.2d 563 (1965).

[38] 149 Conn. 687, 183 A.2d 623, 625 (1962).

[39] N.Y.S.Ct., 67 LC ¶ 52,731.

Still another court vacated an award of an arbitrator who reinstated an employee discharged for stealing four cans of crabmeat. The court held that the issue before the arbitrator was whether the employee was discharged for just cause, but that the arbitrator had involved himself with the justness of the penalty. The court felt that the arbitrator, by limiting his inquiry, had not decided the question submitted—whether there was just cause for the discharge.[40]

(3) Error in Law or Conflict With Federal Policy

At common law, the courts, with near uniformity, refused to set aside an arbitrator's award because of an error in law or fact. The following excerpt from a 1939 New York case is illustrative of the many decisions to this effect:

> "The courts are very much restricted in disturbing an award of an arbitrator. If he has kept within the jurisdiction of the agreement, the award will not be set aside because he may have erred in judgment either upon the law or the facts. . . . Where there was a fair and impartial hearing the arbitrator's determination as to law and facts is conclusive, and his award will not be set aside for mere errors of judgment if he is not guilty of fraud or other misconduct. . . ."[41]

In *Publishers Assn. of New York City v. New York Typographical Union No. 6*,[42] it was held that the judgment of an arbitrator within the submission is not to be impeached for misconception of the law, since errors, mistakes, and departures from strict legal rules are all included in the arbitration risk. However, it has been ruled that where an error of law appears on the face of an award, the award may be set aside.[43] Also, it has been implied that a motion for vacation might be appropriate if the face of an award indicates that the arbitrator

---

[40] *Amalgamated Food & Allied Workers Union Local 56 v. Great Atlantic and Pacific Tea Co.*, 415 F.2d 185 (3d Cir. 1969). See also *Paper Workers v. Allied Paper Co.*, 76 LRRM 2031 (S.D.Ala. 1970) (consideration of racial overtones where irrelevant to issue before arbitrator vacated award).

[41] *In re Pioneer Watch Case Co.*, 4 LRRM 810, 811 (N.Y. Sup. Ct. 1939). *Accord, Fischer v. Guaranteed Concrete Co.*, 276 Minn. 510, 151 N.W.2d 266 (1967); *District 2, Marine Engineers Beneficial Ass'n v. Isbrandtsen Co.*, 233 N.Y.S.2d 408, 38 Misc.2d 617 (Sup.Ct. 1962); *Harris v. R. C. Havenar*, 337 P.2d 832 (Cal.App.Ct. 1959); *Kesslen Bros. v. Board of Conciliation*, 339 Mass. 301 (1959); *Aster v. Jack Aloff Co.*, 155 A.2d 627 (Pa.Super. 1959).

[42] 5 N.Y.S.2d 847, 168 Misc. 267 (Sup.Ct. 1938); see also *Matter of Wilkins*, 169 N.Y. 494 (Sup.Ct. 1902); *Phillips v. American Gas Co. of Reading, Pa.*, 198 N.Y.S.2d 538 (Sup.Ct. 1960); *Delma Engrg. v. Johnson Contracting Co.*, 45 N.Y.S.2d 913 (Sup.Ct. 1944).

[43] *Drug Store Employees Union v. Heid & Yeomans*, 265 A.D. 870, 37 N.Y.S.2d 911 (Sup.Ct. 1942).

intends to follow a particular legal principle and then reaches a "patently erroneous conclusion" as to the effect of such a principle.[44]

But, as the Fifth Circuit emphasized in *Safeway Stores v. American Bakery & Confectionery Workers,*[45] "even if perhaps erroneous," the arbitrator's award should not be overturned. There, the court upheld an arbitrator's decision ordering the employer to pay employees for hours they did not work resulting from a change in the employer's payroll closing date. While holding "that if the reasoning [of an arbitrator] is so palpably faulty that no judge, or group of judges, could ever conceivably have made such a ruling, then the court can strike down the award,"[46] the court emphasized that short of such gross error the award would be enforced. The court held:

> "We emphasize again and again, as we have before, . . . that cases of the type pressed so heavily on us by the Employer must not be read to justify the court resuming its traditional role of assaying the judicial acceptability of the award had it been a court judgment.
>
> "As these admonitions are addressed primarily to ourselves as Judges on the trial and appellate fronts we should heed them by resisting the temptation to 'reason out' a la judges the arbiter's award to see if it passes muster. So it is here. But even under these self-imposed wraps this award shows on its face two things. First, the arbiter was drawing on the collective bargaining agreement as the source both of the dispute and its solution. Second, the award put forward a passably plausible— even if perhaps erroneous—analysis of the interplay of the contractual wage-minimum-day-week provisions, especially in the light of the Employer's long practice of wage payment to the very eve of payment day with no withholding of earned wages.
>
> "If such a result is unpalatable to an employer or his law-trained counsel who feels he had a hands-down certainty in a law court, it must be remembered that just such a likelihood is the by-product of a consensually adopted contract arrangement—a mechanism that can hold for, as well as against, the employer even to the point of outlawing labor's precious right to strike. . . .
>
> "The arbiter was chosen to be the Judge. That Judge has spoken. There it ends." [47]

The interplay between federal substantive law and arbitration has also been the subject of court review. As one court noted, arbitrators, as well as courts, must correctly apply federal substantive laws:

> "[I]t is true that Federal substantive law must be applied by the arbitrator and the State Courts in decisions involving contract violations

---

[44] *Terminal Auxiliar Maritima S.A. v. Winkler Credit Corp.,* 224 N.Y.S.2d 935 (Sup.Ct. 1962).
[45] 390 F.2d 79 (5th Cir. 1968).
[46] *Id.* at 82.
[47] *Id.* at 83.

between an employer and a labor organization representing employees in an industry affecting commerce [citing *Lincoln Mills*]. . . ." [48]

Thus, courts have grappled with numerous attacks on arbitration awards based on alleged conflicts with federal law. In one case, an award enjoining a work stoppage was upheld even though it was argued that it conflicted with the prohibitions of Norris-LaGuardia,[49] and in another case, an alleged conflict with I.C.C. regulations did not bar an award which the court found properly dealt with the statutory question.[50] In still another case, the claim that an award upholding the discharge of an employee was at odds with the Jones Act was rejected on the basis that the arbitrator's ruling was consistent with that legislation.[51]

Where conflicts with applicable law have occurred, however, courts have refused to enforce the arbitrator's award. For example, in *Glendale Mfg. Co. v. Local 520, ILGWU*,[52] the Fourth Circuit affirmed a refusal to enforce an award that would have required an employer to commit an unfair labor practice by bargaining with a union that had become decertified, and in *Puerto Rico District Council of Carpenters v. Ebanisteria Quintara*,[53] the court vacated part of an award on the ground that it required a violation of Section 302(c)(4) of the LMRA.[54]

---

[48] *Ryan Aeronautical Co. v. UAW Local 506*, 179 F.Supp. 1, 4-5 (S.D. Cal. 1959). Arbitrators Russell A. Smith and Dallas Jones concur in the view that courts should be able to review and correct an arbitrator's errors in the application of federal substantive law. They stated in Smith and Jones, *The Supreme Court and Labor Dispute Arbitration: The Emerging Federal Law*, 63 MICH. L. REV. 751, 806 (1965):

> "The basic question is whether the Court, in discharging its role of superintendence of the development of emerging federal law concerning the collective bargaining agreement, will determine for reasons of policy that arbitral as well as judicial decisions should be in conformity with principles approved by the Court. An affirmative view would place issues of this kind in a special category to be differentiated from other kinds of alleged errors of contract interpretation, fact, or law with respect to which the orthodox rule of non-reviewability would obtain."

See also Jav, *Arbitration and the Federal Common Law of Collective Bargaining Agreements*, 37 N.Y.U. L. REV. 448, 457-58, 468 (1962).

[49] *Pacific Maritime Ass'n v. Longshoremen and Warehousemen*, 307 F.Supp. 1315 (N.D.Cal. 1969).

[50] *Auto Sales & Service, Inc. v. Teamsters Local 270*, 311 F.Supp. 313 (E.D.La. 1970).

[51] *Maritime Union v. Federal Barge Lines*, 304 F.Supp. 256 (E.D.Mo. 1969).

[52] 283 F.2d 936 (4th Cir. 1960), *cert. denied*, 366 U.S. 950 (1961).

[53] 56 LRRM 2391 (D.P.R. 1964). To the contrary is a reasonably similar situation where an award directed the employer to pay contributions out of his total payroll (which included nonunion workers) to the union's health, welfare, and retirement funds, and it was enforced in spite of the employer's contention that the payment violated § 302(a) of the Taft-Hartley Act because nonunion members would receive no benefit from the funds. *Kreindler v. Clarise Sportswear Co.*, 184 F.Supp. 182 (S.D.N.Y. 1960). See also *Employees Ind. Union v. Wyman-Gordon Co.*, 314 F.Supp. 458 (N.D.Ill. 1970) (award requiring company to pay employees for processing grievances during working hours did not violate § 302).

[54] 29 USC § 186(c)(4) (1970).

A state court vacated an award which ordered the city to provide hospitalization insurance for policemen's families because the city ordered by the arbitrator to provide such insurance was not within the class of cities which were permitted by the legislature to provide such insurance. In other words, the award was a mandate to the city to do what it could not legally do.[55]

If a court can vacate or refuse enforcement for an error in law, can it vacate or refuse enforcement because the award is against public policy?[56] The Second Circuit said yes:

> "It is no less true in suits brought under Section 301 to enforce arbitration awards than in other lawsuits that the 'power of the federal courts to enforce the terms of private agreements is at all times exercised subject to the restrictions and limitations of the public policy of the United States.' . . ."[57]

And so did the Supreme Court in *Black v. Cutter Laboratories*[58] when it upheld the vacation of an award directing reinstatement of an employee discharged because he was a member of the Communist party on the ground that the award violated public policy.

(4) Error in Fact

Claims that awards should be vacated because the arbitrators did not base their awards on all the evidence have been made, but an assertion that there is newly discovered pertinent evidence usually is not sufficient to vacate an award unless it involves fraud by the arbitrator. A court, in affirming the confirmation of the award, held that the new evidence that the dischargee converted property did not alter the fact that at the time of the arbitration the discharge was not supported by evidence. The court said:

> "We only hold that the parties, having agreed to an arbitration of their differences, are bound by the arbitration award made upon the testimony before the arbitrator."[59]

Consistent with this view, the First Circuit ruled that a federal district court cannot overturn an arbitrator's award on the ground that the arbitrator improperly evaluated the evidence because, under an agreement to arbitrate, arbitrators "have 'jurisdiction' to decide erroneously."[60] Similarly, the Fifth Circuit in *Safeway Stores v. Local*

---

[55] *In re City of Washington,* 259 A.2d 437 (Pa.Sup.Ct. 1969).
[56] See generally Meiners, *Arbitration Awards and "Public Policy,"* 17 Arb. J. 145 (1962); Symposium, *Arbitration and the Courts,* Nw. U.L. Rev. 466, 545 (1963).
[57] *IUE Local 453 v. Otis Elevator Co.,* 314 F.2d 25, 29 (2d Cir.), *cert. denied,* 373 U.S. 949 (1963).
[58] 351 U.S. 2929 (1956).
[59] *Bridgeport Rolling Mills Co. v. Brown,* 314 F.2d 885 (2d Cir. 1963).
[60] *Trailways of New England, Inc. v. Motor Coach Employees,* 353 F.2d 180, 182 (1st Cir. 1965).

111, Bakery Workers[61] held that an arbitrator's decision, ". . . even if perhaps erroneous . . ." should be enforced even though the reviewing court would have arrived at a different decision.[62] However, the court did say, "We may assume, without here deciding, that if the reasoning is so palpably faulty that no judge, or group of judges, could ever conceivably have made such a ruling then the Court can strike down the award. . . ."[63]

(5) Fraud and Corruption

Courts make every legitimate presumption that favors the validity of the award, because they uniformly make the assumption that the award was made honestly and without fraud.[64] However when there is evidence of fraud on the part of the arbitrator, courts have consistently vacated awards. There is basis for this at common law,[65] in the statutory law of a number of states,[66] and in the United States Arbitration Act.[67] For example, the New York statute provides:

"The award shall be vacated on the application of either party who either participated in the arbitration or was served with a notice of intention to arbitrate. If the court finds that the rights of the party were prejudiced by:
"(1) Corruption, fraud or misconduct in procuring the award; or
"(2) Partiality by an arbitrator appointed as a neutral, except where the award was by confession." [68]

---

[61] 390 F.2d 79 (5th Cir. 1968).

[62] *Id.* at 82. See also *Ludwig Honold Mfg. Co. v. Fletcher*, 405 F.2d 1123 (3d Cir. 1969).

[63] 390 F.2d at 82. *Cf. Marble Products Co. of Ga. v. Local 155, United Stone Workers*, 335 F.2d 468 (5th Cir. 1964) (award vacated where arbitrator's reading of the contract was "so unreasonable as to be arbitrary or capricious"); *Firestone Tire & Rubber Co. v. Rubber Workers, Local 100*, 168 Cal. App.2d 444, 335 P.2d 990 (1959).

[64] See generally Note, *Arbitration Awards Vacated for Disqualification of an Arbitrator*, 9 Syracuse L. Rev. 56, 57-58 (1957). But see Hays, *The Future of Labor Arbitration*, 74 Yale L.J. 1019 (1965).

[65] *Withington v. Warren*, 51 Mass. 431 (1845).

[66] Statutory provisions of the following states specify fraud or corruption in procuring the award as grounds for vacating the award: Cal. Civ. Pro. Code § 1286.2 (Supp. 1970); Colo. Rev. Stat. Ann. ch. 18 Rule 109(g) (Supp. 1970); Conn. Gen. Stat. Ann. § 52-418 (1968); Fla. Stat. Ann. § 682.13 (Supp. 1969); Ga. Code Ann. § 7-111 (1936); Idaho Code Ann. § 7-907 (1948); Ill. Ann. Stat. ch. 10 § 112 (1969); Ind. Ann. Stat. § 3-216 (1968); Iowa Code Ann. § 679.12 (1950); Kan. Stat. Ann. § 5-211 (1964); Me. Rev. Stat. Ann. tit. 14 § 5938 (Supp. 1970); Mass. Gen. Laws Ann. ch. 150C § 11 (1965); Minn. Stat. Ann. § 572.19 (Supp. 1970); Miss. Code Ann. § 290 (1957); Mo. Ann. Stat. § 435.100 (1952); Mont. Rev. Codes Ann. § 93-201-7 (1964); Nev. Rev. Stat. § 38.145 (1967); N.H. Rev. Stat. Ann. § 542-8 (1955); N.J. Stat. Ann. § 2A:24-8 (1952); N.Y. Civ. Prac. Law § 7511 (1963); N.C. Gen. Stat. § 1-559 (1953); N.D. Cent. Code § 32-29-08 (1960); Pa. Stat. Ann. tit. 5 § 170 (1963); R.I. Gen. Laws Ann. § 28-9-18 (1969); Utah Code Ann. § 78-31-16 (1953); Va. Code Ann. § 8-506 (1957); W.Va. Code Ann. § 55-10-4 (1966); Wis. Stat. Ann. § 298-10 (1958); Wyo. Stat. Ann. § 1-1048.14 (Supp. 1969).

[67] 9 USC § 10 (1970).

[68] N.Y. Civ. Prac. Law § 7511.

Courts have rightly assumed these provisions are compatible with the federal law under Section 301 and have not been troubled by the fact that the fraud is asserted as a violation of a state statute or the U.S. Arbitration Act, rather than as a violation of the federal labor law being developed under Section 301.

(6) Inconsistency of Award With a Decision of the National Labor Relations Board

Closely related to refusals of courts to enforce awards or to vacate them because of their inconsistency with law or public policy is the refusal by courts to enforce the award because it is inconsistent with a determination by the National Labor Relations Board. This was well demonstrated in *New Orleans Typographical Union No. 17 v. NLBR*.[69] There, the Board had assigned certain disputed work to one of two contesting unions, whereas the arbitrator's award had assigned the disputed work to the other union. The arbitration award was rendered after the International Typographical Union filed a suit to compel arbitration of the work jurisdiction dispute under Section 301 and arbitration was ordered, even though proceedings under Section 10(k) were then pending, but no hearing had been held. The Board's ultimate determination was contrary to the arbitrator's and took precedence over the arbitrator's award under the rule announced in *Carey v. Westinghouse Electric Corp.*[70] There the Supreme Court held that "should the Board disagree with the arbiter, . . . the Board's ruling would, of course, take precedence." [71] Following this mandate, the Fifth Circuit refused to enforce the arbitration award as it was contrary to the Board's Section 10(k) ruling on the work jurisdiction issue.[72]

In *Meyers v. Kinney Motors*,[73] the court refused to enforce an arbitration award requiring the Pleasantville plant employees to be covered by the labor agreement the Amalgamated Union had negotiated on behalf of the Brooklyn plant employees on the ground that the Pleasantville plant was an accretion of the Brooklyn plant. The National Labor Relations Board, however, following the filing of a petition by the United Automobile Workers, found that union to be the

---

[69] 368 F.2d 755 (5th Cir. 1966). *Accord Dock Loaders v. W. L. Richeson & Sons*, 280 F.Supp. 402 (E.D.La. 1968).

[70] 375 U.S. 261 (1964).

[71] *Id.* at 272. An example of a refusal of the NLRB to defer to an award is *Rider Technical Institute*, 199 NLRB No. 85, 81 LRRM 1296 (1972).

[72] 368 F.2d 755 (5th Cir. 1966).

[73] 32 App. Div.2d 266 (N.Y. App. Ct. 1969). See also *Int'l Bhd. of Firemen and Oilers v. Int'l Ass'n of Machinists*, 338 F.2d 176 (5th Cir. 1964) where an award directing a union to desist from efforts to represent maintenance workers was enforced because language of an NLRB order certifying another union was clear enough to justify inclusion of maintenance workers in that other union's unit.

representative of the employees at Pleasantville, and for this reason the award extending the agreement of the Amalgamated was not enforced by the court.[74]

(7) Lateness of the Award

A large proportion of collective bargaining agreements contain clauses establishing a time limitation for the rendition of an award by the arbitrator after final submission of a case by the parties.[75] The purpose of these provisions is generally to cause awards to be rendered promptly. Where a collective bargaining agreement provides a time limit for the rendition of an arbitration award, an award handed down after that time constitutes a violation of the agreement, regardless of what the consequences of this violation may be.[76] A suit by an employer or a union to determine the effect of such a violation is a suit "for violation" of a collective bargaining agreement and within the literal language of Section 301, even though the violation may have been committed by the arbitrator.

At common law, an award rendered after the expiration of such time limit was generally considered void.[77] There are, however, a substantial number of decisions taking a contrary view.[78] Furthermore, some decisions have made a distinction between labor arbitration and commercial arbitration cases, holding that in the former a late award is not necessarily void.[79]

Arbitrator Milton H. Schmidt considered the validity of a prior award claimed by the union to be ineffective because it was rendered after excessive delay. He said:

---

[74] See also *Central General Hospital v. Local 1155, Nursing Home Union,* 74 LRRM 2808 (N.Y.Sup.Ct. 1970) (previously enforced arbitration award vacated following NLRB's unit clarification decision).

[75] See related discussion, Chapter XVI Section B., page 334. Sometimes a time limit rule is adopted by the parties where they adopt the rules to govern an arbitration. Rule 37 of the Voluntary Labor Arbitration Rules of the American Arbitration Association provides:
"The award shall be made promptly by the arbitrator and, unless otherwise agreed by the parties, or specified by the law, not later than thirty days from the date of closing the hearings, or if oral hearings have been waived, then from the date of transmitting the final statements and proofs to the arbitrator."

[76] See generally Givens, *The Validity of Delayed Awards Under Section 301 Taft Hartley Act,* 16 ARB. J. 161 (1961).

[77] See Annot., 154 A.L.R. 1392 (1945); Morse, ARBITRATION AND AWARD 223 (1872); Sturges, COMMERCIAL ARBITRATION AND AWARDS § 83 (1930); 6 Williston, CONTRACTS § 1929 (1938); *Georke Kirch Co. v. Georke Kirch Holding Co.,* 118 N.J. Eq. 1, 176 A. 902 (1935); *General Metals Corp. v. Precision Lodge 1600,* 183 Cal. App.2d 586, 6 CAL. RPTR. 910 (1960).

[78] See *Hegeberg v. New England Fish Co.,* 7 Wash.2d 509, 110 P.2d 182 (1941); *Damon v. Berger,* 191 Pa.Super. 165, 155 A.2d 388 (1959); *Rosenthal v. Tannhauser,* 279 App. Div. 902, 111 N.Y.S.2d 221, aff'd 304 N.Y. 812, 109 N.E.2d 470 (1952); cf. Note, *Procedural Requirements of a Grievance Arbitration Clause: Another Question of Arbitrability,* 70 YALE L.J. 611 (1961).

[79] *Teamsters v. Shapiro,* 138 Conn. 57, 82 A.2d 345, 350 (1951); *Danbury Rubber Co. v. Local 402,* 145 Conn. 53, 138 A.2d 783 (1958); *Local 63 v. Cheney Bros.,* 18 Conn. Supp. 230 (1953).

"The next question is whether the lateness of the award destroyed its validity. My answer to that question is 'no.' . . .

" . . .

"It seems to me a fair guess that had the award been more favorable to the union no attempt would have been made to nullify it—at least no attempt by the union. I cannot speculate what the company might have done in those circumstances. In my view it would be unfair and unreasonable to construe this Agreement to mean that the union (or for that matter, the company) could first look into the package, after asking that it be forwarded, and then decide that since it did not like the looks of the contents, the arbitrator was exceeding his authority when he sent it on. Such a privilege would be tantamount to seeing whether you are dealt a good hand before announcing that the deal is out of turn.

" . . .

"The principles of waiver which I have held to apply here are embodied in the proposed Uniform Arbitration Law drafted and recommended by the National Conference of Commissioners on Uniform Laws (Section 8(b)), 9 U.L.A. pp. 76, 81 (1957), as well as in the proposed United States Arbitration Act adopted by the National Academy of Arbitrators in 1959 (Section 9(B)), 34 L.A. 942, 946." [80]

Schmidt's view appears to be in the mainstream of opinion on this subject which holds that a delayed award should not be considered void. The arbitrator's continued exercise of jurisdiction may be challenged prior to the rendition of the award.[81]

In *IAM v. Geometric Tool Co.,*[82] the fact that the award was not rendered within the mandatory 60 days after the hearing required by the state statute was held by the Second Circuit not to justify its vacation. However, in so holding the court did describe when a vacation would be justified because the award was rendered late. The court said:

"In adopting a uniform federal standard, we ought not to accept an arbitration rule which encourages post-award technical objections by a losing party as a means of avoiding an adverse arbitration decision. . . . Rather, we believe it to be a better rule that any limitation upon the time in which an arbitrator can render his award be a directory limitation, not a mandatory one, and that it should always be within a court's discretion to uphold a late award if no objection to the delay

---

[80] *Bendix-Westinghouse Automotive Air Brake Co.,* 36 L.A. 724, 729-31 (Schmidt, 1961); see also *Modernage Furniture Corp.,* 4 L.A. 314, 315 (Feinberg, 1946).

[81] See *dicta* in *IAM Lodge 725 v. Mooney Aircraft,* 410 F.2d 681 (5th Cir. 1969); *IAM District Lodge 71 v. Bendix Corp., Kansas City Div.,* 218 F.Supp. 742 (W.D.Mo. 1963); *Nathan v. Jewish Center of Danbury,* 20 Conn. Supp. 183, 129 A.2d 514 (1955); *Campbell v. Automatic Dye & Products Co.,* 162 Ohio St. 321, 123 N.E.2d 401, 405 (1954); *Application of Bldg. Service Employees Int'l Union,* 60 N.Y.S.2d 811 (Sup.Ct. 1946); In the *Matter of Arbitration Between Famous Realty and William Savage, Inc.,* 283 App. Div. 957, 130 N.Y.S.2d 281 (1934); *Parks v. Cleveland Ry.,* 124 Ohio St. 79, 177 N.E. 28, 29 (1931); *Fudickar v. Guardian Mutual Life Ins. Co.,* 62 N.Y. 392, 405 (1875).

[82] 406 F.2d 284 (2d Cir. 1968).

has been made prior to the rendition of the award or there is no showing that actual harm to the losing party was caused by the delay.

"In arriving at this standard we are merely restating the rule that has been promulgated in the vast majority of statutes and cases. . . ." [83]

(8) Vacation for Procedural Errors

Somewhat related to those cases where the vacation occurs because of misconduct by the arbitrator are those cases where the award was rendered against a nonparty,[84] or those cases where the appointment of the arbitrator or arbitrators who rendered the award was not in accordance with the procedure in the agreement. For example, under an arbitration clause providing for the appointment of two arbitrators by each party and for the four so appointed to select a fifth, an award rendered by one arbitrator assigned by the Illinois State Department of Labor was vacated because the award was not rendered by a five-member arbitration board.[85]

Courts will usually hold, however, that there has been a waiver of such defects if objection to the award on such a ground is made after the award is received.[86] Furthermore, courts will look to substance when an improper tribunal is asserted. For example, the Supreme Court enforced an award of a joint area cartage committee even though the word "arbitration" did not appear in the collective bargaining agreement. The Court said: "If the award at bar is the parties' chosen instrument for the definitive settlement of disputes under the agreement, it is enforceable under § 301."[87]

Courts hold that most procedural claims raised before the arbitrator are not subject to relitigation in the court. For example, one court said: "It is not the function of the courts to review the board's decision," and a judgment denying the employer's motion to vacate the award was therefore affirmed.[88]

(9) Lack of Fair Representation

Where employees claim an award was issued affecting them and assert and show facts to establish that the union did not fairly represent them, the court has the power to issue an injunction against

---

[83] *Id.* at 286. Accord, *Teamsters Local 560 v. Anchor Motor Freight, Inc.,* 415 F.2d 220 (3d Cir. 1969).

[84] *Livingston v. Cheney-Frantex, Longfordweavers, Inc.,* 14 App. Div.2d 518, 216 N.Y.S.2d 1011 (1961).

[85] *Local 227, Hod Carriers v. Sullivan,* 221 F.Supp. 696 (E.D.Ill. 1963).

[86] *National Cash Register Co. v. Wilson,* 8 N.Y.2d 377, 208 N.Y.S.2d 951, 171 N.E.2d 302 (1960); but see *Consolidated Carting Corp. v. Local No. 282,* 280 N.Y.S.2d 872 (Sup.Ct. 1961) and *Hellman v. Wolbron,* 298 N.Y.S.2d 540 (Sup.Ct. 1969).

[87] *Teamsters Local 89 v. Riss & Co.,* 372 U.S. 517 (1963).

[88] *Avco Corp. Electronics & Ordnance Div. v. Mitchell,* 336 F.2d 289 (6th Cir. 1964).

enforcement of the award which has the effect of vacating it.[89] Unless there is an assertion and proof of unfair representation, individual employees have no standing to challenge an award or ask for its enforcement.[90] Furthermore, if the employee proves in an action against the union and the company that the union did not fairly represent him in an arbitration of his discharge, courts have refused to vacate the award, holding that the employee's remedy is against the union and limited to damages.[91] However, the court will examine into whether the employee made a reasonable effort to protect himself, for if he did not, his objection, based on unfairness in the representation, will be waived. For example, in *Fischer v. Guaranteed Concrete Co.,*[92] an injunction was asked for on the ground that the union breached its duty of fair representation by failing to notify employees prior to an arbitration hearing of its intended neutral position regarding integration of seniority lists of employees of the selling and acquiring companies. At least two employees were present at the hearing, and neither sought a continuance to obtain further representation nor presented additional information during or subsequent to the hearing. Citing *Humphrey v. Moore,*[93] for the proposition that a "union does not breach its duty of fair representation when it does not remain partisan to one single group," the Minnesota Supreme Court stated that "[U]nder the circumstances . . . *Humphrey* requires us to reject plaintiff's argument that they were deprived of their right of fair representation."

Similarly, where individual employees brought an action three years after an award was rendered to set it aside because of the union's alleged failure to represent them properly in not attempting to vacate the award, the court affirmed dismissal of the case, holding that the 100-day state statute of limitations applies to the individual affected by an award as well as to the parties to the arbitration.[94]

A Ninth Circuit grappled with what appeared to be an "agreed" award and found sufficient evidence of an agreed "swap" plus hostility to the grievant to vacate an award. In *Local 13, ILWU v. Pacific*

---

[89] *Davenport v. Kaiser Aluminum & Chemical Corp.,* 206 So.2d 526 (La.App.Ct. 1968). See also *Local 13, ILWU v. Pacific Maritime Ass'n,* 441 F.2d 1061 (9th Cir. 1971).

[90] 206 So.2d 526.

[91] *Hill v. Aro Corp.,* 275 F.Supp. 482 (N.D. Ohio 1967); *Guille v. Mushroom Transportation Co.,* 425 Pa. 607, 229 A.2d 903 (1967); *Afflito v. Estee Frocks, Inc.,* 33 Misc.2d 1066, 226 N.Y.S.2d 854 (1962); *Lorenz-Schneider Co. v. Teamsters Local 802,* 14 App. Div.2d 923, 222 N.Y.S.2d 18 (1961), aff'd, 12 N.Y.2d 186 N.E.2d 191 (1962); *Soto v. Lenscraft Optical Corp.,* 7 N.Y.2d 397, 198 N.Y.S.2d 282 (1960); but cf. *Vaca v. Sipes,* 386 U.S. 171 (1967).

[92] 151 N.W.2d 266 (Minn. Sup.Ct. 1967).

[93] 375 U.S. 335 (1964).

[94] *Archuleta v. IAM,* 68 CAL. RPTR. 694, 262 Cal. App.2d 202 (1968).

Maritime Ass'n,[95] the Ninth Circuit reversed the district court that had refused to set aside an arbitration award which "deregistered" a member of the union, leaving him without an opportunity to obtain longshoreman's work. The award was based on a grievance filed against the member by the Pacific Maritime Association because of his involvement with work stoppages that had occurred while he was an officer of the union. The deregistered member claimed that the arbitrator had erroneously relied upon a section of the labor agreement which did not apply to union officers. The court rejected this argument saying that when an arbitrator erroneously construes a contract, a court has no power to vacate the award. What caused the court of appeals to vacate the award was the evidence of breach of the union's duty of fair representation found in the fact that the arbitrator, on the same day, issued an inconsistent award suggesting that a "swap" took place plus evidence that the "swap" was activated by hostility toward the deregistered member. It appears that it was this combination which justified the vacation and not the mere fact that a "swap" (an agreed award) took place.

B. COURT REMANDS TO THE ARBITRATOR TO CLARIFY OR CORRECT AWARD

Often a party seeking judicial review of an arbitrator's award will allege that the award is ambiguous or indefinite and request the court to interpret or correct the award. In light of the philosophy of deferring to the arbitrator's award expressed in the *Steelworkers Trilogy*,[96] however, the courts have been reluctant to do so. Where the court holds that the award cannot be enforced because of its ambiguity, the court will generally remand the matter to the arbitrator for clarification. For example, in *Hanford Atomic Metal Trades Council v. General Electric Co.*,[97] the court, in remanding an ambiguous award to the arbitrator for clarification, stated:

> "The award must be read in the context of the opinion and the findings of the board of arbitration. We share the view of the district court that the opinion required clarification and interpretation. We also share the view of the district court that this was a task to be first performed by the arbitration committee and not the court, and that the court properly remanded the matter to the arbitration committee for such clarification and interpretation. See *United Steelworkers of America v.*

---

[95] 441 F.2d 1061 (9th Cir. 1971).
[96] *United Steelworkers of America v. American Mfg. Co.*, 363 U.S. 564 (1960); *United Steelworkers of America v. Warrior & Gulf Navigation Co.*, 363 U.S. 574 (1960); *Steelworkers of America v. Enterprise Wheel & Car Corp.*, 363 U.S. 593 (1960).
[97] 353 F.2d 302 (9th Cir. 1965).

American Manufacturing Co., 363 U.S. 564 (1960). It is appellant's position that once the arbitrators have acted, it is the duty of the court to interpret and enforce the award, rather than to send the matter back to the arbitrators, to the end that the further delay involved in sending the matter back can be avoided. We think, however, that all of the foregoing cases accept the philosophy that where the parties have elected to submit their disputes to arbitration, they should be completely resolved by arbitration, rather than only partially resolved. In some cases the carrying out of this philosophy will require remanding the matter to the arbitrators, and we think that this is such a case." [98]

Courts have directed a hearing *de novo* before the *same* arbitrator where the award covered matters beyond submission,[99] *e.g.,* back pay was ordered beyond the expiration date of the agreement,[100] or the meaning of the award was unclear.[101] Courts have directed also a hearing before a *new* arbitrator where proffered evidence was found by the court to be so relevant that its exclusion by the arbitrator denied a fair hearing.[102]

C. ENFORCEMENT OF A COURT'S ENFORCEMENT OF AN AWARD

Thus far, relatively few decisions have arisen involving civil or criminal contempt in connection with the enforcement of an arbitration award. In one case, the Third Circuit in *Philadelphia Marine Trade v. ILA, Local 1291,*[103] affirmed a district court decree imposing a fine of $100,000 per day upon a union for civil contempt of an order enforcing the arbitrator's award. While there are many procedural aspects of contempt proceedings that have not been finally resolved, it would nevertheless appear to be clear that both state and federal courts have authority under Section 301 to find a party in contempt for failure to abide by an arbitration award enforced by the court.

---

[98] *Id.* at 307-08. Accord, *IBEW Local 494 v. Brewery Proprietors,* 289 F.Supp. 865 (E.D.Wis. 1968) (award remanded to board of arbitration for clarification and correction of arithmetic errors); *Todd Shipyards Corp. v. Marine & Shipbuilding Workers, Local 15,* 242 F.Supp. 606 (D.N.J. 1965) (award remanded to arbitrator where there was reasonable ground for disagreement as to what was actually decided); *IAM Winnebago Lodge 1947 v. Kiekhaefer Corp.,* 215 F.Supp. 611 (E.D. Wis. 1963) (award remanded to the arbitrator because the formula for computing vacation payments under certain circumstances was not included).

[99] *Kollsman Instrument Corp. v. Machinists,* 24 App. Div.2d 865, 264 N.Y.S.2d 354 (1965).

[100] *Burt Bldg. Materials Corp. v. Teamsters,* 24 App. Div.2d 897, 264 N.Y.S.2d 993 (1965).

[101] *Kennedy v. Continental Transportation Lines, Inc.,* 230 F.Supp. 760 (W.D.Pa. 1964); *Transport Workers Union of Philadelphia, Local 234 v. Philadelphia Transportation Co.,* 228 F.Supp. 423 (E.D.Pa. 1964).

[102] *Smaglio v. Fireman's Fund Ins. Co.,* 432 Pa. 133, 247 A.2d 577 (1968).

[103] 368 F.2d 932 (3d Cir. 1966), *rev'd on other grounds,* 389 U.S. 64 (1967).

A circuit court held that a district court may grant relief to railroad employees for injuries resulting from a misapplication of an arbitral award. In prior proceedings the district court had enjoined the union from striking as a protest against the misapplication, but allowed the union to seek redress for the misapplication in a subsequent action. The court said that the regular grievance procedure need not be followed when a misapplication of an award is involved because "[e]xhaustion under such circumstances would be a long circuit bypassing the practical and the just."[104]

D. RECOVERY OF ATTORNEYS' FEES AND COSTS IN ENFORCEMENT OR VACATION SUITS

Whether the prevailing party in a suit to confirm or vacate an arbitration award is entitled to attorneys' fees and costs has not yet been definitely settled.[105] In *Lee Co. v. New Haven Printing Pressmen*,[106] attorneys' fees claimed under a provision of a state statute providing for payment of such fees were denied with this statement:

> "[I]t would appear particularly inappropriate, absent specific Congressional authority, for this Court to graft on to the federal remedy a *part* of a state statute to provide attorneys' fees, . . . and to that extent undermining the Act's basic objective of a uniform national labor policy."

Another court held that a union could not recover attorneys' fees against a company which refused to abide by the award where there was sufficient doubt concerning the law to justify the litigation. The court, however, clearly said it had authority to award attorneys' fees to the union and would have if the company's "refusal to abide by the arbitrator's award was arbitrary and without any meritorious basis."[107]

The Fifth Circuit adopts the same view. It said the district court did not abuse its discretion in awarding the union's costs and attor-

---

104 *Southern Pacific Co. v. Bhd. of Locomotive Firemen & Enginemen*, 393 F.2d 345 (D.C.Cir. 1967), *cert. denied* 391 U.S. 913 (1968).

105 In several cases seeking to compel arbitration under Section 301 (as opposed to suits to confirm or vacate an award), the courts have refused the union's request for attorneys' fees where there was nothing to indicate that the employer acted in bad faith in refusing to submit the grievance in question to arbitration. This line of cases would seem to hold implicitly that a request for attorneys' fees may be appropriate if it were found that the employer acted in bad faith. See, *e.g., Office & Professional Employees, Local 105 v. Sheet Metal Workers, Local 249*, 56 LRRM 2529 (E.D.Ark. 1964); *Pulp, Sulphite & Paper Mill Workers, Local 899 v. Hurley & Co.*, 50 LRRM 2652 (W.D.Ark. 1962); *cf. Fruit & Vegetable Packers Local 760 v. NLRB*, 316 F.2d 389 (D.C.Cir. 1963).

106 255 F.Supp. 929, 930 (D.Conn. 1966). Accord, *United Cement, Lime & Gypsum Workers v. Penn-Dixie Cement Corp.*, 216 F.Supp. 667 (E.D.Pa. 1963); *Dallas Typographical Union v. A. H. Belo Corp.*, 372 F.2d 577 (5th Cir. 1967).

107 *UAW Local 149 v. American Brake Shoe Co.*, 298 F.2d 212 (4th Cir. 1962); see also *Local 205 IUE v. General Electric Co.*, 172 F.Supp. 960 (D.Mass. 1959).

neys' fees in light of the employer's unjustified refusal to abide by an arbitrator's award.[108] The arbitration award had ordered reinstatement of a discharged employee and was enforced by the district court, notwithstanding some ambiguity in the arbitrator's decision.

---

[108] *Mine Workers District 50 v. Bowman Transportation, Inc.*, 421 F.2d 934 (5th Cir. 1970). In *United Steelworkers of America v. Butler Mfg. Co.*, 439 F.2d 1110 (8th Cir. 1971), the union was granted attorneys' fees in a suit to recover insurance premiums paid by the union as damages, largely on the basis of a finding that the company's defenses were in bad faith.

CHAPTER XVIII

Special Arbitration Procedures

The previous chapters have dealt with the labor arbitration practice and procedure as it has been shaped by courts and arbitrators during the last 35 years. As has been shown, notions of "due process" must be incorporated into the procedure if the arbitration award is to be sustainable by a court, or if the award is to be deferred to by the National Labor Relations Board.[1] Loosely described, "due process" means that evidence is presented to the arbitrator through witnesses with the opposing party having the right to cross-examine or in agreed to stipulations of facts and with the determination of the arbitrator based upon the evidence contained in the record.

Despite the courts' insistence that labor arbitration hearings conform to "due process" standards, there are certain "labor arbitrations" which do not fit into this mold and no discussion of arbitration practice and procedure would be complete without at least a brief discussion of these different and, hence, special, types of arbitration procedures.

The United Steelworkers union and the basic steel companies agreed in 1971 to experiment with an expedited arbitration procedure to resolve grievance disputes which "do not involve novel problems and which have limited contractual significance and complexity."[2] Under this procedure, there is a hearing and, hence, this experimental expedited procedure still has the elements of due process insisted upon by the courts and the National Labor Relations Board and, therefore, is not an example of the types of arbitration procedure to which attention is being given in this chapter.

Special labor arbitration procedures have most often been developed to resolve disputes over incentive standards and medical questions. Basically, they provide that a neutral industrial engineer, doctor, or clinic, investigate the facts in dispute and then determine the

---

[1] *Spielberg Mfg. Co.,* 112 NLRB 1080 (1955). See also *Collyer Insulated Wire,* 192 NLRB No. 150 (1971).

[2] Appendix 15 to labor agreement between *United Steelworkers of America and United States Steel Corp.*

ultimate question *de novo*. The arbitrators obtain the facts, not at a hearing, but privately and only a minimal factual record of their private investigation is made.[3] Such a procedure, using a clinic to resolve disputes over medical facts is as follows:

"If an employee returns after a sick leave or layoff of thirty days or more, or from any absence due to an occupational injury or occupational illness, or from any absence during which he has been hospitalized, he may be required to take a physical examination by the company's doctor. . . .

". . . [A]ny claim that the company has improperly concluded that reinstatement of the employee in active employment in his regular job classification causes an abnormal health risk . . . shall be resolved . . . by an examination at the diagnostic clinic of the . . . University Hospital.

"If the employee is sent to such . . . clinic, a jointly agreed upon detailed description of the work in the classification or classifications that the employee would perform if he was returned shall be submitted to such doctor or clinic as a basis for a determination of whether the company's action in returning the employee or refusing to return the employee was reasonable. The company doctor and the employee's doctor may submit a statement and copies of medical records or findings to such doctor or such clinic. The costs of such medical examination by such doctor or such clinic shall be paid by the company.

"The findings of such doctor or clinic shall be binding on the company, the union and the employee involved. . . ."

Another example, where the independent diagnostic skill of the neutral doctor is made final, is the following:

"If the two examining physicians disagree concerning whether the employee or pensioner is permanently incapacitated, the question shall be submitted to a third physician selected by such two physicians. The medical opinion of the third physician, after examination of the employee or pensioner and consultation with the two physicians, shall decide such question, and such decision shall be binding upon all interested parties. The fees and expenses of the third physician shall be shared equally by the employer and the local union representing the employee or pensioner."

Some procedures used to resolve industrial engineering disputes actually mix the normal type of arbitration procedure and special fact-finding procedures. Under such procedures, an arbitrator is sometimes permitted to retain an industrial engineer or doctor, not asso-

---

3 Simkin, *The Arbitration of Technical Disputes*, NEW YORK UNIVERSITY SIXTH ANNUAL CONFERENCE ON LABOR 181 (1953). See also Lohoczky, *Industrial Engineering and Collective Bargaining*, 17 LAB. L.J. 393 (1966); Presgrave, *Grievance Arbitration and the Industrial Engineer*, 18 J. OF IND. ENGR. 605 (1967); Sherman, *Arbitrator's Analysis of Job Evaluation Disputes*, 43 PERSONNEL J. 365 (1964); Werner, *Industrial Engineers, Incentive Systems, and the Contract*, 11 J. OF IND. ENGR. 231 (1960).

ciated with either party, to act as his technical assistant, adviser,[4] or fact-finder.[5]

For example, Arbitrator Murray M. Rohman, in an interim award, directed that the grievant, who had had a back operation, be examined by an orthopedic physician to resolve conflicting medical evidence concerning the risk to the grievant if he performed certain work. Thus this arbitrator obtained the aid of a special medical "adviser" or "fact-finder" by his own order in an interim award.[6]

Sometimes an arbitrator will ask an industrial engineer to make an independent measurement of the time required to perform the operation and then, by a subjective judgment, "level" the "measured time" and report an "allowed time" to the arbitrator.

Where such a procedure is used in a situation where the dispute is over the leveling of "measured time" by the company's industrial engineer and the arbitrator's industrial engineer or his fact-finder uses a different method to measure the performance time or to level it, a different allowed time will usually result. This procedure merely substitutes a judgment determination of the arbitrator's industrial engineer for that of the company's industrial engineer. A variation in the allowed time determinations merely proves that such determinations may differ and does not prove that the incentive standard as originally established was arbitrarily or capriciously established, which is the standard usually applied before a management decision is upset.[7]

When the time required to perform the manual elements of an operation is determined by totaling predetermined times for each motion used by the employee performing the operation, the dispute is much easier to resolve than when judgment lending is used. Well-known procedures for determining the "allow time" by totaling predetermined times are Methods Times Measurement and Work Factor. When these procedures are used, no stop watch need be used because the pace at which the employee performs the motions is of no consequence. Hence, no subjective judgment concerning the work pace of the employee being observed need be made. Therefore, when predetermined time techniques are used, the more normal arbitration procedure can be employed to resolve the dispute. The manner in which the "allow time" was computed can be reanalyzed by the arbitrator by a reanalysis of the motions and totaling the predetermined

---

[4] Gomberg, *Arbitration of Disputes Involving Incentive Problems: A Labor View,* CRITICAL ISSUES IN LABOR ARBITRATION 85 (1957); Unterberger, *Technicians as Arbitrators of Wage Disputes,* 4 LAB. L.J. 433 (1953).

[5] Haughton, *Arbitration of Disputes Involving Incentive Problems,* CRITICAL ISSUES IN LABOR ARBITRATION 94 (1957).

[6] *Union Carbide Corp., Linde Div.,* 72-2 ARB ¶ 8382 (Rohman, 1972).

[7] See Chapter XI, *The Burden and Quantum of Proof Requirements.*

time values for each motion. These time values are taken from the motion time chart used with the particular predetermined time system. It is true that the selection of the proper time value for a particular motion from the motion time chart will involve some judgment, but the margin of error is so much less than it is when a stop-watch reading is made and the recorded time is adjusted by the industrial engineer by the use of a subjective judgment.

The following is an example of a special incentive dispute arbitration procedure designed to minimize the small adjustments in time which result when the arbitrator or his technical assistant or fact-finder uses different methods of measuring and leveling time. Under the following procedure, the industrial engineer-arbitrator is required to use the same methods for measuring and leveling the time that were used by the company's industrial engineer. Essentially the industrial engineer-arbitrator's role is to determine whether the company's industrial engineer *properly* used the time measurement procedures which are regularly used *at that plant* to determine the allowed time:

> (a) The Special Arbitrator shall study the entire operation or operations involved, unless it is mutually agreed otherwise. He shall have only the right to determine whether the labor standard was or was not established within the limits of industrial engineering accuracy, to be determined by using the following tests:
> (1) If the element to be measured was established by the Company by a predetermined time value procedure or by a standard data procedure, the Arbitrator shall be required to use the same procedure. If the element to be measured was established by the Company by a stop watch observation, the Arbitrator shall be permitted to level a stop watch observation to daywork pace.
> (2) If the element to be measured is a machine or process-controlled element, the time value shall be established by the determination of the elapsed time required for the machine or process cycle plus a 20 percent process control allowance.

These descriptions of the special arbitration procedures used in disputes involving medical and industrial engineering questions should not cause one to conclude that such disputes are not usually presented for resolution to a regular arbitrator. When they are, the technical aspects of the case are often introduced by industrial engineers or doctors who are called as witnesses by the parties. Those witnesses are then subject to cross examination by the representatives of the other party incorporating the minimal due process which courts require in labor arbitration procedures.[8] Arbitrator William Waite expresses a widely held view that an experienced arbitrator should

---

[8] Miller, *Expert Medical Evidence: A View from the End of the Table*, ARBITRATION AND SOCIAL CHANGE, Proceedings of the Twenty-Second Annual Meeting, National Academy of Arbitrators 135, 138-39 (G. Somers Ed. 1970).

be able to understand and determine disputes involving these questions if he can obtain from expert witnesses the technical information he needs:

"Common sense is still the foremost requirement for an arbitrator, and if he possesses an optimum amount of this quality he need not fear to step in, regardless of technical shortcomings. Common sense should also tell him when he is over his head, and when to go for help if he needs it." [9]

Arbitrators in the evaluation of evidence in industrial engineering disputes have developed certain presumptions. For example, they have learned to refrain from being influenced by earnings information when an incentive standard is under attack. Obviously, when the employees performing the operation are claiming that they are working with incentive effort but cannot make the expected level of earnings, they will not "lose their case" by earning more than the expected level. For example, Arbitrator Ralph Seward said concerning a situation where the employees were not making the expected earnings:

"Such earnings, it is true [measured against an expected earnings level], have not been realized in actual practice. The Umpire has given the Union every opportunity to analyze the time studies and line speed studies on which the rates were based and to point out errors or defects in those studies which would account for the failure to reach target earnings. The Union has failed to make such an analysis or to demonstrate any inadequacy in the studies or any errors in the assumptions which the Company based upon those studies. . . . It has offered the Umpire no grounds for holding that the reason for the failure to reach target earnings lay with the rates rather than with the employees themselves.

"Under these circumstances, the Umpire has no alternative but to hold that the Union has failed to establish that the incentive rates . . . are not in equitable relationship to the old rates and to deny the grievances on that basis." [10]

Similarly, Arbitrator Fred Kindig expressed and applied the normal burden-of-proof concepts so often applied by arbitrators in deciding an industrial engineering dispute:

"The primary question then is as proposed by the parties. Regardless of the validity of the previous standards, do the new standards provide an incentive opportunity of 125 percent? The Arbitrator agrees with the Company; that the burden of proof is with the Union; that a standard created by management should not be overridden by an arbitrator in the absence of clear proof of arbitrariness; that low earnings do not necessarily establish the incorrectness of incentive standards; and that

---

[9] Waite, *Problems in the Arbitration of Wage Incentives,* ARBITRATION TODAY 25 (1955).

[10] *Bethlehem Steel Co.,* 20 L.A. 38, 42-43 (Seward, 1953). See also *Wolverine Shoe & Tanning Corp.,* 15 L.A. 195, 196 (Platt, 1950).

the Arbitrator has no authority to establish a different method of compensating employees, such as, for unavoidable delays." [11]

When normal arbitration procedures are used, the same burden is placed upon the union to show that a medical determination of a company physician was clearly erroneous before it will be upset.[12]

When disputes over "allowed time determinations" of "medical judgments" are resolved by special procedures, the judgment of the special arbitrator (special industrial engineer, doctor, clinic) is final, the fact-finder's investigation is private; no evidence is presented in the normal way as there are no witnesses who may be cross-examined.[13] The determination is *de novo*.

This final chapter is not an attempt to catalog all of the variations of procedure that are used by companies and unions to handle special types of disputes, but merely to record the fact that there are special procedures and to note the essential differences between them and the normal type of labor arbitration procedure.

---

[11] *Fenestra, Div. of the Marmon Group* (unpublished) at 17-18 (Kindig, 1970).

[12] *Ideal Cement Co.,* 20 L.A. 480, 482 (Merrill, 1953); *International Shoe Co.,* 14 L.A. 253, 255 (Wallen, 1950); *Great Lakes Spring Corp.,* 11 L.A. 159, 160 (Gregory, 1948).

[13] As noted elsewhere in this volume, the NLRB will defer to an arbitration award if the due process safeguards were followed and the statutory issue raised and determined. One can only speculate what the Board would do if an employee active in organizing a union claimed he was discharged for his union activities and that his discharge violated Section 8(a)(3) of the Act and the company defended on the ground that a clinic determined he was physically unsuited for the work pursuant to a procedure in a labor agreement which did not provide for the making of a factual record or the cross-examination of the examining physicians.

TABLE OF CASES

INDEX